STANDARD LESSON COMMENTARY
1996-97

International Sunday School Lessons

published by

STANDARD PUBLISHING

Eugene H. Wigginton, *Publisher*

Richard C. McKinley, *Director of Curriculum Development*

Jonathan Underwood, *Senior Editor of Adult Curriculum*

Douglas Redford, *Editor*　　　　Hela M. Campbell, *Office Editor*

Forty-fourth Annual Volume

©1996

The STANDARD PUBLISHING Company

division of STANDEX INTERNATIONAL Corporation

8121 Hamilton Avenue, Cincinnati, Ohio 45231

Printed in U. S. A.

In This Volume

Autumn Quarter, 1996 (page 1)

God's People Face Judgment

Writers

LESSON DEVELOPMENT: Orrin Root
VERBAL ILLUSTRATIONS: Charles R. Boatman

LEARNING BY DOING: Mark A. Taylor
LET'S TALK IT OVER: Kenton K. Smith

Winter Quarter, 1996-97 (page 113)

New Testament Personalities

Writers

LESSON DEVELOPMENT:
Dale Cornett (1, 6), Lloyd Pelfrey (2)
Johnny Pressley (3-5), David Morley (7-9)
Jerran Jackson (10, 11), Dennis Gaertner (12, 13)

VERBAL ILLUSTRATIONS: Richard W. Baynes

LEARNING BY DOING: Alan Weber (1-6)
Jonathan Underwood (7, 12), Mark Plunkett (8, 9, 11)
Phil Haas (10, 13)

LET'S TALK IT OVER: Richard A. Lint

Spring Quarter, 1997 (page 225)

Hope for the Future

Writers

LESSON DEVELOPMENT: Edwin V. Hayden

VERBAL ILLUSTRATIONS: James G. VanBuren

LEARNING BY DOING: Dennis E. Glenn (1-5)
Timothy A. Heck (6-9), Thomas G. May (10-13)
LET'S TALK IT OVER: Kenton K. Smith

Summer Quarter, 1997 (page 337)

Guidance for Ministry (1-5)
A Call to Faithfulness (6-14)

Writers

LESSON DEVELOPMENT: John W. Wade
VERBAL ILLUSTRATIONS: C. Barry McCarty

LEARNING BY DOING: Ronald G. Davis
LET'S TALK IT OVER: David A. Baynes

Artists

TITLE PAGES: James E. Seward

Cover design by Listenberger Design Associates

Lessons based on International Sunday School Lessons © 1993 by the Lesson Committee.

Index of Printed Texts, 1996-97

The printed texts for 1996-97 are arranged here in the order in which they appear in the Bible. Opposite each reference is the number of the page on which it appears in this volume.

Cumulative Index

A cumulative index for the Scripture passages used in the STANDARD LESSON COMMENTARY
for the years September, 1992—August, 1997, is provided below.

V

Autumn Quarter, 1996

God's People Face Judgment

Special Features

Lessons

Unit 1: Responses to Wrong

Unit 2: Judah's Internal Decay

Unit 3: The Fall of Jerusalem

About these lessons

This series of studies focuses on the history of the southern kingdom (Judah) from the time that the north (Israel) fell in 722 B.C. to the fall of Jerusalem in 586 B.C. The reigns of kings Hezekiah and Josiah are highlighted, along with the prophetic ministries of Jeremiah, Habakkuk, and Ezekiel, who tried in vain to turn their countrymen from the path of certain doom.

Sep 1
Sep 8
Sep 15
Sep 22
Sep 29
Oct 6
Oct 13
Oct 20
Oct 27
Nov 3
Nov 10
Nov 17
Nov 24

A Christ for All Time

Two of the most crucial questions to which man seeks an answer are "Who am I?" and "Where am I going?" Because many today are uncertain as to how to address these concerns about the past and the future, the present is saturated with futility.

This year's series of lessons offers a clear, life-enriching perspective on the past, present, and future. The Autumn Quarter, drawn from the Old Testament, focuses on messages of judgment upon the southern kingdom of Judah. It is a history that we should desire not to repeat.

The good news is that even though one's past has been marked by a similar record of defeat and failure, in Christ there is forgiveness of that past and a refreshing hope for the future! Such hope is exemplified in the lives of many of those "New Testament Personalities" highlighted in our Winter Quarter. The theme of hope continues in the Spring Quarter, featuring studies from 1 Thessalonians and Revelation.

The Summer Quarter presents lessons taken from the Pastoral Epistles and Hebrews, under the title, "Guidance for Ministry." Not only does Jesus cleanse us from our past and give hope for the future; He also calls us to a daily experience of fruitful service in His name to a needy world.

May these perspectives on the past, present, and future give you and your students much encouragement throughout the year!

International Sunday School Lesson Cycle
September, 1992—August, 1998

YEAR	AUTUMN QUARTER (Sept., Oct., Nov.)	WINTER QUARTER (Dec., Jan., Feb.)	SPRING QUARTER (Mar., Apr., May)	SUMMER QUARTER (June, July, Aug.)
1992-1993	Old Testament Personalities (Old Testament Survey)	Good News for All (Old Testament Survey)	Believing in Christ (John)	Following God's Purpose (Ephesians, Philippians, Colossians, Philemon)
1993-1994	The Story of Beginnings (Genesis)	The Story of Jesus (Luke)	Good News for God's People (Romans) Set Free by God's Grace (Galatians)	God Redeems a People (Exodus, Leviticus, Numbers, Deuteronomy)
1994-1995	From the Conquest to the Kingdom (Joshua, Judges, 1 and 2 Samuel, 1 Kings)	Jesus the Fulfillment (Matthew)	Christians Living in Community (1 and 2 Corinthians)	A Nation Turns From God (1 and 2 Kings, Amos, Hosea, Micah, Isaiah)
1995-1996	The Story of Christian Beginnings (Acts)	God's Promise of Deliverance (Isaiah) God's Love for All People (Jonah, Ruth)	Teachings of Jesus (Matthew, Mark, Luke)	A Practical Religion (James) God Is With Us (Psalms)
1996-1997	God's People Face Judgment (2 Kings, Jeremiah, Lamentations, Ezekiel, Habakkuk)	New Testament Personalities	Hope for the Future (1 and 2 Thessalonians, Revelation)	Guidance for Ministry (1 and 2 Timothy, Titus) A Call to Faithfulness (Hebrews)
1997-1998	God Leads a People Home (Major Prophets, Minor Prophets, Nehemiah)	God's People in a Troubled World (1 and 2 Peter, 1, 2, 3 John, Jude)	The Gospel of Action (Mark)	Wisdom for Living (Job, Proverbs, Ecclesiastes)

Lessons for Our Learning

by Orrin Root

Most Christians prefer to spend the time that they devote to Bible study in the New Testament. There we find the teaching of Jesus and the apostles, our best guide in Christian living. Yet we know that the Old Testament was also written for our learning (Romans 15:4), so we should want to include it in our study as well. Our Sunday school lessons are planned in accordance with the need to study and learn God's Word in its entirety.

A Long View

The Sunday school lessons that we study are arranged in cycles, each cycle continuing for six years. Each year is divided into three-month quarters, with each quarter focusing on a particular topic. This September we are beginning the fifth year of the current cycle.

Fifteen quarters of this cycle are devoted to the New Testament, and only nine quarters to the Old. This means that more than sixty percent of our time is devoted to the New Testament and less than forty percent to the Old, though the Old offers more than three times as much material as the New does. In proportion to the number of pages in each Testament, we are giving more than five times as much attention to the New Testament.

If the nine quarters of study in the Old Testament were all grouped together, we would have more than two years of Old Testament study only. That is not too long to study the Old Testament, but it is too long to neglect the New. The lessons are arranged to give at least half of each year to the New Testament. In half of the six years of the current cycle, three quarters of the year are devoted to the New Testament and only one quarter to the Old.

Old Testament Lessons

The quarter beginning with this September is one of those devoted to the Old Testament. Before we start, let's look quickly at the other Old Testament studies within the cycle.

Autumn 1992. A quick survey of Old Testament history, each lesson centering on an important person.

Autumn 1993. The book of Genesis, beginning with creation and ending with the migration of Jacob and his family to Egypt.

Summer 1994. The escape from Egypt and the journey to the promised land.

Autumn 1994. The battles that won the promised land, and Israel's life in that land until it became a kingdom and Solomon brought it to the peak of its power.

Summer 1995. The division of Israel and the growth of sin, in spite of urgent warnings by the prophets, until the northern kingdom was destroyed.

Winter 1996. Lessons from Isaiah, Jonah, and Ruth.

Autumn 1996. This is the quarter we are now beginning. It traces the history of the southern kingdom (Judah) after the northern kingdom (Israel) was destroyed, and it ends with Judah's captivity in Babylon. The current cycle contains only two more quarters with lessons from the Old Testament.

Autumn 1997. Lessons from Nehemiah and the prophets concerning Israel's return from Babylon.

Summer 1998. Lessons from Old Testament wisdom literature: Job, Proverbs, Ecclesiastes.

What Now?

Now here is a brief preview of the lessons we shall be studying this quarter.

Unit 1. Responses to Wrong
September

Lesson 1. At the age of twenty-five, Hezekiah became king of Judah. The nation had drifted deep into idolatry and sin, and was facing constant pressure from Assyria. Hezekiah's response to Judah's sin was to get rid of it. Vigorously he restored the worship of Jehovah and led his people in living by Jehovah's Law. The Lord warned that evil would still bring Judah to ruin, but not in Hezekiah's lifetime.

Lesson 2. Two bad kings followed Hezekiah, and idolatry and corruption became the norm once again. During Josiah's reign, however, the forgotten book of the Law was found in the temple, and Josiah enforced it with enthusiasm. Again disaster was delayed.

Lesson 3. While Josiah was king, Jeremiah was called to support his reforms with messages from the Lord. His mission was to proclaim God's messages fearlessly, though many in Judah would oppose him.

Lesson 4. Jeremiah sounded God's call: "Amend your ways and your doings!" If Judah would not do so, the fabulous temple where they pretended to worship would be destroyed. Jeremiah continued to give God's messages after Josiah died, and even after Judah was taken captive to Babylon.

Lesson 5. The prophet Habakkuk spoke during a time when Judah was mired in sin, perhaps after good king Josiah had died. He asked how long the Lord would let this wickedness go on. The answer was grim. Chaldeans from Babylon were going to destroy the nation. This troubled Habakkuk even more; how could God let those wicked Chaldeans do that? But God was firmly in control: Babylon would be destroyed in its turn. Sooner or later, doing wrong always comes back to haunt the wrongdoer.

Unit II. Judah's Internal Decay
October

Lesson 6. This lesson shows how deeply sin was embedded within the people of Judah. Jeremiah was invited to search Jerusalem for a good man, but none could be found.

Lesson 7. This message belongs to the time when ten thousand people of Judah had already been taken captive to Babylon. A false prophet in Jerusalem was preaching that Babylon would soon be crushed and the captives would be free. The true message from God was that the captivity would continue for some time.

Lesson 8. Ezekiel was one of those ten thousand captives in Babylon. God called him to proclaim the truth to his fellow captives, but warned him that they would not welcome his message.

Lesson 9. The captives in Babylon wanted to believe that they were there because of their ancestors' sins, not theirs. God corrected that belief. The exiles were there because they had continued the sins of their fathers. Each person is responsible for what he himself does.

Unit III. The Fall of Jerusalem
November

Lesson 10. In Babylon the prophet Ezekiel made a clay model of Jerusalem being besieged. This was a visualized prophecy of how the Babylonians would one day besiege Jerusalem and capture it. The survivors would then join the captives already in Babylon.

Lesson 11. After a siege of about a year and a half, the city of Jerusalem was captured and destroyed. Most of the survivors were driven away to Babylon to join those already in exile.

Lesson 12. Here we have a sample (from the book of Lamentations) of Jeremiah's sorrow over the disaster that had come to his people. He acknowledged that their fate was due to their sin, but still he prayed that they would be forgiven and restored.

Lesson 13. The nation of Israel was no more; a remnant of its people were helpless captives in a foreign land. Subjection to Babylon would last for seventy years. Yet God gave Ezekiel a clear prophecy of restoration. The nation would live again. God still had a purpose for His people.

Lessons to Be Learned

Mindful of the fact that the Old Testament records were written for our learning, we shall be looking for what they teach us. What do these lessons say to our nation, to our church, and to ourselves?

No other nation was chosen of God as Israel was, but other nations have risen and fallen as it did. Nebuchadnezzar's Chaldean empire took Judah into captivity, yet Nebuchadnezzar's own dream foretold three empires that would follow his (Daniel 2:26-45). History records that they rose and fell, each in its turn: the empire of the Medes and Persians, the Greek empire of Alexander the Great, and the magnificent empire of Rome. Like Israel, each of these was weakened by corruption within before it was destroyed by attack from without. Is there a lesson here for our nation?

Nebuchadnezzar's dream also foretold a kingdom that shall never be destroyed (Daniel 2:44). This is God's kingdom, the kingdom of Heaven. It is eternal, but that does not mean it is immune to corruption. Jesus called His disciples the salt of the earth, but He warned, "If the salt have lost his savor, wherewith shall it be salted? it is thenceforth good for nothing, but to be cast out, and to be trodden under foot of men" (Matthew 5:13). Syria and North Africa once were solidly Christian. But the salt that was present there lost its savor. Officials of the church allied themselves with the secular government and its corruption, until these lands were trodden under the feet of Moslem hordes. Is there a lesson here for the church of today?

Both church and nation are made up of individual people; thus, the corruption of individuals becomes the corruption of church and nation. In a few weeks we shall read God's rebuke to people who wanted to blame others for their troubles. Loud and clear came the message: "The soul that sinneth, it shall die" (Ezekiel 18:4). Through centuries that stern sentence has not been revoked, yet there is a way of escape. In God's kingdom and by His grace there is forgiveness. Sinners can live if their sins are taken away through Jesus, but not if they prefer to continue in their sins. To us the message is as loud and clear as it was to Judah.

The lessons ahead of us are for our learning. Are we ready and willing to listen?

Faithless People, Faithful God

by Terry A. Clark

We are often amazed when objects that are plainly visible to us are virtually invisible to other people. My father had the annoying ability to spot immediately the exact bolt and nut he needed after I had spent twenty minutes looking through the contents of the coffee can I had dumped onto the workshop shelf. Most of us have at one time watched a driver run a red light and wondered how he could have missed something so obvious.

In this quarter's lessons we will witness the unwillingness of the southern kingdom of Judah to see the clear message of God. God wanted them to repent, renew their relationship with Him, and be restored to Him. But the spiritual eyes of the people were blinded by their wickedness. The leadership of good kings such as Hezekiah and Josiah produced evidence of repentance, yet all too soon the people returned to their wicked ways. Great prophets of God such as Jeremiah and Ezekiel warned the people of God's disappointment and impending judgment. Their cries fell on deaf ears and hard hearts.

Not only did the people ignore the proclamations of the prophets, but they also ignored the history of their own people. The northern kingdom of Israel had fallen into the same pattern of sin and idolatry, with tragic results. God had used mighty prophets such as Elijah, Elisha, and Hosea to warn them of judgment to come. They disregarded the prophets' pleas; as a consequence, the Assyrians ravaged their land and took them as captives.

The continued faithlessness of the people of Judah and God's eventual judgment upon them serve as powerful reminders to us. God is truth. He tells us of our sinful condition. He tells us of our need for repentance. He tells us of His longing to restore us. Are we listening? Or will we permit our sin to blind us to God's truth?

A False Faith

The people of Judah claimed to be God's people, yet they remained deeply mired in sin and idolatry. Theirs was a false faith. Jeremiah was instructed to go throughout Jerusalem and see if any genuine truth seeker could be found (Jeremiah 5:1). The people would say, "The Lord liveth," (v. 2), but their actions communicated a very different message. They continued to steal, murder, commit adultery, lie, and participate in idolatry (Jeremiah 7:9).

God spoke to Ezekiel and warned him that he would have to deal with a rebellious people (Ezekiel 2:7). Ezekiel called upon God's people to repent even after he and ten thousand of them had already been taken captive to Babylon. How could those remaining in Jerusalem fail to see the consequences of false faith? Continued rebellion would bring the same dire consequences to the people of Judah. But they chose to remain blind to God's truth. In time His judgment fell upon them.

How often do we see people who profess faith in Christ but fail to live their faith? They adhere to a religion often referred to as "churchianity." Their lives may be filled with church activities, but they have no genuine relationship with Christ. Still other people confuse morality and spirituality. As long as they are tolerant of their mother-in-law or never kick their dog, they consider themselves good Christians. Even patriotism gets confused with true faith. I knew one man who was quite sure he would go to Heaven because he fought for America during World War II. All of these are examples of false faith.

We may not participate in the utter corruption and idolatry of the people of Judah, but any form of false faith will always end in judgment. We must come to God on His terms, not on our own terms.

A False Hope

God called upon men of great faith to serve as His prophets. Theirs was not an easy job. God had to make Ezekiel's head "harder than flint" so that the rebelliousness of the people would not deter him from his calling (Ezekiel 3:9). Unfortunately, there were also false prophets who peddled a false hope to the people of Judah. Hananiah, a contemporary of Jeremiah, was such a man.

The confrontation between Jeremiah and Hananiah gives us a prime example of the kind of opposition that God's prophets often had to face. Jeremiah had placed a yoke around his neck and gone throughout Jerusalem, telling the people that God would bring a yoke of Babylonian oppression upon them if they did not repent. Hananiah broke that yoke and claimed that within two years God would break the dominance of the Babylonians (Jeremiah 28:10, 11). Jeremiah countered Hananiah with the bitter reality of God's truth. God was not "bound" to protect Jerusalem. He would indeed bring Nebuchadnezzar and his army against the city and permit His people to be taken captive. The yoke of wood which Hananiah had broken would be replaced by a yoke of iron (v. 14).

Those who preach false hope are always able to find many who happily accept their teaching. Many religious leaders of today proclaim such a message. They may use the word "hope," but they never confront sin and never call for repentance or the crucifixion of self. Such preaching makes it virtually impossible for the good news of salvation to be heard. As I heard one preacher say, "You've got to get a man lost before you can get him found."

During World War II, a Polish resistance courier named Jan Karski sneaked into the Warsaw Ghetto and later into one of the death camps. After escaping he reported what he had seen to many world leaders. He described the horrible suffering and death of hundreds of thousands of people. President Roosevelt did not believe him. Anthony Eden, the British foreign secretary, did not believe him. Supreme Court Justice Felix Frankfurter, a Jew, heard of the atrocities against his own people but told Karski, "I am unable to believe it." People often refuse to hear bad news, even when that news is the truth.

False hope is wicked and deceitful. Not only does it fail to confront genuine truth, but it makes it impossible to know what changes are necessary for a perilous situation to be resolved.

A False Security

The people of Judah ignored the message of the prophets because they were comfortable with God. They said to themselves, "God won't afflict us. We are His chosen people." The message of false hope lulled them into a sense of false security. They actually believed that they could commit their abominable sins while participating in the temple "worship"—and be spared any punishment from God (Jeremiah 7:9, 10). When the day came on which the Babylonians began to dismantle the temple, the people saw with their own eyes how false their security really was.

False security is one of Satan's favorite tricks. Many non-Christians find false security in their wealth, power, and position in life. Many churchgoers find false security in their outward holiness. They know how to "talk the talk." They pray in public but never in private. They give of their excess but have never made a truly sacrificial gift to God. They know the Bible but never let it speak to their hearts. How does one know if his is a false security? He must seriously examine his relationship with Jesus and give that relationship the attention it deserves. The New Testament offers this simple criterion: "He that hath the Son hath life; and he that hath not the Son of God hath not life" (1 John 5:12). True security is found in Jesus alone.

A True God

God was true to His word. The Babylonians destroyed Jerusalem and took almost all the people as captives. Judgment had to come, even if it was to fall upon God's chosen people. Blindness to truth brings such consequences.

In this quarter's lessons, however, we also see the gracious love of God. He told the people the truth that they needed to believe and obey. He warned them again and again. His desire was for them to repent and renew their relationship with Him. He took no pleasure in their death (Ezekiel 18:32). He pleaded with them to turn from their sin and choose the path of life.

The heart of God has not changed. He wants everyone to repent and live (2 Peter 3:9). The task of the church has never lost its importance. The message we proclaim is life itself—or more accurately, Life Himself, Jesus our Lord. We are still engaged in the glorious work of proclaiming truth to those who are weary of false faith and who long for an alternative to false hope and security. May our minds remain open to God's truth, and may we help others to see His great light.

Answers to Quarterly Quiz
on page 8

Lesson 1—1. The brazen (brass) serpent. 2. Isaiah. **Lesson 2**—1. covenant. 2. Baal, sun, moon, planets, host of heaven. **Lesson 3**—1. child. 2. the north. **Lesson 4**—1. den, robbers. 2. Shiloh. **Lesson 5**—1. just, faith. 2. hind. **Lesson 6**—1. false. 2. lion, wolf, leopard. **Lesson 7**—1. Hananiah. 2. two. 3. iron. **Lesson 8**—1. scorpions. 2. false. **Lesson 9**—1. "The fathers have eaten sour grapes, and the children's teeth are set on edge." 2. sinneth, die. **Lesson 10**—1. the city of Jerusalem. 2. 390 days on his left side; 40 days on his right side. **Lesson 11**—1. Zedekiah. 2. His sons were put to death before his eyes, his eyes were gouged out, then he was bound and taken to Babylon. 3. false. **Lesson 12**—1. black. 2. renew. **Lesson 13**—1. army. 2. the house of Israel. 3. true.

The Prophet and the City

by Earl Grice

The cities of the world have been both exalted and maligned during their history. They have housed extravagance in art, architecture, industry, commerce, government and entertainment. At the same time they have been burdened by corruption, greed, pollution, noise, and the depravity of humanity.

History demonstrates that no city, as renowned as it may be, is invincible. Babylon dominated a vast plain on the banks of the Euphrates, and proudly displayed more than fifty pagan temples at the height of its influence. It was considered the "gate of the gods," yet in 539 B.C. it was captured by the Persians. Even the "city of peace," Jerusalem, experienced massive destruction because of runaway idolatry and rebellion against God. Judgment awaits any people whose "land is full of blood, and the city full of perverseness" (Ezekiel 9:9).

Ascending to the top of a thirty-story skyscraper in a modern city, what might one see? Below are narrow streets, freeways tied up with commuter traffic, mechanical devices pounding the ears—noise, congestion, violence! One can also see finely terraced houses and green lawns, quite a contrast to the squalor of the lower reaches. And lying almost unseen amidst this constant motion is the church building—hidden and, in the minds of many, irrelevant. This is the city! Is it ripe for desolation? Somehow the prophets must be allowed to speak to the city of our time as Jeremiah and Ezekiel spoke to Jerusalem in their time. What is God's message to the city?

Cleansing or Judgment?

Ezekiel addressed Judah while in captivity in Babylon. He and other prophets lived to see Jerusalem ravaged by its own corruption and idolatry, symbolic of what had transpired within the nation. According to Ezekiel, the land was overrun with violence (12:19), false prophecy (13:1, 2), idolatry among the leaders (14:1-5), oppression of the poor and needy (22:7), sexual license (22:9-11), and unbridled greed (22:12). Because of such sins, Jerusalem was laid waste by powers more wicked than she. The parallels to the cities of today are obvious.

Why do human greed and sin congregate in the city? Why are cities centers of moral pollution and contamination? Is it because God's servants have abandoned the city? Unless there is a cleansing, the cities of the world will lead their nations into oblivion. The elderly are locked behind doors because of fear of what lurks in the streets; the poor are trapped in their poverty; the faces of forgotten people can be seen among the homeless. Is it any wonder that some have suggested that the city bear an inscription over its entrance like that of hell in Dante's *Inferno* ("Through me you enter the woeful city, through me you enter eternal grief, through me you enter among the lost")? Is the city beyond help?

Hope for the City

It is no accident that when Paul began his missionary endeavors, he sought out the cities of Europe and Asia. The cities were the places where the Christian gospel crossed swords with the powers of darkness. Within their walls were advanced forms of idolatry, yet Paul saw places of untapped potential for Christ at these crossroads of the Roman world.

When John wanted to paint a sordid picture of the epitome of evil, he alluded to "Babylon the Great, the Mother of Harlots and Abominations of the Earth" (Revelation 17:5). At the same time, when he wished to portray a place filled with hope and righteousness, he saw the "holy city, new Jerusalem, coming down from God out of heaven, prepared as a bride adorned for her husband" (Revelation 21:2). Thus, a city may be a symbol of grace, peace, holiness, and righteousness, or it can represent the garbage pit of humanity. It depends on what the people drink (figuratively), whether the sour vinegar of rebellion or the sweet water of life from above. It is necessary to be in the city but not of the city! The city can be redeemed. There is hope, and if that be true for the city, it is also true for the nation and the world.

The old Babylon and the old Jerusalem are but pointers to the ongoing struggle between the Mother of Harlots and the New Jerusalem. The church must not abandon the city; it must mobilize to reach into its secret enclaves. We cannot afford to be mere observers!

Is there hope? Jeremiah reminds us, "The Lord is good unto them that wait for him, to the soul that seeketh him" (Lamentations 3:25). As our Lord had compassion for the city (Luke 13:34), so must we. Let us enter the city with the "sword of the Lord," for God has many people there!

Quarterly Quiz

The questions on this page may be used in several ways: as a pretest at the beginning of the quarter; as a review at the end of the quarter; or as a review after each lesson. The questions are based on the Scripture text of each lesson (King James Version). **The answers are on page 6.**

Lesson 1

1. What object, which Moses had constructed in the wilderness, did Hezekiah break in pieces? *2 Kings 18:4*

2. Which prophet told Hezekiah of a day when all his goods would be carried to Babylon? *2 Kings 20:16, 17*

Lesson 2

1. King Josiah stood by a pillar and made a _____ before the Lord. *2 Kings 23:3*

2. Name three of the five gods or objects to which the priests in Josiah's day burned incense. *2 Kings 23:5*

Lesson 3

1. Jeremiah's initial response to God's call was, "Behold, I cannot speak: for I am a _____." *Jeremiah 1:6.*

2. From which direction did the Lord tell Jeremiah an enemy would come? *Jeremiah 1:14*

Lesson 4

1. Jeremiah declared that God's house had become a _____ of _____. *Jeremiah 7:11*

2. To what town did Jeremiah tell the people to go for an example of God's judgment? *Jeremiah 7:12*

Lesson 5

1. One of Habakkuk's most notable statements is, "The _____ shall live by his _____." *Habakkuk 2:4*

2. Habakkuk said the Lord would make his feet like those of what animal? *Habakkuk 3:19*

Lesson 6

1. Jeremiah was commanded by God to find ten men who were upright and truthful. T/F *Jeremiah 5:1*

2. Name two of the three animals that Jeremiah said would attack the people because of their sins. *Jeremiah 5:6*

Lesson 7

1. Name the false prophet that opposed Jeremiah. *Jeremiah 28:5*

2. Hananiah said Babylon's yoke would be broken within _____ years. *Jeremiah 28:11*

3. Jeremiah said that God would replace his wooden yoke with a yoke of _____. *Jeremiah 28:14*

Lesson 8

1. To what poisonous creature did God compare the stubborn house of Israel? *Ezekiel 2:6*

2. Ezekiel was told to speak God's message to a people of a strange tongue. T/F *Ezekiel 3:5*

Lesson 9

1. Quote the proverb that was frequently cited by Ezekiel's audience. *Ezekiel 18:2*

2. The soul that _____, it shall _____. *Ezekiel 18:4*

Lesson 10

1. What was Ezekiel to draw upon a tile? *Ezekiel 4:1*

2. How many days was Ezekiel to lay on his left side? *Ezekiel 4:4, 5.* On his right side? *Ezekiel 4:6*

Lesson 11

1. Name the king of Judah whose rebellion against Babylon led to Jerusalem's destruction. *2 Kings 24:20*

2. Describe the punishment that King Zedekiah received from the Babylonians. *2 Kings 25:7*

3. The land of Judah was left completely vacant by Nebuchadnezzar and the Babylonian army. T/F *2 Kings 25:12*

Lesson 12

1. Jeremiah wrote of his and the nation's sad plight, "Our skin was _____ like an oven." *Lamentations 5:10*

2. In hope, Jeremiah prayed, "_____our days as of old." *Lamentations 5:21*

Lesson 13

1. When the bones in the valley came to life, they resembled a great _____. *Ezekiel 37:10*

2. What did the dry bones represent? *Ezekiel 37:11*

3. The Lord promised that the people would return to their own land. T/F *Ezekiel 37:12*

Holding Fast to the Lord

September 1
Lesson 1

DEVOTIONAL READING: **Deuteronomy 10:12-22.**

LESSON SCRIPTURE: **2 Kings 18—20.**

PRINTED TEXT: **2 Kings 18:1-8; 20:16-21.**

2 Kings 18:1-8

1 Now it came to pass in the third year of Hoshea son of Elah king of Israel, that Hezekiah the son of Ahaz king of Judah began to reign.

2 Twenty and five years old was he when he began to reign; and he reigned twenty and nine years in Jerusalem. His mother's name also was Abi, the daughter of Zachariah.

3 And he did that which was right in the sight of the LORD, according to all that David his father did.

4 He removed the high places, and brake the images, and cut down the groves, and brake in pieces the brazen serpent that Moses had made: for unto those days the children of Israel did burn incense to it: and he called it Nehushtan.

5 He trusted in the LORD God of Israel; so that after him was none like him among all the kings of Judah, nor any that were before him.

6 For he clave to the LORD, and departed not from following him, but kept his commandments, which the LORD commanded Moses.

7 And the LORD was with him; and he prospered whithersoever he went forth: and he rebelled against the king of Assyria, and served him not.

8 He smote the Philistines, even unto Gaza, and the borders thereof, from the tower of the watchmen to the fenced city.

2 Kings 20:16-21

16 And Isaiah said unto Hezekiah, Hear the word of the LORD.

17 Behold, the days come, that all that is in thine house, and that which thy fathers have laid up in store unto this day, shall be carried unto Babylon: nothing shall be left, saith the LORD.

18 And of thy sons that shall issue from thee, which thou shalt beget, shall they take away; and they shall be eunuchs in the palace of the king of Babylon.

19 Then said Hezekiah unto Isaiah, Good is the word of the LORD which thou hast spoken. And he said, Is it not good, if peace and truth be in my days?

20 And the rest of the acts of Hezekiah, and all his might, and how he made a pool, and a conduit, and brought water into the city, are they not written in the book of the Chronicles of the kings of Judah?

21 And Hezekiah slept with his fathers: and Manasseh his son reigned in his stead.

GOLDEN TEXT: For he [Hezekiah] clave to the LORD, and departed not from following him, but kept his commandments, which the LORD commanded Moses. —2 Kings 18:6.

> *God's People Face Judgment*
> Unit 1: Responses to Wrong
> (Lessons 1-5)

Lesson Aims

After this lesson a student should be able to:
1. Briefly tell of Hezekiah's reign.
2. Describe the danger of pride.
3. Look ahead and order his life for the benefit of future generations as well as the present.

Lesson Outline

INTRODUCTION
  A. Two Kinds of History
  B. Lesson Background
 I. GOOD KING (2 Kings 18:1-6)
  A. Statistical Summary (vv. 1, 2)
  B. Right Action (vv. 3, 4)
    Twisted Symbols
  C. Right Trust (vv. 5, 6)
 II. REWARD OF GOODNESS (2 Kings 18:7, 8)
  A. National Freedom (v. 7)
  B. National Victory (v. 8)
    Cleaning Up a Mess
III. BAD NEWS AND GOOD (2 Kings 20:16-21)
  A. Bad News (vv. 16-18)
  B. Good News (v. 19)
  C. There's More (vv. 20, 21)
CONCLUSION
  A. Beware of Pride!
  B. Look Ahead
  C. Prayer
  D. Thought to Remember

The visual for lessons 1 and 2 of the visuals packet (see page 13) shows a picture of a copper snake found in southern Palestine. It may be similar to the one destroyed by Hezekiah.

Introduction

There is so much good in the worst of us,
And so much bad in the best of us,
That it ill behooves any one of us,
To find any fault with the rest of us.

That jingle reflects a piece of advice that children used to receive. If someone had nothing good to say about another, it was better to say nothing at all. Adults sometimes ignored that sage advice, and the children would follow their example instead of their advice. Still everyone agreed that the advice was good.

A. Two Kinds of History

In some cases, this advice is applied in a somewhat questionable manner. The way in which history is written is one example. Perhaps as we were growing up, we read about certain individuals who were held up as men and women worthy of respect. Not until years later did we learn that these people possessed certain character flaws. This did not negate the good they achieved, but it did provide a more complete picture of them.

Ancient historians were famous for their attempts to mask the truth about a particular leader. It seems that their purpose was not to record the facts, but to glorify their king—and to be rewarded for it. Some of them shamelessly exaggerated the monarch's triumphs and ignored his defeats.

The inspired men who wrote Bible history were different. Their books "tell it like it is." The sins of Adam and Eve, Abraham, Moses, David, and others are recorded with no attempt to excuse them. And when we come to good king Hezekiah, we see his blunders along with his successes.

B. Lesson Background

Two years ago we began a series of studies that showed how Israel became a kingdom, and how David and Solomon brought that kingdom to the peak of its power and glory. The following summer we saw how that glory faded. The great nation was split into two little ones—Israel in the north and Judah in the south.

Idolatry quickly invaded the northern kingdom. Encouraged by the government, it grew worse and worse. Greed and immorality increased as well.

In Judah, the government swung wildly from bad to good and back again. When the government was bad, the people quickly followed it into evil ways. When it was good, the people were more apt to follow God's ways.

Today's text takes up the story more than two centuries after the kingdom of Israel was divided. Hezekiah was one of Judah's good kings, so good that there was none like him before or after. Yet Hezekiah erred, and the historian does not hide it.

I. Good King
(2 Kings 18:1-6)

Ahaz was one of Judah's worst kings. He turned away from the Lord and became an enthusiastic heathen, even offering one of his sons as a sacrifice (2 Kings 16:1-4). As is always the case, heathen worship was accompanied by all kinds of sin.

When Ahaz died, the new king had the task of turning the government and the whole nation back to the Lord and to honesty, decency, and morality. It was no small task.

A. Statistical Summary (vv. 1, 2)

1. Now it came to pass in the third year of Hoshea son of Elah king of Israel, that Hezekiah the son of Ahaz king of Judah began to reign.

The third year of Hoshea was most likely 729-728 B.C., since in Hoshea's ninth year (722 B.C.) Israel fell to Assyria (2 Kings 17:6). This, however, creates certain problems with the dating of Hezekiah's reign. In this difficult area of chronology, competent scholars disagree.

2. Twenty and five years old was he when he began to reign; and he reigned twenty and nine years in Jerusalem. His mother's name also was Abi, the daughter of Zachariah.

A president of the United States must be at least thirty-five years old, and most presidents have been much older. But in Judah a young man of twenty-five stepped to the throne and resolved to make a change that would reverse the whole course of his country.

The new king's mother is named, probably because his father had more than one wife. *Abi* is a shortened form of *Abijah* (2 Chronicles 29:1). Nothing more is known of either this lady or her father *Zachariah.*

B. Right Action (vv. 3, 4)

3. And he did that which was right in the sight of the LORD, according to all that David his father did.

Thus the general character of Hezekiah's reign is briefly described. The reign of *David* had ended some two hundred fifty years earlier, but he had ruled so well that inspired writers considered him a model for the kings of God's people.

4. He removed the high places, and brake the images, and cut down the groves, and brake in pieces the brazen serpent that Moses had made: for unto those days the children of Israel did burn incense to it: and he called it Nehushtan.

The high places were places of worship on hilltops or artificial mounds. Some of them may have been used for the worship of the Lord; but in the time of Hezekiah's evil father, the high places were devoted mainly to heathen worship. *The images* were idols representing imaginary gods. They were carved of wood or stone, or cast in bronze, silver, or gold.

Most students agree that *the groves* is not an accurate translation of the Hebrew *asherah.* The

---

How to Say It

ABI. *A*-bye.
ABIJAH. Uh-*bye*-juh.
ASHERAH. Uh-*she*-ruh.
EUNUCHS. *you*-nicks.
HOSHEA. Ho-*shay*-uh.
NEHUSHTAN. Nee-*hush*-tun.
NINEVEH. *Nin*-uh-vuh.
PHILISTINES. Fe-*liss*-teens or *Fil*-us-teens.
ZACHARIAH. Zack-uh-*rye*-uh.

---

typical *asherah* was a wooden pole erected at one of the high places to represent an imaginary goddess named Asherah.

We read about *the brazen serpent that Moses had made* in Numbers 21:4-9. The brass serpent provided healing for anyone bitten by the poisonous serpents that the Lord had sent to punish the Israelites for their grumbling. Now, in a time of general idolatry, people had begun to look on this serpent as an idol. They *did burn incense to it.* This was an act of worship, the smoke of the incense representing the prayers of the people. Hezekiah broke this serpent and contemptuously called it *Nehushtan,* meaning "a piece of brass." It was no more a god than any other lump of brass was.

TWISTED SYMBOLS

One December recently, a school board acting in its collective wisdom decided to ban all references to Santa Claus from the classrooms that fell under their authority. The basis for their action was, so they claimed, the principle of the separation of church and state. How ironic that one of the major symbols of the secularization of Christmas in America has come to be seen by some as a religious symbol!

Symbols, by their very nature, only suggest meaning. Thus they can come to symbolize something other than what they were originally intended to mean. Judah's twisting of Moses' serpent of brass into a pagan idol is an example. This serpent had originally symbolized God's power to save the Israelites when they were

---

VISUALS FOR THESE LESSONS

The *Adult Visuals/Learning Resources* packet contains classroom-size visuals designed for use with the lessons in the Autumn Quarter. The packet is available from your supplier. Order No. ST 192.

bitten by poisonous snakes in the wilderness. Jesus would much later refer to this same serpent and give it new meaning as a prophetic symbol of His own death by crucifixion (John 3:14).

The nations of Judah and Israel turned from God to serve idols and became, in themselves, twisted symbols. The people who were to be a sign to the nations of God's providence denied Him and forced Him to bring ruin and desolation upon them. All who wear the name of Christ are symbols of God's redeeming power. Let us wear the name carefully and not twist it into a symbol of hypocrisy or faithlessness.

—C. R. B.

C. Right Trust (vv. 5, 6)

5. He trusted in the LORD God of Israel; so that after him was none like him among all the kings of Judah, nor any that were before him.

Judah had other good kings. Hezekiah's great-grandfather Uzziah was notable among them, and so was his great-grandson Josiah. But the inspired writer put Hezekiah above them all. There was *none like him!*

6. For he clave to the LORD, and departed not from following him, but kept his commandments, which the LORD commanded Moses.

More than seven hundred years had passed since the Lord gave His Law to *Moses;* but that Law was still the law of the land, and King Hezekiah obeyed it.

II. Reward of Goodness (2 Kings 18:7, 8)

A. National Freedom (v. 7)

7. And the LORD was with him; and he prospered whithersoever he went forth: and he rebelled against the king of Assyria, and served him not.

The Lord was with him. With the Lord, a young man of twenty-five became a capable and successful king. *He prospered whithersoever he went forth.* We have seen his great campaign against spiritual enemies (v. 4); verse 8 records another campaign against national enemies (the Philistines).

Verse 7 records that *he rebelled against the king of Assyria.* Assyria was a growing empire with its capital at Nineveh on the Tigris River. With formidable armies, it was pushing to add more nations to its territory. Ahaz, Hezekiah's father, had made a costly treaty with Assyria. Attacked by the combined forces of Israel and Syria, Ahaz did not trust in the Lord but appealed to Assyria for help. Assyria's help cost Ahaz a huge sum of silver and gold, much of it coming from the house of the Lord (2 Kings

16:5-9). Apparently Ahaz had continued to pay tribute to Assyria thereafter; however, Hezekiah refused to pay. That brought the fury of Assyria's intimidating army against him. Hezekiah trusted the Lord, and without a bow or a sword the Lord drove the Assyrians back to Nineveh (2 Kings 18:13—19:36).

B. National Victory (v. 8)

8. He smote the Philistines, even unto Gaza, and the borders thereof, from the tower of the watchmen to the fenced city.

The *Philistines* lived along the coast of the Mediterranean Sea. They were constant enemies of Judah. Probably they had occupied some of Judah's territory while king Ahaz had been busy with the attack by Israel and Syria. Hezekiah not only drove them out, but also followed them into their own territory and defeated them thoroughly. His campaign reached *even unto Gaza,* far to the southwest.

The tower of the watchmen is a phrase symbolizing the most remote rural area. There a tower built in a vineyard provided shelter for workers, and from its top a watchman could see thieves if they entered a secluded part of the vineyard. *The fenced city* was any city with a strong stone wall to protect it from attack. Thus, *from the tower of the watchmen to the fenced city* means "throughout the whole land," from the most isolated part of the country to the biggest city. Hezekiah's victory over the Philistines was complete.

CLEANING UP A MESS

Dolores Zarley's son was not a disorderly adolescent with a messy room. He was a forty-year-old whose sloppiness spilled over into the front yard. There, his collection of junk cars and trucks were an eyesore that grated on his mother's nerves. When her patience wore out, she launched a campaign to get rid of the visual abominations. Her first step was to throw a match into the back seat of the graffiti-covered junker that bothered her the most. Her efforts resulted in a family fight, five stitches on her husband's chin, and her arrest on arson charges!

King Hezekiah, on the other hand, was a *young* man who was embarrassed because his *elders* had allowed Judah to become a religious "junkyard." The people of God had cluttered up their land and their lives with idols of many kinds. The spiritual life of this covenant people was a humiliation to those who loved God. So Hezekiah began cleaning up Judah's "front yard."

Hezekiah got better results than Mrs. Zarley: his cleanup succeeded and he gained an honored reputation for "doing what was right in the sight of the Lord." Our calling as Christians is similar to Hezekiah's: to be a positive influence on God's people and the society in which we worship and work. But let us do it as Hezekiah did—in such a way as to be honored (because our love for God brings needed change), not hated (because of a contentious attitude).

—C. R. B.

visual 1

III. Bad News and Good (2 Kings 20:16-21)

The first part of 2 Kings 20 tells us that Hezekiah was sick and near death. In response to his fervent prayer, the Lord gave him fifteen more years on earth (verse 6). As a sign that this message came from God, the shadow on the sundial moved backward (verses 8-11).

Later, ambassadors from the king of Babylon came to congratulate Hezekiah upon his recovery from his sickness (2 Kings 20:12). They also wanted to know more about "the wonder that was done in the land" (2 Chronicles 32:31). Was that wonder the backward motion of the sundial's shadow (2 Kings 20:11)? Was it the miraculous defeat of the Assyrian army (2 Kings 19:35, 36)? Was it simply Hezekiah's marvelous growth in wealth and power (2 Chronicles 32:27-30)? Any of these was enough to excite the interest of the king of Babylon.

Hezekiah then displayed a regrettable measure of pride. He showed the men from Babylon all he had—his treasures of silver and gold and other precious items, including "the house of his armor" with his battle equipment. "There was nothing in his house, nor in all his dominion, that Hezekiah showed them not" (2 Kings 20:13).

When the emissaries had gone back to Babylon, Isaiah the prophet came to Hezekiah with sharp questions: "Who were those men? Where did they come from? What did you show them?" Hezekiah's answer was plain and honest: "I showed them everything I have." Thus the stage was set for the final scene of our text.

A. Bad News (vv. 16-18)

16. And Isaiah said unto Hezekiah, Hear the word of the LORD.

Isaiah himself had no criticism or comment. He was simply a messenger, bringing *the word of the Lord.*

17. Behold, the days come, that all that is in thine house, and that which thy fathers have laid up in store unto this day shall be carried unto Babylon: nothing shall be left, saith the LORD.

All the wealth that Hezekiah had so proudly shown the Babylonians, all the royal treasures stored up through generations, would finally *be carried unto Babylon.* Babylon would one day take Assyria's place, become the conqueror of Judah, and despoil it.

18. And of thy sons that shall issue from thee, which thou shalt beget, shall they take away; and they shall be eunuchs in the palace of the king of Babylon.

Not only Hezekiah's treasures, but also his *sons* would be included in the spoil taken to Babylon. The princes of Judah would become menial slaves in the palace of a foreign king. In Hebrew literature the word *sons* is frequently used of descendants in later generations. It was more than a century after Hezekiah died when the last of Judah's treasures were taken to Babylon (2 Kings 25:13-17). The king of Judah at that time was Zedekiah. He belonged to the fourth generation after Hezekiah.

The Hebrew word for *eunuchs* is rendered "officers" in 1 Samuel 8:15. In connection with the Babylonians' future treatment of Hezekiah's descendants, the term may imply the actual physical procedure that would make a man a eunuch. Such may have been the treatment to which Daniel and his friends were subjected (Daniel 1:1-7).

B. Good News (v. 19)

19. Then said Hezekiah unto Isaiah, Good is the word of the LORD which thou hast spoken. And he said, Is it not good, if peace and truth be in my days?

Bad as the news was, Hezekiah called it *good.* Of course, even a word of condemnation from the Lord is good in that it is just and right. But Hezekiah found something else that was good. The disaster would be postponed until a later generation. *Peace and truth* would remain as long as Hezekiah lived.

While Hezekiah's reply appears a bit selfish, it seems that Hezekiah overcame his unseemly pride and humbled himself (2 Chronicles 32:26). "Peace and truth" were then granted, and he reigned until the end of the years allotted to him.

C. There's More (vv. 20, 21)

20. And the rest of the acts of Hezekiah, and all his might, and how he made a pool, and a conduit, and brought water into the city, are they not written in the book of the Chronicles of the kings of Judah?

It seems evident that *the book of the Chronicles of the kings of Judah* was not the books of Chronicles that we are acquainted with, but a much more extensive record. Perhaps it was a diary kept by the royal scribes. This longer record may have perished in the flames when Jerusalem was burned about a century later. We must be content with the shorter records we have in Kings and Chronicles, plus chapters 36-39 of Isaiah.

Additional details concerning Hezekiah's reconstruction of Jerusalem's water source are found in 2 Chronicles 32:1-5, 30.

21. And Hezekiah slept with his fathers: and Manasseh his son reigned in his stead.

Slept with his fathers is a gentle way of saying that he died. With but few blunders, Hezekiah had ruled nobly for twenty-nine years (2 Kings 18:2). Sad to say, his son Manasseh proved to be as bad as Hezekiah was good. This bad son of a good father led Judah far down the road to ruin (Jeremiah 15:1-4).

Conclusion

A. Beware of Pride!

A cute little first grader was telling me about her school. "I'm the best reader in my class," she confided. "But that's all right, because I don't know it."

In a second she realized that something was amiss with that statement. Maybe my chuckle tipped her off. "I guess I do know it," she amended, "but I act as if I didn't."

How neatly her alert mind caught one of the lessons we learn from king Hezekiah! Doing well is dangerous. It can make us proud. If you're the best, probably you're smart enough to know you're the best. It's hard to act as if you don't know it, and to act that way without being seen as a hypocrite or a pretender.

Then what? Do you stop being the best? Of course not. You keep on being the best, but you're careful not to brag about it. You're the same sweet, friendly, and helpful person you were before you became the best. Then people like you even if you are the best, and you like them even if they're not. More than that, people admire you and try to be as good as you are—and that may be the best of the good things you do.

B. Look Ahead

"Like father, like son." That's what "they say," but it's not always true. Hezekiah was the best of kings, while his father Ahaz was a bad king and his son Manasseh was even worse. What happened to "Like father, like son"?

Every parent needs to be looking ahead and thoughtfully planning to make the next generation better than this one. The Lord tells how. His words are basic. You cherish them in your heart, and you plant them in the hearts of your children. You talk of them when you're sitting at home, even if you have to turn off the TV sometimes. When you're not at home, you show how they're applied. You think of them when you go to bed and when you get up (Deuteronomy 6:6, 7). And of course you do all this without nagging, for nagging closes the hearts where you're trying to plant God's words. In addition, the way that is best for one child may need to be changed with another. You need the wisdom of Solomon and the patience of Job. Having neither, you do the best you can with what you have.

It isn't easy, but it's your job if you're a parent. The next generation will not be better than this one unless you make it so.

C. Prayer

Our Father in Heaven, we feel small and helpless when we face the task of making tomorrow better than today. In our helplessness we can only trust in You. Bless our efforts, and give us wisdom and patience and power. We beg in Jesus' name. Amen.

D. Thought to Remember

Yesterday is gone, but we can use today to make a better tomorrow.

Home Daily Bible Readings

Monday, Aug. 26—Rabshakeh Mocks the Living God (2 Kings 18:26-36)

Tuesday, Aug. 27—Rabshakeh Rebuked by God (2 Kings 19:1-7)

Wednesday, Aug. 28—Hezekiah Prays for God's Deliverance (2 Kings 19:14-19)

Thursday, Aug. 29—God Promises to Save Jerusalem (2 Kings 19:29-34)

Friday, Aug. 30—God Heals Hezekiah (2 Kings 20:1-6)

Saturday, Aug. 31—The Sign of Hezekiah's Healing (2 Kings 20:7-11)

Sunday, Sept. 1—Hezekiah's Great Riches (2 Chronicles 32:27-41)

Learning by Doing

This page contains an alternate lesson plan emphasizing learning activities.
Classes desiring such student involvement will find these suggestions helpful.

Learning Goals

As students participate in today's class session, they should:

1. List specific ways found in 2 Kings 18 that show how Hezekiah held fast to the Lord.

2. For each of these points, choose at least one practical way in which Christians today can hold fast to the Lord.

3. Decide how they themselves can hold fast to the Lord in at least one of these ways.

Into the Lesson

Before class write the following scrambled sentence on your chalkboard:

"Lord the fast He to held."

Cover the scrambled sentence with a piece of shelf paper taped onto your chalkboard. To begin today's class session, tell class members that you want to have a simple contest to see who can unscramble the sentence first. Uncover the sentence, and let class members shout out the answer when they think they have it. Write, "He held fast to the Lord" (2 Kings 18:6, *New International Version*) on your chalkboard.

Then ask each class member to find a partner and to discuss the following questions together for five minutes:

1. What does it mean to hold fast to the Lord?

2. How does a person hold fast to the Lord?

3. When you think of someone holding fast to the Lord, do you think more often of good times or bad times? Why?

4. Should this be a description only for the turning points in our lives, or for every day?

Tell your group that today's study will look at Hezekiah, the good king of Judah described by this sentence. We will see why the sentence applied to him, and how it can apply to us.

Into the Word

Ask a class member to read aloud 2 Kings 18:1, 2. Briefly present the background for today's lesson. Tell the class that today's Scripture text shows how Hezekiah was a good king of Judah and what he did to hold fast to the Lord.

Ask another volunteer to read aloud 2 Kings 18:3-6. Then ask each of the pairs of students to find another pair, so that they are grouped into fours. These groups should examine verses 3-6 and make a list of all the evidences they find there to show how Hezekiah held fast to the Lord. Give the groups about six minutes, then make a list on your chalkboard as volunteers call out items. They may include:

Did what was right in the eyes of God (v. 3)
Eliminated idolatry (v. 4)
Trusted God (v. 5)
Obeyed God's commands (v. 6)
Enjoyed the Lord's blessings (v. 7)
Defeated the Lord's enemies (v. 8)

If you have time, you may want to highlight Hezekiah's reign for your class members:

• He stood firm against the king of Assyria, and God gave him a miraculous victory (2 Kings 19:35, 36).

• His nation, Judah, grew in wealth and power under his reign (2 Chronicles 32:27-30).

• He became desperately ill, but God heard his tearful prayer for health and granted him fifteen more years of life (2 Kings 20:1-6).

• He asked for a sign from the prophet Isaiah to prove that God would extend his life, and God responded by moving the shadow on the sundial backward (2 Kings 20:8-11).

• The king of Babylon sent messengers and a gift to Hezekiah, to inquire about his recovery (2 Kings 20:12; 2 Chronicles 32:31).

Ask a class member to read 2 Kings 20:13-15. Ask another volunteer to read verses 16-21. Discuss some or all of the following questions:

1. Why did Hezekiah show the Babylonians everything he owned (2 Chronicles 32:25)?

2. What do you suppose was Hezekiah's tone of voice in verse 15?

3. What do you make of Hezekiah's response to Isaiah's prophecy?

4. Are you encouraged or discouraged by Hezekiah's pride and indiscretion? Why?

Into Life

Look again at the class's chalkboard list of ways that Hezekiah held fast to the Lord. Ask class members, in the same groups of four that researched that list, to answer this question for each item on the list: "How can a Christian today follow the example of Hezekiah in this way?"

Give the class several minutes to suggest practical applications for each point. Make a list of these applications. Close with sentence prayers. Encourage class members to commit themselves to acting out at least one of the application points.

Let's Talk It Over

The questions on this page are designed to encourage review of the lesson Scriptures and to promote discussion of the lesson by the class. The answers provided are only discussion starters. Let your class talk it over from there.

1. The lesson writer cites examples of notable Bible people whose sins and failures are recorded. What are some further examples, and why is this significant?

Noah's shameful drunkenness (Genesis 9:20, 21), Abraham's resorting to a half-truth to protect himself (Genesis 20:1-13), and the strife within Jacob's family (Genesis 37:1-11) are early examples. Moses' efforts to excuse himself from God's duty (Exodus 3, 4) and Elijah's fearfulness in response to Queen Jezebel's threats (1 Kings 19:1-3) are other Old Testament examples. In the New Testament, the Gospel writers do not overlook the apostles' weaknesses, such as their preoccupation with which of them was greatest (Mark 9:33, 34) and their craven concealment from the Jews after Jesus' death (John 20:19). This feature of the Bible record underscores the truthfulness of the authors' accounts. Their description of both good and bad characteristics in human heroes is what we would expect in a true narrative.

2. It is remarkable that Hezekiah became a good king, given the example of his wicked father Ahaz. How might this circumstance have come about?

Perhaps Hezekiah's mother Abi had something to do with it. We do not know anything about her, but we are aware that godly mothers sometimes have offset the influence of ungodly fathers. Also, it may be that Hezekiah had advisors who urged him toward a course of righteousness. The effect of godly friends and companions can make a difference in the thinking of a person who has been surrounded by evil. Another answer is that Hezekiah may have observed the disastrous effects of his father's policies and made up his mind that he would take a different course. This last view ties in well with 2 Chronicles 29:1-11. Whatever may be the answer, we can point to Hezekiah as an example of one who rose above his childhood circumstances.

3. Hezekiah's reaction to Isaiah's prophecy regarding coming disaster was a curious question: "Is it not good, if peace and truth be in my days?" (2 Kings 20:19). Why is this a viewpoint we would want to avoid?

Perhaps Hezekiah was not as selfish as this question suggests. He may have been merely expressing gratitude for one favorable aspect of Isaiah's prophecy. For us the idea that our children or grandchildren may have to face disaster is an appalling one. To feel such concern for ensuing generations is surely Christian. It should be our aim to pass on the gospel to the next generation, so that it may continue to bless in the future. It should also be our goal to rid the world of such evils as warfare, crime, poverty, and disease, so that generations to come may be able to worship God without these terrible distractions.

4. What kind of plan can we devise to enable us to avoid the dangers of excessive pride?

First, we need to be aware of just how dangerous pride can be. Proverbs 16:18 says, "Pride goeth before destruction, and a haughty spirit before a fall." We should then take inventory of those personal attributes or talents that tempt us to be proud. We will find that they result from God's goodness to us. Sometimes we also owe what we are and have to our parents or other people who have helped us. Next, we need to take note of those situations in which we tend to feel a proud superiority over other people. Here we should strive to develop the attitude reflected in the words, "There but for the grace of God go I." Finally, we must work at adopting the habit of sincerely praising God and thanking Him for all our attainments and accomplishments.

5. "Like father, like son." This saying has a legitimate counterpart in "Like mother, like daughter." How should the truth behind such sayings affect the performances of Christian parents?

As this lesson demonstrates, these sayings are not always true. However, there is no doubt that children are strongly influenced by their parents' examples. If parents want Jesus Christ to occupy a place of high importance in their children's lives, those parents need to demonstrate their own genuine commitment to Christ. If parents hope that their children will remain active in the church, those parents must give priority to their own attendance, service, and witness. If parents envision a life of purity and honesty for their children, those parents dare not compromise in their own quest for holiness.

Obeying God's Commands

DEVOTIONAL READING: Deuteronomy 30:15-20.

LESSON SCRIPTURE: 2 Kings 22:1—23:20.

PRINTED TEXT: 2 Kings 23:1-8a.

2 Kings 23:1-8a

1 And the king sent, and they gathered unto him all the elders of Judah and of Jerusalem.

2 And the king went up into the house of the LORD, and all the men of Judah and all the inhabitants of Jerusalem with him, and the priests, and the prophets, and all the people, both small and great: and he read in their ears all the words of the book of the covenant which was found in the house of the LORD.

3 And the king stood by a pillar, and made a covenant before the LORD, to walk after the LORD, and to keep his commandments and his testimonies and his statutes with all their heart and all their soul, to perform the words of this covenant that were written in this book. And all the people stood to the covenant.

4 And the king commanded Hilkiah the high priest, and the priests of the second order, and the keepers of the door, to bring forth out of the temple of the LORD all the vessels that were made for Baal, and for the grove, and for all the host of heaven: and he burned them without Jerusalem in the fields of Kidron, and carried the ashes of them unto Bethel.

5 And he put down the idolatrous priests, whom the kings of Judah had ordained to burn incense in the high places in the cities of Judah, and in the places round about Jerusalem; them also that burned incense unto Baal, to the sun, and to the moon, and to the planets, and to all the host of heaven.

6 And he brought out the grove from the house of the LORD, without Jerusalem, unto the brook Kidron, and burned it at the brook Kidron, and stamped it small to powder, and cast the powder thereof upon the graves of the children of the people.

7 And he brake down the houses of the sodomites, that were by the house of the LORD, where the women wove hangings for the grove.

8a And he brought all the priests out of the cities of Judah, and defiled the high places where the priests had burned incense, from Geba to Beersheba.

GOLDEN TEXT: The king [Josiah] stood by a pillar, and made a covenant before the LORD, . . .
to perform the words of this covenant that were written in this book.
And all the people stood to the covenant.—2 Kings 23:3.

God's People Face Judgment
Unit 1: Responses to Wrong
(Lessons 1-5)

Lesson Aims

After this lesson a student should be able to:

1. Briefly describe the great accomplishments of king Josiah's reign in Judah.

2. Mention two ways in which a Christian can help make this world a better world.

3. Mention one specific task that he himself can do this week to glorify God and benefit the world.

Lesson Outline

INTRODUCTION
  A. Drastic Changes
  B. Lesson Background
 I. RENEWING THE COVENANT (2 Kings 23:1-3)
  A. Gathering the People (vv. 1, 2a)
  B. Reading the Law (v. 2b)
  C. Pledging Obedience (v. 3)
    Not Enough Room
 II. REMOVING IDOL WORSHIP (2 Kings 23:4-8a)
  A. Pagan Equipment (v. 4)
  B. Pagan Priests (v. 5)
  C. Pagan Asherah (v. 6)
  D. Pagan Houses (v. 7)
  E. Pagan High Places (v. 8a)
    Destroying the Place Where Evil Was Done
CONCLUSION
  A. Change the King
  B. Change the People
  C. Prayer
  D. Thought to Remember

The visual for lessons 1 and 2 of the visuals packet is a picture of a high place, perhaps resembling one of those destroyed by King Hezekiah. The visual is shown on page 21.

Introduction

During the 1992 presidential election, two of the three candidates clamored for change. Some campaign orators even suggested that we must "reinvent government." But no one suggested that the Constitution be abandoned. No one wanted to abolish the presidency or the Congress or the federal court system. The changes recommended were not very radical.

A. Drastic Changes

When Hezekiah became king of Judah, a series of drastic changes occurred. He did not change Judah's "constitution;" he simply began to govern according to it. The former king (his father Ahaz) had not done that. Hezekiah, however, "did that which was right in the sight of the Lord" (2 Kings 18:3). For most of his reign that was the national policy, as we saw in last week's lesson. Both Hezekiah and Judah prospered (2 Chronicles 32:27-30).

The change was no less drastic when Hezekiah died, but it moved in the opposite direction. His son Manasseh was only twelve years old when he became king, so we must suppose his advisers had much to do with the change. These advisers, however, were not the ones who had helped Hezekiah in his godly rule. They did not abolish the constitution; they simply ignored it. Manasseh "did that which was evil in the sight of the Lord" (2 Kings 21:2). He encouraged idolatry throughout Judah, even in the courts of the Lord's temple. He "shed innocent blood very much, till he had filled Jerusalem from one end to another" (2 Kings 21:16). His reign is recorded in 2 Kings 21:1-18.

In his later years, Manasseh was captured by the Assyrians. While in captivity, Manasseh turned to God in repentance and was restored to the throne of Judah. Earnestly he tried to undo the harm he had done (2 Chronicles 33:10-16), but his time was too short. When he died, his son Amon promptly reverted to the earlier evil policy (2 Kings 21:19-22).

By this time Judah was close to anarchy. Amon ruled only two years, then he was killed in his own house by his own servants. This led to a popular uprising. "The people of the land" arose and executed the killers. They put Amon's son Josiah on the throne (2 Kings 21:23, 24).

B. Lesson Background

We are not told specifically who led the uprising that put Josiah on the throne. We assume those leaders now controlled the government, for the new king was only eight years old. They led well, and the young king "did that which was right in the sight of the Lord" (2 Kings 22:1, 2).

Eighteen years later, at the age of twenty-six, Josiah launched a major project. He planned to repair the temple of the Lord. Manasseh and his evil son had ruled for fifty-seven years, and Josiah himself was in the eighteenth year of his reign before he undertook this project. Thus, for about seventy-five years the temple had been shamefully neglected and polluted by heathen altars and ceremonies. Now it was to be cleaned and repaired (2 Kings 22:3-7).

When the cleanup began, Hilkiah (the high priest) found in the temple the book of the Law, which God had given to Moses more than seven hundred years before. Quite properly the high priest gave it to Shaphan, who was in charge of the cleanup project. Shaphan took it and read it to the king. When king Josiah heard the Law, he must have realized he and his people were breaking it in dozens of ways. The Law prescribed terrible penalties for such violations.

Was Jerusalem doomed to receive the severe punishment the Law demanded? To find an answer, the king and his counselors decided to consult a prophetess of the Lord in Jerusalem named Huldah. She affirmed that Jerusalem indeed was doomed; however, because king Josiah was now doing his best to obey the Law, the punishment would not come during his lifetime (2 Kings 22:15-20). The young king then continued his efforts, as we see in our text.

I. Renewing the Covenant
(2 Kings 23:1-3)

Repairing the temple had appeared to be the primary task, but now it seemed only a tiny part of what must be done. The whole nation must learn of this Law. Every person must be enlisted in the effort to obey it.

A. Gathering the People (vv. 1, 2a)

1. And the king sent, and they gathered unto him all the elders of Judah and of Jerusalem.

Each community of Judah had some mature citizens who were recognized as leaders. Josiah's first step was to secure their cooperation in bringing all the people together.

2a. And the king went up into the house of the LORD, and all the men of Judah and all the inhabitants of Jerusalem with him, and the priests, and the prophets, and all the people, both small and great.

This was a mass meeting of the entire nation —officials and common people, rich and poor, priests and sinners. The meeting place was *the house of the Lord*—probably the porch through which the temple itself was entered.

B. Reading the Law (v. 2b)

2b. And he read in their ears all the words of the book of the covenant which was found in the house of the LORD.

This must have been a long meeting. Years later Ezra conducted a similar reading, which took half a day (Nehemiah 8:2, 3). On that occasion, however, some time was spent in interpre-

---

How to Say It

AMON. *A*-mun.
ASHERAH. Uh-*she*-ruh.
BEERSHEBA. Beer-*she*-buh.
GEBA. *Gee*-buh (g as in *get).*
HILKIAH. Hil-*kye*-uh.
HULDAH. *Hul*-duh.
JEROBOAM. Jair-uh-*boe*-um.
MANASSEH. Muh-*nass*-uh.
SHAPHAN. *Shay*-fan.

---

tation or explanation to help the people understand what was read. We are not told whether Josiah paused for explanation.

Obviously *the book of the covenant* was "the book of the law" mentioned in 2 Kings 22:8. God's Law constituted a covenant (an agreement or contract) between Him and the people who promised to obey it. God agreed to give them peace and prosperity if they kept their promise, but to withhold these if they broke it.

C. Pledging Obedience (v. 3)

3. And the king stood by a pillar, and made a covenant before the LORD, to walk after the LORD, and to keep his commandments and his testimonies and his statutes with all their heart and all their soul, to perform the words of this covenant that were written in this book. And all the people stood to the covenant.

By a pillar indicates some raised place where the king could be seen by all the assembled people. Some students think the Hebrew phrase means *on a platform* rather than *by a pillar*. The Hebrew word for *pillar* literally means "standing place." The question is whether it refers to the place where the pillar stood or the place where Josiah stood.

There in the sight and hearing of all the people, and *before the Lord*, king Josiah *made a covenant.* He vowed *to walk after the Lord,* or to follow His leading. He vowed *to keep his commandments and his testimonies and his statutes.* We need not try to distinguish between these terms; all were included in *the words of this covenant that were written in this book.* Josiah promised to obey them all, with his whole *heart* and *soul.*

And all the people stood to the covenant. Perhaps they had been sitting on the pavement and now literally stood up to indicate that they joined the king in his vow. If not in that way, then in some other manner they demonstrated that all of them were taking the same stand the king was taking.

NOT ENOUGH ROOM

Empty space! When we think of the heavens, most of us think of an infinity of empty space. But the part of that empty space close to the earth is filling up with satellites. Only thirty years ago, the first communications satellite was launched. Now there are some seven hundred of them in orbit, with dozens more scheduled for launch.

For such satellites to be most effective, there should be only 180 of them, each separated from the next by two degrees of arc—about nine hundred miles at the altitude at which they orbit. More satellites result in radio signal interference among them. So strangely enough, there is not enough room in "empty space" for all our satellites!

When king Josiah began his reforms in Judah, he realized that the temple did not have enough room in it to contain idols as well as the God who had created the heavens and earth. That might seem ironic, but only until one considers the truth that Josiah had rediscovered by reading the Law: faith in the true God leaves no room for faith in any other. Thus, he did what was right when he removed the images and utensils of idol worship from the temple and destroyed them.

The gods that compete today for a place in the temple of our hearts (money, fame, power, selfish pride, among others) may be different from the ones that Josiah eliminated, but the principle is still the same: there is not enough room in our hearts for more than one.   —C. R. B.

II. Removing Idol Worship
(2 Kings 23:4-8a)

Places of heathen worship were scattered all over the country. Pagan altars were even in the court of the Lord's house. Most of the people in Judah could not remember a time when heathen worship had not been common. Born in the midst of heathen idols, shrines, and ceremonies, how could the people know all of that was wrong? No one had told them about God's Law.

Now that His Law was known, everything heathen was declared abominable, and it was time to purge the entire country.

A. Pagan Equipment (v. 4)

4. And the king commanded Hilkiah the high priest, and the priests of the second order, and the keepers of the door, to bring forth out of the temple of the LORD all the vessels that were made for Baal, and for the grove, and for all the host of heaven: and he burned them without Jerusalem in the fields of Kidron, and carried the ashes of them unto Bethel.

In *the temple of the Lord,* a cleanup had already begun, during which the book of the Law had been found. Before that, apparently no one had realized that the worst pollution in the temple was the heathen worship occurring there. Now it must stop. This phase of the cleanup was assigned to the people most closely connected with the temple: the high priest, the subordinate priests (*of the second order*), and the temple doorkeepers.

The *vessels* to be removed were not all containers such as jars and pitchers. The Hebrew word can include tools such as knives, tongs, and pokers. Everything that had been used in idolatrous ceremonies had to go. The *New International Version* translates the word "articles."

Baal was chief of the imaginary gods worshiped in Palestine. Different communities represented Baal in different forms, so we often find the plural form of his name, *Baalim,* meaning a number of different idols called Baal.

Grove represents the Hebrew word *asherah.* Apparently the earlier translators thought that this word meant a grove of trees where heathen worship was conducted, but now it is generally agreed that the *asherah* was a pole representing a goddess connected with Baal, whose name was Asherah. The *New International Version* simply uses the Hebrew word and capitalizes it "Asherah," instead of translating it.

The host of heaven refers to the stars. The heathen Hebrews were among those who "worshipped and served the creature more than the Creator" (Romans 1:25).

All the items used in the worship of these false deities were taken out of the temple court and burned *in the fields of Kidron,* a valley east of Jerusalem. Josiah then *carried the ashes of them unto Bethel.* This town was about twelve miles north of Jerusalem. It was one of the places where Jeroboam had introduced idolatry soon after Israel was divided (1 Kings 12:26-30). Already defiled by centuries of idol worship, Bethel was a fitting place for the remains of the idolatry that had defiled God's house. But how tragic it was that Bethel had been so defiled! There Jacob had seen a vision of angels moving between Heaven and earth and had given the place its name—Bethel, meaning "house of God" (Genesis 28:10-22).

B. Pagan Priests (v. 5)

5. And he put down the idolatrous priests, whom the kings of Judah had ordained to burn incense in the high places in the cities of Judah, and in the places round about Jerusalem; them

also that burned incense unto Baal, to the sun, and to the moon, and to the planets, and to all the host of heaven.

Manasseh and Amon, kings of Judah who were Josiah's grandfather and father, had appointed priests to lead in heathen worship *in the high places* dedicated to such activity. Josiah dismissed or "fired" (this is likely the meaning of *put down*) these idolatrous priests.

To burn incense was an act of worship. The smoke of the incense represented the rising prayers of the worshipers. The *sun and moon* and *planets* were also worshiped, as were *Baal,* the stars, and the *asherah*. The *New International Version* has "constellations" instead of *planets;* some students think the twelve signs of the zodiac are meant. These groups of stars have been recognized from ancient times, but God's book made it plain that they were God's creations, not gods themselves.

C. Pagan Asherah (v. 6)

6. And he brought out the grove from the house of the LORD, without Jerusalem, unto the brook Kidron, and burned it at the brook Kidron, and stamped it small to powder, and cast the powder thereof upon the graves of the children of the people.

One might think the *asherah* would have been among the items destroyed as recorded in verse 4, but now the writer returns to mention it specifically. Possibly only the loose tools and vessels were destroyed before, leaving the *asherah* firmly planted in the ground. Now it was cut down or dug up and destroyed. It is thought that the ordinary *asherah* was a plain wooden pole, but perhaps this one in the temple was ornamented with metal. This was crushed to powder, as was the golden calf that Aaron had made at Sinai centuries earlier (Exodus 32:20).

The children of the people probably means the common people or the poor. Their dead were buried in the ground, not in caves or costly chambers hewn in rock. The ground where they lay was already defiled by their dead bodies, so it was a suitable place to scatter the defiled powder of the *asherah*.

D. Pagan Houses (v. 7)

7. And he brake down the houses of the sodomites, that were by the house of the LORD, where the women wove hangings for the grove.

The sodomites are called "male shrine prostitutes" in the *New International Version*. The Hebrew word literally means "consecrated men," but these were consecrated to the wrong cause! Various sexual abuses and perversions were a frequent part of heathen worship. Depraved men available for such purposes were housed conveniently close to the temple. Josiah and his men demolished these structures, perhaps dumping the material in the Kidron Valley where other pagan items had been destroyed.

Some of the houses sheltered women who *wove hangings for the grove.* As noted earlier, the *grove* was actually a simple pole erected to represent an imaginary goddess. We can easily imagine that devoted heathen women dressed their wooden goddess as a lady, with a clean gown every day. Perhaps that is what they did, but the Hebrew word for *hangings* means literally *houses.* Some students therefore conclude that the women made tents or awnings to shelter their idol from sun and rain.

E. Pagan High Places (v. 8a)

8a. And he brought all the priests out of the cities of Judah, and defiled the high places where the priests had burned incense, from Geba to Beersheba.

Josiah not only dismissed these pagan priests, but also destroyed the places of worship where they had officiated. This he did throughout the land of Judah, from *Geba* in the north to *Beersheba* in the south.

Verses 8b-20 continue the record of Josiah's campaign against idolatry. He carried it beyond the northern border of Judah into the territory that had belonged to Israel. Since 722 B.C. the northern nation had been subject to Assyria, but by Josiah's time Assyria was weakened from revolts elsewhere in its empire. Apparently there was no active resistance to Josiah's campaign against idolatry.

DESTROYING THE PLACE WHERE
EVIL WAS DONE

Just one mile west of a small Polish village lies a reminder of the horrible effects of racial pride. The prison blocks, gas chambers, and crematoria of Auschwitz cover fifteen square miles of Polish countryside. This prison camp was a part of the "solution" to what the Nazis called the "Jewish problem."

visual 2

Between 1940 and 1945, some two million Jews and Polish citizens were exterminated in Auschwitz and the neighboring camp, Treblinka. These unfortunate souls, caught in the vise of Nazi hatred, were worked to death, killed in medical experiments, or poisoned in the gas chambers.

During the years after the end of the war, museums were erected at both Auschwitz and Treblinka. In establishing these memorials, the Polish parliament wanted to make sure that the world would never forget the possibility for evil that lurks in the human soul.

Two schools of thought exist on how to deal with such evil places. What the Poles did with Auschwitz is one approach. The second is what king Josiah did to the high places of Baal worship and the centers of "religious" prostitution in Jerusalem. Josiah undoubtedly made the right choice for his time and place. There can be no room for a museum of evil in the place where God is worshiped. The same may be said of our hearts—the temple where God is worshiped today.   —C. R. B.

Conclusion

If you leave your garden alone, weeds will take it. They grow faster than petunias and cabbages. You have to be energetic in weeding.

Your town, your state, or your nation is like a garden. Weeds will take it unless good people are vigilant and vigorous against them.

Weeds seem to be winning in many of our gardens. Moral standards are falling; crime rates are rising. What can we do about it? Hire more police, or build more jails? We have done that until the tax rate appalls us, and look at the weeds! There must be a better way.

Home Daily Bible Readings

Monday, Sept. 2—Josiah Orders Repair of the Temple (2 Kings 22:1-7)

Tuesday, Sept 3—Josiah Receives the Book of the Law (2 Kings 22:8-13)

Wednesday, Sept. 4—Josiah Is Spared From God's Wrath (2 Kings 22:14-20)

Thursday, Sept 5—Josiah Orders the Passover Held (2 Kings 23:21-25)

Friday, Sept. 6—Josiah's Death (2 Kings 23:26-30)

Saturday, Sept. 7—Keep God's Commandments (Psalm 119:1-8)

Sunday, Sept. 8—Live Righteously (Psalm 119:9-16)

A. Change the King

The king set a pattern in Judah. When evil Manasseh was king he encouraged the weeds, and they multiplied. When Josiah took over, the weeding was a big job, but he did it.

When pleasure is king, the weeds grow. When greed is king, they become monstrous. When comfort is king, we lie in the hammock and ignore them.

What if Jesus were honored by all Christians as the King He really is? What if all of us would not only pledge allegiance to Him, but actually obey Him? How beautifully our weedless gardens would bloom!

The best hope—the only hope—of triumphant goodness lies in the kingdom of Christ. The best thing you and I can do for a better world is to bring people to Jesus, make them disciples eager to learn from Him, baptize them into Him, and teach them to do everything He asks.

B. Change the People

In order for a society to be changed, people must be changed. This is not done by law or by force; it is done by persuasion and reason. It is done by winsomely presenting the claims of Jesus, by showing the evidence that He is truly the Son of God, and by demonstrating in our living that it is good to follow Him. Thus it is that men and women are led to be born again and to flourish as flowers.

Why is this so difficult? Why do we shrink from our task? The gospel is good news, not bad. The King eternal is offering life eternal to people condemned to die. We ought to be telling it freely, enthusiastically, joyously. People ought to be accepting it with delight.

How are we doing? Is telling the good news a matter of top priority? Do we need to reexamine our congregation's program of evangelism? Do we need to examine our own way of living?

C. Prayer

Almighty Creator, how happy we are that You are also our Father! How good it is to have from You the rules of healthy and happy and honorable living! How graciously You have provided a way of forgiveness when we have failed to follow Your rules! As we dedicate our lives to You, we ask for wisdom and grace and power to convey Your message in a winsome way to those who need it. May we serve You well for the world's good and Your glory. In Jesus' name we pray. Amen.

D. Thought to Remember

Christ is King.

Learning by Doing

This page contains an alternate lesson plan emphasizing learning activities.
Classes desiring such student involvement will find these suggestions helpful.

Learning Goals

As students participate in today's class session, they should:

1. List the evidences in Josiah's society of an entire generation's ignorance of God's Law.

2. Compare this situation with similar trends in our own society.

3. Choose at least one way to reemphasize the Bible in their world.

Into the Lesson

Begin today's session by asking, "What would our society be like if we had no Bibles?" Divide students into groups of six and let each group choose one of the following activities to answer the question:

Newspaper articles. This group writes one or several headlines describing happenings in your town as a result of no Biblical influence.

Advertisements. This group designs ads for products or services that would be sold in a society where the Bible's influence was absent.

Listing. This group makes a list of *at least fifteen answers* to the question.

Give the groups no longer than ten minutes, then let them share with the entire class.

Discuss with the class: "How much influence does the Bible have on our society today? How close to our members' descriptions has our world already become?" Tell class members that today's study will look at what happened to the nation of Judah when it had ignored the teachings of God's Word for a generation.

Into the Word

Present the lesson background under four headings:

The Bad King Manasseh (2 Kings 21:1-18; 2 Chronicles 33:1-16)

The Bad King Amon (2 Kings 21:19-22)

The Boy Josiah Becomes King (2 Kings 21:23, 24; 22:1-7)

Josiah Finds the Book of the Law (2 Kings 22:8-20)

See the Introduction to the lesson commentary (p. 18) for material to use under each of these four points. If you wish, ask a different class member to prepare a one- or two-minute report for each heading.

Ask a volunteer to read 2 Kings 23:1-3 after you have written these questions on your chalkboard: "What did the king do? What did the people do?" Ask class members to answer the questions.

Divide the class back into the groups that worked together earlier. Ask them to skim verses 4-20 and to write a description of what had happened in the society of Judah when the influence of God's Law had been missing. After four or six minutes, ask volunteers to share items as you make a list on your chalkboard. Beside each of these items, write what Josiah and his people did to remedy each of these problems. Your resulting lists should look something like this:

1. Idols were in the temple and throughout the land (Josiah destroyed them).

2. People participated in prostitution as an act of worship (Josiah tore down their quarters).

3. Pagan priests burned incense to Baal, the sun and moon, and stars (Josiah dismissed them).

4. Places of idol worship had been created (Josiah destroyed them).

5. Human sacrifice was a part of pagan worship (Josiah desecrated the places where this worship had occurred).

6. Horses and chariots were dedicated to worship of the sun (Josiah removed the horses from their places at the entrance to the temple and burned the chariots).

7. Altars for idol worship had been erected in the temple itself (Josiah pulled them down).

Into Life

Ask students to try to think of a counterpart in our society to each of the items from the above list. To prod their thinking, ask questions like these:

1. What items or ideas have become almost like idols in the thinking of some of our countrymen? What would we name as the "places of worship" for these "idols"?

2. How is sexual immorality central to the value system of some people today?

3. What part does a fascination with the sun, moon, and stars play in the lives of many today? How has this become a form of worship?

Ask class members to decide how a reemphasis on the Bible in our society could counteract some of these trends. What can class members do to place a stronger emphasis on the Bible in their society? In their families? In their congregation? In their own lives?

Let's Talk It Over

The questions on this page are designed to encourage review of the lesson Scriptures and to promote discussion of the lesson by the class. The answers provided are only discussion starters. Let your class talk it over from there.

1. The public reading of Scripture preceded the reforms of king Josiah. How can we read the Scripture publicly in such a way as to stir us to renewal of our faith and rededication to service?

Every congregation has some members with the ability to read clearly and with animation. It would be wise to give these people the opportunity to handle the Scripture reading. If elders or deacons or even preachers recognize that they are not effective public readers, it would demonstrate a humble desire to enhance the worship, should they step aside for these better readers. Perhaps we see the Scripture reading as a mere preliminary to a sermon or the Lord's Supper. We need to view it as a potentially powerful act of worship in itself.

2. King Josiah publicly committed himself to accomplish the will of the Lord. This may call to mind the practice of public rededications in our services of worship. How do you feel about such rededications?

Some Christian leaders look with suspicion on the practice of public rededications to the Lord. It is true that people who make such rededications often go back quickly to their habits of poor attendance and general inactivity, as far as the church is concerned. Perhaps the key in this is to make people aware that they will be expected to act on their rededication. In extending this part of the invitation, the preacher may stress that rededication is pointless unless it means commitment to faithful attendance and diligent involvement in the work and witness of the church. In this way rededication could serve a very useful purpose for those people who are sincere in their desire to make a fresh commitment.

3. What are some ungodly influences in our community that we may need to clean up?

Perhaps we have stores in our community that sell pornographic materials. These may be drugstores as well as bookstores. We can make the managers of such stores aware of our opposition to the sale of this material. Another ungodly influence we may encounter is the distribution of illegal drugs. We should do our part to educate the members of the community on the dangers of drug usage and to urge law enforcement officials to combat this plague. Still another ungodly influence may be the presence of a pseudo-Christian cult in our community. Again, we may have to take the lead in educating the community regarding the unhealthy doctrines and practices of such a cult. It may be necessary for us to distribute literature to inform citizens of the cult's true nature.

4. Josiah's reforms extended to the house of God, the temple itself. What are some ungodly influences we may need to combat in the house of God, the church?

We live in a time when many Christians are substituting personal feelings for the Bible as a standard for belief and behavior. The idea is that if a certain doctrine or practice feels right, it must be right. In our church we may need to emphasize constantly that the Bible must remain the ultimate standard for our faith. Another dangerous religious influence that may affect our church members is that teaching which asserts that true believers will achieve material wealth and perfect health. Again, it is important that we combat this by presenting the complete Biblical picture, which shows that God may allow personal afflictions, including physical and economic ones, in order to discipline us and strengthen us spiritually.

5. The lesson writer declares, "The best thing you and I can do for a better world is to bring people to Jesus. . . ." But the people of the world seem increasingly wary of our efforts to bring them to Jesus. What can we do about this?

They are wary in part because they do not see the change Jesus has made in us. When they hear of Christian leaders falling prey to sexual temptations and of churches rent by dissension, it is not surprising that they tend to reject the Jesus we present. We need to get serious about holiness and purity, and demonstrate that Jesus does make a difference. We need to develop the kind of love Jesus envisioned when He said, "By this shall all men know that ye are my disciples, if ye have love one to another" (John 13:35). We need to work for the kind of unity among believers that will accomplish what Jesus prayed for in John 17:21: "that the world may believe that thou hast sent me."

Hearing God's Call

DEVOTIONAL READING: **Galatians 1:11-17.**

LESSON SCRIPTURE: **Jeremiah 1.**

PRINTED TEXT: **Jeremiah 1:4-10, 14-17.**

Jeremiah 1:4-10, 14-17

4 Then the word of the LORD came unto me, saying,

5 Before I formed thee in the belly I knew thee; and before thou camest forth out of the womb I sanctified thee, and I ordained thee a prophet unto the nations.

6 Then said I, Ah, Lord GOD! behold, I cannot speak: for I am a child.

7 But the LORD said unto me, Say not, I am a child: for thou shalt go to all that I shall send thee, and whatsoever I command thee thou shalt speak.

8 Be not afraid of their faces: for I am with thee to deliver thee, saith the LORD.

9 Then the LORD put forth his hand, and touched my mouth. And the LORD said unto me, Behold, I have put my words in thy mouth.

10 See, I have this day set thee over the nations and over the kingdoms, to root out, and to pull down, and to destroy, and to throw down, to build, and to plant.

. . . .

14 Then the LORD said unto me, Out of the north an evil shall break forth upon all the inhabitants of the land.

15 For, lo, I will call all the families of the kingdoms of the north, saith the LORD; and they shall come, and they shall set every one his throne at the entering of the gates of Jerusalem, and against all the walls thereof round about, and against all the cities of Judah.

16 And I will utter my judgments against them touching all their wickedness, who have forsaken me, and have burned incense unto other gods, and worshipped the works of their own hands.

17 Thou therefore gird up thy loins, and arise, and speak unto them all that I command thee: be not dismayed at their faces, lest I confound thee before them.

GOLDEN TEXT: The word of the LORD came unto me [Jeremiah], saying, Before I formed thee in the belly I knew thee; and before thou camest forth out of the womb I sanctified thee, and I ordained thee a prophet unto the nations.—Jeremiah 1:4, 5.

Lesson Aims

After this lesson a student should be able to:

1. Describe Jeremiah's vision of a boiling pot and explain the meaning of it.

2. Explain why Jeremiah might have been afraid to give his message, and tell what reason he had to be fearless.

3. Describe some present-day opposition to Christianity or some evidence of growing godlessness in our country.

4. Resolve to stand firmly for God and His way.

Lesson Outline

INTRODUCTION
    A. Drafted for Service
    B. Lesson Background
  I. COMMISSION (Jeremiah 1:4-8)
    A. The Lord's Prophet (vv. 4, 5)
    B. The Prophet's Objection (v. 6)
    C. The Lord's Insistence (vv. 7, 8)
  II. INSPIRATION (Jeremiah 1:9, 10)
    A. The Lord's Words (v. 9)
    B. The Lord's Power (v. 10)
      A Hidden Power
  III. DANGER (Jeremiah 1:14-17)
    A. Attack (vv. 14, 15)
    B. Judgment (v. 16)
      Trashing the Landscape
    C. Warning (v. 17)
CONCLUSION
    A. Taking the Plunge
    B. Targets for Truth's Sake
    C. Why?
    D. Prayer
    E. Thought to Remember

The visual for lesson 3 of the visuals packet calls attention to the far-reaching plans the Lord had for Jeremiah. It is shown on page 29.

Introduction

At the age of eighteen, Carl was appalled when someone asked him to teach a Sunday school class, and doubly appalled when he heard what class it was. The fourteen-year-old boys! Carl knew that class. He had been in it himself only four years earlier. During those four years, no teacher had stayed with that class more than three weeks. Some had fled in tears before the first session was over. Though its membership changed every year, that class was always incorrigible. It was a "treasured" tradition.

At first Carl refused the request. But the lady pleaded so earnestly and tearfully that he finally gave in. After all, what harm could he do? That class couldn't become any worse. So Carl became a teacher against his will and against his better judgment.

Carl began his task with more vigor than wisdom. During the first session he literally picked up a defiant student and put him in a chair so forcefully that the chair collapsed in a jumble of sticks.

The boys laughed uproariously. That chair had been broken before. They had pieced it together precariously in the place where they hoped the new teacher would sit. When the joke backfired, even Carl joined in the merriment. The boys accepted him as one of the gang, and the class came under control for the first time in years.

A. Drafted for Service

Many Sunday school teachers and other Christian leaders have undertaken their tasks as reluctantly as Carl did. Most of those who have tried earnestly and persistently have become successful.

Reluctant leaders in the Lord's work are not confined to our time. Moses was drafted against his will (Exodus 3:1—4:17), and God made him a magnificent success. Jeremiah likewise was reluctant to take the task assigned to him, but God made him able to do it as well.

If we are doing what the Lord wants us to do, we can be sure He will give us the ability.

B. Lesson Background

The historical setting of Jeremiah is described in the first three verses of his book. He was called to prophesy in the thirteenth year of Josiah's reign in Judah. That was five years before Josiah found the book of the Law and set out to reform the nation.

The teaching of Jeremiah must have been very helpful throughout the period of Josiah's reformation, which we read about last week. But the prophet was not released from service when king Josiah died. Faithfully he proclaimed God's will even when Josiah's evil sons were ignoring it. Courageously he warned that sin would bring disaster, and he kept on doing so while Judah fell under the rule of Egypt, then of Babylon. He continued his warning until his prophecy was fulfilled and most of the people of Judah were driven away to Babylon. Then Jeremiah refused honor and ease in Babylon so he could stay in Judah and help the impoverished few who were left there.

Today's lesson tells of the day when the Lord first "drafted" Jeremiah and called him to the challenging ministry of a prophet.

I. Commission
(Jeremiah 1:4-8)

Jeremiah was a priest of God (Jeremiah 1:1) as well as a prophet. His home was in Anathoth (Jeremiah 29:27), a city of the Levites (Joshua 21:18) only a few miles from Jerusalem.

A. The Lord's Prophet (vv. 4, 5)

4. Then the word of the LORD came unto me, saying.

How did *the word* come? Was there an audible voice heard by Jeremiah's ears, or a silent message to his mind? We are not told, but Jeremiah knew who was speaking. It was *the Lord*, Jehovah, and Jeremiah understood the message clearly.

5. Before I formed thee in the belly I knew thee; and before thou camest forth out of the womb I sanctified thee, and I ordained thee a prophet unto the nations.

The day when the Lord spoke to Jeremiah was not the day when the Lord chose him to be a prophet. That choice was made much earlier. Before he was born, the Lord *sanctified* him or "set him apart" for a special service. Before he was born, the Lord *ordained* him *a prophet unto the nations*. The verbs *formed* and *knew* both describe the intimacy of God's design for Jeremiah. The Lord prepared Jeremiah well in advance for the work he was to do. How blessed is any person who finds and does just what he is designed to do!

B. The Prophet's Objection (v. 6)

6. Then said I, Ah, Lord GOD! behold, I cannot speak: for I am a child.

Immediately Jeremiah protested that he was not adequate for the task. The Hebrew word translated *child* in our text may be compared with our word *youngster*. It can be used of a baby, a child of any age, or a young adult. We do not know how old Jeremiah really was at this time, but he was asked to accept an awesome responsibility. Who would not feel inadequate to be a prophet, a spokesman for the Almighty? Perhaps Jeremiah thought a prophet ought to be an older man, a man with more experience, wisdom, and influence.

C. The Lord's Insistence (vv. 7, 8)

7. But the LORD said unto me, Say not, I am a child: for thou shalt go to all that I shall send thee, and whatsoever I command thee thou shalt speak.

The Lord overruled the prophet's objection and rejected his excuse. Regardless of his youth, the Lord was giving him a job to do. He must do it. Jeremiah's responsibility was to go where the Lord would send him and say what the Lord would tell him to say. Even a child can obey orders.

8. Be not afraid of their faces: for I am with thee to deliver thee, saith the LORD.

Faces would confront Jeremiah: hostile, angry, frowning faces. Politicians would oppose him; priests of Baal would condemn him; false prophets would call him a liar. Behind those faces would be the power of government, the energy of false religion, and the fury of frustrated men. But the Lord would be with Jeremiah and *deliver* him. Centuries later, the apostle John offered a similar assurance to Christians: "Greater is he that is in you, than he that is in the world" (1 John 4:4).

II. Inspiration
(Jeremiah 1:9, 10)

Jeremiah soon had convincing proof that God was with him. First, he felt God's touch on his lips, which placed God's words in his mouth. Isaiah was called of God by a similar experience (Isaiah 6:6, 7). Second, God's power accompanied His words. When Jeremiah said something would happen, it did. This proof of God's presence took somewhat longer, but it was still very convincing.

A. The Lord's Words (v. 9)

9. Then the LORD put forth his hand, and touched my mouth. And the LORD said unto me, Behold, I have put my words in thy mouth.

Did Jeremiah see the Lord's hand? We are not told, and it does not matter. He felt the touch, and he knew what it meant. Jeremiah was inspired like the other prophets and like the apostles of later times. When they were called into court and accused of civil disobedience, they did not have to hire a team of lawyers and plan their defense. In that way the prophets and apostles had an advantage that we do not have as we teach God's Word today. We need to search the Scriptures diligently and deeply. Whether we preach in a pulpit, teach in Sunday school, or talk with a neighbor in the backyard, we need to plan what to say. But we have the inspired Bible to guide us. If we follow it well, our teaching will be true and fruitful.

B. The Lord's Power (v. 10)

10. See, I have this day set thee over the nations and over the kingdoms, to root out, and to pull down, and to destroy, and to throw down, to build, and to plant.

Thus the prophet's task was made even more awesome. He would dominate kingdoms and bring whole nations to destruction—not with bow, sword, or battering ram, but with the Lord's word in his mouth. He announced seventy years of subjugation to Babylon (Jeremiah 25:8-11), and it came to pass. He declared God's wrath upon the nations surrounding Judah (Jeremiah 25:15-29), and they fell under His judgment. He proclaimed the burning of Jerusalem and the capture of the king (Jeremiah 34:2, 3), and these events occurred.

But Jeremiah's mission was not all destructive. He was empowered also *to build, and to plant*. He promised a return from captivity (Jeremiah 30:3), and Judah returned. Looking far into the future, Jeremiah foretold a New Covenant and the forgiveness of sins (Jeremiah 31:31-34). Today Christians rejoice that they are forgiven; they are the people of that New Covenant.

A HIDDEN POWER

In 1856 an Algerian tribe known as the Marabouts (*Mar*-uh-boo) rebelled against their French colonial masters. This tribe practiced religious magic, so Napoleon III sent Robert-Houdin (Roe-*bear* Hoo-*dean*), a French magician, to change their mind.

The magician's most impressive trick was the "Light and Heavy Chest." He told the Marabouts, "A baby can pick up this chest, but at my command, even your strongest man cannot do so." He allowed one of their strongest men to pick up the box and then told him, "Now you are weaker than a woman." At that, the man was unable to lift the box from the floor.

The Marabouts were convinced of French strength and gave up their rebellion. What they did not know was that Robert-Houdin's box had a steel plate in the bottom, while the stage floor had an electromagnet under it that was con-

trolled by the magician. In those days, electricity was still so new that this unseen power seemed magical.

When Jeremiah received God's call to prophesy, he tried to use his youthfulness as an excuse for not accepting God's assignment. However, he was thinking of his own strength, not of the hidden power of God. He did not understand that God's strength could be his if he accepted the prophetic mission. A hidden power is available to us all, greater than we can ever use to its fullest extent. It works for us only if we trust in God as Jeremiah was called to do.   —C. R. B.

III. Danger
(Jeremiah 1:14-17)

The Lord exceeds all experts in the use of visual aids. He needs no blackboard, projector, or object held in His hand. He has a way of showing visual aids, called visions. One of these is mentioned in Jeremiah 1:13. Jeremiah saw a *seething* or boiling pot. He observed that *the face thereof is toward the north.* The Hebrew text reads, "and its face away from the north." Thus, the pot's "face" (opening) was actually toward the south, or, as we say in English, "facing" south. The *New International Version* reads, "tilting away from the north." This boiling pot was thus tilted toward Jerusalem and Judah, indicating that it was ready to pour out a flood of boiling water over the whole country. The meaning of this extraordinary visual aid is explained in the last part of our text.

A. Attack (vv. 14, 15)

14. Then the LORD said unto me, Out of the north an evil shall break forth upon all the inhabitants of the land.

The visionary threat of boiling water symbolized a real evil of a different kind that would come to Judah from *the north*.

15a. For, lo, I will call all the families of the kingdoms of the north, saith the LORD; and they shall come.

Elsewhere Babylon is pictured as the great enemy that would destroy Judah (Jeremiah 20:4-6; 34:2, 3), an event which Jeremiah witnessed (Jeremiah 38:28). Babylon was actually east of Judah rather than north, but the Babylonian army would not come from the east because it could not cross the wide and waterless desert east of Judah. It would go up the Euphrates River and down through Syria to attack Judah from the north. Jeremiah 25:8, 9 also indicates that those *families* would come with Nebuchadnezzar. The Babylonians would not come alone, for Babylon eventually ruled many of the

visual 3

Before I formed you in the womb I knew you, before you were born I set you apart; I appointed you as a prophet to the nations.

(Jeremiah 1:5, NIV)

nations that formerly were ruled by Assyria. Troops from those nations would vastly increase the Babylonian army, so that Judah would be attacked by *all the families of the kingdoms of the north*.

15b. And they shall set every one his throne at the entering of the gates of Jerusalem, and against all the walls thereof round about, and against all the cities of Judah.

The *throne* is the symbol of power. The invaders would establish their rule at the very *gates of Jerusalem*. The *walls* were so strong that the city could not be taken by storm, but the troops would surround it on every side so no one could leave without being captured or killed, and no one could bring in food. In time, starvation would force surrender. The invading troops would also move against the other *cities of Judah*.

B. Judgment (v. 16)

16. And I will utter my judgments against them touching all their wickedness, who have forsaken me, and have burned incense unto other gods, and worshipped the works of their own hands.

The destruction of Judah would not be merely the work of the Babylonians and other invaders who would come with them. All of these would be executing God's *judgments* on the people of Judah. The Babylonians did not believe in the Lord and did not intend to serve Him; nevertheless, He would use them for His purpose.

TRASHING THE LANDSCAPE

America is not the clean place it once was. In a recent two-year period, highway cleanup crews collected enough trash from California freeways to cover a football field with nearly sixty feet of rubbish. In the same period they hauled away 120,000 items ranging in size from suitcases to old sofas.

Just one day's collection of debris included a bicycle, a collection of Elvis tapes, magazines, newspapers, various personal hygiene items, a multitude of pieces of clothing, nearly a dozen species of dead animals, discarded diapers, various kinds and amounts of money, political campaign ads, and a lost history report on Theodore Roosevelt. (Imagine the student's excuse: "The freeway ate my homework.")

In the prophet Jeremiah's time, Judah had polluted its spiritual landscape with idolatry. The people worshiped other gods and bowed before idols they had made with their own hands. Being surrounded by trash gradually deadens our ability to abhor ugliness in our environment. Judah found the same to be true with its spiritual environment. The kingdom had come to the point where the pollution of idols was readily tolerated.

It is important for us all—especially we who claim to know God—to keep alive our ability to be shocked by the evil that surrounds us. Failure to do so will result in the same consequence that Judah suffered: the destruction of our culture and nation.   —C. R. B.

C. Warning (v. 17)

17. Thou therefore gird up thy loins, and arise, and speak unto them all that I command thee: be not dismayed at their faces, lest I confound thee before them.

Gird up thy loins. The usual outer garment was an ankle-length robe of woolen fabric. It was warm and comfortable for resting in an unheated house; but for active work, running, or even rapid walking, the wearer would gather up the robe so the hem was above the knees. He would secure the surplus length at his waist with a girdle or belt. Jeremiah may have done this literally when he went out to deliver God's message, but the phrase came to mean simply "get ready for action." The Lord wanted Jeremiah to strengthen his courage and determination and to get ready mentally for the rigors of giving an unpopular message. The prophet must tell the people and the rulers exactly what God said to tell them. They and their rulers would not be happy to hear that they were vile sinners about to be punished by invaders from the north. They would say that Jeremiah was not patriotic, that he was pessimistic, and that he was on the side of the enemy. They would confront him with scowling faces, threatening him with violence, prison, and even death. He must not become frightened. If he would cave in before hostile faces and refuse to give the message that God gave to him, then he would prove to be a faithless prophet. To such a one, the Lord would be even more frightening than the people would be.

Verses 18 and 19 tell why Jeremiah had no reason to be afraid. God himself would defend him. God would keep him secure through all the attacks of hostile rulers and people.

Conclusion

Thanks to king Josiah's leadership, Judah returned to God's ways and prospered. After Josiah's death, the nation plunged into evil. Jeremiah's life was often in danger during this period, because he spoke for God.

A. Taking the Plunge

Gleaned from newspapers, here are a few indications of a similar decline in our country.

To impress older members of his gang, a twelve-year-old boy opened fire on boys of another gang. He missed them, but killed an eleven-year-old girl who just happened to be passing by. This is one of a swiftly growing number of murders by youths.

In spite of earnest efforts to teach "safe sex," the number of unwanted pregnancies is growing among schoolgirls.

Officers in a major city captured the largest amount of heroin ever seized in a single shipment. They think addicts are returning to heroin after years of favoring cocaine.

In 1994, the Congress passed a highly advertised anti-crime bill, promising billions of dollars for more police and bigger jails. Has crime been conquered?

The 1994 baseball strike brought financial loss to thousands and generated bitterness that is still present. Some think the strike was caused by the owners' greed, while others think it was caused by the players' greed. Most everyone agrees that greed was the primary factor.

You can add to the list of signs indicating that we are "taking the plunge."

B. Targets for Truth's Sake

Because he repeated God's words, Jeremiah became the target of corrupt politicians, depraved priests, and lying prophets. With increasing frequency, conservative Christians are now being branded as ignorant and intolerant bigots, trying to cram their outmoded standards down everyone's throats.

Has anyone noticed how successfully the atheistic evolutionists are cramming their suspect doctrine down the throats of schoolchildren? Who is wailing because militant homosexuals are trying to make all of us accept their lifestyle as normal? Aren't both Republicans and Democrats trying to make all of us accept their policies?

With these and so many other pressure groups striving earnestly for what they think is right, why are earnest Christians singled out for abusive censure? Jesus knew it would be so, but He did not advise His people to stop their efforts. He said, "Blessed are ye, when men shall revile you, and persecute you, and shall say all manner of evil against you falsely, for my sake. Rejoice, and be exceeding glad: for great is your reward in heaven: for so persecuted they the prophets which were before you" (Matthew 5:11, 12). Jeremiah was one of those prophets, and he kept on saying what God told him to say. We too must keep on teaching the Word of God and doing it with joy.

C. Why?

Why was Jeremiah sent to offer God's truth to people who would not accept it? Why are we sent to offer the gospel of salvation to a world where people throng the way that leads to destruction (Matthew 7:13, 14)? So why do we spend time, energy, and money in an effort to avoid what is unavoidable?

The answer is that God is "not willing that any should perish, but that all should come to repentance" (2 Peter 3:9). If we faithfully show the narrow way that leads to life, some precious souls will choose it—and there will be rejoicing in Heaven.

D. Prayer

Almighty God, eternal King, thank You for the truth. Thank You for the honor and privilege and joy of sharing it with others. May we have both wisdom and will to share it well. Amen.

E. Thought to Remember

"Preach the word" (2 Timothy 4:2).

Home Daily Bible Readings

Monday, Sept. 9—God Creates All People (Psalm 139:13-18)
Tuesday, Sept. 10—Israel Forsakes God (Jeremiah 2:4-13)
Wednesday, Sept. 11—God Promises Jeremiah Strength (Jeremiah 1:18—2:3)
Thursday, Sept. 12—Response of an Obedient Servant (Isaiah 50:4-9)
Friday, Sept. 13—Jeremiah Encouraged to Persevere (Jeremiah 15:15-21)
Saturday, Sept. 14—Jeremiah Is Persecuted (Jeremiah 20:7-12)
Sunday, Sept. 15—Jeremiah Laments His Birth (Jeremiah 20:13-18)

Learning by Doing

This page contains an alternate lesson plan emphasizing learning activities.
Classes desiring such student involvement will find these suggestions helpful.

Learning Goals

Students in today's class should:

1. List the emotions Jeremiah felt as God called him.

2. Compare Jeremiah's call with their own perception of God's will for their lives today.

3. Decide what they should do to obey God personally now.

Into the Lesson

Ask the following two questions:

Have you ever felt God was calling you to do something specific?

If you were God, what would you call someone to do for you in this troubled world?

To begin today's session, read the two questions to class members, and ask them, in groups of two or three, to choose one to discuss.

After five minutes, allow a few to share with the entire class. Then tell class members, "Today's lesson looks at how God called one of His prophets to do a difficult task for Him. We'll discuss how the prophet felt and how we may feel when God calls us to do something difficult for Him."

Into the Word

Use material from the Lesson Background (p. 26) to introduce your class members to Jeremiah. Be sure to connect this lesson with the reign of Josiah, which you studied in last week's lesson. Then use one or all three of the following activities to lead your group in Bible study:

List the emotions. Ask class members to write the numbers four through nineteen down one side of a piece of paper. As you or a class member reads Jeremiah 1:4-19, students are to write beside the numbers a word or two to describe Jeremiah's feelings in that verse. Then ask them to share their list of emotions in the same groups of two or three that discussed the first assignment.

Discuss Jeremiah's feelings. Discuss the following questions with the class, or duplicate and distribute them so that the students, in groups of two or three, can discuss them. All of them relate to Jeremiah 1:4-19.

1. When did Jeremiah feel afraid? Why?

2. When might he have felt sad? Why?

3. What about God's assignment to Jeremiah might have been appealing to him?

4. What about God's assignment might have made Jeremiah want to run away?

Scripture matching. Ask a student to read verse 10 aloud again. As you make a list on the chalkboard, class members should name all the tasks for Jeremiah mentioned in this verse.

Next, post a list of the following references from Jeremiah (or point class members to the student book, where they are printed). Again in their groups of two or three, class members should match each of the following references to one of the tasks from your chalkboard list: 25:8-11; 25:17-26; 34:2, 3; 30:3; 33:10, 11; 31:31-34.

Into Life

If your class is large, before class make a handout on which the following sentences are written. If your class is smaller, write each sentence on a slip of paper, so that you have enough slips for each group of two or three students to have one. You will use these sentences to lead class members in thinking about the implications of today's study for their own lives.

The person who speaks for God is often opposed by others.

We must listen to God more than people when we are seeking God's will.

We must trust God's Word more than our feelings when we are choosing how to serve Him.

If you distributed a handout, let class members choose which sentence they want to discuss. Ask them to decide, in the same groups of two or three: (1) how Jeremiah's life illustrates that truth, and (2) how they have seen that truth in action today. Give the small groups at least five minutes, then discuss answers with the entire class.

Next, ask your class the following questions. If you have time, you may discuss them. If you prefer, use them as a prayer guide. Students can pray silently as you read each one:

1. Do you feel God may be calling you to do something that frightens you? How does the experience of Jeremiah affect the answer you will give Him?

2. Are you facing opposition because of a stand you are taking for God? How do you feel about this? How could Jeremiah's experience change the way you feel?

3. Have you turned your back on an assignment from God that you ought to reconsider?

Let's Talk It Over

The questions on this page are designed to encourage review of the lesson Scriptures and to promote discussion of the lesson by the class. The answers provided are only discussion starters. Let your class talk it over from there.

1. God had designed Jeremiah before his birth to be a prophet. Why would it be helpful for us to ponder what God has designed us to be?

This question need not lead us into a discussion of predestination. We are free to choose whether or not we will fit into God's design or one of our own making. Every Christian should examine what he or she is designed to do. The possession of a strong voice and the ability to speak clearly and forcefully may demonstrate God's design for a preacher. A skill at expressing oneself well in prose or poetry may indicate His design for a Christian writer. Looking for God's design in us is the same thing as taking inventory of our gifts and talents. However we put it, it is important to do this, so that we may serve where God wants us to serve in His kingdom.

2. Jeremiah tried to excuse himself from God's call to service on the basis of his youthfulness. What kinds of similar excuses do Christians make when offered a challenge to serve?

Many churches suffer because men and women with years of experience in the Lord's work decide to retire from active service. Even if their physical strength has diminished and their mental prowess is not what it once was, there is surely some valuable work they can still perform. Other excuses that we hear are "I'm not educated enough" or "I'm too busy." Had Jeremiah offered any of these, the Lord would have promptly made clear that He did not accept it. He surely does not accept excuses in the church, but expects His people to serve willingly and zealously.

3. God told Jeremiah, "Gird up thy loins." This was an expression that meant, "Get ready for action." How is this an appropriate exhortation for us?

We find a similar exhortation in 1 Peter 1:13: "Wherefore gird up the loins of your mind." Are our minds ready for action? Too many Christians have their minds cluttered with worldly pursuits. To use another related New Testament verse, some are unable to "run with patience the race that is set before us" because of "the sin which doth so easily beset us"

(Hebrews 12:1). In order to be ready for action, we must focus our minds on the Word of God and let every other communication be secondary. We must commit ourselves to holiness and allow no sin to entangle us. We must dedicate ourselves to serving God and give that service the priority it deserves.

4. The lesson writer handles well the frequent complaint that Christians are always trying to force their religious views on others. How do we respond to such a complaint?

First of all, it is clear that a Christian who takes the New Testament seriously would never try to force others to adopt his or her religious views. The New Testament demonstrates that accepting Christ as Savior and Lord is a personal decision: "Whosoever will, let him take the water of life freely" (Revelation 22:17). Second, we need not apologize for trying to influence others to become Christians. Our society features all kinds of political and educational institutions laboring to influence people's thinking. We have as much right as they to speak out about our convictions. Third, like Peter and John, "We cannot but speak the things which we have seen and heard" (Acts 4:20).

5. Sinful and rebellious as the people of Jeremiah's time were, God pitied them enough to send His prophet to them. How can we view today's world with similar pity?

We remember Paul's experience in Athens. Acts 17:16 tells us that "his spirit was stirred in him, when he saw the city wholly given to idolatry." Today people still have their idols, and it is pitiful to see them focusing their lives around money and material things that will eventually fade away. Another aspect of modern life that should stir us to pity is the almost desperate effort by some to fill their lives with pleasure and thereby escape facing the weighty questions of death and eternity. And how sad we should feel for those who turn to alcohol and drugs in a vain attempt to cope with the pressures and stresses they encounter! We have good news for all these people. Not only should we pity them in their suffering, but we must also share with them the Christ who offers solid, eternal solutions to life's dilemmas.

Proclaiming God's Word

DEVOTIONAL READING: Micah 6:1-8.

LESSON SCRIPTURE: Jeremiah 7.

PRINTED TEXT: Jeremiah 7:1-15.

Jeremiah 7:1-15

1 The word that came to Jeremiah from the LORD, saying,

2 Stand in the gate of the LORD's house, and proclaim there this word, and say, Hear the word of the LORD, all ye of Judah, that enter in at these gates to worship the LORD.

3 Thus saith the LORD of hosts, the God of Israel, Amend your ways and your doings, and I will cause you to dwell in this place.

4 Trust ye not in lying words, saying, The temple of the LORD, The temple of the LORD, The temple of the LORD, are these.

5 For if ye thoroughly amend your ways and your doings; if ye thoroughly execute judgment between a man and his neighbor;

6 If ye oppress not the stranger, the fatherless, and the widow, and shed not innocent blood in this place, neither walk after other gods to your hurt;

7 Then will I cause you to dwell in this place, in the land that I gave to your fathers, for ever and ever.

8 Behold, ye trust in lying words, that cannot profit.

9 Will ye steal, murder, and commit adultery, and swear falsely, and burn incense unto Baal, and walk after other gods whom ye know not;

10 And come and stand before me in this house, which is called by my name, and say, We are delivered to do all these abominations?

11 Is this house, which is called by my name, become a den of robbers in your eyes? Behold, even I have seen it, saith the LORD.

12 But go ye now unto my place which was in Shiloh, where I set my name at the first, and see what I did to it for the wickedness of my people Israel.

13 And now, because ye have done all these works, saith the LORD, and I spake unto you, rising up early and speaking, but ye heard not; and I called you, but ye answered not;

14 Therefore will I do unto this house, which is called by my name, wherein ye trust, and unto the place which I gave to you and to your fathers, as I have done to Shiloh.

15 And I will cast you out of my sight, as I have cast out all your brethren, even the whole seed of Ephraim.

GOLDEN TEXT: Thus saith the LORD of hosts, the God of Israel, Amend your ways and your doings, and I will cause you to dwell in this place.—Jeremiah 7:3.

Lesson Aims

After this lesson a student should be able to:

1. Summarize God's message that Jeremiah was to present at the gate of the temple.

2. Evaluate the changing morality in our country. Is it becoming better or worse?

3. Mention one step that can be taken by himself, the class, or the congregation to help someone obey God better.

Lesson Outline

INTRODUCTION
    A. Learning From the Past
    B. Lesson Background
  I. KEEP YOUR COUNTRY (Jeremiah 7:1-7)
    A. A Place to Preach (vv. 1, 2)
    B. A Call to Amend (v. 3)
    C. False Security (v. 4)
    D. How to Amend (vv. 5, 6)
    E. Real Security (v. 7)
      A Just Society
 II. STOP YOUR SINNING (Jeremiah 7:8-11)
    A. Sins (vv. 8, 9)
    B. Hypocrisy (vv. 10, 11)
      Living With a Lie
III. LOOK AT HISTORY (Jeremiah 7:12-15)
    A. Past Punishment (v. 12)
    B. Present Guilt (v. 13)
    C. Future Disaster (vv. 14, 15)
CONCLUSION
    A. Look at the Past
    B. Look at the Present
    C. Look at the Future
    D. Prayer
    E. Thought to Remember

The visual for lesson 4 of the visuals packet cites examples of God's never-changing call to repentance. The visual is shown on page 37.

Introduction

A. Learning From the Past

In our elementary school, the first warm days of spring brought an epidemic of truancy. It happened every year. The school board and the principal made a rule mandating a whipping for any student who played hooky, but the annual epidemic still went unchecked. Playing hooky brought a boy a certain prestige among his peers, and rugged lads were willing to take a whipping for that.

Then one spring a new truant officer took over. The first time two students failed to appear after lunch, he went in search of them. Wise to the ways of boys, he found them quickly and brought them back to their punishment. Only half an hour later they appeared in class, subdued and humiliated, with tears on their faces. There was no epidemic that year.

People do learn from past events—teachers as well as students. Many of us remember a time when teachers' pay was notoriously low and strikes became popular. In one town a strike resulted in significant raises, and there were three more strikes in the next five years. In another town, the school board fired the strikers and opened the schools within a week with other teachers. There was never even a threat of a strike after that.

B. Lesson Background

Judah was in trouble because its people had failed to learn from their past. For nearly eight hundred years, they had prospered when they had lived by God's Law, and had suffered when disobedience was widespread. The text of our lesson is not dated, but perhaps it belongs to the time after good king Josiah died. At that time Judah was plunging into idolatry and sin.

The first six chapters of Jeremiah expose the sins of Judah; they tell of certain punishment for stubborn sinners; they plead with the people to repent; they promise blessing for obedience. Our text from chapter 7 presents a summary of all these points.

I. Keep Your Country (Jeremiah 7:1-7)

The promised land was God's gift to Israel, along with peace and prosperity as long as the people remained obedient to Him (Deuteronomy 28:1-6, 11, 12). Equally plain was the promise that Israel would lose that land if it did not obey the Lord (Deuteronomy 28:63). We are looking at a time when the northern kingdom had already lost its part of the promised land (2 Kings 17:1-18). The southern tribe of Judah had survived that disaster, because king Hezekiah had led the nation back to the Lord (2 Kings 18:1-8). Hezekiah's great-grandson Josiah likewise had promoted godly ways (2 Kings 22:1, 2). But now we seem to be looking at a time when Josiah was dead; his sons who succeeded him as king were all evil. Judah was on the brink of losing its part of the promised land, but there was still time to avert that loss. Jeremiah pleaded with the people, urging them to do what was necessary to keep their country.

A. A Place to Preach (vv. 1, 2)

1. The word that came to Jeremiah from the LORD, saying.

This book begins, "The words of Jeremiah" (Jeremiah 1:1), but Jeremiah frequently reminds us that he was not the source. He was writing the words that the Lord gave him. The prophet Jeremiah had access to the very counsel of God Himself, in contrast to the false prophets (Jeremiah 23:14-22).

2. Stand in the gate of the LORD's house, and proclaim there this word, and say, Hear the word of the LORD, all ye of Judah, that enter in at these gates to worship the LORD.

The Lord's house was the temple in Jerusalem. Idols and their altars had been set there in the time of King Manasseh (2 Kings 21:4-7), but King Josiah had removed them (2 Kings 23:4-7). Jeremiah was not sent to a temple of Baal or to a gathering of pagans; he was sent to give *the word of the Lord* to members of the chosen people who came into the temple (*the Lord's house*) to *worship the Lord.*

B. A Call to Amend (v. 3)

3. Thus saith the LORD of hosts, the God of Israel, Amend your ways and your doings, and I will cause you to dwell in this place.

To *amend* is to improve, to make better. The Lord did not ask these people merely to improve their worship. He wanted them to improve their *ways* and their *doings,* meaning their whole way of life. That was what it would take to keep their home *in this place,* which could refer to the temple, the city of Jerusalem, or even to the promised land itself. Otherwise they would lose their home; they would die or be deported.

C. False Security (v. 4)

4. Trust ye not in lying words, saying, The temple of the LORD, The temple of the LORD, The temple of the LORD, are these.

The temple of the Lord. The people of Judah kept saying that over and over. Perhaps the repetition contained a symbolic or even magical significance for them. It was their answer to every warning of coming disaster. This temple was God's own holy house; He would not let any disaster come to it. People who worshiped there would be safe, regardless of what they did elsewhere. But these were *lying words,* for the temple of the Lord would not provide safety for those who did not live as God's people.

D. How to Amend (vv. 5, 6)

5. For if ye thoroughly amend your ways and your doings; if ye thoroughly execute judgment between a man and his neighbor.

Now the Lord began to describe the kind of improvements He was requiring. He wanted the people to *thoroughly amend:* no halfway reform would do. The first area to be improved was *judgment,* which here means right judgment or true justice. The courts of Judah were so corrupt that Jeremiah was invited to search Jerusalem and see if he could find anyone dispensing justice (Jeremiah 5:1).

6. If ye oppress not the stranger, the fatherless, and the widow, and shed not innocent blood in this place, neither walk after other gods to your hurt.

A *stranger* or foreigner in Judah had no friends, no influence, and not much knowledge of local customs. He was easy prey for a crooked merchant, employer, tax collector, or moneylender. Orphans and widows were easily victimized because they had no strong man to protect them, no standing with the rulers, and no money to bribe the judges. The Lord wanted fair treatment for all these people who could not secure it for themselves.

Worse than a bit of cheating in business was the shedding of *innocent blood.* A man who had done no wrong might be accused of a terrible crime, convicted by hired perjurers, sentenced by bribed judges, and put to death. Then a creditor could seize his property to pay a debt worth only a fraction of the property's value. This was easy to arrange when the judges were for sale.

The Lord wanted changes that would put a permanent end to all of these evils.

E. Real Security (v. 7)

7. Then will I cause you to dwell in this place, in the land that I gave to your fathers, for ever and ever.

To live *for ever and ever* in the promised land did not mean the people would never grow old and die. It meant they would be safe from invaders who might want to slaughter them or make them slaves. They and their descendants could live securely in the promised land as long as they obeyed the Lord.

A JUST SOCIETY

The Oneida (Owe-*nye*-duh) Community of Christian Perfectionists was one of more than three dozen such communities in nineteenth-century America. A goal shared by most of these utopian communes was the establishment of social justice.

John Humphrey Noyes, who founded the Oneida Community, believed in sharing *everything*. Even children were shared—raised by the commune so their mothers would not love them "idolatrously." Monogamy was forbidden, and a "breeding committee" oversaw sexual relationships in a system of what was called "complex marriage."

Noyes was half a century ahead of the rise of Marxist communism in the Soviet Union. His Oneida Community lasted only thirty years compared to Soviet communism's seventy years, but the two systems were similar in one important respect: both were schemes by which a limited view of social "justice" was imposed on the majority by a tiny minority.

Jeremiah shows us a very different view of the ideal society: a community where true justice reigns is one in which people do good to one and all, because each person is living in covenant relationship with God.

No matter how many utopias are proposed by social visionaries, a truly just society will come only when we live justly in relationship with God. Divine love is both the example and the spirit that empowers us to seek such justice.

—C. R. B.

II. Stop Your Sinning
(Jeremiah 7:8-11)

The security offered in verse 7 could not be realized without the changes demanded in verses 3-6. The Lord proceeded to describe the sins that must be stopped and which would certainly bring destruction if they continued.

A. Sins (vv. 8, 9)

8. Behold, ye trust in lying words, that cannot profit.

Already we have seen one example of *lying words:* the assurance that worshipers in the Lord's temple would be safe regardless of what else they did (v. 4). False prophets specialized in such deceit (Jeremiah 23:25-27).

Of course there were other examples. Every promise of benefit from a false god was a lie. Every promise of allegiance to the Lord was a lie unless it was accompanied by actual obedience. Such lies may fool many listeners and even the liars themselves; they cannot fool God.

9. Will ye steal, murder, and commit adultery, and swear falsely, and burn incense unto Baal, and walk after other gods whom ye know not?

We can see in this cataloging of the people's sins a reflection of those areas of conduct covered in the Ten Commandments. It seems hard to be-

lieve that such repulsive sins were common among those who claimed to be God's people and who worshiped Him in His temple. Yet, even with the advantages we have now (such as the completed Scripture), sometimes a Christian shocks us by falling into gross sin. In all times and places, "Every man is tempted, when he is drawn away of his own lust, and enticed" (James 1:14).

B. Hypocrisy (vv. 10, 11)

10. And come and stand before me in this house, which is called by my name, and say, We are delivered to do all these abominations?

This is the rest of the question that began in verse 9. Can anyone be misled enough to think he is free to indulge in the sins named there, even while he goes through the motions of worshiping in the Lord's temple? Can such a sinner really think his empty words of worship without obedience will cause God to deliver him from enemies that may attack from without or from economic disaster at home? Will God rescue him from every evil so he can go on doing evil? There is no safety for willful sinners!

11. Is this house, which is called by my name, become a den of robbers in your eyes? Behold, even I have seen it, saith the LORD.

Did the men of Judah think the temple was a bandits' hideout? Did they think they could commit such sins as are described in verse 9 and then escape punishment by taking refuge in the temple and pretending to worship the God they disobeyed? No! This temple was the house of God, the holy God, the just God. Yes, He is merciful and gracious, but He will not acquit the guilty (Exodus 34:6, 7). Sinners who repent can find forgiveness with Him, but not those who continue stubbornly in their sins.

LIVING WITH A LIE

In 1894, French army Captain Alfred Dreyfus was convicted of spying. A cleaning woman hired by the French secret service to work in the German embassy had found some classified French military papers on a desk there. Captain Dreyfus was accused of providing the Germans with these papers. Army officials knew their case against Dreyfus was weak, so they created false evidence to convict him. History has proved that he was convicted because of prejudice: he was Jewish and came from the German-speaking district of Alsace in France. Twelve years after Dreyfus began his life sentence on Devil's Island he was exonerated, and his rank was restored.

Even though a major in the army was later found to have committed the crime, the Dreyfus affair is still argued in France a century later. Sometimes a lie takes on a life of its own.

For years the people of Judah persisted in living a lie. While claiming to follow God and going through the motions of temple worship, they were liars, thieves, murderers, adulterers and idol worshipers.

Like Jeremiah's ancient audience and Captain Dreyfus's accusers, we may fool ourselves into thinking we can get away with living a lie. Perhaps, for a while, we can. But eventually the truth will find its way to the surface of the moral swamp we have created for ourselves.

—C. R. B.

III. Look at History (Jeremiah 7:12-15)

The sinners of Judah could have found ample evidence from their past that God had protected His people when they respected His Law, but there was nothing to support the silly notion that they could find protection in His temple when they were disobedient.

A. Past Punishment (v. 12)

12. But go ye now unto my place which was in Shiloh, where I set my name at the first, and see what I did to it for the wickedness of my people Israel.

When the people of Israel divided the promised land among their tribes, *Shiloh* was the central place of worship. There they set up the tabernacle (Joshua 18:1), which remained there until the Israelites removed the ark of the covenant during a battle with the Philistines (1 Samuel 4:3, 4).

The actual destruction of Shiloh is not recorded for us, but from this text it is evident that it had been destroyed, probably by one of the many invaders of the land of Israel. Jeremiah was speaking some time later, but still his hearers could go to Shiloh and see with their own eyes what God had done to that earlier place of worship. From that, they should have known that He would also destroy the place of worship in Jerusalem, if the people who pretended to worship there became too wicked to be tolerated. Holy places can never substitute for a holy people.

B. Present Guilt (v. 13)

13. And now, because ye have done all these works, saith the LORD, and I spake unto you, rising up early and speaking, but ye heard not; and I called you, but ye answered not.

The people of Judah had done *all these works* —the wicked works named in verse 9. They could not say they had no way of knowing those acts were wrong. God had given the Law long

visual 4

before, and later He had spoken through Jeremiah and other prophets. *Rising up early and speaking* means speaking urgently and insistently. The people, however, preferred their sins and closed their ears and minds to what the prophets were saying.

C. Future Disaster (vv. 14, 15)

14. Therefore will I do unto this house, which is called by my name, wherein ye trust, and unto the place which I gave to you and to your fathers, as I have done to Shiloh.

This house was the temple. It was called by the Lord's *name;* it was His house. The people of Judah put their *trust* in it; they said the Lord would take care of them because they worshiped there, in spite of their constant sinning.

The place included Jerusalem and the whole land of Judah. God had given it to the ancestors of the present residents, and He had promised that they and their descendants could keep it forever if they would obey Him. But now they were disobeying, in spite of the constant pleading of the prophets. Therefore the temple, the city, and the nation were to be destroyed as Shiloh had been. Later historians might say the Babylonians had conquered Judah, but they were merely a tool in the Lord's hand.

15. And I will cast you out of my sight, as I have cast out all your brethren, even the whole seed of Ephraim.

Ephraim became one of the more prominent tribes of northern Israel; thus, its name often designates that entire nation. It was also the territory where Shiloh was located. Before the time of Jeremiah, the Assyrians had defeated northern Israel and had settled many of its people in foreign lands (2 Kings 17:1-6). That should have sounded a clear warning to Judah. But Judah had disregarded the message, and was about to be *cast out* as well.

Conclusion

In urging the people of Judah to think of their past, the Lord cited two examples. He had destroyed the earlier place of worship at Shiloh because of the wickedness of His people (see Jeremiah 7:12), and He had destroyed the entire northern nation of Israel because of similar wickedness (v. 15).

Many other examples could have been given. When the people of Israel first approached the promised land, their faithless and fearful rebellion delayed their entrance and made them live as nomads in the desert for forty years (Numbers 13:1—14:35). Led by Joshua, the people then captured the land and settled there. But after Joshua and other faithful leaders died, the people forgot how the Lord had directed their past. Judges 2:6-19 describes a cycle that was repeated throughout the period of the judges. Wickedness brought punishments, poverty, and hardship; these brought repentance; repentance brought deliverance; and then the cycle would begin again.

The people thought a strong central government could stabilize the nation. They clamored for a king, but that did not solve the problem. David and Solomon brought the kingdom to the peak of its wealth and power; but Solomon in his later years reversed its progress, and his son split it in two. Northern Israel went down to destruction in approximately two hundred years, while southern Judah rotated between good and bad kings until its conquest by Babylon.

For nearly eight hundred years, obeying God had brought good results, and disobeying had brought bad results. How could anyone still choose to disobey?

A. Look at the Past

Schoolchildren used to learn much about the intrepid pilgrims who endured severe hardship in order to obey God as they thought they should. Their example is inspiring, but they were not the only emigrants who believed in obeying God. In Virginia some of the Anglicans doubted that Jesus was divine, but they believed in God and in the virtue of doing His will. Catholics in Maryland, Quakers in Pennsylvania, and Baptists in Rhode Island also believed in God and desired to obey Him.

When the British colonies in America declared their independence, they based their declaration on the fact that people are God's creatures, endowed by Him with "certain unalienable rights." They closed the Declaration of Independence "with a firm reliance on the protection of divine Providence." The nation grew and prospered.

B. Look at the Present

Today the fashion in recounting history seems to be to hide the influence of religion in building the nation. The fashion in education seems to be to twist the separation of church and state into an anti-God policy. In news media the trend seems to be to belittle or ridicule earnest Christians. In entertainment, the tendency is to see no difference between right and wrong. Some "comic" productions are characterized by almost constant bickering. Others abound in lies and deceit, and expert lying often is rewarded. Is that what we want our children to learn? With increasing frequency, promiscuous sex is presented as normal. Defenders of such entertainment claim that life is like that; in truth, life is becoming more like that, and popular entertainment is one of the reasons.

Almost any adult will agree that popular standards of morality have been lowered in his time. Evils once abhorred are now tolerated; evils once tolerated are now accepted.

C. Look at the Future

Why did God send Jeremiah to declare that His nation was to be destroyed and its people were to become captives in Babylon? Because that future could be changed! Jeremiah told how it could be changed. Simply by obeying God, Judah could outlive Babylon.

Let's be practical. Let's plan one step that we can take this week to help someone become a Christian, or to help someone obey the Lord better. Let's plan it, and let's do it.

D. Prayer

Father in Heaven, we can't change sinners into saints, but You can. Help us to represent You truly as we try to help people be born again and become Your children. Amen.

E. Thought to Remember

What we do today can change the future.

Home Daily Bible Readings

Monday, Sept. 16—People Refuse to Obey God (Jeremiah 7:16-26)

Tuesday, Sept. 17—People Will Not Listen to Jeremiah (Jeremiah 7:27-34)

Wednesday, Sept. 18—People Are Stubbornly Unrepentant (Jeremiah 8:8-17)

Thursday, Sept. 19—Jeremiah Mourns for the People (Jeremiah 8:18-22)

Friday, Sept. 20—True Wisdom Is in Knowing the Lord (Jeremiah 9:12-24)

Saturday, Sept. 21—People Called to Amend Their Ways (Jeremiah 18:1-11)

Sunday, Sept. 22—The Lord Is the True God (Jeremiah 10:1-10)

Learning by Doing

This page contains an alternate lesson plan emphasizing learning activities.
Classes desiring such student involvement will find these suggestions helpful.

Learning Goals

Today's lesson should lead students to:

1. List all the sins of Judah mentioned in Jeremiah 7:1-15.

2. Decide how those sins are present in our society today as well.

3. Ask God to help them remove those sins from our society.

Into the Lesson

To begin, use one of the following activities:

Newspaper search. Ask students, "How big a problem is sin in our society?" Tell them to search daily newspapers for an answer.

They should look at several articles or advertisements and decide of each, "Does this indicate in any way some sin in our society?" After several minutes, allow class members to share their findings.

Continuum. Draw the following diagram on your chalkboard:

•————————————•————————————•

Totally Sinful   Neutral   Pure

Ask students to duplicate the continuum on a sheet of scrap paper. Ask them to indicate on the line the place they think best characterizes society today. Where would they put a mark to describe the society their parents lived in? Where do they think the mark will go twenty or thirty years from now?

Tell students that today's Scripture study looks at a sinful society and what it could do to move itself to the right on this continuum.

Into the Word

Remind class members that this week's lesson is the second from Jeremiah and the fourth based on the experience of the nation of Judah after the northern kingdom of Israel had fallen to foreign invaders. Remind them that two weeks ago they looked at the reign of the good king Josiah, and that last week's text from Jeremiah was probably written during Josiah's reign. It seems that this week's text looks at a time after Josiah's death, when Judah had once again slipped deep into sin. Today's text shows the seriousness of the sin in the land.

Ask a volunteer to read Jeremiah 7:1-15, while students listen for clues about the sins of Judah. After the text has been read, ask class members

where on the continuum they would put a mark to describe Judah's sinfulness.

Next, ask class members to form groups of about five each. Each group should choose one of the following discussion/study activities:

List the sins. This group makes a list of all the sins plaguing the nation of Judah.

Write the headlines. This group thinks of several popular publications: perhaps your local newspaper, *USA Today, National Enquirer, Reader's Digest, Guideposts, Time,* or others. Suppose the publications they have chosen were published in Jeremiah's time. What would be some of the lead articles or stories in the publication, based on what this text tells us about Jeremiah's society? This group should write headlines or titles for those articles or stories.

Marked Bibles. Students should use photocopies of this text, or the student book. Give them colored pencils, pens, crayons, or markers. Each student should choose one color to represent the sins of the people, another color to represent the warnings of God, and a third color to indicate the promises of God. They should mark their text to show each of these categories.

After several minutes, the groups can share their "creations" and conclusions with each other. Make sure class members understand the vanity of the Jews' reliance on the safety of the temple (v. 4) and the nature of God's warning to them based on His action at Shiloh (vv. 12-15). (See the explanations in the lesson commentary.)

Into Life

If you have listed the sins of Judah, ask class members to decide which of these sins are also present in our society. Beside each sin on your list, students should write evidence or examples of how that sin is present today.

Ask class members to decide what warnings or conditions from God Jeremiah might give if he were speaking to your town or your congregation.

What specific actions could your class members take to move your town to the right on the continuum indicated during "Into the Lesson"? Write these actions on your chalkboard as class members suggest them.

This list will become your prayer request list for the closing activity of your session. Ask a different class member to pray about each of the actions class members have suggested.

Let's Talk It Over

The questions on this page are designed to encourage review of the lesson Scriptures and to promote discussion of the lesson by the class. The answers provided are only discussion starters. Let your class talk it over from there.

1. An often-repeated statement notes, "They who will not learn from the past are doomed to repeat it." What can we do to help ourselves and others to benefit from the mistakes people have made in the past?

Every Christian needs to be a student of history. If we think of all human history as "His story," we will see that God has provided us with an abundance of illustrations of Biblical principles. "Wine is a mocker, strong drink is raging: and whosoever is deceived thereby is not wise" (Proverbs 20:1). "Whatsoever a man soweth, that shall he also reap" (Galatians 6:7). "The love of money is the root of all evil" (1 Timothy 6:10). Old Testament history writers are consistent in showing the results of the foolish mistakes human beings make.

2. Jeremiah was told to stand in the gate of the Lord's house and proclaim His message publicly. How can we gain a public hearing for God's message of sin, righteousness, and judgment to come?

The distribution of tracts and other Christian literature is one way. We dare not let the cults outdo us in the distribution of literature. In addition, the editorial pages of our local newspaper offer us an opportunity to express our Bible-centered viewpoint. Also, as concerned citizens we can make use of opportunities to speak at public meetings and discreetly refer to Biblical principles.

3. The people of Judah took refuge in the phrase, "the temple of the Lord," as though the mere presence of God's temple in their midst would save them from disaster. Can you think of anything similar that people do today?

We may be tempted to think of our nation as a "Christian nation" and therefore conclude that God would never let such a nation be destroyed. However, the term "Christian nation" is hardly appropriate for a land in which Biblical morality is generally spurned. Would a Christian nation sanction abortion on demand? Could a country in which popular entertainment features increasing nudity, vulgarity, and violence be called a Christian nation? It is clear that no such designation would protect us from destruction if God chose to judge us for our sins.

4. What are some examples of "lying words" that people trust in today?

In one form or another we frequently hear the sentiment: "It doesn't matter what you believe so long as you're sincere." This is related to the idea that feelings rather than doctrines are the keys to effective religion. Some people carry this further and assert that, "All religions are merely different roads leading to the same place," apparently meaning Heaven. However, it is as true today as ever that our faith must rest in the never-changing facts of Scripture. God is our Creator, and has exercised His prerogative in giving us laws to heed. Sin is an offense against Him and must be judged. Jesus Christ alone is Savior, and we must trust Him absolutely and obey Him implicitly. There is a Heaven and a Hell, and there will be a day of judgment.

5. The motto, "In God We Trust," is largely forgotten in our society. What are some alternate mottoes that might better describe how people think today?

"In ourselves we trust" is a motto that fits well with the growing influence of humanism. The humanist asserts that man can depend on his own strength and wisdom and has no need for God. It is obvious that "In money we trust" is appropriate for great numbers of people. Contrary to what Jesus said in Luke 12:15, these people believe that life does consist in an abundance of money and possessions. "In education we trust" reflects the far-fetched idea that better education would solve our society's most desperate needs.

6. The lesson writer closes with this observation: "What we do today can change the future." What are some things we can do that could change our future?

This could be the week that we establish a regular practice of Bible study and prayer, if we have not previously done so. Perhaps in the next few days we can take steps to eliminate a bad habit or heal a broken friendship. The time also may be right for us to speak about Christ and His salvation to a neighbor or fellow worker. Any of these could make our future and the future of people around us significantly better. Small as they may be, these are also steps to making the world a better place.

Continuing to Trust

DEVOTIONAL READING: Psalm 31:1-10.

LESSON SCRIPTURE: Habakkuk.

PRINTED TEXT: Habakkuk 2:1-4; 3:17-19.

Habakkuk 2:1-4

1 I will stand upon my watch, and set me upon the tower, and will watch to see what he will say unto me, and what I shall answer when I am reproved.

2 And the LORD answered me, and said, Write the vision, and make it plain upon tables, that he may run that readeth it.

3 For the vision is yet for an appointed time, but at the end it shall speak, and not lie: though it tarry, wait for it; because it will surely come, it will not tarry.

4 Behold, his soul which is lifted up is not upright in him: but the just shall live by his faith.

Habakkuk 3:17-19

17 Although the fig tree shall not blossom, neither shall fruit be in the vines; the labor of the olive shall fail, and the fields shall yield no meat; the flock shall be cut off from the fold, and there shall be no herd in the stalls:

18 Yet I will rejoice in the LORD, I will joy in the God of my salvation.

19 The LORD God is my strength, and he will make my feet like hinds' feet, and he will make me to walk upon mine high places. To the chief singer on my stringed instruments.

GOLDEN TEXT: Although the fig tree shall not blossom, neither shall fruit be in the vines; . . . yet I will rejoice in the LORD, I will joy in the God of my salvation.
—Habakkuk 3:17, 18.

God's People Face Judgment
Unit 1: Responses to Wrong
(Lessons 1-5)

Lesson Aims

After participating in this lesson, a student should be able to:

1. Recall two questions of Habakkuk and the answers that came from the Lord.

2. Tell what made Habakkuk afraid and what assurance reduced his fear.

3. Mention some circumstances that disturb godly people now, and tell what assurance is given to the godly.

Lesson Outline

INTRODUCTION
  A. Habakkuk
  B. Lesson Background
 I. THE LORD'S MESSAGE (Habakkuk 2:1-4)
  A. Waiting for an Answer (v. 1)
  B. Make the Message Plain (v. 2)
  C. Wait for the Time (v. 3)
  D. Life for the Faithful (v. 4)
    Living by Faith
II. JOY IN THE LORD (Habakkuk 3:17-19)
  A. Disaster (v. 17)
  B. Joy (v. 18)
  C. Strength (v. 19)
    When "Everything" Goes Wrong
CONCLUSION
  A. Fear
  B. Assurance
  C. Faith
  D. Prayer
  E. Thought to Remember

The visual for lesson 5 of the visuals packet (see page 44) seeks to provide a current application of Habakkuk's call to trust in God.

Introduction

We all have questions, don't we? Some of them are hard to answer, and some of the hardest ones are about good and evil. If God is in charge and if He is just, why do bad things happen to good people? Why do good things happen to bad people? The Bible gives no clear and complete answer. So we say, "I'm going to ask about that when I get to Heaven." We are sure God knows.

Habakkuk's questions were similar to ours, and he got an answer before he went to Heaven. As sometimes happens, however, the answer raised another question as puzzling as the first one.

A. Habakkuk

Habakkuk was a prophet, so God spoke to him directly. That was how he got an answer without going to Heaven.

The first verse of Habakkuk's book tells us he was a prophet, and that is about all we know of the man himself. In a little note at the end of his book, he speaks of "my stringed instruments." Some students take this as a hint that he was a Levite who served as a temple musician (see 1 Chronicles 23:3-6), but we cannot be sure.

Habakkuk does not say when he received his prophecy, but he gives some clues that help us in fixing the date. To interpret his clues, we need to examine the history of this time. This is recorded in 2 Kings 21—25. Here is a short outline.

697-642 B.C. Evil king Manasseh ruled Judah and brought the country deeper and deeper into wrongdoing, but in his later years he reversed his course and tried to undo the harm he had done.

642-640 B.C. King Amon promptly revived all the evil of Manasseh's earlier years.

640-609 B.C. Good king Josiah restored righteousness and the worship of the Lord, but he was killed in battle with the Egyptian army as it was crossing his country to do battle with the Assyrians.

609 B.C. Josiah's son Jehoahaz became king, but he ruled only three months. Egypt then took charge of Judah, put Jehoahaz in prison, and made his brother Jehoiakim king.

609-598 B.C. Jehoiakim (another son of Josiah) was a very bad king, and the nation sank swiftly into sin. About 605 B.C. Nebuchadnezzar, with an army of Chaldeans (or Babylonians), conquered Judah and compelled it to pay tribute. Jehoiakim paid for three years and then rebelled. Judah was free for a short time, but was harassed by other smaller nations ruled by Babylon.

598-597 B.C. Jehoiachin (Jehoiakim's son) became king, but he ruled only three months. Nebuchadnezzar returned and made him a prisoner along with ten thousand of his people.

597-586 B.C. Zedekiah ruled Judah during this period. He was another son of Josiah (thus an uncle of Jehoiachin). Nebuchadnezzar left him to rule Judah and pay tribute to Babylon. Zedekiah paid for about ten years, then rebelled. Nebuchadnezzar retaliated and besieged Jerusalem for a year and a half.

586 B.C. Nebuchadnezzar destroyed Jerusalem and took most of the survivors to Babylon, leaving a few farmers to occupy the land of Judah. This completed the disaster that Habakkuk foretold.

Now we will try to determine where the prophecy of Habakkuk fits into this outline. First, the prophecy came during a time of widespread sin in Judah (Habakkuk 1:2-4). Manasseh was Judah's most notoriously wicked king, so some students think this points to his reign. On the other hand, the Lord told Habakkuk that a terrible disaster was coming to Judah "in your days"—in the lifetime of the people who heard the prophecy (Habakkuk 1:5, 6). This seems to suggest that the prophecy was given at a time later than the evil part of Manasseh's reign. Manasseh died more than half a century before Jerusalem was destroyed.

Second, the Lord said that the prophecy of destruction would be thought incredible (Habakkuk 1:5). This seems to indicate that the prophecy was given before the Chaldeans became powerful enough to pose a threat to Judah. This would be some time before 605 B.C. So perhaps Habakkuk gave this prophecy soon after good king Josiah died (around 609 B.C.). The nation by then was plunging swiftly into sin (2 Kings 23:31, 32, 36, 37). Surely a godly prophet such as he would be shocked and alarmed.

B. Lesson Background

Habakkuk was distressed and grieved by the rampant sin in his country. He was praying for God to do something about it. His question was this: How long would it be before God would answer that prayer? How long would the Lord let such sinning go on (Habakkuk 1:2-4)?

The Lord did not set an exact time, but He said He would do something "in your days"; that is, in the lifetime of Habakkuk and others who heard His promise. The Lord also told what He was going to do. He would bring the Chaldeans with a huge army to overwhelm Judah and put an end to its corrupt national life (Habakkuk 1:5-9). Chaldea was a territory in southern Baby-

---

How to Say It

CHALDEANS. Kal-*dee*-unz.
HABAKKUK. Huh-*bak*-kuk.
JEHOAHAZ. Jeh-*hoe*-uh-haz.
JEHOIACHIN. Jeh-*hoy*-uh-kin.
JEHOIAKIM. Jeh-*hoy*-uh-kim.
NEBUCHADNEZZAR. *Neb*-uh-kad-*nezz*-er.
  (strong accent on *nezz*).

---

lonia. Its name came to denote all of Babylonia; thus, the Babylonians were often called Chaldeans. These people were going to rule Judah, and they would be brutal masters.

This answer troubled Habakkuk about as much as the sins of Judah did. The Chaldeans were heathens, even more wicked than the people of Judah. How could a just and holy God support them in war, especially when Judah was "more righteous" (Habakkuk 1:13)? Our text begins as Habakkuk was waiting for an answer to that question.

I. The Lord's Message
(Habakkuk 2:1-4)

A. Waiting for an Answer (v. 1)

1. I will stand upon my watch, and set me upon the tower, and will watch to see what he will say unto me, and what I shall answer when I am reproved.

Habakkuk pictured himself as a watchman standing on a tower of the city wall, anxiously looking for a runner to come with a message (see 2 Samuel 18:24-27). Possibly he found a literal tower where he could be alone as he waited.

The phrase *when I am reproved* can be understood in more than one way, and each is possible in light of the Hebrew text. First, Habakkuk may have been thinking about how he would be *reproved* when he announced that the Lord was going to send the Chaldeans to devastate Judah. People would say that the prophet was being disloyal to his country.

Second, it is possible to view the reproof as coming from God. Perhaps Habakkuk expected to be rebuked for his outspoken challenge of the ways of the Lord.

Third, the phrase may be rendered something like "concerning my complaint," an interpretation followed by the *New International Version:* "I will look to see what he will say to me, and what answer I am to give *to this complaint.*"

B. Make the Message Plain (v. 2)

2. And the LORD answered me, and said, Write the vision, and make it plain upon tables, that he may run that readeth it.

Instead of giving the answer immediately, the Lord first told Habakkuk what to do with it. He was to write it plainly *upon tables;* that is, on tablets or placards so *that he may run that readeth it.* Some think this means that the message was to be written so plainly that one running by could read it without stopping. Others think that the message was to be written on tablets so runners could carry it swiftly to readers in different places.

The word *vision* primarily means something that is seen, but it can be used of a revelation from God given in words rather than by something visible (see 2 Samuel 7:17). In our text, the *New International Version* reads, "Write down the revelation" instead of *Write the vision*.

C. Wait for the Time (v. 3)

3. For the vision is yet for an appointed time, but at the end it shall speak, and not lie: though it tarry, wait for it; because it will surely come, it will not tarry.

The *vision* told of an event that would not happen immediately, but at *an appointed time* in the future. That time would come in the lifetime of Habakkuk and other hearers (Habakkuk 1:5), but they did not know how long they must wait. *At the end* of the time of waiting, everyone would see that the revelation was true. No matter how long the event might *tarry*, those who heard the prophecy should trust God and *wait for it*. It surely would *not tarry* beyond the time that God had appointed.

D. Life for the Faithful (v. 4)

4. Behold, his soul which is lifted up is not upright in him: but the just shall live by his faith.

One whose soul is *lifted up* is a proud man. That described the haughty Chaldeans who were to overrun Judah. These words could also describe the arrogant sinners of Judah. They were proud of their ability to do as they pleased, ignoring the law of God. They certainly were *not upright* either.

Verse 5, however, indicates that the king of the Chaldeans was the one whom Habakkuk meant by *lifted up*. He was the "proud man" who did not stay at home, whose desire was unlimited, and who conquered many nations and gathered them into his empire. His soul was not upright; he was an evil man.

In sharp contrast was *the just*, the man who trusted God and did right. Many haughty sinners of Judah would die, and others would be driven to Babylon as captives during the fierce onslaught of the Chaldeans. But the just could expect his life to be preserved.

The rest of the chapter shows that the proud Chaldeans would also in time be destroyed. This was the answer to Habakkuk's second question. The Lord would use the wicked Chaldeans for now to punish the Judeans, but in the end all the wicked would meet disaster. Life and peace were possible only by believing, trusting, and obeying the Lord.

The just shall live by his faith. Paul uses this statement to declare that eternal life is granted

visual 5

Yet I will rejoice in the Lord, I will be joyful in God my Savior.

to those who trust and obey (Romans 1:17; Galatians 3:11). They do not earn eternal life; God gives it to them because of their faith. Therefore we are "continuing to trust," as the title of our lesson puts it. The promise is secure when we are patient in our faith (Hebrews 10:36-39).

LIVING BY FAITH

Today we are just a month and two days away from the 479th anniversary of the beginning of the Protestant Reformation. Martin Luther, a devout German monk, had been deeply distressed. His soul had found no peace in spite of all his study and training in Catholic theology. His rigorous self-discipline had brought him no joy.

Then he found in Paul's letter to the Romans the key to it all: "The just shall live by faith" (Romans 1:17)—a quotation by Paul from the prophet Habakkuk. Luther saw that the good works his superiors had told him would bring salvation were hollow and without meaning when faith was absent.

This new understanding of God's Word galvanized Luther into action. To the door of the Castle Church in Wittenberg, Germany, he nailed a list of ninety-five points in which he challenged the system of works-righteousness from which Scripture and his faith in God had now set him free. The Reformation was born!

God's word to Habakkuk was that *all* we take pride in, *all* we do to make our lives secure, happy, and fulfilling, will be useless if we have no faith in God. However, if faith inspires our attitudes and prompts our good works, we shall find the answer to our souls' deep needs.

When this truth comes alive in our minds, a reformation will be born in our hearts. Living by faith brings freedom and fulfillment! —C. R. B.

II. Joy in the Lord (Habakkuk 3:17-19)

The last chapter of Habakkuk is the prophet's prayer set to music. In times of trouble it is a splendid prayer for all of the faithful to sing. Facing the invasion of hordes of ruthless

Chaldeans, the prophet confessed his fear. Humbly he prayed to the Lord, "In wrath remember mercy" (v. 2). Through most of the prayer he sang of God's irresistible power (vv. 3-15). In the coming time of distress, that power would be aligned with the Chaldeans to punish Judah. The prospect of this filled Habakkuk with fear (v. 16). His prayer concluded, however, with the beautiful assurance found in the last part of our text.

A. Disaster (v. 17)

17. Although the fig tree shall not blossom, neither shall fruit be in the vines; the labor of the olive shall fail, and the fields shall yield no meat; the flock shall be cut off from the fold, and there shall be no herd in the stalls.

This verse describes the devastation that was to come. The invading Chaldeans would either eat the fruit or destroy the trees. For the people of Judah there would be no figs, no grapes, and no olives. The fields would produce *no meat*. In the English of the *King James Version*, *meat* meant food of any kind. Here it meant wheat and barley, which could be made into bread. The crops of these grains would be destroyed or stolen by the invaders. The sheep and cattle would be slaughtered to provide food for the Chaldean army. The people of Judah would become desperately hungry.

B. Joy (v. 18)

18. Yet I will rejoice in the LORD, I will joy in the God of my salvation.

In the midst of utter poverty, close to death from starvation, Habakkuk would still *rejoice in the Lord*. The Lord had said, "The just shall live by his faith" (2:4). Habakkuk's faith in God did not depend on his surroundings. The God of his *salvation* was firmly in control. Thus, Habakkuk could find *joy* in the midst of disaster.

C. Strength (v. 19)

19a. The LORD God is my strength, and he will make my feet like hinds' feet, and he will make me to walk upon mine high places.

Neither the prophet nor the whole nation of Judah had strength enough to resist the overwhelming forces from Chaldea. But *the Lord* had strength enough to do whatever He chose to do, and He would protect the just who lived by faith. *Hinds*, or wild deer, had no fear of invasion. Their *feet* carried them swiftly over the mountains where they grazed on leaves and grasses. Destruction of wheat and barley in the valley would not trouble them. In the same way, the faithful would escape danger by the providence of the Almighty and find food to sustain

them. Well might each faithful one sing with an earlier prophet, "The Lord is my strength and song, and he is become my salvation" (Exodus 15:2).

19b. To the chief singer on my stringed instruments.

This notation, with which the book of Habakkuk concludes, is viewed by some as evidence that the prophet may have served for a time as a temple musician. As noted earlier in the Introduction, this is one of the few pieces of information we have been given about Habakkuk himself.

WHEN "EVERYTHING" GOES WRONG

Pat was definitely a "master teacher," in the words of the elementary school principal who used to supervise her work. During those days, her joy-filled service to God was to introduce children to the wonderful world that opened to them through reading. She had almost completed her doctorate in education. Then, "THE BACK" struck.

There had been two back surgeries before, but this time the villain struck in earnest, and there would be no relief. No more classes of kindergartners or first graders. Instead there was the ordeal of three more surgeries. No more getting out to church. Instead there was pain that came, not as an occasional visitor, but as a permanent, grossly unwelcome resident.

So life continues, day after day. But not all is bleak. Pat has taught herself paralegal skills so that when she feels up to it, she can do work at home for some Christian attorneys. She has found release for her teaching instincts by turning every "grandmothering" opportunity into an educational event for her grandchildren.

The pain is bad *every* day, even with heavy, prescribed doses of medication. But on the days when pain invades her life without mercy, the words of Habakkuk, found in today's text are among those that help Pat to carry on. Even when almost everything seems to be going wrong, "yet I will rejoice in the Lord, . . . the Lord God is my strength."   —C. R. B.

Conclusion

The Chaldeans' final onslaught is recorded in 2 Kings 25:1-21. They besieged Jerusalem for a year and a half, until there was no strength left to resist. The king of Judah tried to break through the Chaldean lines and escape, but he was pursued and captured. The city was burned, and the stone walls that would not burn were battered down. Many people died by the sword and from hunger. Most of the rest were driven to

Babylon, chief city of the Chaldeans. A few were left in Judah, but they soon migrated to Egypt (2 Kings 25:22-26). For half a century Judah lay deserted.

A. Fear

Habakkuk became afraid when he learned of the horrible disaster that was coming to his people (Habakkuk 3:2). Unfortunately, the rulers and the people did not share his fear and change their ways, and so disaster came.

Fear is epidemic in some sections of our cities. Elderly citizens are afraid to leave their homes at night. Many Americans think crime ought to be a major concern of their government. Two years ago Congress responded by passing a costly anti-crime bill. But who responded by turning to God with humility and obedience? Many honest citizens are still afraid to go out at night. The root of the problem is beyond the reach of law.

Big companies are "downsizing" all over the world. As a result, many people are being laid off, and many more are afraid of unemployment and poverty. News media make it plain that cancer and AIDS are frightening many of our people. Multitudes worry about the accident rate, and some are terrified of old age. And of course, thinking people are alarmed by the decay of moral standards.

Within many of our fears looms the same frightful specter that accompanied the fear of a Chaldean invasion—the fear of death. But this is not so frightful to those who trust in the Lord. Paul expressed a desire to depart and be with Christ, "which is far better" (Philippians 1:23). Death loses its terror when we know that the price of our transportation to Heaven has already been paid.

Home Daily Bible Readings

Monday, Sept. 23—Why Does Evil Go Unpunished? (Habakkuk 1:1-11)
Tuesday, Sept. 24—God Will Not Tolerate Wrongs (Habakkuk 1:12-17)
Wednesday, Sept. 25—Woes of the Wicked (Habakkuk 2:5-11)
Thursday, Sept. 26—Fate of the Wicked (Habakkuk 2:12-20)
Friday, Sept. 27—"In Wrath Remember Mercy" (Habakkuk 3:1-8)
Saturday, Sept. 28—God Saves His People (Habakkuk 3:9-16)
Sunday, Sept. 29—God Is Our Refuge and Strength (Psalm 46)

B. Assurance

Habakkuk was afraid, but he knew where to look for assurance. (See Habakkuk 3:18.) How the fears of the world would fade if people would turn to the Lord!

What if the man-hours and dollars used in seeking the lost were as many as those used in policing and jailing them? Most of our economic problems could be solved by massive doses of the Golden Rule. Sickness would be less and health care would be better if everyone loved his neighbor as himself. The accident rate could be lowered by Christian courtesy, and old age would lose its terror as people came to know the Savior.

We ought to be busy bringing people to Christ. Even if some refuse to come, those who do come and those who bring them will find themselves "safe in the arms of Jesus."

"The just shall live by his faith."

C. Faith

Faith is believing. In New Testament Greek, the word *faith* is the noun form of the verb *believe*. Yet faith is more than believing. "Faith is being sure of what we hope for and certain of what we do not see" (Hebrews 11:1, *New International Version*).

Faith is trusting. With such trust, Habakkuk sang of being like a deer in the mountains when the whole valley below was desolate and barren. With such trust, we find security in the Lord when moral standards are falling and crime rates are rising.

Faith is acting, for "faith without works is dead" (James 2:26). By faith Abraham packed up his goods and uprooted his family. He did not know where he was going, but he knew the Lord had told him to go (Hebrews 11:8).

Faith is holding on and keeping on. In both Hebrew and Greek, the word can mean either faith or faithfulness. Confidently the inspired writer says, "But we are not of those who shrink back and are destroyed, but of those who believe and are saved" (Hebrews 10:39, *New International Version*).

D. Prayer

Many things in the world alarm us, our Father, but with David we say, "What time I am afraid, I will trust in thee" (Psalm 56:3). We know Your love is always with us, and Your power is enough to meet our every need. Thank You, Lord. Amen.

E. Thought to Remember

"The just shall live by his faith."

Learning by Doing

This page contains an alternate lesson plan emphasizing learning activities.
Classes desiring such student involvement will find these suggestions helpful.

Learning Goals

As students participate in today's class session, they should:

1. Paraphrase Habakkuk's questions and God's answers from Habakkuk 1 and 2.

2. Analyze Habakkuk's faith in God in spite of the difficulties that would eventually befall Judah.

3. Choose one area of their lives where they most need to trust God.

Into the Lesson

Write one or all of the following open-ended sentences on your chalkboard:

"The hardest time for me to trust God is . . ."

"The person I know who trusts God most is . . ."

"Trusting God is easier to talk about than to do, because . . ."

"It is easier/harder for me to trust God today than ten years ago, because . . ."

Ask class members to group themselves into twos or threes, and have each group complete one of the statements. Allow five minutes or less for this, and then ask volunteers to share with the class.

Tell the class that today's Bible study looks at a prophet who learned to trust God in the midst of a very bleak situation.

Into the Word

Class members will probably need your help to understand who Habakkuk was, when he wrote, and how his book is organized. Develop a mini-lecture, based on the Introduction to the lesson, to deliver before class members do further Bible study. If you wish, you may ask a class member to present this material.

Then divide your class into four groups or sections. (If your class is larger than about thirty, each section could have more than one group.)

Write these assignments on the chalkboard:

1. Question One (1:1-4)
2. Answer One (1:5-11)
3. Question Two (1:12—2:1)
4. Answer Two (2:2-20)

Each section of your class will concentrate on the portion of Habakkuk 1 or 2 indicated by the assignment. Ask a class member to read these chapters aloud while the rest of the class listens carefully. For variety, you might ask more than one person to read.

After the reading, class members, in their groups, should answer the following questions. (Copy these and give them to the groups, or point them to the student book where there is space for them to write answers.)

Question One Group—What was the state of life in Judah? Summarize Habakkuk's question in one or two sentences.

Answer One Group—How would God deal with Judah? Summarize God's answer in one or two sentences.

Question Two Group—How did Habakkuk react to God's use of the Babylonians? Summarize Habakkuk's question in one or two sentences.

Answer Two Group—How would God ultimately deal with the Babylonians? Summarize God's answer in one or two sentences.

Give the groups six or eight minutes to complete their assignment. Let each group share its answers with the class. Then discuss: What did Habakkuk fear? What did he have trouble understanding? How did he relate to God in spite of his fear and confusion?

Tell the class that chapter 3 shows a fuller answer to the last question. Ask another reader or pair of readers to read chapter 3 aloud. As class members listen, they should jot down words that describe Habakkuk's feelings about God.

Allow a few members to tell what words they have written. Discuss: What was Habakkuk's attitude toward God? What was to be the fate of his nation? Why did Habakkuk refuse to give in to despair?

Into Life

Class members should write their own individual paraphrases of Habakkuk 3:17-19. They should consider what situations or problems from their own lives they would put in the "although" half of their sentences (v. 17). Suggest some examples to the class: "Although my cancer may get worse instead of better, still will I rejoice in the Lord." "Even if my son drops out of college instead of finishing his degree, I will trust in God." Class members may write as many sentences as they wish.

You might close the class session by asking volunteers, at random, to read one of their sentences. They should do so, heads bowed, in an attitude of prayer. After many have been read, close with a prayer expressing faith in God.

Let's Talk It Over

The questions on this page are designed to encourage review of the lesson Scriptures and to promote discussion of the lesson by the class. The answers provided are only discussion starters. Let your class talk it over from there.

1. There are certain questions about God and His dealings with man that no person can answer. Is it legitimate for us to say, "We will have to ask God about that when we get to Heaven"? Why, or why not?

Unbelievers sometimes suggest that our inability to answer hard questions about God demonstrates the weakness of our religion. But the Bible makes it clear that we are to "walk by faith" (2 Corinthians 5:7). Such a walk involves accepting truths and enduring trials that we cannot fully understand now. We legitimately hope to gain such an understanding in Heaven. Another consideration here is the fact that in every area of human knowledge, there are questions that experts cannot answer. In medicine, for example, many diseases continue to baffle doctors. In the field of meteorology, we are well aware that forecasters occasionally make inaccurate predictions. Therefore, no person can fault us for an inability to answer every religious question.

2. Habakkuk was shocked by the sins committed in his country. Are we as shocked as we should be by the sins of our era? If not, what can we do about it?

We often find ourselves overexposed to all kinds of shocking sins. Rape, murder, robbery, political corruption, marital infidelity, and the like are brought continually to our attention. Many of our fellow citizens, rather than reacting with shock to these horrors, tend to make jokes about them. Others respond to such sins with little more than indifference. The Bible reminds us of how our transgression of God's laws brings us confusion, fear, and sorrow in this life (see Psalm 107:17; Isaiah 48:22). Beyond that the Bible shows the terrible eternal consequences of sin (see Romans 2:5-11). Pondering these truths will help us view sin as God views it.

3. The Lord commanded Habakkuk, "Write the vision, and make it plain upon tables, that he may run that readeth it" (Habakkuk 2:2). This may mean that a person running by would be able to read the message without stopping. What does this suggest about our presentation of the gospel?

We must find ways of catching the attention of modern human beings who always seem to be "on the run." If we use tracts or other literature in evangelism, they must be eye-catching and both clear and concise in the presentation of our message. The command Habakkuk received also brings to mind the ministry of arranging signs outside church buildings. The persons who do this should pray for wisdom in their task. They need to display messages that will stimulate passersby to ponder their spiritual needs. Some larger churches even rent billboards to catch the eyes of busy people.

4. The lesson writer demonstrates the many ways fear permeates our society. How can we Christians minister to those who are fearful?

If people we meet admit to fear of violence in our neighborhoods and streets, we can point them to Psalm 34. David had faced violence, and he was able to testify, "I sought the Lord, and he heard me, and delivered me from all my fears" (verse 4). When individuals confess to fear of rejection and harshness on the part of others, we can encourage them with Proverbs 29:25: "The fear of man bringeth a snare: but whoso putteth his trust in the Lord shall be safe." People who acknowledge that they are afraid of death give us a golden opportunity to speak of Jesus Christ as the Conqueror of death. We can describe how through His death He is able to "deliver them, who through fear of death were all their lifetime subject to bondage" (Hebrews 2:15).

5. "If every person were a Christian, many of society's problems would vanish." Some people would say a statement like that is unrealistic. What do you think?

Many people now wearing the name Christian are contributing to the problems of society rather than overcoming them. Therefore, we would have to say that only if everyone became a *truly committed* Christian, would it make an impact on human woes. Genuine disciples of Christ could bring His love, compassion, righteousness, wisdom, and power to bear on these woes. The more of such disciples there are, the greater the impact on society's problems. So when we labor to win others to Christ, we are making a powerful contribution to a better world here. We are also providing people with the prospect of a richer life in the world to come.

A Vain Search

DEVOTIONAL READING: Jeremiah 5:20-31.

LESSON SCRIPTURE: Jeremiah 5.

PRINTED TEXT: Jeremiah 5:1-6.

Jeremiah 5:1-6

1 Run ye to and fro through the streets of Jerusalem, and see now, and know, and seek in the broad places thereof, if ye can find a man, if there be any that executeth judgment, that seeketh the truth; and I will pardon it.

2 And though they say, The LORD liveth; surely they swear falsely.

3 O LORD, are not thine eyes upon the truth? thou hast stricken them, but they have not grieved; thou hast consumed them, but they have refused to receive correction: they have made their faces harder than a rock; they have refused to return.

4 Therefore I said, Surely these are poor; they are foolish: for they know not the way of the LORD, nor the judgment of their God.

5 I will get me unto the great men, and will speak unto them; for they have known the way of the LORD, and the judgment of their God: but these have altogether broken the yoke, and burst the bonds.

6 Wherefore a lion out of the forest shall slay them, and a wolf of the evenings shall spoil them, a leopard shall watch over their cities: every one that goeth out thence shall be torn in pieces: because their transgressions are many, and their backslidings are increased.

GOLDEN TEXT: Run ye to and fro through the streets of Jerusalem, and see now, and know, and seek in the broad places thereof, if ye can find a man, if there be any that executeth judgment, that seeketh the truth; and I will pardon it.
—Jeremiah 5:1.

Lesson Aims

After this lesson a student should be able to:

1. Discuss Jeremiah's attempt to find one righteous person in Jerusalem.

2. Promise to read God's Word and follow it.

3. Share his faith with others.

Lesson Outline

INTRODUCTION
  A. Real Live Children
  B. Disobedient Children
  C. Lesson Background
 I. SEARCHING THE CITY (Jeremiah 5:1-3)
  A. Search for a Good Man (v. 1)
    Does Anyone Seek the Truth?
  B. Lying Sinners (v. 2)
  C. Stubborn Sinners (v. 3)
II. THE SEARCH CONTINUES (Jeremiah 5:4-6)
  A. Sinners Among the Poor (v. 4)
  B. Sinners Among the Rich (v. 5)
    Rich and Poor Alike
  C. Punishment for All Sinners (v. 6)
CONCLUSION
  A. You Have to Do It Yourself
  B. Any Nation Can Do It
  C. You Can Be Safe With the Lord
  D. Prayer
  E. Thought to Remember

The visual for lesson 6 of the visuals packet (see page 52) points out that the need for righteous people is as critical now as in Jeremiah's day.

Introduction

The atheist liked to argue with the preacher. One of their conversations went like this:

Atheist: That God of yours must be a monster, if He really exists. First He made a world full of sinners, and then He's going to burn them all in Hell because they're sinners.

Preacher: No, you're off to a bad start. God doesn't make sinners. People who sin make sinners of themselves.

Atheist: They all do it, don't they?

Preacher: Yes, but that's their choice, not God's.

Atheist: And God feels bad about it?

Preacher: Yes. He wants everyone to straighten up and do right.

Atheist: If He's so smart, why didn't He make people who wouldn't sin? He could have saved Himself a lot of grief and them a lot of burning.

Preacher: Phil, how are your boys doing in college this year?

Atheist: My boys? Oh, I get it. You want to change the subject. I don't blame you. I wouldn't want to defend your God either.

Preacher: So tell me about the boys.

Atheist: They're doing all right, I guess. Bill's on the football team. Ed hopes to make it in basketball. Both of them are on the dean's list.

Preacher: I guess neither of them ever did anything wrong.

Atheist: Are you crazy? We used to paddle them nearly every day. Some days we paddled them twice.

Preacher: Didn't that make you feel bad?

Atheist: Millie cried her eyes out.

Preacher: What about you? Weren't you hurting too?

Atheist: Yeah. So what?

Preacher: Before the children were born, didn't you know they would do wrong sometimes? Didn't you know they would hurt you and make Millie cry?

Atheist: Oh, sure. Kids are like that.

Preacher: You could have saved yourself a lot of grief and saved them a lot of paddling just by being childless. Why did you bring children like them into the world?

Atheist: Because there isn't any other kind!

Preacher: Aw, you could have gotten a bunch of marionettes—you know, puppets on strings. With less time than you gave to the boys, you could have them putting on a great show, always doing just what you wanted them to do. You could even put little tape players in them, and they would never say a false or mean word. No paddling, no pain, no grief, and no college tuition.

Atheist: Nuts! Who wants to play with dolls? We wanted real live children.

Preacher: Sure you did—and so did God.

A. Real Live Children

We are not told in the Scriptures about everything God had in mind when He created man, but it is clear that He wanted a family—children He could love and who could love Him in return. If they had no mind and will of their own, if they could not choose their way, or if they were programmed to do always what God wanted them to do, they would be nothing more than puppets, robots, dolls, and toys. God wanted real live children.

So God made people with minds wills, and hearts, who were capable of thinking and choosing. They could obey Him or disobey Him, please Him or grieve Him, love Him or hate Him.

B. Disobedient Children

Very soon God's children chose to disobey. It brought loss to them and grief to God, but still they chose to disobey. Continued disobedience only worsened man's condition: "God saw that the wickedness of man was great in the earth, and that every imagination of the thoughts of his heart was only evil continually" (Genesis 6:5). So God destroyed most of humanity and started over with Noah and his family.

Soon disobedience began again, and once more it grew and multiplied. This time God did not destroy all the sinners. He chose one man of faith and obedience to be the father of a nation that would show the rest of the world how good it is to obey God. To Abraham's children, God gave the special guidance of His Law, the special protection of His power, and the special encouragement of His love. Still they became disobedient children, bringing disaster upon themselves and grieving their Father in Heaven.

Clearly mankind was not going to make itself obedient, even with the help of God's guidance and protection. Then God revealed the plan that would not fail. He sent the Savior, who was both God and man. Jesus gave His spotless life to redeem the disobedient. By His grace the sinners of earth can be forgiven, cleansed, and made ready to live in God's presence as the obedient children He always wanted.

For this lesson, however, we are still looking at the time before the Savior came—a dark and evil time in Judah.

C. Lesson Background

Jeremiah was God's spokesman for more than forty years. The book called by his name is a collection of prophecies he gave to Judah at different times during those years, along with some historical material. The prophecies are not all arranged in the order in which they were given. Some of them are dated; thus we know when

---

How to Say It

BELSHAZZAR. Bel-*shazz*-er.
CHALDEANS. Kal-*dee*-unz.
HABAKKUK. Huh-*bak*-kuk.
MEDES. Meeds.
NEBUCHADNEZZAR. *Neb*-uh-kad-*nezz*-er (strong accent on *nezz*).

Jeremiah delivered them (for example, see Jeremiah 25:1; 26:1; 32:1; 36:1, 9). The one assigned for this lesson is not dated; it may have come about the same time as Habakkuk's prophecy that we considered last week. From the text itself, we see that it came at a time when Judah was deep in sin.

I. Searching the City (Jeremiah 5:1-3)

A. Search for a Good Man (v. 1)

1. Run ye to and fro through the streets of Jerusalem, and see now, and know, and seek in the broad places thereof, if ye can find a man, if there be any that executeth judgment, that seeketh the truth; and I will pardon it.

Other versions have *go* or *roam* instead of *run*. We should not think of a quick and careless search by someone running swiftly. On the contrary, *to and fro* suggests a thorough search by one going back and forth through the streets. *Scour the streets* is the reading in Moffatt's translation. *See now, and know* also suggests a thorough search: look everywhere and make sure.

Houses in a walled city were crowded closely together to make room for many people, but there were some *broad places*—open squares just inside the gates. These areas were to be searched as thoroughly as the streets. No spot in Jerusalem was to be overlooked.

The search was not for a murderer, robber, or other criminal. Any of these could be found easily. This search was for *a man* of a very different kind—a good man. *Judgment* here means justice, or right judgment. Those who heard Jeremiah's message were invited to search the entire city of Jerusalem and see if they could find even one man who did right and really wanted to find *the truth*. If such a man could be found—just one—*I will pardon it*, the Lord said. Jerusalem was nearing destruction because of its wickedness; its only hope was divine pardon.

We are reminded of ancient Sodom. It could have been saved if it had held ten righteous men (Genesis 18:23-32). But ten could not be found; so the one good family was evacuated, and Sodom perished (Genesis 19:15-28). We also think of mankind in the time of Noah: "Every imagination of the thoughts of his heart was only evil continually" (Genesis 6:5). The Lord found eight people worth saving, while all the rest perished (Genesis 6—8). Just one good man could have won pardon for Jerusalem. Where was that man?

In almost any town we can still easily find a good man, or eight or ten of them; but how evil has multiplied in recent years, particularly in our larger cities! Would the search for a righteous man in one of these cities be as desperate as Jeremiah's search in Jerusalem?

DOES ANYONE SEEK THE TRUTH?

The Day America Told the Truth was one of the most revealing books published in 1991. It said a lot about what our "Christian" nation thinks about ethics. On a chosen day the pollsters fanned out across the nation to question a wide cross section of Americans about a number of significant moral issues.

For example, when questioned whether it would be worth $10 million to them to abandon their parents, leave their spouses, or become prostitutes for a week, between one-fourth and two-fifths of non-religious people said, "Yes." People who called themselves "religious" said "yes" only about half as often as others. Maybe there is a *little* consolation in that!

Although 90% of those questioned claimed to believe in God, 93% claimed that they were their own final authority on what is moral and immoral! Only 17% defined sin as "going against God's will."

God's challenge to Jeremiah was to survey the city of Jerusalem and see if there was even one person who practiced justice and sought after the truth. The implication was that no such person could be found. Our situation today is probably not quite that serious, but without question the moral foundation of Western society has some large cracks in it. Those of us who claim to know God must set an example of morality for those who do not know Him.   —C. R. B.

B. Lying Sinners (v. 2)

2. And though they say, The LORD liveth; surely they swear falsely.

In modern courtrooms a witness swears to tell "the truth, the whole truth, and nothing but the truth." To make the oath more solemn, the phrase "So help me God" used to be included. The oath-taking phrase in ancient Judah was *The Lord liveth.* It meant, "I am telling the truth as surely as the Lord is alive." But sinners in Judah thoughtlessly used that oath even when they were lying. Thus they took the name of the Lord in vain, violating one of the Ten Commandments (Exodus 20:7). Lying was bad, and using the Lord's name in the process was worse.

C. Stubborn Sinners (v . 3)

3. O LORD, are not thine eyes upon the truth? thou hast stricken them, but they have not grieved; thou hast consumed them, but they have refused to receive correction: they have

visual 6

made their faces harder than a rock; they have refused to return.

Are not thine eyes upon the truth? The obvious answer was yes. The Lord was looking for *the truth,* expecting His people to speak *the* truth.

Thou hast stricken them. The Lord had *stricken* the lying sinners of Judah with various kinds of punishment. Probably those punishments were similar to those suffered by northern Israel: famine, drought, various types of crop failures, pestilence, and war (see Amos 4:6-11). But the sinners of Judah, like those of northern Israel, had *not grieved:* they were not sorry for their sins, and they continued to do wrong.

Thou hast consumed them. This is parallel to *thou hast stricken them.* By punishments like those named above, the land and nation had been eaten away. Such punishments were meant to make the people see their wrongdoing and correct it, but they had *refused to receive correction.* They had *made their faces harder than a rock.* They were stubborn—firm as a limestone ridge, keeping their faces turned toward evil instead of good. Since various punishments had not been effective, God was driven to a more severe one. He was going to bring the Chaldeans from Babylon to devastate Judah.

II. The Search Continues (Jeremiah 5:4-6)

If no good man could be found, there would be no pardon, and the Chaldeans would invade and ravage the land. So Jeremiah intensified his search.

A. Sinners Among the Poor (v. 4)

4. Therefore I said, Surely these are poor; they are foolish: for they know not the way of the LORD, nor the judgment of their God.

This sounds like the opinion, often expressed by modern sociologists, that poverty breeds ignorance, crime, and other social ills. But Jeremiah was not making a general observation on poverty; he was expressing his frustration at trying to carry out the Lord's command to find just one righteous person. He gave the *poor* the benefit of the doubt and thought that perhaps their status had limited their opportunities to know *the way of the Lord.*

B. Sinners Among the Rich (v. 5)

5. I will get me unto the great men, and will speak unto them; for they have known the way of the LORD, and the judgment of their God: but these have altogether broken the yoke, and burst the bonds.

The great men, such as the elders of the city, the banker and the rich merchant, the priest and the teacher—surely they would be better informed. Surely good men could be found among the wealthy, the rulers, and the scholars.

But these were as bad as the poorer class. They had *burst the bonds* of God's Law; they had *broken the yoke* of service to the Lord. Although they thought such an act set them free, they were merely preparing themselves to bear a truly oppressive yoke (a point to be made in next week's lesson). Clearly sin had permeated all of Judah. It has never recognized class distinctions of any kind.

RICH AND POOR ALIKE

Vultures have long been associated with death. Monuments from the third millennium before Christ show vultures on a battlefield, attacking the corpses of slain soldiers. The vultures that still visit Gettysburg National Military Park are thought to be descendants of those that feasted on horses killed in the Civil War battle. Their history as carrion eaters makes them unwelcome guests.

But vultures are "equal opportunity scavengers." In recent years, large flocks of vultures have been moving to suburbia. They find suburban areas to be very pleasant sources of food. They damage boat seats and lawn furniture and tear roofs from houses. They seem not to care whether they are eating carrion or cars. They are happy with either poor people's garbage or the contents of rich people's garages.

The sin that Jeremiah found in Jerusalem also affected rich and poor alike. He thought to excuse the poor for their sin, because their poverty might have limited their opportunity to know God. But then he saw that the rich were sinners also. The truth he discovered is the same today: disobedience and lack of faith know no social or economic boundaries. Righteousness has far more to do with the contents of our hearts than with the contents of our pocketbooks or bank accounts. —C.R.B.

C. Punishment for All Sinners (v. 6)

6. Wherefore a lion out of the forest shall slay them, and a wolf of the evenings shall spoil them, a leopard shall watch over their cities: every one that goeth out thence shall be torn in pieces: because their transgressions are many, and their backslidings are increased.

A lion is much bigger than a man and armed with frightful claws and teeth. *A wolf of the evenings* is a hungry wolf. All day he has hidden in his lair, and now he is looking for prey. Some students think this should be translated *a wolf of the deserts* instead of *a wolf of the evenings,* but in either case it means a hungry wolf. *A leopard* is also a fearsome beast of prey.

Some students believe this is to be taken literally, as a promise that actual wild beasts would kill the people of Judah. But it is more likely that Jeremiah was speaking figuratively at this point. These savage beasts were symbols of the savage Babylonians or Chaldeans. Their coming is foretold in verses 15-17 of this chapter and in Jeremiah 1:14-16. For other examples of this symbolism, see Jeremiah 4:7; Hosea 13:7, 8; Habakkuk 1:6-8; and Zephaniah 3:3.

Eventually these foes would literally *watch over* the city of Jerusalem, guarding it on every side so no food could be taken to the people inside. Anyone going out would not literally be *torn in pieces* by wild animals, but would be captured or killed by the enemy. After a year and a half of such treatment, the Chaldeans broke through the walls of Jerusalem and captured the entire city (2 Kings 25:1-12).

In the rest of chapter 5, Jeremiah elaborates on the wickedness of Judah and the punishment that was to come because the prophets (other than the Lord's prophets) were false, the priests were no better, and "my people love to have it so" (v. 31).

Conclusion

Boarding a bus in a strange city, a lady asked the driver about her destination.

"It's easy to find," he explained. "You'll see a big Sears store on the right. You want to get off at the next stop after that one."

The lady took a seat near the rear door of the bus. At the proper stop she rose and stood at that door while the front door opened and people poured on. Finally she called to the driver, "Will you please open the back door?"

"Lady," he called back, "you have to do it yourself."

At the touch of her hand the door opened easily, and she went on her way.

A. You Have to Do It Yourself

The Lord gave careful and adequate information to His people. The instructions provided in His Law were marvelously thorough and detailed. He ordered that the Law be read to the nation every seven years (Deuteronomy 31:10-13). He laid on every parent the responsibility of keeping the Law in his heart and passing it on to the next generation (Deuteronomy 6:6, 7). The door was unlocked, and the way was open for everyone to do right; but still each person had to "do it himself."

The nation got into trouble because the people did not do what the Law said to do. When there was no strong national government, "every man did that which was right in his own eyes" (Judges 21:25).

The Israelites then thought that a strong central government would keep them out of trouble. They wanted a king to lead them and fight their battles for them (1 Samuel 8:19, 20). But did they want the king to help them do right, or did they want him to protect them while they went on doing wrong?

After all, kings were only people. Many of them did what was evil in God's sight. The people followed them, selfishly seeking profit and pleasure rather than righteousness. They wanted the government to assure peace and prosperity; they did not want to "do it themselves."

B. Any Nation Can Do It

Some students object to any comparison of our nation with Israel or Judah. Those nations were in a unique position, they say. We are not God's chosen people; our laws are not made by Him. He has not promised to bless us above all the other nations. This is true, but the Scripture says, "All these things happened unto them for ensamples: and they are written for our admonition" (1 Corinthians 10:11). The verses before that list several sins Israel committed that we must avoid (vv. 6-10).

Israel and Judah were not the only nations that rose by integrity and fell by corruption. Consider the Chaldeans who conquered Judah. Heathen though they were, Nebuchadnezzar's troops were strong, dedicated, and well-disciplined. Half a century later, Belshazzar and his nobles were drinking themselves drunk when the alert Medes and Persians took over Babylon and its empire (Daniel 5:1-4, 30, 31). The empire of the Medes and Persians grew corrupt in its turn, and fell before the vigorous forces of Alexander the Great. Alexander's empire was split four ways, then these sections grew tyrannical and corrupt before they were conquered by the armies of Rome. The Roman Empire lasted for centuries, but its end was also due to rottenness within as well as to assault from without.

Having no inspired prophet to instruct us now, we cannot predict when a great nation will fall or when another will rise. But nations still rise through integrity and devotion, and fall through greed and corruption. Any nation can do it.

C. You Can Be Safe With the Lord

Jeremiah was a lonely voice crying in the wilderness of Judah's sin. His pleading went unheeded, and he himself was persecuted. But Jeremiah was faithful, and he was spared when Jerusalem fell to the Babylonians.

Today we hold the good news of the pardon before a world that does not welcome it. We may be ignored, we may be scorned, we may be persecuted; but if we are faithful, we shall be safe when the world is on fire. You can be safe for eternity without a human companion, but you cannot be safe without God.

D. Prayer

Heavenly Father, how grateful we are for Your Word! You yourself have told us what to do. More than that, You have given Your only begotten Son to bear our sins and give us pardon and life. In gratitude we pledge ourselves to follow where He leads. By Your grace and power may we be as faithful as Jeremiah was, and as safe for eternity. Amen.

E. Thought to Remember

A charge to keep I have,
   A God to glorify;
A never-dying soul to save,
   And fit it for the sky.
            —Charles Wesley

Home Daily Bible Readings

Monday, Sept. 30—All Classes Indicted (Ezekiel 22:23-31)

Tuesday, Oct. 1—False Teachers (Titus 1:10-16)

Wednesday, Oct. 2—Judah's Ingratitude (Isaiah 1:2-9)

Thursday, Oct. 3—God Unable to Pardon (Jeremiah 5:7-17)

Friday, Oct. 4—God Judges Stubborn People (Jeremiah 5:18-31)

Saturday, Oct. 5—God Will Destroy Israel (Hosea 13:4-11)

Sunday, Oct. 6—God's Punishment for Falsehood (Jeremiah 6:11-15)

Learning by Doing

This page contains an alternate lesson plan emphasizing learning activities.
Classes desiring such student involvement will find these suggestions helpful.

Learning Goals

As students participate in today's class session, they should:

1. List the sins of Judah mentioned in Jeremiah 5.

2. Compare these sins with sins in their nation and compare the moral state of Judah with the moral state of their country.

3. Choose specific remedies for sins in their country and commit themselves to specific ways to improve the moral fiber of their nation.

Into the Lesson

Ask class members to divide themselves into pairs and tell each other about "the most righteous person I know." Class members may mention anyone they wish, but he or she must be a person the class member actually knows or knew; the person cannot be a person from history or some individual the class member has read about.

After three or four minutes, ask several volunteers to tell about the person they chose. Then read Jeremiah 5:1 to the class. Explain that this was God's challenge to Jeremiah and his condition for saving the city of Jerusalem.

Ask class members to think about your city or town. Suppose God issued the same challenge to you about your community. Who would you suggest as a person whom meets these standards? Can you think of people who are not members of your congregation to suggest?

Tell the class that the nation of Judah and the city of Jerusalem had sunk into such paganism that God had no choice but to destroy them. As we consider this lesson, we might wonder if the spiritual decay in our own country will bring it to a similar judgment.

Into the Word

Give the class a brief summary of Jeremiah's life and ministry. Then lead them into one or both of the following Bible study activities.

Question and Answer. Write the following questions on a poster or on your chalkboard, or point your class members to the student book, where they are written. Challenge students, in groups of three, to write a one-sentence answer to each question:

1. What did God seek (v. 1)?

2. What did the people proclaim (v. 2)?

3. What was the people's attitude (v. 3)?

4. Where did Jeremiah find sinners (vv. 4, 5)?

5. What would be the people's fate (v. 6)?

After a few minutes, discuss with your class the situation in Judah as it is described in our text. What words would your members use to describe that society? How hopeful were the prospects for its future?

Marked Bibles. Class members should use their own Bibles, or distribute photocopies of all of Jeremiah 5. Students should read through the chapter (or you can ask a volunteer to read it aloud) and mark the verses in this way:

Circle the words of God.

Put a box around the words of Jeremiah.

Put an exclamation point in the margin beside descriptions of the sins of the people.

Draw an arrow pointing at sections that describe the punishment of God.

(Note: some verses will be marked twice.)

After a few minutes, class members may compare their papers with each other in pairs, then with the whole class, as you lead the discussion. What general impressions of Judah have the class members gathered? How would they describe the ministry of Jeremiah? The attitude of God? What surprises them about this passage? What frightens them? What encourages them?

Into Life

Read or summarize the material under "B. Any Nation Can Do It" in the Conclusion to the lesson commentary (page 54). Read this sentence or write it on your chalkboard: "Nations rise through integrity and devotion, and fall through greed and corruption." Ask the class to decide, "Is our nation better characterized by the words *integrity and devotion* or *greed and corruption?* Is our nation 'rising' or 'falling'? Why?" Have them give evidence to support their answers.

What can Christians do to help their nation rise through integrity rather than fall through corruption? Surely our nation is not as corrupt as Judah. Your class has already mentioned several righteous people in your own town. What can class members do to build on that trend?

If you have time, make another list on the chalkboard of specific actions class members can take. Then ask a volunteer to pray specifically about each item on the list. End your session with these prayers.

Let's Talk It Over

The questions on this page are designed to encourage review of the lesson Scriptures and to promote discussion of the lesson by the class. The answers provided are only discussion starters. Let your class talk it over from there.

1. The Bible teaches that God has given to all men the gift of free will. We can choose to obey God or to reject His ways. How does this explain much of the evil that exists in our world?

Unbelievers ask, "If God exists, why does He allow so much suffering through poverty, disease, and accidents?" We can answer that God has revealed laws that could prevent much of this suffering, if human beings would heed His laws. Poverty results in part because of the sins of greed and oppression. As for disease, it is sometimes the result of sin. That is true of sexually transmitted diseases and those that come from intemperate eating and drinking. Many accidents happen because of sin. For example, disobedience toward speed limits and other traffic regulations contributes to death and destruction on the highways.

2. We may wonder how many good people in our society a serious searcher would find. Why is this an important matter to ponder?

We tend to think of the majority of our fellow citizens as good people. Quite a few of the individuals we know strike us as honest, truthful, law-abiding, and God-fearing people. That may make it difficult for us to accept the idea that our society is seriously corrupt. Occasionally we receive reminders that people are not as good as they seem. For example, we learn that a highly regarded businessman has been found guilty of fraud or embezzling. We are shocked to find that a trusted schoolteacher has abused some students. We discover that a "model family" has been torn apart by adultery. Beneath the surface, "good people" are still sinners. We see how important it is that we remain steadfast in preaching and teaching the Word of God. It is the only cure for this underlying corruption.

3. The Lord was certainly not pleased with the way the people of Judah used the statement "The Lord liveth" as an oath. How serious is the use of God's name and Christ's name in thoughtless oaths today?

It is a practice that shows up everywhere. In the workplace and in shopping areas people spew out profane language without shame. On television even the family-oriented movies and weekly shows feature careless uses of the name of God. Among Christians one occasionally hears God's name taken in vain or words like "hell" and "damn" used in a thoughtless manner. This is a practice we dare not take lightly. We have no reason to believe that God is any less grieved today than in Biblical times by misuse of His name or His Son's name.

4. While we dare not let poverty be an excuse for crime and other sin, we cannot deny that it does contribute to these evils. What can we do to overcome the effects of poverty?

Jesus said, "For ye have the poor always with you" (Matthew 26:11). Paul recalled in Galatians 2:10 that the Jerusalem church's leaders desired "that we should remember the poor." The poor are still with us today, and we are obligated to minister to them. Obviously we can help by providing food, clothing, and other necessities. Perhaps there is a way that we can aid poor fathers or mothers in obtaining employment. If they are being cheated or oppressed, we must do what we can to assist them. It is vital that we make sure, as Jesus did, that "the poor have the gospel preached to them" (Matthew 11:5). The gospel can give them new life, new hope, and new power to lift themselves out of the clutches of poverty.

5. The lesson writer says of certain Old Testament people, "They wanted the government to assure peace and prosperity; they did not want to 'do it themselves.'" This attitude of "Let the government do it" is still prevalent. How can we answer it?

History has proved that governments do not accomplish many tasks well. Looking back to the previous question, we must say that many government programs designed to help the poor have failed. Churches and individual Christians must do more in this area. Governments often stumble in their efforts to fight crime and protect the innocent. We must take some initiative in working to make our streets and our neighborhoods safer. Government-controlled education for our children is frequently inadequate. We need more parents taking an active role in assuring their children of a quality education, one that is not dictated by "political correctness."

False Hopes for Peace

DEVOTIONAL READING: Jeremiah 30:13-24.

LESSON SCRIPTURE: Jeremiah 28, 29.

PRINTED TEXT: Jeremiah 28:5-14.

Jeremiah 28:5-14

5 Then the prophet Jeremiah said unto the prophet Hananiah in the presence of the priests, and in the presence of all the people that stood in the house of the LORD,

6 Even the prophet Jeremiah said, Amen: the LORD do so: the LORD perform thy words which thou hast prophesied, to bring again the vessels of the LORD's house, and all that is carried away captive, from Babylon into this place.

7 Nevertheless, hear thou now this word that I speak in thine ears, and in the ears of all the people;

8 The prophets that have been before me and before thee of old prophesied both against many countries, and against great kingdoms, of war, and of evil, and of pestilence.

9 The prophet which prophesieth of peace, when the word of the prophet shall come to pass, then shall the prophet be known, that the LORD hath truly sent him.

10 Then Hananiah the prophet took the yoke from off the prophet Jeremiah's neck, and brake it.

11 And Hananiah spake in the presence of all the people, saying, Thus saith the LORD; Even so will I break the yoke of Nebuchadnezzar king of Babylon from the neck of all nations within the space of two full years. And the prophet Jeremiah went his way.

12 Then the word of the LORD came unto Jeremiah the prophet, after that Hananiah the prophet had broken the yoke from off the neck of the prophet Jeremiah, saying,

13 Go and tell Hananiah, saying, Thus saith the LORD; Thou hast broken the yokes of wood; but thou shalt make for them yokes of iron.

14 For thus saith the LORD of hosts, the God of Israel; I have put a yoke of iron upon the neck of all these nations, that they may serve Nebuchadnezzar king of Babylon; and they shall serve him: and I have given him the beasts of the field also.

Oct 13

GOLDEN TEXT: Then shall ye call upon me, and ye shall go and pray unto me, and I will hearken unto you. And ye shall seek me, and find me, when ye shall search for me with all your heart.—Jeremiah 29:12, 13.

God's People Face Judgment
Unit 2: Judah's Internal Decay
(Lessons 6-9)

Lesson Aims

After participating in this lesson students should be able to:

1. Tell about the conflicting prophecies of Hananiah and Jeremiah.

2. Recognize the Bible as their best help in distinguishing truth from falsehood.

3. Resolve to follow the Bible in their own daily living.

Lesson Outline

INTRODUCTION
    A. Sunny Forecasts
    B. True Forecasts
    C. Disaster in Three Phases
    D. Lesson Background
  I. VAIN HOPE (Jeremiah 28:5-9)
    A. Public Place (v. 5)
    B. Earnest Wish (v. 6)
    C. The Lord's Truth (vv. 7-9)
 II. POPULAR PROPHECY (Jeremiah 28:10, 11)
    A. Symbolic Act (v. 10)
    B. Interpretation (v. 11)
      False Predictions
III. TRUE PROPHECY (Jeremiah 28:12-14)
    A. The Lord's Word (v. 12)
    B. From Bad to Worse (v. 13)
    C. Defeat and Bondage (v. 14)
      Trading One Yoke for Another
CONCLUSION
    A. Back to the Bible
    B. Knowing
    C. Talking
    D. Doing
    E. Prayer
    F. Thought to Remember

Use the visual for lesson 7 of the visuals packet to illustrate the unchanging authority of the Word of God. The visual is shown on page 60.

Introduction
A. Sunny Forecasts

We all like sunny forecasts, don't we? Politicians win elections by promising a change for the better, but sometimes the improvement is hard to see. Scientists win fame by proclaiming that we have risen from brutes to human beings, and now are rising to heights not yet imagined. Such rosy forecasts do little to slow the crime rate. Preachers fill their auditoriums by means of glowing sermons picturing growing godliness and the brotherhood of man, but neither of these is seen in the dingy streets on the other side of town.

No one likes the "doomsayer." He becomes the object of derision, contempt, and anger. But doom is as real as triumph.

B. True Forecasts

God's prophets had sunny forecasts too, but such promises were tied to obedience to the Law of God (Deuteronomy 28:1-6). Disobedience was linked to promises of terror (vv. 15-19). Even Jeremiah promised blessing and joy in the future (Jeremiah 31:1-14); that future, however, lay beyond a time of punishment, for the actions Jeremiah saw in his day demanded punishment.

Without the gift of prophecy, we should be cautious about predicting the future. But on the basis of thousands of years of history, we can declare with all confidence that disobeying God has bad consequences, though in God's mercy those consequences may be long delayed. With equal confidence we can declare that doing God's will brings happiness, though in a sinful world that happiness also may be delayed.

C. Disaster in Three Phases

In the first chapter of Jeremiah and again in the first chapter of Habakkuk, we see a gloomy forecast of Judah's disastrous defeat by the Chaldeans, or Babylonians (Jeremiah 1:15,16; Habakkuk 1:6-9). That event was in the future when those prophets wrote about it. Now, as we look back on the events, we see that the disaster came in three phases, each one more severe than the one before it. Mercifully God brought minor disaster first, giving His people time to repent and avoid the greater calamity. But the people did not repent. Stubbornly they continued their evil ways until the destruction was complete.

First phase. About 605 B.C. the Babylonians first subdued Judah. They took a few captives (Daniel 1:1-7). King Jehoiakim was left to rule Judah and pay tribute to Babylon. After three years he rebelled and stopped paying. The Babylonians sent other satellite nations to harass Judah until Nebuchadnezzar was ready to come back (2 Kings 24:1, 2).

Second phase. About 597 B.C. the Babylonians returned to Jerusalem. By then Jehoiachin was king. He quickly surrendered, and the Babylonians took him captive along with ten thousand leading citizens and craftsmen. Zedekiah

How to Say It

CHALDEANS. Kal-*dee*-unz.
HABAKKUK. Huh-*bak*-kuk.
HANANIAH. Han-uh-*nye*-uh.
JECONIAH. Jek-owe-*nye*-uh.
JEHOIACHIN. Jeh-*hoy*-uh-kin.
JEHOIAKIM. Jeh-*hoy*-uh-kim.
NEBUCHADNEZZAR. *Neb*-uh-kad-*nezz*-er
(strong accent on *nezz*).

was made king of Judah and forced to pay tribute to Babylon (2 Kings 24:8-17).

Third phase. About nine years later, Zedekiah rebelled. The Babylonians came to subdue Jerusalem for the third time. Entering the city after a siege of eighteen months, they destroyed it and took most of the survivors to Babylon (2 Kings 24:18—25:21). Thus the disaster was complete about 586 B.C.

D. Lesson Background

The events in this lesson took place during the second phase of disaster. Jehoiachin and ten thousand citizens had been taken to Babylon. Although a bit of confusion exists as to the exact time indicated in Jeremiah 28:1, most students believe that the events recorded therein occurred in Zedekiah's fourth year (approximately 593 B.C.).

Hananiah was a false prophet who cheerfully said what the people wanted to hear. He claimed his message came from God, but that was a lie. His false message was that the power of Babylon would be broken within two years. King Jehoiachin (also called Jeconiah in Jeremiah 27:20 and 28:4) would return along with all the captives and spoil taken from Jerusalem. Judah and the other subject nations would be freed. That message was popular, but it was not true. Our text begins with Jeremiah's response to it.

I. Vain Hope
(Jeremiah 28:5-9)

Jeremiah was in a difficult spot. A lie had been told by one who claimed to speak for God. As God's real spokesman, Jeremiah had to expose it. But the lie was popular; king, officials, and people loved it. Probably they would hate and threaten anyone who would speak against it. A denial would be dangerous, but those who proclaim God's message cannot choose the easy, popular way. They have to say what God says, regardless of what the audience thinks.

A. Public Place (v. 5)

5. Then the prophet Jeremiah said unto the prophet Hananiah in the presence of the priests, and in the presence of all the people that stood in the house of the LORD.

The lie had been told in a public meeting (vv. 1-4); thus, the denial could not be whispered in secret. Priests and people might be angered by the truth, but the truth must be told.

B. Earnest Wish (v. 6)

6. Even the prophet Jeremiah said, Amen: the LORD do so: the LORD perform thy words which thou hast prophesied, to bring again the vessels of the LORD's house, and all that is carried away captive, from Babylon into this place.

Jeremiah took no pleasure in foretelling the coming disaster! His attitude was like that of Jesus, who wept as He foretold the destruction of Jerusalem (Luke 19:41-44). So, before denouncing the lie that had been told, Jeremiah voiced his earnest wish that *the Lord* might indeed bring back all the captives and all the spoil that had been taken to *Babylon.* That spoil included the royal treasury as well as the temple treasury (2 Kings 24:13). The captives included military and civic leaders, along with the blacksmiths who made swords and spears (2 Kings 24:14). Without leaders and without weapons, the men of Judah would not rebel again—or so the Babylonians hoped. Like the rest of the people in Judah, Jeremiah wished that both captives and treasures might return; but he knew they would not. The Lord had told him that.

C. The Lord's Truth (vv. 7-9)

7. Nevertheless, hear thou now this word that I speak in thine ears, and in the ears of all the people.

Even though Jeremiah, Hananiah, all the priests, and all the people fervently wished the captives might come back, they needed to hear what the Lord had to say.

8. The prophets that have been before me and before thee of old prophesied both against many countries, and against great kingdoms, of war, and of evil, and of pestilence.

It was nothing new for a prophet to say that disobedience would bring disaster. Moses had given a lengthy warning on the subject (Deuteronomy 28:15-68). Numerous *prophets* since that time had brought variations of the same message, each speaking as God had directed him. After such warnings, anyone in Judah should have been suspicious when a man like Hananiah announced an end to the people's punishment without an end to their sin.

9. The prophet which prophesieth of peace, when the word of the prophet shall come to pass, then shall the prophet be known, that the LORD hath truly sent him.

Peace is more than the end of war. In the Hebrew way of thinking, it included health, happiness, prosperity, and welfare in general. Most of the prophets foretold increasing trouble, not peace, for sinners. When one promised peace for sinners, as Hananiah did, it would be wise to wait and see if the promise was fulfilled. If it was, then the one who made it could be accepted as God's prophet. Hananiah promised that Babylon would lose its power and that the captives would be home within two years (vv. 2-4). Thus, in two years everyone would know whether or not he was a real prophet.

II. Popular Prophecy (Jeremiah 28:10, 11)

Jeremiah had illustrated his prophecy of judgment by wearing on his neck a yoke such as an ox or donkey might wear when it was pulling a plow or cart. This was a symbol of Judah's subjection to Babylon. The whole nation was "yoked" and compelled to work for Babylon. Though the people were living in their own country and tilling their own soil, a part of their produce had to go to pay tribute to Babylon as punishment for their sins. Jeremiah advised them to accept this yoke, for resistance would only bring more severe punishment. Jeremiah also sent yokes to the kings of surrounding countries with the same advice, for the Lord had delivered all those countries into the hand of Babylon (see Jeremiah 27:1-11).

A. Symbolic Act (v. 10)

10. Then Hananiah the prophet took the yoke from off the prophet Jeremiah's neck, and brake it.

The yoke was merely a symbol to illustrate Jeremiah's messages. Probably it was lighter than a real yoke, so Hananiah was able to break it. Thus the false prophet illustrated his false message in a manner that simultaneously cast doubts upon Jeremiah's message.

B. Interpretation (v. 11)

11. And Hananiah spake in the presence of all the people, saying, Thus saith the LORD; Even so will I break the yoke of Nebuchadnezzar king of Babylon from the neck of all nations within the space of two full years. And the prophet Jeremiah went his way.

Hananiah's act needed no explanation, but he provided one anyway. He repeated his former

visual 7

prediction (vv. 1-4): Babylon's *yoke* would be broken *within the space of two full years,* and Judah and the other "yoked" nations would be free.

While this false prophet made use of the true prophet's illustration and copied his language (*Thus saith the Lord*), his prophecy was still false. In two years everyone would know this. In fact, within two months they would witness the sudden death of Hananiah as punishment for having preached "rebellion against the Lord" (Jeremiah 28:15-17). This was predicted by Jeremiah, thus validating in a most compelling manner his claim to be a true prophet.

For the present, however, the false prophet had the advantage of the last word. Jeremiah left the scene and *went his way.* No doubt the crowd was pleased to have it so, for the false prophecy was the popular one.

FALSE PREDICTIONS

Early in 1988, a false prophet proclaimed the Lord's return later that year. After the Lord failed to come as expected, the teacher clarified his position and said the return would be in 1989. But the "prophet" learned his lesson. After his second failure he said he would not be prophesying anymore.

Another Bible prophecy teacher said Christ would return within a two-week period in September, 1994. Many Christians were taken in by the hoax. In a radio interview on the first day of his two-week "window" of return, the "prophet" announced that the "Great Tribulation" had just ended. More than one Christian was heard to remark that the suffering was not nearly as bad as many prophecy preachers had led them to believe it would be! Of course, it turned out that the prophet was wrong on more than one count.

False prophets are nothing new. In spite of Jesus' words to the contrary, many have claimed to know the day of Christ's return, sometimes using spectacular means to get people's attention. There were false prophets before Christ also. Hananiah fits the classic pattern. Using a vivid method of illustrating his "truth," he misled the people of God. We should search the Scriptures carefully and be wary of those who claim to know too much.   —C. R. B.

III. True Prophecy
(Jeremiah 28:12-14)

A. The Lord's Word (v. 12)

12. Then the word of the LORD came unto Jeremiah the prophet, after that Hananiah the prophet had broken the yoke from off the neck of the prophet Jeremiah, saying.

It is startling to see false Hananiah called *the prophet* exactly as Jeremiah is. How many false teachers are given names and descriptions that properly belong to the true ones! One may be called teacher, preacher, professor, or doctor; but if he teaches falsehood, no title of honor can make what he says true. *The word of the Lord came unto Jeremiah the prophet*, but Hananiah the prophet spoke his own word, a word chosen to please the crowd.

B. From Bad to Worse (v. 13)

13. Go and tell Hananiah, saying, Thus saith the LORD; Thou hast broken the yokes of wood; but thou shalt make for them yokes of iron.

The light wooden yoke that Hananiah broke was a symbol of the tribute Judah was already paying to Babylon. Hananiah promised an end of that, but in so doing he was actually preparing heavier yokes for the people of Judah. The eventual captivity of the people in Babylon would be the *yokes of iron*, heavier than the tribute they were paying while they were in their own country. That harsher bondage would be due in part to Hananiah's misleading prophecy.

C. Defeat and Bondage (v. 14)

14. For thus saith the LORD of hosts, the God of Israel; I have put a yoke of iron upon the neck of all these nations, that they may serve Nebuchadnezzar king of Babylon; and they shall serve him: and I have given him the beasts of the field also.

Although Nebuchadnezzar and his army of Chaldeans had placed the yoke of tribute on Judah and would impose the heavier yoke of captivity, a higher power was involved. *The Lord of hosts*, Jehovah, said, *I have put a yoke of iron upon the neck of all these nations*. He was responsible for what the Babylonians were doing. He had sentenced Judah and other nations to defeat and captivity because of their sins (some of the other nations are named in Jeremiah 27:1-7). All of them were wicked, but the people of Judah were most accountable, because Jehovah

had given them His special care and help (see Amos 3:2). They had received His Law but had chosen to ignore it.

The people of Babylon did not believe in Jehovah; they did not intend to serve Him. Nevertheless, they were His agents to execute the sentence He had pronounced. Into the power of Babylon, the Lord of Heaven and earth was delivering not only all the people of Judah, but even *the beasts of the field*. The rule of Babylon was to be complete.

TRADING ONE YOKE FOR ANOTHER

Many of us adults can remember when the only kind of bread we wanted to eat was that fluffy white stuff that you could compress in your hands into a ball of unappetizing dough. Our parents preached the value of whole wheat bread (ugh!), which seemed to take far too much effort to chew.

Not long ago, *Science* magazine reported that whole wheat toast and some other "healthy" foods had caused cancer in laboratory rats. Natural carcinogens in our food may actually be more dangerous than the artificial chemicals that we have learned to hate in this health-conscious age.

While seeking to avoid one evil, we may have unwittingly opened ourselves to another one! But this would not be anything new.

Hananiah, the false prophet of Judah, viewed Jeremiah as an enemy of his people. Jeremiah had worn a wooden yoke around his neck as a symbol of the Babylonian bondage that the people had suffered because of their sin. Hananiah removed Jeremiah's yoke and broke it to illustrate his prophecy that Babylon's power would soon be broken.

But Hananiah had only made a bad situation worse. Jeremiah declared that Hananiah's false prophecy had not broken a yoke of wood; it had created a yoke of iron for his people. It is better to listen to the facts than to assume what we want to believe.   —C. R. B.

Conclusion

"Relax." said Hananiah. "Take it easy. Go on with your business and your fun. In a couple of years our troubles will be over. Babylon will be out of the picture, and our captive friends will be back home."

"Reform." said Jeremiah. "Quit your greedy, cheating lifestyle. Stop your immoral fun. Otherwise Babylon will be back, and our trouble will be twice as bad as it is now."

How could the people know who was telling the truth? Jeremiah suggested two ways.

1. Wait and see. In two years everyone would know Hananiah was wrong. In seven or eight years everyone would know Jeremiah was right —but by then most of them would be either captives in Babylon "or corpses" in the ashes of Jerusalem.

2. Look at the record. True prophets have always foretold disaster as punishment for sin, and disaster has come. Why should this time be different?

The people of Judah chose the first way. They waited, they saw, and they became captives in Babylon and corpses in the ashes of Jerusalem.

A. Back to the Bible

The people of Jerusalem could have known which prophet was right. They should have recalled the Law that king Josiah had read to them some twenty-five years earlier. According to that Law, sin would lead to disaster. But disaster was always somewhere in the future.

There are many kinds of voices in our world. There is the voice of optimism: "Things are bound to get better." There is the voice of pessimism: "We're on the slippery slope, plunging to our doom." There is the voice of God: "Seek ye me, and ye shall live" (Amos 5:4). Do we want to live?

B. Knowing

The people of Jerusalem were without excuse, though several years had passed since the Law had been taken seriously by their leaders. How shall we be excused if we have a Bible in the living room, but choose to give more time to TV?

A Christian needs to know the Bible. This takes time. We need to read large portions thoughtfully to see what teaching or example we can find for our lives. We need to study the Bible in groups as well as alone. A Sunday school class is great, if we make it so by doing our homework and being ready to contribute. Also great are half a dozen neighbors with open Bibles in someone's living room. It may be greater still if there is a Bible concordance, a Bible dictionary, a Bible commentary, and someone who knows how to use them. It helps if some quiet person thoroughly familiar with the Bible is there, not to teach, but to help the others with their learning.

C. Talking

How long has it been since you heard someone talking about the Bible on a bus, in a car pool, at a baseball game, at a party, over lunch, in a barber shop, or at home? If the Bible is so vital in our lives, why do we talk about it less than about baseball scores, the crime rate, the political campaign, or the latest styles? When do you talk about it? See a suggestion in Deuteronomy 6:7.

D. Doing

Jesus said, "Whosoever heareth these sayings of mine, and doeth them, I will liken him unto a wise man, which built his house upon a rock" (Matthew 7: 24). Perhaps not many people know the Bible very well, but many *know* more than they *do*. A recent television program did a story on honesty. The investigator took short rides in ten taxis. In each cab he left a billfold with a hundred dollars and enough identification so the owner could easily be reached by phone, by mail, or in person. Probably all ten drivers knew the Bible says, "Thou shalt not steal," but only two of them returned the billfold.

Doesn't most every liar know the Bible says, "Thou shalt not bear false witness"? Doesn't nearly every adulterer know it says, "Thou shalt not commit adultery"? Doesn't almost everyone know the Golden Rule, and the commandment, "Thou shalt love thy neighbor as thyself"? Don't you and I both know the Bible says, "Thou shalt not covet"?

Are we building our houses "upon a rock"? Are we *doing* as much as we *know*?

E. Prayer

How good You are to give us the Bible, our Father; and how far we are from making it as useful as You have made it to be! Forgive our neglect, and help us as we try to give Your Word a bigger place in our daily living. Amen.

F. Thought to Remember

"Thy word is a lamp unto my feet" (Psalm 119:105).

Home Daily Bible Readings

Monday, Oct. 7—Do Not Listen to False Prophets (Jeremiah 23:16-22)
Tuesday, Oct. 8—False Prophets Against God (Deuteronomy 13:1-5)
Wednesday, Oct. 9—Do Not Fear False Prophets (Deuteronomy 18:15-22)
Thursday, Oct. 10—False Prophets Speak to Exiles (Jeremiah 29:1-9)
Friday, Oct. 11—God Promises to Hear Prayers (Jeremiah 29:10-14)
Saturday, Oct. 12—Prophets Are the Lord's Servants (Jeremiah 29:15-19)
Sunday, Oct. 13—God Punishes False Prophets (Jeremiah 29:20-32)

Learning by Doing

This page contains an alternate lesson plan emphasizing learning activities.
Classes desiring such student involvement will find these suggestions helpful.

Learning Goals

As students participate in today's class session, they should:

1. Decide why Hananiah lied to the people and why Jeremiah told the truth.

2. List situations in our society where people choose pleasant lies instead of hard truths.

3. List specific ways Christians today can keep a local congregation or a community from making the same error.

4. Choose one of these ways to pursue this week.

Into the Lesson

Before class write the following three sentences on your chalkboard or on a poster:

"He told a popular lie."

"I wanted to believe it, but it wasn't true."

"I was afraid the news would be bad."

To begin today's session, each class member should find a partner. Tell the class you want each person to "tell a story" beginning with one of the above sentences. Give them five minutes to do this, then allow as much as five minutes more to hear several of the "stories."

Tell the class that each of these sentences could have been spoken by or about someone in the story that is in today's Scripture text. Challenge them to find the person or persons characterized by these sentences as they hear Jeremiah 28 read aloud.

Into the Word

Use some part of the Introduction (page 58) to remind class members of the background to this lesson. Then choose some or all of the following Bible study activities to help them explore Jeremiah 28. (If you have time for all the activities, they should be completed in the order indicated here.)

Dramatic reading. Choose four class members to read Jeremiah 28 aloud: a narrator, someone to read the words of the Lord, someone to read the words of Hananiah, and someone to read the words of Jeremiah.

For something different, tell class members to respond out loud, as if they are watching a melodrama. This means they should cheer the hero and boo the villain—even hiss if they want. For a more "reserved" approach to the same idea, have class members make "Cheer" and

"Boo" flash cards to hold up at the appropriate times as the Scripture is read.

Outline. Write on your chalkboard the following verse divisions of Jeremiah 28—1-4; 5-9; 10, 11; 12-14; 15-17. In groups of between three and five, class members should write a heading and a one-sentence summary for each section. Allow six or eight minutes, then let each group share its headings and sentences.

Scriptures and sentences. Write each of the following sentences on your chalkboard, or distribute them on a handout:

Being popular is usually easier than being unpopular.

Many people would rather believe a pleasant lie than a hard truth.

Sooner or later, disobeying God always brings disaster.

Ask class members, in groups of about five, to decide how today's Bible lesson teaches each of these truths. Let them work in groups for several minutes before you discuss all the sentences with the class.

Discussion. Consider these questions:

1. Why did Hananiah lie to the people?

2. Why did Jeremiah risk his reputation to tell them the truth?

3. Why didn't Jeremiah just wait until they could see for themselves what God would do?

Into Life

Challenge class members to look again at the sentences that were found under "Scriptures and sentences." Discuss with them: "How have you seen each of these sentences proven true in our world?"

If you have time, consider the Conclusion to the lesson plan. Ask four class members to read or summarize one section each: "Back to the Bible," "Knowing," "Talking," and "Doing."

Discuss with the class: How can we keep our church from making the same mistake Jeremiah's people made? What actions can one person take to protect his church or his city from falling into this kind of error?

Write specific suggestions on the chalkboard. Ask class members to look at the list and to tell which of the ideas they are willing to pursue. You may want to write their names beside the items they choose. Close with a prayer time, mentioning these commitments as you pray.

Let's Talk It Over

The questions on this page are designed to encourage review of the lesson Scriptures and to promote discussion of the lesson by the class. The answers provided are only discussion starters. Let your class talk it over from there.

1. Writers of self-help books assure us that a more optimistic outlook and a commitment to positive thinking would solve many of our problems. How shall we respond to that?

The Bible endorses certain forms of optimistic, positive thinking. We can be legitimately positive about God's existence, His love for us, His provisions of salvation from sin and the gift of eternal life, and His willingness to hear our prayers. But any approach to positive thinking that ignores the reality of sin and fails to make room for repentance and holiness is foolishness. Jesus pictured a misguided optimist in His parable of the rich fool (Luke 12:16-21). The man was quite positive about the preparations he had made for the future. However, those preparations had not included faith in God and repentance toward sin. As a result, his optimism ended in his sudden, tragic death.

2. Jeremiah used a yoke to illustrate his prophecy regarding subjection to Babylon. What are some symbols that could illustrate our society's subjection to sin?

We could picture a dollar sign weighing us down. The quest for more and more money and material pleasures draws people into various kinds of sin. A syringe would be an appropriate symbol for many individuals. They are in subjection to drugs as a result of the sinful pursuit of ever higher levels of pleasure. A book or magazine cover featuring the familiar skull-and-crossbones symbol could represent those who have enslaved themselves to pornography. Even a knife and fork could appropriately represent those who indulge in the sin of gluttony.

3. Hananiah is described in Jeremiah 28:12 as a prophet. That is a reminder of how deceptive a person's title may be. What are some titles people wear inappropriately today?

When we think about it, it seems absurd that certain individuals wear the title "doctor" while performing abortions. Almost any description of a medical doctor's duties would include saving lives rather than destroying them. A person who calls himself a minister while seeking only his own glory and profit is another example. Such an approach to ministry is wholly out of line with Jesus' model (Mark 10:45). We could also take note of some of those people who call themselves teachers or professors. Instead of leading their students in an unbiased search for truth, they aim to destroy the students' faith with anti-Christian, anti-Biblical propaganda.

4. How well do we need to know the Bible? What can we do to learn it as well as we should?

A good doctor constantly studies medical books and journals, so that he can improve his ability to diagnose and treat diseases. A conscientious teacher familiarizes herself with new literature on her subject material, so that she can make her teaching fresh and thorough. An athlete who desires to excel learns all he or she can from others who have competed in the same sport. It is clear that we need to master the Bible in the same way these people work at mastering their areas of expertise. Our Bible learning would increase if we simply made better use of available opportunities. Do we attend our church's Sunday evening services and midweek prayer and Bible study meetings? Do we make it a priority to participate in special classes, seminars, conventions, and the like in which Bible teaching is featured? Do we purchase and utilize some of the vast array of Bible study aids that are found in Bible bookstores?

5. We hear the Bible preached and taught and we read it for ourselves; but do we take the vital step of acting upon what it says? What can we do to promote the application of Biblical truths?

Christians need to make themselves more accountable to one another. It was so in New Testament times: "But exhort one another daily, while it is called Today; lest any of you be hardened through the deceitfulness of sin" (Hebrews 3:13). We need to ask one another, "How are you doing with your faith? Are you winning over temptation? Do you feel that you understand God's will for you, and are you living up to it?" And as the verse above indicates, we should exhort one another to faithfulness and holiness. This kind of accountability is a feature of many small-group fellowships. Perhaps we need to investigate the possibility of participating in such a group, if we are not already doing so.

A Rebellious People

DEVOTIONAL READING: Ezekiel 3:16-21.

LESSON SCRIPTURE: Ezekiel 2:1—3:21.

PRINTED TEXT: Ezekiel 2:3-7; 3:4-11.

Ezekiel 2:3-7

3 And he said unto me, Son of man, I send thee to the children of Israel, to a rebellious nation that hath rebelled against me: they and their fathers have transgressed against me, even unto this very day.

4 For they are impudent children and stiffhearted. I do send thee unto them; and thou shalt say unto them, Thus saith the Lord GOD.

5 And they, whether they will hear, or whether they will forbear, (for they are a rebellious house,) yet shall know that there hath been a prophet among them.

6 And thou, son of man, be not afraid of them, neither be afraid of their words, though briers and thorns be with thee, and thou dost dwell among scorpions: be not afraid of their words, nor be dismayed at their looks, though they be a rebellious house.

7 And thou shalt speak my words unto them, whether they will hear, or whether they will forbear: for they are most rebellious.

Ezekiel 3:4-11

4 And he said unto me, Son of man, go, get thee unto the house of Israel, and speak with my words unto them.

5 For thou art not sent to a people of a strange speech and of a hard language, but to the house of Israel;

6 Not to many people of a strange speech and of a hard language, whose words thou canst not understand. Surely, had I sent thee to them, they would have hearkened unto thee.

7 But the house of Israel will not hearken unto thee; for they will not hearken unto me: for all the house of Israel are impudent and hard-hearted.

8 Behold, I have made thy face strong against their faces, and thy forehead strong against their foreheads.

9 As an adamant harder than flint have I made thy forehead: fear them not, neither be dismayed at their looks, though they be a rebellious house.

10 Moreover he said unto me, Son of man, all my words that I shall speak unto thee receive in thine heart, and hear with thine ears.

11 And go, get thee to them of the captivity, unto the children of thy people, and speak unto them, and tell them, Thus saith the Lord GOD; whether they will hear, or whether they will forbear.

GOLDEN TEXT: Thou [Ezekiel] shalt speak my words unto them, whether they will hear, or whether they will forbear: for they are most rebellious.—Ezekiel 2:7.

God's People Face Judgment
Unit 2: Judah's Internal Decay
(Lessons 6-9)

Lesson Aims

After this lesson a student should be able to:
1. Briefly review the instructions God gave to Ezekiel.
2. Accept the responsibility of sharing God's Word with others.
3. Describe some way to share God's Word this week.

Lesson Outline

INTRODUCTION
  A. Denial
  B. Lesson Background
  I. COMMISSION (Ezekiel 2:3-7)
  A. Hard Job (vv. 3-5)
  B. Encouragement (vv. 6, 7)
    A Needed Reminder
  II. COMMISSION REPEATED (Ezekiel 3:4-11)
  A. Easy Job Made Hard (vv. 4-7)
    Getting Our Tangues All Tonguled Up
  B. Encouragement Repeated (vv. 8, 9)
  C. Summary (vv. 10, 11)
CONCLUSION
  A. We Hurt Ourselves
  B. God Helps Us
  C. Who Is on the Lord's Side?
  D. Prayer
  E. Thought to Remember

The visual for lesson 8 of the visuals packet illustrates the importance of witnessing for the Lord. The visual is shown on page 69.

Introduction

Susan was hard to awaken in the morning. When her husband shook her gently and spoke to her, she answered sleepily without opening her eyes. Then the husband said, "Honey, your brother has been killed in an accident."

Instantly Susan sat up, wide awake and horrified. "No!" she shouted.

The newspaper reports that a teen-age boy has been sentenced to life imprisonment for killing his father and mother. It seems impossible to doubt his guilt. He admits it freely. Still his aunt insists, "I know that boy. He didn't kill anybody."

A. Denial

Very often, denial is the first response to unwelcome news: "No! That can't be true!" But denial is futile if the news is true. More than that, denial may stand in the way of what needs to be done.

This was illustrated in our lesson last week. Jeremiah told his people they would be captives in Babylon if they did not change their ways. If they had accepted the truth and changed their ways, they could have remained in Jerusalem. But they chose to deny the truth, and so they became captives.

B. Lesson Background

Review the three phases of Judah's disaster as they are described in the Introduction to last week's lesson. That lesson fell in the second phase, and so does this one. King Jehoiachin and ten thousand citizens of Judah were captives in Babylon already; other thousands still lived in Judah. Jeremiah was one of those. Last week we read of his controversy with the false prophet Hananiah.

Ezekiel was one of the captives who had been taken along with the ten thousand. He gave God's message to the other exiles in Babylon. Last week's lesson was dated in the fourth year of king Zedekiah (Jeremiah 28:1). This week's lesson is dated nearly a year later. By then, the captives had been in Babylon nearly five years (Ezekiel 1:1-3).

I. Commission
(Ezekiel 2:3-7)

From the opening verses of Ezekiel, we learn that he was nearly thirty years old when the Lord called him to be a prophet. With other captives he was settled "by the river of Chebar" (Ezekiel 1:1). It is thought that this was actually one of the large irrigation canals in the land of Babylon. The captives may have worked in grain fields, vineyards, and date orchards similar to those in Judah; but the flat plain of Babylon was certainly different from the hills of home. See how their grief was expressed in Psalm 137:1-6.

A. Hard Job (vv. 3-5)

3. And he said unto me, Son of man, I send thee to the children of Israel, to a rebellious nation that hath rebelled against me: they and their fathers have transgressed against me, even unto this very day.

The Lord called Ezekiel to be a prophet, a special messenger of the Almighty. That did not mean he was exalted to a position of divinity.

He was a *son of man*, a human being like the men to whom he was sent.

Immediately the Lord made it clear that His prophet's job would not be easy. He must take God's message to *a rebellious nation*. The Hebrew text reads *nations* here, perhaps alluding to the disunited status of the people. Through generation after generation *the children of Israel* had been breaking God's Law. Ezekiel could not expect them to welcome the Lord's message and obey it. It was more probable that they would viciously persecute him.

4. For they are impudent children and stiffhearted. I do send thee unto them; and thou shalt say unto them, Thus saith the Lord GOD.

Impudent . . . and stiffhearted can be translated *hard of face and obstinate of heart*. The captives in Babylon were accustomed to doing wrong. It would be difficult to turn either their faces or their hearts to the Lord. Nevertheless, the Lord was sending Ezekiel to talk to them, and he had to make it plain that he was bringing God's message, not his own.

5. And they, whether they will hear, or whether they will forbear, (for they are a rebellious house,) yet shall know that there hath been a prophet among them.

Even if Ezekiel's listeners would reject the message and go on stubbornly in their evil way, *yet shall they know that there hath been a prophet among them.* Ezekiel's words about future events would prove to be true. He predicted the continued desolation of Judah at the hands of the Babylonians and the eventual fall of Jerusalem (Ezekiel 11:1-12; 12:17-20; 22:17-31; 24:20-27). This came to pass (33:21).

But Ezekiel was also a prophet of hope, who sought to comfort the discouraged exiles with promises of restoration (11:16-20; 34:20-31; 36:22-38; 37). Those who were alive when the captives were allowed to go home would see yet another validation of Ezekiel's claim to speak as the Lord's prophet. Hopefully they would be ready to obey God and go back to Jerusalem with a firm trust in Him and an earnest desire to do His will.

B. Encouragement (vv. 6, 7)

6. And thou, son of man, be not afraid of them, neither be afraid of their words, though briers and thorns be with thee, and thou dost dwell among scorpions: be not afraid of their words, nor be dismayed at their looks, though they be a rebellious house.

The captives had proved themselves to be a *rebellious house.* They would not cease their rebellion and become obedient to the Lord at Ezekiel's call. Rather, they would attack God's

---

How to Say It

CHALDEA. Kal-*dee*-uh.
CHEBAR. *Kee*-bar.
EZEKIEL. E-*zeek*-yul or E-*zeek*-ee-ul.
HANANIAH. Han-uh-*nye*-uh
JEHOIACHIN. Jeh-*hoy*-uh-kin.

---

prophet with words as sharp as *briers and thorns*, and with hearts as venomous as *scorpions*. Still the prophet must go on fearlessly with his assigned work.

7. And thou shalt speak my words unto them, whether they will hear, or whether they will forbear: for they are most rebellious.

The rebels in Babylon would close their ears to Ezekiel's message. At the same time, their counterparts in Jerusalem would close their ears to Jeremiah's call and continue in their sin. In a few years they too would be deported to Babylon, where they would stay for nearly fifty years. Perhaps Ezekiel wondered why he should keep on giving these *most rebellious* people a message that they would not accept.

The answer is that the Lord was looking far ahead. In a few years He would indeed send the rest of Judah's rebels to captivity in Babylon; but some fifty years later He would open a way for them to go back to Jerusalem. When that way was opened, close to fifty thousand people would make the long trip home to rebuild Jerusalem and the temple (Ezra 2:64, 65). If we faithfully hold forth the gospel of our Lord even when it is rejected, who knows what results may appear in fifty years?

Four times in five verses Ezekiel's hearers are branded as *rebellious*. Twice comes the warning that they are likely to *forbear*, or refuse to listen to Ezekiel's message. Still the Lord insists, *Thou shalt speak my words unto them.* Do we sometimes give up too soon?

A NEEDED REMINDER

Think quickly: what is the name of the statue on top of the Capitol building in Washington, D.C.? Need some hints? It is the figure of a robed goddess bearing a sword and shield. It is the symbolic "protector of Congress." OK, here is the answer: it is called the "Statue of Freedom."

The Statue of Freedom stood atop the Capitol for 130 years until it was removed for repairs in 1993. The statue weighs seven and a half tons, is nineteen feet tall and stands 287 feet above the street. It was originally designed wearing the likeness of a liberty cap worn by freed Roman slaves. But many people in 1863 (when the statue was first erected) thought the "freedom cap" was inappropriate for a nation that still practiced slavery. So the cap was changed to a helmet, with an eagle's head and feathers.

Skeptics of government might say the goddess has not protected Congress from very much, in light of the political scandals and moral hijinks that have so often made Congress a poor example of what freedom is supposed to be about. Nevertheless, the statue is a continuing reminder of the noble ideals on which the nation was founded. We cannot deny the ideals, can we?

The nation of Israel had drifted from the moral ideals upon which God had founded it. The people had become rebellious and wayward when Ezekiel spoke God's word to them. However, even though they did not heed his message, they could not escape the ideals he preached and their own accountability to them.

—C. R. B.

II. Commission Repeated (Ezekiel 3:4-11)

With a touch of His hand, the Lord put His words in Jeremiah's mouth (Jeremiah 1:9). When Jeremiah thought about giving up his hard and thankless mission, those words were in him as a fire; he could not hold them in (Jeremiah 20:9).

The Lord chose another way to implant His words in Ezekiel, but it was no less effective. The Lord gave Ezekiel a "roll" (or scroll) to eat— a scroll inscribed with mournful messages, and promises of punishment yet to come. The prophet ate the scroll (Ezekiel 2:8—3:3). Thus God's message became a part of his very being. He could no more abandon it than he could abandon his stomach or his liver. He could only treasure and proclaim it as the Lord directed.

As we see in the next portion of our text, the Lord then repeated the commission that we have studied in the earlier verses of our text.

A. Easy Job Made Hard (vv. 4-7)

4. And he said unto me, Son of man, go, get thee unto the house of Israel, and speak with my words unto them.

The prophet's preparation was complete. God's message was in him and was a part of him. Now it was time to get to work—to go to *the house of Israel*, as much of it as was in Babylon, and proclaim these *words* that had filled him.

5. For thou art not sent to a people of a strange speech and of a hard language, but to the house of Israel.

Ezekiel was in the land of Babylon, but his mission was not to the Babylonians. He did not

have the language problem that many missionaries have—the problem of learning a language before he could deliver his message effectively. He was sent to *the house of Israel*, to his own people who had come to Babylon with him. He was not going to a people with a *strange speech* (the Hebrew reads *deep of lip*) or a *hard language* (the Hebrew reads *heavy of tongue*). His native language was their native language. It should have been easy to give God's message to them.

6. Not to many people of a strange speech and of a hard language, whose words thou canst not understand. Surely, had I sent thee to them, they would have hearkened unto thee.

In the reports of missionaries, we read of dozens of new Christians in Burma and India, and of new congregations meeting in homes in China. Meanwhile our home churches rejoice with the addition of just one person or two. Likewise, Ezekiel might have found a better reception if he had been sent to the Babylonians with their *strange speech* and *hard language*. But he was sent to the captives from Judah. They had no difficulty in understanding what he was saying, but they certainly were not happy to hear it.

7. But the house of Israel will not hearken unto thee; for they will not hearken unto me: for all the house of Israel are impudent and hard-hearted.

Thus the job that should have been easy was very hard. The problem was not in the language; it was in the people. They were *impudent and hard-hearted*. We are reminded of Jesus' words to the Jews of His day: "Ye will not come to me, that ye might have life" (John 5:40).

GETTING OUR TANGUES ALL TONGULED UP

William Archibald Spooner is one of those unfortunate people whose name has become a household word on the basis of his mistakes rather than his noble accomplishments. The term "spoonerism" refers to Spooner's habit of transposing sounds within words.

For example, a student who was not performing well academically was rebuffed by Spooner: "You have tasted a whole worm. You have hissed my mystery lectures." ["You have wasted a whole term. You have missed my history lectures."] In a sermon he once said, "The Lord is a shoving leopard." ["The Lord is a loving shepherd."] He is reputed to have told a woman looking for a seat in church, "Mardon me, padam, this pie is occupied; allow me to sew you to another sheet" ["Pardon me, madam, this pew is occupied; allow me to show you to another seat."], although Spooner scholars think this one may be fictitious.

Most of us get our "tangues all tonguled up" from time to time, but find that we usually can communicate satisfactorily in our native language. We have more difficulty when trying to converse with someone who speaks a different language from our own.

But at times communication difficulties are caused by other problems, such as a stubborn heart. So it was in Ezekiel's day: Israel failed to hear his message from God, not because of a foreign language or any speech impediments, but because of the impediment of an obstinate heart.
—C. R. B.

B. Encouragement Repeated
(vv. 8, 9)

8. Behold, I have made thy face strong against their faces, and thy forehead strong against their foreheads.

Many *faces* would glower at God's prophet—hard, bitter, hostile faces. To counter this, God had made Ezekiel's *face* as *strong* as any. Ezekiel would still need to exert himself, to do his best to be strong, courageous, and determined; but if he did, God guaranteed that his best would be good enough. He would be able to endure all the opposition and go on with his work.

9. As an adamant harder than flint have I made thy forehead: fear them not, neither be dismayed at their looks, though they be a rebellious house.

The word *adamant* is usually considered an adjective, meaning firm or unyielding. Here it is a noun, describing an object that is unusually hard or impenetrable. The Hebrew word is rendered "diamond" in Jeremiah 17:1. The *New International Version* uses the phrase "hardest stone" in the verse before us.

Among all ten thousand Israelites then in captivity with him, Ezekiel would find few sympathizers. Few stalwart souls would stand by his side to give him courage and support in his stand for truth and right. He would seem to stand alone. Therefore God repeated His encouragement with emphasis. Unseen but Almighty, the Lord would be at Ezekiel's side. The prophet need not be fearful or dismayed. He and the Lord could not be overcome by ten thousand or ten million hostile rebels.

C. Summary (vv. 10, 11)

10. Moreover he said unto me, Son of man, all my words that I shall speak unto thee receive in thine heart, and hear with thine ears.

In this verse and the next one, we see the Lord's summary of the responsibility He was giving His prophet. It was not enough just to hear the message with his ears; Ezekiel was told

visual 8

to receive it *in thine heart,* with willing submission. Whatever the Lord said would be true and whatever He did would be right. Ezekiel's words would reflect these convictions.

11. And go, get thee to them of the captivity, unto the children of thy people, and speak unto them, and tell them, Thus saith the Lord GOD; whether they will hear, or whether they will forbear.

Briefly the Lord repeated Ezekiel's commission. Several points are emphasized in these few words. First, it was time to *go*; Ezekiel must be about his mission. Second, his mission was not to the ruling Babylonians; it was to his own *people,* the ten thousand captives of Judah who were with him in Babylon. Third, he was to make it clear that he was speaking for *the Lord God*—not for himself, for any of his countrymen, or for the Babylonians. Fourth, he was to keep on faithfully with his work, whether his countrymen would listen or not.

Conclusion

Did you ever watch a boy smoke his first cigarette? The first puff starts him coughing. Why does he ever take a second puff?

Because it is forbidden. He wants to prove that he can do as he pleases. So he smokes, though it gives him a quick cough, nausea in half an hour, and lung cancer in fifty years.

Isn't it amazing the way we human beings insist on hurting ourselves?

A. We Hurt Ourselves

"Ye shall be as gods," hissed the snake. With that in mind, Eve ate the one fruit in all the world that would hurt her.

To the Israelites, God gave a detailed Law with specific instructions about what was good for them. They chose to do what was bad for them, and they continued until disaster came.

Ask your doctor just how many of his patients have hurt themselves with self-imposed overwork, stress, or anxiety. Ask how many pleasure seekers have hurt themselves with wild carousing, or how many sober, respectable people have hurt themselves by overeating. Visit an emergency room and ask how many bones have been broken by their owners' reckless driving. Ask Alcoholics Anonymous how many Americans have damaged their abilities and ruined their reputations drinking. Ask the counselors how many people have ruined their marriages and their happiness by carelessness. Search the statistics for the number of people who have destroyed themselves with illegal drugs. The daily papers tell of innocent children who have inherited the HIV virus through no fault of their own, but how many adults are dying of AIDS because of their own misconduct?

Search your church roll for the names of people who have hurt themselves by dropping out of church. Search the faces of your friends for the frowns of those who have hurt themselves by holding a grudge. Search your heart. How have you been hurting yourself?

Jesus gave His life to redeem us from our sins and to give us life instead of death, but most of mankind rejects His offer and chooses the way that leads to destruction (Matthew 7:13,14).

Why?

B. God Helps Us

God gave specific instructions to Adam and Eve: "Leave that fruit alone. It will harm you." To the people of Israel He gave more extensive instructions in the Law, and added the inspired teaching of prophets like Jeremiah and Ezekiel. To people of later ages, including us, He gave Jesus and the apostles. The way of life has never been hidden from human sight. Why do so many people choose to die?

Home Daily Bible Readings

Monday, Oct. 14—Ezekiel Hears a Voice (Ezekiel 1:22-28)

Tuesday, Oct. 15—Ezekiel to Speak for God (Ezekiel 3:12-21)

Wednesday, Oct. 16—Wait for God's Timing to Speak (Ezekiel 3:22-27)

Thursday, Oct. 17—God Gave Ordinances in the Wilderness (Ezekiel 20:1-13a)

Friday, Oct. 18—People Disobeyed Ordinances (Ezekiel 20:18-24)

Saturday, Oct. 19—Look to the Lord (Micah 7:1-7)

Sunday, Oct. 20—Prophets Without Honor in Own Land (Matthew 13:53-58)

God helps us not only by His Word; He helps us also by His presence. Jesus is there when we meet together in His name (Matthew 18:20). When one of us has no Christian friend with him, he is not alone. The Holy Spirit is with him (1 Corinthians 6:19). And God is one: the Father and the Son also abide with us when we love them and obey them. Jesus said, "If a man love me, he will keep my words: and my Father will love him, and we will come unto him, and make our abode with him" (John 14:23). If we love Jesus, we will obey Him. Then both He and His Father will live with us. So we are never alone, and we do not make decisions for ourselves alone. Planning calls for consultation. As I think of what I would like to do today, I ask, "Will Jesus and His Father go along with that?" If they will not, neither will I.

How does God help us? He gives us wisdom, if we value it and ask for it (James 1:5). Do we sometimes fail to ask, because we want to do something foolish?

How does God help us? He gives us protection, if we are willing to use it. He will not let any temptation be too strong for us to resist (1 Corinthians 10:13). If we give in to temptation, it is because we do not do our best. The devil never makes us do anything we really do not want to do.

How does God help us? Praise His name, He forgives us if we honestly confess our sins and beg for mercy (1 John 1:9). If I am burdened with a load of guilt, I have no one but myself to blame.

C. Who Is on the Lord's Side?

The Lord put His words in Jeremiah's mouth and Ezekiel's stomach (Jeremiah 1:9; Ezekiel 2:8—3:3). As Christians, most of us do not claim any such extraordinary experience; but we do have in our hands the Word of God, the Holy Bible. Are we too quiet about it?

Many people do not want to know God's Word. Does that excuse our silence? Christian teaching may be ridiculed by our fellow workers and slandered by people high in education and government. Does that intimidate us? Or do we speak up at every opportunity, trusting the Lord to make our faces as strong as Ezekiel's?

D. Prayer

How patient You have been, our Father, holding forth the Word of life through long centuries! With joy we accept it and treasure it, and we pray for help in sharing it. Amen.

E. Thought to Remember

God's power can overcome our weakness.

Learning by Doing

This page contains an alternate lesson plan emphasizing learning activities.
Classes desiring such student involvement will find these suggestions helpful.

Learning Goals

As students participate in today's class session, they should:

1. Summarize the opposition to Ezekiel's preaching, which God said he would encounter from the Israelites.

2. Decide why Ezekiel faithfully preached an unpopular message.

3. Consider whether God wants them to do something that may be difficult or unpopular.

Into the Lesson

Read the following sentences and ask your class members to raise their hands to indicate whether they agree or disagree with each one.

When a person is doing God's will, he will be successful.

I can determine God's will by deciding what I most enjoy.

A preacher knows he is preaching the truth when his listeners respond positively to his message.

Since God's Word is a source of truth and joy, men and women who truly understand it are happy to obey it.

Class members may discuss each sentence briefly, if you wish. Stop any involved discussion by telling the class that the study of today's Scripture story will shed light on the issues raised by these sentences.

Today class members will look at the ministry of Ezekiel, whose experience contradicts each of these statements.

Into the Word

Before class, copy the following Bible study questions to use as a handout in today's session; or use these questions as they are printed in the student book.

Use the Lesson Background of the lesson commentary to connect this week's study with last week's. Then distribute the Bible study questions to class members. The questions are based on Ezekiel 2:1—3:11.

Class members may answer the questions alone or in groups of between five and seven. After several minutes, discuss answers with the class.

1. List all the words you can find in Ezekiel 2 to describe the Israelites who would receive Ezekiel's message.

2. How would they respond to Ezekiel's preaching?

3. What one word would you use to describe what kind of audience the Israelites would be for Ezekiel?

4. How was Ezekiel supposed to feel about his mission and his audience?

5. What did God tell Ezekiel to do with the document that contained His words? What is the significance of this command? How did Ezekiel come to feel about God's Word? What choice did Ezekiel have about sharing it?

6. Whom does God say might have received His message more readily than the Israelites? What does this tell you about the Israelites?

7. How would God help Ezekiel with his difficult task?

Into Life

Continue your discussion of this passage by considering the following application questions with your class members:

1. How do you suppose Ezekiel may have felt about his orders from God? How do you think you would have reacted?

2. Have you ever felt that you were called by God to do something difficult or distasteful? Did you do it? Why or why not? How did you feel afterward?

3. Have you ever tried to share the message of God with someone who rejected it and hated you for sharing it? What happened? What did you learn from the experience? How does today's study shed light on this experience?

4. Was Ezekiel "successful"? Some Christians today have a tendency to measure their effectiveness for God by how others respond. What does Ezekiel's experience say about that? Have you ever wanted to quit some service for God because your "audience" did not seem to receive your message or service as you expected they would? How do we decide that such a decision on our part is legitimate?

Ask class members to share something they are trying to do for God that is very difficult. Perhaps some will share something they have considered doing, but have hesitated because it seems so hard. Remind them that God demands faithfulness more than "success." Close with sentence prayers, asking God for courage to follow the example of Ezekiel.

Let's Talk It Over

The questions on this page are designed to encourage review of the lesson Scriptures and to promote discussion of the lesson by the class. The answers provided are only discussion starters. Let your class talk it over from there.

1. In our lesson text we see God repeatedly referring to His people as "rebellious." In what ways is this an appropriate description for our modern society?

Rebellion against all forms of authority is rampant today. People want to be "free" from any restrictions or limitations on their behavior. They thumb their noses at civil authority, as they violate traffic regulations, laws prohibiting the sale and distribution of dangerous drugs, and laws designed to halt the spread of pornography. These people delight in trampling on traditional standards of decency and decorum. If God was angry over the rebellion of Judah, He must be even more angry at what He sees today.

2. God wanted Ezekiel to be persistent in delivering His message. Are we persistent enough in presenting the gospel? If not, why?

In the parable of the great supper, Jesus pictured the host saying to his servant, "Go out into the highways and hedges, and compel them to come in" (Luke 14:23). That speaks of persistence, but it is a persistence we sometimes fail to practice. We may fear that we will appear too pushy. Of course, with the destiny of an eternal soul involved, it is better to risk being pushy than to give up too easily. Perhaps we are afraid of rejection or ridicule. As a result we may be almost apologetic in offering the gospel. From pulpit and classroom we need the constant reminder that the gospel is the most precious thing that we can share. We have no reason to be apologetic in doing so.

3. The lesson writer describes how Ezekiel ate the scroll, and "God's message became a part of his very being." What is involved in our "eating" the Word of God?

First, we need to cultivate our appetite for it. Psalm 119 contains an impressive array of "appetizers." If we will give this psalm some significant attention, it will awaken us to the greatness of the Word of God and what it can do for us. A second step is to plan our study. Nutritionists remind us of the importance of a balanced diet. In partaking of the Word of God, we must obtain a good variety of doctrines, commands, warnings, promises, exhortations, and assurances. A related step involves finding a suitable time and place for study. We set times when we can eat our food in a relaxed manner. It is important to take a similar approach to feeding our souls. One more step is to follow our eating with exercise. Spiritual "flabbiness" results from eating God's Word without exercising its principles.

4. God's promise to make Ezekiel's face and forehead strong reminds us that we Christians may have to be a bit hardheaded and thickskinned at times. Why is this so?

The term "hardheaded" describes a stubbornness that can be positive or negative. Some people are hardheaded in resisting the gospel or in refusing to be reconciled to an enemy. But Christians may need to be hardheaded in stubbornly refusing to let disappointment and discouragement keep them from completing their work for God. A person who is thick-skinned may merely be insensitive to the needs of others. In a positive sense we must be thick-skinned in handling criticisms and insults. Any Christian—especially a leader in the church—is likely to be subjected to uncharitable criticisms. We must profit from constructive criticism, but we should learn to overlook that which arises out of jealousy and pettiness.

5. In their quest for fun and excitement, people engage in all kinds of self-destructive behavior. How can we show them that the greatest enjoyment and excitement comes from following Christ?

While Christianity is not a matter of "fun and games," it is true that Christians have more genuine fun than anyone. Our activities of study, service, and fellowship bring enjoyment and do not lead to alcoholic hangovers, broken bones, time in jail, or wrecked families. These are some of the results of the world's brand of "fun." As for excitement, we do not have to risk life and health to have it. No experience can be more exciting than winning another person to Christ. There is abundant excitement in sponsoring a youth group, participating in a vocal ensemble, teaching a lively adult Bible class, attending a great preaching convention, and the like. We also gain personal excitement in discovering Bible verses that speak to our needs and in experiencing answers to prayer.

Personal Responsibility

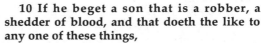

DEVOTIONAL READING: **Psalm 5:1-12.**

LESSON SCRIPTURE: **Ezekiel 18.**

PRINTED TEXT: **Ezekiel 18:1-13, 19, 20.**

Ezekiel 18:1-13, 19, 20

1 The word of the LORD came unto me again, saying,

2 What mean ye, that ye use this proverb concerning the land of Israel, saying, The fathers have eaten sour grapes, and the children's teeth are set on edge?

3 As I live, saith the Lord GOD, ye shall not have occasion any more to use this proverb in Israel.

4 Behold, all souls are mine; as the soul of the father, so also the soul of the son is mine: the soul that sinneth, it shall die.

5 But if a man be just, and do that which is lawful and right,

6 And hath not eaten upon the mountains, neither hath lifted up his eyes to the idols of the house of Israel, neither hath defiled his neighbor's wife, neither hath come near to a menstruous woman,

7 And hath not oppressed any, but hath restored to the debtor his pledge, hath spoiled none by violence, hath given his bread to the hungry, and hath covered the naked with a garment;

8 He that hath not given forth upon usury, neither hath taken any increase, that hath withdrawn his hand from iniquity, hath executed true judgment between man and man,

9 Hath walked in my statutes, and hath kept my judgments, to deal truly; he is just, he shall surely live, saith the Lord GOD.

10 If he beget a son that is a robber, a shedder of blood, and that doeth the like to any one of these things,

11 And that doeth not any of those duties, but even hath eaten upon the mountains, and defiled his neighbor's wife,

12 Hath oppressed the poor and needy, hath spoiled by violence, hath not restored the pledge, and hath lifted up his eyes to the idols, hath committed abomination,

13 Hath given forth upon usury, and hath taken increase: shall he then live? he shall not live: he hath done all these abominations; he shall surely die; his blood shall be upon him.

. . . .

19 Yet say ye, Why? doth not the son bear the iniquity of the father? When the son hath done that which is lawful and right, and hath kept all my statutes, and hath done them, he shall surely live.

20 The soul that sinneth, it shall die. The son shall not bear the iniquity of the father, neither shall the father bear the iniquity of the son: the righteousness of the righteous shall be upon him, and the wickedness of the wicked shall be upon him.

GOLDEN TEXT: The son shall not bear the iniquity of the father, neither shall the father bear the iniquity of the son.—Ezekiel 18:20.

God's People Face Judgment
Unit 2: Judah's Internal Decay
(Lessons 6-9)

Lesson Aims

After this lesson a student should be able to:

1. Describe the mistaken belief of the captives in Babylon.

2. State the true principle that corrected that mistaken belief.

3. Tell how it is possible for sinners to have eternal life.

Lesson Outline

INTRODUCTION
  A. Responsibility
  B. Lesson Background
I. PROVERB AND PRINCIPLE (Ezekiel 18:1-4)
  A. God's Word (v. 1)
  B. Useless Proverb (vv. 2, 3)
  C. Useful Principle (v. 4)
    It's Not My Fault!
II. ONE WHO SHALL LIVE (Ezekiel 18:5-9)
  A. Justice (v. 5)
  B. No Idolatry or Immorality (v. 6)
  C. Honesty and Generosity (vv. 7, 8)
  D. Obedience to God (v. 9)
III. ONE WHO SHALL DIE (Ezekiel 18:10-13)
  A. Crooked and Violent (v. 10)
  B. Idolatrous and Immoral (v. 11)
  C. Greedy and Oppressive (vv. 12, 13a)
  D. Doomed to Die (v. 13b)
    Making Lemonade
IV. PRINCIPLE REEMPHASIZED (Ezekiel 18:19, 20)
  A. Question and Answer (v. 19)
  B. Summary (v. 20)
CONCLUSION
  A. The Catch
  B. The Solution
  C. Prayer
  D. Thought to Remember

The visual for lesson 9 of the visuals packet illustrates the principle, "The soul that sinneth, it shall die." It is shown on page 77.

Introduction

Two-year-old Annie was very interested in the daffodils that grew in a long box under a sunny window. When the first flower opened, she was delighted. Seeing that it came from a bud, she hastened to help another bud open and display its glory.

Daddy interrupted her effort, explaining that some processes of nature are not to be hurried. The bud must be allowed to open in its own good time.

Annie stayed away for a while, but she was not convinced. Soon she came back to pick a bud apart with her tiny fingers. This time Daddy spoke with the voice of authority: "I'll spank you if you do that again."

Annie tried to take an interest in other things; but Daddy was hidden behind a newspaper, and the lure of unopened buds was irresistible.

Daddy's face was invisible, but his voice was stern: "Are you picking at those buds again?"

"Yes."

"Didn't I tell you I would spank you?"

"Yes."

"So do I have to spank you?"

"I guess so." The tot trotted over to Daddy and bent her little form over his knee.

A. Responsibility

Annie was an intelligent child. She learned early that actions have consequences. She was an honest child. She acknowledged her guilt and accepted the consequences. Some older wrongdoers are not so honest. They deny the facts; or, if that is impossible, they deny their responsibility.

Today we have a message from God about actions, consequences, and responsibility.

B. Lesson Background

In 597 B.C. Nebuchadnezzar of Babylon subdued Judah for the second time. He took king Jehoiachin back to Babylon with him, along with ten thousand citizens of Judah (see the outline in the Introduction to Lesson 7 on page 58).

One of those ten thousand captives was Ezekiel the prophet. He gave God's word to his fellow exiles in Babylon (Ezekiel 1:1-3), while Jeremiah was continuing to speak for God in the homeland of Judah. Today's lesson looks at one of God's messages to the captives in Babylon.

I. Proverb and Principle
(Ezekiel 18:1-4)

The Lord's message began by quoting a proverb. It was not one of the proverbs of Solomon, but an uninspired saying often repeated by the people of Judah. Apparently the people held such sayings in higher esteem than the word of God. On other occasions, Ezekiel's messages consisted of responses to the conventional wisdom expressed by these proverbs

(Ezekiel 11:2, 3; 12:21-28). Ironically, one of the criticisms leveled against Ezekiel was that his own messages consisted of nothing more than proverbs or "parables" (Ezekiel 20:49).

Such popular sayings appear in any society. "Time and tide wait for no man" is one of ours. "A stitch in time saves nine" is another. Such sayings are often repeated because they are true and because they can be applied in many situations. But some of these sayings are not completely accurate. An example is "Clothes make the man." We know this is not really so, but the clothes a man wears do help us shape our opinion of him, and thus the saying remains popular.

A. God's Word (v. 1)

1. The word of the LORD came unto me again, saying.

This indicates the beginning of a new revelation from *the Lord,* not a continuation of the one recorded in chapter 17.

B. Useless Proverb (vv. 2, 3)

2. What mean ye, that ye use this proverb concerning the land of Israel, saying, The fathers have eaten sour grapes, and the children's teeth are set on edge?

"What do you mean?" can constitute a rebuke for something done rather than a request for information. The question seems to ask for an explanation, but it really means that no explanation or excuse is sufficient for what has been done. *What mean ye* is used in a similar manner. The proverb quoted here was apparently well known in Judah (Jeremiah 31:29). The captives in Babylon had been using it in a way that was wrong and which could not be justified.

Sour grapes (or anything sour) can produce a peculiar and unpleasant sensation that is described in the phrase, *teeth are set on edge*. As the captives in Babylon were using the proverb, that painful sensation represented the pain and shame of their captivity. The sour grapes that caused it were the sins of Judah. The captives claimed, however, that they were being punished for the sins of former generations, not for their own sins. Like many modern wrongdoers, they wanted to avoid responsibility when cir-

cumstances worsened. They were saying, "It's not our fault."

It was true that Judah's punishment had come "for the sins of Manasseh" (2 Kings: 24:3), and Manasseh had died forty-five years before these captives were taken. But these captives were punished because they themselves continued to commit those sins.

3. As I live, saith the Lord GOD, ye shall not have occasion any more to use this proverb in Israel.

Ye shall not have occasion any more to use this proverb in Israel. Here the Hebrew idiom is so different from ours that it is hard to put into our language. Translating some of the words more literally, we read, *It will not be for you anymore to use this proverb.* The meaning seems to be that it will not be right or proper for you to keep on using this proverb as you have been using it. In the next few verses the Lord will show that such use is mistaken.

C. Useful Principle (v. 4)

4. Behold, all souls are mine; as the soul of the father, so also the soul of the son is mine: the soul that sinneth, it shall die.

Here the word *souls* means persons. Each individual person belongs to God, the Creator. Each one is accountable to Him, and each one must take the responsibility for his actions.

This principle calls for some careful thinking. At an earlier time, God clearly described himself as "visiting the iniquity of the fathers upon the children unto the third and fourth generation of them that hate me" (Exodus 20:5). The message we see in Ezekiel seems so different that some students suggest that God now was amending His older law. But we need not see either a contradiction or an amendment.

The sins of parents do affect their children. Many innocent babies died when God destroyed most of the world's population with a flood, when He destroyed Sodom with fire, and when He destroyed Jericho with the swords of the Israelites. In today's world, children also suffer for the sins of their parents. A sinner is put in jail, leaving his family in poverty. Sinful parents neglect their children; the children grow up in the streets and become thieves and murderers. A drunken father takes the wheel to drive home with his family, and all of them are killed in an accident. Obviously, *the soul that sinneth* does not always die alone. What then does it mean to say, "The soul that sinneth, it shall die"? Two thoughts emerge.

First, while children share some of the results of their parents' sins, they do not share the guilt of those sins. Therefore they share only the earthly results of their parents' sins, not the eternal results.

Second, He who said, "All souls are mine," is not only our Creator and our Judge; He is also our loving Father. He not only visits the iniquity of the fathers upon the children; He also shows mercy to thousands who love Him and keep His commandments (Exodus 20:6). The dawn of the Christian era brought a flood of light upon matters dimly foreshadowed in the Law and the Prophets. Now we know that God is not willing for any to perish and that sinners can live forever if they repent and obey Jesus.

IT'S NOT MY FAULT!

For many years now, it seems that some people have excused almost every lapse from standards of decent or moral behavior by saying that the sinner is a victim of something.

This folly has been satirized nicely by a newspaper comic strip. "Modern Ethics 101" was written on the door of a college classroom. Inside, the professor pointed to the blackboard, which read, "DON'T BLAME ME, IT'S: my victim's fault, society's fault, television's fault, the government's fault, the school system's fault, my parents' fault, my victim's parent's fault, my religion's fault, your religion's fault, your race's fault." The bottom line on the blackboard read, "Choose one for misdemeanors, any combination of two for felonies."

We started down this slippery path in an attempt to save every person's dignity. But by ignoring the truth of personal responsibility, we have not dignified people; we have dehumanized them. The Israelites of Ezekiel's day had a proverb, "The fathers have eaten sour grapes, and the children's teeth are set on edge," and they were paying the price for forgetting about personal responsibility. History seems to repeat itself, doesn't it? By now, we should have learned!   —C. R. B.

II. One Who Shall Live (Ezekiel 18:5-9)

God then gave to Ezekiel a description of one who would not die but "surely live"—a description drawn from the Law and the Prophets.

A. Justice (v. 5)

5. But if a man be just, and do that which is lawful and right.

The way of life was not a secret. The Law of God had been before Israel for centuries. Plainly it set forth the regulations "which if a man do, he shall live in them" (Leviticus 18:5; Galatians 3:12).

B. No Idolatry or Immorality (v. 6)

6. And hath not eaten upon the mountains, neither hath lifted up his eyes to the idols of the house of Israel, neither hath defiled his neighbor's wife, neither come near to a menstruous woman.

To eat *upon the mountains* was to join in a heathen feast, eating the meat of the animals sacrificed to Baal or some other imaginary god. To lift up one's *eyes to the idols* was to look to them in worship instead of to the Lord. The reference to *his neighbor's wife* indicates adultery. The last portion of the verse calls attention to a requirement stated in Leviticus 18:19 and 20:18.

C. Honesty and Generosity (vv. 7, 8)

7. And hath not oppressed any, but hath restored to the debtor his pledge, hath spoiled none by violence, hath given his bread to the hungry, and hath covered the naked with a garment.

"Mistreated" would be a good synonym for *oppressed*. One hoping to receive life should be careful not to take unfair advantage of anyone.

Hath restored to the debtor his pledge. To buy daily food for his family, a very poor man might pawn his outer garment, hoping to earn enough that day to redeem it. The Law said that the garment must be returned at night, even if the debt was not paid, for the borrower would need it to keep him warm as he slept (Exodus 22:26, 27).

Hath spoiled none by violence. It seems that greedy men sometimes simply took the property of defenseless victims (Micah 2:1, 2). They could escape punishment by bribing corrupt judges, but they would still die for their sin.

Hath given his bread to the hungry, and hath covered the naked with a garment. One seeking life should be more than fair; he should be generous in sharing food and clothing with the needy. Certainly Christians, who have experienced God's love in Jesus, should demonstrate this same measure of compassion (Matthew 25:31-46; 1 John 3:17, 18).

8. He that hath not given forth upon usury, neither hath taken any increase, that hath withdrawn his hand from iniquity, hath executed true judgment between man and man.

In modern business, *usury* means interest at an exorbitant rate; but in the English of our version, it referred to any interest at all. According to God's Law, His people were to make loans to the needy without charging interest (Exodus 22:25). Of course, interest was *increase*, but the latter word may have included profit made by selling produce at a price above the cost of production. The Law regarded the nation of Israel as a family in which the members generously helped each other instead of trying to make a profit.

Iniquity is a general name for wrongdoing of all kinds. The man hoping for life should avoid any kind. If called on to mediate a dispute between others, he must do it with *true judgment*, not favoritism.

D. Obedience to God (v. 9)

9. Hath walked in my statutes, and hath kept my judgments, to deal truly; he is just, he shall surely live, saith the Lord GOD.

Hath walked in my statutes, and hath kept my judgments both refer to living by God's laws. That is the way *to deal truly,* to do right, to be *just.* According to the Law, that is the way to *live* and escape the sinner's punishment of death.

III. One Who Shall Die (Ezekiel 18:10-13)

A. Crooked and Violent (v. 10)

10. If he beget a son that is a robber, a shedder of blood, and that doeth the like to any one of these things.

It was quite possible for the good man described in verses 5-9 to have a son who was very different.

B. Idolatrous and Immoral (v. 11)

11. And that doeth not any of those duties, but even hath eaten upon the mountains, and defiled his neighbor's wife.

The bad son of a good father might neglect all the *duties* to God and man that his father had done so well. He might join in riotous pagan feasts *upon the mountains,* and indulge in the adultery that often accompanied such feasts.

C. Greedy and Oppressive (vv. 12, 13a)

12, 13a. Hath oppressed the poor and needy, hath spoiled by violence, hath not restored the pledge, and hath lifted up his eyes to the idols, hath committed abomination, hath given forth upon usury, and hath taken increase.

The father described in verses 5-9 was not only honest—he was kind, generous, and helpful to people in need. The son now being described was greedy for gain. For his own profit he was utterly heartless in mistreating those who had no way of resisting. Worshiping idols instead of God, he forsook all the moral standards of divine law in his pursuit of profit and pleasure.

D. Doomed to Die (v. 13b)

13b. Shall he then live? he shall not live: he hath done all these abominations; he shall surely die; his blood shall be upon him.

Certainly this wicked man would not be allowed to escape punishment because his father was good. Probably those who heard this message would have agreed with that. It would be unthinkable for a father's goodness to excuse the badness of his son, or for a righteous son to be punished on account of his father's evil deeds (vv. 14-18). Still, Ezekiel's hearers wanted to believe they were suffering because of their fathers' sins. This convenient belief enabled them to deny their own sin and claim that God's ways were unjust. God responded to this claim in verses 25-32.

MAKING LEMONADE

George F. Will, the political commentator, wrote a column about his son Jonathan on Jon's twenty-first birthday. Jon has Down syndrome, the defect in one's chromosomes that causes physical abnormalities and mental retardation in varying degrees of severity.

Jon could make excuses about his inability to function at a normal level, but he does not. As his father writes, "He does not 'suffer from' Down syndrome. It is an affliction, but he is happy. . . . Although Jon would be forgiven for shaking his fist at the universe, he has been equable. I believe his serenity is grounded in his sense that he is a complete Jon and that is that."

In other words, instead of complaining about his lot in life, Jonathan Will has gone about being the best person he can be, given the chromosomal limitations with which he was born. He is a good example of the old proverb, "When life gives you lemons, make lemonade."

The Israelites of old seemed to delight in excusing their moral failures and violations of God's Law by blaming their parents. But Ezekiel held up the Law as the moral norm and said that

The son shall not bear the guilt of the father, nor the father bear the guilt of the son.

visual 9

each person had the responsibility to live up to it, regardless of the heritage he had received at birth. The principle still stands: accept what you have been given and then do your best to please God by the way you live. By the grace of God, make some nice, sweet lemonade!   —C. R. B.

IV. Principle Reemphasized (Ezekiel 18:19, 20)

A. Question and Answer (v. 19)

19. Yet say ye, Why? doth not the son bear the iniquity of the father? When the son hath done that which is lawful and right, and hath kept all my statutes, and hath done them, he shall surely live.

The Lord's declaration in verses 4-18 was plain. Each person is judged by what he himself does, regardless of what his father did. Still the captives clung to their opinion: their captivity was due to their ancestors' sins, and they themselves were not responsible for it.

The answer of God remained unmistakably clear. None of the people's arguments could nullify the principle of personal responsibility. Regardless of what his father did, if a son obeys God and does right, *he shall surely live.*

B. Summary (v. 20)

20. The soul that sinneth, it shall die. The son shall not bear the iniquity of the father, neither shall the father bear the iniquity of the son: the righteousness of the righteous shall be upon him, and the wickedness of the wicked shall be upon him.

Thus the principle from verse 4 is repeated, and the point of the illustrations in verses 5-19 is reemphasized. A father's sins may bring loss and grief to his son, but they bring the son no guilt. Likewise, a son's sins may disturb his father greatly, but they do not make the father guilty. There is no way for anyone to escape responsibility for what he does.

Conclusion

"The soul that sinneth, it shall die." If a soul is just and right, keeping the Law of God, that soul shall live. All this is clear, isn't it? But there is a catch.

A. The Catch

No one is just and righteous enough to merit life. No one has kept God's Law so well that he deserves no punishment—not Moses the lawgiver, not David, the man after God's own heart, not Hezekiah, the best of Judah's kings.

This was known even during the Old Testament times: "There is none that doeth good, no, not one" (Psalm 53:3). It is also stated emphatically in the New Testament: "All have sinned, and come short of the glory of God" (Romans 3:23).

B. The Solution

Through the prophet Jeremiah, God promised a New Covenant by which sins can be forgiven (Jeremiah 31:31-34). He sent His Son to establish that covenant. The one sinless man in all history offered His life to atone for all the sins of the world (1 John 2:1, 2). He who did not deserve to die suffered the death that all sinners deserved. This is what makes the grace of God the wonder that it is. Those who accept His offer become truly righteous, not by doing no wrong, but by being forgiven. Their righteousness is not attained by their own efforts; God gives them His righteousness because of their faith (Philippians 3:8-11). Thus, even sinners can live, if they renounce their sins and follow Jesus. Eternal life is a free gift of God through Jesus Christ (Romans 6:23), but even so we do not escape our responsibility. We must decide to trust and obey Jesus, and we must do it.

C. Prayer

Almighty God, Father of mercies and God of all comfort, we are thankful for Your Word that shows us the way to live. We are thankful for Your Son the Savior who opens that way for us. Dedicating our lives to You, we beg for the wisdom and strength and courage to walk always in the way everlasting. In Jesus' name we pray. Amen.

D. Thought to Remember

I am responsible.

Home Daily Bible Readings

Monday, Oct. 21—Ezekiel Made Watchman (Ezekiel 33:1-9)
Tuesday, Oct. 22—Promise of a Righteous Branch (Jeremiah 33:10-16)
Wednesday, Oct. 23—The Righteous Shall Live (Ezekiel 33:17-22)
Thursday, Oct. 24—Righteousness Is Rewarded (Psalm 18:17-22)
Friday, Oct. 25—Trust in God (Psalm 3)
Saturday, Oct. 26—Turn From Sinful Ways (Ezekiel 18:21-28)
Sunday, Oct. 27—Each Person Must Test Own Work (Galatians 6:1-5)

Learning by Doing

This page contains an alternate lesson plan emphasizing learning activities.
Classes desiring such student involvement will find these suggestions helpful.

Learning Goals

As students participate in today's class session, they should:

1. List the questions and answers in Ezekiel 18:1-20.

2. Decide why the parable of Ezekiel 18:2 is false and how it relates to the truth of Exodus 20:5.

3. Choose one way they will avoid a sin of their parents in their own lives now.

Into the Lesson

Ask class members to write a three-sentence description of their fathers, and then a three-sentence description of their mothers. When they finish, each should find a partner (not one's spouse), and the partners should share the descriptions with each other.

Next, the partners should talk with each other about how each is like the parents he has just described. Either a person can volunteer how he is like one or both of his parents, or his partner can tell him some way he resembles the description he has written.

Discuss with the class: "Are you aware of how you resemble your parents? Was anyone surprised by his partner's assessment of his similarity to his parents? How do you feel about being like your parents? How many are pleased to be like their parents? How many work to be different from their parents?"

Tell the class that today's Scripture challenges us to consider the relationship of our parents' strengths and weaknesses to our own.

Into the Word

Remind the class of the historical setting for this passage of Scripture (see "B. Lesson Background," page 74). Tell the class that one way to analyze today's text is to see it as a series of questions and answers. Tell the class to listen for the questions and answers as class members read aloud from Ezekiel 18.

Divide the reading into the following sections: Question One (vv. 1, 2); Answer One (vv. 3, 4); Question Two (vv. 5-13a); Answer Two (v. 13b); Question Three (implied, vv. 14-17a); Answer Three (vv. 17b, 18); Question Four (v. 19a); Answer Four (vv. 19b, 20).

Now ask class members, in groups of three or four, to paraphrase each question and answer on a sheet of scrap paper (or in the student book, where space for this activity has been included).

Give the groups at least five minutes to discuss and write, then ask for some members to share what they have written. Ask, "Why do you suppose Ezekiel delivered this message to the Israelites? What did they need to learn? What misconception about themselves and their captivity did they hold?"

Display two posters. On the first, write the text of Ezekiel 18:2. On the second, write the text of Exodus 20:5. Ask class members to tell you what the proverb in Ezekiel 18:2 means. (See the discussion in the lesson commentary. Remind the class that this was not an inspired proverb of God, but a popular saying of the time.) Then ask them to explain what God meant by His declaration in Exodus 20:5, especially since God said that the proverb is not true.

Into Life

Ask class members to return to their small groups and to share with each other situations where one generation has felt the effects of the previous generation's sins. They may either relate general examples or personal stories.

Let several members respond, then discuss: "Is it inevitable that we will repeat the mistakes and the sins of our parents? What does Ezekiel's teaching tell us about personal responsibility for our own sins?"

Next, ask the class (continuing in their small groups) to discuss a situation in which a person intentionally avoided the sin of his parents or his ancestors. Again, they may tell someone else's story or their own. Allow a few volunteers to share, then ask class members to write responses to the following open-ended sentences:

1. One mistake my parent(s) made that I want to avoid is . . .

2. A negative quality in my parent(s) that I've seen myself repeating is . . .

3. One way I've avoided a sin of my parent(s) is . . .

4. A sin of my parent(s) that I need to watch out for in my own life is . . .

These responses are meant to be kept private. But as class members return to their small groups for closing sentence prayers, they may share what they have written, if they wish.

Let's Talk It Over

The questions on this page are designed to encourage review of the lesson Scriptures and to promote discussion of the lesson by the class. The answers provided are only discussion starters. Let your class talk it over from there.

1. Actions have consequences, yet it seems that many people fail to recognize this simple fact. What are some examples today of people engaging in actions without regard for the serious consequences?

It is obvious that many people give no thought to the consequences of illicit sexual activity. Illness, unwanted pregnancies, and the terrible decision to abort an unplanned or unwanted child are among the results. Some of those who have engaged in careless sexual activity could identify with the sobering assessment Solomon gives in Proverbs 5. Another category of actions is that of experimenting with addictive substances. Enslavement to tobacco, alcohol, or drugs is the result. If people could see their bodies as temples of the Holy Spirit (1 Corinthians 6:19, 20), they could avoid the tragic consequences of such bondage. One other category is crime. Many individuals commit crimes without pondering the punishment that will follow.

2. "The fathers have eaten sour grapes, and the children's teeth are set on edge" (Ezekiel 18:2). This popular proverb of Ezekiel's time was not true. What are some proverbs or sayings of our time that are not true?

How about, "Nice guys finish last"? This seems to suggest that in order to get ahead we must cheat, lie, and take advantage of others. But plenty of honest, conscientious, caring people have achieved success. Here is a related one: "It's not what you know, but who you know." This proposes that the key to success is in currying favor with people in high positions. Such efforts at manipulation are less effective than hard work and diligent attention to duty. Another is, "You have to grab for all the gusto you can." Some people feel that life's purpose lies in packing as much pleasure in it as possible. There is greater satisfaction in serving God and man.

3. The *New International Version* translates Ezekiel 18:17 in this way: "He withholds his hand from sin and takes no usury or excessive interest." Should Christians who loan money charge any interest at all?

If Israel was a family in which no one endeavored to make a profit from another, as the lesson writer suggests, how much more should that be

true of the church? Of course, it could be argued that ancient Israel did not experience the kind of inflation we do today. The one thousand dollars a Christian lends to another Christian may not be worth that much several months later. A congregation of Christians may be in a position to maintain a supply of money that is made available at little or no interest for emergency situations. In Matthew 5:42 Jesus was speaking on the subject of how we treat our enemies. His words may apply here as well: "Give to him that asketh thee, and from him that would borrow of thee turn not thou away." Whether to enemies or friends, we should practice generosity.

4. "The soul that sinneth, it shall die" (Ezekiel 18:20). Why do we need to emphasize this simple truth today?

Perhaps no previous generation has marshaled more excuses for sin than ours has. We blame it on our parents, our society, the little quirks in our personality, and the terrible pressures we face. The statement God made to Ezekiel emphasizes each person's responsibility for his own sin. It leaves no room for excusing ourselves or justifying our behavior. And it gives us a sobering reminder of the seriousness of all sin. In the New Testament we read a similar truth: "The wages of sin is death" (Romans 6:23). Those are wages we may deny having earned, but they are undeniable and unavoidable.

5. In light of the New Testament revelation, we could alter the statement in Ezekiel 18:20 to read, "The soul that followeth Jesus, it shall live." How is this a legitimate statement?

It focuses on Jesus Christ. In Ezekiel's time, sin and death were linked together by a system of animal sacrifices that atoned for sin. Perhaps the people dimly realized that "it is not possible that the blood of bulls and of goats should take away sins" (Hebrews 10:4). Only in the perfect atonement provided by Christ can the power of sin and death be broken. The statement also emphasizes following Jesus Christ. That signifies trust, commitment, and obedience. Finally, the statement promises that we shall live. In Ezekiel's day the people's primary concern was for the preservation of earthly life. We know that following Jesus leads to life eternal.

A Portrayal of Doom

DEVOTIONAL READING: Acts 10:9-16.

LESSON SCRIPTURE: Ezekiel 3:22—5:17.

PRINTED TEXT: Ezekiel 4:1-13.

Ezekiel 4:1-13.

1 Thou also, son of man, take thee a tile, and lay it before thee, and portray upon it the city, even Jerusalem:

2 And lay siege against it, and build a fort against it, and cast a mount against it; set the camp also against it, and set battering rams against it round about.

3 Moreover take thou unto thee an iron pan, and set it for a wall of iron between thee and the city: and set thy face against it, and it shall be besieged, and thou shalt lay siege against it. This shall be a sign to the house of Israel.

4 Lie thou also upon thy left side, and lay the iniquity of the house of Israel upon it: according to the number of the days that thou shalt lie upon it thou shalt bear their iniquity.

5 For I have laid upon thee the years of their iniquity, according to the number of the days, three hundred and ninety days: so shalt thou bear the iniquity of the house of Israel.

6 And when thou hast accomplished them, lie again on thy right side, and thou shalt bear the iniquity of the house of Judah forty days: I have appointed thee each day for a year.

7 Therefore thou shalt set thy face toward the siege of Jerusalem, and thine arm shall be uncovered, and thou shalt prophesy against it.

8 And, behold, I will lay bands upon thee, and thou shalt not turn thee from one side to another, till thou hast ended the days of thy siege.

9 Take thou also unto thee wheat, and barley, and beans, and lentils, and millet, and fitches, and put them in one vessel, and make thee bread thereof, according to the number of the days that thou shalt lie upon thy side; three hundred and ninety days shalt thou eat thereof.

10 And thy meat which thou shalt eat shall be by weight, twenty shekels a day: from time to time shalt thou eat it.

11 Thou shalt drink also water by measure, the sixth part of a hin: from time to time shalt thou drink.

12 And thou shalt eat it as barley cakes, and thou shalt bake it with dung that cometh out of man, in their sight.

13 And the LORD said, Even thus shall the children of Israel eat their defiled bread among the Gentiles, whither I will drive them.

GOLDEN TEXT: Therefore thou shalt set thy face toward the siege of Jerusalem, and thine arm shall be uncovered, and thou shalt prophesy against it.—Ezekiel 4:7.

Lesson Aims

After participating in this lesson, a student should be able to:

1. Describe the teaching helps used by Ezekiel and tell what he taught by means of them.

2. Renew his dedication to God and His Word.

3. Give more attention to Bible study.

Lesson Outline

The visual for lesson 10 of the visuals packet is a chart that helps summarize and explain what God commanded Ezekiel to do in today's text. It is shown on page 85.

Introduction

A. Visual Aids

In Lesson 7, we saw a yoke used as a visual aid by the prophet Jeremiah to symbolize Judah's slavery to Babylon. The false prophet Hananiah broke this yoke to try to validate his claim that the bondage would end within two years.

This week we are to consider some visual aids that were used by Ezekiel the prophet. These were highly unusual visual aids; probably those who saw them were both surprised and puzzled.

B. Lesson Background

In the land of Babylon many of the captives from Judah lived in a settlement called Tel-abib, meaning "hill (or heap) of grain ears." It may have received its name from the fertility of the area. Modern Israel has a town of the same name, but usually it is written as Tel Aviv. The town in Babylon was by a "river" called Chebar, which was actually a large irrigation canal. There Ezekiel came with God's message (Ezekiel 3:15). The exiles were now in the fifth year of their captivity (Ezekiel 1:2, 3).

I. Picture of Siege (Ezekiel 4:1-3)

The Lord had taken away Ezekiel's voice, promising to restore it when it was time for him to speak (Ezekiel 3:26, 27). Such times occurred in Ezekiel 11:24, 25 and again in 33:21, 22, when Jerusalem fell to the Babylonians. Apparently the message in our lesson text was given without a word, using only visual aids. The prophecy of siege could be understood without any explanation.

A. The City (v. 1)

1. Thou also, son of man, take thee a tile, and lay it before thee, and portray upon it the city, even Jerusalem.

The Hebrew word for *tile* is often translated *brick*. This object was probably made of clay, which was the most frequently used writing material in Babylon. A stylus was used to inscribe a message on a slab of soft clay, and the writing became permanent when the clay dried. Ezekiel could take such a slab and *portray upon it the city* by drawing a map with a stylus, or he could shape the soft clay into a more elaborate relief map. This would quickly be recognized by captives who had lived in Jerusalem only five years before.

B. The Enemy (v. 2)

2. And lay siege against it, and build a fort against it, and cast a mount against it; set the camp also against it, and set battering rams against it round about.

Thus Ezekiel was to build a prophecy in clay. Probably using sticks along with the soft clay, he was to construct models of the items that the Babylonians would use about five years later to besiege Jerusalem. They would *build a fort*. The

Hebrew term denotes a system of towers used to besiege a city and to protect the soldiers from a surprise attack by men from the city. This same word (translated *forts*) is used in 2 Kings 25:1 during the actual siege of Jerusalem by Nebuchadnezzar.

The Babylonians would also *cast a mount* or mound (perhaps a ramp) to the top of the city wall. They would *set the camp*, pitching their tents on all sides of the city to be sure no one from inside would escape and no one from outside would be able to bring in provisions. They would then prepare *battering rams* to break down the gates after the defenders were weakened by starvation.

C. The Iron Pan (v. 3)

3. Moreover take thou unto thee an iron pan, and set it for a wall of iron between thee and the city: and set thy face against it, and it shall be besieged, and thou shalt lay siege against it. This shall be a sign to the house of Israel.

The description of Babylonian siege works seems to be finished with verse 2; *moreover* signals the addition of something else. *An iron pan* might be found in someone's kitchen. It was the object on which loaves of dough were placed before they were shoved into an oven (see Leviticus 2:5). This was to symbolize *a wall of iron*.

A number of views exist as to what this wall represented. Some see it as a symbol of Jerusalem's wall in which the people were trusting. Others see it as depicting the severity (like iron) of the Babylonian siege. Still another view is that the wall stood for the barrier that the people's sins had erected between themselves and God. Thus, the separation of the model city from God's prophet indicated that the real Jerusalem was cut off from God's help. Ezekiel must *lay siege* against the model city, for God Himself was now the enemy of the real city. The coming destruction by the Babylonians would be punishment by the Lord Himself.

This shall be a sign to the house of Israel. Apparently the model of Jerusalem besieged was to be built in a public place, perhaps in the marketplace of Tel-abib. There it would be seen by members of *the house of Israel* who were captives in that area. They would tell others about it, and thus what Ezekiel was doing would become *a sign* to the whole nation—a sign that clearly foretold the siege of Jerusalem.

LEARNING FROM THE "ANCIENT ONES"

We call them the Anasazi (An-uh-*sah*-zee)—the "ancient ones." The remains of their civilization may be found preserved in national parks and monuments across the American southwest.

The Anasazi inhabited the canyons and plateaus of that region for over a thousand years and then simply disappeared about A.D. 1300. No one today knows whether drought, disease, or hostile tribes drove them into oblivion.

The mute testimony that remains to tell us of the Anasazi civilization is found in paintings on countless "newspaper rocks" and on a multitude of dwellings and grain storage "kivas." A few of these remains are in good condition; some have been restored; most are in various stages of decay. In several of the national parks, archaeologists and artists have created elaborate dioramas or scenic representations to help us see what life was like among these ancient ones.

To help his people see the *future* rather than the past, God told the prophet Ezekiel to create a simple diorama that would illustrate the siege and destruction coming against the city of Jerusalem. The Old Testament message is a verbal "diorama" through which we may learn from the sins of Israel and Judah—the "ancient ones" of the Christian faith. By it we know both the cause of Israel's demise and the means by which God's judgment was accomplished. Let us learn from Scripture the lesson that Israel did not. —C. R. B.

II. Pictures of Punishment (Ezekiel 4:4-8)

Ezekiel had just represented himself as an enemy besieging the city of Jerusalem and its sinful people. Now he was to represent the sinful people.

A. Israel's Punishment (vv. 4, 5)

4. Lie thou also upon thy left side, and lay the iniquity of the house of Israel upon it: according to the number of the days that thou shalt lie upon it thou shalt bear their iniquity.

The sun rising in the east provided the basis for the Israelites' sense of direction. "East" was considered the "front," thus "north" was the direction on their *left side*. Here *the house of Israel* meant the northern kingdom, separated from the southern nation of Judah. The prophet was to lie on his left side, facing north, as if crushed by the weight of Israel's sin laid upon him. He must continue to lie in that position for the number of days specified in the next verse.

5. For I have laid upon thee the years of their iniquity, according to the number of the days, three hundred and ninety days: so shalt thou bear the iniquity of the house of Israel.

For *three hundred and ninety days* (about thirteen months) Ezekiel was to lie prone, bearing *the iniquity of the house of Israel*. Each day meant a year in which Israel would have to bear her iniquity, or be borne down by the weight of her sin. Apparently this meant the number of years that Israel sinned plus the number of years she would be punished by captivity. Ezekiel was to lie helpless on the ground as a symbol of Israel lying helpless in sin and captivity.

The northern nation had become separated from the south in the year 931 B.C. Almost immediately its *iniquity* had begun, with king Jeroboam's introduction of pagan worship and practices (1 Kings 12:25-33). Moving forward 390 years from that point brings us to 541 B.C., very close to the time when the captives in Babylon were liberated by the Persian emperor Cyrus (Ezra 1:1-4). These captives likely included people of both the northern and southern kingdoms.

B. Judah's Punishment (v. 6)

6. And when thou hast accomplished them, lie again on thy right side, and thou shalt bear the iniquity of the house of Judah forty days: I have appointed thee each day for a year.

After picturing the punishment of Israel by lying on his left side, Ezekiel was to picture the punishment of Judah by lying on his *right side*, facing the south. This he must do for *forty days*, indicating that Judah's punishment would continue for forty years.

How should this forty-year period be understood? What time does it cover? It is difficult to speak with certainty. If we count from the final stage of Judah's captivity, which occurred in 582 B.C. (Jeremiah 52:30), then forty years later brings us to 542 B.C., which once again is very close to the time of the release of the captives by Cyrus. Perhaps the number forty was used to call to mind the period of Israel's wandering in the wilderness.

Others have observed that the two numbers given, 390 and 40, total 430. This was the number of years Israel spent in bondage in Egypt, according to Exodus 12:40, 41. The longer period of punishment allotted to the north would seem to reflect its greater guilt, due to its quicker acceptance of heathen ways.

C. Picture of Power (v. 7)

7. Therefore thou shalt set thy face toward the siege of Jerusalem, and thine arm shall be uncovered, and thou shalt prophesy against it.

In this verse, Ezekiel returned to the role of a warrior coming to destroy Jerusalem. Just as we roll up our sleeves to undertake a hard or dirty job, the prophet's uncovered arm represented strength at work (see Isaiah 52:10). It was the Lord's strength that was coming against Jerusalem, though the army of Babylon was the weapon in His hand. The prophet's *face toward the siege of Jerusalem* represented the Lord's face turned in anger toward the sinful city.

D. Picture of Persistence (v. 8)

8. And, behold, I will lay bands upon thee, and thou shalt not turn thee from one side to another, till thou hast ended the days of thy siege.

In some way, the Lord was going to restrain His prophet and keep him lying in the assigned position, first on the left side and then on the right, for the required number of days. Perhaps this symbolized the unrelenting efforts of the Babylonians during the *siege*. Some students think that Ezekiel was physically paralyzed, unable to move. If the Lord chose, however, He could control the man's mind and muscles without actually paralyzing him.

It does not seem necessary to suppose that Ezekiel lay motionless through twenty-four hours of every day. His mission would be accomplished and his prophecy would be given, if he were there in position only a part of each day. He must have risen for the activities ordered in the following verses of our text. He may have been free to engage in normal activities at night, when there would be no one to see his visualized prophecies. But the daily picture had to be continued without fail for the allotted time.

III. Picture of Hunger (Ezekiel 4:9-13)

The last part of out text presents a visualized prophecy that pointed to both of the events already pictured—the siege and the captivity.

A. Mixed Bread (v. 9)

9. Take thou also unto thee wheat, and barley, and beans, and lentils, and millet, and fitches, and put them in one vessel, and make thee bread thereof, according to the number of the days that thou shalt lie upon thy side; three hundred and ninety days shalt thou eat thereof.

Usually *wheat* was ground and sifted to make a fine flour, with which a delicate bread was baked. *Barley* provided a much coarser bread. Ezekiel was told to picture a time when food would be so scarce that all kinds of grain and seed would be mixed with wheat and barley to make an inferior kind of bread. *Fitches*, for example, is a lesser quality of wheat (it is called "spelt" in the *New International Version*).

This act suggested the severity of existence during the siege pictured in verses 1-3. Ezekiel was to eat this inferior bread for *three hundred and ninety days*—the time of punishment pictured in verses 4 and 5. Why the forty days of verse 6 (representing the punishment of Judah) were not included in this set of commands is difficult to ascertain. It may have been another way to show that the treatment of the northern kingdom would be more severe than that of the south.

B. Small Rations (vv. 10, 11)

10. And thy meat which thou shalt eat shall be by weight, twenty shekels a day: from time to time shalt thou eat it.

In modern English, *meat* is not bread, but a very different kind of food. In the *King James Version*, however, *meat* meant food of any kind. Here it seems that the only kind Ezekiel was to eat was the inferior bread made of mixed grains. He was to allow himself only a limited amount of that—*twenty shekels a day*. A footnote in the *New International Version* estimates twenty shekels to be about eight ounces. Ezekiel was not to eat the daily ration all at once, but *from time to time*, probably at the usual meal times. Thus Ezekiel was to picture conditions during the coming siege of Jerusalem.

11. Thou shalt drink also water by measure, the sixth part of a hin: from time to time shalt thou drink.

The *New International Version* notes that *the sixth part of a hin* of *water* is about two-thirds of a quart. That would be less than an eight-ounce glass of water with each meal, with none between meals. Such rationing would add to the suffering of the people in Jerusalem during the coming siege and would be especially harmful in a hot climate. When the people were living on such inadequate amounts of food and water, each one would be appalled to see how he and his companions were wasting away (vv. 16, 17).

C. Defiled Food (vv. 12, 13)

12. And thou shalt eat it as barley cakes, and thou shalt bake it with dung that cometh out of man, in their sight.

The bread of mixed grains was to be prepared and eaten as *barley cakes* were; that is, in small

visual 10

flat loaves more like our hamburger buns than our loaves of bread.

During a long siege, lack of fuel frequently became a serious problem. Ezekiel was to illustrate this by using dried human *dung* for fuel to bake his bread. At Ezekiel's horrified protest he was allowed to use cow's dung instead (vv. 14, 15). That was a little less revolting (cow's dung was often used for fuel in the ancient Near East), but still the bread was defiled.

13. And the LORD said, Even thus shall the children of Israel eat their defiled bread among the Gentiles, whither I will drive them.

Not only during the siege, but all through the long captivity, the people of Israel would have to eat *defiled bread.* It would not always be defiled in the same way Ezekiel's bread was, but in various ways it would not comply with the strict regulations of God's Law. The people of Judah had ignored that Law so long and so flagrantly that He was going to drive them into captivity among heathen *Gentiles*, where food approved by the Law would not always be available.

AN EPIDEMIC OF MORAL DEFILEMENT

Cholera is a plague that still haunts vast areas of the world. Outbreaks of the disease remain common in those Third World countries where proper sanitation of food and water supplies does not exist. The disease is always acquired by consuming food or water that is contaminated by human waste. Without prompt treatment by antibiotics and intravenous infusion of fluids, death comes rapidly to the victim.

During the period of 430 days that Ezekiel lay bound on his side as a demonstration of the moral pollution and bondage of Israel and Judah, he survived on bread and water. That was bad enough, but the circumstance that was calculated to draw the attention of the people to their sins was the fact that his bread was to be baked over human dung!

Although Ezekiel was permitted to use cow's dung instead of human dung, the picture is still an unpleasant one. Yet wasn't that just the point? Somehow, Israel and Judah had to be shocked into seeing that their spiritual pollution had reached the epidemic stage. May God's warnings about their moral defilement not be lost on us.   —C. R. B.

Conclusion

A. Optimist and Pessimist

When ten thousand captives of Judah were marched away to Babylon, Hananiah remained in Jerusalem with a cheery assurance. Babylon would be crushed and the captives would be back home in less than two years (Jeremiah 28:2-4). Perhaps Hananiah became the most popular prophet in Jerusalem.

On the other hand, Jeremiah advised the captives to settle down for a long stay in Babylon. Judah would be subject to that nation for a total of seventy years, he wrote in a letter to the exiles (Jeremiah 29:4-10). Furthermore, Jerusalem would be burned and the rest of its people would become captives (Jeremiah 34:1-3). That was not a popular message. Powerful men in Jerusalem wanted the king to have Jeremiah killed; but when the king told them to kill him themselves, they decided to put him in a dungeon to silence his voice (Jeremiah 38:1-6).

B. Getting Attention

Ezekiel was one of the ten thousand captives in Babylon. There he gave the same message Jeremiah was giving in Jerusalem. He must have been as unpopular as Jeremiah was. The other captives had no authority to put him in a dungeon, but they could walk away instead of listening.

God told Ezekiel how to get attention. Can't you imagine some of the comments? "Hey, that's a little map of Jerusalem. What's the idea of that?" Soon the little battering rams around the miniature city gave the answer. "Why is he lying out there on the ground day after day?" "It's a symbol of us lying here in captivity." "Why does he cook that outlandish bread and nibble such a little bit of it?" "It's a picture of the hunger when Jerusalem will be under siege."

Some Christians are suspicious of a preacher who recruits a band, gathers a crowd in a tent, and shouts his message. We are no less suspicious of one who stages a spectacular show on national television. In some cases our suspicions have been justified. But a preacher is not to be judged by how noisy he is. A better question is this: Is his message true? Truth deserves respect, whether the telling of it is loud or soft, modest or spectacular, conventional or unconventional.

C. Testing for Truth

Hananiah said he was speaking for God, but that was a lie. Jeremiah and Ezekiel made the same claim, and it was true. How could the hearers tell truth from falsehood?

An earlier prophet in Jerusalem told where to go for an answer: "To the law and to the testimony: if they speak not according to this word, it is because there is no light in them" (Isaiah 8:20). Plainly the Law told what was right and what was wrong. Powerfully it promised blessing for doing right and disaster for doing wrong. Anyone should have known Hananiah was a liar when he promised blessing to open and unrepentant sinners. Anyone should have known Jeremiah and Ezekiel were truthful when they preached what the Law said.

We Christians are not under the Law, but the Christian teaching recorded in the New Testament is the standard by which teachers are tested. If we do not know that standard well enough to conduct a test, we are in danger of being duped by teachers who teach their own word, not the Word of God. If their teaching does not agree with that of Jesus, Peter, John, and Paul, it is because there is no light in them.

D. Prayer

In a time when dozens of voices are calling us to dozens of ways, how good it is to know that one voice is always calling to the way that leads to life! Dear Father, we thank You for Your Word, for we know we can depend on it. Help us to find in our busy lives the time to know it better, and help us to have in our selfish hearts the will to follow it better. Amen.

E. Thought to Remember

God's Word is truth.

Home Daily Bible Readings

Monday, Oct. 28—Ezekiel Ordered to Shave Hair (Ezekiel 5:1-4)

Tuesday, Oct. 29—Jerusalem's Fate for Sinning (Ezekiel 5:5-9)

Wednesday, Oct. 30—The Lord Speaks in Anger (Ezekiel 5:13-17)

Thursday, Oct. 31—High Places to Be Destroyed (Ezekiel 6:1-10)

Friday, Nov. 1—The Lord Known by His Judgments (Ezekiel 6:11-14)

Saturday, Nov. 2—Days of Punishment (Hosea 9:1-9)

Sunday, Nov. 3—God Rejects Israel (Hosea 9:10-17)

Learning by Doing

This page contains an alternate lesson plan emphasizing learning activities.
Classes desiring such student involvement will find these suggestions helpful.

Learning Goals

Students in today's class session should:

1. List Ezekiel's prophecies in Ezekiel 4 and the meaning of each.

2. Evaluate how open they are to the challenge to repent.

3. Choose an area in their own lives where they need to repent.

Into the Lesson

Begin today's class session with a word association game. Give class members slips of paper, and ask them to write down the first word that comes to mind as you read each of the following words: defeat, repentance, change, error, punishment, disaster.

Next (or instead), ask class members to write a sentence using any combination of at least two of these words.

This activity is meant to point out the importance of change in order to avert the negative consequences of certain acts. Tell the class that today's Scripture text contains some dramatic, visualized prophecies that showed the Israelites the dire consequences that would come to them because of their sin. But they ignored these warnings. Would we ignore such prophecies if they came to us today?

Into the Word

Deliver a brief lecture to your class to explain the visual aids God told Ezekiel to use to portray His message to the exiles in Babylon. If you prefer, ask a class member to make this explanation. Or recruit four from your group; each person can explain a different point:

1. The clay tablet (vv. 1-3)
2. Lying on the left side (vv. 4, 5)
3. Lying on the right side (vv. 6-8)
4. Unclean bread (vv. 9-13)

As the rest of your group listens to the lecture, they should make notes under the following headings, which they should write across the top of a paper:

Ezekiel's actions

Ezekiel's words

What they symbolized

The lesson they taught

(These headings form a chart in the student book, which you may choose to use. If you prefer, you can make this a small group activity.

Option. After reading Ezekiel 4:1-13 and receiving a brief explanation from you, students are to write imaginary diary entries of Israelites who witnessed Ezekiel's prophecy. Students should choose one of the four prophecies, indicated by the four headings above. They should write a diary entry that summarizes the prophecy and expresses the feelings of the Israelite who saw and heard it. Class members may work in groups, producing one diary entry per group, or alone.

Discuss: How do you suppose the Israelites reacted to Ezekiel's prophecy? What was offensive or outrageous about it? What was intimidating or convicting about it? Do you believe it stimulated repentance? Why or why not?

Into Life

Before class prepare a poster or overhead projector transparency with the following open-ended statement and possible responses (or write them on your chalkboard ahead of time):

Think of a time when . . .

• Someone did something dramatic to get my attention.

• I was wrong, and I did something to make it right.

• Someone corrected me, and I took it to heart.

• I lost, but I learned an important lesson.

• I was defeated by defeat.

• I refused to take good advice.

In groups of two or three, class members should talk with each other about these sentences. Each person should choose one of them to discuss with his or her small group.

After six or eight minutes, allow volunteers to share responses. Then discuss with the class:

1. How do these sentences relate to today's Bible study?

2. Do you know someone with an obvious character or temperament flaw? Do you know someone who makes the same error again and again in his life? Why is it so difficult for some adults to change?

3. Do you believe it is difficult or easy to repent of sin? Why?

Remind the class that God allowed Jerusalem to fall to the Babylonian invaders because the Jews would not repent of their obvious sins. Ask each class member to consider: What sin in my life would cause God to challenge me to repent?

Let's Talk It Over

The questions on this page are designed to encourage review of the lesson Scriptures and to promote discussion of the lesson by the class. The answers provided are only discussion starters. Let your class talk it over from there.

1. Ezekiel 4 is an interesting chapter with its description of the "visual aids" God told the prophet to use. What are some other interesting features in the Old Testament books of prophecy? Why is it important that we note these features?

People sometimes complain that the writings of the prophets are dull and difficult to read. It is true that these books contain frequent pronouncements of judgments on nations that no longer exist. The prophets repeatedly expose the same sins of idolatry, greed, and oppression of the poor. But the present chapter is one of many portions of prophetic material that make for interesting reading. Isaiah's abundance of Messianic prophecies (for example, 7:14; 9:6, 7; 35:1-10; 53:1-12; 61:1-3), Jeremiah's account of king Jehoiakim's burning of the scroll of judgment (chapter 36), and Ezekiel's vision of the valley of dry bones (37:1-14) are among these.

2. What are other examples in the Scriptures of the effective use of visual aids?

We need look no further than Jesus the Master Teacher. For example, He used a little child to teach His disciples a much-needed lesson about greatness (Matthew 18:1-4). The Sermon on the Mount was likely delivered during a time of year that made such an outdoor teaching session possible and provided Jesus with certain visual aids. Perhaps birds and wild flowers were visible when Jesus told His hearers to behold them (Matthew 6:26-30). There may have been a sower nearby to whom Jesus could point when He said, "Behold, a sower went forth to sow" (Matthew 13:3). Jesus also used visual aids not actually seen, but easily imagined, such as a lost sheep and a lost boy (Luke 15:3-7, 11-24).

3. Why do we see so many more visualized prophecies during the ministry of Ezekiel than we do with other Old Testament prophets?

The circumstances of Ezekiel and his audience may provide an answer. God told Ezekiel, "And I will make thy tongue cleave to the roof of thy mouth, that thou shalt be dumb, and shalt not be to them a reprover: for they are a rebellious house" (Ezekiel 3:26). These people had become captives in a foreign land because of their rebellion against God and His spokesmen.

They had failed to heed the message of the Lord when it had been plainly and repeatedly proclaimed to them. Ezekiel's "dumbness" and his frequent use of visualized messages may have been a part of the people's punishment. They had paid no attention to God's clear word; now they would receive it only by means of symbols. Perhaps this was the time of which Amos had spoken, when he predicted a "famine . . . of hearing the words of the Lord" (Amos 8:11).

4. Ezekiel's "visual aids" surely drew some attention from the Jewish captives in Babylon. How can we use modern media in order to draw people's attention to the gospel?

It is disturbing how so much of the art, literature, and music produced today is anti-Christian and immoral. But instead of merely protesting it, we need to produce something better with a Biblically sound message. How we need to encourage our Christian young people with artistic talents to produce works that will glorify God! What a potential there is for Christian writers who can gear their literary skills to the task of retelling God's message! Because music has such a significant impact, think of what Christian musicians can do to exhibit the power and love of Christ! In the church we can utilize art, music, and drama, along with powerful preaching, to attract people to the gospel.

5. What kind of Bible study do we need, so that we can test the claims that some preachers, teachers, and writers make today?

In Ephesians 4:14 Paul expresses his vision that Christians "will no longer be infants, tossed back and forth by the waves, and blown here and there by every wind of teaching and by the cunning and craftiness of men in their deceitful scheming" (*New International Version*). Paul indicates that only a Christ-centered kind of spiritual growth will bring that vision to reality. Our Bible study should be concerned with who Jesus Christ is, the details of His life on earth, the realities and results of His death and resurrection, and the certainty of His coming again. When we study the Old Testament, we should aim to see it as Jesus did. When we study the New Testament, we should aim to see Jesus as His disciples saw Him.

Jerusalem Falls

DEVOTIONAL READING: Psalm 74:1-12.

LESSON SCRIPTURE: 2 Kings 24, 25.

PRINTED TEXT: 2 Kings 24:20b—25:12.

2 Kings 24:20b

20b Zedekiah rebelled against the king of Babylon.

2 Kings 25:1-12

1 And it came to pass in the ninth year of his reign, in the tenth month, in the tenth day of the month, that Nebuchadnezzar king of Babylon came, he, and all his host, against Jerusalem, and pitched against it; and they built forts against it round about.

2 And the city was besieged unto the eleventh year of king Zedekiah.

3 And on the ninth day of the fourth month the famine prevailed in the city, and there was no bread for the people of the land.

4 And the city was broken up, and all the men of war fled by night by the way of the gate between two walls, which is by the king's garden: (now the Chaldees were against the city round about:) and the king went the way toward the plain.

5 And the army of the Chaldees pursued after the king, and overtook him in the plains of Jericho: and all his army were scattered from him.

6 So they took the king, and brought him up to the king of Babylon to Riblah; and they gave judgment upon him.

7 And they slew the sons of Zedekiah before his eyes, and put out the eyes of Zedekiah, and bound him with fetters of brass, and carried him to Babylon.

8 And in the fifth month, on the seventh day of the month, which is the nineteenth year of king Nebuchadnezzar king of Babylon, came Nebuzaradan, captain of the guard, a servant of the king of Babylon, unto Jerusalem:

9 And he burnt the house of the LORD, and the king's house, and all the houses of Jerusalem, and every great man's house burnt he with fire.

10 And all the army of the Chaldees, that were with the captain of the guard, brake down the walls of Jerusalem round about.

11 Now the rest of the people that were left in the city, and the fugitives that fell away to the king of Babylon, with the remnant of the multitude, did Nebuzaradan the captain of the guard carry away.

12 But the captain of the guard left of the poor of the land to be vinedressers and husbandmen.

Nov 10

GOLDEN TEXT: If ye will not hear it, my soul shall weep in secret places for your pride; and mine eye shall weep sore, and run down with tears, because the LORD's flock is carried away captive.—Jeremiah 13:17.

God's People Face Judgment
Unit 3: The Fall of Jerusalem
(Lessons 10-13)

Lesson Aims

After this lesson a student should be able to:
1. Tell about the siege of Jerusalem.
2. Explain why Jerusalem was destroyed.
3. Compare obedience to God in his town or city with the obedience in Jerusalem.
4. Improve his own obedience to God.

Lesson Outline

Use the time line for lesson 11 of the visuals packet to call attention to the time of Jerusalem's fall. It is shown on page 92.

Introduction

It will be helpful to refer once again to the material provided in the Introduction to Lesson 7 on page 58 (under the heading "C. Disaster in Three Phases"). This is a summary of the significant events leading up to the fall of Jerusalem in 586 B.C.—the focus of our Scripture for today.

A. Getting What We Deserve

Although prophets such as Jeremiah, Habakkuk, and Ezekiel had been warning their audiences repeatedly that the destruction of Jerusalem was imminent, these men did not rejoice to see the city fall. Theirs was not an "I told you so" attitude, as they watched Jerusalem's residents leaving their homes in tears.

No type of discipline, whether coming from parents, judges, church elders, or prophets is easy to administer. But in a fallen world, such discipline is necessary to maintain order in a home, a church, and a society. Those who fail to heed the clear warnings they have been given should expect no other treatment except that of punishment.

Perhaps we should pause at this point to consider how unparalleled the message of the cross continues to be. The Son of God, who did nothing to deserve punishment, took upon Himself the treatment that we had coming to us. In mercy God has provided a way for sinful man to be saved. A way was also provided for the people of Judah. They simply refused to accept it.

B. Lesson Background

During October we read how Jeremiah continued to give God's word to the people who stayed in Judah, and how Ezekiel did the same for the captives in Babylon. In last week's lesson we read that Ezekiel built a model city in clay to foretell the end of Jerusalem. Now we are to see how that prophecy was fulfilled.

I. Defeat
(2 Kings 24:20b—25:4)

We can understand why Nebuchadnezzar's patience was wearing thin when king Zedekiah rebelled against Babylonian rule. Nebuchadnezzar's army was having to march against Jerusalem for the third time. He realized that the only way to deal with this problem was to eliminate it.

A. Rebellion (v. 20b)

20b. Zedekiah rebelled against the king of Babylon.

Zedekiah was the native king whom Nebuchadnezzar had left to rule Judah after the ten thousand captives had been removed in 597 B.C. He was an uncle of the king (Jehoiachin) who had been taken to Babylon (v. 15).

Zedekiah had been made to swear allegiance to Nebuchadnezzar (2 Chronicles 36:13), but now he *rebelled*. Perhaps it distressed him to pay the heavy tribute to Babylon year after year.

He may have thought Nebuchadnezzar and his army were busy with troubles elsewhere in the empire. He may have hoped for an alliance with other small kingdoms, which would be strong enough to break off the yoke of Babylon. It is also possible that he thought that Egypt would come to help him, especially since a new, more aggressive pharaoh had recently assumed power in Egypt. Whatever his reasons were, and in spite of the warnings of Jeremiah, Zedekiah broke his oath and rebelled.

B. Siege (vv. 1, 2)

1. And it came to pass in the ninth year of his reign, in the tenth month, in the tenth day of the month, that Nebuchadnezzar king of Babylon came, he, and all his host, against Jerusalem, and pitched against it; and they built forts against it round about.

The *ninth year of his reign* refers to Zedekiah, thus placing the beginning of the siege around 588 B.C. *All his host* means that Nebuchadnezzar's entire army was involved in this campaign. Of course he had other troops in other parts of his empire. We are not told how many soldiers came *against Jerusalem*, but surely the number was so overwhelming that the men of Judah would not dare to meet them in open battle. The people of Judah could only take refuge behind the strong walls of Jerusalem.

The Babylonians surrounded the city and *pitched* their camp on every side, so that no one could sneak in with food for the hungry defenders or escape from the besieged city. They also *built forts against it round about*. The Hebrew word rendered *forts* is the same word translated *fort* in Ezekiel 4:2, which was part of last week's lesson text. There Ezekiel visualized the coming siege of Jerusalem; here his prophecy came to fulfillment. The word denotes the assault towers manned by archers by which a besieged city was attacked. These towers were sometimes as much as twenty stories high.

2. And the city was besieged unto the eleventh year of king Zedekiah.

From the dates given in verses 1 and 3, we see that the siege continued about a year and a half.

C. Crisis (v. 3)

3. And on the ninth day of the fourth month the famine prevailed in the city, and there was no bread for the people of the land.

Within a year and a half, the siege reached a critical stage. The food stored in the city was all gone. The starving people had no strength or will to resist the invaders. Inside their strong walls they were safe from Babylonian swords, but they were about to die of starvation.

D. Attack and Flight (v. 4)

4. And the city was broken up, and all the men of war fled by night by the way of the gate between two walls, which is by the king's garden: (now the Chaldees were against the city round about:) and the king went the way toward the plain.

Some of the starving people "fell away" (v. 11); that is, they slipped out of the city and surrendered. From such defectors the Babylonians knew how terrible the famine was becoming. When they judged that the people were too weak to resist, they brought up a battering ram and broke into the city. Probably they smashed a gate on the north side, where the ground was nearly level. Officers of the Babylonian army then came in and established their headquarters at "the middle gate" (Jeremiah 39:3).

Judah's *men of war*, the soldiers who were there to defend the city, thought resistance was useless. They tried to escape by night through the other side of the city at the southeastern corner, near which was located *the king's garden*. The king went with them (Jeremiah 39:4), likely accompanied by the other officials of Judah.

Chaldees is another name for the Babylonians. When their troops, who had surrounded the city, joined in the effort to break through the walls, they left some unprotected sections through which Zedekiah and those with him could escape. The compact body of Judah's soldiers found such an opening and fled eastward, down the mountain road to the narrow *plain* beside the Jordan River.

COURAGE AND COWARDICE

The annals of warfare are filled with stories of both unbelievable courage and unspeakable cowardice. Out of World War II came the story of the bravery of Corrie Ten Boom and her family,

---

How to Say It

CHALDEES. Kal-*deez*.
GEDALIAH. *Ged*-uh-*lye*-uh (G as in get; strong accent on *lye*).
HABAKKUK. Huh-*bak*-kuk.
JEHOIACHIN. Jeh-*hoy*-uh-kin.
MEDITERRANEAN. *Med*-uh-tuh-*ray*-nee-un (strong accent on *ray*).
NEBUCHADNEZZAR. *Neb*-uh-kad-*nezz*-er (strong accent on *nezz*).
NEBUZARADAN. *Neb*-uh-zar-*ay*-dun (strong accent on *ay*).
RIBLAH. *Rib*-luh.

who risked their lives in saving countless Jews from extermination by the Nazis.

Other names live on in infamy from that terrible time. Marshal Philippe Petain (Pay-*tan*) was a World War I hero who disgraced his name by leading the Nazi puppet government in France. On a single day in 1942, Petain's forces sent thirteen thousand Jews to the Nazi death camps.

Vidkun Quisling was a Norwegian politician who sympathized with Nazi principles. He returned home from Germany just three days before the Nazis invaded Norway in 1940. Quisling's aid to the German occupational forces gained him a dishonorable distinction in history: his name is now used to describe a traitor.

Judah had its cowards too. When Babylon laid siege to Jerusalem, king Zedekiah and his soldiers found a way to escape, leaving behind those whom they should have protected. No doubt they had a good rationale; cowards usually do.

Sometimes it is difficult to determine whether an act is true bravery or mere bravado. But our tendency to look for the easy way out of difficult situations should make us wary of the temptation and cause us to honor true courage when we find it.
—C. R. B.

II. Capture
(2 Kings 25:5-7)

At the point of escape, the Babylonians were too few to stop the fugitives, but they knew which way they went. Quickly they assembled a force strong enough to go in pursuit.

A. Pursuit (v. 5)

5. And the army of the Chaldees pursued after the king, and overtook him in the plains of Jericho: and all his army were scattered from him.

Those who escaped had a head start while the pursuers were gathering their forces. The pursuers, however, were well fed; the fugitives were weak from hunger.

It was about twenty miles to *the plains of Jericho*. Possibly dawn had come by the time the

men of Judah reached this territory, so they could see the Babylonians gaining on them. It is likely that the morale of the army was so low at this point that the soldiers simply deserted their king and scattered, with every man looking out for himself. It was easy for the Babylonians to round up the king and the other important men.

B. Judgment (v. 6)

6. So they took the king, and brought him up to the king of Babylon to Riblah; and they gave judgment upon him.

By this time in history, Nebuchadnezzar dominated all the countries at the east end of the Mediterranean Sea. It seems that he began the siege of Jerusalem (v. 1), then left his generals to conduct it while he made his headquarters at *Riblah*, two hundred miles to the north in what is now Syria. From there he directed the affairs of all these western territories in his empire. King Zedekiah was taken there as a prisoner, and tried, judged, and condemned. Having broken his oath of allegiance to Nebuchadnezzar, he was considered a traitor.

C. Punishment (v. 7)

7. And they slew the sons of Zedekiah before his eyes, and put out the eyes of Zedekiah, and bound him with fetters of brass, and carried him to Babylon.

Nebuchadnezzar and his officers saw no reason to be merciful to this petty rebel who had caused them so much trouble. The punishment was severe. First, *Zedekiah* had to watch while his *sons* were killed. Jeremiah 39:6 adds that the other leading men ("nobles") of Judah were also killed. Apparently all these had been captured along with the king. Then Zedekiah's eyes were gouged out, and he was taken to *Babylon* in chains—a dismal journey of nearly a thousand miles.

BEASTLY BEHAVIOR

For years, the decrepit old cannery of Monterey, California, was an eyesore to the community. Then about a decade ago, the structure was turned into a world-class marine aquarium and study center. One of the startling findings of a research team at the Monterey Bay Aquarium is that sea otters can be as vicious as humans. More correctly, we might say that humans are sometimes as violent as the dumb beasts.

Most of us think of otters as charming creatures, which lie on their backs on the surface of the sea. But scientists at Monterey have discovered that male otters will sometimes kill prospective mates by biting them or drowning them. Researchers have also observed male

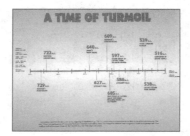
visual 11

otters kidnapping otter pups, holding them for "ransom" until the mother gives up the food she has found for her offspring.

This is very much like human behavior, isn't it? Violence is a terrible and all-too-common phenomenon of human life also. We see this in the way Zedekiah was treated by his captors. They forced him to watch as they murdered his sons, and then humiliated him by putting out his eyes. The last sight he would remember for the rest of his days would be the violent death of his sons. Today, with increasing frequency, we see such beastly behavior in those who neither honor God nor respect His creation. —C. R. B.

III. Destruction
(2 Kings 25:8-10)

Having thus disposed of the rebels, the Babylonians proceeded to make sure that Jerusalem would not be a place of refuge for any future troublemakers.

A. Fire (vv. 8, 9)

8. And in the fifth month, on the seventh day of the month, which is the nineteenth year of king Nebuchadnezzar king of Babylon, came Nebuzaradan, captain of the guard, a servant of the king of Babylon, unto Jerusalem.

This was nearly a month after the end of the siege (v. 3). Apparently the people of Judah had been living under Babylonian military government for that month. Now came a special envoy, probably from Riblah, to direct the destruction of Jerusalem.

9. And he burnt the house of the LORD, and the king's house, and all the houses of Jerusalem, and every great man's house burnt he with fire.

First, *the house of the Lord* was set on *fire*. Verses 13-17 tell of the valuable items that were removed from the temple and taken as spoil by the Babylonians. When all of this had been removed, the temple itself, which had taken seven years to build (1 Kings 6:37, 38), was torched. Such was also the fate of *the king's house*, which had taken thirteen years to build (1 Kings 7:1), and all the other houses in Jerusalem. Apparently special attention was given to the more elegant homes (*every great man's house*).

B. Demolition (v. 10)

10. And all the army of the Chaldees, that were with the captain of the guard, brake down the walls of Jerusalem round about.

When the fire had burned itself out, *all the army of the Chaldees* had the arduous task of tearing down the massive stone walls. It must have taken quite some time to turn a well-protected city into a pile of rubble. By such drastic measures, the Babylonians sought to insure that the city of Jerusalem would never again rebel against their authority.

UTTERLY DESTROYED

Dresden was once known as "the Florence of Germany," in reference to the Italian city's famous architecture. But then, on the night of February 13, 1945, Allied bombers dropped thousands of tons of incendiary bombs on Dresden in retribution for Nazi Germany's devastation of Europe. The city became an inferno.

Estimates of fatalities in the bombings ranged from thirty-five thousand to two hundred thousand people. Most of the city, including the marvelous *Frauenkirche (Frow*-un-keer-kih), was utterly destroyed. This Protestant church had been one of northern Europe's finest examples of Baroque (Buh-*roke*) architecture. For nearly fifty years, the pile of debris and a couple of standing portions of the walls were left as silent reminders of the horrors of war. Then, in 1993, city officials began rebuilding the church. They hope to have it completed by the year 2006, sixty-one years after it was destroyed.

Modern weapons of warfare devastated Dresden and decimated its populace, but the primitive weapons of the Babylonians destroyed Jerusalem just as completely. The temple, the palace, and all the houses were burned, and the city walls were leveled. And so they would remain until the Jews returned and possessed the means and the leadership necessary to rebuild them. The destruction of Jerusalem was God's retribution on Judah for generations of unfaithfulness. The testimony of the Bible stands as a witness of the wages of sin to all who will see.
—C. R. B.

IV. Captivity
(2 Kings 25:11,12)

The people of Judah had lost their homes; now they were to lose their homeland as well.

A. Taken to Babylon (v. 11)

11. Now the rest of the people that were left in the city, and the fugitives that fell away to the king of Babylon, with the remnant of the multitude, did Nebuzaradan the captain of the guard carry away.

Now began the long, dreary march of nearly a thousand miles to Babylon. The same official who had supervised the demolition took charge of the deportation. He assembled the people who were still alive in Jerusalem after the siege, those who had gone out and surrendered during the siege, and *the remnant of the multitude*. This last phrase may include some people of Judah who had not been in Jerusalem during the siege, but had stayed out in the hills or down in the Jordan Valley.

B. Left Behind (v. 12)

12. But the captain of the guard left of the poor of the land to be vinedressers and husbandmen.

The Babylonians did not want the land of Judah to be entirely uninhabited. They left some people to till the ground and to produce some revenue for Babylon. Those left behind were some of *the poor of the land*. Without wealth, influence, or leadership, they would not be likely to stage another rebellion. Nebuzaradan "gave them vineyards and fields" (Jeremiah 39:10), hoping that they would peacefully till their farms and pay whatever taxes they were asked to pay. A man named Gedaliah was put in charge of the remnant, with the title of governor rather than king (Jeremiah 40:5).

Probably these farmers found homes in the villages that had not been destroyed along with Jerusalem. Men of Judah who had been in hiding now joined them, and many came back from foreign countries where they had found refuge.

Conclusion

"Everything that was written in the past was written to teach us, so that through endurance and the encouragement of the Scriptures we might have hope" (Romans 15:4, *New International Version*). So what does the history of Israel teach us?

Home Daily Bible Readings

A. Prosperity Can Be Dangerous

With rare exceptions, the people of Israel were loyal and obedient to God when they were fighting their way into the promised land and risking their lives every day. God gave them victory. Then they became prosperous, at ease, and comfortable. Soon the more prosperous ones found that they could become even more prosperous by cheating poorer neighbors. They found pleasure in the heathen feasts of their godless neighbors. In prosperity they drifted away from God, but then their prosperity began to vanish. Crops failed, or bandits invaded the land and stole harvests and livestock. This brought poverty and misery. In their suffering the people sought God again and begged Him for help. Prosperity returned—and then they drifted away from God again.

Such was the history of Israel for some eight hundred years. What does it teach us? It teaches us to put obedience to God and helpfulness to others above our own profit and pleasure. Have we learned?

B. Misinterpreting Mercy

God did not destroy His people as soon as they began to drift away from Him. In mercy He gave them time to turn back to Him in worship and obedience. But they misinterpreted His mercy. They took it as permission to keep drifting away.

How many are drifting away from God now? In mercy God delays punishment, yet drifters continue in their path.

We are warned that some will doubt Jesus' promise that He will come again. "He's not coming," they say. "We can forget about Him and do as we please." But He is coming, and so is disaster to those who disobey Him (2 Peter 3:3-10).

What does Israel's history teach us regarding this? It teaches us that God always keeps His promises. It teaches that He lives and rules. It teaches that our ultimate success depends on doing His will. Have we learned?

C. Prayer

Father in Heaven, King eternal, Ruler of Heaven and earth, we give You thanks for Your faultless Word. In its perfect light we see and confess our sins. For these we beg forgiveness as we dedicate anew our lives to Your service. May we be guided by Your wisdom and strengthened by Your power to do Your will. In Jesus' name we pray. Amen.

D. Thought to Remember

God lives; God knows; God rules.

Learning by Doing

*This page contains an alternate lesson plan emphasizing learning activities.
Classes desiring such student involvement will find these suggestions helpful.*

Learning Goals

As students participate in today's class session, they should:

1. Discover the terrible consequences that finally came to Jerusalem because of the sins of the Jews.

2. Recognize that God is a God of both mercy and wrath.

3. Understand their need for God's continued mercy.

Into the Lesson

Ask the class to make a list of "Everyday Warnings." As class members suggest ideas, write them on your chalkboard. These should be warning signals that anyone might hear or see in a normal week. If your group needs some ideas to get started, suggest a speed limit sign, a railroad crossing flasher, or a warning light on an automobile dashboard.

After you have completed as long a list as possible in a few minutes, ask the class, "What happens when each of these warnings is ignored?" If you wish, you may jot down the consequences in a column beside the first list. If you have time, you may ask members to tell what happened to them when they ignored one of the warnings.

Tell the class that today's lesson on the fall of Jerusalem shows the terrible consequences of ignoring God's warnings.

Into the Word

Use material from the Introduction to the lesson commentary to set the historical context for today's lesson. Last week's study looked at Ezekiel's dramatic prophecies of the fall of Jerusalem. This study examines the fall itself.

The student book contains the following list of events from 2 Kings 25:1-21 (prepare a handout if you prefer). The sentences are not in order, and the number before each sentence has been removed. Ask class members, in groups of two or three, to examine the text and to put the sentences in order.

(1) Nebuchadnezzar marched against Jerusalem.

(2) Nebuchadnezzar's army kept Jerusalem under siege.

(3) Famine in Jerusalem left the people with nothing to eat.

(4) The Babylonians broke the wall and entered the city.

(5) Zedekiah, king of Judah, fled Jerusalem with his army, because they decided resistance against the Babylonians was useless.

(6) Zedekiah, king of Judah, was captured by Babylonian forces in the plains of Jericho.

(7) Zedekiah watched as his own sons were killed.

(8) Zedekiah was blinded by the Babylonians, put into shackles, and taken to Babylon.

(9) A Babylonian official burned down the temple, the palace, and every other important building in Jerusalem.

(10) All the walls surrounding Jerusalem were destroyed.

(11) All but the poorest residents of Jerusalem were taken into exile in Babylon.

(12) The Babylonians looted the temple, transporting valuable bronze, gold, and silver items back to Babylon.

(13) The king of Babylon executed the chief priest, as well as other priests and officials from the land of Judah.

After several minutes review the sentences with the class, making sure everyone has the order correct. Ask the class to brainstorm a list of words that describe how they feel after reading this story.

Into Life

Write these two sentences on your chalkboard: "God is a God of mercy." "God is a God of wrath." Ask the class to decide how our study so far this quarter, and in particular our study this week, illustrates each of these truths. If you have time, let half of the class, in groups, discuss the first sentence while the other half discusses the second sentence.

Let several members share their thoughts. You may want to add some of the material from the Conclusion to the lesson commentary, particularly under the heading, "B. Misinterpreting Mercy."

Ask the class members to put together a list for your chalkboard under the heading, "Our Country Needs God's Mercy Because . . ." As members suggest items, write them under the heading.

End with sentence prayers for God's mercy upon our country.

Let's Talk It Over

The questions on this page are designed to encourage review of the lesson Scriptures and to promote discussion of the lesson by the class. The answers provided are only discussion starters. Let your class talk it over from there.

1. For Jerusalem, the long-prophesied judgment finally came when the Babylonian armies laid siege to the city. How can we compare this with the certainty of judgment upon our society?

The time of judgment will at last arrive. It may seem to the careless sinner that he will avoid reaping the fruits of his immoral and ungodly behavior, but the moment of harvest will come. Peter describes some of these careless ones as "scoffers, walking after their own lusts, and saying, Where is the promise of his coming? for since the fathers fell asleep, all things continue as they were from the beginning of the creation" (2 Peter 3:3, 4). Judgment will come with Jesus' return to earth. It may also come as a result of military defeat, economic collapse, or moral chaos. One way or another, it is inevitable, and we need to warn sinners of it.

2. We may wince as we read of the punishment king Zedekiah received from the Babylonians. Why did God allow him to be treated so cruelly? Does this apply in any way to our own time?

The Babylonians blinded Zedekiah. Prior to that they made sure that the last scene his eyes would behold was the brutal execution of his sons. Then they carried him off in chains to Babylon. But it was a punishment he deserved. He had rejected God and God's prophets. His rebellion against Nebuchadnezzar was foolish and presumptuous, since he had ignored prophetic counsel in the matter. In our time Christians differ on the subject of capital punishment. Perhaps we will not want to debate that in class. But one point needs to be made: If it seems cruel to strap a criminal in an electric chair or administer a lethal injection to him, it is no more cruel than the crime that led to his sentencing.

3. Can we appreciate the horror of exile from one's homeland, such as the people of Judah experienced? What can we do to deepen our awareness of it?

Psalm 137 gives us a glimpse into the hearts of the exiles. We see the weeping, the desolation, the longing for home, and the bitterness toward the Babylonians that they experienced. Aside from what the Bible shows us, we can draw upon our own circumstances. If we have ever been homesick, we know how painful that can be. Remembering that experience and then imagining our separation from home as a permanent, irrevocable act can aid us in understanding the exiles' suffering. If we have lost our home or valuable possessions in a disaster, we also have a hint of the exiles' desolation. Many of them had witnessed the complete devastation of their homes. From a positive standpoint, let us thank God that we have not undergone all that the people of Judah suffered. And let us pray for Christians in other parts of the world who are suffering such deprivation because of their faith.

4. The lesson writer states, "Prosperity can be dangerous." How is this so, and how can we guard against this danger?

In Proverbs 30:8, 9 we find this prayer: "Give me neither poverty nor riches, but give me only my daily bread. Otherwise, I may have too much and disown you and say, 'Who is the Lord?'" (*New International Version*). This is a prayer that we would do well to pray. If we have too much money and too many possessions, we may become so self-sufficient and comfortable that we will tend to forget God. In a famous statement in 1 Timothy 6:10, Paul notes that "the love of money is the root of all evil." Can we be sure that our heart is strong enough to resist that kind of love? Thus it is wise for us to pray, "Lord, give me enough, but not too much."

5. Why are people today prone to misinterpret God's mercy? That is, why do they assume that His slowness to punish their sins gives them permission to continue in those sins?

We human beings sometimes think that God is like us. We can easily excuse ourselves for wrongdoing, and we assume that He does the same. On occasion we forget to carry out the threats we make, and we seem to regard God as equally forgetful. We procrastinate and sometimes never get around to fulfilling our intentions, and we may hope that God is also such a procrastinator. But we should not presume upon God's mercy. His delay in giving us the punishment we deserve should lead us instead to repentance (see Romans 2:4).

A Cry of Anguish

November 17
Lesson 12

DEVOTIONAL READING: Psalm 13:1-6.

LESSON SCRIPTURE: Lamentations.

PRINTED TEXT: Lamentations 5:1-10, 19-22.

Lamentations 5:1-10, 19-22

1 Remember, O LORD, what is come upon us: consider, and behold our reproach.

2 Our inheritance is turned to strangers, our houses to aliens.

3 We are orphans and fatherless, our mothers are as widows.

4 We have drunken our water for money; our wood is sold unto us.

5 Our necks are under persecution: we labor, and have no rest.

6 We have given the hand to the Egyptians, and to the Assyrians, to be satisfied with bread.

7 Our fathers have sinned, and are not; and we have borne their iniquities.

8 Servants have ruled over us: there is none that doth deliver us out of their hand.

9 We gat our bread with the peril of our lives, because of the sword of the wilderness.

10 Our skin was black like an oven, because of the terrible famine.

. . . .

19 Thou, O LORD, remainest for ever; thy throne from generation to generation.

20 Wherefore dost thou forget us for ever, and forsake us so long time?

21 Turn thou us unto thee, O LORD, and we shall be turned; renew our days as of old.

22 But thou hast utterly rejected us; thou art very wroth against us.

GOLDEN TEXT: Turn thou us unto thee, O LORD, and we shall be turned; renew our days as of old.—Lamentations 5:21.

**Nov
17**

God's People Face Judgment
Unit 3: The Fall of Jerusalem
(Lessons 10-13)

Lesson Aims

After this lesson a student should be able to:

1. Describe the condition of the people of Judah who were left there after Jerusalem was destroyed.

2. Explain what brought them to that sad condition.

3. Tell how today's sinners can be restored to God's favor.

Lesson Outline

INTRODUCTION
  A. Lamentations
  B. Lesson Background
 I. LOSS (Lamentations 5:1-4)
  A. Plea for Attention (v. 1)
  B. Loss of Home (v. 2)
  C. Loss of Family (v. 3)
  D. Loss of Produce (v. 4)
II. ANGUISH (Lamentations 5:5-7)
  A. Overwork (v. 5)
  B. Submission (v. 6)
    History Repeating Itself
  C. Sin (v. 7)
III. MISERY (Lamentations 5:8-10)
  A. Helplessness (v. 8)
  B. Danger (v. 9)
  C. Hunger (v. 10)
IV. HOPE (Lamentations 5:19-22)
  A. Statement of Faith (v. 19)
  B. Plea for Restoration (vv. 20, 21)
  C. The Last Word (v. 22)
CONCLUSION
  A. Back to the Lord!
  B. A Greater Blessing
  C. Prayer
  D. Thought to Remember

The visual for lesson 12 of the visuals packet (see page 101) shows a person praying in a manner perhaps similar to Jeremiah in today's text.

Introduction

Can you recall the last time you studied a Sunday school lesson from Lamentations? Obviously this is not the most popular part of the Bible for study or for reading; but it is nonetheless a wonderful book. It is deeply emotional and filled with human sorrow, but it is also filled with trust in the Lord and brightened with gleams of hope.

A. Lamentations

The book of Lamentations is a collection of five sad lyric poems, mourning the downfall of Judah and the destruction of Jerusalem. There are graphic pictures of horror (4:10). There is frank confession of the sin that brought the disaster (1:5). There are calls to turn from sin to God (3:40, 41). There is recognition of God's mercy, and there is bright hope of a better day (3:22-26, 31, 32).

Following an ancient custom, the first word of the book was placed above it as a title. Because the book begins with a cry of anguish, it received a title that would be rendered in English, "Alas!" or "How!" (as in the opening verse, "How doth the city sit solitary"). Nearly three hundred years later, some scholars translated it with a word meaning *Lamentations*. Probably not long after that it received the expanded title, *The Lamentations of Jeremiah.*

B. Lesson Background

Last week we saw how the Babylonians completed their conquest of Judah. They slaughtered the chief men of government; they blinded the king and took him to Babylon in chains. They burned Jerusalem, and tore down the stone walls that could not be burned. They drove the survivors of Judah away to captivity in Babylon, leaving some of the poorer class to till the soil.

Today we turn our attention to those who continued to live in Judah. Although these people had been given fields and vineyards by the Babylonians (Jeremiah 39:10), they were still in a despondent condition. Their lives had been completely disrupted; their city and the temple of their God now lay in ruins. Spiritually and materially, they were devastated.

Our text includes a bit of the mournful poetry of that tragic time of poverty and desperation.

I. Loss
(Lamentations 5:1-4)

Mournful times lay ahead, but Jeremiah grieved first for the past, and for the terrible loss that had been suffered.

A. Plea for Attention (v. 1)

1. Remember, O LORD, what is come upon us: consider, and behold our reproach.

The prophet began by asking God to *remember* and *consider* the terrible disaster that had come upon the people of Judah. This does not mean that Jeremiah thought God was unaware of anything that had happened. Today when someone leads in public prayer, he often begins by calling attention to a specific need or request. Such a statement is not made to inform God; it is made to introduce a subject of prayer, so all the congregation may join in the prayer. The opening verse of our text served the same purpose. Probably this carefully worded poem (as well as the other portions of Lamentations) was not written to be the writer's private prayer, but the united prayer of a group.

B. Loss of Home (v. 2)

2. Our inheritance is turned to strangers, our houses to aliens.

The land where these people lived had been given to the tribe of Judah nearly eight hundred years earlier, when Israel had come from Egypt to the promised land. Through the centuries each family's homestead had been passed on from generation to generation. A farmer might sell his property if he was deep in debt, but the Law stated that every fifty years, during the year of Jubilee, there was to be a redistribution of real estate. Each tract was then restored to the original owner or his heirs, so that a family's *inheritance* could not be lost forever.

Now the inherited land belonged to the people of Judah no more. It had been turned over to heathen foreigners. People of Judah were allowed to live on the land and cultivate it, but they were not owners. They were renters or sharecroppers. The "tax man" would be around at harvest time to collect the owners' share, and the Babylonians did not intend to give the property back in the year of Jubilee.

C. Loss of Family (v. 3)

3. We are orphans and fatherless, our mothers are as widows.

Probably every person now living in Judah was bereaved. Countless people had died of starvation during the long siege. Brave men had died in feeble and futile resistance when the enemy had broken into Jerusalem. Leaders of the nation had been slaughtered after being captured. Most of the survivors had been taken to Babylon. Those who remained were stricken with grief.

How to Say It

LAMENTATIONS. Lam-un-*tay*-shunz.
MESOPOTAMIA. Mes-uh-puh-*tay*-me-uh.

D. Loss of Produce (v. 4)

4. We have drunken our water for money; our wood is sold unto us.

The wood that grew in Judah (which was used to make tools, provide heat, and supply other necessities) was *our wood;* the water from Judah's wells and springs was *our water.* But now even these most basic resources had been taken by the Babylonians. "We, the people of Judah, must buy what rightfully belonged to us."

It is not necessary to suppose that the Babylonians set up a store and *sold* these items over the counter. More likely the people of Judah still gathered wood from the forests and drew water from the springs and wells. They could use these products of the land, but they would pay a price assessed through taxation.

II. Anguish
(Lamentations 5:5-7)

"Every cloud has a silver lining," says a popular maxim; but when clouds are darkest it is hard to see the lining. The people living in Judah had many reasons to be thankful. They were alive. They were still in their homeland. Water and firewood were available. They could plant seed and reap harvests. They could increase their flocks of sheep and herds of cattle. For a time, however, their blessings were hidden under their tremendous loss, and they could see nothing else clearly.

A. Overwork (v. 5)

5. Our necks are under persecution: we labor, and have no rest.

The mention of *necks* suggests a yoke of hard labor. The Hebrew word for *persecute* also means *pursue* or *drive.* By stern necessity the people of Judah were driven to continual hard work. Seed for planting must be brought from far away, and quickly. Fields must be plowed and planted; that too must be done without delay. Perhaps plows must be made, along with yokes for the oxen (since the Babylonians may have used such necessities for firewood). Neglected grapevines and fruit trees must be pruned. Cattle and sheep must be taken to pasture. Perhaps every family had lost some of its members, so those who were left had to work longer hours, without the benefit of needed *rest.*

B. Submission (v. 6)

6. We have given the hand to the Egyptians, and to the Assyrians, to be satisfied with bread.

The Assyrian empire had been taken over by the Babylonians approximately twenty-five years before the destruction of Jerusalem. Thus, the word *Assyrians* is used here in a general way to mean the people living in Mesopotamia. The people of Judah had to go to them or to the *Egyptians* for grain to plant or with which to make *bread*.

To modern Americans, *given the hand* suggests a friendly handshake between a buyer and seller, but the term has a different meaning here. It may indicate a gesture of submission or surrender. In Jeremiah 50:15, the phrase is used in a verse describing the collapse and surrender of Babylon. Today, for someone to "come out with their hands up" would be the likely equivalent of "giving the hand" in submission.

Others suggest that since the people of Judah had no money, they therefore had to "give their hands" to work for the Assyrians and Egyptians in exchange for grain. In any case, they had to rely on heathen foreigners for help. That was distressing to a proud people, who probably thought of the glorious time when king Solomon ruled over many such foreigners.

HISTORY REPEATING ITSELF

Twelve hundred years before the text of today's lesson was written, the ancestors of Jeremiah's audience experienced severe famine in Canaan. Jacob sent his sons to Egypt to buy grain so they would not starve. The family moved to Egypt and later became enslaved there. They became so accustomed to living in an idol-worshiping culture that after God miraculously delivered them from slavery, they fashioned a golden calf to worship at Sinai while Moses was on the mountain with God. Their life in the promised land would turn out to be a tragic tale of continuing flirtation with idolatry.

And now, because they had forgotten God, the people of Judah were looking again to Egypt for their bread (Lamentations 5:6). Many actually migrated there, seeking a more peaceful existence, in spite of the warnings of the prophet Jeremiah (Jeremiah 42:7—43:7).

What causes us to repeat the past? George Santayana, the twentieth-century American philosopher, is credited with saying, "He who does not learn from history is condemned to repeat it." The children of Israel are proof of this.

We have much more of the past to learn from than did the people of Israel and Judah (including the inspired Scripture). Nevertheless, "each generation has to learn for itself that the stove is hot," as someone has said. Modern idolatries of many sorts would lure us away from God, and we have our own spiritual famines with which to contend. We should hear again the lessons of the children of Israel.   —C. R. B.

C. Sin (v. 7)

7. Our fathers have sinned, and are not; and we have borne their iniquities.

Jeremiah knew that the misery of the people was caused by sin. He had urged the people to turn from their sins, but had met with only stubborn resistance. The *iniquities* of the *fathers* included those of evil king Manasseh; years after he died, the Scripture says, Judah was destroyed for his sins (2 Kings 24:1-4). Now, that punishment had come to its climax. In poverty, grief, and misery, the people were bearing the punishment for the sins of their fathers.

We should, however, consider our lesson for October 27. There we read that some of the captives in Babylon were saying they were innocent, but were suffering for the sins of former generations. Ezekiel set them straight in no uncertain terms. They were not suffering because their fathers had sinned, but because they themselves had continued in the sins of their fathers (Ezekiel 18).

This was equally true of the people of Judah who were left behind in their homeland. They were in poverty and misery, not because their fathers had sinned (as they were lamenting), but because of their own sins. Jeremiah stated this in no uncertain terms: "The crown is fallen from our head: woe unto us, that we have sinned!" (Lamentations 5:16).

At the same time, the tragic consequences of the destruction of Jerusalem and the collapse of the nation were being felt particularly by those who remained in the land. Certainly they were suffering the effects of the nation's sins in a way their fathers had not.

III. Misery (Lamentations 5:8-10)

After acknowledging that the misery of his people was due to sin, Jeremiah went on to describe some other aspects of that misery.

A. Helplessness (v. 8)

8. Servants have ruled over us: there is none that doth deliver us out of their hand.

God's people should have been masters of the heathen, not their servants. They should have dominated the ungodly nations as they had done in the days of David and Solomon. But their sins had caused them to lose their high standing. Now they were servants of the heathen, who should have been their servants—and there was nothing they could do about it. They had no power to resist the Babylonians, and no other nation was able and willing to help them.

visual 12

Restore us to yourself, O Lord.

In bygone times God had delivered them *from* all enemies, but now He had delivered them *to* the Babylonians. They were helpless.

B. Danger (v. 9)

9. We gat our bread with the peril of our lives, because of the sword of the wilderness.

Gat is simply an Old English form of the verb "get." *The sword of the wilderness* may refer to the sword of nomad tribes living in the desert. People going to Assyria or Egypt to get food were in danger of being killed and robbed by such bandits. Another danger was that such tribes would invade Judah to steal food left by the Babylonians, brought from abroad, or produced in Judah. The men in Judah were few in number, and surely the Babylonians had not left them well armed.

C. Hunger (v. 10)

10. Our skin was black like an oven, because of the terrible famine.

The word translated *black* can mean black from burning, or it can simply mean *heated*. Here it may describe the fever that comes when one is near death from starvation. The *New International Version* reads, "Our skin is hot as an oven, feverish from hunger." This may look back to *the terrible famine* during the siege of Jerusalem, or perhaps it describes some of the people who were starving in the aftermath of the siege. Verses 11-18 continue to portray the dark cloud of anguish over the people left in Judah. The last part of our text, which is also the conclusion of the book of Lamentations, offers a glimpse of the silver lining.

IV. Hope
(Lamentations 5:19-22)

The lament we have been reading provides the background for the main points of the prayer. They are two: a declaration of steadfast faith, and a plea for restoration.

A. Statement of Faith (v. 19)

19. Thou, O LORD, remainest for ever; thy throne from generation to generation.

Even though the temple, which had symbolized God's presence, was demolished, God still lived and ruled. He would continue to do so forever. He had brought affliction to His people because they had not acted as His people ought to act. They had turned away from Him, ignored His Law, and persecuted His prophets. For centuries they had chosen to do wrong rather than right, and now they were paying the price for their choice.

But hope was not dead. God had brought anguish to unrepentant sinners; He could bring restoration if they would repent, and once again trust Him and obey Him. He still had power to bless His righteous people. Such was Jeremiah's faith, by which he desired to encourage his countrymen.

B. Plea for Restoration (vv. 20, 21)

20. Wherefore dost thou forget us for ever, and forsake us so long time?

In view of God's unchanging sovereignty, recognized in verse 19, Jeremiah then expressed his continued anguish at the condition of his people. In the midst of trying circumstances, those who suffer often raise the troubling question, "If God is in control, why are we suffering as we are?" Jeremiah pleaded that God in His mercy put an end to the *long time* of the people's affliction. Such an anguished cry often appears in the book of Psalms (see 10:1; 13:1, 2; 22:1; 74:1; 88:14).

21. Turn thou us unto thee, O LORD, and we shall be turned; renew our days as of old.

Now came the main plea of the prayer. Jeremiah was asking the Lord to bring back the "good old days"—the days of peace, prosperity, and blessing that His people had enjoyed when they had been loyal to Him and His Law. Obviously there could be no such restoration unless the people who had turned away from God would turn back to Him. Here the writer prayed that the Lord Himself would do this. But these people had a will of their own. They had turned away from God by their own will, not His. How could the Lord turn them back? There are two possible answers.

First, He could turn them by means of the inspired preaching of Jeremiah. Jeremiah would point out their continuing sin. He would remind them that it was the cause of their present agony. He would tell them that God was eager to bless them with peace and joy, but must wait for them to trust and obey.

Second, if such pleading would not turn the people back to God, He could allow the present agony to continue, and they would turn to God for relief. So perhaps God's man was praying, "If nothing but continued agony will turn these people back to You, then let the agony continue!"

C. The Last Word (v. 22)

22. But thou hast utterly rejected us; thou art very wroth against us.

As we see it in the *King James Version*, this last word seems to be a word of utter despair. There is no silver lining. There is no hope. The people cannot be turned back to God: *Thou hast utterly rejected us.* Yet this does not seem to be in accord with the hope that gleams so brightly in verses 19 and 21.

It is possible to render the Hebrew phrase at the beginning of this verse in other ways besides *but.* Several versions have *unless;* for example, the *New International Version* reads, "Renew our days as of old unless you have utterly rejected us and are angry with us beyond measure." This recognized the possibility of utter rejection for unrepentant sinners. God did utterly reject most of humanity in the days of Noah. He utterly rejected the sinners of Sodom in the days of Abraham. He utterly rejected the depraved tribes of Canaan and sent Israel to wipe them out. He would have been entirely within His rights if He had utterly rejected the people of Judah and left them to die in their sorrow.

But the man of God dared to pray that it would not be so. He prayed that the people of Judah would indeed be turned back to God and would be restored to the former days of peace and joy. There was a silver lining. There was hope. There could be restoration.

Conclusion

Though they were deeply saddened, the people of Judah were still blessed. God was taking vigorous action to turn them back to Him. Once He had blessed them with prosperity and comfort, and they had turned away from Him. Now He had taken away their prosperity and comfort, so that they would see their need for Him and come back to Him. If they utterly refused to return, they would be utterly rejected. The choice was theirs.

A. Back to the Lord!

The people of Judah are typical of all mankind. In paradise Adam and Eve turned away from God, and paradise was lost. The rest of us have followed their example. Blessed with sunshine and rain, with a fruitful earth and a loving God, "all have sinned, and come short of the glory of God" (Romans 3:23). Some have seen their mistakes and turned back quickly; others have waited for affliction to prod them. In prison, in sickness, in poverty or in grief, they have seen their need and have turned back to the loving Father—and have given thanks for the agony that turned them back.

B. A Greater Blessing

The people of Judah were blessed to have been prodded by anguish, but now we have a greater blessing. We are called by the glad gospel of salvation. We are privileged to know that God sent His only begotten Son to redeem us. We know that Jesus died in our place, paid the penalty for our sin, and opened wide the way for us to turn back to God. We can walk through all our days on earth with our Father's unseen presence beside us, and we can know that we will see His face forever in Heaven. The choice is ours. Why would anyone choose to be utterly rejected?

C. Prayer

How good You are, our Father! How deeply You have loved us, how mercifully You have called us, and how greatly You have blessed us! "All we like sheep have gone astray," but upon the Savior You have laid the iniquity of us all. Forgive our repeated straying, we pray, and strengthen our resolve to stray no more. In Jesus' name we pray. Amen.

D. Thought to Remember

Turn us unto thee, O Lord.

Home Daily Bible Readings

Monday, Nov. 11—Prophet's Lament (Lamentations 3:1-9)
Tuesday, Nov. 12—Prophet Bitter Over Conditions (Lamentations 3:10-20)
Wednesday, Nov. 13—Prophet Recalls God's Mercies (Lamentations 3:21-30)
Thursday, Nov. 14—Prophet Acknowledges Need for Punishment (Lamentations 3:31-39)
Friday, Nov. 15—Prophet Examines the Situation (Lamentations 3:40-48)
Saturday, Nov. 16—Prophet Urges Vengeance on Enemies (Lamentations 3:55-66)
Sunday, Nov. 17—Assurance of God's Deliverance (Psalm 13)

Learning by Doing

This page contains an alternate lesson plan emphasizing learning activities.
Classes desiring such student involvement will find these suggestions helpful.

Learning Goals

Students in today's class session should:

1. Categorize the suffering of Judah because of its sin.

2. Write a contemporary set of "lamentations" describing the effect of sin on our society.

3. Ask God to forgive our country for its sin and to help them make our society less sinful.

Into the Lesson

Choose one of the following activities to get a discussion started in this session. Each activity is meant to be completed by a group of between four and six of your class members. If you prefer, suggest all the options to your class and let groups choose the activity they want to do.

Acrostic. Students should write the word *sorry* vertically down a sheet of paper. Then for each letter in the word, they should find a word that they associate with the word *sorry.*

Newspaper search. Give a stack of newspapers to the class, and ask members to find examples of situations where people were sorry for their sin. When they are ready to report, ask them if they found instances where people were not sorry for their sin.

Sentence writing. Put the following words on the chalkboard: *sin, sorry, punishment.* Students are to write sentences that contain at least two of the words. Each small group should produce at least four sentences, and each of these words should be used in at least one of the sentences.

After any or all of these activities, discuss the following questions with your group: "What is the attitude toward sin in our society? Does sin always lead to sorrow? Give examples to support your answer. How would our society change if more people were more sorry about sin?"

Tell the class that today's lesson looks at the situation in Judah after the fall of Jerusalem. Our text shows a society devastated by the results of its sinfulness. Could such a document be written by anyone in our day?

Into the Word

Begin with a bit of background about the book of Lamentations itself (see Lesson Background, page 98). Read all of Lamentations 5 aloud. Because of its poetic nature, this text lends itself to some sort of "creative" reading. You could read it responsively; that is, alternate reading the verses between the men, the women, and yourself. Or prepare a choral reading before class. Photocopy the Scripture and mark phrases for different readers, following the thought patterns of the text instead of just the verse divisions.

Next, ask class members to analyze the text. Have them categorize the punishments of the people under the headings, Emotional Suffering and Physical Suffering (space has been provided for this activity in the student book). Have them work in pairs for several minutes before you discuss as a class.

If you have time, ask students to answer individually the following questions, all based on Lamentations 5 (these are also included in the student book):

1. What is the saddest verse in this chapter?

2. What is the most serious punishment the people are suffering?

3. What is the climax of the chapter?

4. What is hopeful about the chapter?

5. What verse most reminds you of a contemporary situation?

After a few minutes, let several class members share their answers to each question. Discuss with the class: "Who suffered in Jerusalem (see verses 11-18)? Who was responsible for the suffering of the Jews? How can we reconcile verse 7 with verse 16? Why is the confession of verse 16 important?"

Ask how this chapter would be different if it were not for verses 19-22. Do they believe the chapter ends with hope or with despair? Why?

Into Life

Lamentations 5 contains the cries of the people of Judah suffering for their sin. Ask the class: "Are people in our society suffering because of their sin? Suppose we were to write a list of 'lamentations' recorded by a contemporary sufferer in our society. What would it contain?"

Ask the class to prepare such a list, in groups of four or six. After they have listed ways in which people today suffer because of their sin, perhaps they will have time to write a more poetic version, in the style of Lamentations 5.

Ask each group to read its "lamentations." Then close with prayers concerning the sinfulness of our society. Prayers should both express repentance for society's sins and vow to take steps to make our society more holy.

Let's Talk It Over

The questions on this page are designed to encourage review of the lesson Scriptures and to promote discussion of the lesson by the class. The answers provided are only discussion starters. Let your class talk it over from there.

1. It seems presumptuous for anyone to ask God to "remember," as Jeremiah did in Lamentations 5:1. How can we explain Jeremiah's use of this plea? How does this apply to us?

This is one of several places in the Old Testament in which a speaker or writer called on God to "remember." Psalms 25:6, 74:2; and 119:49 contain other examples. It is interesting to observe that in another portion of our lesson text (Lamentations 5:20), Jeremiah expresses concern that God had forgotten His people. These seem to be merely reflections of human frailty. From our earthly standpoint, it seems that God does sometimes forget us. Our prayers go unanswered; we encounter problems and look in vain for divine guidance; we see wicked people prospering while we suffer. But God has no memory lapses. Often when He seems to have forgotten us, we later find it to be a time of discipline or testing.

2. Had the people of Judah understood better that all their property belonged to God, they might have handled better the loss of it to the Babylonians. Why is it important that we develop a clearer recognition of God's ownership of our property?

We remember Job's reaction when all that he had owned was lost: "The Lord gave, and the Lord hath taken away; blessed be the name of the Lord" (Job 1:21). At some time we are likely to lose some valuable property. A fire, an accident, theft, or other such occurrence will suddenly take it from us. It will be easier for us to handle that loss, if we see the possession as something God gave us, and something that is still ultimately His. That recognition of God's ownership will also keep us from undue pride based on our possessions.

3. The preaching of the prophets was designed in part to turn people back to God. How can the preaching of the Word accomplish that in our time?

What kind of preaching do church members expect? Do they desire to be entertained? Do they want to be made to feel good? Are they looking only for some intellectual stimulation or emotional gratification? The preaching that calls for repentance and real purity of life, the kind that emphasizes God's judgment and Hell, does not appear to be very popular right now. We need to encourage those who preach to tell us what God wants us to hear, even if it makes us feel uncomfortable. We need to pray for those who preach, that they will issue a bold and uncompromising call to obedience. We need to avoid supporting those radio and television preachers who proclaim a flawed, unscriptural message. This answer deals mostly with preaching to the church, but the same principles apply to preaching to the unsaved.

4. People frequently do not seem to be open to God unless they experience some kind of suffering. How should we pray about such suffering?

Sometimes we pray a little too hastily for an unsaved friend who is suffering. We may petition God for healing, when God wants to use the suffering to draw the person to Him. Perhaps we should get into the habit of praying, "Lord, whatever it takes to awaken my friend to his or her need for Your salvation, then do that." In Acts 16 we read of the Philippian jailer's moment of "awakening." After the earthquake had rocked the prison, he feared that his prisoners had escaped. Paul called out to him in time to keep him from suicide. The man's traumatic experience led him to ask Paul and Silas, "Sirs, what must I do to be saved?" (Acts 16:30). Later he and the members of his household were baptized into Christ. We might do well, therefore, to pray that our friends would have a "Philippian jailer experience."

5. To be rejected by God—surely no prospect is more frightening than that. How can we use the idea of God's rejection of sinners in our evangelistic efforts?

God has shown us in many places in the Scripture that He will reject those who reject Him and His Son. Many people do not have that kind of picture of God. They are aware of His love, but they have no concept of His holiness; they know God is merciful, but they give no thought to His judgment. These same people think of themselves as decent, honest individuals worthy of a place in Heaven. We must help them see that failure to follow Jesus Christ is rejection of God. And we must show them how God's holiness and justice require rejection of those who do not come to Him through Jesus Christ.

God's Power to Restore

DEVOTIONAL READING: Hosea 14:1-9.

LESSON SCRIPTURE: Ezekiel 37.

PRINTED TEXT: Ezekiel 37:1-14.

Ezekiel 37:1-14

1 The hand of the LORD was upon me, and carried me out in the Spirit of the LORD, and set me down in the midst of the valley which was full of bones,

2 And caused me to pass by them round about: and, behold, there were very many in the open valley; and, lo, they were very dry.

3 And he said unto me, Son of man, can these bones live? And I answered, O Lord GOD, thou knowest.

4 Again he said unto me, Prophesy upon these bones, and say unto them, O ye dry bones, hear the word of the LORD.

5 Thus saith the Lord GOD unto these bones; Behold, I will cause breath to enter into you, and ye shall live:

6 And I will lay sinews upon you, and will bring up flesh upon you, and cover you with skin, and put breath in you, and ye shall live; and ye shall know that I am the LORD.

7 So I prophesied as I was commanded: and as I prophesied, there was a noise, and behold a shaking, and the bones came together, bone to his bone.

8 And when I beheld, lo, the sinews and the flesh came up upon them, and the skin covered them above: but there was no breath in them.

9 Then said he unto me, Prophesy unto the wind, prophesy, son of man, and say to the wind, Thus saith the Lord GOD; Come from the four winds, O breath, and breathe upon these slain, that they may live.

10 So I prophesied as he commanded me, and the breath came into them, and they lived, and stood up upon their feet, an exceeding great army.

11 Then he said unto me, Son of man, these bones are the whole house of Israel: behold, they say, Our bones are dried, and our hope is lost: we are cut off for our parts.

12 Therefore prophesy and say unto them, Thus saith the Lord GOD; Behold, O my people, I will open your graves, and cause you to come up out of your graves, and bring you into the land of Israel.

13 And ye shall know that I am the LORD, when I have opened your graves, O my people, and brought you up out of your graves,

14 And shall put my Spirit in you, and ye shall live, and I shall place you in your own land: then shall ye know that I the LORD have spoken it, and performed it, saith the LORD.

GOLDEN TEXT: I shall put my Spirit in you, and ye shall live, and I shall place you in your own land: then shall ye know that I the LORD have spoken it, and performed it, saith the LORD.—Ezekiel 37:14.

God's People Face Judgment
Unit 3: The Fall of Jerusalem
(Lessons 10-13)

Lesson Aims

After this lesson a student should be able to:

1. Describe Ezekiel's vision of dry bones and tell the meaning of it.

2. Give a good reason to be joyful when troubles come.

3. Take pleasure in facing difficulties.

Lesson Outline

INTRODUCTION
  A. Quick Review
  B. Lesson Background
  I. VALLEY OF DRY BONES (Ezekiel 37:1-6)
    A. Vision (vv. 1, 2)
    B. Question (v. 3)
    C. Answer (vv. 4-6)
      Hope for Life
  II. LIFE FOR DRY BONES (Ezekiel 37:7-10)
    A. Bodies for the Bones (vv. 7, 8)
    B. Life for the Bodies (vv. 9, 10)
  III. MEANING (Ezekiel 37:11-14)
    A. Dry Bones Represent People (v. 11)
    B. People to Be Restored (v. 12)
    C. Knowledge to Be Restored (vv. 13, 14)
      Bringing the Dead to Life
CONCLUSION
  A. Our Own Fault
  B. Look at Results
  C. Prayer
  D. Thought to Remember

The visual for lesson 13 of the visuals packet tries to capture the joy of restoration in the Lord. It is shown on page 109. Use the time line (Visual 11) to review this quarter's lessons.

Introduction

The Old Testament has accurate records of important events, but sometimes it is hard to learn exactly when those events happened. Looking at several scholarly works, we often find different dates assigned to the same event, although in some cases the dates do not vary by more than a year or two. The following dates help provide an outline of the time we have been studying. The dates printed in boldface type apply to our lessons for the past three months.

1407 B.C. The people of Israel arrived in the promised land after forty years of nomadic life in the desert. The Lord guaranteed peace and prosperity if they would obey His Law, but their frequent disobedience brought punishment instead. Finally they decided they needed a king. The Lord consented, though He warned that a king would not solve their problems (1 Samuel 8:10-22).

1051 B.C. Saul became Israel's first king. He was followed by David, then Solomon, and Israel built a magnificent empire. While David was a man after God's heart (Acts 13:22), Solomon eventually strayed from the Lord. God promised him that the kingdom would be divided. The reigns of these three kings are covered in 1 Samuel 10:1—1 Kings 11:43.

931 B.C. After Solomon died, Israel was split into two kingdoms (1 Kings 12:1-17). The northern part was still called Israel; the southern part was called Judah. Most of the nation's power was lost, and so was much of its devotion to the Lord.

722 B.C. The Assyrians conquered Israel and scattered most of its people in foreign countries (2 Kings 17:1-6). In September the lessons we studied took up the history of Judah from that time.

605 B.C. Nebuchadnezzar of Babylon conquered Judah and took a few captives to Babylon (Daniel 1:1-7). The rest of the people were left with a native king (Jehoiakim) to rule them and pay tribute to Babylon (2 Kings 24:1-7).

597 B.C. Nebuchadnezzar's army returned after Judah rebelled and stopped paying tribute. This time the Babylonians took king Jehoiachin and ten thousand captives to Babylon. Another native king (Zedekiah) was left to continue paying tribute (2 Kings 24:8-17).

586 B.C. After Judah rebelled again, the Babylonians destroyed Jerusalem and took most of the surviving people to Babylon (2 Kings 24:18 —25:12).

539 B.C. An alliance of Medes and Persians conquered Babylon and took control of its empire (Daniel 5:28-31). A year later the captives were liberated (Ezra 1:1-4), and about fifty thousand of them went back home to rebuild Jerusalem and the temple (Ezra 1:5-8; 2:64, 65).

A. Quick Review

In September our lessons focused on efforts by both kings and prophets to stem the rising tide of evil in Judah. Two great kings (Hezekiah and Josiah) led Judah in doing right; but when these monarchs died, their successors quickly turned to evil, and the people followed. Jeremiah responded to God's call and gave warning to the nation, but the nation did not repent. Habakkuk revealed that while Judah was to be destroyed, its punisher (the Babylonians) would also be destroyed. God was still in control.

The October lessons showed the prophet Jeremiah faithfully continuing to preach God's message, in spite of opposition from false prophets such as Hananiah. Ezekiel was called to serve as God's spokesman to those already exiled in Babylon.

Thus far in November, the lessons have told how Ezekiel used a clay model to foretell the siege of Jerusalem. We have seen how Jerusalem was captured and destroyed, and we have read from Jeremiah's poetic cry of anguish in Lamentations, which ended with a glimmer of hope. Now the closing lesson of the series tells of "God's Power to Restore."

B. Lesson Background

Ezekiel 33:21 records how news came to Ezekiel that Jerusalem had been destroyed. Chapter 34 blames this disaster on the shepherds of Israel, the leaders who had practiced and promoted evil ways instead of good. It adds that the Lord will still care for His sheep. Chapter 35 proclaims woe upon a long-time enemy of Israel (Edom), then chapter 36 declares that Israel will be restored. Our text illustrates this restoration with a dramatic vision.

I. Valley of Dry Bones
(Ezekiel 37:1-6)

Instructed by the Lord, Ezekiel sometimes used visual aids in his teaching. We saw some examples in an earlier lesson (November 3). In a similar manner, the Lord Himself sometimes used visions to give His messages to Ezekiel. Chapter 1 records an impressive vision to emphasize the glory of the Lord. Chapters 8-11 tell of a series of visions concerning the temple and the abuses going on there. Now we come to a dramatic vision that illustrated the restoration of Israel and Judah after their captivity.

A. Vision (vv. 1, 2)

1. The hand of the LORD was upon me, and carried me out in the Spirit of the LORD, and set me down in the midst of the valley which was full of bones.

The hand of the Lord seems to mean the power of the Lord, which took possession of Ezekiel to give him a message. The phrase is also used in Ezekiel 1:3; 3:22; 8:1; and 40:1. Each time it introduces a visionary experience.

The Spirit of the Lord was also involved in this. Several times in Ezekiel, the Spirit "lifted,"

"entered into," or "brought" Ezekiel to another place (2:2; 3:12, 14, 24; 8:3; 11:1, 24; 43:5). In our text Ezekiel was *carried* to *the valley which was full of bones.* Perhaps this was the same location where Ezekiel had earlier seen a vision (3:22, 23), although there the word used is "plain." The Hebrew word, however, is the same as that which is rendered *valley* in the verse before us.

2. And caused me to pass by them round about: and, behold, there were very many in the open valley; and, lo, they were very dry.

The Lord, by His hand and Spirit, led Ezekiel about the valley so he could inspect the bones thoroughly. Two facts were notable: they were *very many*, and they were *very dry*. It was as if a tremendous battle had been fought in the valley long before, as if countless thousands of men had been slain (v. 9). It appeared that the bodies had not been buried, but left until lions, jackals, and vultures had stripped all the flesh from the bones. The bones had then been dried and bleached by the sun.

B. Question (v. 3)

3. And he said unto me, Son of man, can these bones live? And I answered, O Lord GOD, thou knowest.

An ordinary *son of man*, an ordinary human being, might have answered quickly, "Of course not!" But God's prophet knew that God's power was unlimited. He would not try to answer the question that God alone could answer.

C. Answer (vv. 4-6)

4. Again he said unto me, Prophesy upon these bones, and say unto them, O ye dry bones, hear the word of the LORD.

The prophet was to speak to the bones as if they could hear. He was to give them *the word of the Lord,* just as he had been giving it to his fellow captives in Babylon.

5. Thus saith the Lord GOD unto these bones; Behold, I will cause breath to enter into you, and ye shall live.

This answered the question that the Lord had raised in verse 3. Although receiving the *breath*

How to Say It

HABAKKUK. Huh-*bak*-kuk.
HANANIAH. Han-uh-*nye*-uh.
JEHOIACHIN. Jeh-*hoy*-uh-kin.
JEHOIAKIM. Jeh-*hoy*-uh-kim.
NEBUCHADNEZZAR. *Neb*-uh-kad-*nezz*-er
  (strong accent on *nezz*).

of life would be the final step in the process of restoring the dry bones (v. 10), it was probably mentioned here to emphasize God's primary intention.

6. And I will lay sinews upon you, and will bring up flesh upon you, and cover you with skin, and put breath in you, and ye shall live; and ye shall know that I am the LORD.

The bones would live, but not as bare bones or skeletons. God would provide them with *sinews*, the ligaments that hold bone to bone and the tendons that attach bone to muscle. He would provide *flesh*. Here this term refers to the muscles and various internal organs of the human body. God would then supply *skin* to cover the assembled bodies. To these completed bodies He would give *breath*, and they would become alive. Their restoration to life would prove to them and everyone else that the One who restored them was *the Lord*, Jehovah, the one true and living God, and the Creator and Giver of life.

HOPE FOR LIFE

Colma, California, is the town that for several years has been called "more dead than alive." The city got this unusual claim to fame in 1937, when San Francisco found itself running out of building room and decided to move all its cemeteries to Colma.

This little town, ten miles south of San Francisco, has no schools, churches, or grocery stores, but it has more than a dozen cemeteries (including Pet's Rest, a pet cemetery with its own "nondenominational" chapel!). The cemeteries cover eighty percent of the two square miles of land within the town limits. The 1,100 living residents are outnumbered by some two to three million deceased ones. The official tongue-in-cheek slogan for the town is, "It's great to be alive in Colma."

It may be great to be alive in Colma, but that is no consolation for the millions who lie buried there. No slogan, however catchy, can bring them back to life.

When God showed Ezekiel the valley of dry bones, he said to the prophet, "Can these bones live? . . . Prophesy upon these bones, and say unto them, O ye dry bones, hear the word of the Lord. . . . Ye shall live; and ye shall know that I am the Lord" (Ezekiel 37:3, 4, 6).

To a world that is dead in its sin, the message is still the same: "Hear the word of the Lord, and live!" Today we do not have to receive a vision to know that God can raise the dead; God has spoken to us through the risen Christ, confirming our faith and giving hope to the world.

—C. R. B.

II. Life for Dry Bones
(Ezekiel 37:7-10)

At this point, the dry bones had no ears and no minds, but Ezekiel was to speak to them as if they could hear and understand. That seemed absurd, but Ezekiel trusted God and spoke the message God gave him.

A. Bodies for the Bones (vv. 7, 8)

7. So I prophesied as I was commanded: and as I prophesied, there was a noise, and behold a shaking, and the bones came together, bone to his bone.

The prophet's word brought quick results. Even before he finished his message, the bones were in motion. *There was a noise,* or *a sound,* or possibly *a voice.* The Hebrew word can have any of these meanings. Some students suppose that there was a dramatic sound like a great clap of thunder or the blast of a trumpet. Some think a voice may have shouted something like, "Bones, get up!" Others suppose there was only the sound of bones moving on the ground and clicking against each other as each bone found those that must be joined to it to form a skeleton.

There was also *a shaking* that is not fully described. Some students think this was an earthquake; others think it was merely the multitude of bones shaking themselves free from the earth and moving to find and join other bones. The *New International Version* takes *a shaking* to be a description of the noise just mentioned. It reads, "There was a noise, a rattling sound." Whatever the noise sounded like, and whatever the shaking looked or sounded like, the bones came together. Each one joined another so that complete skeletons were formed.

8. And when I beheld, lo, the sinews and the flesh came up upon them, and the skin covered them above: but there was no breath in them.

Perhaps what Ezekiel witnessed was like watching a movie with impressive special effects. Ligaments fastened the bones together, and muscles appeared on them along with all the necessary glands and organs of human bodies. Then skin appeared on the bodies. We wonder if the bodies were clothed, but we are not told. They were like corpses lying on the ground.

B. Life for the Bodies (vv. 9, 10)

9. Then said he unto me, Prophesy unto the wind, prophesy, son of man, and say to the wind, Thus saith the Lord GOD; Come from the four winds, O breath, and breathe upon these slain, that they may live.

Translators have difficulty with this verse because the same Hebrew word can mean either *wind, breath,* or *spirit.* The *New International Version* says, "Prophesy to the breath" instead of *unto the wind.* If we translate *Prophesy unto the wind,* as the *King James Version* does, then it is proper to translate, "Come from the four winds, O wind, and blow upon these slain." Another possible translation is, "Prophesy unto the Spirit . . . Come from the four winds, O Spirit, and breathe upon these slain."

With any of these translations, the intent of the order is clear. The *spirit* or *breath* of life was to enter the lungs of the lifeless bodies; they were to become alive and start breathing. The breath, wind, or spirit was to *come from the four winds,* or from all directions. This suggests that there was to be an abundant supply of it, enough for all the uncounted thousands of bodies in the valley.

10. So I prophesied as he commanded me, and the breath came into them, and they lived, and stood up upon their feet, an exceeding great army.

God's order given through His prophet was obeyed promptly. *The breath* or *spirit* of life came into the lifeless bodies, and the valley of dry bones was filled with living human beings standing upright.

III. Meaning
(Ezekiel 37:11-14)

Sometimes a visual aid is so captivating that the watchers lose sight of the truth it teaches. Even a story told to illustrate a point may so fascinate the hearers that they forget the point it illustrates. So the Lord promptly and clearly explained the meaning of the dramatic vision of dry bones that came to life.

A. Dry Bones Represent People (v. 11)

11. Then he said unto me, Son of man, these bones are the whole house of Israel: behold, they say, Our bones are dried, and our hope is lost: we are cut off for our parts.

The dead and dried bones represented *the whole house of Israel.* This included the people of Judah who recently had been taken to Babylon, the ten thousand who had been taken with Ezekiel a few years earlier, and the people of northern Israel who had been scattered among foreign lands for more than a century. At this point in history, both parts of the divided nation had been destroyed and scattered; but they would be restored to life and be united again (vv. 15-23).

As individuals, the captives in Babylon were living and active, but as a nation they were as dead as bare bones bleached by time. They real-

visual 13

I will put my Spirit in you and you will live.

ized this and expressed their desperation through the statement quoted in the last half of this verse. The odd expression *cut off for our parts* is more literally rendered *cut off to ourselves.* The captives in Babylon still had one another, but the holy temple and the holy city no longer existed. The people were separated from their homeland by nearly a thousand miles of travel. They also felt themselves separated from the holy God and they thought the separation was permanent—as permanent as it would be if they were dead and buried.

B. People to Be Restored (v. 12)

12. Therefore prophesy and say unto them, Thus saith the Lord GOD; Behold, O my people, I will open your graves, and cause you to come up out of your graves, and bring you into the land of Israel.

To the captives, Babylon was their grave. They could no more escape than a dead man could dig his way out of the ground. But the Lord knew better. In this verse the word *God* represents the Hebrew word that has come into English as *Jehovah.* He was the One who promised to break the grip of Babylon, set His people free, and bring them again *into the land of Israel.*

C. Knowledge to Be Restored
(vv. 13, 14)

13. And ye shall know that I am the LORD, when I have opened your graves, O my people, and brought you up out of your graves.

Here the words *the Lord* represent the name *Jehovah.* After a time, He was going to rescue His people from their captivity and take them back to their homeland. Then they would realize who He was—the only true God, who can foretell the future and do wonders.

14. And shall put my Spirit in you, and ye shall live, and I shall place you in your own land: then shall ye know that I the LORD have spoken it, and performed it, saith the LORD.

Again we see the Hebrew word that can mean either *spirit* or *breath*. By His Spirit or by His breath, Jehovah was going to restore life to the dead nation of Israel. Israel again would possess the ancient homeland.

The history of later centuries shows that the Israelites learned well from their captivity. They learned who their God was, and they were far less prone to the worship of idols. They fell into sins of other kinds; for example, some of them married heathen women (Malachi 2:11), some of them mistreated their wives (Malachi 2:14), and some of them selfishly robbed God by withholding the tithes and offerings required by the Law (Malachi 3:8-10). But they did not fall into idolatry as they had before the captivity.

BRINGING THE DEAD TO LIFE

Just a few years ago Hollywood found a way to capitalize on the popular interest in dinosaurs. "Jurassic Park" was a Tyrannosaurus-size hit movie. The premise of the film was that scientists had discovered a way to extract the genetic stuff of dinosaur DNA trapped in the dinosaur blood they had found in the remains of prehistoric mosquitoes. From this DNA, scientists recreated several species of dinosaurs in frightening form. With the help of some amazingly realistic, computerized special effects, the filmmakers created an exciting film, even though the premise was farfetched.

The message of Ezekiel was that God would restore to life the "dead bones" of Israel—a nation whose faith had long been dead. God *still* has that power: He needs no cinematic sleight of hand to bring the dead to life. His Spirit is the source of life-giving power, which can revive the souls of all who, in faith, place themselves in the hands of their Creator and Redeemer.

—C. R. B.

Conclusion

A. Our Own Fault

When the ten thousand captives were taken to Babylon along with Ezekiel, they were quick to say, "It's not our fault" (see the lesson for October 27). They claimed they were suffering unfairly for the sins of their ancestors. Only when disaster was complete, only when Judah had fallen, and only when hope was gone were they ready to acknowledge the bitter truth: "It's our own fault."

How quickly we all blame someone else when something goes wrong! How hard it is to say, "It's my own fault"! But one vital step toward better times is to see our own mistakes and correct them.

B. Look at Results

Some of our troubles are not our own fault. A crippling accident may be entirely the fault of someone else. Sickness comes to good people as well as to bad. A hurricane or a drought afflicts the innocent as well as the guilty.

It then becomes important to think about results. For example, read the story of the blind man in John 9. This man was blind from birth, and Jesus' disciples asked about the cause. Was he blind because his parents sinned? Could he be blind from birth because of his own sins?

Jesus turned their thinking from cause to effect. As a result of this man's blindness, the work of God was seen in his healing.

The Bible often encourages us to look at the results of our trials rather than the cause of them. James writes, "Consider it pure joy, my brothers, whenever you face trials of many kinds" (James 1:2, *New International Version*). Joy in trouble? Why? Because we know that keeping on in spite of trouble will develop perseverance, and with perseverance we can grow spiritually and become what a Christian ought to be (read James 1:3, 4 as well). So be faithful through your trials! But correct your faults.

C. Prayer

Father in Heaven, by marvelous grace You have saved us from the greatest of all troubles, the torment of Hell. Help us then to find joy in the lesser troubles that come our way, and by them to grow into what You want us to be. In Jesus' name we pray. Amen.

D. Thought to Remember

God's power can restore those who are dry and dead because of sin.

Home Daily Bible Readings

Monday, Nov. 18—Israel and Judah Reunited (Ezekiel 37:15-22)

Tuesday, Nov. 19—They Will Worship One God (Ezekiel 37:23-28)

Wednesday, Nov. 20—Israel Delivered From Captivity (Zechariah 9:11-17)

Thursday, Nov. 21—Restoration of Davidic Kingdom (Amos 9:11-15)

Friday, Nov. 22—God Redeems His People (Zechariah 10:1-12)

Saturday, Nov. 23—God Comforts His People (Isaiah 49:8-15)

Sunday, Nov. 24—Sing Praise to the Righteous Lord (Psalm 98)

Learning by Doing

This page contains an alternate lesson plan emphasizing learning activities.
Classes desiring such student involvement will find these suggestions helpful.

Learning Goals

As students participate in today's class session, they should:

1. Discover that God's prophecy to the dry bones was a picture of His promise of restoration to Israel.

2. Decide where new spiritual vitality is necessary in several areas of contemporary life.

3. Pray for renewed vitality in their lives.

Into the Lesson

If you can find a recording of the well-known spiritual that recounts Ezekiel 37, play it for the class. Ask class members if they know where the spiritual came from and what it means. How many class members have read the Biblical account that is the basis for the spiritual?

Option. Bring a skull or a skeleton (or a picture of one) to class. Ask class members what ideas or words they would associate with it.

After either activity, tell the class that today's study, after looking at the Jews' failure because of sin, looks at God's promise of hope and new life. His promise reminds us of the spiritual life He makes available to all of us.

Into the Word

Ask a class member to summarize or read the paragraphs in the Introduction on page 106 of the lesson commentary. Then use the material under "A. Quick Review" on page 106 to summarize this quarter's lessons. When you have finished, have the class discuss these questions:

1. What have we learned this quarter about sin?

2. What have we learned about God's patience and mercy?

3. What have we learned about His wrath?

4. What have you decided about everyday life today in light of what we have learned from these studies?

Before this week's study, explain to the class the context of Ezekiel 37 (use "B. Lesson Background," page 107). Then distribute the following list of statements (also found in the student book). Class members are to decide whether each statement is true or false and to cite a verse to prove their conclusion. (Answers, for the teacher's reference, are included here.)

1. Ezekiel lived in the valley of the dry bones (false, vv. 1, 2).

2. Ezekiel knew at once that the bones would be transformed into living bodies (false, v. 3).

3. God told Ezekiel to take His message to the bones (true, vv. 4-6).

4. God prophesied that the bones would be destroyed because of their sin (false , vv. 5, 6).

5. Ezekiel did not want to take God's message to the bones (false, v. 7).

6. The bones immediately became bodies, with voices that prophesied and praised God (false, vv. 7-9).

7. The bones represented the twelve apostles and the church (false, vv. 11, 12).

8. The revived bones represented a restored nation in Israel (true, vv. 11-14).

Give students a few minutes to answer the statements, then discuss each statement with the class, explaining why it is true or false if there is disagreement in the group.

Into Life

Write on your chalkboard as many of the following headings as you wish to discuss:

The church in our society   Government
Families in our country   The court system
Our local congregation   Education

Ask class members, in groups of about four each, to choose at least one of these topics and to decide, "What 'dry bones' do we see in this area?" They are to discuss, for their category, how spiritual vitality has dried up because people have forsaken God. Give groups at least six or eight minutes to discuss, then ask them to share with the class.

Next, ask class members to return to their groups and respond to this topic: "A time in my life when I felt very dry spiritually." After a few minutes, without reporting back to the class, group members should consider this topic: "How God 'brought me back to life.'"

After several minutes, ask for volunteers to share their responses with the class.

In your closing prayer time, ask different class members to pray, with each using one of the following prayers as the basis for his thoughts:

"God, help us to see the dry bones in our country, our congregation, and our lives."

"God, thank You for breathing spiritual vitality into our lives, just when we needed it."

"God help us to 'come alive' for You in this place right now!"

Let's Talk It Over

The questions on this page are designed to encourage review of the lesson Scriptures and to promote discussion of the lesson by the class. The answers provided are only discussion starters. Let your class talk it over from there.

1. "He asked me, 'Son of man, can these bones live?' I said, 'O Sovereign Lord, you alone know'" (Ezekiel 37:3, *New International Version*). How is Ezekiel's attitude, shown here, worth imitating?

At first glance it may seem to us that Ezekiel was evasive. We may feel he should at least have expressed his opinion. Instead we have here a demonstration of the man's humility and teachableness. It is wise for us to admit that we are still ignorant about God and His Word, and that we have a great deal yet to learn. Ezekiel was an example of what James later exhorted Christians to be: "Let every man be swift to hear, slow to speak. . ." (James 1:19).

2. The lesson writer points out, "Sometimes a visual aid is so captivating that the watchers lose sight of the truth it teaches." Why is this an important reminder for both speakers and hearers?

Preachers are troubled if they gain the impression that their humorous anecdotes are all that people remember from their sermons. Teachers do not like it if their visual aids are so interesting in themselves that they draw students' attention from their lessons. Both must be very careful to emphasize the life application they want their listeners to make. But hearers also have a responsibility. We dare not become so distracted by a visual aid, an interesting story, or the rich voice and the dramatic gestures of a speaker that we miss the message he is presenting. Jesus said, "Take heed therefore how ye hear" (Luke 8:18). Let us aim to be conscientious hearers.

3. Some churches may identify with the exiled Israelites' feelings of being dead and dried up. What can leaders do when members of the church complain that the congregation is dead?

If you were to ask your members which of the seven churches of Asia in Revelation 2 and 3 your congregation most closely resembles, how would they respond? Would they see it as another Laodicea, "the lukewarm church," or as another Sardis, "the dead church"? The complaint may not be legitimate. Some members tend to identify life in the church with an excess of emotion. Others are so inactive that they have no idea what is happening in the church. If the complaint is legitimate, however, the leaders must determine why the deadness and dryness exist. Are leaders and members grieving the Holy Spirit through sin? Has the church become too comfortable, failing to reach out in active faith? Are there conflicts within the congregation that have not been resolved? Leaders must deal prayerfully with problems like these.

4. How often do we hear someone say when caught in an error, "It was my own fault"? Why is this refreshing to hear?

No one is ever guilty of a crime or responsible for an error, or so it seems. People almost always find something else or someone else to blame. But on certain rare occasions an individual faces up to his responsibility and declares, "I am the one who did it. It is my fault, and mine alone." This is refreshing in part, because it eliminates a good deal of confusion. When a person accused of wrongdoing says, "It is *not* my fault," then we must ask, "Whose fault is it?" When the individual accepts his responsibility, that settles the issue. Another refreshing aspect of this is that it encourages others to be similarly honest. When we see someone else own up to his mistakes, we are more likely to put away our excuses and our finger-pointing.

5. Our personal troubles give us the opportunity to develop perseverance. Why is that to our advantage?

It is tempting to envision a time in life that will be trouble-free. Everything will go smoothly, and any problems that arise will be minor. But when we think this through, we know better. As long as we live, we shall have to face problems, pressures, crises, and difficult decisions. The sooner we develop the habit of perseverance, the better off we will be. We can even welcome the less serious troubles we face now, because they give us the occasion to forge the tough-mindedness and coolness under pressure that we may need for more rigorous trials later. Paul spoke of this in Romans 5:3, 4: "We also rejoice in our sufferings, because we know that suffering produces perseverance; perseverance, character; and character, hope" (*New International Version*).

Winter Quarter, 1996-97

New Testament Personalities

Special Features

Lessons

Unit 1: Persons of Jesus' Nativity and Early Life

Unit 2: Persons in Jesus' Ministry

Unit 3: Persons of the New Testament Church

About these lessons

This series of lessons highlights individuals who appear within the pages of the New Testament record. Some are quite prominent; others may appear for only a short time. Some exhibit a strength of spiritual character; others illustrate the heartache of failure. All remind us of how important it is to follow Jesus and to make His cause our cause.

Dec 1
Dec 8
Dec 15
Dec 22
Dec 29
Jan 5
Jan 12
Jan 19
Jan 26
Feb 2
Feb 9
Feb 16
Feb 23

Quarterly Quiz

The questions on this page may be used in several ways: as a pretest at the beginning of the quarter; as a review at the end of the quarter; or as a review after each lesson. The questions are based on the Scripture text of each lesson (King James Version). **The answers are on page 120.**

Lesson 1

1. What was Zechariah doing when the angel of the Lord appeared to him? *Luke 1:9*
2. On what occasion did the neighbors and relatives of Elisabeth and Zechariah gather to name the couple's child? *Luke 1:59*

Lesson 2

1. The angel told Mary that the Lord would give to her son the throne of his father ____. *Luke 1:32*
2. Elisabeth told Mary, "Blessed art thou among ____, and blessed is the ____ of thy ____." *Luke 1:42*

Lesson 3

1. What three titles of Jesus are found in the angel's announcement to the shepherds? *Luke 2:11*
2. After traveling to Bethlehem, the shepherds told no one of what they had witnessed. T/F *Luke 2:17*

Lesson 4

1. Herod spoke with the ____ ____ and the ____ to determine where Christ was to be born. *Matthew 2:4*
2. What was the age of the children whom Herod sought to kill? *Matthew 2:16*

Lesson 5

1. Simeon was promised that he would not die before doing what? *Luke 2:26*
2. To whom was Simeon speaking when he said, "A sword shall pierce through thy own soul also"? *Luke 2:34, 35*
3. Anna is described as a (temple musician, prophetess, Samaritan). *Luke 2:36*

Lesson 6

1. What two foods did John the Baptizer eat? *Mark 1:6*
2. Jesus said, "And blessed is he, whosoever shall not be ____ in me." *Luke 7:23*

Lesson 7

1. To whom did Jesus say, "Thou art careful and troubled about many things"? *Luke 10:41*
2. What type of ointment did Mary use to anoint Jesus' feet? *John 12:3*

3. What disciple complained about Mary's anointing of Jesus? *John 12:4, 5*

Lesson 8

1. Jesus was in the "coasts" of what city when He asked His disciples about who He was? *Matthew 16:13*
2. When Jesus announced His upcoming death in Jerusalem, Peter kept silent. T/F *Matthew 16:22*

Lesson 9

1. For how much did Judas betray Jesus? *Matthew 26:15*
2. When Jesus announced that one of the twelve would betray Him, what question did each of them ask Him? *Matthew 26:22*
3. What was the act in the upper room by which Jesus said His betrayer would be known? *Matthew 26:23*

Lesson 10

1. What country was Barnabas's home? *Acts 4:36*
2. What does the name Barnabas mean? *Acts 4:36*
3. To what city did Barnabas bring Saul, that he might teach the church there? *Acts 11:25, 26*

Lesson 11

1. Before the council, Stephen's face resembled that of an ____. *Acts 6:15*
2. Where was Jesus when Stephen looked into Heaven and saw Him? *Acts 7:56*

Lesson 12

1. In what city did Paul first meet Aquila and Priscilla? *Acts 18:1, 2*
2. Whom did Aquila and Priscilla instruct "more perfectly"? *Acts 18:24, 26*

Lesson 13

1. Give the names of Timothy's mother and grandmother. *2 Timothy 1:5*
2. The brethren in the two cities of ____ and Iconium spoke highly of Timothy. *Acts 16:1, 2.*
3. To the Corinthians, Paul described Timothy as "my ____ ____." *1 Corinthians 4:17*

Learning From People of the Past

by David Morley

Most Christians would love to visit the lands of the Bible and walk where the great Bible heroes walked. What a thrill it would be to visit Nazareth and recall Gabriel's visit to Mary, announcing the coming birth of Jesus the Messiah. How moving to sit in the Garden of Gethsemane and visualize Jesus praying, the disciples sleeping, and the betrayer approaching the gate. How interesting to walk the streets of Corinth and imagine walking with Paul, Timothy, Aquila, and Priscilla.

Many Christians actually do visit such places and are greatly inspired by their visits. But wouldn't it be even more exciting if somehow we could travel back through time and actually walk and talk with Jesus? What an overwhelming thrill that would be! What would we ask the Lord? What lessons would He teach us? How could we minister to Him and help in the work of His kingdom?

Unfortunately, time travel will remain forever in the realm of science fiction. None of us will ever have the chance to go back to those days—except, that is, in our imaginations. However, this is exactly what we are invited to do in the lessons for this quarter. We will participate in sort of a "time travel of the mind," as we study the topic, "New Testament Personalities."

Each lesson in this series is about one or more persons who were associated with Jesus or with the early church. The lessons are divided into three units. Each unit includes characters from a specific historical period. The first unit is entitled, "Persons of Jesus' Nativity and Early Life." The people who are studied include Elisabeth and Zechariah, Mary, the shepherds, the wise men and Herod, and Simeon and Anna. These people were privileged to live during the time when God fulfilled the words of the prophets and sent His promised Deliverer and Messiah into the world as a baby. Most of them were filled with joy to witness such an event. Herod, in contrast, saw this child as a threat to his power and sought to kill Him.

The second unit is called, "Persons in Jesus' Ministry," a section that includes lessons on John the Baptizer, Mary and Martha, Peter, and Judas Iscariot. These people all had close contact with Jesus during His adult years. Theirs were the privileges of seeing Jesus work miracles and of hearing Him teach and preach. They found Jesus to be so much more than they expected, and also so much different from what they expected the Messiah to be. All but Judas learned valuable lessons from the Lord.

The third unit highlights "Persons of the New Testament Church." The characters studied are Barnabas, Stephen, Priscilla and Aquila, and Timothy. Each of these played an important role in the early church. They possessed varied talents and were called to various works, but each made a significant contribution to the kingdom of the Lord.

Learning From Bible Characters

Some of the great riches of the Bible are found in the stories of individuals and their walks with God. Some are examples of good (to be imitated) and others are examples of evil (to be avoided), but we can learn lessons from all. The reason we can do this is that spiritual principles never change. Actions that brought spiritual growth and God's blessing then do the same today. Actions that led to spiritual disaster then cause spiritual disaster today as well. The key to learning from the lives of Bible characters is to strive to see how we are like them and how our situations parallel theirs. Then we can learn from their experiences and decisions. Several comparisons are useful as we seek to identify with these people of long ago.

1. *Attitude.* With the exception of Herod, the people associated with Jesus' birth displayed an attitude of spiritual sensitivity and of joy and wonder at the workings of God. Perhaps it was because they had such an attitude that they received special guidance from angels, dreams, and a star.

As you teach these lessons, challenge your students to evaluate their attitudes. Try to get them to feel the excitement of Zechariah, Elisabeth, Mary, and the others. Do they ever feel excited about God's works? Do they have eyes to see God's working in the lives of people today? Do they have ears to hear when God calls them? Do you have such spiritually sensitive eyes and ears? Do you get excited about what God is doing in your church and community? We all need to feel excitement over what God has done in the past and what He continues to do today. When we are filled with wonder at God's works, the natural response is worship and obedience, just as in the case of the shepherds and wise men.

2. *Challenges.* Several of the individuals in these lessons were faced with daunting challenges. Mary was challenged to allow her entire world to be turned upside down. Peter was challenged to leave all to follow Jesus. Stephen was challenged to keep preaching in the face of persecution. All knew the costs, but they were willing to make the sacrifices. When they accepted the challenges, God walked with them and cared for them. It is only because they accepted their challenges that they were used of God.

Try to lead your students to identify with these characters in their moments of decision, as they weighed the cost of God's call and chose to follow Him. Every Christian faces challenges to his faith and dedication, some of them quite momentous. It is likely that some of your class members are facing such challenges now. We are strengthened to respond to God's call when we remember those who have answered His call before us. It may be a call to teach a class, serve as a leader, call on visitors, or go to a foreign field as a missionary. God did not desert any of these people in our lessons when they answered His call, and He will not desert anyone who answers His call today.

3. *Strengths and Weaknesses of Character.* Just like us, these New Testament personalities possessed both strengths and weaknesses. Peter was bold, but he was impulsive. Martha was industrious and generous, but she had some of her priorities out of order. Judas had zeal, but he also had the fatal flaw of greed. Jesus worked with these people, taught them, and helped them build on their strengths and overcome their weaknesses. When we compare Peter and Judas, we see how important it is to overcome our weaknesses lest they overcome us.

As you study these lessons, help your students look for similarities between themselves and the Bible characters. Encourage them to identify and develop their own individual strengths. Warn them to be aware of their weaknesses and to work very hard to overcome them. God still works with us, one by one, to guide us and refine us. However, we must submit to His leading, teaching, and discipline.

4. *Talents.* These people had a variety of talents. Several were powerful preachers. Barnabas had a real talent for encouragement. Martha was an organizer and hostess. Priscilla and Aquila could make tents, but they also could teach effectively. Whatever talents each individual had, they gladly used them in the Lord's service. As they did so, their talents became even more refined and powerful. These individuals made very important contributions to the work of the kingdom.

Each person in your class possesses some talent or talents that can be used for the Lord. Whether they are the same talents as those of the Bible characters is not important. (You are not likely to have any tentmakers in your class.) What matters is that the people in our lessons enthusiastically used their talents. As your students see the joy that these people felt in using their talents for the Lord, they will be encouraged to use their talents as well. As they understand that God can use ordinary people and talents to do His work, they will be more confident to volunteer to serve. The people in your class can make a difference. They can make valuable contributions to the work of the church.

Growing in Faith

The character studies that make up our lessons this quarter are much different from lessons in history or doctrine. The specific goal of studying people is to grow as a person. Remember to make this your emphasis in each lesson. Ask yourself what each person did and what characteristics each person possessed that are worthy of imitation. On the other hand, you should also identify mistakes and negative characteristics that we must avoid.

Challenge each of your class members to make personal Christian growth a goal for this lesson series. Perhaps they can pick one of the Bible characters and say, "I want to be like that." They may want to identify one strong trait in each person and work to build those traits in themselves. They can analyze a lesson that the person learned and apply that lesson to themselves.

However you and your students approach the lessons, do not forget that the goal is growth—change for the better. If you or your students are just the same at the end of the quarter as you were at the beginning, then you have not really learned the lessons, no matter how well you can recite the facts and tell the stories. At the same time, do not expect to reach perfection in three months. Zechariah, Elisabeth, Simeon, and Anna did not reach their high levels of devotion without many years of discipline. Barnabas did not become a wonderful encourager overnight. Priscilla and Aquila did not become effective teachers until they had spent long hours being taught by Paul.

Keep in mind that the people you will study this quarter were not supermen or superwomen. They were just ordinary people who (except for Herod and Judas) put spiritual interests first and who submitted their lives to the Lord. Ordinary people like us can grow as well if we do the same.

Being of Value to God

by Bill D. Hallsted

I AM SURE he must have thought his usefulness to God was finished. The stroke had left him unable to use his right hand or to speak. Only by the aid of braces on his right leg could he walk. All of this meant that he could no longer work, so he was placed on permanent, total disability. Certain tasks that he had done for the church were now out of the question: he could no longer teach his Sunday school class, serve as an elder, or do the calling the church had come to expect of him.

Finding himself with much more time on his hands, this man learned to compensate for his sudden limitations, and began to take care of those little chores around the church that needed done. He worked early in the morning and late at night. He came when no one else was normally around, so that he would not be embarrassed about his inability to speak, or the clumsiness of his one-handed efforts. Over the next few years, however, it was amazing what he was able to do.

Not until he died did the church fully realize how much he did, or why the grounds and building were always in perfect condition and immaculately kept. It took almost a year, and the efforts of three or four people, to begin doing the tasks he had been doing. This man did his work quietly—unasked and unannounced. He did it without credit or praise. He did as much of it as he could with no one's knowledge. He did it for God.

God had used this man in so many ways before his stroke. Yet what stands out most strongly in my memory of him is that his usefulness to God was not altered by that tragedy. Only the avenue of that usefulness was changed.

God Is Not Predictable

Sometimes the avenue of service God has mapped out for us coincides with our desires, almost as though we were allowed to write the script. At other times it is the very opposite, and the avenue of service He desires of us is the path we most dread.

When Gabriel announced to Zechariah and Elisabeth what God's plan was for them, it seemed too good to be true. They had probably hoped and prayed for a child during all the years when their wish might have come true. Now they were old, and had resigned themselves to remaining a childless couple. In fact,

Gabriel's news was so good that Zechariah found it impossible to believe, and asked for a special sign that it was true. The sign he received (of dumbness and probably deafness as well) was not pleasant, but it served a purpose.

With Mary, the opposite was true. On the surface, the news that Gabriel brought could not have been worse. To become pregnant outside of marriage meant the end of her dream of marrying Joseph. He would never consider marrying her when she was pregnant by someone else! The news also meant the end to her good standing in the community. Unwed mothers were not just frowned upon in her society—they were ostracized or even stoned to death. And what would others think of her explanation for what had happened? Who would believe her when she said that it was God who made her pregnant? If being pregnant and single were not enough to merit being stoned to death, the blasphemy of blaming it on God surely would be!

Yet we can see that the perfect will of God was carried out in the lives of both Mary and Elisabeth. The fact that their situations were so different did not affect their importance to God.

It can be so difficult for us to accept that anyone who is different from us, or from our ideas of usefulness, could be of value to God. Yet if any portion of Scripture teaches us such a lesson, it is the story of the birth of Christ. The humble peasant couple from the obscure town of Nazareth, the stable in Bethlehem, the shepherds (who were considered social outcasts in their time), and the wise men (foreign dignitaries who apparently had an interest in Jewish prophecy) are all details that impress upon us how unpredictable God is.

Had we been in charge of orchestrating the birth of Christ, we would probably have arranged for Him to have been ushered into the household of a godly and powerful king, cared for with the very best of everything, pampered in every way, and acknowledged with great fanfare as God's very special emissary. We would probably have had Him protected by the finest soldiers, schooled by the finest scholars, and instructed by the most prominent members of the priesthood.

Instead, God chose the poorest of the poor to be the Messiah's mother. He chose an obscure priest's aged wife to confirm that this was indeed from God. He chose rustic shepherds and foreign astrologers to receive word of His birth. To a feeble old man and an aged widow He gave the privilege of viewing the Messianic child in the temple. Simple fishermen, not members of the sophisticated, knowledgeable temple hierarchy, were called to be His disciples. No, God is certainly not predictable!

The problem of expecting God to act according to our own expectations is present in the story of Mary and Martha as well. Martha was certain that Mary could not be of value to Jesus unless she was in the kitchen doing her share of the work. It must have been troubling to her when Jesus said that Mary's choice of how to spend her time was better. It flew directly in the face of Martha's own expectations.

It is exactly because God is not predictable that we must always be open to the leading of His Spirit. We must always be in prayer that He will open doors of opportunity for us to be of value to Him. We must never ignore an opportunity to serve because we are waiting for one that better fits our expectations!

God's Idea of Importance

We should also notice, as we study the lives of the people highlighted in this quarter's lessons, that God's criteria and man's criteria for determining importance are vastly different.

How important would John the Baptizer be in our scheme of things? Consider his unique and unorthodox appearance. His long hair probably had never been trimmed in his whole life. He wore a smelly garment made out of camel's hair and held on by a leather strap. He lived on a diet of locusts and wild honey. He dared to call the religious leaders (they constituted the "Greater Jerusalem Clergy Association") a "generation of vipers." By man's values, he would not have been rated very highly.

When one of our daughters was about to be married, we were expecting the arrival of a couple of our future son-in-law's closest friends. They planned to stay at our house. About all we knew of them was that they worked to bring young people to Christ out of the drug culture and off the streets. That made them both preachers, right? I know what preachers look like—I am one!

When their arrival was imminent, our daughter took special pains to tell us not to be taken aback by their appearance. Even so, I was not prepared for the two who stood on our doorstep. I was not ready to meet John the Baptizer in person, let alone in tandem! Long, scraggly hair, bushy and unkempt beards, strange clothing, and backpacks that substituted for suitcases, were not what I expected. Without her warn-

ings, I'm not sure I would have let them in the door! Yet within the first hour's conversation, it was readily apparent that here were two of the most committed Christian men I had ever known. They are also two of the most effective in accomplishing the very difficult work God has called them to do.

Sometimes, instead of getting beyond the world's idea of importance, we need to move beyond our own. All of Jesus' disciples struggled with this idea throughout His ministry. Simon Peter stands as one of the classic examples of this ongoing conflict. In order to be of value to Jesus, he thought he had to be more important than any of the others. When he successfully answered Jesus' question about His identity, he was certain that he had climbed to a higher rung on the ladder of importance than all the other disciples. When Jesus then singled him out to be given "the keys of the kingdom of heaven," he must have felt certain he had a lock on the number one spot.

Before he could truly be of value to Jesus, however, Peter had to lose all sense of his own importance. When he totally denied any involvement with Jesus, or even any knowledge of Him, it must have appeared to Peter that he had destroyed whatever usefulness to Jesus he had possessed. Yet only then was Peter in a position where he could learn to become what Jesus wanted him to be, and to do what He wanted him to do.

Putting Christ First

Our final unit, entitled "Personalities of the New Testament Church," covers only four lessons, yet think of the range of personalities covered! There is Stephen, unfazed by the angry faces of the Sanhedrin and fearless in his proclamation of the gospel. In contrast, we see Timothy, who required encouragement from Paul not to be too timid in standing for his faith. How different they were—yet each carried out the job God had for him to do, and did it well.

As you study the lessons of this quarter, make special note of the primary ingredient that makes people truly important and of great value to God. That ingredient is the deliberate placing of Jesus, and the will of God, first above all else.

We must never fall into the trap of trying to press ourselves or others into some mold of personality or talent in order to be important to God. Whoever we are, and whatever gifts God has or has not given us, we can be of inestimable value to Him. The most important question any of us can ask as we study these lessons is, "How can I make serving Jesus a matter of top priority in my life?"

The Greatest Personality of All

by Steve Wyatt

THE WORD *PARADOX* is defined as "a statement that is seemingly contradictory or opposed to common sense and yet is perhaps true." It can also mean "something (as a person, condition, or act) with seemingly contradictory qualities or aspects." A paradox seems to defy "logical" explanation, yet it (or he or she) conveys a measure of truth.

Certain statements of Jesus fall into this category. We think of His words recorded in Matthew 16:25: "Whosoever will save his life shall lose it: Whosoever will lose his life for my sake shall find it." On the subject of greatness, He taught, "And whosoever shall exalt himself shall be abased; and he that shall humble himself shall be exalted" (Matthew 23:12). In other cases, statements made by the Master on separate occasions can leave a reader a bit bewildered. How do we understand and apply, "These things I have spoken unto you, that in me ye might have peace" (John 16:33), in light of, "Think not that I am come to send peace on earth: I came not to send peace, but a sword" (Matthew 10:34)?

Even more challenging to our minds is the fact that Jesus *Himself* constitutes a paradox. His character transcends every attempt at definition. On one occasion, He is quieting a storm on the Sea of Galilee; on another, He is tenderly welcoming children to come to His side. In one instance, He is denigrating the Pharisees, calling them a "generation of vipers"; in another, He is coming to the defense of a woman caught in the very act of adultery.

No wonder the scribes and Pharisees had such a frustrating time trying to figure Him out! Not only did Jesus fail to fit into their neatly organized "boxes"; He failed to fit into anyone's "box."

Leadership According to Jesus

What if Jesus were to visit our world today? If He did so, I do not think that we would be surprised by His physical appearance. He would probably look like most every other man looks. Neither do I think that we would be startled by His power, for we are quite familiar with Jesus' miracles. We would expect to see His power manifested in some manner. Nor would we be surprised by His teaching. The message of Jesus has been carefully preserved for nearly twenty centuries of earth's history.

Perhaps the most striking aspect of Jesus' appearance (and the most paradoxical) would be His demeanor, or, if you will, His *style*. For Jesus simply did not fit the stereotypical image of a strong leader, nor does He fit such an image today.

We live in the day of the "high roller." We are accustomed to leaders and heroes who strut. We expect our executives to ride in limousines, eat in private dining quarters, and bark out orders to a huge retinue of underlings. We have grown so accustomed to that kind of leadership style that we find it hard to accept any other. We like the aggressive type. We are attracted to speakers who have some "pizzazz."

This is not to say that Jesus would be an embarrassment. Jesus was strong! But His strength was never posed; His power was never designed to impress. Jesus never did a miracle and then looked over His shoulder to see if the audience liked it. He was not interested in maintaining solid public relations or in "working the crowd." He seemed to prefer individual encounters—speaking to a burdened woman beside a well in Samaria, visiting a scorned tax collector in his home, or challenging a searching young man who had inquired about eternal life. Even though He is clearly presented to us in the New Testament as the absolute and ultimate Lord—indeed the very Lord of lords—and even though such a title may conjure up images of royalty and assertiveness, Jesus was never characterized by such qualities.

What *was* the nature of Jesus' leadership style? Thankfully, He did not leave that to our own flawed analysis; it is not a matter to be settled by our own speculation or guessing. He spoke forthrightly about the focus of His life and ministry: "Even the Son of Man did not come to be served, but to serve, and to give his life as a ransom for many" (Mark 10:45, *New International Version*). Jesus was not the kind of leader who fretted unless He was grabbing the spotlight or attracting attention to Himself. Jesus came *to serve.*

When we scan the Gospel records, we see on nearly every page that Jesus carried out His ministry in exactly this manner. He was a connected Savior who was moved with compassion for the needs of the masses. He was seen quickly and enthusiastically responding to the heartfelt cries of a harassed and helpless people. Jesus never measured His effectiveness by the size of His congregation; such concerns mattered little to Him. His greatest passion was servanthood. He was at His best while kneeling by the bed of someone who needed Him.

That is why the crowds thronged to follow Jesus. They came, not because of any personal charisma He possessed, but because when they came for healing, He healed them. When they were hungry, He fed them. When they were brokenhearted, He comforted them. Often going without proper nourishment and adequate rest, Jesus continually gave Himself in service to others. He was not locked away in isolation or stationed on a high mountain that seekers had to climb in order to draw from His wisdom. He was in the streets where the people were. And because the people had finally found a spiritual leader who genuinely cared for them (as opposed to the scribes and Pharisees), they loved Him! There was no one else like Jesus.

Real Leadership Demonstrated

Even on the night before His humiliating public execution, Jesus was still serving. His disciples had just entered the upper room with dirty feet. Yet they were so caught up in the "burning issue" of who would be the greatest in Jesus' kingdom, that not one of them was willing to do the humble but necessary task of washing the others' feet. So our Lord, no more than eighteen hours from the cross, took a basin and a towel and performed the act that the disciples were too busy and important to consider: He washed their feet.

When He had completed the task, He assumed His position with the group. Although Jesus was on the threshold of the most horrifying experience of His life—indeed, of all history—He was still demonstrating a servant's heart.

This unforgettable lesson was delivered to a group of would-be leaders who thus far had showed almost no comprehension of Jesus' style of servanthood. Apparently Judas had become so disenchanted with Jesus' failure to act as he thought He should that Judas had struck a deal with the Jewish leaders to turn Jesus over to them at a convenient moment. James and John were preening themselves in preparation of a place of honor, right next to Jesus. Peter no doubt pictured himself a member of the "inner circle" and figured that he would be among Jesus' most trusted advisors. Anxious for power, fame, and status, these men who had sat at Jesus' feet for nearly three years were more than willing to sit at His throne. They did not realize that followers of Jesus were (and are) called to hold a towel, not a scepter.

A Time for Servants

Such words as those Jesus spoke in the upper room can be hard to swallow, especially in a world that seems totally obsessed with personal pleasure, piles of possessions, and plenty of perks. Whether we are teachers, accountants, attorneys, homemakers, businessmen, or preachers, we are often caught up in the fast lane of life in the nineties. We dash through airports, sit through meetings, dial our cellular phones, make heavy-duty decisions, attend "power lunches," and change dirty diapers. All the while we barely take time to even acknowledge the people around us. Their needs, their heartaches, and their burdens are all but ignored. Like the disciples in the upper room, we are far too busy and "important" to serve.

Yet if Jesus, who possessed the power to work miracles, still considered service the heartbeat of His ministry, who are we to shirk this responsibility? Have we "thrown in the towel" just when the world needs it the most?

The word "service" must mean more to us than just worship on Sunday. It must describe what we are all about between Sundays. Dietrich Bonhoeffer, the renowned German preacher and theologian, stated the issue in these words: "The church does not need brilliant personalities; it needs faithful servants." Do not suppose that such a leadership style is optional. It is essential! Our times thirst for it, our churches need it, and our Lord absolutely demands it!

Answers to Quarterly Quiz
on page 114

Lesson 1—1. burning incense in the temple. 2. the child's circumcision. **Lesson 2**—1. David. 2. women, fruit, womb. **Lesson 3**—1. Saviour, Christ, Lord. 2. false. **Lesson 4**—1. chief priests, scribes. 2. two years old and under. **Lesson 5**—1. seeing the Lord's Christ (Messiah). 2. Mary. 3. prophetess. **Lesson 6**—1. locusts and wild honey. 2. offended. **Lesson 7**—1. Martha. 2. spikenard. 3. Judas. **Lesson 8**—1. Caesarea Philippi. 2. false. **Lesson 9**—1. thirty pieces of silver. 2. "Lord, is it I?" 3. dipping his hand in the dish with Jesus. **Lesson 10**—1. Cyprus. 2. "son of consolation." 3. Antioch (of Syria). **Lesson 11**—1. angel. 2. standing on the right hand of God. **Lesson 12**—1. Corinth. 2. Apollos. **Lesson 13**—1. His mother was Eunice; his grandmother, Lois. 2. Lystra. 3. beloved son.

Elisabeth and Zechariah

DEVOTIONAL READING: Luke 1:18-24.

LESSON SCRIPTURE: Luke 1:5-25, 57-80.

PRINTED TEXT: Luke 1:5-13, 24, 25, 59-64.

Luke 1:5-13, 24, 25, 59-64

5 There was in the days of Herod, the king of Judea, a certain priest named Zechariah, of the course of Abijah: and his wife was of the daughters of Aaron, and her name was Elisabeth.

6 And they were both righteous before God, walking in all the commandments and ordinances of the Lord blameless.

7 And they had no child, because that Elisabeth was barren; and they both were now well stricken in years.

8 And it came to pass, that, while he executed the priest's office before God in the order of his course,

9 According to the custom of the priest's office, his lot was to burn incense when he went into the temple of the Lord.

10 And the whole multitude of the people were praying without at the time of incense.

11 And there appeared unto him an angel of the Lord standing on the right side of the altar of incense.

12 And when Zechariah saw him, he was troubled, and fear fell upon him.

13 But the angel said unto him, Fear not, Zechariah: for thy prayer is heard; and thy wife Elisabeth shall bear thee a son, and thou shalt call his name John.

. . . .

24 And after those days his wife Elisabeth conceived, and hid herself five months, saying,

25 Thus hath the Lord dealt with me in the days wherein he looked on me, to take away my reproach among men.

. . . .

59 And it came to pass, that on the eighth day they came to circumcise the child; and they called him Zechariah, after the name of his father.

60 And his mother answered and said, Not so; but he shall be called John.

61 And they said unto her, There is none of thy kindred that is called by this name.

62 And they made signs to his father, how he would have him called.

63 And he asked for a writing table, and wrote, saying, His name is John. And they marveled all.

64 And his mouth was opened immediately, and his tongue loosed, and he spake, and praised God.

GOLDEN TEXT: They [Zechariah and Elisabeth] were both righteous before God, walking in all the commandments and ordinances of the Lord blameless.
—Luke 1:6.

New Testament Personalities
Unit 1: Persons of Jesus' Nativity
and Early Life (Lessons 1-5)

Lesson Aims

As a result of this lesson students should:

1. Understand that God chooses godly persons to receive His greatest blessings.

2. See that godliness is not always immediately rewarded.

3. Resolve to give God their best and then, in patient and serene trust, await God's best.

Lesson Outline

INTRODUCTION

  A. A Well-Run Kindergarten?

  B. Lesson Background

 I. PROMISE TO A RIGHTEOUS COUPLE (Luke 1:5-13)

  A. Good Character (vv. 5-7)

  B. Good Timing (vv. 8-10)

  C. Good News (vv. 11-13)

 II. BLESSINGS ON AN ELDERLY COUPLE (Luke 1:24, 25)

  A. Conception (v. 24a)

  B. Joyful Seclusion (vv. 24b, 25)

  Whose Disgrace?

III. OBEDIENCE FROM A BLESSED COUPLE (Luke 1:59-64)

  A. The False Assumption (v. 59)

  B. Elisabeth's Correction (vv. 60, 61)

  C. Zechariah's Confirmation (vv. 62-64)

  Parental Consensus

CONCLUSION

  A. "If I Were God"

  B. Prayer

  C. Thought to Remember

The visual for Lesson 1 in the visuals packet (see page 124) shows a map of Palestine highlighting most of the places covered in Lessons 1-9.

Introduction

A. A Well-Run Kindergarten?

In his book, *Your God Is Too Small*, J. B. Phillips observes that some people are disappointed with God because He fails to run His world like the ideal kindergarten teacher runs her classroom: the diligent and cooperative student receives immediate praise and reward, while the uncooperative and rowdy child is scolded and quickly sent to the corner. Perhaps the analogy is somewhat dated (discipline is not what it used to be); but it is true that we humans frequently find ourselves pushing God to reward goodness immediately (especially if it is ours) and punish badness just as swiftly (as long as it is someone else's).

However, God does not usually work that way. Very often He reserves His best blessings and opportunities for those believers who have faithfully endured long periods of trial and testing. God allows painful times in our lives, not because He is punishing us, but because it is the hardships that build our Christian character—our faith, our strength, our endurance, our humility, our sympathy, our appreciation, and our reliance upon God.

Nor should we think that God no longer loves us when He fails to answer our prayers with haste. The examples of Joseph in Egypt, Job, the grieving sisters of Lazarus, Paul with his "thorn in the flesh," and John in exile on Patmos, teach us that pleas to God for deliverance are often denied so that God can give an even greater blessing in His "due time." Someone has observed, "We ask for silver, and God sends His denials wrapped in gold."

B. Lesson Background

Luke's Gospel serves as an excellent bridge between the Old and New Testaments. The last writer of the Old Testament, Malachi, had recorded the Lord's promises that He would send someone to "prepare the way" before Him (3:1) and that He would send Elijah before the "day of the Lord" (4:5, 6—the last two verses of the Old Testament). Both of these prophecies were fulfilled by John the Baptizer (Mark 1:2-4; Matthew 11:13, 14); thus, it is with his birth that the methodical historian Luke begins.

God had been silent for some four hundred years. As the time neared for the birth of the Savior, He suddenly broke His silence by a succession of revelations and miracles. And He

---

How to Say It

ABIJAH. Uh-*bye*-juh.

DEUTERONOMY. Due-ter-*ahn*-uh-me.

EDOMITES. *E*-duh-mites.

ELISHEBA. Eh-*lish*-eh-buh.

GABRIEL. *Gay*-bree-ul.

IDUMEAN. Id-you-*me*-un.

JEHOHANAN. Jeh-hoe-*hay*-nun.

MALACHI. *Mal*-uh-kye.

OUCHI (Greek). oo-*kee*.

ZECHARIAH. Zek-uh-*rye*-uh.

chose, as the recipients of this series of special blessings, a handful of special people who had been humbly serving Him and waiting for Him to act. The first of this select group was a dedicated elderly couple whose example teaches us that we should never give up on God.

I. Promise to a Righteous Couple
(Luke 1:5-13)
A. Good Character (vv. 5-7)

5. There was in the days of Herod, the king of Judea, a certain priest named Zechariah, of the course of Abijah: and his wife was of the daughters of Aaron, and her name was Elisabeth.

Luke sets his Gospel historically in the final years of the reign of *Herod*, the Idumean (Edomite) founder of the Herodian dynasty in Palestine. The Edomites possessed historical ties to the children of Israel (Esau, their ancestor, was Jacob's brother); however, relations between the two groups generally had been hostile. That Herod came to be called "the Great" by no means reflects anyone's estimate of his character or morals, but only that he was a shrewd politician who, despite his cruelty, was able to bring prosperity and order to Palestine. Though he energetically supported the construction of numerous cities and buildings (including the impressive renovation of the temple in Jerusalem), most Jews hated him.

Here *Judea* probably means all of Palestine (the entire land of the Jews), and is not limited to the province below Galilee and Samaria as it usually is elsewhere in the Gospels. Herod ruled from 37 to 4 B.C.; the events of this lesson probably should be dated around 6 B.C.

Both *Zechariah* and *Elisabeth* were of priestly lineage, able to trace their ancestry back to Israel's first high priest, *Aaron*. Since the days of David there had been twenty-four "courses," or divisions of priests (see 1 Chronicles 24:1-19), which took turns, a week at a time, performing the required priestly functions in the temple (sacrificial duties and the proper care of such items as offerings, altars, candlesticks, and showbread). Only four of these divisions returned from the Babylonian captivity (Ezra 2:36-39), but they were then redivided into twenty-four courses and given the original names. Zechariah belonged to the eighth course, *the course of Abijah*, which took its turn two weeks a year.

Priests who married into another family of the priestly line were accorded special honor. Such was the case with Zechariah. Elisabeth, too, was a *daughter* (or descendant) of Aaron, with the same name as Aaron's wife (Exodus 6:23, where the spelling is *Elisheba*).

6. And they were both righteous before God, walking in all the commandments and ordinances of the Lord blameless.

Certainly this couple was not morally perfect in every aspect of their lives (Romans 3:23), but over the years they had done their best to keep the stated *commandments and ordinances* of God's laws. Words such as *blameless*, perfect, and just are used in the Scriptures to describe such individuals, who, though not sinless, were still considered faithful to the will of God revealed to them. Examples include Noah (Genesis 6:9), Job (Job 1:1), Joseph (Matthew 1:19), and Simeon (Luke 2:25). Zechariah and Elisabeth had served God faithfully, yet, as the next verse shows, it appeared that He had overlooked them.

7. And they had no child, because that Elisabeth was barren; and they both were now well stricken in years.

Sadly, Elisabeth had been unable to give her husband a *child*. Her barrenness was more than disappointing; most Jews considered childlessness a disgrace for a woman, and usually saw it as a sign of God's displeasure with her. After all, Scripture taught that children were blessings from God to the obedient (see Deuteronomy 7:12-14; Psalm 127:3). Childlessness was a punishment for sin (as in Leviticus 20:20, 21), although it did not (and does not) follow that every instance of barrenness was a sign of God's disfavor.

Though verse 6 shows that Elisabeth was not barren because of any personal wrongdoing, her neighbors would naturally suspect that she was not as devout as she seemed. Legally, barrenness was considered sufficient grounds for divorce if a husband so chose. But Zechariah loved his wife, and, knowing better than anyone how godly she was, had kept her as his wife until they were now *well stricken in years*. Since sixty was considered the beginning of old age (see 1 Timothy 5:9), these two were likely in their seventies or eighties at least.

B. Good Timing (vv. 8-10)

8. And it came to pass, that, while he executed the priest's office before God in the order of his course.

The week came for the division of Abijah to perform its service in the temple, so Zechariah traveled to Jerusalem from whatever "city of Judah" was his home (Luke 1:39, 40).

9. According to the custom of the priest's office, his lot was to burn incense when he went into the temple of the Lord.

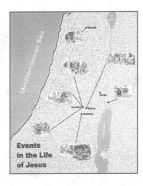

visual for
lessons 1, 2

Except on the Sabbath, when all the priests in a division would serve, there was only a handful of tasks to be performed daily in the *temple*. However, there were hundreds of priests (estimates vary from about 330 to around a thousand) in each course. Therefore, each course of priests would cast lots each day of their week of service to see which of them would be privileged to carry out the sacred duties that day.

Both priests and people considered the most solemn and honorable duty of the daily service to be the preparing and burning of the *incense* on the golden altar. This altar was located near the veil of entrance into the Holy of Holies, so the incense service would bring an ordinary priest the closest to the Holy of Holies that he could ever come. Selection for such a ministry as this was a once-in-a-lifetime opportunity. A priest could be so honored only once, after which he was considered "rich and holy." Many priests were never chosen, and those who were, considered it the highlight of their lives. After years of waiting, the lot finally had fallen to Zechariah. Since a priest never retired, his age had not disqualified him for this honor.

10. And the whole multitude of the people were praying without at the time of incense.

Whenever the priest entered the Holy Place *at the time of incense*, a signal was given which told the people in the courts of the temple to begin their *praying*. Thus, while the priest offered the incense inside the Holy Place, the people outside in the courts prayed, until he came out and dismissed them with a benediction. This normally happened rather quickly, but today's priest would be delayed.

C. Good News (vv. 11-13)

11. And there appeared unto him an angel of the Lord standing on the right side of the altar of incense.

The *right side of the altar of incense* would be just in front of the veil that led into the Holy of Holies. This *angel*, who later identified himself

as Gabriel, had come directly from the presence of God (v. 19) with a divine message.

12. And when Zechariah saw him, he was troubled, and fear fell upon him.

Fear is the usual response in the Bible to the sudden appearance of angels (see Judges 6:22; Mark 16:5, 6; Luke 1:30; 2:10; Acts 10:3, 4). Apparently angels did not resemble the soft, effeminate, or baby-like figures often created by artists' imaginations. As God's mighty warriors, they were likely imposing and intimidating figures.

13. But the angel said unto him, Fear not, Zechariah: for thy prayer is heard; and thy wife Elisabeth shall bear thee a son, and thou shalt call his name John.

For what had Zechariah been praying? A son? Perhaps—and if so, what a lesson for Christians to persevere in prayer, even when everything looks as if the prayer will not be answered. Perhaps this was a prayer Zechariah had not prayed since many years earlier, yet it was still answered. Perhaps Zechariah had been praying, along with other righteous Jews, for the coming of the Messiah and His kingdom. Maybe he had just then, as a priest, interceded for Israel, asking that her sins be forgiven. The birth of Zechariah's son would be the first in a series of redemptive events that would, in fact, grant all of the above requests.

God-given names always seem to possess a special meaning. The name *John*, a shortened form of the Hebrew *Jehohanan*, means "Jehovah's gift," or "Jehovah is gracious." The coming of John—and even more, the coming of his greater Kinsman—showed just how gracious God really was, not only to this godly couple but to the entire world.

According to verses 14-20, Gabriel went on to tell Zechariah that his son would become a great prophet who would prepare people for the coming of the Lord. The old priest, in a moment of doubt, asked Gabriel for a sign that this unbelievable news was true. The sign that he got was his own dumbness (and perhaps deafness as well) until the time that the angel's prophecy would be fulfilled.

II. Blessings on an Elderly Couple (Luke 1:24, 25)

A. Conception (v. 24a)

24a. And after those days his wife Elisabeth conceived.

Just as God had promised, through Gabriel, Elisabeth did become pregnant, thus illustrating the meaning of her own name, "God is an oath" (that is, He is absolutely faithful to His word).

B. Joyful Seclusion (vv. 24b, 25)

24b, 25. And hid herself five months, saying, Thus hath the Lord dealt with me in the days wherein he looked on me, to take away my reproach among men.

Luke does not say why Elisabeth stayed out of sight for such a long period as *five months*, but he suggests that it was a time of excitement and joy. Perhaps she wanted to enjoy these months privately with her husband for as long as possible, with the two of them offering up unhindered praise to God for a time before they created a stir in their happy news. Perhaps she knew that no one would believe her anyway until she started to "show," and that an announcement before that time would only cause doubt, speculation, and further humiliation from her neighbors. Instead, Elisabeth would savor these private moments until the time when all could recognize that God had taken away from her the *reproach* of barrenness.

WHOSE DISGRACE?

William J. Bennett's book, *The Index of Leading Cultural Indicators*, contains some disturbing statistics about the state of American society. In 1990, for example, more than two-thirds of all births to teens were to unmarried girls, compared with less than one-third in 1970. In 1991 some thirty percent of all births in this country were illegitimate. In 1994 it was estimated that nearly twenty-five percent of all pregnancies ended in abortion.

Elisabeth thought her *barrenness* was a disgrace. Our present disgrace is *fertility without responsibility*. Elisabeth was ashamed that she had borne no children, a condition that was hardly a sin. Yet millions today commit fornication, adultery, and the murder of abortion with little trace of remorse, let alone guilt. The public conscience has been seared by years of permissiveness, promiscuity, and perversion.

If "godly sorrow worketh repentance" (2 Corinthians 7:10), America is not likely to repent soon. Too many have lost their capacity for shame. They sense no disgrace in sinful behavior, thus they exhibit no contrition. Until our national disgrace is acknowledged, we shall continue to degrade ourselves, plummeting into ultimate dissipation and self-destruction. "Righteousness exalteth a nation: but sin is a reproach to any people" (Proverbs 14:34).

—R. W. B.

III. Obedience From a Blessed Couple (Luke 1:59-64)

A. The False Assumption (v. 59)

59. And it came to pass, that on the eighth day they came to circumcise the child; and they called him Zechariah, after the name of his father.

The Law commanded that a boy be circumcised on the eighth day after his birth (Leviticus 12:3). Circumcision was a solemn ceremony by which a male became part of the covenant people of God. At the same time, his parents pledged to rear him in accordance with the Law of God. Circumcision on the *eighth day* was part of a Jewish man's "blameless" pedigree (Philippians 3:5, 6). The procedure took place in the child's home, and was usually performed by either the head of the family or a physician.

It had also become the custom to give a boy his name on the day of his circumcision, perhaps because Abram had received his new name, Abraham, on the day of his circumcision (Genesis 17:5, 9, 10, 26). It was rather common to name a son after his grandfather or *his father*, and the family and friends assumed Zechariah and Elisabeth would want to perpetuate the elderly father's name by calling the boy *Zechariah*.

B. Elisabeth's Correction (vv. 60, 61)

60. And his mother answered and said, Not so; but he shall be called John.

In the original Greek, the answer of Elisabeth begins with the strong negative *ouchi*, meaning "No, indeed!" God had commanded that the name be *John*, and so the matter was settled for this obedient couple. Zechariah evidently had made regular use of his "writing table" (v. 63) over the past nine or ten months, communicating to his wife (among other matters) the revelations of Gabriel.

Home Daily Bible Readings

Monday, Nov. 25—Hannah Prays for a Child (1 Samuel 1:9-20)

Tuesday, Nov. 26—Hannah's Joy Completed (1 Samuel 2:1-10)

Wednesday, Nov. 27—Priestly Duties (1 Chronicles 23:28-32)

Thursday, Nov. 28—Angel Promised Great Joy (Luke 1:14-18)

Friday, Nov. 29—Zechariah Struck Dumb (Luke 1:19-23)

Saturday, Nov. 30—Praise God for His Works (Psalm 111:1-9)

Sunday, Dec. 1—John Grows Strong in Spirit (Luke 1:76-80)

61. And they said unto her, There is none of thy kindred that is called by this name.

The family and friends questioned Elisabeth's name selection, unaware of any relatives (*kindred*) by that name, and perhaps thinking that she had not consulted Zechariah. The father, after all, had the final say in all such matters.

C. Zechariah's Confirmation
(vv. 62-64)

62. And they made signs to his father, how he would have him called.

This would seem to indicate that Zechariah was deaf as well as dumb. By sign language those present asked him his choice of name for his son.

63. And he asked for a writing table, and wrote, saying, His name is John. And they marveled all.

Zechariah's *writing table* or tablet was probably a wooden board covered with wax or sand, on which one could write a message with a sharp stylus and then smooth it out afterward to erase the message. Zechariah confirmed the name *John*, but apparently neither he nor Elisabeth explained the reason for their choice at this time. Their friends *marveled* at such an unexpected development.

PARENTAL CONSENSUS

Billy comes to Mom and asks, "Can I spend the night at Jimmy's tonight?"

"Well, I guess so, if your father says OK."

Billy then goes to his father and says, "Dad, Mom says I can spend the night at Jimmy's tonight if you say, 'Yes.' So can I?"

Most conscientious parents go through this routine dozens of times as their children grow up. It is important for mothers and fathers to agree, even on relatively small decisions, and to present a "united front" in parent-child relationships. Just discussing issues as they arise can help a couple avoid serious mistakes in parenting. "Two are better than one," Solomon reminds us (Ecclesiastes 4:9). (This can present somewhat of a dilemma for single parents, since at times they must make decisions with no other adult input.)

Elisabeth and Zechariah agreed on their new baby's name. Though relatives and neighbors could not understand their choice, they insisted on the name that God had ordained. Their example is instructive. When parents agree, especially when they agree in the Lord, parenting becomes the blessing God intended it to be.

Parents, take note! Successful parenting is guaranteed when there is consensus in the context of godliness.   —R. W. B.

64. And his mouth was opened immediately, and his tongue loosed, and he spake, and praised God.

What praise must have been bound up in this old man turned new father! How he must have radiated a joy and excitement uncharacteristic of a man his age! With the curse on his speech now withdrawn, he immediately proceeded to give glory to his miracle-working God. Probably the prayer of verses 68-79 was part of his praise offered here.

Conclusion
A. "If I Were God"

Someone once said, "If I had the power of God for just one day, I'd do things much differently; but if I had His wisdom as well, I'd probably do things just as He does." During the difficult times of our lives, we often wonder why God responds to our plight as He does. Why does He not remove the burdens and trials from us if He really loves us? Why does He not answer when we pray? Is He aware of our struggles to remain faithful and to trust Him?

Yes, He is fully aware. But God cares for our character more than our comfort. He knows that our character needs the refinement of fire (1 Peter 1:6, 7). Painful as that might be for the moment, God is preparing us for glory to come (2 Corinthians 4:17; Romans 8:18). "The refiner is never very far from the mouth of the furnace when it's his gold in the fire" (Charles Spurgeon).

B. Prayer

Father, teach us to trust You more. Let us never forget that someday we will be glad for each deprivation and each trial, when we can see how You used them to accomplish Your will, and how they were always for our ultimate good. Amen.

C. Thought to Remember

"Folks are always saying how horrible this world is. But the fact of the matter is, this world is perfect for God's purpose: the development of character" (Anonymous).

VISUALS FOR THESE LESSONS

The *Adult Visuals* packet contains classroom-size visuals designed for use with the lessons in the Winter Quarter. The packet is available from your supplier. Order No. 292.

Learning by Doing

This page contains an alternate lesson plan emphasizing learning activities.
Classes desiring such student involvement will find these suggestions helpful.

Learning Goals

After this lesson, students will be able to:

1. List reasons why God may not answer their prayers as quickly as they might expect.

2. Appreciate God's timing in answering their prayers and the prayers of others.

3. Make a commitment to accept and trust God's timing in their lives.

Into the Lesson

Open today's lesson by asking for prayer requests. List these requests on poster board or on the chalkboard.

Review the list, focusing on *when* it would be best for these requests to be answered. Ask (but hold any discussion until later): "Are we allowed to put suggestions about timing into our prayer requests? Why isn't God's timing the same as ours?"

Today we will examine the life of a couple who had made repeated prayer requests, but had to wait on the Lord's timing for an answer.

Assure the class that we will pray for the needs they have listed a bit later in the lesson.

Into the Word

Early in the week, ask one person to prepare a brief oral report for the class on the organization and function of the temple priests. Have the student include information about the responsibility of preparing and burning incense on the golden altar. Resources for the report can be found in this week's lesson commentary and in most Bible dictionaries. Displaying a photo of the temple or of a priest will add interest to this report. Begin this portion of class with the student's presentation.

After the report, display a poster with the words, "Word Pictures of Elisabeth and Zechariah's Godliness." Ask the students to listen for descriptive words or phrases that give evidence of this couple's godliness.

Read today's Scripture text aloud. Allow students to suggest ideas for the poster, such as, "righteous before God" (v. 6), "walking in all the commandments and ordinances of the Lord" (v. 6), "blameless" (v. 6), and Zechariah "praised God" (v. 64).

From verse 6, ask, "What does 'blameless' mean? Is 'blameless' the same as 'sinless'? Does this mean that Elisabeth and Zechariah were morally perfect?" Refer to the lesson commentary (page 123) for information to guide this discussion.

Remind the students that here was a godly couple who had to wait patiently for God's blessing. They must have experienced much personal anguish in the process. In addition, they probably had to bear the social stigma that accompanied being childless in that time. Not until they had reached their senior years did God finally answer their prayer. This is a real lesson on perseverance in prayer. Just because our prayer is not answered immediately does not necessarily mean that God has rejected our prayer (even though that is His option).

Into Life

Ask the class: "Do you sometimes wonder about God's timing? There were other Biblical women besides Elisabeth who had to wait to have children." Ask the class to name some (Sarah, Rachel, Hannah, and Samson's mother are examples).

Repeat the question: "Why does God sometimes wait to answer our prayers?" Allow the class to discuss the question. Remember, there may be numerous or different reasons for different situations. God knows what timing is best for us.

Ask, "Can our relationship with the Lord sometimes affect the timing of His answers to our prayers?" Yes. Sometimes He may want our character to be refined. See the Conclusion in the lesson commentary for a discussion of this concept.

There are so many instances when we ask for God's help. Ask the class to resolve to be patient while waiting for God's answers. We must continually trust His wisdom. Our commentary writer includes this quote: "If I had the power of God for just one day, I'd do things much differently; but if I had His wisdom as well, I'd probably do things just as He does."

Conclude with a group prayer (or divide the class into groups, depending on the size). Have each group pray for a portion of the prayer list made at the beginning of class. Also ask each group to make a commitment to patience as members wait for God's timing in answering prayer.

We must trust Him. He is God.

Let's Talk It Over

The questions on this page are designed to encourage review of the lesson Scriptures and to promote discussion of the lesson by the class. The answers provided are only discussion starters. Let your class talk it over from there.

1. Many devout Christians struggle with disappointments and failures. Others experience almost continual suffering and grief. Still others live on the ragged edge of poverty. Why doesn't God reward righteousness with material benefits?

Whether we admit it or not, we are influenced by the values of a secular society. So we tend to think of God's rewards in terms of money, success, and happiness, almost as if they were bonuses for a job well done. However, while God always rewards righteousness, His rewards are not always what we expect.

The rewards that God promises to give us are primarily spiritual and emotional: spiritual growth and enlightenment, a closer walk with Jesus, increased sensitivity to the needs of others, awareness of divine approval, and emotional health and wholeness. God has also promised that our basic material needs will be met (Matthew 6:33). We should keep in mind, however, that fullness of life in God's eyes is measured in terms of the quality of our character and our relationship with Christ, not the size of our bank account or the number of "toys" we have.

2. If our prayers are not answered immediately, how can we know God hears us?

The Bible emphasizes that God hears our prayers. When the enslaved Hebrews cried out in Egypt, "God heard their groaning" (Exodus 2:24). The psalmists repeatedly affirmed that the Lord heard their cries (Psalms 6:9; 34:4; 66:19; 118:21). The angel Gabriel assured Zechariah, "Thy prayer is heard" (Luke 1:13).

Believing that God hears us when the answer fails to come immediately or when events do not happen the way we think they should is part of faith. We must believe that God hears and will answer in His way and in His time. His answer may not be what we want, but it will be what we need.

3. Zechariah was disciplined when he asked the angel for a sign. At what point does honest doubt become unbelief?

God invites our questions, and He welcomes honest doubt. Through the prophet Isaiah, He urged the Israelites, "Come now, and let us rea-

son together" (Isaiah 1:18). God is not offended when we seek more information or even if we are skeptical (as the example of Thomas clearly shows). The primary consideration is whether our attitude is sincere and whether we are really willing to examine the available evidence.

4. Zechariah and Elisabeth's relatives wanted to follow tradition and name the newborn child Zechariah, after his father. What are some benefits of following tradition? Why are we often reluctant to break tradition and try something new?

Tradition can be either positive or negative, beneficial or harmful, depending on our point of view and how tradition is used. On the positive side, tradition has been tested and proved by time, so it represents something trustworthy and dependable. Tradition is also a valuable link to the past. Tradition represents our heritage. It provides a solid foundation on which we can build for the future.

But tradition can have a harmful and negative influence. Honoring tradition can become more important than helping people. In addition, tradition can be used as an excuse for blocking progress ("But we've *always* done it this way!"). Tradition also becomes an obstacle rather than a foundation stone, if we interpret the Bible in the light of tradition, thereby giving tradition more authority than the Scriptures.

We tend to hold on to traditional practices— even after we know they no longer work— because they are safe and comfortable. Breaking with tradition means taking a risk, and we are not always willing to do that.

5. Zechariah "spake, and praised God" (Luke 1:64). Besides speaking, what are some other ways we can praise God?

We can praise God through music, both singing and playing instruments. We can praise God through giving gifts and offerings. We can praise Him through acts of service.

However, God is praised most by a life lived daily and consistently according to the teachings of Jesus. God is glorified and the world receives a powerful testimony when we stand firm for Christ in the midst of adversity, temptation, and the pressures of everyday life.

Mary, Mother of Jesus

DEVOTIONAL READING: Luke 1:24-56.

LESSON SCRIPTURE: Luke 1:26-56.

PRINTED TEXT: Luke 1:26-42.

Luke 1:26-42

26 And in the sixth month the angel Gabriel was sent from God unto a city of Galilee, named Nazareth,

27 To a virgin espoused to a man whose name was Joseph, of the house of David; and the virgin's name was Mary.

28 And the angel came in unto her, and said, Hail, thou that art highly favored, the Lord is with thee: blessed art thou among women.

29 And when she saw him, she was troubled at his saying, and cast in her mind what manner of salutation this should be.

30 And the angel said unto her, Fear not, Mary: for thou hast found favor with God.

31 And, behold, thou shalt conceive in thy womb, and bring forth a son, and shalt call his name JESUS.

32 He shall be great, and shall be called the Son of the Highest; and the Lord God shall give unto him the throne of his father David:

33 And he shall reign over the house of Jacob for ever; and of his kingdom there shall be no end.

34 Then said Mary unto the angel, How shall this be, seeing I know not a man?

35 And the angel answered and said unto her, The Holy Ghost shall come upon thee, and the power of the Highest shall overshadow thee: therefore also that holy thing which shall be born of thee shall be called the Son of God.

36 And, behold, thy cousin Elisabeth, she hath also conceived a son in her old age; and this is the sixth month with her, who was called barren.

37 For with God nothing shall be impossible.

38 And Mary said, Behold the handmaid of the Lord; be it unto me according to thy word. And the angel departed from her.

39 And Mary arose in those days, and went into the hill country with haste, into a city of Judah;

40 And entered into the house of Zecharias, and saluted Elisabeth.

41 And it came to pass, that, when Elisabeth heard the salutation of Mary, the babe leaped in her womb; and Elisabeth was filled with the Holy Ghost:

42 And she spake out with a loud voice, and said, Blessed art thou among women, and blessed is the fruit of thy womb.

GOLDEN TEXT: Mary said, Behold the handmaid of the Lord; be it unto me according to thy word.—Luke 1:38.

Lesson Aims

After this lesson each student should:

l. Be able to describe Mary's reactions to the message of the angel.

2. Resolve to imitate Mary's submissive attitude to God's opportunities for service.

3. Determine to keep alive the joy associated with celebrating the birth of Jesus.

Lesson Outline

INTRODUCTION

    A. Parental Discretion

    B. Lesson Background

  I. GABRIEL VISITS MARY (Luke 1:26-38)

    A. The Angel's Assignment (vv. 26, 27)

    B. The Angel's Acknowledgment (v. 28)

    C. Mary's Apprehension (v. 29)

    D. The Angel's Announcement (vv. 30-33)

    E. Mary's Appeal (v. 34)

    F. The Angel's Answer (vv. 35-37)

      Accident or Surprise?

    G. Mary's Affirmation (v. 38)

 II. MARY VISITS ELISABETH (Luke 1:39-42)

    A. Mary's Sojourn (v. 39)

    B. Mary's Salutation (v. 40)

    C. Elisabeth's Statement (vv. 41, 42)

CONCLUSION

    A. The Place of Mary

    B. Accepting the Challenge

    C. Let Us Pray

    D. Thought to Remember

Use the map of Palestine (mentioned in Lesson 1) to note the places mentioned in this lesson and to trace Mary's journey to see Elisabeth.

Introduction

A. Parental Discretion

She was a student at a state university, and she asked her minister this question: "Do you know what we talk about during our reflective hours in the dorm?" He waited for her to answer and she said, "We ask ourselves if we should be a part of bringing children into this world." That was a generation ago, and almost every statistic related to the values of America has moved in the wrong direction.

A recent survey of young people from evangelical homes revealed these rather surprising statistics: 66% lied to their parents in the last three months; 36% cheated during the same period; 57% did not affirm moral absolutes to govern behavior.

The thoughtful couple faces many challenges as they consider parenting in today's world. Will their children become a part of the negative statistics? Do they want to subject their children to a world of turmoil? Does moral decline dictate that godly parents should determine to have even more children as a means of reversing the trend?

The subject of today's lesson is the Lord's announcement to Mary that she had been chosen to be the mother of the Messiah. As we shall see, Mary had to face her own fears and apprehensions about fulfilling such a challenging task. Parents today can take heart from the fact that the God who used this humble and devoted Jewish maiden from Nazareth can likewise use us to dispel the darkness of our time through raising godly children.

B. Lesson Background

Elisabeth, one of the two personalities mentioned in last week's lesson, is also a part of today's lesson. She was a relative of Mary, the primary focus of our Scripture text.

The lesson text is again from Luke 1. Luke was more than a physician. He was a careful historian who investigated "all things from the very first" (Luke 1:3). We, as well as Theophilus (to whom Luke directed his writing), can "know the certainty of those things, wherein [we have] been instructed" (Luke 1:4).

I. Gabriel Visits Mary
(Luke 1:26-38)

A. The Angel's Assignment
(vv. 26, 27)

26. And in the sixth month the angel Gabriel was sent from God unto a city of Galilee, named Nazareth.

This was the *sixth month* of the pregnancy of Elisabeth (see last week's lesson), but it was also much more than that. It was the beginning of that "fulness of the time" when God would send "his Son, made of a woman" (Galatians 4:4).

This "fulness of the time" was to impact a world that was on the verge of moral collapse. The Roman and Greek gods were recognized by many people for the false gods that they were. Religion had degenerated into observance of tradition, and spiritual apathy was the result. Roman oppression created a negative outlook on life. Slaves had no status, and women were often treated as chattel.

The "fulness of the time" also meant that *the angel Gabriel* had yet another mission. In the past he had been sent to Babylon to provide understanding for the prophet Daniel (Daniel 8:16; 9:21). He had appeared to Zechariah at the temple in Jerusalem, as we observed last week. Now he was sent from God one more time—not to a capital city, but to an obscure *city of Galilee, named Nazareth.*

Galilee was in the northern third of Palestine. It was commonly held that nothing "good" would ever "come out of Nazareth" (John 1:46). That was about to change!

27. To a virgin espoused to a man whose name was Joseph, of the house of David; and the virgin's name was Mary.

Gabriel's assignment was to a specific individual—*a virgin* whose *name was Mary.* The "fulness of the time" demanded that the Messiah be born of a virgin (Isaiah 7:14). The fact that Luke, a physician, gives such unequivocal testimony about Mary's virginity is especially valuable.

Mary was a frequent name then, as it is now. In the "fulness of the time" she became *espoused* (engaged) to *Joseph, of the house of David.* That Mary was also a descendant of David is seen from the genealogy found in Luke 3:23-38, which is generally considered to be that of Mary (Matthew 1:1-17 records Joseph's). It was necessary that an actual descendant of David be the Messiah and occupy David's throne (see 2 Samuel 7:12-16; Psalm 132:11; Matthew 1:1; 9:27; 22:41, 42).

B. The Angel's Acknowledgment (v. 28)

28. And the angel came in unto her, and said, Hail, thou that art highly favored, the Lord is with thee: blessed art thou among women.

Gabriel appeared to Mary directly as he had to Zechariah. This was not a dream or a vision. In both instances, however, the angel's manifestations were in private, not in public.

The statement that was made by the angel included a descriptive phrase about Mary: she was *highly favored.* This expression was much more than just a courteous greeting or a congratulatory word about her engagement to Joseph. Mary had been chosen to give birth to the Messiah and to raise and nurture Him during His early years.

The final phrase, *blessed art thou among women*, does not appear in the oldest Greek manuscripts, and some recent translations do not include it. The same words are a part of Elisabeth's greeting in the last verse of today's lesson text (v. 42).

How to Say It

CYRUS. *Sigh*-russ.
GABRIEL. *Gay*-bree-ul.
MAGNIFICAT. Mag-*nif*-ih-cot.
SHUNEM. *Shoo*-nem.
THEOPHILUS. Thee-*ahf*-ih-luss.
ZECHARIAH. Zek-uh-*rye*-uh.

C. Mary's Apprehension (v. 29)

29. And when she saw him, she was troubled at his saying, and cast in her mind what manner of salutation this should be.

As Luke later tells us, Mary was someone who "pondered" (2:19) and "kept" certain matters "in her heart" (2:51). She tended to think issues through carefully, rather than rush to a conclusion. At first, she did not respond verbally to the angel's *salutation*, but *in her mind* a variety of thoughts must have been present. The angel's comforting words helped her to remain calm, but she was still *troubled.*

D. The Angel's Announcement (vv. 30-33)

30. And the angel said unto her, Fear not, Mary: for thou hast found favor with God.

The angel was aware of Mary's apprehension, and he provided comfort to her in three ways. First, *Fear not* brought immediate calm. These words were often used when heavenly beings spoke to humans (as in Genesis 21:17; Matthew 28:5; Luke 1:13; 2:10; Acts 27:23, 24). Second, he called her by name. This was likely done in a compassionate way that relieved Mary's anxieties. Third, the thought that Mary had *found favor* was repeated. This brought further reassurance, for God's messengers, whether angels or prophets, often pronounced judgment on those who were disobedient to God's commands.

31. And, behold, thou shalt conceive in thy womb, and bring forth a son, and shalt call his name JESUS.

This is the announcement that the angel was commissioned to give. Each part provided a more specific detail: Mary would be with child; the baby would be *a son;* and she would give him a particular name. The fact that Joseph is said to give the child his name in Matthew 1:21 is not a contradiction; rather, it may be considered evidence that there was harmony between both the man and the woman in following God's direction. The same spirit of agreement is seen in Zechariah and Elisabeth's naming of John (Luke 1:60, 63).

Perhaps Mary had thrilled at the accounts of the women in the Scriptures who had been blessed with sons in special ways: Sarah (Genesis 18:13, 14), the unnamed mother of Samson (Judges 13:3), Hannah (1 Samuel 1:9-20), and the woman of Shunem (2 Kings 4:16). In each case, however, the woman involved already had a husband.

The name *Jesus* in Greek is the equivalent of *Joshua* in Hebrew, and it means "the Lord is salvation," or "salvation is of the Lord." Two factors combined to give it special significance: its meaning, and the fact that it was specifically chosen by God for the Messiah.

32. He shall be great, and shall be called the Son of the Highest; and the Lord God shall give unto him the throne of his father David.

The phrases describing the promised Son continue to build. The adjective *great* had become incorporated into the name by which "Great" rulers (such as Cyrus and Alexander) were known. The current ruler, Herod, was also designated as "Herod the Great." Whatever greatness these men possessed, however, would pale in comparison with that which would be bestowed upon the promised son of Mary.

Son of the Highest is a phrase that suggests a special association with deity. This was confirmed by the angel's words in verse 35. It is noteworthy that John the Baptist is referred to as the "prophet of the Highest" in Luke 1:76. John was a spokesman for God; Jesus was the Son of God.

Mary's son would occupy *the throne of his father David*. This phrase confirmed the significance of David, which was implied in verse 27. Gabriel promised that Mary's son would be a King and would fulfill the promises made to and about David in the Old Testament.

33. And he shall reign over the house of Jacob for ever; and of his kingdom there shall be no end.

The *kingdom* of the Messiah had three distinctive characteristics: it was spiritual (John 18:36), universal (Daniel 7:14), and eternal (Daniel 2:44; 7:14). The term *house of Jacob* (or Israel) would take on a new meaning that included far more than national or geographical Israel. It embraced all peoples who would enter the kingdom by faith in the Messiah, regardless of physical ancestry (see Paul's use of the phrase "Israel of God" in Galatians 6:16).

E. Mary's Appeal (v. 34)

34. Then said Mary unto the angel, How shall this be, seeing I know not a man?

Mary's response was different from Zechariah's unbelief (Luke 1:20) and Sarah's doubting laughter (Genesis 18:12). Her question indicates acceptance, but she was puzzled and perplexed with a natural bewilderment. The universal experience of mankind was that a woman must *know* (a term for sexual intimacy) a man. The *New International Version* interprets the last phrase of the question in this way: "since I am a virgin."

F. The Angel's Answer (vv. 35-37)

35. And the angel answered and said unto her, The Holy Ghost shall come upon thee, and the power of the Highest shall overshadow thee: therefore also that holy thing which shall be born of thee shall be called the Son of God.

The angel's answer highlighted two factors: the creative power of God, and the nature of the child who was to be born. As the Spirit of God was active in the original creation (Genesis 1:2), so He would be the agent in Mary's conception. We are not informed how the *Holy Ghost* accomplished this. If the angel's explanation had been phrased according to our present understanding of genetics, it would have baffled men in the succeeding centuries and produced confusion rather than wonder. It was not deemed essential for Mary (or for us) to understand completely the ways of God. Her task was, and ours is, simply this: "The just shall live by faith" (Romans 1:17).

The child was given two designations: *holy* and the *Son of God. Holy* impresses upon us the sacredness of the entire account of Jesus' birth. The sneering and snickering of the skeptics are totally out of place. For them to claim, "This is not the way children are normally conceived," is precisely the point! This was not a normal conception.

During December it is appropriate to emphasize Jesus' birth and to focus once more on the simple yet beautiful accounts of his birth in Matthew and Luke. But in so doing, we should not overlook the impact of *all* of Jesus' life, including His teachings, miracles, death, resurrection, and promised return. One can imagine how strange it would seem to observe the birthday of Abraham Lincoln, for example, by focusing only on his birth and childhood and ignoring all of the accomplishments of his adult life. The same is true of Jesus. At Christmas we should recognize that God has given us one glorious package —one matchless life. It is ours to open and to treasure.

J. Gresham Machen states the issue in these terms: "If Jesus was at all the sort of person that He is represented as being in the whole New Testament, then it is the most probable thing imaginable that He came into the world in the manner described in the early chapters of Matthew and Luke." Something would seem terribly wrong if Jesus had been born in a spectacular fashion, and then had settled down to live a simple carpenter's life and die a simple carpenter's death. We would then have good reason to question the accuracy of the birth accounts. However, the New Testament challenges us not only with a "special delivery," but also with a totally unique life. It is one awe-inspiring Christmas package.

ACCIDENT OR SURPRISE?

Too often, parents speak of unplanned pregnancies as "accidents." Sometimes they do so even in the presence of their children. Despite the teasing tone, youngsters hardly like to think of their conception as some sort of mishap. Such "accidents" are much better called "surprises." If a child has to know at all, his self-esteem will suffer less if he is referred to as a "surprise."

Mary's pregnancy was a surprise—most certainly not an accident. The conception was planned by God, and effected by the Holy Spirit. It was "on purpose"—God's purpose, in "the fulness of the time" (Galatians 4:4). Those connected with the circumstances surrounding the birth of Christ were surprised, but generally they were surprised and *pleased*. The ones who were well acquainted with Messianic prophecies were more pleased than surprised. For people such as Simeon and Anna the birth of the long-expected Jesus in their lifetime was a most joyous turn of events.

This same observation can be made concerning the second coming of Christ. His return certainly will not be an accident. Though the timing will be a surprise, the faithful will be *pleasantly* surprised. What a joy it will be if this "blessed event" should occur in our lifetime!

—R. W. B.

36. And, behold, thy cousin Elisabeth, she hath also conceived a son in her old age; and this is the sixth month with her, who was called barren.

Gabriel provided confirmation for his message in the form of astounding news about *Elisabeth*, a relative (not necessarily an actual *cousin*) who had been childless. These personal details were new and exciting to Mary, and served to address the concerns she had expressed through her question (v. 34).

37. For with God nothing shall be impossible.

God can do more than the "laws" of nature allow man to do. He is the one who established the laws, and He can set them aside or override

them to accomplish His purposes. The angel's final remark referred primarily to Elisabeth, but it gave further assurance to Mary.

G. Mary's Affirmation (v. 38)

38. And Mary said, Behold the handmaid of the Lord; be it unto me according to thy word. And the angel departed from her.

Mary's affirmation of acceptance is an outstanding declaration of faith, trust, and devotion. The verbal exchange between her and the angel shows that she was not naive. She had the ability to assess the immediate future, and no doubt she recognized some of the sensitive situations she would likely have to confront: Joseph's reaction, the townspeople's skepticism toward her explanation of her pregnancy, and the resultant rumors that were certain to surface. Aware of these possibilities, Mary still gave her unqualified acquiescence to God's plan.

II. Mary Visits Elisabeth (Luke 1:39-42)

A. Mary's Sojourn (v. 39)

39. And Mary arose in those days, and went into the hill country with haste, into a city of Judah.

We may wonder about the timing of some of these events with those recorded in Matthew 1. Did Mary share her news with Joseph immediately, and is that why "he had in mind to divorce her quietly" (Matthew 1:19, *New International Version*)? Or did she delay informing him until she returned from her journey *into the hill country*? The divine record does not tell us.

Mary's inner joy about Elisabeth's news, coupled with the excitement of her own, prompted her to make her trip to Judah *with haste*. Whenever two women in the same family are both pregnant, a special bond tends to develop between them. How much more so with these women whose conceptions were in the realm of the "impossible"!

The *city of Judah* (Judea) is not identified. It was customary for priests such as Zechariah to live within a day's walk from Jerusalem.

B. Mary's Salutation (v. 40)

40. And entered into the house of Zechariah, and saluted Elisabeth.

When Mary *saluted* Elisabeth, it was surely more than a formal greeting such as that used by Gabriel to address Mary. This must have been a joyous exchange between the young virgin and the aged woman, each of whom was miraculously carrying a son who would fulfill prophecies given hundreds of years before.

C. Elisabeth's Statement (vv. 41, 42)

41. And it came to pass, that, when Elisabeth heard the salutation of Mary, the babe leaped in her womb; and Elisabeth was filled with the Holy Ghost.

Mary's *salutation* produced three immediate and dramatic reactions. John, though still unborn, *leaped* in his mother's *womb* in such a way that she knew something unusual had transpired. Some have proposed that John was already giving homage to the Son of God, but it is more probable that God prompted the movement as a sign to Elisabeth.

Second, *Elisabeth was filled with the Holy Ghost*, prior to making an inspired utterance. We may question why such inspiration is ascribed to the statements of Zechariah (Luke 1:67) and Elisabeth, but not to Mary's response, known as the Magnificat, in vv. 46-55. This does not make Mary's words any less significant. In the cases of Elisabeth and Zechariah, the Holy Spirit was providing information and insight not naturally discerned. The record specifically states that Zechariah "prophesied" (Luke 1:67). Mary's words of praise acknowledged God's special care for her and the singular role her child would play. These were matters already revealed to her through Gabriel's message. Mary's words also exhibit similarities to the prayer of Hannah, the mother of Samuel (1 Samuel 2:1-10), whose conception was also orchestrated by God.

42. And she spake out with a loud voice, and said, Blessed art thou among women, and blessed is the fruit of thy womb.

The third reaction was Elisabeth's pronouncement of blessing on Mary and on Jesus. Chronologically these are the first beatitudes of the New Testament, and the very first one is upon Mary.

This incident also highlights a contrast between the faith of Mary and that of Zechariah. Mary's faith enabled her to enter into a home with a salutation. Zechariah's unbelief resulted in his inability to speak.

Conclusion

A. The Place of Mary

It has been well said that Mary was blessed *among* women, not *above* women. Through the centuries, however, men have added much to the simple teaching of the New Testament. Mary has been declared sinless along with Jesus, and is said to have been a perpetual virgin. It is also believed that her body did not decay, for it experienced an "assumption" into Heaven at her death. Some have supposedly heard "prophetic"

utterances from her. A recent headline in a newspaper read: "Book Compiles the Prophecies of Mary."

On the other hand, some have gone to the opposite extreme and ignored this one who was declared *blessed*. As today's lesson has indicated, Christians have much to learn from the unshakable faith and commitment of Mary. She should be accorded the honor that Scripture grants to her.

B. Accepting the Challenge

Believers of today need to move beyond being just "Sunday Christians," and to accept the challenges and invitations for special service and sacrifice. Many need to progress from always being fed, to being one of those who "feed" others—by teaching a class, serving as a youth sponsor, increasing financial stewardship, leading a Bible study, participating in one of many types of calling programs, supporting a missionary, becoming a missionary, or becoming a foster parent. There will be some heartaches, rejections, and disappointments—just as there must have been for Mary. The determined Christian will understand this, and he will continue faithfully in the service of Christ.

C. Let Us Pray

God in the highest, lead me today into paths of righteousness that also include paths of service. May my eyes be opened to see the opportunities that I have avoided in the past. Amen.

D. Thought to Remember

It was not essential for Mary (nor is it for us) to understand completely the ways of God. Her task was, and ours is, simply this: "The just shall live by faith" (Romans 1:17).

Home Daily Bible Readings

Monday Dec. 2—Accepting God's Plan (Psalm 138:1-8)

Tuesday, Dec. 3—Joseph Accepted Mary (Matthew 1:18-25)

Wednesday, Dec. 4—Mary's Song of Praise (Luke 1:46-56)

Thursday, Dec. 5—Mary and Joseph Go to Bethlehem (Luke 2:1-7)

Friday, Dec. 6—Mary and Joseph Go to Egypt (Matthew 2:13-18)

Saturday, Dec. 7—Mary and Joseph Go to Nazareth (Matthew 2:19-23)

Sunday, Dec. 8—Jesus Provides for Mary's Care (John 19:23-27)

Learning by Doing

This page contains an alternate lesson plan emphasizing learning activities.
Classes desiring such student involvement will find these suggestions helpful.

Learning Goals

As a result of this lesson, students should be able to:

1. Describe Mary's reactions to the message of the angel.

2. Express a desire to imitate Mary's submission to God's will for them.

Into the Lesson

Before class begins, prepare a large poster board with the following events from the Christmas story listed vertically. Be sure to allow plenty of space between each event. You may need to use two sheets.

Gabriel's visit to Mary
Mary's visit to Elisabeth
The virgin birth
The Bethlehem nativity scene
The shepherds
The impact of Jesus' birth

Open today's lesson by asking the class to cite the names of Christmas carols or phrases from Christmas carols that reflect each of these events from the Christmas story. Have a class member write the song titles or phrases beside the events they depict. After the activity is completed, point out that few or no songs or phrases refer to Gabriel's announcement to Mary or to Mary's visit with Elisabeth. These important scenes in the Christmas story receive little attention in music, Christmas cards, and nativity scenes. Yet God has recorded them for us.

Into the Word

Divide the class into groups of four to six. Each group is to work on one of the following two tasks. Give each group an instruction sheet for their task and a piece of large poster board to record their answers. If your class is large, you will have more than one group working on the same task.

Task 1. Read today's text, then list all the words or phrases describing the promised Son to whom Mary would give birth. Also list one or two phrases in songs (preferably Christmas songs) that reflect these descriptions of Jesus. For example, verse 35 calls Him "Son of God." The last verse of a familiar carol uses that title as follows: "Silent night, holy night, Son of God, love's pure light." Other descriptions include

"great," "Son of the Highest," "throne of his father David," "he shall reign," "of his kingdom there shall be no end," and "that holy thing."

Task 2. Read today's text, then on poster board, list phrases or words from it that highlight Mary's character and godliness. Be ready to share the significance of these characteristics with the class. Discuss verse 38 and the implications of Mary's model for women today and for all Christians.

Ask the groups to report their findings. If more than one group has been working on a task, compare their answers. As the group working on Task 1 lists their descriptions of Jesus and the accompanying song titles, focus on the significance of these descriptions as discussed in the lesson commentary. After the reports on Task 2, include the remarks from the section of the lesson commentary entitled, "The Place of Mary" on page 134.

Into Life

Ask the class: "If you had to record Mary's reaction to Gabriel's announcement in just one word, what word would you use?" Probably someone will mention "submissive" or "willing" (as seen from v. 38). Focus on that attitude as the key word for application into life. Mary was not naive. Remind the class that Mary knew the implications of a virgin birth. She knew the questions people would raise. She knew people would have trouble believing her explanation about her pregnancy. Yet she yielded herself to God's will and plan. Her willing submission to God's will is a model for us.

Have the small groups write a brief prayer expressing the desire to be submissive to the will of God. They should try to write this prayer in the form of an acrostic (where each line of the prayer begins with a letter from a certain word). Those groups who did Task 1 should write their prayer using the word "Yield." The other group should do the same with the word "Trust." You may want to display the following acrostic/ prayer (based on the word "Love") as an example on a transparency or on poster board.

Lord, I often find life challenging.
Over and over I must give myself to Your will.
Very often I need Your wisdom.
Encourage me to stay close to You!

Let's Talk It Over

The questions on this page are designed to encourage review of the lesson Scriptures and to promote discussion of the lesson by the class. The answers provided are only discussion starters. Let your class talk it over from there.

1. Luke's Gospel opens with an angel making surprise visits and dramatic announcements. Why don't angels deliver God's messages today?

Extraordinary angelic activity marked the transition from the Old Testament era based on the Law to the New Testament era based on faith in Christ. An angel broke a four-hundred-year prophetic silence by bringing prophetic messages to Zechariah and Mary. An angel also announced the birth of Jesus to lowly Bethlehem shepherds.

In our day, we have the completed Scriptures, which contain God's full message of salvation. Also, as believers we have the indwelling Holy Spirit, who provides us with power and direction in applying the Scriptures. So we do not need dramatic messages from angels.

At the same time, we should keep in mind passages such as Hebrews 1:14 and 13:2, which indicate that angels do function in a special (though often unrecognized) way on behalf of believers.

2. God chose for special honor a humble peasant maiden from a culturally backward area of the world. Why does He often use ordinary people?

The apostle Paul said that God delights in using "the foolish things of the world to confound the wise" (1 Corinthians 1:27). God looks for people who are willing and responsive. A proud and arrogant person puts his confidence in his education, his talents, his intelligence, or his ability. But God wants someone who is humble enough to recognize that any success he has is only because God is working through him and using him (1 Corinthians 1:26-29).

Of course, this does not imply that the intelligent, educated, and scholarly are therefore excluded from the kingdom. Paul himself was such a man. But before God could use him, he had to be humbled by an encounter with the living Christ.

3. Mary was told she had found favor with God. How should Christians seek to find favor with God in our day?

After posing the question, "What doth the Lord require of thee?" the prophet Micah answered it himself: "To do justly, and to love mercy, and to walk humbly with thy God" (Micah 6:8). This is the essence of finding favor with God in any age and at any age.

We may think that favor with God involves an act of noble service, a great personal sacrifice, or a strict observance of a long list of *dos* and *don'ts*. But God is more concerned with our character and conduct than He is with praiseworthy deeds done for selfish motives. Read the "love chapter" of 1 Corinthians 13.

4. Since God is omnipotent (all-powerful), why do we often doubt when He promises to do something "impossible"?

While the spiritual side of our nature reaches out to God in faith, our human side wants to keep one foot firmly on the ground. Because of this, we have a tendency to believe only what we can touch and see and taste. Believing that the "impossible" can be done requires a level of trust in God that takes time and experience to develop. Even so great a man of faith as Abraham had a hard time accepting the "impossible." He tried to help God keep His "impossible" promise to give him a son by using a totally human solution (Genesis 16:1-3).

We should remember that "impossible" is a term that relates only to our limited experience and understanding. It becomes a part of our vocabulary when we learn to "walk by faith, not by sight" (2 Corinthians 5:7).

5. Mary received confirmation of the angel's message when she visited her relative Elisabeth. What are some of the ways in which we can receive confirmation of something we believe to be God's will?

First, we can look to the Scriptures for direction. If the Bible contradicts something we believe is God's will, this is sure proof that we need to change our thinking.

Often God will use other Christians to provide the counsel that we need. He may use a minister, a Sunday school teacher, or a trusted Christian friend to offer a helpful perspective; or, as was true with Mary, the advice may come from some family member. We must also make such decisions a matter of daily and fervent prayer.

The Shepherds

DEVOTIONAL READING: Micah 5:2-9.

LESSON SCRIPTURE: Luke 2:1-20.

PRINTED TEXT: Luke 2:8-20.

Luke 2:8-20

8 And there were in the same country shepherds abiding in the field, keeping watch over their flock by night.

9 And, lo, the angel of the Lord came upon them, and the glory of the Lord shone round about them; and they were sore afraid.

10 And the angel said unto them, Fear not: for, behold, I bring you good tidings of great joy, which shall be to all people.

11 For unto you is born this day in the city of David a Saviour, which is Christ the Lord.

12 And this shall be a sign unto you; Ye shall find the babe wrapped in swaddling clothes, lying in a manger.

13 And suddenly there was with the angel a multitude of the heavenly host praising God, and saying,

14 Glory to God in the highest, and on earth peace, good will toward men.

15 And it came to pass, as the angels were gone away from them into heaven, the shepherds said one to another, Let us now go even unto Bethlehem, and see this thing which is come to pass, which the Lord hath made known unto us.

16 And they came with haste, and found Mary and Joseph, and the babe lying in a manger.

17 And when they had seen it, they made known abroad the saying which was told them concerning this child.

18 And all they that heard it wondered at those things which were told them by the shepherds.

19 But Mary kept all these things, and pondered them in her heart.

20 And the shepherds returned, glorifying and praising God for all the things that they had heard and seen, as it was told unto them.

GOLDEN TEXT: The shepherds returned, glorifying and praising God for all the things that they had heard and seen, as it was told unto them.—Luke 2:20.

New Testament Personalities
Unit 1: Persons of Jesus' Nativity
and Early Life (Lessons 1-5)

Lesson Aims

As a result of studying this lesson the students should:

1. Appreciate how the grace of God shines forth in the Christmas story.

2. See good reason for giving God praise during this Christmas season.

3. Desire to share the good news of our Savior's birth with others as best they can.

Lesson Outline

INTRODUCTION
    A. Beloved Characters
    B. Lesson Background
 I. A DAY OF GRACE (Luke 2:8-12)
    A. A Gift for All Men (vv. 8-10)
      Communication Barriers
    B. A Remedy for Our Sin (vv. 11, 12)
 II. A NIGHT OF GLORY (Luke 2:13-16)
    A. A Sound of Praise (vv. 13, 14)
    B. A Scene of Promise (vv. 15, 16)
III. A TIME OF GOOD NEWS (Luke 2:17-20)
    A. A Message Worth Retelling (vv. 17, 18)
      Unlikely Prospects
    B. A Story Worth Remembering (vv. 19, 20)
CONCLUSION
    A. A Day of Good Tidings
    B. Let Us Pray
    C. Thought to Remember

The visual for Lesson 3 in the visuals packet is appropriate for the Christmas season, showing a traditional nativity scene. It is shown on page 141.

Introduction

A. Beloved Characters

The story is told of a kindergarten teacher who asked each of her students to tell the class what his father did for a living. One young girl said that she thought her father was a shepherd. When asked why she believed this, she responded, "Because he usually walks around the house in his bathrobe."

For many of us our knowledge of the shepherd's life does not extend much beyond the impressions we receive from our Christmas pageants and live nativity scenes. Shepherding is not a vocation we teach in school or see around us in our daily life. We may know something about modern livestock farming, but we have difficulty identifying with people who used to live in open fields "keeping watch over their flocks by night."

Nevertheless, the shepherds of Luke 2 are a favorite part of the Christmas story. We enjoy visualizing a quiet night, gentle sheep, an angelic visit, and a trip to the stable. We may know few facts regarding shepherds, but we are familiar with these shepherds. Now, as we study the Biblical text for today, let us learn from their experience.

B. Lesson Background

Last week's lesson focused upon Gabriel's announcement to Mary that she would give birth to the promised Messiah. This week's lesson moves approximately nine months forward to the events surrounding that birth.

Bethlehem, where Jesus was born, was about ninety miles south of Nazareth, the hometown of Joseph and Mary. The couple was away from home at this awkward time because a decree by the Roman emperor Augustus required that they, along with every other citizen, return to their family place of origin long enough to register for a new tax. For Joseph and Mary, that meant a trip to Bethlehem (Luke 2:1-5).

The lack of housing in Bethlehem was likely due to a large influx of visitors from all over the Roman Empire who, like Joseph, had come to register. Because of this overcrowding, the Son of God was born in a stable (Luke 2:6, 7).

I. A Day of Grace
(Luke 2:8-12)

A. A Gift for All Men (vv. 8-10)

8. And there were in the same country shepherds abiding in the field, keeping watch over their flock by night.

On the day Jesus was born, a band of shepherds was *in the same country*; that is, in the vicinity of Bethlehem. For the most part shepherds were nomadic people. They could have a permanent home base, as the shepherd David had in his father's house in Bethlehem (1 Samuel 16:10-13). But much of their time was spent moving their flock of sheep and goats throughout the open countryside in search of grass. At night shepherds would herd their animals together into a makeshift fold or pen, temporarily constructed from pieces of wood or the sides of natural rock formations. Once the flock was secure, the shepherds could take turns sleeping while one of them remained on guard.

Some have suggested that the birth of Jesus could not have occurred in December, based on the assumption that shepherds would not be sleeping outdoors during the winter. However, the work of a shepherd is a year-round duty. Sheep must be led to pasture for feeding even in winter. On a Christmas tour of Bethlehem today, it is still possible to see shepherds tending sheep in the nearby fields.

God's decision to make the first announcement of the birth of His Son to shepherds vividly illustrates the gracious nature of God. In Biblical times shepherds were on the low end of the social scale. Their living and working conditions did not measure up to urban standards. One may recall, for example, how the patriarch Jacob and his family had to settle in the land of Goshen outside the cities of Egypt, because shepherds were a reproach to the Egyptians (Genesis 46:31-34). But God is no such respecter of persons. The privilege of first hearing of the long-awaited birth of the Messiah was bestowed upon a group viewed by the world as outcasts.

9. And, lo, the angel of the Lord came upon them, and the glory of the Lord shone round about them; and they were sore afraid.

The text does not identify this angel by name, but it may very well have been Gabriel. Gabriel was the *angel of the Lord* who (as we have seen in the last two lessons) first appeared to Zechariah (Luke 1:11, 19) and later to Mary (Luke 1:26, 27). The *glory of the Lord* was apparently a radiant light shining forth from the angel, probably symbolizing the fact that he had just come from the glorious presence of God with a divine message to deliver.

It was a natural response for the shepherds to be very (*sore*) afraid of the angel. Under normal circumstances, shepherds were accustomed to facing dangerous situations. David, for example, boldly confronted a lion and a bear even as a boy (1 Samuel 17:34-36). But these anticipated dangers would not fully prepare one for confronting in the dark of night a celestial being who radiated a heavenly glory. The picture of fear gripping Zechariah (Luke 1:12, 13), Mary (Luke 1:29, 30), and the shepherds makes them seem like common people with whom we can easily identify.

10. And the angel said unto them, Fear not: for, behold, I bring you good tidings of great joy, which shall be to all people.

The phrase *good tidings* is a translation of a Greek word that means "to deliver good news." In other passages this word is often translated by the Old English word "gospel," derived from "god" (good) and "spel" (tale). Thus, we could speak of the angel proclaiming the "gospel" of

---

How to Say It

AUGUSTUS. Aw-*gust*-us.
GABRIEL. *Gay*-bree-ul.
SYNOPTIC. Sin-*op*-tick.
SYRIA. *Seer*-e-uh.
ZECHARIAH. Zek-uh-*rye*-uh.

Jesus Christ when he announced the good news of Jesus' birth.

The grace of God was emphasized again when the angel declared that the birth of Jesus was good news for *all people*. When mankind sinned, God was under no obligation to save anyone, and certainly not at so great a cost as the suffering experienced by His Son at Calvary. To save even one sinner by this means would be a monumental act of grace. Consider the boundless measure of God's grace in that He sent His Son to provide a means of salvation for every person who has ever lived on this earth (John 3:16; 1 John 2:2). That is truly *good tidings of great joy* for *all people*.

COMMUNICATION BARRIERS

Nearly all missionaries experience the frustration of communication barriers. Language and cultural differences erect huge hurdles to anyone ministering on "foreign soil." Often, suspicion and other forms of fear must be overcome.

The Judean shepherds, not surprisingly, were "sore afraid" at the unexpected visit of the Lord's angel. The supernatural sights and sounds accompanying the event could have short-circuited the transmission of a vital message. Thus, the first words from the divine messenger were, "Do not be afraid" (Luke 2:10, *New International Version*).

In a sense, every Christian faces similar challenges in personal evangelism. Prospects may be "fearful" of Christians because of an unfortunate personal experience in the past, the questionable actions of "televangelists," or some other negative impression of the church that they have received.

Whatever the cause, such fears are real to unbelievers, and must be overcome by modern messengers of God. Our words, attitudes, and actions should communicate the message: "Do not be afraid."   —R. W. B.

B. A Remedy for Our Sin (vv. 11, 12)

11. For unto you is born this day in the city of David a Saviour, which is Christ the Lord.

Three of our most popular titles for Jesus are introduced in this passage. While other New

Testament books, particularly the epistles, often refer to Jesus as *Saviour*, Luke 2:11 is the only verse in the Synoptic Gospels (Matthew, Mark, and Luke) to use this title in reference to Jesus. At the same time, the concept of Jesus as Saviour pervades the Synoptics, perhaps most notably in the angel's message to Joseph: "Thou shalt call his name Jesus: for he shall save his people from their sins" (Matthew 1:21).

The title *Christ* is the Greek equivalent of the Hebrew word *Messiah*. Both terms mean *the anointed one*; that is, the one God has chosen to perform a certain task. In Biblical times, prophets, priests, and kings were typically installed into their office with a ceremony in which a small amount of oil was placed upon the head. This symbolized their selection and calling by God for the task at hand. Jesus was the ultimate Anointed One, performing the ultimate task at Calvary; thus, He wears the title *Christ* or *Messiah* in a way that is unique.

The title *Savior* highlights the work of Jesus. The title *Christ* implies God's appointment of Jesus. But it is the title of *Lord* or King that calls attention to our personal obligation to Jesus. We owe Him a complete submission to His revealed will. By virtue of His victory over the forces of Satan and death, Jesus now lays claim to "all power . . . in heaven and in earth" (Matthew 28:18). "God . . . hath highly exalted him," so much so that "every knee should bow . . . and . . . every tongue should confess that Jesus Christ is Lord" (Philippians 2:9-11). If we want the child who was born in Bethlehem as our Savior and Christ, we must also make Him our Lord.

12. And this shall be a sign unto you; Ye shall find the babe wrapped in swaddling clothes, lying in a manger.

The *swaddling clothes* were strips of cloth somewhat comparable to our cloth diapers or baby blankets. Apparently Mary was prepared for the possibility of a birth during her trip south. These cloths in and of themselves would not serve to identify the Messiah, for such would be the appropriate care for any baby the shepherds would find in crowded Bethlehem. The *sign* was the oddity of finding a child being loved and cared for (as indicated by the clothing) in a *manger* or feeding trough. Not only did this clue narrow the shepherd's search to stables, but it also provided an indicator so distinctive it could not be missed.

Though the angel's words did not explicitly say, "Go seek the child," that assignment was clearly implied in the giving of a sign. A heart that is eager to serve the Lord does not require much more than just a suggestion from the Lord that there is work to be done.

II. A Night of Glory
(Luke 2:13-16)

A. A Sound of Praise (vv. 13, 14)

13, 14. And suddenly there was with the angel a multitude of the heavenly host praising God, and saying, Glory to God in the highest, and on earth peace, good will toward men.

As suddenly as the first angel had appeared, a *multitude* of angels joined him. Perhaps the timing is an indication of the kindness of God toward the shepherds. To begin this encounter with one glorious angel was frightening enough. To have begun with a great company of angels might have thrown the shepherds into a state of panic.

Our Christmas carols typically depict the angels as "singing" their praise to God. The terms *praising* and *saying* are consistent with this idea, though they do not necessarily indicate a musical expression of praise. However, there is a sense of balance in the way the angels' words are constructed. *Glory to God* is paralleled by *peace, good will toward men. In the highest* is balanced by *on earth*. This is the kind of poetic or literary arrangement that one might expect to find in a song.

This passage also illustrates the twofold meaning of the word *glory* in Scripture. There is the *glory of the Lord* (v. 9), which is the radiant light that shone from the angel, as well as the *glory to God*, which refers to the praise that was spoken by the angels. God is worthy of having both kinds of glory attributed to Him.

The final phrase has lent itself to two different translations. Our text wishes *peace* and *good will* to all men. More recent translations understand *good will* to be a description of the kind of *men* who are to receive peace. Thus, readings such as "peace to men on whom his favor rests" (*New International Version*) and "peace among men with whom He is pleased" (*New American Standard Bible*) are suggested. Such an approach is probably a better rendering of the Greek text, but both translations express equally the idea that mankind is under God's good will and grace through Jesus Christ.

B. A Scene of Promise (vv. 15, 16)

15. And it came to pass, as the angels were gone away from them into heaven, the shepherds said one to another, Let us now go even unto Bethlehem, and see this thing which is come to pass, which the Lord hath made known unto us.

We can only imagine the excitement that must have filled the souls of the shepherds as they reflected upon their heavenly experience. For them there was no question but that they must go immediately to Bethlehem and search the stables for the Messianic child. This is the kind of enthusiasm we associate with people when they first come into contact with Jesus Christ. It is an enthusiasm we would do well to rekindle afresh during this Christmas season.

The shepherds did not need to worry about losing their sheep while they were away in Bethlehem. The sheep could remain in their pen under the watch of a single shepherd, as was the case each evening when the men took turns sleeping.

16. And they came with haste, and found Mary and Joseph, and the babe lying in a manger.

This description is so basic and simple. It is perhaps much less than we might have anticipated, given the drama of the angelic announcement. Yet what else would the shepherds have expected to find in a stable? Surely not a throne with royal attendants, much less the radiant glory of God displayed by the angels. They were not seeking a man ready to lead them—only a baby asleep in a manger. But that was enough. For with that sleeping baby God's salvation had finally arrived on earth. The waiting was over. As it still does for so many of us, that first nativity scene filled hearts with hope and promise for the future.

III. A Time of Good News
(Luke 2:17-20)

A. A Message Worth Retelling
(vv. 17, 18)

17. And when they had seen it, they made known abroad the saying which was told them concerning this child.

The shepherds had seen too much of the working of God to keep it all to themselves. In a manner of speaking they became "evangelists," for the basic definition of "evangelist" is one who "proclaims good news to others." The angel had delivered *good tidings* to the shepherds (v. 10), and they in turn felt compelled to share that good news with others.

Here is an example that should challenge us. The shepherds knew very little about the Messiah. They had not yet witnessed His ministry, His death, or His resurrection. They had not had the opportunity to enjoy the benefits of Jesus' work, to mature within the fellowship of His church, or to read the New Testament Scriptures. But they were ready to witness to what they did know regarding Jesus. We have a great number of advantages over the shepherds, and

visual for
lesson 3

yet we are often so quiet among non-Christians that one might not even know that we have good news within us. We can learn much from the enthusiasm and forthrightness of these simple shepherds.

UNLIKELY PROSPECTS

An outreach tool used by increasing numbers of churches today is the demographic report. This is a set of statistics that defines the average person in a church's "sales territory." Such information guides churches in designing strategies for evangelism. Programming, publications, and promotions are aimed at the statistical composite of the average constituent in a given geographical radius.

If pollsters in New Testament times had surveyed the "Greater Bethlehem Metropolitan Area," the demographics would not have suggested that shepherds on the Judean hillside were the ideal market for angelic "sales promotion" of the news of Jesus' birth. Shepherds were uneducated, unsophisticated, with little disposable income. Consumer-conscious marketers would have considered them to be unlikely prospects. The preliminary announcement of the good news would have been made to people of position, power, and substance.

Evangelistic outreach is a major concern of the church. To whom should we go with the truth of God? How can we most efficiently and effectively use our time and resources to help the kingdom grow? We must be "wise as serpents" as we determine our strategy, but we must not compromise the gospel to accommodate our culture. And we must not ignore "unlikely prospects," for, as the angel said, the good news is for *all* people.
—R. W. B.

18. And all they that heard it wondered at those things which were told them by the shepherds.

Is it any surprise that people *wondered* in amazement and curiosity at this strange story told by the shepherds? Many may have proceeded to ignore the shepherds' message, just as they would have normally written off the shepherds themselves, because of their rustic background. And yet those who heard the shepherds' account must have *wondered* about the possibilities.

It is not likely that the shepherds revealed the name of the young Messiah or His parents, since there is no indication in the Gospels that Jesus' identity was known prior to His revealing Himself at His baptism. What is more likely is that the shepherds simply reported what they had seen and heard in the field and in the stable. This "rumor" that the Messiah had been born in Bethlehem would then serve to stir up a Messianic expectation that both John the Baptist and Jesus could later tap into when they began their ministries.

B. A Story Worth Remembering
(vv. 19, 20)

19. But Mary kept all these things, and pondered them in her heart.

The Greek literally reads that Mary "treasured" the events of that first Christmas Day and continually "reflected" upon them. For most parents the birth of their first child is a precious and memorable experience. But imagine being in Mary's place and participating in a miraculous conception of the Son of God, a providential move to the "city of David," a hasty birth in a stable, and an unexpected visit by shepherds, who had been guided by angels. There was much here that could be *kept* and *pondered*.

20. And the shepherds returned, glorifying and praising God for all the things that they had heard and seen, as it was told unto them.

The shepherds also did not soon forget this experience. They had a story worth remembering and retelling for the rest of their lives.

Conclusion

A. A Day of Good Tidings

Second Kings 6 and 7 record a time when the city of Samaria was under siege by an army from Syria. The people within were starving to death because their food supply had been cut off. Outside the walls of the city were four lepers with little prospects for survival. If they entered the city, they would starve to death with those inside. If they surrendered to the enemy, they would likely be killed. The latter option at least held the prospect that they might be taken captive and fed. So one night the lepers ventured into the enemy camp.

It was then that they discovered that God had frightened off the Syrians with the sound of an approaching army. The lepers began to enjoy a bounty of food and supplies that had been left behind. However, in the midst of their celebration they realized that they should have been sharing their good fortune with the people starving within the city. "We do not well: this day is a day of good tidings, and we hold our peace" (2 Kings 7:9).

Is it not amazing that those whom society casts off, such as lepers and shepherds, can sometimes teach us great lessons regarding our spiritual duty to God? Perhaps it is their lowly stature that helps them to appreciate more fully the depths of the grace of God and the importance of witnessing to others about what they have experienced. Have we become too familiar with the Christmas story, to the point that we have lost our sense of wonder at the events recorded in the Gospels? Are we so busy giving gifts to others that we have failed to concentrate on *receiving* the Gift that God has given us? Are we "holding our peace" during a time when the world desperately needs "good tidings"?

As we reflect upon the nativity story, let us humble ourselves with a spirit akin to that of the shepherds.

B. Let Us Pray

Father, help us to see more clearly the fullness of the grace You have bestowed upon us through Jesus Christ. May we then be faithful witnesses of what we have seen and heard in Your Word and in our lives. Amen.

C. Thought to Remember

This Christmas season is once again a day of "good tidings of great joy . . . to all people." Let us share this good news with all who need "a Saviour, which is Christ the Lord."

Home Daily Bible Readings

Monday, Dec. 9—Don't Be Afraid of Adversaries (Isaiah 41:11-16)
Tuesday, Dec. 10—Don't Be Afraid of Criticism (Isaiah 51:4-8)
Wednesday, Dec. 11—Don't Be Afraid of Changes (Isaiah 54:4-8)
Thursday, Dec. 12—Don't Be Afraid of Adversities (Haggai 2:4-9)
Friday, Dec. 13—God Can Free Us From Fear (Luke 12:22-31)
Saturday, Dec. 14—God Is Our Shield (Genesis 15:1-6)
Sunday, Dec. 15—Everything Praise the Lord! (Psalm 150:1-6)

Learning by Doing

This page contains an alternate lesson plan emphasizing learning activities. Classes desiring such student involvement will find these suggestions helpful.

Learning Goals

As a result of this lesson, the students should:

1. Know that God's coming to earth to be our Savior is a message to be shared with the whole world.

2. Appreciate the enthusiastic witness of the shepherds.

3. Make a commitment to share the good news of our Savior's birth and His gift of grace whenever possible.

Into the Lesson

Open the lesson by reminding the class that last week we listed songs and choruses that tell about various events surrounding the birth of Jesus. There are very few that tell about the angel's announcement to Mary, but there are many carols that contain a reference to the shepherds. Ask the class to recall some of the songs or lines in the songs that mention the shepherds. Then ask why it seems that so many songs have been written focusing on the shepherds. After some discussion, remind everyone that one possible reason is that it is easier to view the nativity through the eyes of common, ordinary shepherds. We will do that today.

Into the Word

Recruit a man to play the part of a costumed shepherd to be interviewed in front of the class. He does not need to be a member of your class. He should also read the lesson commentary and a Bible encyclopedia's entry on "shepherds" to prepare his answers for the interview. Ask the following questions during the interview.

1. You've been a shepherd for some time, haven't you? Tell me, just what does a shepherd do? What is a typical day like for you?

2. Where does the shepherd fit on the social scale?

3. I'm told you had an interesting visitor the other night. Tell me about the visitor. Where did he come from? What message did he bring?

4. After the visitor left, what did you do?

5. Now let me ask you something personal: What do *you* think of this baby? And what message would you give to others about this baby? (The shepherd should recall how he and his companions enthusiastically told everyone they met about the baby. His advice for Christians: do the same!)

After the shepherd leaves, take three or four minutes to present the lesson background from page 138. Next, read the printed text. Present a brief lecture on it from the lesson commentary. Special items to highlight or explain include:

Verse 10. "To all people." The good news is not for only a certain few, it is for everyone.

Verse 11. Explain the significance of the three titles for Jesus mentioned in this verse.

Verse 12. The "sign" was the manger, not the swaddling clothes.

Verses 13, 14. Explain the "balance" in the angels' words as explained in the lesson commentary.

Verses 17, 18, 20. Emphasize the shepherds' enthusiasm about sharing their experience.

Into Life

The coming of the Savior has always been "good news." Anyone who has ever had anything to do with this news has had the responsibility to pass it on. What about us? Are we being faithful to our responsibility?

There is a passage from the Old Testament that serves as a powerful illustration of the importance of sharing the gospel. Have the class find 2 Kings 7:9 in their Bibles. Explain the background of this story, using the Conclusion on page 142 of the lesson commentary.

Allow class members to apply this challenge by giving each a prepared self-evaluation and commitment sheet with the following items on it. Ask each person to complete it to help determine his or her effectiveness in sharing the good news.

1. I am alert to opportunities to share my faith and my Lord.

Always   Usually   Seldom

2. I find I have anxieties when it comes to talking about Jesus, my faith, and God's grace to people who are not Christians.

Always   Usually   Seldom

3. I am comfortable in inviting people to worship with me at our church.

Always   Usually   Seldom

4. I am determined to be the witness that God wants me to be.

Always   Usually   Seldom

Close with prayer for strength to grow and improve in the important area of witnessing about the good news.

Let's Talk It Over

The questions on this page are designed to encourage review of the lesson Scriptures and to promote discussion of the lesson by the class. The answers provided are only discussion starters. Let your class talk it over from there.

1. The announcement of Jesus' birth was made to lowly shepherds. What does this tell us about God's system of values?

While their menial occupation put them near the bottom of the social ladder, the Bethlehem shepherds were important to God. His announcement was a gracious gesture showing that He values the condition of the heart more than social status. He appreciated their devout hearts and open minds, and knew they would be willing to believe a message from an angel.

Consider some symbolic implications of the announcement. The shepherds were watching sheep in the hills near Bethlehem; David, the man after God's own heart, and the Jews' favorite king, had herded sheep in those same hills. Also, it is quite possible that the shepherds were tending sheep that would be used for temple sacrifices, making them an appropriate audience for the announcement of the birth of the Lamb of God.

2. The birth of Jesus means good news for all people of the world. So why do we sometimes keep the gospel to ourselves?

Based on Jesus' warning not to cast "pearls before swine" (Matthew 7:6), some believers feel that the gospel should not be exposed to ridicule by sharing it with people who are likely to reject it. This might be a legitimate policy if we knew in advance who would accept and who would reject the good news of salvation, but we simply do not know that. Sometimes the most unlikely person responds eagerly, while a seemingly ideal prospect turns away with contempt. (What Jesus was probably teaching in Matthew 7:6 is that we are not obligated to continue presenting the gospel to those who repeatedly and scornfully reject it.)

Others want to protect the gospel from becoming contaminated and diluted. While we certainly should treat the gospel with dignity and respect, it is not a treasure to be stored in a safe deposit box. It is a tool to be taken out and used. The more we use it, the brighter and sharper and more valuable it becomes.

3. How does God send us messages today?

As the living Word, Jesus Christ is God's primary and foremost message for us today. We find out about the living Word by reading the written Word, the Bible.

While God's revelation is closed and no new truths are being revealed, God has ways of explaining and teaching us about what He has already revealed. He provides guidance through the Holy Spirit, through ministers, through Sunday school teachers, through Christian literature, through Christian music, through certain events, and through Christian friends.

4. Jesus was born in order to bring peace and goodwill. But we still live in a world dominated by war, conflict, violence, and crime. What went wrong?

Jesus' birth set in motion the final phase of God's plan of salvation, which has been in operation for almost two thousand years. The goal of that plan is the defeat of Satan and the destruction of his kingdom, his power, and his influence. However, Satan is not going down without a fight. He is powerful, and he has many followers. He knows his very existence is at stake, so he is firmly committed to doing anything to thwart God's plan.

From our human perspective, it may appear as if God's plan has been thwarted—that Satan is in control and God is on the defensive. But from God's perspective, His plan is right on time. At present, He is waiting for the right time to send His Son back to earth.

5. The shepherds were enthusiastic witnesses to what they had seen and heard concerning Jesus. This is the kind of zeal new converts often have. Why do we lose that "just saved" enthusiasm?

Excitement and enthusiasm result from any new experience. Beginning a relationship with Jesus is no exception. We are excited. We are enthusiastic. We want to tell everyone about it, regardless of how they may react.

But no one can stay on that kind of emotional high indefinitely. When the newness wears off, we settle into a more normal routine of living the day-to-day Christian life. Some give in and return to the old life. The challenge we face as Christians is similar to that which married couples face: to keep the daily routine from becoming mundane and boring.

The Wise Men and Herod

Dec 22

DEVOTIONAL READING: Matthew 2:13-23.

LESSON SCRIPTURE: Matthew 2.

PRINTED TEXT: Matthew 2:1-12, 16.

Matthew 2:1-12, 16

1 Now when Jesus was born in Bethlehem of Judea in the days of Herod the king, behold, there came wise men from the east to Jerusalem,

2 Saying, Where is he that is born King of the Jews? for we have seen his star in the east, and are come to worship him.

3 When Herod the king had heard these things, he was troubled, and all Jerusalem with him.

4 And when he had gathered all the chief priests and scribes of the people together, he demanded of them where Christ should be born.

5 And they said unto him, In Bethlehem of Judea: for thus it is written by the prophet,

6 And thou Bethlehem, in the land of Judah, art not the least among the princes of Judah: for out of thee shall come a Governor, that shall rule my people Israel.

7 Then Herod, when he had privily called the wise men, inquired of them diligently what time the star appeared.

8 And he sent them to Bethlehem, and said, Go and search diligently for the young child; and when ye have found him, bring me word again, that I may come and worship him also.

9 When they had heard the king, they departed; and, lo, the star, which they saw in the east, went before them, till it came and stood over where the young child was.

10 When they saw the star, they rejoiced with exceeding great joy.

11 And when they were come into the house, they saw the young child with Mary his mother, and fell down, and worshipped him: and when they had opened their treasures, they presented unto him gifts; gold, and frankincense, and myrrh.

12 And being warned of God in a dream that they should not return to Herod, they departed into their own country another way.

· · · · · · · · · · · ·

16 Then Herod, when he saw that he was mocked of the wise men, was exceeding wroth, and sent forth, and slew all the children that were in Bethlehem, and in all the coasts thereof, from two years old and under, according to the time which he had diligently inquired of the wise men.

GOLDEN TEXT: When they were come into the house, they saw the young child with Mary his mother, and fell down, and worshipped him: and when they had opened their treasures, they presented unto him gifts; gold, and frankincense, and myrrh.
—Matthew 2:11.

Lesson Aims

This lesson should produce within each student a desire to imitate the wise men of Matthew 2 in the following ways:

1. In their desire to seek out God's will no matter where He leads them.

2. In their eagerness to worship Christ as Lord and King.

3. In their willingness to give an offering to the Lord of what they value.

Lesson Outline

INTRODUCTION
    A. Scavenger Hunts
    B. Lesson Background
  I. THE SEARCH FOR CHRIST (Matthew 2:1-8)
    A. Visitors From the East (vv. 1-3)
      The Great Disturber
    B. Prophecy of a Birth (vv. 4-6)
    C. Deception by the King (vv. 7, 8)
 II. THE DISCOVERY OF CHRIST (Matthew 2:9-11)
    A. Light From the Star (vv. 9, 10)
    B. Gifts for a King (v. 11)
      Gifts for God
III. THE ATTACK AGAINST CHRIST (Matthew 2:12, 16)
    A. Warning From a Dream (v. 12)
    B. Violence Against the Young (v. 16)
CONCLUSION
    A. Wise Men Still Seek Him
    B. Let Us Pray
    C. Thought to Remember

The visual for Lesson 4 challenges us to honor Jesus as our King by crowning Him Lord of all. It is shown on page 149.

Introduction

A. Scavenger Hunts

One of the great party pastimes is the scavenger hunt. Participants are divided into teams and then sent out to look for objects of varying degrees of difficulty to obtain. Usually some items can be borrowed and some purchased, while others are simply too hard to locate.

The most exciting part of a scavenger hunt is the hunt itself. The search process stimulates imagination and creativity; it fosters competition and team spirit. On the other hand, those items that are found tend to lose their significance when the game is over. They become junk to be discarded.

When the wise men of Matthew 2 searched for the newborn King, they faced a challenge that tested their skill and knowledge. There was surely some excitement in the hunt itself. In their case, however, the end of the hunt was far more exciting. For what they discovered was not an item to be casually discarded, but a baby to be worshiped, adored, and remembered for the rest of their lives. They had found their Savior and Lord.

B. Lesson Background

Matthew's account of the birth of Jesus does not simply repeat what we have learned from the Gospel of Luke. Whereas Luke focuses upon the mother Mary and her relatives Zechariah and Elisabeth, Matthew highlights Joseph. While Luke describes a visit by nearby shepherds, Matthew is interested in a visit by foreign sages. Together these two different accounts give us a fuller picture of the birth of Jesus.

Even the genealogies presented in these two Gospels exhibit a difference in focus. Luke does not present his genealogy until Jesus begins His Messianic ministry in the third chapter. Then Luke traces Jesus' lineage all the way back to Adam, perhaps to emphasize the identity all people have with this Savior. Matthew, on the other hand, puts his genealogy at the very beginning as he opens both his Gospel and his nativity account. Matthew's purpose in doing this becomes clear as his story unfolds. He wants to establish Jesus' regal descent from David (Matthew 1:1) as a prelude to his account of the wise men seeking the "King of the Jews" (Matthew 2:2). Jesus' royal lineage in chapter 1 lays the groundwork for His royal treatment in chapter 2.

I. The Search for Christ (Matthew 2:1-8)

A. Visitors From the East (vv. 1-3)

1. Now when Jesus was born in Bethlehem of Judea in the days of Herod the king, behold, there came wise men from the east to Jerusalem.

The identity of these *wise men* is quite a mystery for us today. Their name in Greek is *magoi*, and in Latin *magi*. They were literally "the mighty ones," not in physical strength or political authority, but in knowledge; thus, our popular translation of *wise men*.

Their specific origin in the *east* is not certain. The ancient Medes and Persians (who lived in what is modern-day Iran) had their "wise men" who specialized in several scholarly disciplines including astrology. The ancient Babylonians (who lived in what is now Iraq) also had "wise men" who studied astronomy and developed charts for planetary and stellar orbits as well as accurate astral calendars. These and other areas east of Palestine could have produced the wise men of Matthew 2.

The knowledge and interest of these men in the Jewish hope for a coming Messiah can be attributed to the dispersion of the Jews following both the Assyrian conquest of Israel and the Babylonian conquest of Judah. The Assyrians relocated many Jews in the cities of the Medes (2 Kings 17:6), while the Babylonians later took back to their home the finest among the young Jewish men, such as Daniel and his three friends (Daniel 1:1-7). These wise men may not have practiced Judaism, but they at least had an awareness of and appreciation for Jewish Messianic prophecies.

Many of our modern-day assumptions regarding the wise men cannot be confirmed either by the Biblical text or by other historical sources. For example, we often sing about the "three kings." Matthew, however, does not indicate the number of these men, nor does he suggest that they possessed a royal status. In fact, in most of the Eastern cultures the wise men were not kings; rather, they served as counselors to kings. It is only a church tradition that supplies the names of Melchior, Balthasar, and Caspar to these men and claims that they originated from India, Egypt, and Greece (two of these three locations are not even east of Palestine). No more credible than this is the claim of several cathedrals throughout church history to possess the bones of the wise men. The truth is that we do not know as much about the wise men as we often think we do.

2. Saying, Where is he that is born King of the Jews? for we have seen his star in the east, and are come to worship him.

The nature of this *star* is not explained in our lesson text, and many theories concerning it abound today. Many planetarium shows present a natural explanation from the field of astronomy. One view is that there was an alignment of certain stars and planets, such as Jupiter the "king planet," that was interpreted as signaling the birth of a new king. It is also suggested that there may have been an unusual amount of meteoric activity, which became the subject of astrological interpretation. Given the precise movements of the star in conjunction with the

---

How to Say It

BALTHASAR. Ball-*tay*-sar.
CASPAR. *Kass*-par.
EDOMITES. *E*-duh-mites.
MAGI. *May*-jye.
MAGOI (Greek). *Mah*-goy.
MELCHIOR. *Mel*-key-or.
MICAH. *My*-kuh.
ZECHARIAH. Zek-uh-*rye*-uh.

---

wise men's search and Jesus' location, the only plausible explanation is that God created this particular star to guide the wise men to Palestine. In so doing, He could have created and used one of the astronomical phenomena that is described above.

Whatever it was that the wise men saw, it apparently served only to initiate their search, and not to provide precise guidance. After all, Jerusalem was not the actual location of Jesus' birth, but simply the logical place to look for a Jewish king.

Our curious nature wants to know more about this star. But Matthew's interest is not in the mechanics of the star, but in the intent of the wise men: *we . . . are come to worship him.*

3. When Herod the king had heard these things, he was troubled, and all Jerusalem with him.

Matthew mentions the reaction of King *Herod* the Great, who ruled Israel from 37 B.C. to 4 B.C. There were other members of his family who wore the name "Herod," but none with accomplishments worthy of the title "the Great." Herod was known as a clever political strategist and a patron of great art and architecture. In Jerusalem alone Herod built a theater, an amphitheater, a hippodrome, and a palace, and initiated a major reconstruction of the Jewish temple.

This reference to Herod gives us a historical peg on which to "hang" the date of the birth of Jesus. Herod died in March or April of 4 B.C. Jesus' birth was some time shortly before Herod's death, perhaps in the winter of 5 B.C. Thus our traditional date of December 25 is not unreasonable. It may not be the exact date, but it provides us with an important opportunity to celebrate our Savior's birth and draw the attention of others to Him.

The words of the wise men *troubled* Herod. The Greek literally says he was "shaken" by what he heard. The primary reason for this was Herod's constant insecurity regarding his position as king of Israel. Herod's family was not of Jewish descent; they were Edomites. The

Edomites were a people who, even though they could claim Jacob's brother Esau as their ancestor, had been hostile toward Israel for most of their history. Herod practiced the Jewish religion somewhat, but he was not a true Jew. Throughout his reign he feared that the people would revolt against him, and so he tried to safeguard his position with generous favors, such as his building projects. When that tactic seemed ineffective, he resorted to physical force and deadly intimidation.

For this reason, *all Jerusalem* was also *troubled* or "shaken" when the wise men arrived, asking about a newborn "King of the Jews." They knew what Herod's likely response would be. Already he had killed several of his own family members, including sons, because he suspected that they wanted his throne. In fact, shortly after this episode, and only five days before his death, Herod killed one more son out of fear and suspicion. What the people feared when they heard the mention of a new king would soon be realized through the slaughter of the babies in and around Bethlehem.

THE GREAT DISTURBER

Those who are supposed to know tell us that the average modern churchgoer wants only to feel good when he leaves worship. "Yuppies" and "baby boomers" belong to the "feel-good generation," and most of them will not knowingly subject themselves to experiences that bring them discomfort.

Dana Eynon once suggested in a workshop setting that many moderns have adopted an "Eleventh Commandment": *Thou shalt not suffer.* Personal comfort is a priority in our affluent, pampered society. Worshipers expect only to be soothed and encouraged, never to be confronted, challenged, or chastised.

Herod and "all Jerusalem" were troubled by the advent of King Jesus. The coming of Christ can be disturbing to those who are possessed by pride, selfish ambition, and/or the love of money, sex, and power. He is the Light, exposing all who live in sinful darkness. He is the living Word, whose person and purity disturb us by forcing us to confront the reality of our own shortcomings.

The gospel is designed not only to comfort the disturbed, but also to disturb the comfortable. The church must not proclaim God's promises to the exclusion of God's punishments. We must both share His love and warn of His wrath. Christian preaching will always be distinguished not only by the good news, but also by the "bad news" that goads us toward God and goodness. —R. W. B.

B. Prophecy of a Birth (vv. 4-6)

4. And when he had gathered all the chief priests and scribes of the people together, he demanded of them where Christ should be born.

Herod's minimal ties with the Jewish heritage made him ill-equipped to handle the kind of Messianic question posed by the wise men. He had to seek an answer from the leaders of the Jewish religion. We should note that *Christ* is being used here according to the Biblical definition—not as the last name of Jesus, but as the Greek title for *Messiah.*

5, 6. And they said unto him, In Bethlehem of Judea: for thus it is written by the prophet, And thou Bethlehem, in the land of Judah, art not the least among the princes of Judah: for out of thee shall come a Governor, that shall rule my people Israel.

The chief priests and scribes referred to Micah 5:2 to locate the birthplace of the Messiah. Though Herod was ignorant of the significance of this passage, the average Jew understood its importance. In fact, one of the reasons so many Jews rejected Jesus' claims was their mistaken assumption that He had been born in His hometown of Nazareth rather than in Bethlehem (John 7:42). But God in His providence had arranged for the fulfillment of Old Testament prophecy. How appropriate that the Messianic successor to King David should be born in Bethlehem, the "city of David."

C. Deception by the King (vv. 7, 8)

7. Then Herod, when he had privily called the wise men, inquired of them diligently what time the star appeared.

The devious nature of Herod is well portrayed in this passage. What Herod actually wanted to find out was the age of the child his soldiers should kill when he sent them to Bethlehem. To get this information, he feigned an interest in the wise men's investigation of the new king's star. By knowing the date when the star first *appeared*, Herod could estimate the age of his rival.

This discussion with the wise men had to be conducted *privily*, or in secret, so that Herod would not appear to have too much interest in their news of another king. It would be in the best interest of his rule not to further alarm the citizens of Jerusalem or to tip off the parents of the child he was seeking to kill.

8. And he sent them to Bethlehem, and said, Go and search diligently for the young child; and when ye have found him, bring me word again, that I may come and worship him also.

Knowing the child's birthplace and guessing his age would not automatically lead to a discovery of the child. There would be many families to interview in Bethlehem in order to locate the child in question. And it was possible that the family was no longer in Bethlehem. Thus Herod could not send his soldiers just yet. The best plan for now would be to persuade the wise men to do the searching for him and inform him of the results. Herod's craftiness and guile were worthy of the devil himself, as he cloaked his real intentions in pious language: *that I may come and worship him.*

II. The Discovery of Christ (Matthew 2:9-11)

A. Light From the Star (vv. 9, 10)

9. When they had heard the king, they departed; and, lo, the star, which they saw in the east, went before them, till it came and stood over where the young child was.

This is the first time that Matthew mentions any unusual movement related to the star. But once again he provides no explanation. The star apparently gave the appearance of moving toward Bethlehem and of stopping over a specific building. Artists have typically portrayed this scene with a ray of light shining down from the star to the house where Jesus and His family were now residing. However all this happened, it is clear that at this point something supernatural was occurring. It is possible that when the wise men first began their search, they attributed what was happening to natural movements in the sky. But to move forward and then stand still over a location is not natural for stars and planets. The Biblical language makes it clear that this was a miraculous work of God.

10. When they saw the star, they rejoiced with exceeding great joy.

The joy of the wise men was not so much at seeing an "old friend," but in receiving supernatural assistance and confirmation for their search. What could have been a lengthy process was completed in short order. Now at last they had reached the goal of their searching.

B. Gifts for a King (v. 11)

11. And when they were come into the house, they saw the young child with Mary his mother, and fell down, and worshipped him: and when they had opened their treasures, they presented unto him gifts; gold, and frankincense, and myrrh.

The shepherds found Jesus lying in a manger in a stable. But the wise men found him in a *house.* Obviously Joseph had moved his family

to more appropriate quarters just as soon as something became available. Our modern nativity scenes with both shepherds and wise men surrounding the manger are historically inaccurate, but are usually done for the sake of convenience in telling the story.

The wise men honored the newborn King with three valuable *gifts.* The value of *gold* requires no explanation. *Frankincense* (literally, "pure incense") refers to an expensive incense derived from the resin of a milky white tree. This was usually burned in a bowl to release a sweet aroma in a room. *Myrrh* was also made from a tree resin and was quite expensive. It was not used as an incense, but as a pain reliever or anesthetic. It was also used in embalming the dead. Some have observed that such gifts as these may have helped provide for the material needs of Joseph and his family during their journey to and from Egypt.

Consider the actions of the wise men toward Jesus. They presented Him with expensive gifts and with acts of worship and homage—and all of this before Jesus had actually done anything for them. He was just a baby, the promise of a King and a Savior. We can see His work from a different perspective, as already completed. Yet, with this advantage, do we seek Him and honor Him with the same diligence and eagerness of these men? Truly they deserve the title "wise men."

GIFTS FOR GOD

What do you give to someone who has everything? Many of us resort to giving gift certificates, from stores, restaurants, and theaters. No matter what we give, gracious recipients are pleased and thankful. They recognize that "it's the thought that counts." Thus, we who give are blessed as much as or more than the receivers.

The toddler Jesus could hardly appreciate the fine gifts of the wise men, though his parents surely were grateful for such valuable treasures. God Incarnate did not need gold, frankincense

visual for lesson 4

CROWN HIM LORD of ALL

and myrrh. He owns "the wealth in every mine." But the "thought" that prompted the giving was what was meaningful. The Magi expressed reverence, worship and submission, and they were blessed more than Jesus.

God does not need our paltry tithes and offerings. "He owns the cattle on a thousand hills." But He knows how blessed we will be by giving. In His eyes, our thoughts count supremely. When we share our resources with thoughts of love, loyalty, and worship, God is pleased.

—R. W. B.

III. The Attack Against Christ (Matthew 2:12, 16)

A. Warning From a Dream (v. 12)

12. And being warned of God in a dream that they should not return to Herod, they departed into their own country another way.

This is the first indication of God actually speaking to the wise men. He had been guiding them before, but in a manner that had required them to seek out additional information from the Jewish leaders in Jerusalem. This time clear instructions were needed. God could not allow the wise men to assist Herod unwittingly in his murderous plot; therefore, He spoke through a *dream* to move the wise men away from Herod. At about the same time, He also used a dream to instruct Joseph to flee with his family to Egypt (Matthew 2:13).

B. Violence Against the Young (v. 16)

16. Then Herod, when he saw that he was mocked of the wise men, was exceeding wroth, and sent forth, and slew all the children that were in Bethlehem, and in all the coasts thereof, from two years old and under, according to the time which he had diligently inquired of the wise men.

Unable to stand the thought of having been *mocked* (the *New International Version* reads, "outwitted") by the *wise men*, Herod moved swiftly to insure that the newborn King would not slip from his grasp. The depth of his depravity is seen in his reckless slaughter of innocent *children*. It is a sobering reminder that Jesus entered a world darkened by sin—a world that needed what He alone could provide.

The order to kill all children *two years old and under* does not imply that Jesus was now about two years old. It is more likely that Herod was cleverly minimizing the margin for error by using a figure higher than the actual age. Matthew does not say how many children were killed, but in a town the size of Bethlehem it probably would have been a dozen or more.

The end results of Herod's mad scheme may be summarized as follows: innocent lives were wasted, the Messianic plan continued unhindered, and Herod died shortly thereafter.

Conclusion

A. Wise Men Still Seek Him

A popular slogan for billboards, bumper stickers, and songs is the phrase, "Wise Men Still Seek Him." Such a sentiment is understandable. The men we have considered today were genuine seekers of truth and God. They put much effort and personal expense into finding the Messiah. When they did find Him, they treated Him in the royal manner He deserves, giving Him a rich measure of homage and allegiance.

After the events of Matthew 2, the wise men disappear from the pages of Biblical history. They should not disappear from our reflections upon Christmas. They symbolize what this season really means. They challenge us to follow their example, to be "wise" like them in our relationship with Jesus Christ.

Indeed, wise men do still seek Him.

B. Let Us Pray

Father, rekindle within us the spirit of enthusiasm we once felt when we first encountered our Lord and Savior Jesus Christ. May we honor the newborn King with the worship, offerings, and devotion He so richly deserves. Amen.

C. Thought to Remember

Wisdom is not to be measured in the amount of knowledge one has, but in the manner in which one uses his knowledge. The truly wise person is the one who uses his knowledge to serve the Lord.

Home Daily Bible Readings

Monday, Dec. 16—Prophecy of a Savior (Jeremiah 23:1-8)

Tuesday, Dec. 17—Prophecy of a Victorious King (Zechariah 9:9-11)

Wednesday, Dec. 18—All Kings Will Worship Him (Psalm 72:1-11)

Thursday, Dec. 19—The Lord Has Done Great Things (Psalm 72:12-20)

Friday, Dec. 20—The Messiah Is Born (Isaiah 9:2-7)

Saturday, Dec. 21—Unbelievers Will Bow to Christ (Isaiah 60:10-16)

Sunday, Dec. 22—Present Our Talents to God (Ephesians 4:9-16)

Learning by Doing

This page contains an alternate lesson plan emphasizing learning activities. Classes desiring such student involvement will find these suggestions helpful.

Learning Goals

After this lesson, students will be able to:

1. Identify and separate the facts from the traditions surrounding the visit of the wise men.

2. Appreciate the sacrifice made by the wise men to visit and worship the Christ child.

3. Make a commitment to treasure and honor the privilege of worshiping the Lord.

Into the Lesson

Begin with a brief quiz to sort out the facts from the traditions regarding the visit by the wise men. The results of the quiz will not be discussed until the end of the lesson. You can either type out the questions and make copies for the students, or have them use the student book page on which the questions appear. Give the students two or three minutes to do the quiz.

The Visit of the Magi

Mark each statement as "F" for Fact or "T" for Tradition. "Fact" means the information is in the Bible. "Tradition" means we have assumed this idea from other sources.

___There were three wise men from the East who came to worship Jesus.

___The wise men found the baby Jesus at the stable where they presented him gifts of gold, frankincense, and myrrh.

___The names of the wise men were Melchior, Balthasar, and Caspar.

___A star led the wise men all the way from the East to the stable where Jesus was resting.

___The wise men were recognized as kings in their native land.

Into the Word

Early in the week, ask two persons to make brief reports to the class on the following assignments. One person should identify the wise men from the East. The other person should prepare a report on the star that appeared to them. Give each person copies of the appropriate material from the lesson commentary and a copy of a Bible dictionary as resource material. The *New Unger's Bible Dictionary* has especially fine articles on both subjects.

Open this part of the lesson with the reports on the wise men and the star. Then read the text for today's lesson with the class.

Follow this with a mini-lecture and appropriate questions. An outline and questions for the lecture are given below. Fill in the outline with information from the lesson commentary.

A. Herod the Great
   1. His title and family background.
   2. The dating of Jesus' birthday.
Questions: Why do you think Herod was "troubled"? Why was all of Jerusalem "troubled"?
B. Herod's Inquiry
   1. Bethlehem: a fulfillment of prophecy.
   2. Herod's devious trickery.
Question: Why do you suppose Herod asked at what time the star appeared?
   3. Herod's lie: "That I may . . . worship him."
C. Finding the Christ Child
   1. The star's supernatural movement.
   2. Finding Jesus at the "house."
Questions: Why do you think so many nativity scenes include the wise men at the stable? What are frankincense and myrrh?
D. The Slaughter of Infants
   1. The reason Herod used the time of "two years old and under."
   2. The outcome of Herod's plot and its impact on the child he tried to kill.

Into Life

At this time, review the quiz used at the beginning of the lesson. All answers should be "Tradition." Some of the traditions are clearly untrue while some are entirely possible.

Write the often-used saying, "Wise Men Still Seek Him," on the chalkboard.

Use the following discussion questions to help class members make this lesson personal:

Why did the wise men seek Jesus? (To worship Him and bring gifts.)

What indications in our text are there of the sacrifice that these important men made in order to worship Jesus? (They traveled a long distance, brought expensive and carefully chosen gifts, and risked Herod's wrath.)

It is clear that these men held the worship of Jesus as something important and made a great sacrifice to do it. Such is not always true of today's Christian. What are some indications of a lower view of worship among believers today? What can we do to teach the priority of joyful (even sacrificial) worship to our families?

Close with a prayer that all may become better models in teaching the privilege of worship to our children and youth in our churches.

Let's Talk It Over

The questions on this page are designed to encourage review of the lesson Scriptures and to promote discussion of the lesson by the class. The answers provided are only discussion starters. Let your class talk it over from there.

1. Since the wise men were astrologers, God communicated with them through the stars. Why did He make that accommodation to convey a message to these men? What are some examples of His communicating in the same way today?

The wise men were astrologers—people who studied the stars and read meaning into their positions and alignment. As they scanned the heavens day after day, God used their interest in and knowledge of astrology to send a message to them. Seeing a spectacular display in the heavens, and perhaps knowing the Hebrew Scriptures (specifically Numbers 24:17), they believed that the display meant that a king had been born in Judea.

Romans 1:20 reminds us, "For the invisible things of him from the creation of the world are clearly seen, being understood by the things that are made." To the biologist God reveals Himself in the intricate complexity of living organisms. To the astronomer He reveals Himself in the limitless vastness of the heavens. To parents He reveals Himself as the loving Father. To rebellious teens He reveals Himself as the only begotten Son who willingly submitted to His Father.

2. Some people believe that the star of Bethlehem was a miracle. Others believe it was a natural phenomenon. What difference does it make?

Whether God created a star or used an existing bright star or cluster of stars or alignment of stars makes no difference in terms of what God intended and how the wise men responded. However, if we say the wise men interpreted an existing phenomenon as a sign from God, *even though God had nothing to do with it*, this is an entirely different issue. Then it comes down to a matter of divine involvement versus human interpretation.

This is the central issue. Do we see God as the One in control of the event and give Him the praise, honor, and glory? If we do, then we see the event as a miracle.

3. Some people believe Jesus was born on December 25. Others are not so sure. How important is it for us to celebrate Christmas on the right day?

The Bible gives neither the day nor the year of Jesus' birth. Since Herod the Great died in 4 B.C., Jesus must have been born not long before that—perhaps in the winter of 5 B.C. Christmas was first celebrated on December 25 in the middle of the fourth century A.D.

If it were important for us to know the precise date of Jesus' birth, the Bible would tell us. Since it does not, we can conclude that the issue is one that is not crucial to our salvation.

This is not to say that celebrating Christmas is not important. But in all our celebrations, the focus should not be on the day but on what (and whom) that day represents.

4. The wise men traveled over a thousand miles to find Jesus, while the priests and scribes refused to go just a few miles—from Jerusalem to Bethlehem. Why are some people more willing to seek Jesus than others?

The noted theologian Augustine (A.D. 354-430) said, "Thou hast made us for Thyself, and the heart of man is restless until it finds its rest in Thee." However, that restlessness is often numbed (but never really satisfied) by an inferior substitute for God. Some (like the priests and scribes in Jesus' day) try to satisfy it through institutional religion. As long as they have power, prestige, and status in the church, they have no desire for a real relationship with Christ. After all, He may make demands that they are not willing to accept.

5. Because the wise men gave gifts to the baby Jesus, gift giving has become an important part of Christmas. What are some advantages of this feature of Jesus' birthday? What are some drawbacks?

Gift giving serves a valuable function by reminding us that since God gave His Son, the primary theme of Christmas should be giving. To honor God's gift, the wise men gave gifts to Jesus. For us, honoring God's gift means giving Jesus what He really wants—our hearts in loving obedience. Gift giving is carried to harmful extremes when the gifts become the most important part of Christmas. Some have completely lost sight of what Christmas is all about, and even resent attempts to infuse Christmas celebrations with religious emphases.

Simeon and Anna

DEVOTIONAL READING: Psalm 42:1-11.

LESSON SCRIPTURE: Luke 2:21-40.

PRINTED TEXT: Luke 2:22, 25-38.

Luke 2:22, 25-38

22 And when the days of her purification according to the law of Moses were accomplished, they brought him to Jerusalem, to present him to the Lord.

· · · · · · · · · · ·

25 And, behold, there was a man in Jerusalem, whose name was Simeon; and the same man was just and devout, waiting for the consolation of Israel: and the Holy Ghost was upon him.

26 And it was revealed unto him by the Holy Ghost, that he should not see death, before he had seen the Lord's Christ.

27 And he came by the Spirit into the temple: and when the parents brought in the child Jesus, to do for him after the custom of the law,

28 Then took he him up in his arms, and blessed God, and said,

29 Lord, now lettest thou thy servant depart in peace, according to thy word:

30 For mine eyes have seen thy salvation,

31 Which thou hast prepared before the face of all people;

32 A light to lighten the Gentiles, and the glory of thy people Israel.

33 And Joseph and his mother marveled at those things which were spoken of him.

34 And Simeon blessed them, and said unto Mary his mother, Behold, this child is set for the fall and rising again of many in Israel; and for a sign which shall be spoken against;

35 (Yea, a sword shall pierce through thy own soul also;) that the thoughts of many hearts may be revealed.

36 And there was one Anna, a prophetess, the daughter of Phanuel, of the tribe of Asher: she was of a great age, and had lived with a husband seven years from her virginity;

37 And she was a widow of about fourscore and four years, which departed not from the temple, but served God with fastings and prayers night and day.

38 And she coming in that instant gave thanks likewise unto the Lord, and spake of him to all them that looked for redemption in Jerusalem.

GOLDEN TEXT: It was revealed unto him [Simeon] by the Holy Ghost, that he should not see death, before he had seen the Lord's Christ. . . . She [Anna] coming in that instant gave thanks likewise unto the Lord, and spake of him to all them that looked for redemption in Jerusalem.—Luke 2:26, 38.

New Testament Personalities
Unit 1: Persons of Jesus' Nativity
and Early Life (Lessons 1-5)

Lesson Aims

This lesson should produce within the students:

1. A greater appreciation for the faithfulness of the saints of old as they awaited the fulfillment of God's promise to send the Messiah.

2. A recollection of the joy many experienced when they met Christ for the first time.

3. A renewed spirit of joy in their relationship with Christ and an eager anticipation for the work He has yet to do in their lives.

Lesson Outline

INTRODUCTION
    A. Fifteen Minutes of Fame
    B. Lesson Background
  I. THE PARENTS' DUTY (Luke 2:22)
    A. Mary's Purification (v. 22a)
    B. Jesus' Presentation (v. 22b)
      Trust and Obey
  II. SIMEON'S FAITH (Luke 2:25-35)
    A. God's Promise (vv. 25, 26)
    B. Simeon's Song (vv. 27-32)
    C. Jesus' Destiny (vv. 33-35)
 III. ANNA'S WITNESS (Luke 2:36-38)
    A. Anna's Devotion (vv. 36, 37)
    B. Anna's Declaration (v. 38)
      How Long, Lord?
CONCLUSION
    A. Backstage Helpers
    B. Let Us Pray
    C. Thought to Remember

The visual for Lesson 5 in the visuals packet is an artist's depiction of Simeon in the temple. It is shown on page 157.

Introduction

A. Fifteen Minutes of Fame

In a critique of modern Western culture, with its orientation toward high-tech communications and mass media, one of our artists is reported to have said that we now live in an age in which anyone can have "fifteen minutes of fame." Ordinary people become overnight news sensations because of heroic acts, scandalous crimes, or unusual stunts. But their notoriety is short-lived. Just as quickly as the attention comes, it shifts to other interesting people, and former news stories fade away, never to be heard again.

These cultural dynamics of our day have little to do with Biblical times, yet there is one interesting parallel. The Bible often gives readers a brief glimpse of fascinating characters, with no prelude or follow-up. Many times all we are given is a "fifteen-minute" picture. The classic example in the Old Testament is Melchizedek, who appears but briefly (Genesis 14:18-20) and leaves us with many questions. The same could be said regarding the various characters in the Christmas story: Zechariah and Elisabeth, the shepherds, the wise men, and Simeon and Anna. We are intrigued by the brief descriptions given by Matthew and Luke and wish we knew more about these individuals. As it is, we have to content ourselves with the information we are given and try to appreciate fully what we do know about them.

B. Lesson Background

After the Gospel of Luke describes the birth of Jesus and the visit by the shepherds, it records the circumcision and naming of the child (Luke 2:21). We are then told about a visit to the temple in Jerusalem by Joseph, Mary, and the baby Jesus. We know nothing about what transpired between these two occasions, except to guess that Joseph moved his family to more appropriate quarters than a stable just as soon as possible. Why they had not headed back home to Nazareth becomes clear in today's lesson. The parents had a duty under the Mosaic Law to present themselves in the temple at this time with their newborn child.

I. The Parents Duty
(Luke 2:22)

A. Mary's Purification (v. 22a)

22a. And when the days of her purification according to the law of Moses were accomplished.

The *law of Moses* specified in Leviticus 12 that a woman was to be considered ceremonially unclean for a specified period of time following childbirth. During this time she was not to participate in public worship services or other activities outside the home. This period of being "unclean" was not intended to be a negative reflection upon women nor upon childbearing, but was essentially a time of recuperation.

To mark the end of this time of uncleanness, the couple was expected to take a designated offering to a priest. While this could be done at home in the local synagogue, the ideal location for this act of *purification* was the temple. Since Jesus had been born in Bethlehem, just a few miles from Jerusalem, Joseph apparently decided to remain in the area for a while in order to take advantage of their close proximity to the temple.

The Mosaic Law stipulated a period of uncleanness of forty days following the birth of a boy and eighty days after the birth of a girl (Leviticus 12:4, 5). Therefore, we can date Mary and Joseph's temple visit by knowing that the *days* of Mary's *purification . . . were accomplished* forty days after Jesus' birth. The forty-day period included the eight days during which circumcision occurred, as the Leviticus 12 passage shows.

Verse 24 indicates that Joseph and Mary offered two birds for Mary's purification—either two turtledoves or two pigeons. The Mosaic Law actually preferred a lamb and one bird, but allowed the substitution of a second bird if a couple could not afford a lamb (Leviticus 12:6-8). Apparently after the expense of their trip to Bethlehem and their extended stay in the vicinity, Joseph and Mary did not have the financial means to afford a lamb. This suggests that the visit of the wise men occurred at some point *after* this purification ceremony, because Joseph and Mary certainly could have afforded a lamb had they earlier received the gifts of gold, frankincense, and myrrh.

B. Jesus' Presentation (v. 22b)

22b. They brought him to Jerusalem, to present him to the Lord.

The purification ceremony for the mother took on an additional significance when she had given birth to her firstborn son. In the last of the ten plagues upon Egypt, according to the book of Exodus, God's death angel killed every firstborn male of man and beast, except in those families whose front door had been smeared with the blood of a slain lamb (Exodus 12:7, 13). From that point on, God laid claim to every firstborn male among the Israelites (Exodus 13:2, 12, 13). Luke 2:23 quotes the command God gave to Moses, found in Exodus 13:1, 2. With livestock an owner had the option of either killing the firstborn male animal as an offering to God or redeeming the animal through a substitute offering. In the case of children there was only one option. Every Jewish couple was required *to present* their firstborn son *to the Lord* in the presence of a priest and redeem him with a lamb. A couple with limited means could do as Joseph and Mary did and let the bird offerings satisfy both the purification and presentation requirements.

How to Say It

MELCHIZEDEK. Mel-*kizz*-ih-dek.
MICAH. *My*-kuh.
PHANUEL. *Fan*-you-el.
SIMEON. *Sim*-e-yun.
ZECHARIAH. Zek-uh-*rye*-uh.

TRUST AND OBEY

Marriage has fallen into disrepute in America. An alarming number of couples are opting for "unholy matrimony" (living together without marriage), with no regard for whether such a decision is right or wrong.

Why are so many choosing to live in sin? Millions flaunt God's absolutes to conform to adulterous lifestyles. They may be ignorant of God's Word; more likely, they feel that the Biblical teaching is irrelevant to modern culture.

Perhaps Mary and Joseph wondered if God's Law applied to their special child. After all, should the Messiah be bound by Mosaic statutes? Presenting God's Son to God might have seemed like a trivial formality. How could a religious ceremony consecrate Jesus any more than His unique conception and miraculous birth had done? In spite of whatever questions and doubts they had, Joseph and Mary "brought him to Jerusalem, to present him to the Lord" (Luke 2:22).

Trusting God, even when His way fails to make sense, requires hard-core faith. It means submitting to His authority and obeying His absolutes, despite the popularity and acceptance of more permissive behavior.

There is still "no other way to be happy in Jesus, but to trust and obey." —John H. Sammis
—R. W. B.

II. Simeon's Faith
(Luke 2:25-35)

A. God's Promise (vv. 25, 26)

25. And, behold, there was a man in Jerusalem, whose name was Simeon; and the same man was just and devout, waiting for the consolation of Israel: and the Holy Ghost was upon him.

From this brief description we get almost no biographical details regarding *Simeon*, but we learn much about his moral and spiritual character. He was a *just* man; that is, one who was committed to doing what was right and fair in all of his dealings with both man and God. Simeon was also *devout*. The basic idea of the

Greek word used here describes one who has a religious attitude at all times, even when he is not doing something religious.

Simeon was awaiting *the consolation of Israel.* For some reason, near the end of the first century B.C. there was an unusual number of Jews who believed that the arrival of the Messiah was no longer in the distant future, but was actually going to happen in their day. Both John the Baptist and Jesus were able to take advantage of this Messianic enthusiasm and draw large crowds to them as they preached that Jesus was this long-awaited Messiah. It is likely that God's providence was at work here, stirring up this expectancy of an imminent arrival, and selecting this time as the occasion to send His Son to earth. Simeon was one of those who eagerly anticipated the Messiah.

Yet Simeon was quite different from others of like mind. He had the *Holy Ghost . . . upon him.* Simeon was blessed with a revelation from the Holy Spirit. Probably his Messianic enthusiasm did not derive from this working of the Holy Spirit, but, more likely, the Spirit blessed him with the means and opportunity for meeting the Messianic child in response to his desire to see the Messiah finally come to his people.

26. And it was revealed unto him by the Holy Ghost, that he should not see death, before he had seen the Lord's Christ.

Simeon enjoyed a privilege unparalleled among the saints of old. Hebrews 11 speaks of the Old Testament saints as men and women of faith who looked forward to something far better that God was preparing, but they died without experiencing the fulfillment of His Messianic promise (Hebrews 11:39). Simeon was guaranteed that he would live long enough to see the Messiah.

As great as were the deeds and blessings of men like Abraham, Isaac, Jacob, David, and Elijah, none of what they experienced could match the special gift granted to Simeon.

B. Simeon's Song (vv. 27-32)

27. And he came by the Spirit into the temple: and when the parents brought in the child Jesus, to do for him after the custom of the law.

It was no coincidence that Simeon arrived in the *temple* at the same time Jesus' *parents* were there. He was specifically led *by the Spirit.*

28. Then took he him up in his arms, and blessed God, and said.

Imagine the shock of having a stranger approach you and request to hold your child. Luke's simple account does not indicate how much persuasion it took (if any) for Simeon to convince Jesus' parents to trust him. But with all

of the unusual events that had already occurred surrounding Jesus' birth, Joseph and Mary were apparently open to granting this unusual request.

29-31. Lord, now lettest thou thy servant depart in peace, according to thy word: for mine eyes have seen thy salvation, which thou hast prepared before the face of all people.

These words suggest the possibility that Simeon was an old man nearing death, though it should be acknowledged that no indication of his actual age is given. Simeon was apparently a man of great vision. He looked at a baby and saw *salvation* for *all people.* This is somewhat similar to what Jesus did in His first recorded encounter with Simon Peter. He saw the potential within Simon and gave him the name "Peter," from the Greek word meaning "rock." We should be challenged by the example of Simeon to look beyond the external appearances of the people we meet, and imagine the possibilities and potential that could emerge from their lives with the appropriate encouragement and support.

32. A light to lighten the Gentiles, and the glory of thy people Israel.

Simeon exhibited an insight into God's plan of salvation that was uncommon among the Jews. The Jewish people were not an evangelistic people, sending missionaries among the *Gentiles.* Even the early church had difficulties understanding the full import of Jesus' Great Commission.

Simeon, however, spoke like the Old Testament prophets (see, for example, Isaiah 42:6, 7 and Micah 4:1, 2) who anticipated the salvation of Gentiles as well as Jews. The words he chose were quite appropriate for these two categories of people. Since the Gentiles had lived for ages in darkness, outside the knowledge of Jehovah God, the Messiah would bring them *light.* But the Jews had known the true God and had even witnessed His *glory* through His mighty works, His righteous Law, and the imagery within the tabernacle and temple. For them, the Messiah would bring an even greater view of the glory of God.

C. Jesus' Destiny (vv. 33-35)

33. And Joseph and his mother marveled at those things which were spoken of him.

To read this verse by itself could be misleading. As we know from the context, the phrase *Joseph and his mother* does not refer to Joseph's mother but to Jesus' mother Mary.

Being strangers in Jerusalem, Joseph and Mary had been blending in anonymously with the temple crowd. It was highly unusual for a stranger to pick them out of the crowd and know the true identity of their son. But what astonished them most were the words of Simeon: the special promise that he would live to see the Messiah, his insight into their son's Messianic mission, and his exceptional grasp of the broad extent of God's plan of salvation.

34. And Simeon blessed them, and said unto Mary his mother, Behold, this child is set for the fall and rising again of many in Israel; and for a sign which shall be spoken against.

Simeon was mindful of the Old Testament prophecies that spoke of the Messiah's rejection by His own people. For example, the prophet Isaiah portrayed the Messiah as a stone upon which the faithful would build and be saved, while for those who kick at it the stone would become a "stumbling-block," causing them to *fall.* (Isaiah 8:13-15; 28:16). Isaiah also pictured the Messiah as a *sign* or visible object lesson from God that would be understood by the faithful but rejected as meaningless by most (Isaiah 8:16-18; 53:1-3).

35. (Yea, a sword shall pierce through thy own soul also;) that the thoughts of many hearts may be revealed.

Here Simeon introduced the ominous thought that the Messiah's mission would include suffering—the first time such a thought appears in Luke's narrative of the birth. Joseph and Mary's son was to be rejected by His own people and pierced. This is implied by the statement that the soul of Mary herself would be pierced *also.*

This was a difficult concept for the Jews of Jesus' day to grasp. They could not imagine a Messiah who, rather than conquering His enemies, would in fact be conquered by them. They had rejected all references to the Messiah suffering (such as Isaiah's "suffering servant" passages), and had interpreted them as applying to some other servant of God. This bias was still evident many years later when Paul spoke of the cross as a "stumblingblock" to most Jews (1 Corinthians 1:23).

With the benefit of the New Testament witness, we understand how suffering figured into God's plan for Jesus. It was through Jesus' death that the atonement and forgiveness of our sins was accomplished. The victory over death that He promised occurred shortly thereafter in His resurrection. These events and the questions they raise have always challenged individuals to look closely at themselves and to confront the genuine issues of life. Thus, whenever the gospel is proclaimed, *the thoughts of many hearts* are still *revealed.*

We do not know if Joseph and Mary had previously understood the aspect of suffering in the Messianic plan any better than the rest of their countrymen. But certainly now, through Simeon, they were given a more descriptive picture of their son's ultimate mission, and in addition, of the hurt that Mary would one day experience. It is almost as though Simeon could see her standing before the cross, watching her son die there.

The faithful commitment of Joseph and Mary to the will of God is evident throughout the Christmas story. From this point on, however, their commitment would need to be especially strong, as they reared and prepared their son for a ministry that would be accompanied by pain and suffering.

III. Anna's Witness
(Luke 2:36-38)

A. Anna's Devotion (vv. 36, 37)

36. And there was one Anna, a prophetess, the daughter of Phanuel, of the tribe of Asher: she was of a great age, and had lived with a husband seven years from her virginity.

A second person now approached Joseph and Mary in the temple on this occasion. *Anna* was a member of the ancient *tribe of Asher,* one of the original twelve tribes of Israel. We know nothing of her father *Phanuel,* but his mention implies that he had some prestige in that day. Anna had been married *seven years* before her *husband* died.

37. And she was a widow of about fourscore and four years, which departed not from the temple, but served God with fastings and prayers night and day.

It is possible that Anna had been a *widow* for *fourscore and four years,* or eighty-four years, but that would make her well over one hundred years old. It is more likely that Luke is stating that Anna was currently a widow and currently eighty-four years old. To say that she *departed not from the temple* could mean that she had made some kind of arrangements for living in a residence on the temple grounds. But since this was not usually done for single women, the phrase may simply mean that she made long visits to the temple each day. Whatever the case, it

visual for lesson 5

Lord, now lettest thou thy servant depart in peace, according to thy word: for mine eyes have seen thy salvation, which thou hast prepared before the face of all people; a light to lighten the Gentiles, and the glory of thy people Israel.

Luke 2:29-32

is clear from the description that Anna possessed a spiritual character comparable to that of Simeon.

B. Anna's Declaration (v. 38)

38. And she coming in that instant gave thanks likewise unto the Lord, and spake of him to all them that looked for redemption in Jerusalem.

Luke does not specifically indicate what prompted Anna to approach Joseph and Mary and begin speaking about their special child. Perhaps she heard what Simeon said. Perhaps the Holy Spirit was pointing her toward the Messianic child just as He had done for Simeon. In either event, Anna's devotion to God shines through. From that point on she began testifying to others who anticipated the coming of the Messiah (who *looked for redemption in Jerusalem*) that He had finally arrived, for she had seen Him with her own eyes.

It is not likely that either Simeon or Anna revealed the names of Jesus and His parents, since later, when Herod attempted to locate Jesus, his only clue for finding Him was a birthplace and an approximate age. What these two people did was initiate a "rumor" like that of the shepherds, which would stir up a Messianic expectation. This in turn would prepare people for the preaching of John the Baptist and Jesus that would come later.

How Long, Lord?

For several years, I ministered to a Christian man who was incurably ill. His lungs were almost "burned up" due to occupational hazards of chemical dust and smoke fumes. He had to be hospitalized every few months, sometimes for a week or so, sometimes longer.

Home Daily Bible Readings

Monday, Dec. 23—Our Hope Is in God (Psalm 42:1-11)

Tuesday, Dec. 24—Honor Older Widows (1 Timothy 5:3-10)

Wednesday, Dec. 25—Firstborn Son Redeemed (Exodus 13:11-16)

Thursday, Dec. 26—The Mission of the Servant (Isaiah 42:1-9)

Friday, Dec. 27—The Hope of Salvation (1 Thessalonians 5:1-11)

Saturday, Dec. 28—Salvation Through Jesus Christ (Acts 4:5-12)

Sunday, Dec. 29—A Sure Salvation (Romans 8:31-39)

Toward the end of his life, he would frequently ask in his misery, "Why doesn't the Lord take me?" As his minister and shepherd, I frankly was stymied. I dreaded the question, because I had no answer. His desire was not only for death; he was also longing for life, for deliverance, and for the Lord's promised "consolation."

Anna herself must have wondered, "How long must we wait, Lord? How long?" Her temple vigil is a classic model of patient perseverance. For years she had faithfully pursued her single purpose of prayer and preparation. When the Lord arrived, she immediately recognized Him as the long-awaited Redeemer.

Why is Christ delaying His return? He promised: "I will come again, and receive you unto myself" (John 14:3). Especially when we are sick, sad or lonely, we wonder, "How long, Lord?" But just as surely as Anna's faith was finally rewarded, so will ours be, for Jesus' second coming is as certain as was His first. My deceased friend has been ushered already into His presence.

—R. W. B.

Conclusion

A. Backstage Helpers

Sometimes we wonder why we are given a long list of credits at the end of theater and concert guidebooks, television programs, and movies. Why not list only the main performers and singers? Because as important as the main characters are, there would be no production without the labor of those who work behind the scenes. They deserve some recognition for the finished product.

Simeon and Anna are minor characters in the drama of the life of Jesus Christ. Their names are not as prominent in our minds as Joseph, Mary, Peter, James, and John. Yet a careful look at their story reminds us that the true significance of our labors is not in the size of our tasks but in the size of the faith that performs those tasks.

B. Let Us Pray

Father, help us to humbly commit ourselves to Your service in whatever capacity You present before us. And help us to remain ever expectant for the work that Jesus Christ our Messiah has yet to do in our lives. In Jesus' name we pray, amen.

C. Thought to Remember

God has a service for each one of us to perform when we are ready to yield ourselves completely to the leading of His Spirit and His Word.

Learning by Doing

This page contains an alternate lesson plan emphasizing learning activities.
Classes desiring such student involvement will find these suggestions helpful.

Learning Goals

Because of this lesson students should:

1. Know and understand the descriptions of Jesus given by Simeon and Anna.

2. Appreciate the vast number of descriptive words and phrases given to help us understand the character, will, and work of Jesus.

3. Offer a personal description of what Jesus means in their lives.

Into the Lesson

Ask class members to "brainstorm" and try to recall every word or phrase they can think of from Scripture that describes Jesus. Have two people ready to list these on a large visual. Next, go back through the list and ask the class to place a check mark beside each description that comes from the Old Testament. Class members may discover that more of these have Old Testament roots than they realized! Clearly, those who knew these Scriptures had enough to fill them with a hope and a longing for the Messiah's coming. We will discover the richness of some of these descriptions as cited by Simeon and Anna when they saw the baby Jesus.

Into the Word

Begin the Bible study by appointing two "listening teams." Team 1 is to listen for any information that tells us something about Simeon and Anna (such as age, occupation, or spiritual character). Team 2 is to listen for words that describe the purpose and life of Jesus.

Read today's text. Afterward, do a brief lecture on the days of purification for Mary (their purpose and length), the purification ceremony, and the presentation of the firstborn son. Notes in the lesson commentary will be helpful.

Ask listening team 1 to report what they have discovered about Simeon and Anna. Record these on a large visual (poster board, flip chart, etc.). Items team 1 might note about Simeon could include his personal righteousness ("just and devout"), spiritual life ("the Holy Ghost was upon him"), patience ("waiting for the consolation of Israel"), old age (some feel he was elderly because of his statement that he was now ready to "depart in peace"), his special promise from God (that he would not die until he had seen the Messiah), and his ability to prophesy about the future of Jesus and Mary.

Remarks about Anna would include her calling (a prophetess), her lineage ("daughter of Phanuel, of the tribe of Asher"), her age (elderly, eighty-four years old), her marital status (married seven years, then widowed), and her devotion (spent much time in the temple fasting and praying.)

Ask listening team 2 to report the words and phrases they have found that describe the purpose and life of Jesus. Write their findings on a large visual (perhaps the same kind used by team 1). Their report should be identical to the one in the student book, which includes: "the consolation of Israel" (v. 25), "the Lord's Christ" (v. 26), "thy salvation" (v. 30), "a light to lighten the Gentiles" (v. 32), "the glory of thy people Israel" (v. 32), "set for the fall and rising again of many in Israel" (v. 34), "a sign which shall be spoken against" (v. 34), and "redemption" (v. 38).

Discuss the significance of each of these descriptions of Jesus. Use the lesson commentary to help explain their meaning. Questions you might ask include: "What does 'consolation of Israel' mean?" "Why did Simeon feel the time was near for the appearance of the Messiah?" "What is the significance of the description, 'the Lord's Christ'?" "Why the special mention of 'Gentiles' in verse 32?" Be sure to mention the reference to the Messiah's suffering in verse 34 (see the discussion in the lesson commentary).

Into Life

Tell class members that the student book asks them to do an acrostic with the word "Messiah." This means taking each letter of the word and thinking of a description of Jesus that begins with that letter. Here is a sample:

My Redeemer

Expiation (He paid the penalty for my sin)

Suffering

Savior

In Heaven preparing my home

Always (or eternal)

Herald of God's grace

You may want to show this on a transparency or on poster board to help give class members some ideas. When they are finished, ask a few class members to share their acrostics with the rest of the class. Close with a prayer of thanks for all that Jesus means in our lives.

Let's Talk It Over

The questions on this page are designed to encourage review of the lesson Scriptures and to promote discussion of the lesson by the class. The answers provided are only discussion starters. Let your class talk it over from there.

1. Joseph and Mary followed the prescribed ritual when they brought the infant Jesus to the temple in Jerusalem. What is the role of ritual in the lives of Christians today?

The dictionary defines a ritual as "the established form for a ceremony." Rightly understood and observed, religious rituals serve a valuable purpose in our lives and in our churches. Such traditions link us to the past and with the faith of the previous generation. Rituals can provide a sense of stability and continuity in a world that often is anything but stable.

Sadly, some Christians look with disdain on religious rituals, fearing they make worship too formal and liturgical. Certainly there is a danger that a ritual can become a substitute for genuine, heartfelt worship. But that can happen to any worship form, even the "unstructured" format used in some churches today.

2. Expectancy and anticipation are important themes in the story of Simeon and Anna. What are some blessings that we as Christians anticipate with expectancy?

In the short term, we anticipate answers to prayer. We anticipate growing in grace and in spiritual maturity. We anticipate getting to know Jesus better as we walk with and serve Him. We anticipate the joy that comes from joining with other believers in worshiping and praising God. We anticipate receiving God's blessings.

In the long term, we anticipate the return of Christ and living with Him eternally.

3. No doubt there were other devout and faithful Jews in Jerusalem besides Simeon and Anna. Why does God single out some people for special honor and blessings?

We certainly cannot begin to understand why God does all that He does or why He uses the specific people He does. His ways are far beyond our limited powers of comprehension (Isaiah 55:8, 9). We can, however, affirm that God rewards with special blessings those who are faithful to Him. Faithfulness puts us in positions where we can be chosen and used by God. We have seen that quality in Mary, who proved by her actions that she was devout, God-fearing, and obedient. In this lesson, we see it in Simeon, who was "just and devout" (Luke 2:25). We see it

also in Anna, who "served God with fastings and prayers night and day" (v. 37). This shows that it is important for us to be the kind of persons God can bless and use.

4. What is the basis of prophetic utterance? What is its purpose? Are prophets still prophesying today?

Genuine prophetic utterance is inspired, motivated, and directed by the Holy Spirit. Originally, prophecy was both *fore*telling future events and *forth*telling a message from God. Indeed, the Old Testament prophets spent more time telling the people God's messages directed toward them than they did predicting the future.

Those two aspects—foretelling and forthtelling—carried over into the prophetic office in the church. In the first-century church, prophets declared God's messages. But on some occasions they also predicted future events (Acts 11:27, 28; 21:10, 11).

In our day, ministers of the gospel declare God's messages, but the foretelling aspect of the prophetic office has disappeared. The Scripture reminds us, "In the past God spoke to our forefathers through the prophets at many times and in various ways, but in these last days he has spoken to us by his Son" (Hebrews 1:1, 2, *New International Version*). The responsibility is ours to hear, understand, and respond to that message of the Son, for it is God's final word to mankind.

5. What are some behind-the-scenes supporting roles we can fill in helping others to communicate the gospel?

Paul said that the less glamorous roles in the body of Christ are just as important as the prominent roles (1 Corinthians 12:21-25). Not everyone can be a minister, but everyone can be a helper in some way. Some can teach a Sunday school class; others can set up and take down chairs. Not everyone feels comfortable making phone calls or visiting prospective members, but what about making cookies or helping with a repair job at the church? Not everyone can sing a solo, but what about lifting a voice in prayer? Not everyone can work in a class with children, but what about giving them a ride to church? Everyone can do something.

John the Baptizer

DEVOTIONAL READING: Matthew 11:7-17.

LESSON SCRIPTURE: Mark 1:1-15; Luke 7:18-30.

PRINTED TEXT: Mark 1:4-11, 14, 15; Luke 7:18-23.

Jan 5

Mark 1:4-11, 14, 15

4 John did baptize in the wilderness, and preach the baptism of repentance for the remission of sins.

5 And there went out unto him all the land of Judea, and they of Jerusalem, and were all baptized of him in the river of Jordan, confessing their sins.

6 And John was clothed with camel's hair, and with a girdle of a skin about his loins; and he did eat locusts and wild honey;

7 And preached, saying, There cometh one mightier than I after me, the latchet of whose shoes I am not worthy to stoop down and unloose.

8 I indeed have baptized you with water: but he shall baptize you with the Holy Ghost.

9 And it came to pass in those days, that Jesus came from Nazareth of Galilee, and was baptized of John in Jordan.

10 And straightway coming up out of the water, he saw the heavens opened, and the Spirit like a dove descending upon him:

11 And there came a voice from heaven, saying, Thou art my beloved Son, in whom I am well pleased.

. . . .

14 Now after that John was put in prison, Jesus came into Galilee, preaching the gospel of the kingdom of God,

15 And saying, The time is fulfilled, and the kingdom of God is at hand: repent ye, and believe the gospel.

Luke 7:18-23

18 And the disciples of John showed him of all these things.

19 And John calling unto him two of his disciples sent them to Jesus, saying, Art thou he that should come? or look we for another?

20 When the men were come unto him, they said, John Baptist hath sent us unto thee, saying, Art thou he that should come? or look we for another?

21 And in that same hour he cured many of their infirmities and plagues, and of evil spirits; and unto many that were blind he gave sight.

22 Then Jesus answering said unto them, Go your way, and tell John what things ye have seen and heard; how that the blind see, the lame walk, the lepers are cleansed, the deaf hear, the dead are raised, to the poor the gospel is preached.

23 And blessed is he, whosoever shall not be offended in me.

GOLDEN TEXT: I [John the Baptist] indeed have baptized you with water: but he shall baptize you with the Holy Ghost.—Mark 1:8.

New Testament Personalities
Unit 2: Persons in Jesus' Ministry
(Lessons 6-9)

Lesson Aims

As a result of this lesson students should:

1. See that God's essential gospel message remains the same: Jesus the Christ must be trusted and obeyed for salvation.

2. Realize that honest doubts about their Christian faith are not sinful, but, when resolved, can become the entryways to a stronger faith.

Lesson Outline

INTRODUCTION
   A. Doubt and Faith
   B. Lesson Background
 I. JOHN'S MINISTRY TO THE MULTITUDES (Mark 1:4-8)
   A. John's Message (vv. 4, 5)
   B. John's Dress and Diet (v. 6)
     Would You Hire This Preacher?
   C. John's Messianic Predictions (vv. 7, 8)
 II. JOHN'S MINISTRY TO JESUS (Mark 1:9-11)
   A. Jesus' Baptism (v. 9)
   B. Heaven's Response (vv. 10, 11)
III. JOHN'S MINISTRY GIVES WAY TO JESUS (Mark 1:14, 15)
   A. John's Arrest (v. 14a)
   B. Jesus' Arrival in Galilee (vv. 14b, 15)
IV. JESUS' MINISTRY TO JOHN (Luke 7:18-23)
   A. John's Doubts (vv. 18-20)
   B. Jesus' Reassurance (vv. 21-23)
     Of Pudding and Fruit
CONCLUSION
   A. Healthy Doubting
   B. Prayer
   C. Thought to Remember

The visual for Lesson 6 in the visuals packet shows how John's doubts about Jesus were answered. It is shown on page 165.

Introduction

A. Doubt and Faith

Lew Wallace was a doubter. Though an accomplished lawyer, esteemed Civil War hero, and former governor and ambassador, he started research in the late nineteenth century on a historical novel to be set in the first century. At the time, he believed Jesus Christ to be no more than a mere man. But because Wallace intended to incorporate some material about Jesus into his book, he began for the first time to read the Biblical accounts of Jesus' life. By the time his Bible reading and his historical research were complete, Lew Wallace was a believer. His novel, *Ben Hur: A Tale of the Christ*, reflected his firm conviction that Jesus was, in fact, the Son of God and the Savior of the world.

Neither Christ nor Christianity has anything to fear from honest doubt. The Bible itself disapproves of religious gullibility and recommends a healthy skepticism in the consideration of religious claims (Acts 17:11; 1 Thessalonians 5:21; 1 John 4:1).

Today's study shows John the Baptizer as a powerful proclaimer and forerunner of the Messiah, but it also illustrates how even a spiritual giant such as John can experience genuine doubts. Jesus knew, however, that John's misgivings were honest, and He challenged him: "Look at the evidence; am I the Messiah or not?"

B. Lesson Background

The lesson today moves us forward about three decades from the time when the first five lessons in this series took place, as we begin a look at four key personalities during the ministry of Jesus. We start with Jesus' stalwart forerunner, John the Baptizer, who began to announce publicly the Messianic kingdom's arrival in about A.D. 26.

It is important to see that John's brief ministry was actually a transition period between the Law and the gospel. Jesus said, "The Law and the prophets were until John: since that time the kingdom of God is preached" (Luke 16:16; see also Matthew 11:13; Acts 10:36-38). Mark (1:1-4) says that John's preaching was "the beginning of the gospel." That John would prepare the way for the Lord had been determined by God centuries earlier (Isaiah 40:3; Malachi 3:1) and had been reaffirmed at his birth (Luke 1:17, 76, 77).

I. John's Ministry to the Multitudes (Mark 1:4-8)

A. John's Message (vv. 4, 5)

4. John did baptize in the wilderness, and preach the baptism of repentance for the remission of sins.

John did not carry on his work in the sacred city of Jerusalem; he was a man of the *wilderness*. He roamed the uninhabited and mostly desolate areas of the wilderness of Judea (this more specific location is mentioned in Matthew 3:1), which extended northward from the area north-west of the Dead Sea to the southern part of the Jordan River valley.

John baptized (immersed in water) men and women who committed themselves to *repentance*—a genuine change of mind and heart, leading to a change of life. *Baptism* seems to be a totally new rite introduced by John. There is no convincing evidence to link baptism to the ceremonial washings and bathings of the Jews, the Essenes (a sect of the Jews known for its simplicity and strictness of lifestyle), or the Qumran community (the group most famous for producing what we know as the Dead Sea Scrolls). Nor can it be shown that the baptism of converts to Judaism (who were known as "proselytes") was practiced this early. The unusual nature of John's act was the reason he came to be designated as "the Baptizer."

John's baptism promised a *remission* or forgiveness, *of sins*. Evidently submission in faith to John's baptism granted a forgiveness that prepared for Christian baptism, through which a more permanent forgiveness, secured by Jesus' death and resurrection, would be available. John offered a forgiveness similar to that secured by obedience to the Old Testament sacrificial demands (see, for example, Leviticus 4:26, 31; 5:16), but which also looked forward and called attention to what the Messiah who was to follow him would accomplish. This illustrates John's ministry as a transition from the Law to the gospel.

5. And there went out unto him all the land of Judea, and they of Jerusalem, and were all baptized of him in the river of Jordan, confessing their sins.

John certainly fulfilled his appointed task of arousing the nation of Israel to righteousness. His unique personality, his powerful preaching, and his unique rite of baptism combined with the expectant atmosphere in Palestine (Luke 2:25, 38; 3:15) to set the whole region ablaze with excitement. The imperfect tense (indicating repeated action) of the verb *were . . . baptized* suggests a constant flow of penitent Israelites turning to God in obedience, *confessing* and renouncing *their sins.*

B. John's Dress and Diet (v. 6)

6. And John was clothed with camel's hair, and with a girdle of a skin about his loins; and he did eat locusts and wild honey.

John's appearance reflected the poor but rugged wilderness man that he was. Dressing like his prototype Elijah (2 Kings 1:7, 8), John wore a coarse, itchy robe woven from *camel's hair*, and a leather *girdle* or "belt" (*New International Version*) around his waist.

John's diet also reflected the lifestyle of the wilderness. The *locusts* were likely the large grasshoppers that have always been a part of the diet of the Near East. Leviticus 11:22 declares locusts "clean," or permissible to eat, and the Jews were known to eat several varieties of them, roasting or frying them after removing the legs and wings.

WOULD YOU HIRE THIS PREACHER?

Sometimes pulpit committees look for ministers who possess a pleasant if not handsome appearance, a ready smile, and the ability to "dress for success." They want a leader who is up-to-date, fashionable, and non-controversial. After all, preachers must appeal to the "baby boomer" crowd. And they must look good in public, in case the congregation wants to televise its worship services someday.

John the Baptizer would have failed to qualify in nearly every one of these areas. He seemed rather eccentric with his strange style of dress and his even stranger eating habits. His preaching was often controversial and rarely accommodating to prevailing political philosophy. Like his Old Testament counterpart Elijah, his demeanor and tone were austere and dogmatic. Not many of today's pulpits would be available to him.

The surprise is that so many ("all the land of Judea") came to the Jordan valley to hear John—and scores of those who came and heard were baptized. Who would have guessed? John seems to have been all wrong for the part. But his convictions, his passion, and his guileless humility shone through the rough facade of his exterior.

Is it possible that pulpit committees tend to look for the wrong qualifications in leadership?

—R. W. B.

C. John's Messianic Predictions (vv. 7, 8)

7. And preached, saying, There cometh one mightier than I after me, the latchet of whose shoes I am not worthy to stoop down and unloose.

John humbly confessed that he was not the Christ (many were wondering if he were) and pointed to a *mightier* One who would come after him. This One was so great that John was not even *worthy* to be His slave. One of the slave's jobs was to undo the *latchet* and remove the sandals of his master or of an honored guest after travel, and then to clean them.

8. I indeed have baptized you with water: but he shall baptize you with the Holy Ghost.

Some interpreters believe that this promise was fulfilled in the miraculous outpouring of the

---

How to Say It

ANTIPAS. *Ant*-ih-pus.
BAPTIZO (Greek). bap-*tidz*-owe.
ESSENES. Ess-*eenz*.
HERODIAS. Heh-*roe*-dee-us.
JOSEPHUS. Joe-*see*-fuss.
MACHAERUS. Muh-*keer*-us.
MALACHI. *Mal*-uh-kye.
PROSELYTE. *prahs*-uh-light.
QUMRAN. Koom-*rahn*.

Holy Ghost on the apostles on the Day of Pentecost (Acts 2:1-4). But the promise here seems broader than that, made to the multitudes and not just to the few who would later become apostles. Perhaps a better interpretation is that Jesus, after His death and resurrection, would *baptize* in the power of the Holy Spirit all who would trust and obey Him. The fulfillment of this began with the apostles in a special way on the Day of Pentecost (Acts 1:5), but was expanded to include all subsequent baptized believers (1 Corinthians 6:11; 12:13). All of this would constitute a new working of the Spirit, which would clearly distinguish the Messiah's ministry from John's.

II. John's Ministry to Jesus (Mark 1:9-11)

A. Jesus' Baptism (v. 9)

9. And it came to pass in those days, that Jesus came from Nazareth of Galilee, and was baptized of John in Jordan.

This occasion marked the climax of John's ministry and the beginning of Jesus' ministry. After thirty years of obscurity, Jesus was ready to introduce Himself to the public. Leaving His family and His carpentry work in *Nazareth of Galilee*, He traveled down to the Jordan River to be *baptized of John* (Matthew 3:13). He did not need to be convinced of His duty; He knew that it was time for Him to begin His work.

In Jordan is literally, in the Greek, "*into the* Jordan." This indicates immersion as the mode of Jesus' baptism. This fact is further supported by the basic meaning of the Greek word *baptizo*, as well as the "coming up out of the water" in verse 10.

It is not completely clear why Jesus submitted to John's baptism. Jesus was sinless, so He did not need a "baptism of repentance for the remission of sins" (v. 4). Matthew quotes Jesus' explanation that He did it "to fulfil all righteousness" (3:15), which perhaps means that He wanted to

identify Himself with what was right for all people to do, even though He Himself might actually be exempt from those requirements (compare the temple tax incident in Matthew 17:24-27).

B. Heaven's Response (vv. 10, 11)

10. And straightway coming up out of the water, he saw the heavens opened, and the Spirit like a dove descending upon him.

The word *straightway* is characteristic of Mark's Gospel. Mark uses it nineteen times, far more than any other Gospel writer. It distinguishes his account as one of constant activity.

Literally, the *heavens* were "torn open" (the reading in the *New International Version*), and the Holy *Spirit* took upon Himself the bodily form of a *dove* (see Luke 3:22) and descended upon Jesus. From this moment Jesus would be full of the Holy Spirit and of power (Luke 4:1, 16-21; Acts 10:38), just as the Old Testament had predicted (Psalm 45:7; Isaiah 11:1, 2; 42:1; 61:1). Apparently this is the anointing that made Jesus the *Christ* ("Anointed One").

Why the form of a dove was chosen is hard to determine with certainty. Among the common suggestions are the dove's association with qualities such as gentleness, innocence, hope, peace, and love. Regardless, this was the sign given to John, by which he recognized that Jesus was indeed the Messiah and the Son of God (John 1:32-34).

11. And there came a voice from heaven, saying, Thou art my beloved Son, in whom I am well pleased.

Thus, the three personalities of the Trinity (the Father, the Son, and the Holy Spirit) were all present for this pivotal event. The Father's words of approval recall two Messianic prophecies: Psalm 2:7 says, "Thou art my Son; this day have I begotten thee"; and Isaiah 42:1 calls God's suffering Servant "mine elect, in whom my soul delighteth." Probably John heard and understood the *voice* as part of the confirmation he received concerning Jesus (John 1:32-34).

III. John's Ministry Gives Way to Jesus (Mark 1:14, 15)

A. John's Arrest (v. 14a)

14a. Now after that John was put in prison.

Mark later provides the details of John's arrest and subsequent murder at the hands of Herod Antipas and his wife Herodias (6:14-29). The Jewish historian Josephus also speaks of this arrest and locates the place of the imprisonment at Herod's castle at Machaerus, which was in Perea, just east of the Dead Sea.

B. Jesus' Arrival in Galilee
(vv. 14b, 15)

14b, 15. Jesus came into Galilee, preaching the gospel of the kingdom of God, and saying, The time is fulfilled, and the kingdom of God is at hand: repent ye, and believe the gospel.

The first eight months of Jesus' ministry had been conducted in Judea. A combination of three factors now led Him to leave Judea: (1) He knew that the Pharisees had learned of His successes and would be increasing their scrutiny of and opposition to Him (John 4:1-3); (2) He received the news that John had been arrested (Matthew 4:12); and (3) He was following the leading of the Holy Spirit (Luke 4:14).

While Jesus preached the same message that John had (see Matthew 3:2), He no doubt added many of His own details to the themes His forerunner had first introduced. The Messianic *kingdom of God* was near, and these Galilean hearers needed to commit their lives to the gospel Jesus was announcing to them. In almost no time, Jesus' fame had spread all over Galilee and people everywhere were shouting His praise (Luke 4:14, 15).

IV. Jesus' Ministry to John
(Luke 7:18-23)

A. John's Doubts (vv. 18-20)

18. And the disciples of John showed him of all these things.

Apparently Herod's restrictions on his prisoner were not so great as to disallow periodic visits from John's *disciples*. They described to him the great miracles Jesus had been performing and the enthusiastic reception He had received among the Galileans.

19. And John calling unto him two of his disciples sent them to Jesus, saying, Art thou he that should come? or look we for another?

Some interpreters think that John was not showing signs of doubt, as it might appear, but was asking this question for his disciples' sake; that is, he wanted them to hear Jesus affirm that He was the Messiah. Others think that John was impatient and was trying to prod Jesus to hurry up and publicly declare Himself as Messiah and eliminate all doubts among the Jews. The prevailing view that Jesus was just a "great prophet" (v. 16) was simply not good enough. John wanted all to know who Jesus really was.

Most likely, however, the faith of John himself was starting to waver. This seems apparent from Jesus' response in verse 22, which was directed specifically to John. By this time, John may have been in Herod's prison for slightly

visual for
lesson 6

more than six months. Where was the powerful Deliverer for whom John had so willingly stepped aside? When would He baptize the obedient in the Spirit and burn the wicked "with fire unquenchable" (Luke 3:17)? Alone in his dark dungeon cell, John's discouragement with what appeared to be Jesus' delay seems to have created some measure of doubt. If Jesus really were the Christ, why had He not vindicated John's preaching and shown Himself plainly to the world?

20. When the men were come unto him, they said, John Baptist hath sent us unto thee, saying, Art thou he that should come? or look we for another?

John's two disciples traveled approximately seventy miles from the prison to Galilee and faithfully carried out their assigned task.

B. Jesus' Reassurance (vv. 21-23)

21, 22. And in that same hour he cured many of their infirmities and plagues, and of evil spirits; and unto many that were blind he gave sight. Then Jesus answering said unto them, Go your way, and tell John what things ye have seen and heard; how that the blind see, the lame walk, the lepers are cleansed, the deaf hear, the dead are raised, to the poor the gospel is preached.

Jesus prefaced His verbal answer to the two men by offering a visual answer through a series of miracles. He then called attention to certain Old Testament prophecies about the coming Messiah's ministry (see Isaiah 29:18, 19; 35:4-6; 42:6, 7). In effect, His response to John's query was, "I am doing the Messiah's work. Yes, I am He."

Perhaps John had misapplied the prophecies of judgment to Christ's first coming, whereas they properly describe His second. He appeared the first time to be, in John's own words, "the Lamb of God, which taketh away the sin of the world" (John 1:29). He will come the second time to judge and destroy the wicked.

OF PUDDING AND FRUIT

Do you know a good cook when you see one? Skilled chefs are not recognizable by their appearance. Anyone can wear a chef's hat and apron. All of us have come across impersonators at one time or another. Most people who dine out frequently (and some who do not!) have discovered impostors in the kitchen.

Good cooks are identified primarily by the food they prepare. "The proof is in the pudding," as the saying goes. The same principle applies to carpenters, car manufacturers, seamstresses, and Messiahs. All are evaluated by the product of their labors. Uniforms, vocabulary—even diplomas and degrees—are not necessarily proofs of competence. Until one "tastes the pudding," one cannot be certain that a person who calls himself "cook" deserves the title.

Jesus taught that teachers and leaders (and everyone else, actually) are to be evaluated by inspection of their "fruit." "By their fruits ye shall know them" (Matthew 7:20).

When John asked for proof of Jesus' messiahship, the Lord invited him to inspect the fruit of His labor. His many miraculous deeds and His preaching were the "proof of His pudding" (see also John 10:37, 38).

We believe Christ's claims because we have inspected the fruits of His ministry and have determined, like Nicodemus, that He is "from God: for no man can do these miracles . . . except God be with him" (John 3:2).   —R. W. B.

23. And blessed is he, whosoever shall not be offended in me.

Jesus sent the disciples back to John with words that were both a gentle rebuke and a firm encouragement. "John, keep your faith no matter

Home Daily Bible Readings

Monday, Dec. 30—The Ministry of John the Baptizer (Luke 3:1-9)

Tuesday, Dec. 31—People Seek John's Counsel (Luke 3:10-18)

Wednesday, Jan. 1—John's Witness to Jesus (John 1:29-34)

Thursday, Jan. 2—John Baptizes Jesus (Matthew 3:13-17)

Friday, Jan. 3—Jesus Affirms John's Ministry (Matthew 11:7-19)

Saturday, Jan. 4—People Believe John Was a Prophet (Luke 20:1-8)

Sunday, Jan. 5—The Death of John the Baptizer (Matthew 14:1-12)

what the circumstances; it is well founded. Do not stumble now. Be assured that your message about Me is true, no matter how little you understand the details or the timing of My program." John's faith was no doubt renewed, and it provided him with the assurance he needed as he faced his untimely death (Mark 6:27-29). His ministry had not been in vain.

Conclusion

A. Healthy Doubting

John's doubts were honest doubts. After John's two disciples had left Jesus, He proceeded to defend John's character and commend him to the multitudes (Luke 7:24-28). John was not "a reed shaken with the wind," in spite of his apparent wavering. His confusion caused him to doubt, but he addressed his doubts. It was, in fact, his dissatisfaction with his confusion that had compelled him to send the two disciples to Jesus. He had to be sure that he was preaching the truth about Jesus.

Most Christians—even church leaders—have tinges of doubt at times. Is what I believe really true? Does it deserve my life's devotion? Am I leading others astray? Such doubts are nothing to be ashamed of, *if* they are followed by a renewed examination of the evidence. Lazy, dishonest doubt is content to be unsure; sometimes it even prefers the darkness. Honest or healthy doubt seeks more light. Its reward is a firmer conviction about what it believes. May we doubt as John doubted—with integrity, refusing to rest until our doubt is turned into firm conviction.

Jesus' challenge to John must also challenge us to consider the evidence. In light of what Jesus did and spoke, particularly concerning His resurrection from the dead, is it not much easier to believe than to disbelieve that He is the Christ, the Son of God and the Savior of the world?

B. Prayer

Father, I believe; help my unbelief. When I do find myself vacillating, make me restless until I have searched Your Word and Your world for the convincing truths that are there. Do not let me be lazy with my doubts. Thank You for understanding, and for providing all the proofs I need to find a "blessed assurance." Amen.

C. Thought to Remember

Really honest doubts are those which seek to be resolved. As someone has observed, "Merely having an open mind is nothing. The object of opening the mind, as of opening the mouth, is to shut it again on something solid."

Learning by Doing

This page contains an alternate lesson plan emphasizing learning activities.
Classes desiring such student involvement will find these suggestions helpful.

Learning Goals

As a result of today's lesson, students should:

1. Know that honest doubts about Jesus may lead to a firmer conviction about what they believe.

2. Identify ways to resolve their doubts.

3. Make a commitment to seek an answer to unresolved doubts.

Into the Lesson

Before the class begins, have a large poster prepared that reads: "What do these four persons have in common: Thomas, John the Baptist, Nathanael, and Lew Wallace?" Answer: They all possessed a healthy skepticism about Jesus. To encourage a correct answer, ask for the identity of each of these persons or call attention to well-known characteristics of each.

Nathanael was a skeptic who was told, "Come and see." Having done so, he proclaimed Jesus as the Son of God. Thomas was a doubter who, after seeing Jesus' wounds, proclaimed Him as "my Lord and my God" (John 20:28). Lew Wallace was the author of *Ben Hur: A Tale of the Christ.* At first, he doubted whether Jesus was anything more than a mere man. But as he began to do research for his novel, he read the Biblical accounts of Jesus' life. His research convinced him that Jesus is the Son of God.

Remind the class that it is not uncommon for people to have doubts about Jesus. How we handle those doubts, however, will make a great deal of difference in what happens to our faith. Today we will discover that John the Baptizer had his own doubts about Jesus—even after he had baptized Jesus and witnessed God's Spirit descending upon Him.

Into the Word

Divide the class into small groups of four to six, and give each group one of the sets of assignments, Scriptures, and materials listed below (the assignments and Scriptures are included in the student book). Find an article on John the Baptizer in a Bible dictionary for Group 1 to use. The *New Unger's Bible Dictionary* has an article divided into sections that would be especially helpful for this assignment. Group 2 should be given a copy of the lesson commentary on verse 8 and an article from a Bible dictionary on John's baptism. Again, the *New*

Unger's Bible Dictionary has informative sections marked "John's Baptism" and "Baptism of Jesus" under the general topic of "Baptism." Group 3 should be given a copy of the lesson commentary on Luke 7:18-23.

Group 1: Read the article about John the Baptizer from the Bible dictionary. Summarize his life for the class by having one person report on his birth and early life, another person report on his personal life and ministry, and a third person report on his imprisonment and death.

Group 2: Your task is to report on the purpose of John's baptism and the reason Jesus submitted Himself to baptism. Read Mark 1:7-11 and the information on John's baptism from the Bible dictionary entry.

Group 3: Read Luke 7:18-23. What were the indications that doubts were surfacing in John and his disciples? Can you describe the doubts they were experiencing? Why would such doubts have arisen at this particular time? How did Jesus offer reassurance to John and his disciples? The attached notes from the lesson commentary will be helpful in preparing your report.

Allow eight to ten minutes for the groups to prepare their reports. Then call them together to share their findings. Permit others outside the groups to ask questions or make comments.

Into Life

Focus on life application by using the following discussion questions (see the lesson commentary Conclusion for assistance in guiding this discussion):

1. Most Christians—even church leaders—have tinges of doubt: "Is what I believe really true? Does it deserve my life's devotion?" What will determine if these doubts are helpful to our faith or if they will be destructive?

2. What are some of the common doubts or questions that adults raise about their faith today, or that may remain unanswered from their teen years?

3. How can we turn people's questions toward healthy skepticism rather than destructive doubt?

Conclude by reading the prayer in the lesson commentary. Probably you do not often "read" prayers. But this one may well reflect the heart's desire of each class member.

Let's Talk It Over

The questions on this page are designed to encourage review of the lesson Scriptures and to promote discussion of the lesson by the class. The answers provided are only discussion starters. Let your class talk it over from there.

1. How do some preachers and teachers blunt the effectiveness of their messages?

The popular expression "tell it like it is" applies here. The message of the Scriptures needs to be preached and taught forthrightly and without compromise. Most of us will listen to a message that rings true, but we are turned off by shallow, simplistic platitudes.

We are also turned off by a minister or teacher who says one thing but does another. A minister who lives a lavish and extravagant life-style cannot convincingly call for sacrifice and self-denial. A teacher who employs questionable business practices in his personal life cannot expect us to take him seriously when he tells us to be ethical and honest in our relationships.

We can learn a lot about effective ministry by looking at John the Baptizer. People listened to John because he lived his message. He was genuine and authentic.

2. Why do we often feel uncomfortable around people (like John the Baptizer) whose life-style differs from the norm?

John the Baptizer was his own man—accountable to no one but God, and not concerned with what other people thought of him. If John came to our church, we probably would feel a bit uncomfortable. He was not the kind of man most of us like to have around. He tended to be too outspoken, too different, too unpredictable, and too abrasive.

Sometimes it is difficult to see beneath the exterior of one who looks or acts "different," to the person underneath. John proves that "different" does not always equal "bad." Beneath John's unconventional and nonconformist exterior was a man of unflinching courage, deep conviction, and great piety.

3. Why is humility difficult for a Christian minister? Why is it important to cultivate humility?

Because we like to feel important and like others to think of us as special, humility is difficult for all of us. This is especially true for a minister. People look up to him and admire him. They call on him to help them, and when he does, they are appreciative and tend to heap praise on him.

However, pride can be extremely destructive in the life of a minister. If his church is growing, he may feel he deserves the credit, not God. If a troubled couple decides not to get a divorce as a result of his counseling, he may feel it was all because of him. If he uses his influence to convince the city to redefine some zoning laws, he may begin to feel that his standing in the community is rising.

My father often said, "A lot of good can be done if we don't care who gets the credit." A humble minister is willing to work hard, then give God all the credit for the results.

4. What does true repentance involve?

Essentially, repentance means a turning around. We are walking in one direction, and then we turn around and begin walking in the opposite direction.

Awareness is the first step in repentance. Through the convicting work of the Holy Spirit, we become aware that we are living in sin. We then respond to conviction with *confession*. We admit that we are sinners who need to be saved, and we call upon Jesus to save us. The final step is obedience to Christ in Christian baptism, which brings *forgiveness*. When He forgives our sins, they are wiped away—never to be held against us again. At baptism, we also receive the Holy Spirit, who gives us the power to change and to bring our lives more completely under the lordship of Jesus.

5. Why are we so fearful of the word "doubt"? What are some effective ways to deal with honest doubt?

Doubt suggests unbelief or an unwillingness to believe. But such is not always the case. We can have doubts even when we want to believe and actually do believe. Honest doubt asks questions that need to be resolved. The father of a demon-possessed boy told Jesus, "Lord, I believe; help thou mine unbelief" (Mark 9:24). So we see that belief and honest doubt can coexist in the same heart.

The Lord is patient in dealing with our sincere doubts. Jesus answered John's doubts with evidence, not arguments. That seems to be the most effective procedure for resolving honest doubt.

Mary and Martha

DEVOTIONAL READING: Psalm 27:1-6.

LESSON SCRIPTURE: Luke 10:38-42; John 12:1-8.

PRINTED TEXT: Luke 10:38-42; John 12:1-8.

Luke 10:38-42

38 Now it came to pass, as they went, that he entered into a certain village: and a certain woman named Martha received him into her house.

39 And she had a sister called Mary, which also sat at Jesus' feet, and heard his word.

40 But Martha was cumbered about much serving, and came to him, and said, Lord, dost thou not care that my sister hath left me to serve alone? bid her therefore that she help me.

41 And Jesus answered and said unto her, Martha, Martha, thou art careful and troubled about many things:

42 But one thing is needful; and Mary hath chosen that good part, which shall not be taken away from her.

John 12:1-8

1 Then Jesus six days before the passover came to Bethany, where Lazarus was which had been dead, whom he raised from the dead.

2 There they made him a supper; and Martha served: but Lazarus was one of them that sat at the table with him.

3 Then took Mary a pound of ointment of spikenard, very costly, and anointed the feet of Jesus, and wiped his feet with her hair: and the house was filled with the odor of the ointment.

4 Then saith one of his disciples, Judas Iscariot, Simon's son, which should betray him,

5 Why was not this ointment sold for three hundred pence, and given to the poor?

6 This he said, not that he cared for the poor; but because he was a thief, and had the bag, and bare what was put therein.

7 Then said Jesus, Let her alone: against the day of my burying hath she kept this.

8 For the poor always ye have with you; but me ye have not always.

GOLDEN TEXT: Martha, Martha, thou art careful and troubled about many things: but one thing is needful; and Mary hath chosen that good part, which shall not be taken away from her.—Luke 10:41, 42.

New Testament Personalities
Unit 2: Persons in Jesus' Ministry
(Lessons 6-9)

Lesson Aims

At the conclusion of the lesson the students should:

1. Be able to evaluate their own priorities in the light of what Jesus taught Martha.

2. Understand that love for the Lord ought to move all of His followers to sacrificial acts of devotion.

3. Rejoice in the gifts that other Christians give to the Lord.

Lesson Outline

INTRODUCTION
   A. First Give Yourself
   B. Lesson Background
 I. A LESSON IN PRIORITIES (Luke 10:38-42)
   A. Martha's Gracious Hospitality (v. 38)
   B. Mary at Jesus' Feet (v. 39)
   C. The Exasperated Hostess (v. 40)
   D. Choose What Is Necessary (vv. 41, 42)
      The Need for Marthas
II. AN ACT OF DEVOTION (John12:1-8)
   A. A Supper With Friends (vv. 1, 2)
   B. Mary's Extraordinary Act (v. 3)
   C. Judas's Outrage (vv. 4-6)
   D. Jesus Defends Mary (vv. 7, 8)
      Good, Better, Best
CONCLUSION
   A. Giving Jesus the Best
   B. Let Us Pray
   C. Thought to Remember

The visual for Lesson 7 in the visuals packet is an artist's portrayal of the incident in today's lesson text. It is shown on page 174.

Introduction

A. First Give Yourself

We have all heard of parents who worked very hard to give their children the finest clothes, toys, and education, yet neglected to give them the most necessary items of all: time and love. Even though the gifts the parents gave may well have been motivated by love, such gifts are less than useless if the parents have not first given themselves to talk to their children, listen to them, and play with them.

Today's lesson is about two sisters, Mary and Martha, and the gifts that they gave to Jesus. Their example teaches us that the most important gift we can give to Jesus is ourselves.

B. Lesson Background

Mary and Martha, along with their brother Lazarus, were some of Jesus' closest friends. John specifically mentions Jesus' love for them (John 11:5). The sisters are mentioned in three different incidents in the Gospels, and two of them form this lesson's printed text. The other one in John 11 tells of the raising of Lazarus.

The precise time of the first incident is uncertain, but it likely occurred during the fall of the year preceding Jesus' death. The occasion was a visit to Bethany by Jesus and the disciples. Certainly Jesus was welcome in the sisters' home, but Mary and Martha reacted quite differently to the visit. Jesus used the opportunity to teach Martha a valuable lesson on priorities.

The second event took place the day before Jesus' triumphal entry into Jerusalem and six days before the Passover during which Jesus was crucified (John 12:1, 12). The setting was a supper that had been prepared for Jesus and the disciples. This was a very tense time. The Jewish leaders were seeking to kill Jesus and had given orders that anyone who knew where Jesus was should report His whereabouts so that He could be arrested (John 11:57). Moved by her love for the Lord and perhaps by her anxiety for His safety, Mary presented Jesus a valuable gift in a very dramatic way.

The experiences and actions of these two sisters teach us important lessons about the place the Lord should have in our hearts and lives and how we should express our love to Him.

I. A Lesson in Priorities
(Luke 10:38-42)

A. Martha's Gracious Hospitality (v. 38)

38. Now it came to pass, as they went, that he entered into a certain village: and a certain woman named Martha received him into her house.

The phrase *as they went* includes the twelve disciples, and perhaps others, who were traveling with Jesus as He went about preaching and teaching. Their journey brought them to *a certain village*. This was Bethany, which is located less than two miles east of Jerusalem on the eastern slope of the Mount of Olives. While the text says that *Martha received him into her house*, it is likely that the disciples were included as well. The fact that the house belonged to Martha placed upon her the responsibility of being hostess to the group. As we shall see, she took this responsibility very seriously.

Martha did well to welcome Jesus and His followers into her home. Her hospitality revealed a kind heart and a sincere interest in the kingdom of God. What a blessing gracious hospitality is to those who receive it and to those who offer it.

B. Mary at Jesus' Feet (v. 39)

39. And she had a sister called Mary, which also sat at Jesus' feet, and heard his word.

Martha's *sister* was *Mary.* Apparently both sisters lived in Martha's house. John 11:1 mentions "Bethany, the town of Mary and her sister Martha." The phrase *sat at Jesus' feet* calls to mind the relationship of student to teacher. Paul spoke of being taught at the feet of Gamaliel (Acts 22:3). Mary stayed in Jesus' presence because she wanted to hear what He said. Perhaps He was taking this time to teach the disciples or to answer questions people were asking.

What a thrill it would have been to sit at Mary's side! Surely all of us could sit at Jesus' feet and listen to Him for hours—or could we? In our day our churches are blessed with great numbers of godly preachers, who have invested a lifetime studying God's Word and walking with the Lord. Yet we sometimes have a hard time listening to them for just half an hour while they open the Word to us. We have at our disposal all kinds of books and magazines to help us grow in our faith and understanding, but we seldom find the time to read them. We all need to imitate Mary, who put everything else aside to take advantage of the opportunity to learn from the Lord.

C. The Exasperated Hostess (v. 40)

40. But Martha was cumbered about much serving, and came to him, and said, Lord, dost thou not care that my sister hath left me to serve alone? bid her therefore that she help me.

Cumbered means distracted or flustered. To be *about much serving* involved preparations for at least thirteen guests—a lot of work! Martha's "cumberedness" would have increased if they had come unexpectedly; after all, they could not phone ahead! At any rate, the entire undertaking became too much for Martha, who found herself quite frustrated.

Dost thou not care? Martha must have been very upset indeed to make such an accusation against Jesus. Why was He to blame? Perhaps she felt that Jesus should have excused Mary and told her to help. Martha's words, *My sister hath left me to serve alone,* bring us to the heart of the matter. Martha did not seem to mind the preparations as much as she resented the fact

---

How to Say It

GAMALIEL. Guh-*may*-lee-ul.

---

that Mary was not giving her any help. Mary may have been ignoring Martha's beckoning motions and her stern looks. Martha felt justified in expressing her sentiments to Jesus: *bid her therefore that she help me.*

Martha's irritation with Mary arose in part because Mary did not share her priorities. To Martha it was perfectly obvious that meals must be prepared and other arrangements made. To Mary, it was perfectly obvious that the most important matter at the time was to sit down and listen to Jesus.

We often wrestle with this same conflict today. It is natural for each person to feel that the ministry he or she fulfills is a high priority and that it should be a priority for everyone else as well. If others do not place the same degree of importance on it, hard feelings sometimes result. We must recognize that the church has need of many different ministries and learn to value them all.

D. Choose What Is Necessary
(vv. 41, 42)

41. And Jesus answered and said unto her, Martha, Martha, thou art careful and troubled about many things.

As we would expect, Jesus remained calm and composed in the face of this criticism. *Martha, Martha:* the repeating of her name served to emphasize Jesus' affection for her and to soften the rebuke that followed. The words *careful and troubled* are rendered in the *New International Version* as "worried and upset." The *many things* about which Martha was troubled might have included such thoughts as, "Is the meat done yet?" "The bread is burned!" or "Where am I going to put everyone?" Her mind must have been racing as she made a mental check of how all the necessary preparations (at least in her mind) were going.

42. But one thing is needful; and Mary hath chosen that good part, which shall not be taken away from her.

Martha was worried about many things; yet only *one thing is needful,* and Martha was giving no attention to it. She was concerned with food, accommodations, and similar matters. These had crowded out the much more important opportunity to spend time with Jesus. Mary, on the other hand, had *chosen that good part* when she sat to listen to Jesus. Contrary to Martha's request, Jesus did not tell Mary to help but gave her permission to stay with Him.

Even though Jesus' words were spoken tenderly, they were nonetheless a rebuke. It was not that Martha's activities were unimportant or unappreciated, for her guests did need life's necessities. Perhaps Martha was too obsessed with time. Would it really have mattered if they had eaten two or three hours later? Perhaps she was "going overboard" and making needlessly elaborate preparations. In some way Martha was placing undue importance on what she was doing. Ministering to physical concerns is important, but the *one thing* that is truly necessary is to feed the spirit.

We all have responsibilities like Martha's that press upon us every day. Besides the basic duties at work and at home, there are a thousand other seemingly endless chores and demands on our time, all of which appear absolutely necessary. To a certain extent they are necessary; however, they must not be allowed to determine our priorities and control our outlook. Specifically, we must not allow such items to crowd spiritual concerns out of our lives.

All Christians face this challenge. It is not that we have no love for Jesus. We say to ourselves that as soon as we get everything done, we will set a fixed time for prayer or Bible study, or start going to that new midweek class. But somehow we never get caught up. We need to learn that the yard can be mowed tomorrow, supper can be an hour later, the dust on the coffee table will wait, and other similar duties can be skipped altogether—if that is what it takes to spend time feeding ourselves spiritually.

THE NEED FOR MARTHAS

Jesus' comments to Martha in our lesson text were not meant to disparage Martha's value, nor the value of her worthwhile contribution to His visit. He simply and softly rebuked her judgmental attitude toward her sister, and gave her the divine perspective on what seemed to be an unfair circumstance.

This needs to be kept in mind in today's world, where cultural forces have seemingly reduced the rank of any woman without a "career" to second-class citizen. Stay-at-home wives and mothers should not be ashamed to declare the worthiness of their vocation. Someone should be demonstrating on behalf of those who cook, clean, launder, counsel, encourage, administrate, schedule, train, comfort, discipline, transport, and carry out scores of other tasks. These women who do necessary household chores, superintend their homes, hold together their families, and successfully rear the children of the world are involved in perhaps the most demanding and least appreciated of careers.

Martha's spiritual descendants, for whom we should be eternally grateful, are legion. Their leadership may be hardly noticed by the church, just as it is often taken for granted in the home. The cooks, the flower arrangers, the Communion preparers, the nursery attendants—these are vital though unsung heroes and heroines in God's family. Their ministries are invaluable to the success of kingdom enterprises. God bless them every one!
—R. W. B.

II. An Act of Devotion
(John 12:1-8)

A. A Supper With Friends (vv. 1, 2)

1. Then Jesus six days before the passover came to Bethany, where Lazarus was which had been dead, whom he raised from the dead.

At this point, Jesus was headed to Jerusalem for a final confrontation with His enemies. *Six days* later, at the time of the *passover*, He would be crucified. Indeed, His primary purpose for coming to Jerusalem at this precise time was so that He might die in fulfillment of prophecy and of God's will.

Before entering Jerusalem, Jesus stopped and stayed in *Bethany*, the village where the incident in our first Scripture occurred. Sometime between that earlier visit and this one He had come to Bethany and raised Lazarus from the dead.

2. There they made him a supper; and Martha served: but Lazarus was one of them that sat at the table with him.

Jesus' friends *made him a supper*. Matthew mentions that this took place in the house of a man called Simon the leper (Matthew 26:6). Even though it was not at her house, *Martha served*. The fact that she would do this even at someone else's home seems to indicate that she was prominent in the village and among Jesus' followers. It also shows that she had a heart and a talent for serving. *Lazarus* and Mary also were present.

B. Mary's Extraordinary Act (v. 3)

3. Then took Mary a pound of ointment of spikenard, very costly, and anointed the feet of Jesus, and wiped his feet with her hair: and the house was filled with the odor of the ointment.

Since this was not her home, Mary must have come prepared with the *ointment*. The term *a pound* is rendered "about a pint" in the *New International Version*. *Spikenard* was a fragrant ointment of the highest quality, which had to be imported from northern India; thus it was *very costly*.

Whereas John states that Mary *anointed the feet of Jesus*, Matthew (Matthew 26:7) and Mark (Mark 14:3) say that Jesus' head was anointed. Evidently Mary did both, starting with His head and finishing with His feet. It was common courtesy to wash and anoint a guest's feet, but it was very unusual to use such expensive ointment. Mary then wiped Jesus' feet *with her hair*.

This extraordinary act showed Mary's genuine humility in the presence of Jesus. Her compelling desire to minister to Him and show her love for Him overrode any feelings of pride or embarrassment. The great cost of the gift did not matter to her. She did not care that all eyes were upon her as she knelt at Jesus' feet and wiped them with her hair, if she thought about that at all. What mattered to her at that moment was Jesus. Her only thought was to minister to Him and to do as much for Him as she could.

It is only when we focus on Jesus that we do extraordinary tasks for Him. If we dwell too much on the cost or the sacrifice involved with a particular act, we may become unwilling to do it. But if we remember the One to whom we offer the gift or service and what He did for us at such great cost to Himself, then we will dedicate everything we have and are to His service.

When we focus on Jesus, we do not hear or care what others say. They may call our service foolish, extravagant, or dangerous, but their opinion is irrelevant. We care only about Jesus' approval.

C. Judas's Outrage (vv. 4-6)

4, 5. Then saith one of his disciples, Judas Iscariot, Simon's son, which should betray him, Why was not this ointment sold for three hundred pence, and given to the poor?

Far from being moved by Mary's beautiful act, Judas was indignant, and railed at what he considered a blatant waste of such a valuable commodity. He estimated that the ointment was worth *three hundred pence*. This was almost a year's wages for a common laborer—a great deal of money indeed! Judas suggested a more practical use: the money should have been *given to the poor*.

6. This he said, not that he cared for the poor; but because he was a thief, and had the bag, and bare what was put therein.

With the advantage of hindsight, John shone the light of truth upon Judas's professed concern *for the poor*. He was a thief who cared nothing for the suffering of the unfortunate. His protest resulted from the thought of how much money

had slipped through his fingers when Mary used the ointment for something as foolish as anointing Jesus' feet. That he *had the bag* means that the money given to Jesus and the disciples was kept in a single bag, over which Judas was in charge. He also *bare what was put therein;* that is, he not only carried the bag, but also used its contents for his own purposes.

Judas is the subject of a future lesson (January 26), and he will be discussed in more detail there. However, we can see from this text that Judas's greed made it impossible for him to appreciate Mary's gift to the Lord. The jaundiced viewpoint of his selfish heart twisted and perverted his outlook on a beautiful gesture.

So it is with every sin that finds a home in a person's heart. The heart filled with prejudice cannot recognize the value of individuals. The heart filled with envy cannot rejoice when others are blessed. The heart filled with lust cannot appreciate beauty and innocence. Sin always twists and perverts the eyes of the mind.

D. Jesus Defends Mary (vv. 7, 8)

7. Then said Jesus, Let her alone: against the day of my burying hath she kept this.

By His words *Let her alone*, Jesus rebuked Judas and anyone else who thought Mary's actions absurd and wasteful. By defending her He gave His approval to what she had done.

Jesus then added, *Against the day of my burying hath she kept this.* He knew that His death and burial were only a few days away. With this in mind He considered Mary's anointing to be a preparation for this event. He may have meant that the Father intended the ointment to be used in this way, though it is possible that Mary herself grasped to some degree the significance of her act.

Home Daily Bible Readings

Monday, Jan. 6—Mary and Martha Send for Jesus (John 11:1-16)

Tuesday, Jan. 7—Martha Believes in the Resurrection (John 11:17-27)

Wednesday, Jan. 8—Mary Believes in Jesus' Power (John 11:28-32)

Thursday, Jan. 9—Jesus Raises Lazarus From the Dead (John 11:33-44)

Friday, Jan. 10—Jesus Anointed in Simon's Home (Mark 14:3-9)

Saturday, Jan. 11—Women Minister to Jesus' Body (Mark 15:42-47)

Sunday, Jan. 12—Be Confident in the Lord (Psalm 27:1-6)

GOOD, BETTER, BEST

"Enter to worship; depart to serve." This is often seen on church bulletins and outdoor signs. Whether worship or service is more important is not subject to debate. For the church, it is not an *either/or* option; it is a *both/and* obligation. We are commanded to worship, and we are compelled to serve.

In this lesson's texts, Martha served while Mary worshiped. Generalities, however, should not be concluded from one or two instances. It surely must not be assumed that Martha *never* worshiped, nor that Mary *never* served. Both did what seemed best to them at the time.

Jesus favored the choice of worship on these occasions. But remember the profound lesson He taught while celebrating His last Passover with His disciples? Under those particular circumstances (where feet needed washing), the Lord emphasized humble service as a key to His kingdom. After He had washed the feet of His followers, He instructed them to do likewise. We should follow Christ's example.

Occasionally we must choose, from *good* things to do, the *best* thing to do. Sometimes that will be worship, sometimes service, sometimes both—but never neither.   —R. W. B.

8. For the poor always ye have with you; but me ye have not always.

Jesus was not callous toward *the poor*. He often ministered to them and always treated them with kindness. His words indicate that poverty will exist until the end of the world, and so His disciples will always have opportunity to minister to the poor. Jesus, on the other hand, would be among His followers for only a short time. The opportunity to minister to Him (as Mary had just done) was soon to end.

Conclusion

A. Giving Jesus the Best

Mary and Martha demonstrate an important lesson: we should always give Jesus what is best. This means allowing Him to define what "best" really means.

Martha wanted to give to Jesus, and she set about to render a useful and practical service to Him by ministering to His physical needs. She did not realize that this was not a priority item. What Jesus wanted most was Martha herself. He would have been delighted for her to sit at His feet too. This was not an either/or situation; Martha could have addressed both the physical and the spiritual concerns. Perhaps after Jesus' rebuke she did take time to sit down with Him.

visual for
lesson 7

Have you chosen the better way?

We must learn to give Jesus that which He knows is best and most important for us to give. True, we must give Him our money and our physical labors. But in addition to these, and even before these, we must give Him ourselves. We must spend time with Him—not just time working for Him. Because items such as prayer, worship, and Bible study usually do not yield the tangible, visible results that actual *work* seems to do, it is easy to become careless about these matters. We must remember that *one thing is needful*, as Jesus taught.

When Mary wanted to give Jesus a gift, she gave Him the very best that she had. This was a unique situation, but it demonstrates that we must not give the Lord our leftovers. In the Old Testament, the Israelites were taught to bring burnt offerings to the Lord that were "without blemish" (Leviticus 1:3, 10). The prophet Malachi rebuked God's people for bringing inferior offerings to Him: "Ye brought that which was torn, and the lame, and the sick; thus ye brought an offering: should I accept this of your hand? saith the Lord" (Malachi 1:13).

David expressed his degree of commitment to the Lord in these words: "I will not sacrifice to the Lord my God burnt offerings that cost me nothing" (2 Samuel 24:24, *New International Version*). When we give a gift that truly costs us something, and do it joyfully, then we have given an acceptable gift. We have performed an act of true devotion.

B. Let Us Pray

Father above, help us to give our best to You. As we spend time in worship and in prayer, increase our faith and understanding. When we labor for You, help us do it with a cheerful heart even when we grow weary. Accept our gifts. In the name of Your perfect Gift, Amen.

C. Thought to Remember

The best gift we can give to the Lord is ourselves.

Learning by Doing

This page contains an alternate lesson plan emphasizing learning activities. Classes desiring such student involvement will find these suggestions helpful.

Learning Goals

As students participate in today's class session, they should:

1. Compare the gifts of Mary with the service of Martha and the criticism of Judas.

2. Suggest principles for acceptable service.

3. Get involved in a ministry, or evaluate their participation in a current ministry, so that they pursue what is best.

Into the Lesson

Before class, write the following words on the chalkboard or on poster board: *fuel, lubrication, spark plugs, tires.* When class begins, ask, "Which of these is most important for operating an automobile? Why?" In your discussion, observe that while each item is essential, timing is usually what makes one item more important than the others. When the tank is nearly empty, fuel is most important; when the tires are poorly inflated, they receive priority.

Sometimes we compare ministries in the church. We may have a tendency to believe that what *we* do for the Lord is especially important. We may even believe *our* gift is more important than another's. We need to see that each gift is important. When we do that, we can better appreciate each other's service and more humbly evaluate our own.

Into the Word

Ask the class to form two groups. Ask one group to study Luke 10:38-42. As the group examines the passage, the following questions should be answered:

1. What was Martha's gift to Jesus on this occasion?

2. What was Mary's gift to Jesus?

3. What was Martha's complaint?

4. Had Martha realized that Mary had chosen "that good part," what would she have done?

The second group is to study John 12:1-8 and answer the following questions:

1. What was Martha's gift to Jesus on this occasion?

2. What was Mary's gift?

3. What was Judas's complaint?

4. Why did Jesus disagree with Judas?

5. If Mary had sold the ointment, bought a cheaper anointing oil to use, and given the remainder of the sale price to the poor, would that have been an acceptable gift? Why or why not? What if she had kept the balance for herself (she still gave more than anyone else)? Would that have been acceptable? Why or why not?

Allow about ten minutes for the two groups to work, then ask for reports from each group. Discuss the last question from each group in the larger group: What should Martha have done—sit with Jesus or serve with joy? Why? What about Mary's gift: could she have given less and still have been commended? Why or why not?

Into Life

Mary gave herself completely to Jesus. She did not miss an opportunity to hear the words of eternal life (John 6:68) from His lips. She gave no less than her best—and all of it—in anointing Him.

How can we give our best? To consider this with the class, distribute the following list of "complaints." Ask each student to suggest how he or she would answer each complaint in light of today's Scriptures.

1. I work in the church nursery during every Sunday school session. None of the other mothers ever helps out; they just go to class every week and enjoy themselves. I'm tired of it!

2. Why should we give all the money we got from the Hendersons' estate to missions? Don't the elders know there are things we need right here? Our kitchen looks like it was designed in the fifties! Let's get it up to date!

3. Every time we have a work night at church, just a few of us show up. Where are the elders and deacons? Where is the preacher? If the leaders won't participate, why should we?

As you discuss each situation, list some general principles about service that can form a set of guidelines for acceptable service. Write these on the chalkboard or on poster board.

Ask the students to call out the names of ministries in which they participate. Write these down. Note the variety of ministries represented just by the people in your class. Say something about the importance of each one to the overall work of the church. Observe how people can follow the principles on the chalkboard as they participate in these ministries. Challenge class members to get involved in a ministry if they are not already, and to follow the principles for acceptable service if they are.

Let's Talk It Over

The questions on this page are designed to encourage review of the lesson Scriptures and to promote discussion of the lesson by the class. The answers provided are only discussion starters. Let your class talk it over from there.

1. How can we let Jesus know that He is welcome in our homes?

We can let Jesus know He is welcome in our homes by making them places where He would want to be and where He would feel comfortable. This means that the conversation around the dinner table would be the kind He would like to hear and in which He could participate. We would not be ashamed to have Him read the magazines in our homes. The television shows we would be watching are the kind He could watch without being offended. He would not be grieved by the way we talk to other family members or by the vocabulary we use. We could take Him along to the places we go for entertainment and recreation.

Jesus stands at the door of our homes and our hearts and knocks. But He will not force His way in. He will not enter unless He is invited.

2. Martha wanted Jesus to tell Mary to get to work and stop loafing. Do we ever feel this way about members of our church who may not be doing their "fair share"?

Perhaps we are tempted to be critical of those in our congregation who do not appear to be shouldering their part of the responsibilities. How many do we feel are wasting their time on items that are not important?

Before we start making a list, we should pause a moment to consider that people are different. Not everyone has the same skills. Some work well with their hands; some are good with people; others are artistic and creative. The people we criticize may be serving Jesus in ways that are appropriate for their temperaments, talents, aptitudes, and personalities. In fact, Jesus may want to talk to us about our critical attitude, just as He wanted to speak to Martha.

3. Mary literally sat at Jesus' feet to learn from Him. How may we sit at Jesus' feet today?

We sit at Jesus' feet when we have personal devotions—when we make time to read and study the Bible, and then meditate on what the Word says. We sit at Jesus' feet when we pray—when we talk to Him, praise Him, tell Him how much we love Him, and bring Him our burdens and requests. We sit at Jesus' feet when we listen to a sermon or a Sunday school lesson that increases our understanding of the Scripture and challenges us to apply it. We sit at Jesus' feet when we worship Him with other believers in Christian fellowship.

4. Why are we usually more willing to spend time working for Jesus than listening to and learning from Him?

Most Christians find service personally fulfilling and rewarding. Also, service makes us feel we are doing something to help others. We may be reluctant to sacrifice that positive feeling to engage in what often seems like a passive or unproductive exercise.

However, if we fail to sit at the feet of Jesus to worship Him and learn from Him, we will not be adequately equipped to be involved in Christian service. Our good deeds will amount to no more than a "resounding gong or a clanging cymbal" (1 Corinthians 13:1, *New International Version*).

5. What can we do to show Jesus our devotion?

Throughout history, there have been a variety of methods to express religious devotion. Some have been extreme, such as total isolation from the world, self-mutilation, and vows of celibacy. In most cases, these were attempts to substitute acts of devotion for genuine, heartfelt devotion. The act of devotion that Jesus desires most is the sacrifice of ourselves (Romans 12:1). This means a heart filled with love for Him and a life devoted to living by His teachings.

6. What can we do if others criticize our acts of devotion?

Sometimes criticism is motivated by jealousy, sometimes by greed, and sometimes by a desire to stir up trouble. If our acts of devotion are criticized, we should do what Mary did: just keep on expressing our love for Jesus. There will always be those who criticize. His approval is what we need to be concerned about, not the nit-picking of those who sit on the sidelines and refuse to get involved themselves. Being criticized by others should also make us more careful to avoid being critical ourselves and more willing to support, encourage, and defend those who are criticized.

Peter

DEVOTIONAL READING: Luke 22:54-62.

LESSON SCRIPTURE: Matthew 4:18-20; 16:13-23.

PRINTED TEXT: Matthew 4:18-20; 16:13-23.

Matthew 4:18-20

18 And Jesus, walking by the sea of Galilee, saw two brethren, Simon called Peter, and Andrew his brother, casting a net into the sea: for they were fishers.

19 And he saith unto them, Follow me, and I will make you fishers of men.

20 And they straightway left their nets, and followed him.

Matthew 16:13-23

13 When Jesus came into the coasts of Caesarea Philippi, he asked his disciples, saying, Whom do men say that I, the Son of man, am?

14 And they said, Some say that thou art John the Baptist; some, Elijah; and others, Jeremiah, or one of the prophets.

15 He saith unto them, But whom say ye that I am?

16 And Simon Peter answered and said, Thou art the Christ, the Son of the living God.

17 And Jesus answered and said unto him,

Blessed art thou, Simon Barjona: for flesh and blood hath not revealed it unto thee, but my Father which is in heaven.

18 And I say also unto thee, That thou art Peter, and upon this rock I will build my church; and the gates of hell shall not prevail against it.

19 And I will give unto thee the keys of the kingdom of heaven: and whatsoever thou shalt bind on earth shall be bound in heaven; and whatsoever thou shalt loose on earth shall be loosed in heaven.

20 Then charged he his disciples that they should tell no man that he was Jesus the Christ.

21 From that time forth began Jesus to show unto his disciples, how that he must go unto Jerusalem, and suffer many things of the elders and chief priests and scribes, and be killed, and be raised again the third day.

22 Then Peter took him, and began to rebuke him, saying, Be it far from thee, Lord: this shall not be unto thee.

23 But he turned, and said unto Peter, Get thee behind me, Satan: thou art an offence unto me: for thou savorest not the things that be of God, but those that be of men.

Jan 19

GOLDEN TEXT: Simon Peter answered and said, Thou art the Christ, the Son of the living God.—Matthew 16:16.

New Testament Personalities
Unit 2: Persons in Jesus' Ministry
(Lessons 6-9)

Lesson Aims

At the conclusion of the lesson the students should:

1. Be able to explain ways in which Jesus "sculpted" Peter to prepare him to be a leader in the church.

2. Express what their personal belief in Jesus as God's Son means.

3. Submit themselves to be "sculpted" for the Lord's service.

Lesson Outline

INTRODUCTION
    A. The Master Sculptor
    B. Lesson Background
I. A FISHER OF MEN (Matthew 4:18-20)
    What's Your Line?
II. KEEPER OF THE KEYS OF THE KINGDOM
    (Matthew 16:13-23)
    A. Peter's Good Confession (vv. 13-17)
    B. The Keys of the Kingdom (vv. 18, 19)
    C. A Stinging Rebuke (vv. 20-23)
    Caring Yet Tough
CONCLUSION
    A. Masterful Sculptures
    B. Let Us Pray
    C. Thought to Remember

The visual for Lesson 8 in the visuals packet (see page 181) calls attention to the "rock" on which the church is built: "Thou art the Christ."

Introduction

A. The Master Sculptor

Michelangelo was one of the greatest artists of all time. Though he lived and worked more than four centuries ago, his creations still inspire us with their beauty and power. Two of his most famous works are sculptures. One, known as the Pieta, depicts Mary holding Jesus' lifeless body in her arms after He was taken down from the cross. Another is a figure of king David, whose perfect physique stands tall and proud. Both of these pieces are so lifelike that they look as if the real people have been turned into marble.

Like all other sculptures, these two works began only as large blocks of stone. In his mind's eye Michelangelo saw Mary, Jesus, and David in the stone. Carefully he chiseled and polished until only the magnificent figures remained.

When Jesus first met Peter, Peter strongly resembled one of the large blocks of stone with which Michelangelo began. But Jesus, like Michelangelo, was able to see what this rock of a man could become. Slowly, patiently, masterfully, Jesus chiseled and polished Peter until he became the great leader and apostle of the early church.

Michelangelo worked with stone and canvas to produce masterpieces. Jesus worked with people to produce His masterpieces. He continues to work on hearts and lives today to transform individuals into creations of beauty and strength.

B. Lesson Background

Today's lesson text consists of two selections from the Gospel of Matthew. The first records Jesus' call to Peter to become a full-time follower and disciple. Peter had met Jesus earlier, thanks to his brother Andrew (John 1:40-42), and perhaps had had the opportunity to listen to Him teach and watch Him perform miracles. Now, however, Jesus was calling Peter to leave his life as a fisherman, never to return to it again. This event took place rather early in Jesus' public ministry.

The second portion records an event that happened as much as two years later in Jesus' ministry, after the disciples had walked with Him for many months. The Lord asked them whom they believed Him to be. Peter, speaking for the group, declared that they believed Jesus to be the Christ, the Son of God. We call this Peter's Good Confession.

I. A Fisher of Men
(Matthew 4:18-20)

18. And Jesus, walking by the sea of Galilee, saw two brethren, Simon called Peter, and Andrew his brother, casting a net into the sea: for they were fishers.

We have noted in the Lesson Background that Jesus was already familiar with these *two brethren*. *Simon* was *called Peter*. While Jesus had given him the name of Cephas (John 1:42), which is an Aramaic word meaning "rock," he became known by the more familiar Greek name of Peter, which has the same meaning. We shall see, in the second portion of our lesson text, why the name Peter became so significant.

19. And he saith unto them, Follow me, and I will make you fishers of men.

How to Say It

ARAMAIC. Air-uh-*may*-ick.

AUGUSTUS. Aw-*gust*-us.

CAESAREA PHILIPPI. Sess-uh-*ree*-uh Fuh-*lip*-pie or *Fil*-uh-pie.

CAPERNAUM. Kuh-*purr*-nee-um.

CEPHAS. *See*-fus.

HADES. *Hay*-deez.

MICHELANGELO. *Mike*-uh-*lan*-jell-owe (strong accent on *lan*).

PANIUM. *Pan*-e-um.

PETRA (Greek). *peh*-trah.

PETROS (Greek). *peh*-tross.

Follow me was a call to a life-changing commitment. Peter and some of the other disciples had accompanied Jesus on other occasions before this (at the wedding in Cana, for example, according to John 2:1, 2). They may even have been with Him for several days at a time, but they always went back home and back to their work. Now, Jesus was inviting them to make a complete break with their old lives. He was asking them to leave their business, their home, and their family to follow Him.

For now, Jesus told the two brothers that He would make them *fishers of men.* This figure is easily understood, yet challenging to apply. Peter and Andrew knew about fishing. They knew it involved hard work, long hours, uncertain results, and even danger. It would be the same for a fisher of men. McGarvey explains the elements of the figure in this way: "Disciples are fishers, human souls are fish, the world is the sea, the gospel is the net, and eternal life is the shore whither the catch is drawn" (*Fourfold Gospel,* p. 162).

20. And they straightway left their nets, and followed him.

Peter and Andrew did not hesitate, but *straightway* (immediately) *left their nets.* They had seen and heard enough of Jesus to convince them that He was from God and that following Him was the most important decision they could make.

WHAT'S YOUR LINE?

The TV game show, "What's My Line?" was popular for several years during the '50s and '60s. A panel of celebrities would question guests who had odd or unlikely occupations. In those days, it was unusual for a woman to be employed in a typically male job. So, the "line" of a female guest would be a police officer, sewer cleaner, company executive, or other pro-

fession generally associated with men. Men who were featured sometimes held typically female positions, or rather strange jobs, such as snake charming, dog walking, or stunt skydiving. The television viewers of that era found the show fascinating and entertaining.

Most of us still find consideration of different job options interesting, especially if we are not content with our current employment. Surveys reveal that a sobering percentage of today's workers are dissatisfied with their jobs. Only a fortunate few work at something truly fulfilling. All the coffee breaks, profit sharing, and other perks in the world will not suffice if you are unhappy with what you do to earn a living.

Peter may have liked his fishing career, but it did not take long for him to leave the nets behind when Christ called. He changed abruptly from fisherman to fisher of men and subsequently found true fulfillment.

Jesus still calls all of us to some "line" of personal ministry. Some heed the call to full-time Christian service, but all disciples, no matter how they earn their living, can be fishers of men.

—R. W. B.

II. Keeper of the Keys of the Kingdom (Matthew 16:13-23)

A. Peter's Good Confession
(vv. 13-17)

13. When Jesus came into the coasts of Caesarea Philippi, he asked his disciples, saying, Whom do men say that I, the Son of man, am?

At this time the disciples had been with Jesus for about two years. They had traveled the length of Palestine with Him. Now Jesus led them to *Caesarea Philippi,* which was to the extreme north, about twenty-five miles north of the Sea of Galilee. He appears to have led them to where the crowds would be less likely to interrupt, so that He could have some privacy with the disciples. They did not enter into the city itself, at least not at once, but remained in the *coasts,* or general vicinity.

The history behind Caesarea Philippi is noteworthy, given what was about to occur there. The city was very ancient and for centuries was called Panium, because it was a center of worship for the Greek god Pan. A son of Herod the Great, named Philip, rebuilt the city and renamed it in honor of the Roman emperor and himself. It then became a center of worship for Caesar Augustus (mentioned in Luke 2:1). Thus, in a place where pagan worship had become the accepted practice, Jesus challenged His disciples to consider the crucial question of His identity.

14. And they said, Some say that thou art John the Baptist; some, Elijah; and others, Jeremiah, or one of the prophets.

The apostles had heard many speculations about Jesus' identity. The general populace seemed confused and uncertain. Many guessed that Jesus was *John the Baptist* returning from the dead after being beheaded by Herod, or that He was *Elijah*, *Jeremiah*, or another of the *prophets* who had come back to life. Of course, all these conjectures were wrong, but they show that the common people regarded Jesus as someone sent by God and on a par with the greatest prophets.

15. He saith unto them, But whom say ye that I am?

Whom say ye that I am? Jesus next asked the disciples to express their own convictions about His identity. Did they share the popular ideas or did they have greater faith? More than anyone else, the disciples had had ample opportunities to observe Jesus and form an accurate idea as to who He was.

16. And Simon Peter answered and said, Thou art the Christ, the Son of the living God.

Although Jesus addressed the whole group, *Simon Peter answered.* In typical fashion he spoke out first: *Thou art the Christ. Christ,* or *Messiah,* is a title that was given to the individual who was expected to fulfill the Old Testament prophecies of a coming Deliverer and King. The word means "anointed." The Old Testament records the anointing of prophets, priests, and kings when they were installed into office. Jesus came to fill all three of these positions.

Peter went on to state his belief that Jesus was *the Son of the living God.* This meant that Peter considered Jesus to be more than a mere human; He was divine. This was a dramatic confession. The Jews did not expect the Messiah to be God Himself coming to deliver them, but Peter and the others had heard and seen enough of Jesus to reach this radical but correct conclusion. *The living God* means the true, active, personal God of creation as opposed to the false gods and dead idols worshiped by the heathen. When one considers the pagan background of Caesarea Philippi (noted under verse 13), Peter's confession of Jesus stands out even more distinctly.

17. And Jesus answered and said unto him, Blessed art thou, Simon Barjona: for flesh and blood hath not revealed it unto thee, but my Father which is in heaven.

Simon Barjona was Peter's original name (meaning Simon, son of Jonah). *Blessed art thou* expressed Jesus' approval of what Peter had just affirmed. Although he had answered Jesus'

question correctly, Peter did not understand all the implications of his words, as verse 22 will indicate.

Flesh and blood hath not revealed it unto thee. Peter had not learned this spiritual truth through human wisdom or agency, but from the *Father which is in heaven.* This does not mean that Peter had suddenly and miraculously been given the answer to Jesus' question as soon as He asked it. More likely Jesus meant that God had revealed Jesus' identity and nature through His words and miracles. Other men and women had experienced much of what Peter and the other disciples had seen and heard, yet they did not believe as Peter did.

B. The Keys of the Kingdom
(vv. 18, 19)

18. And I say also unto thee, That thou art Peter, and upon this rock I will build my church; and the gates of hell shall not prevail against it.

The meaning of the name *Peter* ("rock") was discussed earlier. In the Greek text this word is masculine (spelled *petros*), and describes a small piece of rock (something like a pebble). The word used in the phrase *upon this rock* is feminine (spelled *petra*) and describes a large boulder or a mass of rock such as that found at the cliffs along the seacoast. Although some have proposed that Peter was to become the rock on which the church would be built, it appears that Jesus was making a play on words which, in effect, made the very opposite point. We might paraphrase Jesus' words in this way: "You're a small rock, Peter, but upon the greater rock that you have confessed, the truth of who I am, I will build my church."

This verse, the first reference in the New Testament containing the word *church*, tells us much about this unique institution. Jesus' church is like no other kingdom because He, God's Anointed and chosen One, indeed God's own Son, is its founder and Lord. If this were not true, His kingdom would not survive. Because it is true, His kingdom has grown throughout the world and will continue into eternity.

The phrase *gates of hell* is more accurately rendered, according to the Greek text, *gates of Hades.* Hades refers to the realm of death and the dead, not to the place of eternal punishment. Hebrews 2:14, 15 describes the devil as having held the power of death at one time. Jesus, by virtue of His death and resurrection, took control of death. He now holds the "keys of death and Hades" (Revelation 1:18, *New International Version*).

Jesus' words in this verse pictures two kingdoms locked in fierce combat. His promise was that the gates of Satan's kingdom *shall not prevail* against the kingdom of Heaven. Jesus' words portray the church as on the offensive, attacking Satan's domain, much as He Himself attacked and shattered the gates of the devil's kingdom, opening the way for sinners to return to the family and fellowship of God. The Lord's soldiers plunder Satan's kingdom every time a person is led to believe in Jesus and accept Him as Lord and Savior.

19. And I will give unto thee the keys of the kingdom of heaven: and whatsoever thou shalt bind on earth shall be bound in heaven; and whatsoever thou shalt loose on earth shall be loosed in heaven.

Jesus now stated that He would give Peter, as the leader of the disciples, *the keys of the kingdom of heaven*. Peter used the "key" of the gospel message to open the doors of the kingdom to the Jews on the Day of Pentecost when he preached the first gospel sermon (Acts 2:14-39). Several years later he used the same key when he opened the kingdom to the Gentiles by preaching to Cornelius and his household (Acts 10:34-48).

Whatsoever thou shalt bind on earth shall be bound in heaven. *Bind* and *loose* refer to the acts of establishing and revoking the commandments and ordinances of Jesus' kingdom. We must not think that Peter and the other apostles had the authority to make up any rules they wanted, and that these would then be approved in Heaven. Rather, as spokesmen filled with and inspired by the Holy Spirit, they proclaimed what the Lord had established as binding upon His followers.

C. A Stinging Rebuke (vv. 20-23)

20. Then charged he his disciples that they should tell no man that he was Jesus the Christ.

For the time being it was sufficient that only *his disciples* know that Jesus was *the Christ*. They needed to hear this explicitly affirmed by Jesus Himself, so that He could proceed to explain His mission to them. Jesus did not want the crowds to be told just yet, and so he *charged*, or strictly instructed, the disciples *that they should tell no man*. The disciples were to have a hard enough time understanding what Jesus would tell them (as we shall see shortly); the multitudes would not understand at all.

21. From that time forth began Jesus to show unto his disciples, how that he must go unto Jerusalem, and suffer many things of the elders and chief priests and scribes, and be killed, and be raised again the third day.

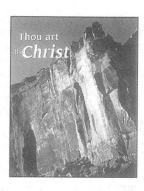

visual for
lesson 8

Up to this time Jesus had worked to convince the disciples to believe in Him and trust Him. Peter, representing the group, had just expressed their faith. *From that time forth*, Jesus began to tell them about coming events that would threaten to shatter that belief and trust. Although Jesus would *be killed* at the hands of the ruthless, jealous leaders of the Jews, He would *be raised again*.

22. Then Peter took him, and began to rebuke him, saying, Be it far from thee, Lord: this shall not be unto thee.

Peter took him implies that Peter took Jesus aside. The very thought of Jesus suffering and dying was so shocking, so incomprehensible, so abhorrent to the disciples that they recoiled from it in horror and disbelief.

Boldly Peter *began to rebuke him*. In doing so, Peter clearly overstepped his bounds. He may have been emboldened by Jesus' earlier praise, but now he was leaving his place as a disciple and presuming to instruct his Master. Peter's plea, *Be it far from thee, Lord*, revealed how far he himself was from the Father's will. It is clear that he did not grasp the full meaning of his earlier "confession."

23. But he turned, and said unto Peter, Get thee behind me, Satan: thou art an offense unto me: for thou savorest not the things that be of God, but those that be of men.

Get thee behind me, Satan. Peter was not literally Satan, or possessed by Satan, but his words certainly reflected the interests of Satan. In the wilderness, Satan had tempted Jesus to avoid the path of suffering; now Peter was offering the same temptation. In speaking out of turn and trying to dictate to the Master, Peter had become *an offense*. This was because he did not "savor" or have proper respect for *the things that be of God*. Most Jews thought of the Messianic kingdom as one that would cast off Roman rule and reestablish the glorious era of David and Solomon. These were only the speculations *of men*; they did not reflect the plans *of God*.

At this point, Peter surely had much upon which to reflect. Jesus had verified that He was indeed the Messiah. What joy and excitement! He then promised that Peter would have an important place in the work of His kingdom. What an honor and a privilege! Then came a stinging rebuke. What hurt and humiliation! Clearly, Jesus had not yet completed His chiseling and shaping of Peter.

CARING YET TOUGH

"Tough love" is recommended for parents, spouses, teachers, and others who want to demonstrate genuine concern for the objects of their affection. It means caring enough for people that you will confront them with their unacceptable words or behavior, that you will clearly communicate your disagreements with them, that you will discipline them when appropriate, and that you will intervene when they engage in self-destructive activities.

Tough love always affirms with positive reinforcement when possible, but never sidesteps confrontation when conflict occurs. A child gains a sense of security when parents both praise and punish appropriately. Neither abuse nor permissiveness produces wholesome attitudes and behavior. Tough love balances actions and reactions for the total good of any relationship.

Peter's emotions must have soared when he was pronounced "blessed" by Jesus (Matthew 16:17-19). They plummeted just as quickly when, moments later, he was strongly reprimanded by Jesus (v. 23). Yet Jesus loved Peter—unconditionally. He praised him when his thinking and speaking demonstrated maturity. He rebuked him when his attitude and counsel were carnal and offensive. Jesus' love is a tough love, and He still chastens those whom He loves (Revelation 3:19).   —R. W. B.

Conclusion

A. Masterful Sculptures

Michelangelo did not go to the quarry to sculpt. First the piece of marble was cut loose from the ground so that it could be fashioned. Then the great artist could begin the work of chiseling away the unwanted stone until only the final sculpture remained.

In a similar way, when Jesus called Peter to leave his home and job to follow Him, He cut the disciple loose so that He could begin the work of sculpting him. If Peter had been unwilling to leave the comfort, familiarity, and security of his surroundings, he could not have been shaped by Jesus into the great leader of the apostles. But Peter was willing, and so day by day Jesus worked to sculpt him. He chiseled away false ideas and improper attitudes. He cut away Peter's pride. He taught Peter to bring himself under control. He gave him responsibilities. He encouraged him. He rebuked Peter when he wandered "out of bounds" and tried to dictate, rather than defer, to Jesus. Some of Peter's training and teaching must have been exhilarating, while some of it was surely excruciating.

In the end, when Jesus was finished with Peter, he was a masterpiece. The great apostle was strong and courageous. He was a true leader. He was a rock.

Peter is not the Lord's only masterpiece. Through the centuries He has sculpted multitudes of men and women into spiritual works of art, and He continues to do so today. The process is the same as with Peter. Jesus cannot begin to sculpt and shape us until we leave the world behind and place ourselves in His hands. Then He begins the work of cutting off destructive beliefs and attitudes, sinful habits, selfishness, pride, and similar defects until He has shaped us into His own glorious image.

May all of us submit consciously and deliberately to the sculpting of the Master's hands.

B. Let Us Pray

Dear Father, we place ourselves in Your hands to do with as You wish. Shape us and change us into what You would have us to be even if the process is painful. Make us instruments to be used in Your service. Perfect the image of Your Son in us. Amen.

C. Thought to Remember

If we submit ourselves to His hands, God will fashion us into individual masterpieces.

Home Daily Bible Readings

Monday, Jan. 13—The Calling of Simon Peter (Mark 1:14-18)

Tuesday, Jan. 14—Peter's Pentecost Sermon (Acts 2:14-21)

Wednesday, Jan. 15—Peter Confirms Jesus' Resurrection (Acts 2:22-36)

Thursday, Jan. 16—Peter Works Two Miracles (Acts 9:32-42)

Friday, Jan. 17—Peter's Vision of Food (Acts 10:9-16)

Saturday, Jan. 18—Peter Visits Cornelius (Acts 10:23-33)

Sunday, Jan. 19—Peter's Sermon to Cornelius (Acts 10:34-43)

Learning by Doing

This page contains an alternate lesson plan emphasizing learning activities.
Classes desiring such student involvement will find these suggestions helpful.

Learning Goals

As students participate in today's class session, they should:

1. Describe the qualities that make someone a good leader.

2. Find examples of these qualities in the life of Peter.

3. Commit themselves to becoming better followers of Jesus Christ in one specific area of their lives.

Into the Lesson

Before class, write the following open-ended sentence on a chalkboard or on poster board before your students arrive:

The kind of leader I am most willing to follow is . . .

Note: if you usually have your classroom arranged in small groups—in circles or around tables—this activity may be more effective if you print this phrase on a card and place it in the middle of the table or give it to someone in the circle of chairs. This way each group can begin sharing ideas without needing to turn toward a chalkboard.

If your class is not arranged so that the students are in small groups, ask them to get together in groups of two or three and make a list of the qualities of a good leader.

After a few minutes, ask the class members to share their thoughts about what the qualities of a good leader should be while you record them on the chalkboard or on poster board. When you have finished recording most of the responses, make the transition into the Bible study by saying: "Today we are going to take a close look at the life of Peter, a leader in the early church, to see what we can learn about the process of becoming a leader."

Into the Word

Ask the class to use the chart in the student book to study specific examples from the life of Peter that demonstrate his qualities of leadership. As your students participate in this Bible study, keep track of any qualities of leadership that they find in the life of Peter, which correspond to those listed in the earlier activity. (It may be easiest to put a check mark next to them as they are mentioned.)

If your students do not have access to a student book, a smaller version of that chart appears below. You may want to make one copy for each group, or simply assign a different passage of Scripture to several people in the class and conduct the activity as one large group.

Scripture Reference	Quality Demonstrated
Matthew 4:18-20	
Matthew 14:22-33	
John 13:3-9	
John 20:1-9	
Acts 3:1-7	
Acts 8:14-25	
Acts 10:25-29	
Acts 15:6-11	

After completing the Scripture study, draw your students' attention to Matthew 16:23-25. Ask them if they think it is possible to be a good leader without first being a good follower. Spend some time discussing their responses. Encourage them to refer to the events from Peter's life, recorded in the above Scriptures, for examples of Peter's submission to his Lord. Point out that Peter became a good leader only as he learned to become a good follower of Jesus.

Perhaps the priority of following Jesus comes through most clearly in verse 23, where Jesus responds to Peter's demand that He lay aside all thoughts of suffering and dying. Ask, "What did Jesus mean by, 'Get thee behind me, Satan'?" Point out that Peter needed to get *behind* Jesus, where a follower should be. It was not his place (nor is it ours) to try to go in front of Jesus and show Him the way.

Into Life

Provide a small piece of paper for each member of the class. Ask them to think of one area of their lives that needs to be submitted to the leadership of Jesus. Point out that even though we may have confessed Jesus with our words (as Peter did in Matthew 16:16), we must also confirm this Lordship by continually submitting ourselves to Him in our thoughts and actions.

Close the session by asking the members of the class to pray for one another in small groups. Ask them to pray specifically for the need of each member of the group to yield all aspects of his life continually to the leadership of Jesus.

Let's Talk It Over

The questions on this page are designed to encourage review of the lesson Scriptures and to promote discussion of the lesson by the class. The answers provided are only discussion starters. Let your class talk it over from there.

1. What bait should fishers of men use?

"Bait" may sound a bit crude, but as fishers of men there are certain lures we can use to entice sinners into the gospel "net." Jesus Himself is the most effective lure. When Jesus is presented in all His compassion, power, and glory, sinners will be drawn to Him (John 12:32).

Becoming a follower of Christ identifies us with a cause and a purpose bigger than ourselves and beyond ourselves. For many sincere adults, this carries a strong appeal. The hope of Heaven is another lure. This can be especially effective with elderly people or people who suffer in this life. Sometimes a more negative approach works. The threat of Hell can cause some people to think seriously about the kind of life they are living. They are then prepared to understand that Christ came to save them from such a destination.

2. What qualities of a good fisherman can make us good fishers of men?

The noted Bible commentator William Barclay suggests six of those qualities:

(a) *Patience.* Fishermen never wade into the water with a club. They cast a line and wait. Fishers of men can learn a lesson here. We should not drive people away through undue pressure.

(b) *Perseverance.* Patience and perseverance go together. Even if there is no success, we keep trying.

(c) *Courage.* While fishing isn't a dangerous activity, there are certain risks. A sudden storm can come up, as it often did on the Sea of Galilee (Mark 4:37). As fishers of men, we face risks too. Our witness may be rejected. The people to whom we witness may be hostile and belligerent.

(d) *Alertness.* Good fishermen have an eye for the right moment. Christian educators call this the "teachable moment"—the time when a person is most receptive to the gospel.

(e) *Perceptiveness.* Fishermen use different lures for different fish and different conditions. We need to be perceptive enough to see what approach and appeal will work best.

(f) *Humility.* Boisterous, gaudy fishermen drive the fish away. As wise fishers of men we must exalt Christ, not ourselves.

3. Why are some people unwilling to accept Jesus as who He really is?

One possible reason is intellectual snobbery. They may claim that it is not intellectually sophisticated to believe in a divine/human miracle worker who says He is able to forgive sins. Fear is another possible factor. Some may feel that if they accept Jesus as who He really is, this decision will force them to make some drastic changes in their lives. Still another reason is unbelief. Sin darkens minds and hardens hearts to the truth. As a result, some people would rather believe an enslaving lie than the liberating truth.

4. Why is what we think of Jesus so important?

We act on what we believe. No matter what we claim to believe or say we believe, our actions reflect our belief system.

If we think that Jesus was an impostor, we will want nothing to do with Him. If we think He was a misguided zealot, we will simply write Him off as another of history's tragedies. If we think He was a good and just man, we may respect and admire Him, but we will stop short of putting our faith and trust in Him.

In his defense before the Sanhedrin, Peter put the matter bluntly: "There is none other name under heaven given among men, whereby we must be saved" (Acts 4:12). If we believe this, we will offer Jesus our total allegiance, for there is no other means of salvation open to us.

5. How can we become Satan's tool without even knowing it?

The word Satan means "adversary." We become Christ's adversary by doing or saying anything that sets human desires and interests above God's desires and interests. This was the reason Jesus rebuked Peter (Matthew 16:23).

Satan is extremely wily. He may not tempt us to become his active helpers, but he knows that if he can get us to look at issues solely from a human perspective rather than from God's will, we will actually be helping him. On the other hand, we may be quite correct concerning a certain issue. If in the process we demonstrate a haughty or divisive spirit, we are again employing one of Satan's techniques.

Judas Iscariot

DEVOTIONAL READING: Matthew 27:1-10.

LESSON SCRIPTURE: Matthew 26:14-16, 20-25, 47-50; 27:1-5.

PRINTED TEXT: Matthew 26:14-16, 20-25, 47-50; 27:1-5.

Matthew 26:14-16, 20-25, 47-50

14 Then one of the twelve, called Judas Iscariot, went unto the chief priests,

15 And said unto them, What will ye give me, and I will deliver him unto you? And they covenanted with him for thirty pieces of silver.

16 And from that time he sought opportunity to betray him.

. . . .

20 Now when the even was come, he sat down with the twelve.

21 And as they did eat, he said, Verily I say unto you, that one of you shall betray me.

22 And they were exceeding sorrowful, and began every one of them to say unto him, Lord, is it I?

23 And he answered and said, He that dippeth his hand with me in the dish, the same shall betray me.

24 The Son of man goeth as it is written of him: but woe unto that man by whom the Son of man is betrayed! it had been good for that man if he had not been born.

25 Then Judas, which betrayed him, answered and said, Master, is it I? He said unto him, Thou hast said.

. . . .

47 And while he yet spake, lo, Judas, one of the twelve, came, and with him a great multitude with swords and staves, from the chief priests and elders of the people.

48 Now he that betrayed him gave them a sign, saying, Whomsoever I shall kiss, that same is he; hold him fast.

49 And forthwith he came to Jesus, and said, Hail, Master; and kissed him.

50 And Jesus said unto him, Friend, wherefore art thou come? Then came they, and laid hands on Jesus, and took him.

Matthew 27:1-5

1 When the morning was come, all the chief priests and elders of the people took counsel against Jesus to put him to death:

2 And when they had bound him, they led him away, and delivered him to Pontius Pilate the governor.

3 Then Judas, which had betrayed him, when he saw that he was condemned, repented himself, and brought again the thirty pieces of silver to the chief priests and elders,

4 Saying, I have sinned in that I have betrayed the innocent blood. And they said, What is that to us? see thou to that.

5 And he cast down the pieces of silver in the temple, and departed, and went and hanged himself.

Jan 26

GOLDEN TEXT: Judas, which betrayed him, answered and said, Master, is it I? He said unto him, Thou hast said.—Matthew 26:25.

New Testament Personalities
Unit 2: Persons In Jesus' Ministry
(Lessons 6-9)

Lesson Aims

At the conclusion of this lesson the students should:

1. Understand the primary factors that led to Judas's act of betrayal.

2. Examine their own hearts and lives to detect any sins or doubts that might lead them to turn away from Jesus.

Lesson Outline

INTRODUCTION
    A. What Went Wrong?
    B. Did Judas Have a Choice?
    C. Lesson Background
I. JUDAS'S HEINOUS PLOT (Matthew 26:14-16, 20-25, 47-50)
    A. The Plot Conceived (vv. 14-16)
        Is Your Price Right?
    B. The Plot Exposed (vv. 20-25)
    C. The Plot Executed (vv. 47-50)
II. JUDAS'S WRETCHED END (Matthew 27:1-5)
    Sorry Is Not Enough
CONCLUSION
    A. What Might Have Been
    B. Let Us Pray
    C. Thought to Remember

Today's visual for Lesson 9 focuses on the question that each disciple asked of Jesus in the upper room: "Lord, is it I?" It is shown on page 189.

Introduction

A. What Went Wrong?

How often people have wondered, "What went wrong?" when it appeared that everything should have gone right! The passengers on the Titanic surely wondered what went wrong with the great "unsinkable" ship, causing it to plummet to the bottom of the ocean. During the "crash" of 1929, Wall Street investors asked themselves what went wrong with the stock market, causing their fortunes to disappear overnight.

More puzzling than these examples is the question of what goes wrong when people who have an abundance of advantages become failures and prodigals, wasting their own lives and shattering the lives of others. Many parents, even good Christian parents, have agonized over the tragedy of a wayward child.

Today's lesson concerns Judas—a sobering example of someone who seemed to possess the ultimate advantage and still went wrong. We wonder how anyone who had walked for so long as a close friend of Jesus could betray Him.

It is important for us to understand what occurred in Judas's case and why so many choose the same path today. Such tragedies as his are possible because all people have freedom of will—the freedom to make their own choices for good or for evil. A chain of wrong choices will lead to disaster, and in some cases the impact of that disaster is experienced during a person's earthly life. Even the most mature Christian must not let down his guard for a moment, lest he find himself asking, "What went wrong?"

B. Did Judas Have a Choice?

Some may ask, "Did Judas really have a choice? Was he little more than a puppet on a string?" We must address this issue before proceeding to the lesson text. Among the numerous Messianic prophecies in the Old Testament was the prediction that Jesus would be betrayed. Zechariah prophesied the amount of thirty pieces of silver and added that this sum would be given to the potter (11:12, 13). Long before it even entered Judas's heart to do so, Jesus knew that Judas would betray Him and called him a devil, though without naming him explicitly (John 6:64, 70, 71). According to today's lesson text, Jesus revealed to Judas that He knew what he intended to do (Matthew 26:25). But knowing what a person will do is not the same as causing him to do it.

It is probable that Judas was not always a betrayer. We assume that when Jesus chose the twelve, Judas possessed a faith, zeal, and trust that was similar to that of the other disciples. However, as soon as Jesus chose these men, Satan began to look for ways to destroy them. He attacked them all by appealing to their pride, fear, lust for power, and greed. In one case, that of Judas Iscariot, he succeeded.

Some may ask why Jesus did not choose someone else who would have been spiritually stronger than Judas. It does not appear to be God's policy to prevent us from sinning by keeping us from tempting situations, even when He knows that we will fall. Though He promises not to allow us to be tempted to the point that we have no chance of resisting (1 Corinthians 10:13), the Lord still requires us to make our own choices, and we all sometimes fail. Step by step, through his own choices, Judas came to the terrible decision to betray his Master.

At the same time, God's sovereignty should not be overlooked. He knew in advance that Judas would become a traitor, and inspired His prophets to record some of the details of the betrayal. Jesus was fully aware that He would be betrayed. These facts tell us that God was not surprised, nor were His plans thwarted or altered by Judas's actions (see John 13:18, 19). Jesus' eventual arrest and crucifixion were part of the "determinate counsel and foreknowledge of God" (Acts 2:23).

C. Lesson Background

Today's lesson text covers four events in the life of Judas. They all occurred during the last few days before Jesus' death. Matthew indicates that soon after Jesus rebuked Judas for criticizing Mary's "wasteful" use of expensive perfume to anoint Him (see lesson 7), Judas went to the chief priests and plotted to betray Jesus. This is recorded in the first section of our printed text.

The second portion of text relates an event that took place in the upper room when Jesus ate the Passover with the disciples on the night He was betrayed. There Jesus revealed to Judas that He knew what he was plotting to do. The third passage records the actual betrayal, which took place later that same night in the Garden of Gethsemane.

The final portion of the lesson text tells of Judas's remorse and suicide. This happened on the morning of the day on which Jesus was crucified.

I. Judas's Heinous Plot
(Matthew 26:14-16, 20-25, 47-50)

A. The Plot Conceived (vv. 14-16)

14. Then one of the twelve, called Judas Iscariot, went unto the chief priests.

The word *then* follows the incident of Mary's anointing of Jesus in the home of Simon the leper (vv. 1-13). This occurred "six days before the passover" (John 12:1) and the day before the triumphal entry (John 12:12)—thus, on the Saturday prior to the beginning of Jesus' final week. Jesus had reprimanded the disciples for their criticism of Mary's act. John's Gospel specifically mentions Judas as the source of the criticism (John 12:4, 5).

Judas Iscariot was chosen as *one of the twelve* at the same time as the other eleven apostles (Matthew 10:2-4). The name *Iscariot* means "man of Kerioth," which probably referred to his hometown (a town by this name was located in southern Judah). Like the others, Judas was

---

How to Say It

GETHSEMANE. Geth-*sem*-uh-nee (*G* as in *get*).
ISCARIOT. Iss-*care*-e-ut.
KERIOTH. *Care*-e-awth.
TIBERIUS. Tie-*beer*-ee-us.

---

commissioned to preach the arrival of the kingdom of Heaven. He was given power to heal the sick, raise the dead, cleanse lepers, and drive out demons (Matthew 10:7, 8).

It is impossible for us to know exactly what happened in Judas's heart to change him from one of the loyal twelve to a betrayer. Students have made many suggestions, including disillusionment with Jesus when He did not set up an earthly kingdom as Judas might have expected. Others believe that Judas may have been attempting to "force the hand" of Jesus. In other words, by putting Jesus in a life-threatening situation, Judas may have hoped that Jesus would move with more urgency to establish His kingdom. It is quite clear, from Judas's response to Mary's anointing of Jesus, and from John's additional comment about Judas's thievery (John 12:6), that he was a man often driven by selfishness and greed. Perhaps Judas's dissatisfaction with Jesus had been building for some time prior to that point; the incident with Mary was the proverbial "last straw."

From the standpoint of the *chief priests*, Judas's timing could not have been better. It should be noted that we cannot be certain when Judas approached the chief priests with his scheme, whether late on the Saturday after the anointing by Mary, or after Jesus' last day of teaching (probably Tuesday of the final week). During this day of teaching, the priests and their cohorts had tried to embarrass Jesus in public through a series of supposedly "hard" questions. Instead, on each occasion Jesus had given an answer that left His critics silenced and the multitudes even more enthralled with Him.

It became apparent to the chief priests that they and their companions would succeed in arresting Jesus only "by subtilty" (Matthew 26:4). When one of Jesus' own followers approached them with an offer, they must have been quite surprised, but pleased nonetheless.

15. And said unto them, What will ye give me, and I will deliver him unto you? And they covenanted with him for thirty pieces of silver.

Thirty pieces of silver was not a great amount of money; it was the approximate price of a slave. Greedy though he was, Judas betrayed the

Lord for a pittance. One wonders to what degree anger, resentment, or even hatred motivated Judas's action. Jesus' enemies surely would have paid much more than this to be rid of their nemesis.

16. And from that time he sought opportunity to betray him.

The cold-blooded nature of the plot is evident in this verse. Judas began a diligent search for a way to *betray* Jesus into the hands of the chief priests.

IS YOUR PRICE RIGHT?

From time to time, we are provided with new evidence that our world is becoming increasingly warped and weird. For example, a survey was conducted among people representing a cultural cross section of the American public. Respondents were asked to select from a list of possible answers to the question, "What would you do for $100,000?" The reported results were sobering, even frightening. Several women indicated that they would become prostitutes for a day. Some parents answered that they would put their children up for adoption. A few participants even said they would kill a stranger for $100,000!

Cynical criminal types in movie and TV dramas often say, "Everyone has his price; what's yours?" Are they right? Will people really do anything for money? If that is the rule, then Judas was certainly no exception. Apparently his relationship with Jesus had become (or possibly always was) superficial and hypocritical. He actually sold out to the enemies of the Lord for a few coins—the equivalent of the price of a slave.

Does your love for and loyalty to Christ carry a price tag? Sometimes professed disciples sell Him out for far less than Judas's blood money. Nominal Christians have betrayed the Lord for as little as a few moments of carnal pleasure, a few winks of sleep on Sunday morning, or a part of a tithe withheld for personal use.

No price is right when one is trying to bargain over eternal matters. In fact, it is futile to do so. "What shall a man give in exchange for his soul?" (Matthew 16:26).   —R. W. B.

B. The Plot Exposed (vv. 20-25)

20. Now when the even was come, he sat down with the twelve.

The even was the evening of the Passover, during which Jesus was betrayed and arrested. The location was in the upper room that Jesus had told Peter and John to prepare (Luke 22:8). All of *the twelve* were present, including Judas, who no doubt realized that here was an opportu-

nity to carry out the agreement he had made with the priests. His problem was finding an opportunity to slip away and inform them of Jesus' location.

21. And as they did eat, he said, Verily I say unto you, that one of you shall betray me.

The disciples had been shocked on other occasions when Jesus spoke about dying or being killed (as in Matthew 16:21, 22). Now came the almost unbelievable news that one of them would be the instrument in making this happen. The atmosphere must have been extremely tense.

22. And they were exceeding sorrowful, and began every one of them to say unto him, Lord, is it I?

Exceeding sorrowful describes the disciples' reaction to Jesus' announcement. It is noteworthy that rather than suspecting each other, each wondered if he would do this unthinkable deed: *Lord, is it I?*

23. And he answered and said, He that dippeth his hand with me in the dish, the same shall betray me.

This was the fulfillment of a prophecy in Psalm 41:9. John, who gives a more detailed account of this portion of the meal, adds that Jesus took some bread ("sop"), dipped it in the dish (which usually contained a sauce or gravy), and handed it to Judas (John 13:25, 26).

To dip one's *hand* in a *dish* with another was an act symbolizing the closeness of friendship that existed between the two individuals. This was part of the heinous nature of Judas's betrayal of Christ. It is reflected in the somber words of Psalm 41:9: "Yea, mine own familiar friend, in whom I trusted, which did eat of my bread, hath lifted up his heel against me." John notes that immediately after this gesture of friendship, "Satan entered" into Judas (John 13:27).

24. The Son of man goeth as it is written of him: but woe unto that man by whom the Son of man is betrayed! it had been good for that man if he had not been born.

The Son of man goeth as it is written of him. The events of this last week were not a series of accidents or coincidences. Neither Judas nor the chief priests were in control of the outcome. Jesus' sacrificial death was predicted throughout the Old Testament, even though the Jews did not recognize it at the time. One purpose of the Gospel of Matthew was to point out many of the ways in which Jesus fulfilled prophecy, in order to demonstrate to the Jews that He was indeed the Messiah.

Although Jesus' death on the cross fulfilled God's plan for mankind's salvation, this did not excuse Judas from responsibility for his actions.

Jesus still pronounced *woe unto that man by whom the Son of man is betrayed.* Perhaps Jesus' sobering words served as one last warning to the betrayer of the severity of what he had chosen to do.

25. Then Judas, which betrayed him, answered and said, Master, is it I? He said unto him, Thou hast said.

Judas, who knew full well that he was the guilty party, must have been reluctant to ask the fateful question, *Is it I?* But the others had, and he no doubt felt compelled to ask it as well and to continue his pretense. Jesus, however, knew exactly what Judas was doing. *Thou hast said* was actually an emphatic way of saying, "Yes! It is you!" or "You said it!"

This was Judas's last chance. Before him stood the most important decision of his life. Knowing now that Jesus was aware of his scheme, Judas could have fallen down at the Lord's knees and confessed. Instead, he brazenly hardened his heart one final and fateful time. Now there was no turning back.

C. The Plot Executed (vv. 47-50)

47. And while he yet spake, lo, Judas, one of the twelve, came, and with him a great multitude with swords and staves, from the chief priests and elders of the people.

The setting has now shifted to the Garden of Gethsemane. Jesus had just returned from praying for the third time and found Peter, James, and John asleep. Shortly thereafter, *Judas* entered the garden with *a great multitude with swords and staves.* Jesus' enemies were taking no chances. They did not know what Jesus might do, and they could not be certain what kind of resistance they might encounter.

48. Now he that betrayed him gave them a sign, saying, Whomsoever I shall kiss, that same is he; hold him fast.

The *kiss* was another act of despicable hypocrisy, similar to Judas's dipping his hand in the dish with Jesus. Judas's kiss identified Jesus for the soldiers, who may not have known Him by sight. Fearful that He might escape, they wanted quick and positive identification.

49. And forthwith he came to Jesus, and said, Hail, Master; and kissed him.

Forthwith (quickly) Judas consummated his betrayal. To say *Hail, Master* was yet another hypocritical gesture. Judas had rejected all that Jesus was, all that He taught, and all that He represented. Judas had submitted to the control of another master.

50. And Jesus said unto him, Friend, wherefore art thou come? Then came they, and laid hands on Jesus, and took him.

visual for
lesson 9

"Lord, is it I?"

Only the Son of God could have addressed Judas in such a kind manner as *Friend. Wherefore art thou come?* means, "Why are you doing this, Judas?" Luke's account indicates that Jesus knew full well Judas's intent: "Judas, betrayest thou the Son of man with a kiss?" (Luke 22:48).

The soldiers then *laid hands on Jesus, and took him.* Judas apparently had succeeded. The other disciples, who had earlier pledged unswerving loyalty to Jesus, fled in panic (Matthew 26:56).

II. Judas's Wretched End
(Matthew 27:1-5)

1, 2. When the morning was come, all the chief priests and elders of the people took counsel against Jesus to put him to death: and when they had bound him, they led him away, and delivered him to Pontius Pilate the governor.

By *morning* the Jewish leaders had begun to implement their plan to kill Jesus. They could not do this without Roman approval (John 18:31), so they took Jesus to *Pontius Pilate the governor.*

3. Then Judas, which had betrayed him, when he saw that he was condemned, repented himself, and brought again the thirty pieces of silver to the chief priests and elders.

It is hard to imagine what else Judas thought would happen, except that Jesus would be *condemned.* He knew that the chief priests were seeking to kill Jesus. Nonetheless, when Jesus' condemnation became evident, *Judas repented himself.* Perhaps some spark of the love and faith that had once moved him to follow Jesus was rekindled. Perhaps he realized that in his desire to "make something happen," he had become merely a pawn in the hands of the Jewish leaders. At any rate, Judas was filled with an overwhelming sense of guilt. His repentance was not the kind that moves a person to reform his life, such as when one becomes a Christian. This repentance was the remorse and grief that arise from the pangs of a guilty conscience. Its end is self-loathing and self-destruction.

To seek to relieve his guilt, Judas *brought again the thirty pieces of silver*. That which Judas formerly had coveted so much now became utterly detestable to him.

4. Saying, I have sinned in that I have betrayed the innocent blood. And they said, What is that to us? see thou to that.

Finally, Judas acknowledged his wrongdoing: *I have sinned*. He saw his treacherous act for what it was. He also saw himself as he really was. On the other hand, the chief priests felt no such remorse. They had gotten what they needed out of Judas and had no more use for him. The betrayer himself had been betrayed.

5. And he cast down the pieces of silver in the temple, and departed, and went and hanged himself.

Judas could not undo what he had done. In utter blackness of soul, he *went and hanged himself*. He could not live with his guilt and remorse. Thus ends one of the world's greatest tragedies.

SORRY IS NOT ENOUGH

In one episode of the once-popular TV series, *The Waltons*, John Walton was running for the public office of county supervisor. He left his son Ben in charge of operations at the family sawmill. Ben and a helper took the opportunity to bid on a large lumber contract for a new residential development, still pending approval by the county commissioners. This, of course, posed a conflict of interests for John, and seemed to compromise his personal integrity.

When father confronted son with the dilemma, the dialogue was heated. John Walton was disappointed, frustrated, and angry. Ben was contrite and said, "I'm sorry, Daddy." But the conflict was not that easily resolved. John's fiery retort was: "*Sorry* is not enough, Ben. You have made me and our family look bad. You have disgraced our name in the community. This kind of reputation doesn't go away quickly."

Judas wanted desperately to undo his deed. Though "seized with remorse" (Matthew 27:3, *New International Version*), his attempt to reverse the outcome of his betrayal was unsuccessful. Sometimes *sorry* is not enough. Even the "godly sorrow" that leads to repentance and forgiveness can leave lasting temporal damage. Not every consequence of human error can be fixed.

All sins literally have "Hell to pay," but in some cases a portion of that Hell is experienced in this life. —R. W. B.

Conclusion
A. What Might Have Been

The renowned poet John Greenleaf Whittier wrote, "For of all sad words of tongue or pen, The saddest are these: 'It might have been.'"

This was certainly true in Judas's case. His life might have been—indeed should have been—so much different. Yet Judas is only one of millions who have chosen to follow the road to destruction and ruin. To avoid a similar path, we must heed the admonition of Scripture: "Keep thy heart with all diligence; for out of it are the issues of life" (Proverbs 4:23). All of us must take a serious look at our lives on a regular basis to see if any sin is finding (or has the potential to find) a permanent home in our lives. If so, we must do whatever it takes to eliminate that sin before it controls us. Jesus even spoke of a person gouging out an eye or cutting off a hand rather than continuing to subject himself to a temptation that he cannot resist (Matthew 5:29, 30).

May each of us resolve to live each day making the choices that Jesus would have us make. Then we will have no regrets about our conduct and no laments over "what might have been."

B. Let Us Pray

Dear Father, we tremble to think of Judas's destruction. We tremble even more when we realize that each of us could follow in his path. Help us to discern the sins in our hearts and to cast them out with Your help. Refine and increase our faith. Help us to accept Your discipline. In Jesus' name, amen.

C. Thought to Remember

Destruction is only a few steps away from each of us.

Home Daily Bible Readings

Learning by Doing

This page contains an alternate lesson plan emphasizing learning activities.
Classes desiring such student involvement will find these suggestions helpful.

Learning Goals

As students participate in today's class session, they should:

1. Identify several characteristics that can create barriers between ourselves and others (including God).

2. Identify the characteristics in Judas's life that hardened his heart and finally led him to betray Jesus.

3. Examine their own lives to see if any of these barriers exist and ask God for help in removing them.

Into the Lesson

As your class session begins, ask half of the students to work together to make a list of the characteristics of a trustworthy friend, based on their experiences. Ask the other half of the class to create a list of the characteristics of an untrustworthy friend.

If you have a large class, you will want to create several groups so that each one is small enough to allow everyone an opportunity to participate. If your class is small, you will need only two groups. Allow the groups several minutes to complete this activity so that they have time to tell some of their personal experiences with friendships (either good or bad).

When the groups have had enough time to create their lists, ask each group to share its list of characteristics with the entire class. Have someone record the responses on a chalkboard or on poster board. When each group has had an opportunity to add to the list, ask the class members to explain why they feel some of these characteristics might make someone either trustworthy or untrustworthy.

Make your transition into the Bible study portion of the lesson by explaining that even Jesus had at least one friend who did not prove to be trustworthy.

Into the Word

For the first Bible study activity, you will need three groups to work independently. If your class is not too large, you may complete this portion of the Bible study as one large group. Assign each group the Scripture passage(s) listed below (or, if the entire class is working on this together, ask someone to read each passage so that everyone can hear).

Group One: Matthew 26:6-16
Group Two: John 12:1-6
Group Three: Mark 14:10; Luke 22:47, 48

Ask each group to identify at least one characteristic in Judas, based upon the passage(s) it was assigned, that would make him untrustworthy. Your students may suggest several characteristics; however, they should notice at least the following:

Group One: Greed
Group Two: Hypocrisy and Dishonesty
Group Three: Treachery

After discussing the character of Judas, point out that we know Judas as "Judas Iscariot." Ask the class if anyone knows the meaning of the word "Iscariot." If no one knows (or no one has a study Bible or other reference that might provide the answer), point out that the term means "the man from Kerioth." Most likely this refers to a town located in southern Judah. This would make Judas the only non-Galilean disciple. Ask the class, "Do you think being an 'outsider' made it easier for Judas to distance himself from Jesus and the others until he ultimately betrayed Him? Do you think being 'different' might explain his behavior?"

Into Life

Point out that there are many objects and attitudes in each of our lives that can make us untrustworthy friends, building barriers rather than bridges between ourselves and others. Likewise there are objects and attitudes that can become barriers to fellowship with our Father in Heaven. Each of these has the potential to harden our hearts slowly, until we reach the point where we have betrayed the One who gave His all for us.

Ask your students to use the illustration that is given in the student book to write names on some of the "stones" that have become barriers in their lives. (If you do not have access to a student book, draw an illustration of a wall made of stones large enough that your students can write single words in them, such as greed, jealousy, pride, etc. Photocopy the illustration and have copies ready to distribute during this activity.)

Close the class session in prayer that our hearts might be softened and that we might remove some of the stones from our walls.

Let's Talk It Over

The questions on this page are designed to encourage review of the lesson Scriptures and to promote discussion of the lesson by the class. The answers provided are only discussion starters. Let your class talk it over from there.

1. When God sees that we are heading for disaster, why doesn't He do something to stop us and prevent it?

Since God is sovereign, all-knowing, and all-powerful, He could perform a miracle every time He sees us heading for trouble, making a wrong decision, or yielding to temptation. He could protect us from every sin, error, blunder, and mistake—yet He does not.

God has given us the power to choose, and He has a healthy respect for our free will. He uses other means than miraculous intervention to influence us to decide on our own to reject the wrong and do the right. His Word, for example, contains numerous warnings about the consequences of choosing to follow sin. But we must decide to do right on our own. Anything else would make us no better than robots.

2. Why do we think we can keep our "secret" sins secret?

This is just another of Satan's tricks. One of his most persuasive arguments is, "No one will ever know."

It is true that some secret sins can be kept secret for a long time. Sometimes even those who know us best (husband, wife, family member, co-worker, close friend) have no idea of what is going on. Jesus' other disciples had no idea that Judas was dipping his hand into the group's "treasury." But even if no one else knows about our secret sins, God knows. As far as He is concerned, nothing is ever secret. Jesus said, "There is nothing covered, that shall not be revealed; neither hid, that shall not be known" (Luke 12:2). And even before our private sins become public, the results of those sins have a negative impact on our lives by polluting the wellspring of our souls.

3. Judas became a betrayer without any of the other disciples knowing about it. Do we have any responsibility to probe and monitor the spiritual lives of other members of the church? If so, how do we exercise it?

While they were at Oxford University, John and Charles Wesley were leaders of a support group for Christians, called the Holy Club. At meetings of the Holy Club, the members examined each other with penetrating and probing questions. Such questions as, "How is it with thee?" "How is it with thy soul?" and, "Dost thou have the victory?" were common.

The purpose of the questions was not to embarrass or humiliate or ridicule anyone, but to provide mutual accountability. If there was a problem, it could be confessed in a safe, non-threatening, and supportive environment of fellow believers. Then they could all pray about the problem.

Many Christians are afraid to confess a spiritual weakness or failure, because they are afraid they will be condemned or criticized. We need to provide an atmosphere where believers can talk about their spiritual problems and battles and confess their failures. Then we need to support struggling believers with prayer.

4. How might we betray Jesus without meaning to do so?

The classic betrayal model is a person intentionally doing something to harm his friend, as Judas did when he betrayed Jesus. However, there are several variations of that basic theme that apply to us. We can betray Jesus by failing to say we are Christians, because we fear the ridicule of those around us. We can betray Jesus by remaining silent when others are taking His name in vain. We can betray Jesus by saying we love and serve Him at church, but then carelessly violating His teachings during the week. We can betray Jesus by willfully and repeatedly sinning.

5. When we know we have sinned, what should we do?

We can follow the counsel given by Peter to Simon the sorcerer. This consisted of two commands: "repent" and "pray" (Acts 8:22). Repentance involves not only a confession of one's sin, but also a change of mind and a change of life. If at all possible, we also need to do what we can to right the wrong we did. This usually involves some form of restitution, which may include meeting with the person we wronged.

Judas experienced deep sorrow and regret for what he did, but that did not address his real need. He could have been forgiven if he had genuinely confessed and repented.

Barnabas

DEVOTIONAL READING: Acts 15:1-11.

LESSON SCRIPTURE: Acts 4:32-37; 9:23-31; 11:19-30.

PRINTED TEXT: Acts 4:32, 36, 37; 9:26, 27; 11:22-30.

Acts 4:32, 36, 37

32 And the multitude of them that believed were of one heart and of one soul: neither said any of them that aught of the things which he possessed was his own; but they had all things common.

. . . .

36 And Joses, who by the apostles was surnamed Barnabas, (which is, being interpreted, The son of consolation,) a Levite, and of the country of Cyprus,

37 Having land, sold it, and brought the money, and laid it at the apostles' feet.

Acts 9:26, 27

26 And when Saul was come to Jerusalem, he assayed to join himself to the disciples: but they were all afraid of him, and believed not that he was a disciple.

27 But Barnabas took him, and brought him to the apostles, and declared unto them how he had seen the Lord in the way, and that he had spoken to him, and how he had preached boldly at Damascus in the name of Jesus.

Acts 11:22-30

22 Then tidings of these things came unto the ears of the church which was in Jerusalem: and they sent forth Barnabas, that he should go as far as Antioch.

23 Who, when he came, and had seen the grace of God, was glad, and exhorted them all, that with purpose of heart they would cleave unto the Lord.

24 For he was a good man, and full of the Holy Ghost and of faith: and much people was added unto the Lord.

25 Then departed Barnabas to Tarsus, for to seek Saul:

26 And when he had found him, he brought him unto Antioch. And it came to pass, that a whole year they assembled themselves with the church, and taught much people. And the disciples were called Christians first in Antioch.

27 And in these days came prophets from Jerusalem unto Antioch.

28 And there stood up one of them named Agabus, and signified by the Spirit that there should be great dearth throughout all the world: which came to pass in the days of Claudius Caesar.

29 Then the disciples, every man according to his ability, determined to send relief unto the brethren which dwelt in Judea:

30 Which also they did, and sent it to the elders by the hands of Barnabas and Saul.

Feb 2

GOLDEN TEXT: When he came, and had seen the grace of God, [Barnabas] was glad, and exhorted them all, that with purpose of heart they would cleave unto the Lord. For he was a good man, and full of the Holy Ghost and of faith.
—Acts 11:23, 24.

New Testament Personalities
Unit 3: Persons of the
New Testament Church
(Lessons 10-13)

Lesson Aims

After this lesson, students should be able to:

1. List ways Barnabas lived up to the meaning of his name.

2. Measure Barnabas's impact on the early church.

3. List ways they can encourage others in their congregation and in other congregations.

4. Plan an act of encouragement this week.

Lesson Outline

INTRODUCTION

  A. The Power of One

  B. Lesson Background

I. ENCOURAGEMENT BY GENEROSITY (Acts 4:32, 36, 37)

  A. A Generous Church (v. 32)

  B. A Generous Individual (vv. 36, 37)

II. ENCOURAGEMENT BY SUPPORTIVE WORDS (Acts 9:26, 27)

  "A Friend in Need"

III. ENCOURAGEMENT BY TEACHING (Acts 11:22-30)

  A. Barnabas Comes to Antioch (vv. 22-24)

  B. Barnabas Brings Saul to Antioch (vv. 25, 26)

  Safety Net

  C. Barnabas Carries an Offering to Jerusalem (vv. 27-30)

CONCLUSION

  A. Encouragers Wanted

  B. Prayer

  C. Thought to Remember

Lesson 10's visual (see page 196) challenges each Christian to "be a Barnabas." Use the map for Lesson 11 to refer to sites in today's lesson.

Introduction

A. The Power of One

Perhaps you have heard the proverbial statement: "For the want of a nail, a shoe was lost; for the want of a shoe, a horse was lost; for the want of a horse, a rider was lost; for the want of a rider, a message was lost; for the want of a message, a battle was lost; for the want of a battle, a kingdom was lost; and all for the want of a nail!" Little details can make a big difference.

This applies to the Christian life as well. The above statement could be rewritten as follows: "For want of a Christian, a kind word or deed is lost; for want of a kind word or deed, an influence is lost; for want of an influence, a soul is lost; and all for the want of a Christian!" One individual firmly committed to Jesus can make a big difference.

B. Lesson Background

Throughout this quarter, we have been studying people whose lives of active faith had a significant impact. The unit we begin with today's lesson (which is also the final unit of this quarter) looks at people who made a difference in the early church through their faithful service for Christ.

The first of these individuals is Barnabas. His contribution to the early church was substantial. The three passages from Acts 4, 9, and 11 in today's lesson text all show how he provided needed encouragement at critical times in the life of the early church. As we study these examples, we should give serious consideration to how we can follow his example by being encouragers of others. This is a ministry in which every Christian can participate, Like Barnabas, every believer can make a significant difference through encouragement.

I. Encouragement by Generosity (Acts 4:32, 36, 37)

A. A Generous Church (v. 32)

32. And the multitude of them that believed were of one heart and of one soul: neither said any of them that aught of the things which he possessed was his own; but they had all things common.

Verse 31 mentions that the believers "were all filled with the Holy Ghost, and they spake the word of God with boldness." Their bold preaching was one result of the Holy Spirit's presence. Their *one heart* and *one soul* was another sign of the Spirit's influence. This oneness manifested itself in a willingness to share their possessions with those in need. These Christians did not consider *aught*, or any, of their property to be private; the needs of others were more important to them than their own.

B. A Generous Individual (vv. 36, 37)

36. And Joses, who by the apostles was surnamed Barnabas, (which is, being interpreted, The son of consolation,) a Levite, and of the country of Cyprus.

We know *Joses* (the Greek form of Joseph) by his more familiar nickname, *Barnabas,* which was given to him *by the apostles*. Barnabas is an Aramaic name meaning *son of consolation*, or "son of encouragement." *Bar* is the Aramaic word for "son," as in the name Simon Barjona (Matthew 16:17). The phrase *son of* is a Hebrew idiom often used to describe a person's character or characteristics. For example, Judas, who was the subject of last week's lesson, is referred to by Jesus as a "son of perdition" in John 17:12. This meant that Judas was a man characterized by evil thoughts, words, and actions, all of which contributed to his downfall.

Barnabas's background as a Levite meant that he would have been quite knowledgeable of the Mosaic Law. In addition, Barnabas was a Jew whose home was outside of Judea amidst the influence of Greek culture. He was *of the country of Cyprus*, a large island located in the eastern Mediterranean Sea. These ingredients in Barnabas's background helped to prepare him for the important role he would play in encouraging and aiding the spread of the gospel throughout new territories.

37. Having land, sold it, and brought the money, and laid it at the apostles' feet.

Barnabas's *having land* may seem strange, since Levites, according to the Law of Moses, were not to be landowners (Numbers 18:20-24; Deuteronomy 10:9). By this time, however, such regulations were apparently no longer recognized or enforced.

The sale of property and the giving of the money from the sale to the church was purely voluntary. As Peter told Ananias in Acts 5:4, "While it remained, was it not thine own? and after it was sold, was it not in thine own power?" At this point, the benevolent work that the church accomplished through these funds was handled primarily by the *apostles*. Acts 6 tells of how the apostles came to delegate this ministry to another group of men, so that they could give themselves more fully "to prayer, and to the ministry of the word" (Acts 6:4).

How to Say It

AGABUS. *Ag*-uh-bus.
ANTIOCH. *Ann*-tee-ock.
ARAMAIC. Air-uh-*may*-ick.
CHRESTOS. *Crest*-awss.
CHRESTUS. *Crest*-us.
CLAUDIUS. *Claw*-dee-us.
JOSEPHUS. Joe-*see*-fus.
ORONTES. Or-*ahn*-teez.
PISIDIA. Puh-*sid*-e-uh.
SUETONIUS. Soo-*toe*-nee-us.

Some have proposed that the practice of having "all things common" (Acts 4:32) was a form of communism, in agreement with the dictum pronounced by Karl Marx: "From each according to his ability; to each according to his needs." But Marx's program was to be achieved through the use of government force. The early church's giving and receiving was based upon a common devotion to Christ, who taught and modeled self-sacrifice.

II. Encouragement by Supportive Words (Acts 9:26, 27)

Another important role that Barnabas played in the early church was that of companion to Saul (later Paul).

26. And when Saul was come to Jerusalem, he assayed to join himself to the disciples: but they were all afraid of him, and believed not that he was a disciple.

This was apparently the visit to which Paul refers in Galatians 1:18. He *assayed*, or tried, to enter the fellowship of the *disciples* in Jerusalem. But Saul's role in Stephen's murder and his relentless persecution of the church (see Acts 7:57—8:3) no doubt continued to weigh heavily upon the disciples' minds, and influenced their attitude toward Saul. It is not surprising that they were quite skeptical about the news of his alleged conversion. How could they be sure he was not pretending to be one of them in order to infiltrate their ranks?

27. But Barnabas took him, and brought him to the apostles, and declared unto them how he had seen the Lord in the way, and that he had spoken to him, and how he had preached boldly at Damascus in the name of Jesus.

Barnabas courageously stood up for Saul and encouraged the *apostles* to accept him. Saul *had seen the Lord*—the same Lord whom they knew and followed. Saul had accepted their Lord as his. He was now their brother in Christ and no longer their enemy.

Later Paul wrote that he spent only fifteen days in Jerusalem (Galatians 1:18). Apparently it did not take long for opposition to Saul to become a serious threat. Sensing the danger to Saul's life, the Christians in Jerusalem arranged for him to quickly leave the city (Acts 9:29, 30). Barnabas may have come under close scrutiny from Saul's opponents as well, because of his role in giving Saul's voice an opportunity to be heard.

Although Saul returned to his hometown of Tarsus (Acts 9:30), he would not remain there. Another opportunity to serve would present itself, as our next portion of Scripture shows.

"A FRIEND IN NEED"

Shadowlands is the moving story of well-known Christian author C. S. Lewis, and his double marriage to Joy Gresham. Their first ceremony was merely a legal formality for convenience. Joy Gresham was in London on a visitor's visa, and Mr. Lewis consented to marry her so that she and her son could stay in England by virtue of Lewis's citizenship. It was an act of genuine friendship: she was a "friend in need," and he was a "friend indeed." Later, these two friends married again, this time for love and commitment, until they were separated by Joy's untimely death.

Shadowlands is a poignant love story, but it is much more than mere romance. It is the true account of a beautiful friendship that finally, and almost incidentally, was consummated in marriage. Such true and loving relationships are so rare that they become unforgettable.

Joses possessed such a capacity for brotherly love that the apostles called him by a new name —Barnabas, the "son of encouragement." When a new Christian named Saul confronted the suspicious resistance of believers in Jerusalem, Barnabas came to his defense, vouching for his integrity. Later, when Paul had retreated to Tarsus, Barnabas coaxed him back to active ministry in Antioch. Paul was a friend in need; Barnabas was a friend, both "indeed" and "in deed."   —R. W. B.

III. Encouragement by Teaching (Acts 11:22-30)

A. Barnabas Comes to Antioch (vv. 22-24)

After persecution had scattered believers out of Jerusalem (Acts 11:19), Barnabas's ministry of encouragement helped to maintain significant growth in one of the new congregations.

22. Then tidings of these things came unto the ears of the church which was in Jerusalem: and they sent forth Barnabas, that he should go as far as Antioch.

The book of Acts mentions two cities named *Antioch*, one in Syria and one in the territory of Pisidia in southern Asia Minor, where Paul preached during his first missionary journey (Acts 13:14). The Antioch in this passage was Syrian Antioch, located fifteen miles inland from the Mediterranean Sea on the left bank of the Orontes River (near the northern border of modern Lebanon). Antioch had become a very cosmopolitan city, whose population included many Jews and Gentiles. It was an appropriate setting for a new church.

visual for
lesson 10

Among the Christians who settled in Antioch were some "men of Cyprus," which was Barnabas's home, and others from Cyrene in northern Africa (Acts 11:20). These believers told their new Gentile neighbors about Jesus, and a great number of them believed (v. 21). The *Jerusalem* church then *sent forth Barnabas* to visit and inspect the new community of believers. Perhaps they chose Barnabas because of his understanding of Greek culture and his common bond with the believers from Cyprus. The primary reason, however, may have been his character. The new believers in Antioch needed encouragement in maintaining their new faith, and Barnabas was just the person to provide this.

23. Who, when he came, and had seen the grace of God, was glad, and exhorted them all, that with purpose of heart they would cleave unto the Lord.

Barnabas *exhorted* or encouraged the church in Antioch. He was gladdened to see *the grace of God* at work in Antioch, and he encouraged the church to continue to *cleave* (follow closely) *unto the Lord*.

24. For he was a good man, and full of the Holy Ghost and of faith: and much people was added unto the Lord.

This description of Barnabas parallels Luke's description of Stephen in Acts 6:5: "a man full of faith and of the Holy Ghost." The ministry of Barnabas made a recognizable difference in the growth of the new church at Antioch.

B. Barnabas Brings Saul to Antioch (vv. 25, 26)

Barnabas's encouragement of the church at Antioch was demonstrated in yet another act: he recruited Saul of Tarsus to come to Antioch and help build up the church.

25. Then departed Barnabas to Tarsus, for to seek Saul.

Tarsus, Saul's hometown, lay north and west of Antioch, less than one hundred miles by boat.

Saul had returned to Tarsus after the believers helped him escape death threats in Jerusalem (Acts 9:29, 30).

26. And when he had found him, he brought him unto Antioch. And it came to pass, that a whole year they assembled themselves with the church, and taught much people. And the disciples were called Christians first in Antioch.

The church at *Antioch* proved to be fertile ground for the teaching ministry of Barnabas and Saul. *Much people* had been added to the church (v. 24); now *much people* were being taught.

In Antioch, Barnabas and the other *disciples were called Christians*. The Christians themselves tended to use other terms, such as disciples (as in this verse), believers (Acts 5:14), brethren (Acts 6:3), beloved of God (Romans 1:7), saints (Philippians 1:1), or the faithful (Ephesians 1:1). *Christian* describes one as a follower of Christ; the title thus recognized the change that set these followers apart from nonfollowers.

The specific motive behind this new name has been the subject of much study. Some have proposed that *Christian* may actually have been a term of ridicule based upon the common slave name "Chrestos," meaning "useful." Others cite the Roman historian Suetonius who speaks of riots that broke out within the Jewish community at Rome "at the instigation of Chrestus." Suetonius may have been referring to Christ Jesus and to a disturbance that had arisen in Rome because of the preaching of the gospel.

Others believe that *Christian* was a name given by God to the followers of Jesus. They note that the Greek word translated *called* in this verse is used elsewhere in the New Testament of God's calling, warning, or speaking to someone. It is translated "warned from God" in Acts 10:22 and "admonished of God" in Hebrews 8:5. Many who hold to this view also see this new name as the fulfillment of a prophecy found in Isaiah 62:2: "And the Gentiles shall see thy righteousness, and all kings thy glory: and thou shalt be called by a new name, which the mouth of the Lord shall name." The "new name" of *Christian* would have been particularly appropriate for the believers in Antioch, where the gospel had begun to make significant inroads among Gentiles.

Regardless of the source of the term, *Christians* accurately describes the people Barnabas and Saul were teaching. Barnabas's ministry of encouragement continued to make an observable difference in the life of a congregation (Antioch) and in the life of an individual (Saul).

SAFETY NET

The National Church Growth Research Center, headquartered in Washington, D.C., has developed a program to restore "ministerial dropouts" to the pulpit. The "Safety Net," as it is named, encourages preachers who have resorted to secular work (or are about to), to reconsider their decision. The program works through a network of Barnabas-type Christian counselors across the nation, who are committed to rescuing God's servants from the deep despair that has resulted in too many quitting the cause. The Safety Net is truly a worthy ministry.

Apparently Barnabas had caught this concept, even in the first century. He threw a "safety net" beneath Saul by involving him in a congregation where his talents could be used fruitfully. Saul's call to ministry was honed and polished through the friendship and encouragement of Barnabas. Barnabas was not content just to *send* for Saul or to *invite* him to serve at Antioch; he personally went to Tarsus, sought out Saul, and brought him back. Later, these fast friends became a most effective missionary team.

The gift of encouragement is one worth developing. This can be done through prayer and practice. Speak a word, send a card, or make a call today to some Christian servant who may be discouraged. Perhaps you hold the "safety net" that could rescue a ministry. —R. W. B.

C. Barnabas Carries an Offering to Jerusalem (vv. 27-30)

Both Barnabas's character and his familiarity with the Jerusalem church made him a natural choice to undertake yet another ministry of encouragement.

27. And in these days came prophets from Jerusalem unto Antioch.

The communication between the church at Jerusalem and the church at Antioch continued in the form of *prophets* who traveled *from Jerusalem unto Antioch*. As Ephesians 4:11, 12 notes, God gifted some to be prophets for the building up of the church. These prophets were especially important at that time, because the New Testament Scriptures were not in any completed written form.

28. And there stood up one of them named Agabus, and signified by the Spirit that there should be great dearth throughout all the world: which came to pass in the days of Claudius Caesar.

The prophet *Agabus* also appears in Acts 21:10, 11, where he warned Paul of his coming arrest in Jerusalem. Here Agabus forewarned the church of an impending *dearth*, or shortage, of food. The fact that Agabus *signified* this prediction may mean that he presented some kind of visualized message, much as he did when he foretold Paul's arrest (Acts 21:11). Again, the Roman historian Suetonius reports that "a series of droughts had caused a scarcity of grain" during the reign of *Claudius*, who ruled Rome from A.D. 41 to A.D. 54. The Jewish historian Josephus refers to a famine in Judea that occurred in the year A.D. 46.

29. Then the disciples, every man according to his ability, determined to send relief unto the brethren which dwelt in Judea.

The relatively new Christians in Antioch showed that they were genuine followers of Christ by responding to Agabus's message with action. From *every man according to his ability*, *the disciples* in Antioch gave *unto the brethren which dwelt in Judea.* It is noteworthy that the first benevolent offering taken by a church was sent from a mission church to its "mother church." The Gentile-Jewish congregation at Antioch obviously felt an indebtedness to the Jerusalem church (see Paul's words in Romans 15:27).

30. Which also they did, and sent it to the elders by the hands of Barnabas and Saul.

At this point, the *elders*, not the apostles (as in Acts 4:34-37), received the money given to the Jerusalem church. Perhaps the persecution initiated by Saul had necessitated some measure of reorganization in these matters. *Barnabas*, mentioned first in this verse, appears to have led the delegation from Antioch. Involving *Saul* in taking the offering to Judea may have been another effort by Barnabas to encourage Saul's acceptance by the Jerusalem church. Again, Barnabas appears in the role of encourager for both a church and an individual.

Conclusion

A. Encouragers Wanted

Barnabas is a marvelous example of how one person can make an enormous difference. One wonders what the early church might have been like without Barnabas. The church in Jerusalem might have had a more difficult time caring for its needy members; perhaps morale among the believers would have been lower. Saul probably would have been accepted much more slowly by the Jerusalem church. The church in Antioch might not have been encouraged to grow as it did. The gospel's advancement into the Gentile world may have been hampered. Saul may not have come to Antioch. Looking beyond our lesson text, Saul and Barnabas might not have been sent out on their missionary journey.

Everyone makes some difference. Every Christian can have a significant impact on his church and on his community by following Barnabas's example.

What are some of the ministries of encouragement available to church members? Here are some suggestions: writing notes of encouragement, asking people about circumstances in their lives that need prayer, giving small gifts of food or money, sending care packages to missionaries, greeting people each Sunday, writing poetry about others, inviting others home for a meal, visiting residents in the nursing home, calling people on the phone, taking pictures of new members or of members at work for Christ, spending time with children who have no father or mother at home, and making craft items to give to people.

Every congregation has its own needs and circumstances that must be addressed, but perhaps these suggestions have given you some ideas. Like Barnabas, every believer can have a positive influence for Christ through the encouragement of others.

B. Prayer

Dear God, thank You for the many people who have encouraged us and lifted us to where we are. Thank You for the encouragement we receive from Scripture. Open our eyes to see the people around us. Open our ears to their needs and hardships. And open our hearts to opportunities to encourage them. May we, like Joses, become known as sons and daughters of encouragement. In Jesus' name we pray, amen.

C. Thought to Remember

Encourage one person every day and make a difference in the world for Jesus' sake.

Home Daily Bible Readings

Learning by Doing

This page contains an alternate lesson plan emphasizing learning activities.
Classes desiring such student involvement will find these suggestions helpful.

Learning Goals

Students in today's class should:

1. Describe how Barnabas earned his nickname, "son of encouragement."

2. Recognize the importance of being an encourager.

3. Put into practice at least one action that will make them encouragers.

Into the Lesson

Before class, write on the board, "Everyone needs encouragement." Ask the class whether they agree or disagree with this statement. Your class should reach a consensus on our common need for encouragement. Next, point out that encouragement means "to give courage, hope, or confidence." Encouraging others is one of the most dominant themes in the New Testament. It is a concept presented numerous times in the book of Acts and the epistles.

Then lead a brainstorming session during which class members create a list of encouraging acts that they have observed recently. Record the responses on the board.

Into the Word

Barnabas made a number of significant contributions to the life of the early church. In order to measure his impact, we will observe Barnabas in action, according to the record in the book of Acts. Each time we read about Barnabas, we will find him busy providing needed encouragement.

Divide the class into four smaller groups. Assign each group a section of Scripture from Acts that features Barnabas (or you can divide the Scriptures differently, depending on the size of your class). Listed below are the sections that should be studied.

Group	Scripture	Subject
1	Acts 4:32, 36, 37	Barnabas encourages the Jerusalem Church
2	Acts 9:26-28	Barnabas encourages Saul
3	Acts 11:22-30	Barnabas encourages the church at Antioch
4	Acts 15:36-41	Barnabas encourages Mark

Instruct the groups to read their Scripture texts and then discuss the following questions:

1. What did Barnabas do in this scene?

2. Why were Barnabas's actions encouraging?

3. How could we imitate Barnabas today?

Each group should appoint a reporter who will summarize the group's findings for the whole class later.

Allow approximately ten minutes for the groups to do their assignments, then have the reporter from each group summarize its group's discussion. You may want to keep track of the answers to Question 3 to suggest to students when you challenge them to put the idea of encouragement into practice.

If time permits, after the groups have completed their reports, you may want to ask the class to try and imagine the early church without Barnabas. What would have been missing? See the Conclusion to the lesson commentary on page 198 for responses to this question.

Into Life

Ask class members, "Who specifically has been a source of encouragement to you in your walk with the Lord?" Answers might include a particular Christian author, or a Christian worker whom the individual has never met. Challenge class members to think of individuals in the congregation who have been a source of inspiration or encouragement to them.

Barnabas's encouraging words and actions were very significant in the life of the early church. Like Barnabas, every Christian can have a similar impact on his or her congregation. Ask class members to consider how they can be like Barnabas this week. Challenge each student to choose at least one encouraging act learned from the life of Barnabas and put it into practice. Remind them that studies have shown that it takes approximately twenty-one days to form a habit, so they will need to repeat this act at least twenty-one times to make it a good habit. How about doing an encouraging act once a day for the next three weeks?

Close the class session with prayer for class members and their response to situations they may encounter where encouragement is needed. Pray that God will help each student to be sensitive to people's needs for encouragement in the upcoming weeks.

Let's Talk It Over

The questions on this page are designed to encourage review of the lesson Scriptures and to promote discussion of the lesson by the class. The answers provided are only discussion starters. Let your class talk it over from there.

1. Barnabas was someone who became well-known for his compassion for the needy. How can we help the homeless, the hungry, and other needy people without demeaning them or making them feel like charity cases?

Perhaps most important is the attitude we have when we give the help. A superior, condescending attitude will always be harmful and will be more likely to drive needy people away. Pity is not an appropriate attitude either. In some cases, the needy do not want our pity. They want to be treated with dignity, and as persons of worth who have suffered a temporary setback and who need a helping hand to get back on track. Respect, thoughtful attention, genuine caring, and Christian compassion—these are the keys.

2. When it comes to assisting those with material and financial needs, at what point does the church's responsibility end and the state's begin?

Caring for people with needs should be the responsibility of the family first and then the church, not the state. Many today, however, have become almost totally dependent upon government to take care of their needs. This does not relieve the church of its responsibility. There are some specific needs we can meet within the congregation and the community. Has a husband and father lost his job? Is a long-term illness putting a severe strain on a family's financial resources? Does an elderly widow on a fixed income need help with repairs to her home? Does a single mother need someone to take care of her children so she can get a job?

Beyond our own congregation are food banks and clothing distribution centers run by other churches. In addition, many communities have church-sponsored homeless facilities. Such places can always use more money and help.

3. What are the risks of accepting into the church's fellowship a person who has been a flagrant sinner but who claims to have found Christ? What are the blessings and benefits?

The greatest risk is one that may have concerned the Jerusalem church when faced with accepting Saul: that the new convert is just pretending and has his own agenda. However, since we cannot see into people's hearts, it can be argued that the risk is worth it. The other option is to reject and turn away a person because of his past history. But Jesus never did that.

While the acceptance of a new convert must be open and unconditional, it is wise to include him or her in the church's leadership and ministry programs on a gradual basis. For example, it would not be appropriate to assign such a person to teach a Sunday school class. A new Christian who was rescued from deep sin likely will be excited and will have a vivid and thrilling testimony. This can be a real plus—as long as he is not treated as a sort of "celebrity" because of his "colorful" past.

4. What do new believers need most?

New believers need love and unconditional acceptance. They need to feel that they belong and that they are part of the church fellowship. They need a friend—someone who will introduce them to other members, just as Barnabas did for Saul. They also need a mentor to give them mature guidance and instruction. Most new believers have only a hazy idea of what the Bible says, what the church teaches, and how to live as a Christian. Someone needs to familiarize them with such matters.

5. The church at Antioch was a new congregation with great potential. What are some advantages of attending a "new church"—that is, a church that has recently started operating? What are some disadvantages?

A new church is not bound to the past. No one can say, "This is the way we've always done it." Of course, that can also be a disadvantage. A new church cannot draw strength and inspiration from its history and tradition, or look with gratitude to the influence it has had in the community.

In addition, a new church does not have a reputation. Against this fact can be both a plus and a minus. On the plus side, a new church does not need to deal with any scandals caused by hypocritical members or philandering preachers. On the negative side, it cannot count on people in the community saying, "Oh, yes, I know that church well; its members are some of the most dedicated Christians I've ever seen."

Stephen

DEVOTIONAL READING: Matthew 5:43-48.

LESSON SCRIPTURE: Acts 6:1—8:3.

PRINTED TEXT: Acts 6:8-15; 7:54-60.

Acts 6:8-15

8 And Stephen, full of faith and power, did great wonders and miracles among the people.

9 Then there arose certain of the synagogue, which is called the synagogue of the Libertines, and Cyrenians, and Alexandrians, and of them of Cilicia and of Asia, disputing with Stephen.

10 And they were not able to resist the wisdom and the spirit by which he spake.

11 Then they suborned men, which said, We have heard him speak blasphemous words against Moses, and against God.

12 And they stirred up the people, and the elders, and the scribes, and came upon him, and caught him, and brought him to the council,

13 And set up false witnesses, which said, This man ceaseth not to speak blasphemous words against this holy place, and the law:

14 For we have heard him say, that this Jesus of Nazareth shall destroy this place, and shall change the customs which Moses delivered us.

15 And all that sat in the council, looking steadfastly on him, saw his face as it had been the face of an angel.

Acts 7:54-60

54 When they heard these things, they were cut to the heart, and they gnashed on him with their teeth.

55 But he, being full of the Holy Ghost, looked up steadfastly into heaven, and saw the glory of God, and Jesus standing on the right hand of God,

56 And said, Behold, I see the heavens opened, and the Son of man standing on the right hand of God.

57 Then they cried out with a loud voice, and stopped their ears, and ran upon him with one accord,

58 And cast him out of the city, and stoned him: and the witnesses laid down their clothes at a young man's feet, whose name was Saul.

59 And they stoned Stephen, calling upon God, and saying, Lord Jesus, receive my spirit.

60 And he kneeled down, and cried with a loud voice, Lord, lay not this sin to their charge. And when he had said this, he fell asleep.

Feb 9

GOLDEN TEXT: Stephen, full of faith and power, did great wonders and miracles among the people.—Acts 6:8.

New Testament Personalities
Unit 3: Persons of the New Testament Church
(Lessons 10-13)

Lesson Aims

After this lesson, students should be able to:

1. Explain the charges brought against Stephen by his opponents.

2. Summarize Stephen's defense before the Sanhedrin and why his audience reacted as it did.

3. Relate Stephen's courageous witness to the need for the courageous witness of Christians today.

Lesson Outline

INTRODUCTION

   A. The Courage to Speak Up

   B. Lesson Background

  I. COURAGE AMONG THE PEOPLE (Acts 6:8-11)

   A. Wonders and Miracles (v. 8)

   B. Wisdom in Speaking (vv. 9-11)

 II. COURAGE BEFORE THE COUNCIL (Acts 6:12-15)

   A. Stephen Arrested (v. 12)

   B. Stephen Accused (vv. 13-15)

     Hunting for Little Bears

III. COURAGE IN THE FACE OF DEATH (Acts 7:54-60)

   A. A Vicious Crowd (v. 54)

   B. Stephen's Vision (vv. 55, 56)

   C. A Vengeful Crowd (vv. 57, 58)

   D. Stephen's Victory (vv. 59, 60)

     Messianic Martyrdom

CONCLUSION

   A. Stephen's Impact and Ours

   B. Prayer

   C. Thought to Remember

Use the map for Lesson 11 in the visuals packet to locate some of the places mentioned in today's lesson. It is shown on page 204.

Introduction

A. The Courage to Speak Up

When Nikita Khrushchev was invited to the United States nearly thirty-five years ago, he gave a press conference at the Washington Press Club. The first question directed to Khrushchev was passed on to him by his interpreter: "Today you talked about the hideous rule of your predecessor, Stalin. You were one of his closest aides and colleagues during those years. What were

you doing all that time?" Khrushchev's face turned red. "Who asked that?" he roared. All five hundred reporters peered down into their notepads. "Who asked that?" he shouted again. No one spoke or moved. "That's what I was doing," Khrushchev concluded.

To do what is right when everyone around you chooses wrong demands courage. To stand up and speak up for what you believe when an angry crowd disagrees with you demands courage. It is the kind of courage that our Lord requires from those who are His witnesses. "Be not afraid of their terror, neither be troubled; but . . . be ready always to give an answer to every man that asketh you a reason of the hope that is in you" (1 Peter 3:14, 15).

Stephen courageously witnessed about Christ to a hostile crowd. He did not change his message to please his listeners, but spoke the truth with courage even though it cost him his life. His witness is a powerful example for us.

B. Lesson Background

Last Sunday we considered the pivotal role that Barnabas played in the early church as an encourager. In today's lesson we will learn about the pivotal role that Stephen played in the outreach of the church.

Jesus had told His followers, "Ye shall be witnesses unto me both in Jerusalem, and in all Judea, and in Samaria, and unto the uttermost part of the earth" (Acts 1:8). Nevertheless, during the time covered by the first seven chapters of the book of Acts, only Jews in Jerusalem had heard the good news of Jesus. Christianity was still little more than a sect within Judaism. While Jewish leaders had challenged the Christians' preaching and even had the apostles beaten (Acts 5:40), there had been no recognized break between Judaism and Christianity. Stephen boldly changed all of this.

Stephen is listed as the first of seven men chosen by the Jerusalem church to administer the distribution of food to needy widows. All of the seven were chosen because they were "men of honest report, full of the Holy Ghost and wisdom" (Acts 6:3). Stephen is especially noted as "a man full of faith and of the Holy Ghost" (v. 5). All seven men had Greek names, a factor that probably helped to reassure the Grecian widows who had been neglected (v. 1). These men took over the daily food distribution, providing more time for the apostles to engage in prayer and the ministry of the word. As a result, "the word of God increased; and the number of the disciples multiplied in Jerusalem greatly; and a great company of the priests were obedient to the faith" (Acts 6:7).

The apostles, however, were not the only ones responsible for the increase of the word of God. Although he was one of those who had been designated to oversee the ministry to the widows, Stephen certainly did his part to spread the gospel.

I. Courage Among the People
(Acts 6:8-11)

A. Wonders and Miracles (v. 8)

8. And Stephen, full of faith and power, did great wonders and miracles among the people.

The Greek text literally reads, *full of grace and power.* G. Campbell Morgan described Stephen as a man "full of sweetness and strength." Stephen's *power* was demonstrated in his ability to work *great wonders and miracles among the people.* This ability came from the laying on of the apostles' hands (see v. 6 and compare with Acts 8:18).

B. Wisdom in Speaking (vv. 9-11)

9. Then there arose certain of the synagogue, which is called the synagogue of the Libertines, and Cyrenians, and Alexandrians, and of them of Cilicia and of Asia, disputing with Stephen.

Apparently Luke was describing one *synagogue* comprised of Jews from several different countries. Since Stephen's name was Greek rather than Hebrew, it is not surprising to find him speaking to Jews whose homes or ancestors were from lands outside of Palestine. He himself may have been at one time a member of one of these synagogues.

The *Libertines* were either freed slaves or the descendants of freed slaves. The Roman general Pompey took many Jewish prisoners when he invaded Judea in 63 B.C. He released them all when he reached Rome. These Libertines may then have settled in Cyrene (in northern Africa), Alexandria (in northern Egypt), *Cilicia and Asia.* The latter two territories were provinces in Asia Minor. Cilicia was the province in which Saul's hometown of Tarsus was located; thus, he may have been a member of this particular synagogue.

10. And they were not able to resist the wisdom and the spirit by which he spake.

The Libertines' dispute with Stephen probably led to a formal public debate. Stephen's courageous witness calls to mind the assurance Jesus gave His disciples: "I will give you a mouth and wisdom, which all your adversaries shall not be able to gainsay nor resist" (Luke 21:15).

It is likely that the word *spirit* in this verse should be capitalized in order to indicate the Holy Spirit (though it could simply describe the attitude of conviction with which Stephen defended his faith). That Stephen was filled with the Holy Spirit and with power is given special emphasis (Acts 6:5, 8; 7:55). The *New International Version* reads, "They could not stand up against his wisdom or the Spirit by whom he spoke."

11. Then they suborned men, which said, We have heard him speak blasphemous words against Moses, and against God.

The word *suborned* means to persuade someone to commit perjury. The Libertines who had taken part in the debate with Stephen had no argument that could successfully answer his witness about Jesus. Therefore they recruited other men who claimed that they heard Stephen *speak blasphemous words.* The Jewish Mishnah, a collection of teachings compiled in the second century A.D., stated, "The blasphemer is not guilty until he has expressly uttered the Name." But in the first century, the charge of blasphemy was understood in a much broader sense to include any words uttered against something or someone considered holy.

II. Courage Before the Council
(Acts 6:12-15)

A. Stephen Arrested (v. 12)

12. And they stirred up the people, and the elders, and the scribes, and came upon him, and caught him, and brought him to the council.

The *people, and the elders, and the scribes* are mentioned as part of this crowd, but not the priests. This may be due in part to the fact that "a great company of the priests were obedient to the faith" (Acts 6:7). This crowd dragged Stephen before the *council,* which was called the Sanhedrin. The Sanhedrin was the highest ruling body of the Jewish nation, composed of seventy members plus the high priest, who served as its president. This was the group that had condemned Jesus to death.

How to Say It

CAESAREA. Sess-uh-*ree*-uh.
CILICIA. Suh-*lish*-e-uh.
CYRENE. Sigh-*ree*-nee.
CYRENIANS. Sigh-*ree*-nee-uns.
KHRUSHCHEV. *Kroosh*-shef.
LIBERTINES. *Lib*-er-teens.
POMPEY. *Pom*-pea.
SANHEDRIN. San-*heed*-run or *San*-heh-drun.

It is significant to note that Stephen's preaching resulted in the loss of public favor through the agitation of *the people*. The Christians had previously enjoyed such "favor with all the people" (Acts 2:47; see also 4:21; 5:13, 26).

B. Stephen Accused (vv. 13-15)

13. And set up false witnesses, which said, This man ceaseth not to speak blasphemous words against this holy place, and the law.

The Libertines used the same tactics against Stephen that the priests and council members had used against Jesus: "And the chief priests and all the council sought for witness against Jesus to put him to death; and found none. For many bare false witness against him, but their witness agreed not together" (Mark 14:55, 56). Stephen's accusers, however, appeared more united. These *false witnesses* twisted Stephen's words to make him appear to speak against *this holy place* (the temple), *and the law*.

14. For we have heard him say, that this Jesus of Nazareth shall destroy this place, and shall change the customs which Moses delivered us.

The assertion that *Jesus of Nazareth shall destroy this place* (the temple) was similar to the charge made against Jesus Himself (Mark 14:57, 58). John records Jesus' actual words: "Jesus answered and said unto them, Destroy this temple, and in three days I will raise it up. . . . But he spake of the temple of his body" (John 2:19, 21). Stephen may have quoted Jesus in order to prove Jesus' messiahship by His resurrection. Stephen may also have suggested that the Jerusalem temple was not God's true dwelling place, a point that he made quite clear in his later defense (Acts 7:48-50).

The charge that Jesus had come to *change the customs which Moses delivered* was also an instance of misinterpretation. Jesus did seek to change many of the Jewish customs that were based upon tradition, not upon Moses' teaching. The Jews, however, held these traditions in as high a regard as the Law itself.

The Jerusalem temple and the Law of Moses were the pillars of the Jewish faith. To speak about changing or destroying them was to speak against God's will. This was considered blasphemy, a capital crime.

15. And all that sat in the council, looking steadfastly on him, saw his face as it had been the face of an angel.

Saul of Tarsus was likely Luke's source for this particular detail. Perhaps the closest Biblical parallel to Stephen's *face of an angel* is Moses' face when he descended from Mount Sinai (Exodus 34:29, 30).

visual for lesson 11

HUNTING FOR LITTLE BEARS

Excusing an unproductive life on the basis of small or inadequate resources is always a temptation. "I could have accomplished that much too, if I had his money, his charisma, his good looks, etc." One of my favorite stories comes from a "Mutt and Jeff" cartoon, in which the two friends are camping by a forest in grizzly country. Mutt (the little guy) says, "Man, if I was as big as you are, I'd go into the woods, find the biggest bear in there, and kill him with my bare hands!" Jeff (the big guy) replies, "Well, there's a lot of *little bears* in there!"

Stephen's record shows a man who was respected by his peers and who experienced success in whatever he undertook. As the adage says, "Cream rises to the top." From among thousands of disciples in Jerusalem, Stephen was selected as one of only seven men to administer the first "food pantry" of the church. Shortly thereafter, we find him preaching and debating in the local synagogue. He rose from waiter to witness overnight, it seems. He performed "great wonders and miracles among the people" (Acts 6:8).

When we contrast our puny personal evangelistic efforts with Stephen's, we may be tempted to excuse ourselves on the basis of his apostolic blessing and his resulting possession of the special powers of the Holy Spirit. Truthfully, however, Stephen's biggest advantage is described by the phrase *full of faith*. Besides, we should never forget that a lot of "little bears" live in our neck of the woods. —R. W. B.

III. Courage in the Face of Death (Acts 7:54-60)

The next portion of our lesson text is preceded by Stephen's defense before the Sanhedrin (Acts 7:1-53). The contents of this address reveal Stephen's understanding of the radical difference between the Old Covenant and the New Covenant established by Jesus. As indicated in the Lesson Introduction, prior to Stephen's speech, Christianity was still considered little more than a Jewish sect. But Stephen's speech drew a clear and unmistakable "line in the sand" between Judaism and Christianity, and that is why Luke includes this message in its entirety in his record. The gospel meant the end of the system of laws and sacrifices that the Jews held dear. That they were adamant about not letting go of this system is evident from their reaction to Stephen's incisive discourse.

A. A Vicious Crowd (v. 54)

54. When they heard these things, they were cut to the heart, and they gnashed on him with their teeth.

To this point, Stephen's speech had traced God's activity on behalf of Israel. It appears that Stephen's audience interrupted his message before he had the opportunity to move forward in time and speak of Jesus. But they had heard all they could stand. The phrase *cut to the heart* indicates extreme anger and annoyance (Acts 5:33). The assembly ground their *teeth* and snarled at him like a pack of wild animals.

B. Stephen's Vision (vv. 55, 56)

55. But he, being full of the Holy Ghost, looked up steadfastly into heaven, and saw the glory of God, and Jesus standing on the right hand of God.

The *Holy Ghost* had been guiding Stephen thus far (Acts 6:5, 8), and Stephen continued to follow His leading. He *looked up* and *saw the glory of God, and Jesus standing on the right hand of God.* This confirmed Jesus' resurrection and ascension, and demonstrated that the *glory of God* was not to be associated with the temple, but with the person of Jesus.

56. And said, Behold, I see the heavens opened, and the Son of man standing on the right hand of God.

Stephen's words bring to mind the testimony of Jesus before the Sanhedrin when asked if He were the Christ: "I am: and ye shall see the Son of man sitting on the right hand of power, and coming in the clouds of heaven" (Mark 14:62). Stephen was now declaring that he agreed with these words of Jesus. Thus, he was opening himself up to the same charges of blasphemy leveled against Jesus.

That Stephen saw Jesus *standing* may be of some significance, since the words of Jesus quoted above refer to Him as *sitting*. Some propose that Jesus stood as a witness on Stephen's behalf. Because Stephen had faithfully and unashamedly confessed Christ before men, Jesus was now confessing His servant before the Father (Matthew 10:32). Others believe that Jesus was standing to greet this brave disciple, who was about to join Him in glory.

C. A Vengeful Crowd (vv. 57, 58)

57. Then they cried out with a loud voice, and stopped their ears, and ran upon him with one accord.

The Jews *stopped their ears* so that they would not hear such "blasphemy" as this. The Sanhedrin now ceased from being a court of law and turned into an enraged mob. This must have been a frightening scene.

58. And cast him out of the city, and stoned him: and the witnesses laid down their clothes at a young man's feet, whose name was Saul.

This was clearly not a civil action; it had turned into a mob reaction. Still, in accordance with Deuteronomy 17:7, the proper *witnesses* took part in Stephen's execution. Stephen was also taken *out of the city* (Leviticus 24:13, 14; Numbers 15:32-36) to be *stoned*. Roman law did not allow the Jews to execute anyone. But Pilate, the Roman governor of Judea, usually lived in Caesarea, which was nearly sixty miles from Jerusalem. The unruly mob was in no mood to go through proper channels.

In this verse, Luke introduces *Saul*, who had just heard Stephen's defense. Saul stood watching and approving of the stoning. He never forgot this scene: "And when the blood of thy martyr Stephen was shed, I also was standing by, and consenting unto his death, and kept the raiment of them that slew him" (Acts 22:20). The witnesses *laid down their clothes* at Saul's feet. This act probably involved the heavier outer garments that might have hampered the throwing of stones.

D. Stephen's Victory (vv. 59, 60)

59. And they stoned Stephen, calling upon God, and saying, Lord Jesus, receive my spirit.

In the face of death, Stephen did not recant, but continued his courageous witness. A more accurate translation of this verse might read, "And as they were stoning him, Stephen was calling out and saying, 'Lord Jesus, receive my spirit.'" This was similar to Jesus' prayer from the cross: "Father, into thy hands I commend my spirit" (Luke 23:46).

60. And he kneeled down, and cried with a loud voice, Lord, lay not this sin to their charge. And when he had said this, he fell asleep.

Stephen's *loud voice* was for the benefit of the crowd, not Jesus. He wanted them to know that he held no bitterness toward them. Like Jesus, Stephen prayed for the forgiveness of those who murdered him. Shortly thereafter, Stephen became the first Christian to die for the sake of Jesus. In one sense, Stephen lost his life; but by virtue of Jesus' resurrection, he gained it. The victory belonged to him, not to his accusers. He did not die; he simply *fell asleep*. Such language testifies to the impact of Christ's resurrection. As a hurricane is eventually "downgraded" to a tropical storm, so has death been "downgraded" to a falling asleep for all believers in Jesus.

MESSIANIC MARTYRDOM

Psychoanalysts were the first, I suppose, to coin the term *messianic complex*. It has been used to describe the obsession of certain charismatic leaders, particularly religious leaders who have assumed the speech and behavior of a Messianic figure, or who have presumed to possess His authority and power. "Father Divine," Jim Jones and David Koresh are examples.

Stephen, the first Christian martyr mentioned in Acts, spoke words as he was dying that resembled some of the words Jesus uttered from the cross. Did Stephen purposely provoke the stoning to draw attention to himself? Was he deluded as to his own identity? Did Stephen suffer from a messianic complex?

The more likely explanation is that just as Jesus quoted Scripture on the cross, Stephen quoted his Lord. He felt privileged to share the sufferings of Christ. His dying words matched the Lord's because he was spiritually linked by love and commitment to the Savior. As he honored Him in life, he desired to honor Him in death.

Paul possessed this outlook and described it in these words: "I want to know Christ and the power of his resurrection and the fellowship of sharing in his sufferings, becoming like him in his death, and so, somehow, to attain to the resurrection from the dead" (Philippians 3:10, 11, *New International Version*).   —R. W. B.

Home Daily Bible Readings

Monday, Feb. 3—Stephen Chosen to Be Deacon (Acts 6:1-8)
Tuesday, Feb. 4—Stephen's Testimony Before the High Priest (Acts 7:1-10)
Wednesday, Feb. 5—Stiff-necked People Resist the Holy Spirit (Acts 7:54-60)
Thursday, Feb. 6—Gain True Life by Enduring Persecution (Luke 21:12-19)
Friday, Feb. 7—Take Refuge in God (Psalm 57:1-11)
Saturday, Feb. 8—Pray for Those Who Persecute You (Matthew 5:43-48)
Sunday, Feb. 9—Acknowledge God Before People (Luke 12:4-12)

Conclusion
A. Stephen's Impact and Ours

Luke's purpose in including Stephen's message and death in such detail was not to satisfy interest in the first Christian martyr. Luke wanted to show Stephen's pivotal role in the development and spread of the church's witness.

Inspired by the Holy Spirit, Stephen advanced the church's understanding of how Jesus made the Law of Moses and the temple obsolete. Up to this point, not even the apostles had pressed the gospel to this conclusion. It is significant that Saul of Tarsus was present to hear Stephen's courageous testimony. In the years to come, Saul himself would take up Stephen's message and advance it even more.

Although Stephen could not have realized it, his death resulted in the expansion of the church's witness beyond Jerusalem. Following Stephen's death, Luke records that "there was a great persecution against the church . . . [believers] were all scattered abroad throughout the regions of Judea and Samaria, except the apostles" (Acts 8:1). He then adds, "Therefore they that were scattered abroad went every where preaching the word" (v. 4). In this way, Stephen helped fulfill Jesus' commission to send "witnesses . . . in all Judea and in Samaria" (Acts 1:8). What was said of Abel in Hebrews 11:4 could have been applied to Stephen: "He being dead yet speaketh."

We can see what a pivotal role Stephen played in the early church because of his courageous witness. What about us today? What courageous role does God want us to play?

Ask each class member to think of at least one person to whom he would like to witness. What message does that person need to hear? What fears or apprehensions arise when thinking about witnessing to this person? Ask your class members to pray specifically for a courageous witness to those they have in mind. Also ask them to share examples of courageous Christian witnessing that they have observed or in which they have participated. These examples will encourage you and other members of the class.

B. Prayer

Lord, when I am afraid to speak up for You, remind me of Stephen's courageous witness. Remind me that You will be with me just as You were with Stephen. Help me not to be intimidated by opponents or critics, but to be courageous in standing up and speaking up for You. Amen.

C. Thought to Remember

The Lord wants you to speak up for Him.

Learning by Doing

This page contains an alternate lesson plan emphasizing learning activities.
Classes desiring such student involvement will find these suggestions helpful.

Learning Goals

As students participate in today's class session, they should:

1. Describe what made Stephen a courageous witness.

2. Identify one situation in which they plan to be a more courageous witness for Jesus Christ.

Into the Lesson

As you begin your class session, divide the students into two groups, explaining that you will be giving each group a different assignment.

Ask members of the first group to think of a time when someone told a terrible lie about them. Ask them to share with the group what effect the lie had on them personally and on their relationships. Was the lie ever exposed? What happened? Did you ever forgive the person who told the lie? What did you tell him?

Ask those in the second group to think about someone who makes them desire to serve Christ more faithfully. Ask them to share with their group the identity of this person and what it is about him or her that causes this reaction. Allow both groups plenty of time to complete their assignments. When everyone has had an opportunity to respond, ask each group to elect someone to tell one of its stories to the class.

Ask class members how they would feel if a terrible lie was told about a person who, up to that point, had been a great example of faith to them. Would they believe it? How would they refute it? How would it hurt the church?

Make the transition into the lesson by saying that Stephen was one of the most courageous believers in the first-century church. So compelling was his testimony that the Jewish leaders found it necessary to fabricate a lie about him to try to rid themselves of his witness.

Into the Word

As you move into the Scripture text for today's lesson, use the Lesson Background in the commentary to create a mini-lecture about the events in Acts 6 and 7. Outline what we know from the Bible about the life of Stephen and why the Jewish leaders plotted to kill him. Note especially the material in the commentary under Acts 6:13, 14. Do not go into great detail; be sure that enough time is allotted for the students to complete the following activity.

Next, ask your students to divide into groups of two or three. When they have done so, ask them to use the chart in the student book to learn about the character of Stephen and to reflect on their own Christian character. If you do not have access to a student book, write the following passages on a chalkboard or on poster board, and ask each of the groups to read them to find out what "filled" Stephen's life. Then ask them to discuss within their groups which of these qualities they need most in their lives.

(Acts 6:5—full of faith; Acts 6:3, 10—full of wisdom; Acts 6:8—full of power; Acts 6:3, 5; 7:55—full of the Holy Spirit; Acts 7:55, 56—fullness of vision; Acts 7:60—fullness of love and forgiveness for his enemies.)

Into Life

Use either of the following sets of questions to apply today's study of Stephen. The final paragraph can be used to conclude the session, regardless of which set is used.

1. Tackling Tradition. Use the material in the lesson commentary (p. 204) to explain why Stephen's defense, recorded in Acts 7:1-53, caused such an angry reaction from the Sanhedrin. Stephen's words were attacking many of the traditions these men held dear. Ask, "What are some religious 'traditions' that make it difficult for people to accept the gospel? How does one cut through the misunderstandings that often accompany such traditions, without antagonizing someone?"

Ask if any of the class members had to overcome an attachment to certain traditions to come to Christ. Was it a long and difficult process? What was the most important factor in helping them make their decision?

2. Firmness Under Fire. Ask the class whether any have ever been persecuted for trying to witness for Jesus. If some have experienced ridicule, lies, or other forms of persecution, allow them to share the circumstances briefly.

Before you close, ask each class member to think of one person to whom they need to make a bold witness about Jesus, or to think of a situation in which they need to be more courageous in their witness. Then lead the class in a time of prayer in which all have the opportunity to commit themselves to be more courageous in speaking for Christ.

Let's Talk It Over

The questions on this page are designed to encourage review of the lesson Scriptures and to promote discussion of the lesson by the class. The answers provided are only discussion starters. Let your class talk it over from there.

1. Witnessing to hostile people can easily develop into a confrontation. How can we keep this from happening?

One sure way to avoid a confrontation is to avoid hostile people. Jesus said we are not to give what is sacred to "dogs" (Matthew 7:6). This may mean that we are not to witness to people who are likely to attack us or make fun of Christ.

At the same time, avoiding a confrontation may not always be possible. The gospel goes against the grain of contemporary culture and values, which is sure to make some people angry. If the choice is between confrontation and backing down, we must follow Stephen's example and speak up for Christ.

2. What are the credentials for being effective witnesses for Jesus?

The primary requirement is that witnesses for Christ must truly know Him. We can talk about and witness to only what we have personally experienced.

We must also live each day in a manner that is in harmony with our belief in Christ. In a court trial, a witness who lies or exaggerates reflects badly on the person he is trying to help. The same is true of our witness for Christ. Unreliable and untrustworthy witnesses for Christ do more harm than good. We must be authentic and genuine.

3. Why are religious debates usually angry and seldom productive?

When it comes to religion, many people are not willing to consider other views. This may be because they feel that if another view is right, they must be wrong. They do not even want to think about the possibility that they may have invested a good portion of their lives in a belief that is wrong. Others maintain that religion is a highly personal matter, and that it is absolutely no one else's business what they believe. Such a view is commonly expressed in the erroneous maxim: "We are all going to Heaven—just by different roads."

It is better to build a friendship with an individual and pray for the right opening to come, so that Jesus can be considered in an atmosphere of honest inquiry, not useless debate.

4. What motivates people to oppose God's truth?

People may oppose God's truth because it threatens their financial interests. Jesus was confronted by the Gergesenes when He sent a legion of demons into a herd of pigs (Matthew 8:28-34). Instead of rejoicing because a demon-possessed man had been set free, the townspeople were upset over the loss of their pigs. Paul ran into a similar situation in Philippi. He faced opposition when he cast a demon out of a slave girl who was being used to tell the future, thus depriving her masters of "much gain" (Acts 16:16-24).

Other people simply love sin and hate righteousness. They oppose the gospel because it tells them that their current life-style is wrong and needs to be changed.

5. Why doesn't God protect us when our witnessing exposes us to harm and danger?

The Greek word for "witness" is the source of our English word "martyr." In fact, the word is translated "martyr" in Acts 22:20 and Revelation 2:13. There is something in the very nature of being a witness that exposes the witness to risk and danger.

The government has a witness relocation program to protect its witnesses from retaliation, but God does not. He asks us to expose ourselves to ridicule and possible harm by telling the truth to those who may not want to hear it. He does not promise to protect us from all harm, but He does promise to fill our mouths with the right words.

Seeing us take the risk to speak up for Christ might be the best witness a sinner can receive. If we are willing to put our lives on the line, it proves we really believe what we say.

6. How are we able to have courage in the face of hostility and opposition?

Courage in the face of danger comes from a firm conviction that we are right and that what we are doing is God's will. Any lesser conviction will not stand up under pressure. The source of our courage is Christ Himself. As we lean on Him, He supports and encourages us. Such a view sustained Stephen as he was being martyred for his witness.

Priscilla and Aquila

DEVOTIONAL READING: 1 Thessalonians 5:12-22.

LESSON SCRIPTURE: Acts 18:1-4, 18, 19, 24-26; Romans 16:3-5a.

PRINTED TEXT: Acts 18:1-4, 18, 19, 24-26; Romans 16:3-5a.

Acts 18:1-4, 18, 19, 24-26

1 After these things Paul departed from Athens, and came to Corinth;

2 And found a certain Jew named Aquila, born in Pontus, lately come from Italy, with his wife Priscilla, (because that Claudius had commanded all Jews to depart from Rome,) and came unto them.

3 And because he was of the same craft, he abode with them, and wrought: (for by their occupation they were tentmakers.)

4 And he reasoned in the synagogue every sabbath, and persuaded the Jews and the Greeks.

. . . .

18 And Paul after this tarried there yet a good while, and then took his leave of the brethren, and sailed thence into Syria, and with him Priscilla and Aquila; having shorn his head in Cenchreae: for he had a vow.

19 And he came to Ephesus, and left them there: but he himself entered into the synagogue, and reasoned with the Jews.

. . . .

24 And a certain Jew named Apollos, born at Alexandria, an eloquent man, and mighty in the Scriptures, came to Ephesus.

25 This man was instructed in the way of the Lord; and being fervent in the spirit, he spake and taught diligently the things of the Lord, knowing only the baptism of John.

26 And he began to speak boldly in the synagogue: whom when Aquila and Priscilla had heard, they took him unto them, and expounded unto him the way of God more perfectly.

Romans 16:3-5a

3 Greet Priscilla and Aquila, my helpers in Christ Jesus:

4 Who have for my life laid down their own necks: unto whom not only I give thanks, but also all the churches of the Gentiles.

5a Likewise greet the church that is in their house.

Feb 16

GOLDEN TEXT: Greet Priscilla and Aquila, my helpers in Christ Jesus: who have for my life laid down their own necks: unto whom not only I give thanks, but also all the churches of the Gentiles.—Romans 16:3, 4.

New Testament Personalities
Unit 3: Persons of the
New Testament Church
(Lessons 10-13)

Lesson Aims

Today's lesson should seek to achieve the following goals:

1. Help married adults understand some of the advantages of serving Christ as a married team.

2. Help singles realize how Christian friendships can enhance service in the church.

3. Motivate believers to use their own homes to advance the gospel.

Lesson Outline

INTRODUCTION
    A. Faithful and Fearless
    B. Lesson Background
 I. ASSISTING PAUL (Acts 18:1-4)
    A. Arriving in Corinth (vv. 1, 2)
    B. Supporting Paul (vv. 3, 4)
      Movers and Shakers
 II. TEACHING IN EPHESUS (Acts 18:18, 19, 24-26)
    A. Beginning Again (vv. 18, 19)
    B. Instructing Apollos (vv. 24-26)
III. MINISTERING IN ROME (Romans 16:3-5a)
    A. Risking Their Necks (vv. 3, 4)
    B. Hosting a Church (v. 5a)
CONCLUSION
    A. Service and Teamwork
    B. Cooperation and Communication
    C. Courage and Hospitality
    D. Prayer
    E. Thought To Remember

The visual for Lesson 12 in the visuals packet (see page 213) challenges every Christian to use his home for Christ, as Priscilla and Aquila did.

Introduction

A. Faithful and Fearless

The early church would not have made the significant strides that it did, were it not for the willing and sacrificial spirit that characterized so many. Today's lesson focuses on how a godly couple, Priscilla and Aquila, demonstrated that same spirit. As a matter of fact, the entire book of Acts is full of accounts of how men and women of faith refused to be silenced concerning the gospel of Christ. They spoke the word without flinching, and they shared with other believers without complaining. Together these early saints "turned the world upside down" for Christ (Acts 17:6) within just a couple of decades.

B. Lesson Background

Priscilla and Aquila are mentioned (always together, never separately) six times in the New Testament (three times in Acts and three times in Paul's letters). Priscilla's name occurs first in four of the six instances—perhaps an indication of a higher social status than her husband, or of a wider reputation in the church. Aquila was originally from the Roman province of Pontus in Asia Minor, located along the southern shore of the Black Sea.

Luke, the author of the book of Acts, consistently uses Priscilla as the name of Aquila's wife. On the other hand, Paul uses the more formal name of Prisca when he refers to her in his letters. One should keep in mind that this distinction is made in the Greek text of these passages, but it is not always maintained in the English translations.

I. Assisting Paul
(Acts 18:1-4)

At this point of the record in Acts, Paul was in the middle of his second missionary journey, which had brought him into Macedonia and Achaia (territories located in modern Greece). Thus far, he had met with beating and imprisonment in Philippi (Acts 16:22-24), rioting in Thessalonica (17:5), and ridicule in Athens (17:32). His disposition is described as very distressed in Athens because of the grip that paganism seemed to have on that city (17:16).

A. Arriving in Corinth (vv. 1, 2)

1. After these things Paul departed from Athens, and came to Corinth.

The city of *Corinth* was one of the commercial giants of the Roman world. By the first century it had become a thoroughly pagan city, housing temples dedicated to such deities as Aphrodite, the Roman goddess of love. The worship of this goddess included acts of prostitution and gave rise to Corinth's reputation as a center of immorality. Making inroads in such an atmosphere would be difficult.

Paul had come to Corinth from *Athens*, where he had been deeply disturbed over the predominance of idolatry (17:16) and where some had mocked his preaching of the resurrection (17:32). It was a period in Paul's ministry when he might have become quite discouraged.

2. And found a certain Jew named Aquila, born in Pontus, lately come from Italy, with his wife Priscilla, (because that Claudius had commanded all Jews to depart from Rome,) and came unto them.

When Paul arrived in Corinth, *Priscilla* and *Aquila* were already living there. Their home had been in *Rome*, but an edict from Emperor *Claudius* had forced them to leave. This edict is mentioned by the Roman historian Suetonius in his *Life of Claudius.* He says that Claudius (who ruled A.D. 41-54) took this action because of riots in Rome that were instigated because of one "Chrestus." This name is probably a corrupted form of the name "Christ," written by a historian who knew very little about Christianity.

The edict of Claudius, dated at about A.D. 49, forced Jews to leave the city of Rome, but made no distinction between Jews and Jewish Christians. The role that Priscilla and Aquila may have played in the disturbance in Rome is unclear. Perhaps their preaching about Jesus helped spark the backlash from the Jews, which then provoked Claudius to take the drastic action that he took. At any rate, Priscilla and Aquila were forced to leave Rome and find a new home.

For the apostle Paul, the presence of Priscilla and Aquila in the city of Corinth was like an answer to prayer. The fact that he *found* this couple reminds us of the providential manner in which God works out His will in our lives and ministries. Can it be considered mere coincidence that the events driving Priscilla and Aquila from Rome occurred at just the right time to bring them to Corinth and then into contact with Paul? The Master of life knows how to bring to us the right friendships at just the right time!

B. Supporting Paul (vv. 3, 4)

3. And because he was of the same craft, he abode with them, and wrought: (for by their occupation they were tentmakers.)

Priscilla and Aquila's *occupation* was tentmaking, which usually amounted to leather working. This trade involved long hours of punching holes in cloth or leather with an awl, and then stitching the materials together to serve as awnings or tents. These could then be sold to merchants for their booths in the marketplace. Priscilla and Aquila may have rented a two-story structure in the marketplace of Corinth, using the lower level for the workshop and the upper level for living quarters.

4. And he reasoned in the synagogue every sabbath, and persuaded the Jews and the Greeks.

How to Say It

ACHAIA. Uh-*kay*-uh.
APHRODITE. Aff-roe-*dye*-tee.
APOLLOS. Uh-*pahl*-us.
AQUILA. *Ack*-will-uh.
CENCHREAE. *Sen*-kree-uh.
CLAUDIUS. *Claw*-dee-us.
EPHESUS. *Eff*-uh-sus.
GALLIO. *Gal*-lee-owe.
MACEDONIA. Mass-uh-*doe*-nee-uh.
PHILLIPI. Fuh-*lip*-pie or *Fil*-uh-pie.
PHOEBE. *Fee*-bee.
PRISCILLA. Prih-*sill*-uh.
SEPTUAGINT. Sep-*too*-ih-jent.
SUETONIUS. Soo-*toe*-nee-us.
THESSALONICA. *Thess*-uh-low-*nye*-kuh
   (strong accent on *nye*).

Though somewhat limited by his hours spent in making tents, Paul's efforts to preach the gospel of Christ continued uninterrupted. He did not fail to take every opportunity to go to the *synagogue.* True to his "manner" (see Acts 17:2), Paul focused on persuading the *Jews* that Jesus is the Christ (18:5).

Paul's presence in the synagogue also brought him into contact with *Greeks.* These were the "God-fearers"—Gentiles who had not been circumcised, but had become participants in synagogue worship and instruction (see the example of Cornelius in Acts 10:1, 2).

By offering Paul their support at a critical time, Priscilla and Aquila shared in the birth of the Corinthian congregation. When they first heard of the decree from Claudius that forced them from Rome, they could not have known how God would use this unwelcome change. But they kept their hearts open to any door the Lord might open.

MOVERS AND SHAKERS

Contemporary society is characterized by mobility. People move much more frequently than in former years. Often church directories become outdated even before they are distributed. Changes of address change constantly! Those in the business world who want to be "upwardly mobile" usually must be geographically mobile as well. A sad sequel to this story is that many Christian "movers" do not continue to be Christian "shakers."

Aquila and Priscilla led a rather nomadic life, moving from Rome to Corinth, then to Ephesus, and finally back to Rome. Through it all, the Biblical record reveals that they maintained their faith, their witness, and their service. Their support of Paul, their efforts in teaching Apollos, and their church-planting ministry in Rome all testify to their consistent commitment to Christ.

When Christians move, their first priority should be finding, or beginning, a fellowship of believers with whom to worship and serve. We are promised that if we give the kingdom of God priority, all other necessities will be supplied (Matthew 6:33). If we are to be the "salt of the earth," we must be "shakers" as well as "movers."

—R. W. B.

II. Teaching in Ephesus (Acts 18:18, 19, 24-26)

Eventually, opposition against Paul reached a fever pitch in Corinth (as it often did elsewhere). His eighteen-month ministry (Acts 18:11) came to a turning point. Jewish opponents forced Paul to account for himself before Gallio, proconsul of Achaia. Priscilla and Aquila's loyalty to the cause of Christ may have been severely tested during this time. Gallio ruled, however, that the issues raised by the Jews against Paul had nothing to do with maintaining law and order in Corinth (18:14-17).

A. Beginning Again (vv. 18, 19)

18. And Paul after this tarried there yet a good while, and then took his leave of the brethren, and sailed thence into Syria, and with him Priscilla and Aquila; having shorn his head in Cenchreae: for he had a vow.

After remaining in Corinth for a period of time not specifically stated (*yet a good while*), Paul determined to travel back to the Roman province of *Syria*. Eventually he hoped to return to Jerusalem by the time of a particular "feast" (v. 21).

Luke explains that another motivation for Paul's journey was a *vow* he had taken. As a part of this vow, Paul had his hair *shorn*, or cut in *Cenchreae*, the eastern seaport of Corinth. If this vow was a temporary version of the Nazirite vow, Paul would have thirty days after having cut his hair to go to Jerusalem and conclude the vow by offering a sacrifice in the temple, and then throwing his hair into the burnt offering. It is noteworthy that Paul saw no conflict in participating in this Jewish ceremony, though he was now a Christian.

Paul did not go alone on this return trip; he invited *Priscilla and Aquila* to go with him. For them this would mean being uprooted once more. They would have to relocate their business and establish contacts with believers all

over again. But this challenge did not prevent them from agreeing to leave with Paul.

19. And he came to Ephesus, and left them there: but he himself entered into the synagogue, and reasoned with the Jews.

Always prepared to seize new opportunities for service, Priscilla and Aquila began a ministry in *Ephesus*, the most important city of the province of Asia (located in what is today western Turkey). This commercial city was dominated by the worship of the goddess Diana (Artemis was her Greek name), and proudly displayed a temple to her, which was considered one of the seven wonders of the ancient world. The Ephesians adored Diana, which meant that evangelizing this city would not be easy.

The phrase *left them there* means that Paul parted company with Priscilla and Aquila in Ephesus, apparently ceasing his tentmaking arrangement. He began his ministry in the usual manner, by making contact with the *Jews* in the *synagogue*. Priscilla and Aquila proceeded to use their home once more to further the gospel, as 1 Corinthians 16:19 shows.

B. Instructing Apollos (vv. 24-26)

24. And a certain Jew named Apollos, born at Alexandria, an eloquent man, and mighty in the Scriptures, came to Ephesus.

Paul had already departed for Jerusalem when *Apollos* arrived in Ephesus. He was from *Alexandria*, the capital city of Egypt, and may have traveled to Ephesus for business purposes. Alexandria was a city that placed a strong emphasis on learning, and this probably helped to make Apollos *an eloquent man*. One should keep in mind that Alexandria was also the city in which the Greek translation of the Old Testament (called the Septuagint) was made. This may have contributed to Apollos's familiarity with the *Scriptures*. His skill in expounding them to shed light on the gospel of Christ became invaluable, although at this point his understanding of the Scriptures was deficient in a crucial area.

25. This man was instructed in the way of the Lord; and being fervent in the spirit, he spake and taught diligently the things of the Lord, knowing only the baptism of John.

Not only did Apollos have training in the Old Testament Scriptures, but he had also been taught certain truths of the gospel. He knew *the way of the Lord*, and he could teach many of the truths that Jesus had spoken. But his knowledge was imperfect. He did not know about baptism into the Lord Jesus or about the gift of the Holy Spirit (Acts 2:38). In this shortcoming he resembled those disciples in Ephesus whom Paul later baptized (19:1-7). Nevertheless, Apollos was devoted to proclaiming *the things of the Lord*. If only his grasp of God's plan of salvation could be improved, his presence in Ephesus would be of great value in advancing the gospel.

The phrase *fervent in the spirit* should not be considered a reference to the Holy Spirit, whom Apollos would not have possessed at this point. It is more likely describing the fervency with which Apollos taught. The *New International Version* reads, "He spoke with great fervor."

26. And he began to speak boldly in the synagogue: whom when Aquila and Priscilla had heard, they took him unto them, and expounded unto him the way of God more perfectly.

Soon after Apollos arrived at Ephesus, Aquila and Priscilla heard him speaking in the *synagogue*. They immediately saw the potential in him, and instead of being revolted at his doctrinal differences, they looked for an opportunity to speak with him. They realized how delicate this situation might be, so they took him aside in private, probably inviting him to their home. This approach would protect the dignity of this promising preacher of the gospel.

The remarkable sensitivity of Aquila and Priscilla in handling this matter with Apollos is an example that modern Christians should not overlook. Unfortunately, some today react to any type of doctrinal difference with an attitude of hostility toward the person who espouses the other viewpoint. To consider speaking with someone who may hold a different teaching is taken as compromise. Speaking *about* the doctrinal position of others is much more convenient than actually speaking *to* those who hold that position. In refusing to address such individuals directly, we may be missing the opportunity to mold another Apollos—a preacher with powerful skills for advancing the cause every believer holds dear.

Aquila and Priscilla focused on the potential of Apollos, rather than on his inadequate doctrinal views. They arranged for a meeting that

visual for
lesson 12

would produce the best results. They carried out their mission in such a way that Apollos, far from being offended, was convinced of the truth of what they presented. Later he traveled to Corinth and became a powerful influence for Christ in that city (Acts 18:27, 28).

In this way, the providential work of God came full circle. Paul instructed Aquila and Priscilla at Corinth, they instructed Apollos at Ephesus, and then Apollos went to Corinth to "water" where Paul had planted (1 Corinthians 3:6).

III. Ministering in Rome (Romans 16:3-5a)

When Paul returned to Ephesus from Syria (during his third missionary journey), he spent more time there (three years) than in any of the other cities that Acts says he visited (Acts 20:17, 31). Aquila and Priscilla worked by his side through many dangerous circumstances during these years.

It appears that when Paul moved on from Ephesus, Aquila and Priscilla returned to Rome, arriving some time after the death of Claudius in A.D. 54. Some months after their return, Paul wrote the letter to the Romans. Among those to whom he desired to send greetings were Aquila and Priscilla.

A. Risking Their Necks (vv. 3, 4)

3. Greet Priscilla and Aquila, my helpers in Christ Jesus.

Romans 16 concludes a letter that Paul wrote to a church he had never visited. By the time of its writing, he was ministering in Corinth once again. Coming to Rome, however, was something he earnestly hoped to do (see Romans 1:9-15; 15:23-33).

In bringing the long letter to the Romans to a close, Paul's mind turned to familiar faces of believers he had met in other cities of the Roman Empire. Some twenty-six names are included in this list of greetings. Near the top of the list (immediately after Phoebe, the woman who carried his letter from Corinth to Rome), the names of Priscilla and Aquila appear. The Greek text renders Priscilla's name with the more formal Prisca, and the two are cited for their labors on Paul's behalf.

4. Who have for my life laid down their own necks: unto whom not only I give thanks, but also all the churches of the Gentiles.

Perhaps Paul was recalling incidents such as the riot in Ephesus (Acts 19:23-41), which had jeopardized the whole missionary team. Priscilla and Aquila had stood courageously beside Paul during this difficult time. Their strength under pressure in such situations created in Paul not only a sense of his own debt to them, but also the conviction that *all the churches of the Gentiles* owed a great debt to this Jewish Christian couple. Faith such as theirs had kept the gospel going to people who otherwise would have remained lost without Christ.

B. Hosting a Church (v. 5a)

5a. Likewise greet the church that is in their house.

Here we see another illustration of Priscilla and Aquila's intense commitment to spreading the gospel and building the church. They had opened *their house* to believers in Rome. Such an act was nothing new for Priscilla and Aquila. We have already noted how they made room for Paul when he came to Corinth (Acts 18:3). First Corinthians 16:19 indicates that in Ephesus ("Asia") a church had been meeting "in their house." Now, in Rome, this courageous couple was using their home once again to further the work of the Lord.

Conclusion

A. Service and Teamwork

As a married couple committed to Christ, Priscilla and Aquila found in their business and in the use of their home opportunities to participate in the proclamation of the gospel. They used their relationship as a married couple to support and encourage devoted workers in the kingdom. They illustrate that marriage can present advantages to those seeking to contribute to the building of the church, and that Christian spouses have the privilege of blending their talents for the glory of God.

Home Daily Bible Readings

Monday, Feb. 10—Priscilla and Aquila Host a Church (1 Corinthians 16:15-24)
Tuesday, Feb. 11—Priscilla and Aquila Support Paul's Teachings (Acts 18:5-11)
Wednesday, Feb. 12—Each Person Has a Special Duty (1 Corinthians 3:5-9)
Thursday, Feb. 13—Support Others' Christian Work (Romans 12:1-8)
Friday, Feb. 14—Share Christian Lifestyles (Romans 12:9-21)
Saturday, Feb. 15—Fulfill the Law of Love (Romans 13:8-14)
Sunday, Feb. 16—Respect Your Leaders (1 Thessalonians 5:12-22)

The partnership of Priscilla and Aquila with Paul also demonstrates how a single Christian can join with a married couple to accomplish things together that could not be accomplished separately. Marriage need not become the great divide to prevent married believers from associating with the unmarried in promoting the gospel. Singles who sense clearly the call of the Lord to take up His cross may find friendships among married couples that will encourage both to become more effective workers in the church.

B. Cooperation and Communication

The sensitivity that Aquila and Priscilla demonstrated in their counseling of Apollos shows modern believers that doctrinal differences can be handled in a positive manner, without having to resort to mutual accusations. Because the issue of baptism could not be ignored, Aquila and Priscilla knew that action had to be taken. Their handling of the matter shows their maturity and their ability to see the larger good of the kingdom.

When a more experienced teacher lovingly speaks the truth to a newcomer in the faith, wonderful results can happen. Such an alliance can multiply the power of each person's testimony for Christ.

C. Courage and Hospitality

Priscilla and Aquila also made hospitality a cornerstone of their faith. At a time when opening their home to Christians was not only inconvenient but also dangerous, they repeatedly placed themselves in the position of hosts.

Modern Christians with far less to lose are challenged to do likewise. In many cases, our homes have come to resemble entertainment centers, in which we have invested thousands of dollars in equipment and resources. If our homes are considered a gift from the Lord, then using them for His service should be a natural consequence. We cannot afford to miss the opportunity to contribute our households so that the "household of faith" is advanced.

D. Prayer

Father, we thank You for sending into our lives brothers and sisters in Christ, who came to us at just the time we needed them. Their encouragement lifted our spirits and reminded us that we are never alone. Help us to be that kind of brother or sister to someone else. In Jesus' name, amen.

E. Thought To Remember

May God help us to see our homes and our relationships as blessings meant for His service.

Learning by Doing

This page contains an alternate lesson plan emphasizing learning activities.
Classes desiring such student involvement will find these suggestions helpful.

Learning Goals

As students participate in today's class session, they should:

1. List some of the contributions of Priscilla and Aquila to the cause of Christ.

2. Identify the attitude that seems to have motivated their service.

3. State some ways Christians today can imitate the faithfulness of Priscilla and Aquila.

Into the Lesson

As students arrive, give each a piece of paper on which is written, "The worst thing about moving is. . . ." Ask the students to think about how they would complete that sentence. They may discuss the idea with others as more people come to class, or you may have them think about it individually.

Call the class to order and ask for some answers. List the responses on the chalkboard or on poster board so everyone can see them. You should get answers like, "Finding a new doctor," "Getting the kids enrolled in a new school," "Packing," "Unpacking," "Finding a good church." If no one mentions church, bring up the subject yourself. Discuss the problems of finding a church: doctrine, location, programming, worship styles, and other factors one might consider. Ask, "What if you moved to a city that had no church at all?" After a brief discussion, point out that the New Testament personalities you will be studying today faced that challenge.

Into the Word

Position three posters around the room—one labeled Corinth, one Ephesus, and one Rome. Ask the students to form three groups, one near each poster. Have a member of the Corinth group read Acts 18:1-11 aloud. Someone from the Ephesus group should then read Acts 18:18, 19, 24-26 aloud. Finally, ask a reader from the Rome group to read Romans 16:3-5a aloud. Ask each group to write on its poster the contributions of Priscilla and Aquila to the church in that city. Be prepared to assist each group with background information from the lesson commentary, or from other research.

Corinth

Giving Paul a place to stay and an opportunity to support his preaching while in Corinth is all that is mentioned, so this, we must assume, was Priscilla and Aquila's major contribution. Another Christian, Justus, provided a place for Paul to preach (18:7). We can be sure that Priscilla and Aquila were also active in the life of the church, since Paul wanted them to come with him to Ephesus (18:18, 19).

Ephesus

Helping to establish the church in Ephesus is certainly notable, and must have been the reason Paul later left Priscilla and Aquila in Ephesus and sailed to Jerusalem (18:19-21). Their greater work, however, may have been their teaching of Apollos, who would go on to touch many more lives than they probably could have imagined. Who knows what far-reaching influence we may have today when we touch the life of even one individual for Christ?

Rome

Paul says a church met in Priscilla and Aquila's home, and that is all we know for certain about their labors in Rome. This, of course, became more and more risky as time went on. Within six years of the writing of the letter to the Romans, Rome would be burned. The Christians were blamed, and those who stood out as their leaders were especially vulnerable to retribution. If Priscilla and Aquila had "laid down their own necks" before, they may have literally laid down their necks before a Roman executioner when the persecution intensified.

Into Life

Ask the class members to suggest one-word descriptions of Priscilla and Aquila. Words such as *courageous*, *dedicated*, *hospitable*, and *selfless* should be mentioned. Make a list of all the suggestions. Then ask, "How did these qualities advance the cause of Christ in their day?" After a few minutes discussion, ask, "How can our practice of the same qualities advance the cause of Christ today?"

Ask the class to form groups of three or four. Ask each group to think of one specific way we can imitate the faithfulness of Priscilla and Aquila. The group should suggest a plan of action, not just a character trait or attitude. After four or five minutes, ask for reports.

Close with a challenge to students to act with the same faithfulness to the cause of Christ as did this committed Christian couple.

Let's Talk It Over

The questions on this page are designed to encourage review of the lesson Scriptures and to promote discussion of the lesson by the class. The answers provided are only discussion starters. Let your class talk it over from there.

1. Paul came to Corinth, having just experienced a measure of rejection at Athens. Aquila and Priscilla had traveled to Corinth after being expelled from Rome. When situations fail to work out the way we think they should, what can we do to keep from becoming discouraged or depressed?

We need to know that the "grin and bear it" approach usually does not help. This tends to mask the problem without dealing with it. Nor can we try to forget our problems by throwing ourselves into our work or taking a vacation.

A first step is to realize that we have no guarantee of a trouble-free life. Bad things happen to us, just as they happen to others. When they happen, we need to grieve. It often helps to talk to a trusted Christian friend about our disappointment and the pain we are feeling. We should also remember that Christ is able to comfort and support us because He too experienced grief and sorrow (John 11:35; Hebrews 4:14-16).

2. The fact that Paul and Priscilla and Aquila met one another in Corinth was a circumstance used by God to bless all three. How can we tell if some unexpected event is a happy coincidence or the result of God's intervention?

With unexpected good or happy events, our tendency is likely to thank God. When unexpected difficulties arise, perhaps we are not as quick to thank God or to see His hand at work. Romans 8:28 reminds us, however, that "in all things God works for the good of those who love him, who have been called according to his purpose" (*New International Version*). Quite often, particularly when tragedy strikes, we are not able to discern God's design until a certain amount of time has passed (as was the case with Joseph, according to Genesis 50:20).

We should seek to acknowledge God's hand in the normal flow of events from day to day, so that we can learn to trust Him when the "abnormal" occurs, whether good or bad.

3. What is the value of a "tentmaking" ministry, such as that of the apostle Paul in Corinth?

Today, many countries disapprove of missionaries entering their borders. In such situations, one of the most creative and fruitful responses has been through "tentmakers"—people who enter the country to work at a specific job or industry and seek to influence others for Christ while engaged in such work. Such a tentmaker may find a broad range of opportunities to communicate his faith in Christ. In addition, he may encounter less resistance than would "professionals" (such as ministers or missionaries), since some people have a negative mindset toward such Christian workers.

4. What can we do if we hear a Sunday school teacher teaching something that does not measure up to what the Bible says?

The direct approach is to confront the teacher during class and point out the error. This is rude and tactless and probably will result in the teacher's becoming defensive and even belligerent. There is also the "everyone's entitled to his own view" approach. If we follow this method, we do nothing. The "talebearer" approach involves running around and telling everyone what the teacher said and how wrong he was. Of course, this helps no one, least of all the teacher.

The mature approach safeguards the teacher's feelings and does not seek to embarrass him publicly. This is what Priscilla and Aquila used. They took Apollos aside privately and talked to him kindly.

5. Priscilla and Aquila seemed to use their home for Christ wherever they were living. How can we use our homes for Christ more effectively?

To some degree, this depends on our surroundings or the specific needs we see that must be addressed. Perhaps our home can be the meeting place for a congregation, as was Priscilla and Aquila's in Ephesus (1 Corinthians 16:19) and in Rome (Romans 16:3-5). Perhaps we can host a missionary, as Priscilla and Aquila hosted Paul in Corinth (Acts 18:3). If our home is located near the church building, it may serve as a place for a Sunday school class or Bible study group to meet.

The Scripture also instructs all to be hospitable (1 Peter 4:9). Certainly the ministry of hospitality can be an influential one in today's society, where fear and distrust often keep people isolated.

Timothy

DEVOTIONAL READING: 1 Timothy 4:6-16.

LESSON SCRIPTURE: Acts 16:1-5; 1 Corinthians 4:14-17; Philippians 2:19-24; 2 Timothy 1:3-7; 3:14, 15.

PRINTED TEXT: Acts 16:1-5; 1 Corinthians 4:14-17; Philippians 2:19-22; 2 Timothy 1:3-7.

Acts 16:1-5

1 Then came he to Derbe and Lystra: and, behold, a certain disciple was there, named Timothy, the son of a certain woman, which was a Jewess, and believed; but his father was a Greek:

2 Which was well reported of by the brethren that were at Lystra and Iconium.

3 Him would Paul have to go forth with him; and took and circumcised him because of the Jews which were in those quarters: for they knew all that his father was a Greek.

4 And as they went through the cities, they delivered them the decrees for to keep, that were ordained of the apostles and elders which were at Jerusalem.

5 And so were the churches established in the faith, and increased in number daily.

1 Corinthians 4:14-17

14 I write not these things to shame you, but as my beloved sons I warn you.

15 For though ye have ten thousand instructors in Christ, yet have ye not many fathers: for in Christ Jesus I have begotten you through the gospel.

16 Wherefore I beseech you, be ye followers of me.

17 For this cause have I sent unto you Timothy, who is my beloved son, and faithful in the Lord, who shall bring you into remembrance of my ways which be in Christ, as I teach every where in every church.

Philippians 2:19-22

19 But I trust in the Lord Jesus to send Timothy shortly unto you, that I also may be of good comfort, when I know your state.

20 For I have no man likeminded, who will naturally care for your state.

21 For all seek their own, not the things which are Jesus Christ's.

22 But ye know the proof of him, that, as a son with the father, he hath served with me in the gospel.

2 Timothy 1:3-7

3 I thank God, whom I serve from my forefathers with pure conscience, that without ceasing I have remembrance of thee in my prayers night and day;

4 Greatly desiring to see thee, being mindful of thy tears, that I may be filled with joy;

5 When I call to remembrance the unfeigned faith that is in thee, which dwelt first in thy grandmother Lois, and thy mother Eunice; and I am persuaded that in thee also.

6 Wherefore I put thee in remembrance, that thou stir up the gift of God, which is in thee by the putting on of my hands.

7 For God hath not given us the spirit of fear; but of power, and of love, and of a sound mind.

GOLDEN TEXT: I [Paul] sent unto you Timothy, who is my beloved son, and faithful in the Lord, who shall bring you into remembrance of my ways which be in Christ, as I teach every where in every church.—1 Corinthians 4:17.

Lesson Aims

Today's lesson should seek to achieve the following goals:

1. Help believers understand that adults of differing ages can work together for Christ.

2. Motivate adults to find ways of encouraging the service of younger believers.

3. Encourage Christian parents to provide foundations at home for future church leaders.

Lesson Outline

INTRODUCTION
    A. The Truth About Youth
    B. Lesson Background
  I. TIMOTHY'S REPUTATION (Acts 16:1-5)
    A. Credentials for Service (vv. 1, 2)
       Surviving the Odds
    B. Invitation From Paul (vv. 3-5)
 II. TIMOTHY'S UNSELFISH SPIRIT (1 Corinthians
      4:14-17; Philippians 2:19-22)
    A. Ministry to a Troubled Church (1
      Corinthians 4:14-17)
    B. Ministry for the Welfare of Others
      (Philippians 2:19-22)
       Genuine Friendship
III. TIMOTHY'S FOUNDATIONS OF FAITH (2 Timothy
      1:3-7)
    A. Childhood Training (vv. 3-5)
    B. Using a Spiritual Gift (vv. 6, 7)
CONCLUSION
    A. Unselfish Leadership
    B. Bridging the "Gap"
    C. Developing Leaders at Home
    D. Prayer
    E. Thought to Remember

Use the visual for Lesson 13 in the visuals packet to highlight Paul's challenge to Timothy in 2 Timothy 1:7. It is shown on page 221.

Introduction

A. The Truth About Youth

What can we say about the younger generation? Do they seem too restless, too lazy, too frivolous, too wasteful, too superficial, too worldly? All of these charges have been made against today's youth.

The irony of this is that almost every younger generation has received the same criticism. Older Christians have expressed these concerns for years. Yet God has always raised up faithful believers to guarantee that the church would advance. Among these believers have been younger disciples such as Timothy, the subject of our final lesson in this unit and in this quarter. His example should encourage us to believe that God will raise up young people from this present generation as well, who will faithfully uphold the cause of Christ.

B. Lesson Background

Timothy became one of the most beloved coworkers of the apostle Paul. His name means "one who honors God," and his ministry with Paul lived up to this description. The two were partners on most of Paul's second and third missionary journeys recorded in Acts.

The frequency with which Timothy is mentioned in the letters of Paul illustrates the important role he played in the apostle's life and ministry. Timothy was with Paul when he wrote the following epistles (as indicated in the opening verse of each): 2 Corinthians, Philippians, Colossians, 1 Thessalonians, 2 Thessalonians, and Philemon.

That an intimate friendship developed between Timothy and Paul is obvious from the terminology the apostle uses of his younger companion in those letters addressed to him. Paul describes Timothy as his "own son" in 1 Timothy 1:2 ("true son" in the *New International Version*), and as his "dearly beloved son" in 2 Timothy 1:2. In Romans 16:21, Paul uses the term "workfellow" of Timothy, and in 1 Thessalonians 3:2 he calls Timothy "our brother, and minister of God, and our fellow laborer in the gospel of Christ."

I. Timothy's Reputation
(Acts 16:1-5)

A. Credentials for Service (vv. 1, 2)

1. Then came he to Derbe and Lystra: and, behold, a certain disciple was there, named Timothy, the son of a certain woman, which was a Jewess, and believed; but his father was a Greek.

Paul was conducting his second missionary journey, traveling with Silas, when he arrived at *Derbe and Lystra*. These two cities were located in southern Galatia (what is today south central Turkey). On Paul's previous missionary journey, he and Barnabas had visited these cities. They had succeeded in establishing churches in both locations, returning a short time later to Lystra

How to Say It

APOLLOS. Uh-*pahl*-us.
DERBE. *Der*-bee.
EUNICE. *You*-niss.
ICONIUM. Eye-*koe*-nee-um.
LYSTRA. *Liss*-truh.
PROSELYTE. *prahs*-uh-light.

to see that elders were ordained in that church (Acts 14:21-23).

It is likely that *Timothy*, a native of Lystra, became a *disciple* of Jesus during Paul's earlier visit there. Timothy's mother, *a Jewess*, had married a *Greek*, or Gentile. Such a decision was not uncommon among Jews living outside of Palestine, though it would have brought criticism from many Jews in Palestine. The fact that Timothy's father is not described as a proselyte or "God-fearer" probably means that he had little personal interest in promoting the influence of the gospel in his family.

Paul's preaching of Jesus as the Messiah struck a chord with Timothy. He was probably in his teens at the time, since Paul refers to him as a young man some twenty years later (1 Timothy 4:12).

SURVIVING THE ODDS

Children of "unequally yoked" parents generally must leap high hurdles to find and keep personal faith. Their circumstances can be confusing and inhibiting. They may love both parents, yet their parents do not serve the same Master. The believing parent (often the mother) may be a strong influence during early childhood years, but too often a child in a spiritually divided home will make no personal commitment to Christ. He sees his decision as favoring one parent or the other. If he chooses to believe, his choice can be perceived as a negative judgment upon the unbelieving parent. The dilemma immobilizes him.

Timothy's Jewish mother and Greek father created a potentially paralyzing situation for him. But somehow, perhaps through the additional influence of a believing grandmother, Timothy survived the odds and developed not only *saving* faith, but *serving* faith as well.

Christians must take very seriously the Biblical cautions against marrying unbelievers. Spiritually divided homes jeopardize marital harmony, and escalate the odds against offspring making and keeping personal vows to God. Timothy was more than just lucky; he was unusually blessed.   —R. W. B.

2. Which was well reported of by the brethren that were at Lystra and Iconium.

Timothy's reputation as a young man who was serious about his faith had spread throughout the church at *Lystra,* and even to *Iconium* some twenty miles away. Believers in these cities considered his spiritual development to be quite impressive.

B. Invitation From Paul (vv. 3-5)

3. Him would Paul have to go forth with him; and took and circumcised him because of the Jews which were in those quarters: for they knew all that his father was a Greek.

So interested was Paul in this promising young man that he wanted him to become a permanent member of the missionary team. But Paul usually began his evangelistic work in any city by going to the synagogue and preaching to the Jews there (Acts 17:1, 2). This posed a potential problem with *the Jews which were in those quarters* who knew of Timothy's background and upbringing. They were aware of the fact that *his father was a Greek,* and that he apparently had refused to have Timothy *circumcised* as an infant. This could constitute a significant stumbling block in their minds and give them reason to oppose Paul's efforts (no doubt many of them would be quite pleased to have such grounds). In order to keep this from becoming a barrier to his evangelistic work, Paul *took and circumcised* Timothy in accordance with the Old Testament regulation.

It is important to note the distinction between this situation and that involving Titus, to whom Paul refers in Galatians 2:3-5. There Paul was contending that circumcision should not be imposed on Gentiles who accepted Christ (5:6-12). Timothy's circumcision was not being forced upon him; it was a voluntary act, performed out of a desire to become "all things to all men, that I might by all means save some" (1 Corinthians 9:22; see vv. 19, 20).

4. And as they went through the cities, they delivered them the decrees for to keep, that were ordained of the apostles and elders which were at Jerusalem.

The *cities* covered by Paul, Silas, and their new companion included those locations covered during the first missionary journey. Within these predominantly Gentile churches, the question of whether Gentile Christians were required to be circumcised and keep the Law of Moses had arisen. This issue had been addressed by the Jerusalem conference (Acts 15:22-29). The *decrees*, decided upon by *the apostles and elders* attending that conference, were now *delivered* by the missionaries as they traveled. Timothy's presence, and how circumcision had been handled in his case, probably helped clarify additional questions that were raised.

5. And so were the churches established in the faith, and increased in number daily.

Paul's choice of Timothy to accompany the missionary team and his handling of the sensitive question of circumcision contributed to the continued growth of the *churches.*

II. Timothy's Unselfish Spirit (1 Corinthians 4:14-17; Philippians 2:19-22)

One of Paul's most critical needs was for missionary companions who would be able to travel to churches needing help with special problems. Not only did this require workers with a sterling reputation; it also required individuals with a servant spirit, who were willing to suffer inconvenience for the good of the church.

Both the Corinthian and the Philippian churches were congregations founded by Paul during his second missionary journey, with the help of Timothy. Over the next few years of Paul's ministry, these churches faced severe challenges. Paul needed the help of his trusted companion to address these situations.

A. Ministry to a Troubled Church (1 Corinthians 4:14-17)

14. I write not these things to shame you, but as my beloved sons I warn you.

With these words, Paul concluded the first section of his first letter to the Corinthian church. Four segments of the congregation were in conflict (see 1 Corinthians 1:12). The Corinthians were showing more loyalty to favorite preachers and the factions that had built around them than they were to Jesus alone.

Although Paul's tone may have seemed sharp and severe, he did not consider the Corinthians his enemies, but his *beloved sons.* He wanted *to warn* them of the consequences of their divisive spirit.

15. For though ye have ten thousand instructors in Christ, yet have ye not many fathers: for in Christ Jesus I have begotten you through the gospel.

The *instructors* mentioned by Paul referred to the other preachers and teachers who had played a part in establishing the Corinthians in the gospel. Paul wanted to acknowledge the role of these instructors in the progress of the Corinthians, but he reminded them that he was the only one among them who had worked to bring the church into existence. Even though the instructors might number as many as *ten*

thousand, none of them could fill the position Paul held. When he initially arrived in Corinth, he was virtually alone in his missionary work, and thus he had *begotten* or "fathered" the church all by himself. He had "planted," later Apollos had "watered," but only God had given "the increase" (1 Corinthians 3:6).

16. Wherefore I beseech you, be ye followers of me.

If Paul was the Corinthians' "father" in the faith, this should constitute sufficient grounds for them to accept his counsel. He urged them to be *followers* of his by seeking unity among themselves and putting to rest their contentions.

17. For this cause have I sent unto you Timothy, who is my beloved son, and faithful in the Lord, who shall bring you into remembrance of my ways which be in Christ, as I teach every where in every church.

Paul knew that Timothy could provide the leadership necessary to heal the divisions within the Corinthian church. Though he was sending Timothy with some reservations about how he would be received (see 1 Corinthians 16:10, 11), Paul was confident in his *beloved son.*

B. Ministry for the Welfare of Others (Philippians 2:19-22)

The book of Acts concludes with Paul living under house arrest in Rome (Acts 28:16, 30, 31). During this time, Paul was able to preach the gospel to "the whole palace guard" (Philippians 1:12, 13, *New International Version.*)

Despite the limitations that he faced during his imprisonment, Paul did his best to keep in contact with the churches. The "prison epistles" of Ephesians, Philippians, Colossians, and Philemon represent Paul's communications during this period. Timothy's name appears with Paul's in the opening verse of each of these letters, except for Ephesians. Paul was able to use his trusted companion to travel to places where he could not go.

The Philippian church held a special place in Paul's heart. These saints had aided him financially at some difficult moments (Philippians 4:10-19). News had come, however, that false teachers were making inroads among the believers (3:2), and that friction had developed between some prominent church members (4:2, 3). The church needed the encouragement that someone like Timothy could offer.

19. But I trust in the Lord Jesus to send Timothy shortly unto you, that I also may be of good comfort, when I know your state.

Paul's sense of responsibility for the welfare of the churches did not end with his imprisonment. He felt a burden for all congregations wherever he was (see 2 Corinthians 11:28). Timothy's journey to Philippi would give him the opportunity to learn about the current *state* of the believers.

20, 21. For I have no man likeminded, who will naturally care for your state. For all seek their own, not the things which are Jesus Christ's.

Here Paul expressed the highest level of confidence in Timothy. This confidence was based on Timothy's unselfish character. Such a spirit was just the kind of influence the Philippians needed to solve their problems.

GENUINE FRIENDSHIP

Dale Carnegie lists "six ways to make friends" in his classic book, *How To Win Friends and Influence People*. One of his suggestions is, "Become genuinely interested in other people." Perhaps he borrowed that principle from Philippians 2:19, 20, found in today's lesson text (many of Carnegie's concepts are Biblical).

Timothy was a standout among Paul's companions and co-workers, because he took a genuine interest in the welfare of those he served. His priority was to act in the interest of Christ and all Christians. His giving was without guile; his ministry was free of ulterior motives.

If we want to win friends to Christ and influence people for God, we too must demonstrate a genuine interest in others. We must become "people persons." We must add to our faith those qualities listed in 2 Peter 1:5-7. These virtues will open many doors of opportunity, and will help us to be effective and productive in every ministry. They must, however, be real. The world already has been disillusioned by too many hypocrites. —R. W. B.

22. But ye know the proof of him, that, as a son with the father, he hath served with me in the gospel.

Paul illustrated Timothy's qualification for service with terminology appropriate to a family business. Timothy had learned to serve with Paul in a subservient role, much like a *son* who learns the family business while his *father* supervises him. Timothy had submitted himself in such a way that he could faithfully carry out the wishes of the apostle.

If great things are to be accomplished in the church today, then believers will need to imitate the unselfishness of Timothy. This means that believers will not be concerned with getting due recognition or proper rewards for their efforts. Through such a spirit, unity in the church will be preserved, and the gospel will never be hampered by embarrassing church quarrels.

III. Timothy's Foundations of Faith

(2 Timothy 1:3-7)

Timothy's trademark of unselfishness was no accident. Paul's words in this portion of our printed text make clear that Timothy's character was formed in the early years of his life.

Perhaps close to twenty years had passed since the apostle Paul first met young Timothy in Lystra. Throughout these years, Paul and Timothy had served side by side in taking the gospel to place after place where the news of Jesus had never been heard. Now, Paul was a prisoner in Rome. He knew he was nearing the end of his earthly life; he was "ready to be offered" and prepared for his "departure" (2 Timothy 4:6). He wrote this final letter to Timothy, hoping that his young friend would come to visit him one last time in his prison cell. His words offer a number of personal reflections on Timothy's life and service.

A. Childhood Training (vv. 3-5)

3. I thank God, whom I serve from my forefathers with pure conscience, that without ceasing I have remembrance of thee in my prayers night and day.

Imprisonment may have kept Paul from staying in touch with various congregations, but it never kept him out of touch with God. Despite his surroundings, Paul's *prayers* for Timothy continued *night and day*. His reference to his *forefathers* included Abraham, Moses, and other outstanding men of faith from Israel's history. Paul recognized that his faith in Christ had its roots in their faith in the promises of God.

4. Greatly desiring to see thee, being mindful of thy tears, that I may be filled with joy.

Paul's *desiring* for Timothy sprang from the apostle's awareness that his opportunities to see his young friend were quickly vanishing. Timothy's *tears* were probably his reaction to his awareness that Paul's days on earth were indeed numbered.

5. When I call to remembrance the unfeigned faith that is in thee, which dwelt first in thy

"God hath not given us the spirit of fear; but of power, and of love, and of a sound mind."

visual for
lesson 13

grandmother Lois, and thy mother Eunice; and I am persuaded that in thee also.

Paul proceeded to reflect on Timothy's roots in the faith. *Lois* (his *grandmother*) and *Eunice* (his *mother*) were given credit for implanting within Timothy the knowledge of the truth that led him to his faith in Christ. This knowledge began with instruction in the Old Testament Scriptures (2 Timothy 3:15). It was solidified by the *unfeigned,* or sincere, *faith* of Lois and Eunice themselves.

B. Using a Spiritual Gift (vv. 6, 7)

6. Wherefore I put thee in remembrance, that thou stir up the gift of God, which is in thee by the putting on of my hands.

Paul reminded Timothy to use the *gift* he had been given by *God*. This was probably a spiritual gift passed on to Timothy when Paul laid his hands on him (see the example of the disciples in Ephesus in Acts 19:6), but the use and fruitfulness of such gifts depended on the eagerness of the believer. Timothy had to *stir up* the "coals" of this gift, so that it might be useful in his ministry.

7. For God hath not given us the spirit of fear; but of power, and of love, and of a sound mind.

As a young man, Timothy appears to have struggled with the temptation of being too timid in the Lord's work (see 1 Corinthians 16:10, 11; 1 Timothy 4:12). Paul's words to Timothy have much to offer today's believer, who often finds himself encountering intimidating situations. Believers have nothing to fear when God's *power* and *love* energize them, whatever the trial or difficulty. When they keep their minds *sound* (the *New International Version* has "self-discipline"), they are continually prepared for service to the Lord.

Conclusion

A. Unselfish Leadership

Timothy's example speaks volumes concerning the qualities needed for effective spiritual service. His unselfish concern for the welfare of other believers set him apart in the church. Skill, creativity, and intelligence are all important ingredients for leaders in the church, but nothing is as crucial as the kind of mature Christian temperament possessed by Timothy.

Leaders who hope to build the church on a lasting foundation will turn their attention to the spiritual qualities exhibited by Timothy. Such a leader will build with materials that will stand not only the test of public scrutiny, but of God's judgment as well.

B. Bridging the "Gap"

Frequently people of the older generation question whether they can "relate" to youth or help them become mature Christians. Paul's acceptance of Timothy and his constant encouragement of this young soldier for Christ point out how older church members can make a difference in the lives of younger followers of Jesus. In many cases, we who are more experienced in the faith cannot know the influence we might have when we put our effort into building our youth. They will not be the "church of tomorrow" unless we teach them the faith today.

C. Developing Leaders at Home

Just as Timothy's upbringing equipped him to become an exceptional minister of the gospel, so the homes of young people today can provide the motivation that enables them to answer the call of God. Parents should never underestimate the role they play in lighting the spark of spiritual interest in young people. This mission can be accomplished in spite of conditions at home, which may be less than perfect.

May God give us the foresight to see every young person as a potential leader who could one day be used by God.

D. Prayer

Father, how thankful we are for those who cared enough for us to assist and encourage us in our spiritual growth. Help us to make a difference in the life of another, as Paul did in the life of young Timothy. In Jesus' name. Amen.

E. Thought To Remember

Good vision includes the ability to see what another person can become.

Home Daily Bible Readings

Monday, Feb. 17—Timothy's Work in Corinth (1 Corinthians 16:5-12)
Tuesday, Feb. 18—Timothy to Teach Sound Doctrine (1 Timothy 1:3-11)
Wednesday, Feb. 19—Speak Out for the Lord (2 Timothy 1:8-14)
Thursday, Feb. 20—Be Strong for the Lord (Ephesians 6:10-20)
Friday, Feb. 21—Be True to God's Call (1 Corinthians 1:26-31)
Saturday, Feb. 22—Timothy's Mission (2 Timothy 4:1-5)
Sunday, Feb. 23—Defend the Faith (2 Timothy 3:10-17)

Learning by Doing

This page contains an alternate lesson plan emphasizing learning activities.
Classes desiring such student involvement will find these suggestions helpful.

Learning Goals

As a result of this study, students should be able to:

1. Suggest ways Christian parents can develop the faith of their children at home.

2. Describe what adults can do to help younger believers develop their faith.

3. Identify one person they plan to influence this next week.

Into the Lesson

Write the following names on the chalkboard or on poster board before students arrive: *Timothy, Lois, Eunice,* and *Paul.* Instead of writing the names correctly, scramble them. Begin class by asking the students to unscramble the names. You may need to give some hints from the information provided in the lesson commentary.

After the class has successfully unscrambled the names, ask them to describe Timothy's relationship with each of the other three people. (Timothy was Lois's grandson, Eunice's son, and Paul's spiritual "son.")

Then make some brief comments about the background of the letter of 2 Timothy. Use the notes in the commentary that are found just prior to the printed text from 2 Timothy (page 221). Highlight the fact that Paul's ministry was coming to a close. It was up to the next generation of Christians, including people like Timothy, to "receive" the torch and continue the work of spreading the gospel.

Into the Word

Divide the class into two groups. Each group will be given a list of Scripture references and a key question to guide discussion. Instruct the groups to appoint a reader, a recorder, and a reporter. The reader will read the Scriptures aloud. The recorder will take notes on the group's discussion of the Scriptures and the answers to its assigned question. The reporter will summarize the group's discussion when called upon by the teacher.

Before you give the groups their assignments, point out that God created two important institutions—the family and the church. Both of these institutions are vital to the development of mature believers and leaders. The family trains the next generation of believers and leaders, and the church develops younger believers into mature leaders.

Group One

Let this group know that they will be considering the family's role in training more Timothys who are ready to receive the torch of ministry from the older generation. Have members of this group read the following Scriptures: 2 Timothy 1:3-7; Proverbs 22:6; and Deuteronomy 6:4-9. The key question for this group is: *What can Christian families do to pass a genuine faith on to their children and to train them to become future leaders in the church?*

Group Two

This group will be considering the church's role in training more Timothys who are ready to receive the torch of ministry from the older generation. Have members of this group read the following Scriptures: Acts 16:1-5; Romans 16:21; 1 Corinthians 4:14-17; and Philippians 2:19-22. The key question for this group is: *What can the church do to develop younger believers into mature leaders?*

Allow approximately fifteen minutes for the groups to work on their assignments. Give them a five-minute warning before asking them to stop. Write the question from Group One on the chalkboard or on poster board, and then have its reporter summarize the group's discussion. Repeat the same procedure for Group Two.

Into Life

Make the following statement: *Good vision includes the ability to see what a young person can become.* We have seen how young Timothy became a respected leader in the New Testament church by following the instruction of his family and the footsteps of a mature church leader—the apostle Paul. Ask the class to think of the people who influenced them to become followers of Jesus, to get involved in the church, or to accept a leadership position. As time permits, have class members share their responses.

Close the class session by challenging your students to select someone to influence in the weeks ahead. Have a moment of silent prayer during which they pray for this person, Then offer a prayer of thanksgiving for those people whom God has provided to guide us in our journey of faith.

Let's Talk It Over

The questions on this page are designed to encourage review of the lesson Scriptures and to promote discussion of the lesson by the class. The answers provided are only discussion starters. Let your class talk it over from there.

1. Why do some Christians seem better suited to full-time Christian service than do others?

Every Christian has at least one gift, talent or skill. What we are able to do for Christ depends on whatever gift, talent, or skill we possess. Some gifts, such as preaching, teaching, or leadership (Romans 12:6-8) equip a person for full-time service. Other gifts (such as serving and encouraging) may enable one to serve Christ in the secular world and to work in the church on a volunteer basis. Both types of gifts are necessary for the church to have an impact upon its surroundings; "secular" Christians are just as vital to the kingdom as full-time workers.

2. How can the Christian community support a young person whom God has called to full-time Christian service?

The local church of which the young person is a part can validate his call to the ministry by affirming that he is living a clean moral life and has a good reputation. We should also be able to affirm that the candidate for ministry has demonstrated the fruit of the Spirit, the knowledge of the Scriptures, and the appropriate gifts for such a calling.

Beyond such validation and confirmation, we can also support such an individual by giving our prayers, our financial resources (particularly during the time when the individual is enrolled in Bible college), and our encouragement.

3. What effect does parental influence have on the character of a child? As parents, what can we do to influence our children for good?

A father glowed with pride as his young son imitated his walk, his expressions, and his mannerisms. But he was horrified when his son went through the motions of taking out a cigarette and lighting it up. The father immediately threw away his pack of cigarettes and vowed to stop smoking.

Children pick up our bad habits as well as our good habits. Clearly it is not enough to tell children what is right. We must set a positive example by the choices we make, the words we speak, the way we live, and the manner in which we respond to trouble and adversity. This is how children really learn what it means to live as Christians.

4. Timothy was often Paul's emissary to troubled churches. Why do some churches have problems? What can we do to help if we belong to a church that is having problems?

Churches are made up of people just like us. Although we have been forgiven of our sins and have received the Holy Spirit, we are still human. We will have differences of opinion and disagreements. There are times when selfishness rears its ugly head.

When Paul counseled troubled and feuding churches, he urged the members to think of others and put others first. Writing to the Philippians, he pointed them to the example of Christ, who was willing to serve even at the expense of Himself (Philippians 2:1-8). Within troubled churches, sometimes even "little things" done out of a serving spirit can be of great value in soothing tensions and healing divisions. In addition, we should never forget the importance of praying for the congregation.

5. What responsibility do we have to the person who led us to Christ?

It is noteworthy to consider the bond between Paul and Timothy, which deepened until the two men became as close as a father and son. While the relationship between most Christians and the people they win may not grow quite that close, there should still be a sense of heartfelt gratitude on one's part toward that individual who was instrumental in leading him to the Savior. Perhaps on the occasion of his spiritual "birthday" he could write or call that person and thank him once again.

6. How does Christ improve the quality of a Christian family's home life?

Christ is the glue that holds a family together. When family members live by the teachings of Christ, they think first of others and put others first. They go out of their way to help, encourage, and support. They turn the other cheek when insulted, and go the second mile when not asked to do so. Even in such a family as this, there will still be problems, disagreements, and arguments. But the problems will not become divisive, because the family members have a commitment to Christ and to each other and are willing to work things out.

Spring Quarter, 1997

Hope for the Future

Special Features

Lessons

Unit 1: Stand Fast in the Lord

Unit 2: Letters to Churches

Unit 3: A Message of Hope

About These Lessons

The lessons for the Spring Quarter challenge Christians to acknowledge God's control of the future and their need to prepare for that future by living faithfully for Him in the present. The Scripture texts are taken primarily from Paul's two letters to the Thessalonians and from the book of Revelation. They remind us that the second coming of Jesus is a doctrine that should thrill, motivate, and encourage Christians to live each day in anticipation of *the* day!

Mar 2
Mar 9
Mar 16
Mar 23
Mar 30
Apr 6
Apr 13
Apr 20
Apr 27
May 4
May 11
May 18
May 25

Quarterly Quiz

The questions on this page may be used in several ways: as a pretest at the beginning of the quarter; as a review at the end of the quarter; or as a review after each lesson. The questions are based on the Scripture text of each lesson (King James Version). **The answers are on page 232.**

Lesson 1

1. Before coming to Thessalonica, Paul and his companions had been shamefully treated in what city? *1 Thessalonians 2:2*

2. Paul told the Thessalonians, "We were gentle among you, even as a _____ cherisheth her _____." *1 Thessalonians 2:7*

Lesson 2

1. "God hath not called us unto uncleanness, but unto _____." *1 Thessalonians 4:7*

2. Concerning what subject did Paul have no need to write to the Thessalonians? *1 Thessalonians 4:9*

Lesson 3

1. Name the three men mentioned in the opening verse of 2 Thessalonians. *2 Thessalonians 1:1*

2. The apostle Paul wrote 2 Thessalonians out of a concern that the Thessalonians had failed to grow in their faith and love. T/F *2 Thessalonians 1:3*

Lesson 4

1. Paul told the Thessalonians to pray that something might have "free course." What was it? *2 Thessalonians 3:1*

2. Paul's counsel to the church at Thessalonica was that if any did not _____, he should not _____. *2 Thessalonians 3:10*

Lesson 5

1. The angel who told the women that Jesus had risen said that He would be going to (Samaria, Bethany, Galilee). *Matthew 28:7*

2. Jesus will descend from Heaven, with the voice of the _____ and with the _____ of God. *1 Thessalonians 4:16*

Lesson 6

1. On what island was John exiled? *Revelation 1:9*

2. John directed his writing to the seven churches in (Macedonia, Asia, Judea). *Revelation 1:4*

Lesson 7

1. For how long did Jesus say the saints in Smyrna would undergo trial? *Revelation 2:10*

2. Within the church at Pergamos were those who held to the doctrine affiliated with what Old Testament character? *Revelation 2:14, 15*

Lesson 8

1. What was the name of the woman who was troubling the church at Thyatira? *Revelation 2:20*

2. Jesus said of the evil Jezebel, "I gave her space to _____." *Revelation 2:21*

3. Jesus promised that the one who overcomes will rule the nations with a _____ of _____. *Revelation 2:27*

Lesson 9

1. To the church at Philadelphia, Jesus refers to Himself as having the key of _____. *Revelation 3:7*

2. Complete these words to Laodicea: "Because thou art _____, and neither _____ nor _____, I will _____ thee out of my mouth." *Revelation 3:16*

Lesson 10

1. Who asked the question, "Who is worthy to open the book?" *Revelation 5:2*

2. Jesus is called the _____ of Judah and the _____ of David. *Revelation 5:5*

Lesson 11

1. In what portion of their bodies were the servants of God to be sealed by the angels? *Revelation 7:3*

2. The multitude dressed in white and standing before the throne of God had come out of _____ _____. *Revelation 7:14*

Lesson 12

1. What did the One riding upon the white horse have on His head? *Revelation 19:12*

2. The lake of fire is called the _____ death. *Revelation 20:14*

Lesson 13

1. The holy city is called the new _____. *Revelation 21:2*

2. John heard a voice say, "Behold, the _____ of God is with men." *Revelation 21:3*

3. The _____ of the earth will bring their glory and honor into the city of God. *Revelation 21:24*

A Season and a Reason for Hope

by Edwin V. Hayden

SPRING IS AN APPROPRIATE SEASON for a lesson series entitled, "Hope for the Future." For those who have had to endure a long, cold winter, the warmth and beauty of springtime have been anticipated with great hope. More important, however, spring carries within itself both the promise and the provisions of fruitful harvests yet to come. The blossoms of springtime are the beginnings of the fruit to be harvested during summer. The spring sun that soothes winter-stiffened joints also warms the soil, preparing it to receive the seed that will one day supply a variety of grains and vegetables. This bounty will sustain us through another winter season, until spring again arrives to pave the way for another harvest.

Beyond What Is Seen

Hope always looks beyond the range of present vision, for "hope that is seen is not hope: for what a man seeth, why doth he yet hope for? But if we hope for that we see not, then do we with patience wait for it" (Romans 8:24, 25). Patient waiting distinguishes the confidence of Christian hope from the vague wishfulness that is commonly called hope, but may be nothing more than postponed frustration. Hope's value depends upon *what* one hopes for, and *why* he hopes for it. James urges patient endurance until Christ comes again, and compares this attitude with a farmer's patient expectation of the "early and latter rain" that will aid in producing his crops, thus providing a living for himself and his family (James 5:7).

Hope—the expectation of future and unseen benefits—is strong motivation, and people do act on it. The motivation may lie in the *certainty* of the coming good, as in the assurance of tomorrow's sunrise or next week's paycheck. Equally strong may be the *value* of the expected benefit, though the fulfillment is somewhat less certain. Thus we invest our lives and possessions in the upbringing and education of our children, expecting them to "turn out well" and prove to be the best of all investments.

Then there is the lottery, which entraps millions of victims with the lure of great wealth, although the basis of expectation is virtually nonexistent. The "hope" lies solely in the size of the bait. Let us consider, in contrast, the Christian's hope—as sure as the reality of God and as vast as the treasures of Heaven.

So Many Are Hopeless

Tragically, much of the modern world lives in a state of hopelessness. Increasing numbers of young people, who can find no purpose in life and see no relief from its meaninglessness, are committing suicide, either suddenly or by throwing their lives away in small pieces.

If there is no God, no resurrection, and no life beyond the physical and the material, what real hope is there? For even those with aspirations to leave the world a better place for their having lived here, what ultimate hope exists if people have nothing beyond material existence? Hear the triumphant cry of Paul at the conclusion of his seemingly "hopeless" imprisonment: "I am now ready to be offered, and the time of my departure is at hand. I have fought a good fight, I have finished my course, I have kept the faith: henceforth there is laid up for me a crown of righteousness, which the Lord, the righteous judge, shall give me at that day: and not to me only, but unto all them also that love his appearing" (2 Timothy 4:6-8).

Faith and Hope

Hope depends on faith, and both rest ultimately in God, and what He has revealed through His Son. God "raised him up from the dead," writes Peter, "that your faith and hope might be in God" (1 Peter 1:21). John Ruskin, the nineteenth-century essayist, referred to hope as the child of faith and as the most distinctive Christian virtue. He went on to say that faith makes the *present* visible, while hope makes the *future* visible. Faith *inspects*, but hope *expects*. Faith looks *at*, but hope looks *up*. Faith *sees*, and hope *foresees*. Faith *realizes*, but hope *idealizes*. Faith is quiet in *possession*, but hope trembles with *expectation*. Faith *holds on* to what *is*, but hope *leaps out* to what *shall be*. Faith is a *conviction;* hope is a *dream* of the very highest kind.

The circumstances during which much of the New Testament was written were extremely perilous for Christians. Our lessons for this quarter, dealing with the theme of "Hope for the Future," come from the writings of Paul to the Thessalonians and from the visions delivered to John that are found in the book of Revelation. It should be noted that the Thessalonian letters are among the earliest of the New Testament writings, while Revelation may well have been the last of the New Testament books written. Yet both men were emboldened by the same hope, and sought to empower their readers with that hope. Of course, those readers include us.

Implementing Hope

The five lessons in March, under the general title, "Stand Fast in the Lord," speak of Jesus as the basis of our hope, and they point the way toward building a life of hope securely on Him. All of the lesson texts in this unit are taken from Paul's letters to the Thessalonians. These Scriptures reflect the Thessalonians' need for additional instruction concerning the second coming of Christ, so that they may live in proper preparation for that day.

Lesson 1. "Proclaim the Gospel!" The proclamation of Christ requires Christlike conviction, character, and caring on the part of the proclaimers. Paul and his partners manifested these qualities as they established the church in Thessalonica.

Lesson 2. "Live in Love and Holiness!" If the hearers of the gospel are to realize their hope in Christ and convey it to others, they must reflect the Christian character and love that Jesus commanded and the apostles demonstrated.

Lesson 3. "Pray for Others!" The believer's hope in Christ sustains him through difficulties, including persecutions. Members of God's family are to pray for one another, that their faith may be adequate for such testings.

Lesson 4. "Do What Is Right!" The Christian's hope of Heaven does not exempt him from the responsibility to be a good and productive citizen on earth. If anything, his commitment to Christ gives him a greater capacity to live as such a citizen. It also lays on him a greater responsibility to honor his Lord by representing Him well.

Lesson 5. "The Resurrection Hope." Our Easter lesson focuses on the basis of our hope in Jesus, and upon the promise of resurrection to all who believe and follow Him. Jesus' resurrection is recounted from Matthew's Gospel; the promise of the saints' resurrection at Jesus' return comes from 1 Thessalonians 4:13-18.

Assurance to the Faithful

Our April lessons, "Letters to Churches," revolve around the Lord's promise, "Be thou faithful unto death, and I will give thee a crown of life" (Revelation 2:10). They are taken from five of the seven letters to churches, which John was commanded to write from his exile on the island of Patmos.

Lesson 6. "Commanded to Write." John's vision of the glorified Christ includes Jesus' command for him to write letters as dictated to "the seven churches which are in Asia" (Revelation 1:4).

Lesson 7. "To Smyrna and Pergamos." The church at Smyrna was spiritually rich, though materially poor. The congregation at Pergamos was a more affluent church, endangered by false teaching. To both of these groups of saints, the Lord promises glory with Him on the condition that they faithfully overcome their present difficulties.

Lesson 8. "To Thyatira." The rewards of victory are promised to a church seriously threatened by vicious and seductive leadership. Jesus challenges these believers to remain faithful to what they already possess in Him.

Lesson 9. "To Philadelphia and Laodicea." A church with limited strength (Philadelphia) is promised a reward for its faithfulness, while a proud and self-satisfied church (Laodicea) is rebuked, warned, and tenderly invited to repent.

Visions of Heaven

Our lessons for May develop the theme, "A Message of Hope," using passages from the book of Revelation that depict the Lamb of God in all His glory, and the city of God in all its unparalleled magnificence.

Lesson 10. "The Redeeming Lamb." Jesus Christ, glorified after His sacrificial death, is found to be the only One worthy to receive and open the sealed record of divine mysteries.

Lesson 11. "Provision for the Redeemed." Protection from the "wrath of the Lamb" (Revelation 6:16) is provided for multitudes who have come faithfully through great tribulation, having washed their robes white in the blood of the Lamb.

Lesson 12. "The Victorious Christ." The Lamb of God is presented as a triumphant Warrior, having conquered all the enemies of God, and as the Judge of all the earth, meting out eternal reward and punishment according to everyone's works.

Lesson 13. "A New Heaven and Earth." The Holy City, new Jerusalem, is depicted in terms of glorious and immeasurable grandeur. It is a place free from evil and all its consequences, providing tender intimacy with God forever.

May these lessons give us renewed confidence to sing Edward Mote's familiar words:

"My hope is built on nothing less
Than Jesus' blood and righteousness;
I dare not trust the sweetest frame,
But wholly lean on Jesus' name.
On Christ, the solid Rock, I stand;
All other ground is sinking sand,
All other ground is sinking sand."

Living in Hope

by Stephen K. Nash

MANY BELIEVE THAT OUR WORLD is running out of hope. Every thoroughfare seems to have a "No Exit" sign thrown across it. As one pundit put it, "Nature has let us down, God seems to have left the receiver off the hook, and time is running out." Much of today's art reflects this feeling of meaninglessness. If you were to go to a contemporary art exhibit and view the works of the noted painter, Jackson Pollock, you might think to yourself that someone just randomly splattered paint upon a canvas. Believing that surely there is something more profound to it than that, you ask a museum guide how Pollock created his "masterpieces." The guide would tell you that Pollock's method of painting was to rig a scaffolding from which buckets of paint were tipped, spilling paint onto a canvas placed below. Was Pollock making a joke? No, he was making a statement, and a loud one at that. His "art" was random, chaotic, and meaningless, reflecting his view of life and history. When there is no sense of purpose or destination, we tend toward despair and cynicism, which can be expressed in many ways.

The gospel, however, is a message of ultimate hope in the face of despair. It is a message that the divine Creator has not abandoned His creation, but has worked to redeem it. History is God's story, and it is moving toward a future consummation. The old order corrupted by sin will pass away, and a new Heaven and a new earth will be established forever. This is the good news of the gospel. This is our hope.

Distortions of Christian Hope

One of the fundamental ingredients in Paul's preaching was his conviction that the present age will one day end, to be replaced by the rule of God over His creation. This rule will be ushered in by the return of Jesus—an event that could happen any day, since no one knows the exact time when Jesus will return.

Although the early Christians possessed this hope, there were certain misunderstandings among some of the believers as to how this hope was to impact their daily living. In particular, troubling questions arose among the Thessalonian Christians. Their faith had been shaken by the fact that some of their members had died without having seen the expected coming of Christ. Would they miss the fulfillment of what God had promised?

Paul sought to address these fears in his first letter to the Thessalonians. The term he uses in 1 Thessalonians 3:13 and 4:15 to refer to Christ's coming is *parousia* (par-oo-*see*-uh). This word was used in New Testament times to describe someone who was present to exercise power on behalf of another, as when an officer deputized by the emperor made his appearance in one of the Roman provinces to settle a dispute or to demand fulfillment of an obligation. As God's "deputy," Jesus will appear to establish God's eternal rule. "The dead in Christ shall rise first" (1 Thessalonians 4:16). Then the living Christians will join them to "meet the Lord in the air" (v. 17). "So shall we ever be with the Lord," writes Paul (v. 17). No Christian will miss the glories awaiting the redeemed.

2 Thessalonians tells of another related problem that arose within the same church. Apparently some of the believers had decided that the "day of the Lord" (meaning the *parousia* of Christ) had already taken place, and that they had been left behind (see 2 Thessalonians 2:1, 2). Paul balances the picture of immediate expectation that he had sketched in 1 Thessalonians 4 by explaining that there were certain events that would take place before the coming of Christ (2 Thessalonians 2:1-12). Thus, Christians would have some measure of warning regarding the end of the age.

Paul's counsel to those preoccupied by the coming of Christ is twofold. First, they should not be led to think that believers who have died will not share in the joys of the age to come. Second, they should not use the fact that the present age is coming to an end as an excuse to become lazy and complacent. Rather, they are to act responsibly toward one another and toward their leadership within the Christian community. Christians in Thessalonica were fixing their eyes on the Lord's coming, not as a source of hope and inspiration for more effective ministry in the world, but as a form of escape from the world. This is a temptation contemporary Christians must resist as well.

End-Times Fanaticism Versus True Christian Mission

The futility of end-times speculation has been demonstrated again and again throughout the history of the church, but many groups within the body of Christ have been slow learners. All of us are aware of individuals who received a high degree of publicity by claiming to know the specific day on which Jesus would return. This fallacy has been repeated untold times, in spite of Jesus' clear teaching to the contrary: "But of that day and hour knoweth no man, no, not the angels of heaven, but my Father only" (Matthew 24:36).

Today eager speculators continue to be preoccupied by apocalyptic ideas about the end of the world. In becoming fixated on Christ's coming as a centerpiece of spirituality, some have become guilty of treating the second coming as the Thessalonians treated it. Their error may not be exactly like that of the Thessalonians, but their obsession with certain details of Jesus' return has smothered the hope and comfort that His coming is meant to offer to all His followers.

In trying to prepare for the second coming of Christ, many have embraced a misunderstanding of the need to separate oneself totally from the world and to set one's mind on the things of God. They have forgotten that the world is the object of God's love and the arena to which the church is to direct its message. The gospel places its focus on the world. God's concern is directed toward the world, as John 3:16 clearly tells us. The ministry of Jesus Christ was on behalf of the sins of the whole world (1 John 2:2). The church of Jesus Christ is the company of disciples whom He has sent into the world to serve; indeed, our primary "field" of service is the world (Matthew 13:38). The leaders whom God gives to the church have been given to it in order that it may fulfill its mission in the world. The church exists, in large measure, not for its own sake, but for the sake of the world.

Christians are not pessimists, fatalists, or cynics regarding the future, but partners with God in forming a beachhead in this world for the establishment of God's kingdom—the "presence of the future." Can we bring this about through human effort? Certainly not, for it is God's work in the present, and it will be God's work when He brings history to its ultimate destiny. But this does not mean that we are to remain passive, expecting God to work in this world apart from our endeavors. While looking forward in hope to God's "exclamation point" that will be brought about by Christ's return, we nevertheless work to transform our present culture as if that fulfillment were still thousands of years in the future, which it may well be. The world is important to us because, though estranged from God because of sin, it is still important to Him.

A truly Biblical theology of the world might be summarized in three brief affirmations. First, the world as a creation of God is good. All that encompasses physical and spiritual life in the world has been given to us by God to enjoy (1 Timothy 6:17). We must recognize that its source is God, for only then can we enjoy the world to its fullest.

A second affirmation must be that the world is a distorted or fallen world. It is a world of broken laws, broken relationships, estrangement, alienation, addiction, disease, and idolatry, where evil often has a firm foothold. Therefore, we find negative evaluations of "the world" in such texts such as John 18:36, Galatians 6:14, and 1 John 2:15. The third affirmation has to do with God's relationship to the world of humanity. God wills the redemption of all mankind (1 Timothy 2:3, 4). This is the Biblical message of salvation.

Hope: Our Sustaining Motive

The Christian's hope is that history is heading toward the end that God has planned for it. Such a hope empowers and sustains our ongoing efforts to be God's agents in this world. "We are saved," asserts Paul in Romans 8:24, "by hope." Some claim that the hope for God's eternal future leads to escapism from this world and its needs. But as C. S. Lewis observed, a careful reading of history will demonstrate that those who did the most for the present are those who thought most about the future. Citizens of Heaven make earth a better place.

Leslie Weatherhead once related that during a long sea journey, he began thinking what would happen if one day the captain, in the middle of the Pacific Ocean, summoned all of the passengers to the dining hall and said something like this: "There is plenty of food and water on board. Life will proceed as before. Meals will be served, games played, dances arranged, concerts provided, but I have decided not to make for port. We shall just cruise around and around in the ocean until our fuel is exhausted, and then I shall sink the ship." Weatherhead concluded that the next few days would come and go just as those that preceded them. Only one thing would be different. The captain's speech would have snatched from every mind the concept of purpose, meaning, and direction. In all probability, very soon afterward on a dark night, first one and then another passenger would jump overboard. No one can live without hope.

The *why* of life is as important as the *how*. The resurrection hope proclaimed by the gospel gives us our "why." Ours is not simply a hope for personal survival, but a conviction that we are co-laborers with God, who will one day by His power make all things new. Maranatha! Even so, come, Lord Jesus.

Our Enduring Hope

by Kenn Filkin

EVERYONE LOVES A WINNER, especially one that overcomes seemingly insurmountable challenges to win. Many said that Jim Abbott, a one-armed pitcher, could never win or succeed in major league baseball, but who couldn't help but be excited when he threw his first no-hitter on September 4, 1993, against the Cleveland Indians? Jim Abbott is an overcomer.

What tends to be the exception for athletic overcomers with disabilities, should be the norm for Christians. We are called to overcome our most serious "disability"—the power and presence of sin—not by our own might or power, but by Christ's provision, God's Spirit, and our heavenly Father's word of victory. The theme of overcoming is nowhere more prominent in Scripture than in the book of Revelation.

Although the apostle John never uses the word *hope* in Revelation, every chapter exudes hope for "him that overcometh." In the Bible hope is not a wish. Hope is an assurance, a knowledge of God's victory. The Bible does not speak of the *wish* for Christ's return, like one wishing it would quit raining, but rather of the *assurance* of His coming. The Christian does not have an uncertain wish for the future; he has a hope that endures hardship with the knowledge of God's future victory. Revelation boldly proclaims that victory.

Our Three Companions

Our three companions for our journey to Christlikeness are hope, endurance, and trials. These three are inseparable. Overcomers are always tested with trials, and "the testing of your faith produces endurance" (James 1:3, *New American Standard Bible*). Our trials result in endurance, which produces character. That Christlike character in turn produces hope (Romans 5:2-5).

Writing about the levels of Christian maturity, Vance Havner has observed that there are four classes of maturity: freshman, sophomore, junior, and senior. The freshman knows not, and knows not that he knows not. The sophomore knows not, and knows that he knows not. The junior knows, but knows not that he knows. The senior knows, and knows that he knows.

How and whether we grow from one level to the next depends upon how we respond to trials and struggles similar to those encountered by the seven churches in Revelation. The church at Ephesus (2:1-7) rejected evil, exhibited patience, and endured its trials, but it had lost its first love. The Christians at Smyrna (2:8-11) gracefully endured suffering from the "synagogue of Satan," and were promised a "crown of life" if they were "faithful unto death." The saints at Pergamos (2:12-17) kept their faith, but tolerated immorality and heresies. Still, if they repented, they would receive the "hidden manna" and a white stone with a "new name written." Thyatira (2:18-29) demonstrated love, service, faith, endurance, and works that were more abundant than before, but the church also tolerated cults of idolatry and immorality. If the faithful ones in Thyatira were able to "hold fast" and keep the faith until Jesus came, they would receive the "morning star." Sardis (3:1-6) was a "dead" church where only some had kept the faith, but if they could "strengthen the things which remain," the faithful would be honored and clothed in white. The Christians in Philadelphia (3:7-13) had endured all their trials in faith; if the believers there continued to keep the faith, they would receive a new name and a place in the temple of God. Laodicea (3:14-22) was self-satisfied and indifferent to God and His will, but if they repented and recaptured their zeal, they too could share Christ's throne.

These seven churches were at different levels of Christian maturity. The trials they endured had the potential to "make or break" them. Let us consider the part trials play in shaping us, using Havner's four "classes."

The Freshman

The freshmen Christians intellectually know about the hope of Christ, but theirs is a head knowledge only—a kind of "hearsay" knowledge from other believers. Freshmen think they know, but they know not that they have no personal knowledge or experience of Christ's power. Thus when they encounter trials, like the "stony ground" in Jesus' parable (Mark 4:16, 17), they are blind to the real significance of their circumstances. Laodicea's freshmen were told, "Thou sayest, I am rich, and increased with goods, and have need of nothing; and knowest not that thou art wretched, and miserable, and poor, and blind, and naked" (Revelation 3:15-17). They knew not that they knew not.

The freshman's endurance has no backbone of hope, so he falls flat and wonders why. But if the freshman responds to his failure in faith, and looks to God for strength, he will soon realize that he understands nothing. He is then prepared to stand up and walk again in the Lord's strength.

The Sophomore

The sophomore knows not hope, but because of failure in times of trial, he knows that he knows not. Freshmen resist change and stumble back into the old life. Sophomores struggle and fail, then recognize just how much they need to learn. They begin to recognize that trials do not indicate God's absence, but His presence.

James and May, a couple of my acquaintance, had been Christians less than a year before they encountered a severe time of testing. One night James, an engineer for a railroad, saw a drunk walking out onto the tracks. He tried to stop but could not. The drunk was killed, though James was not at fault. James's response to this tragedy was to start fighting with May and to resume his drinking. James knew not, and by resisting God's guidance he remained a freshman—he still knew not that he knew not. May, on the other hand, was crushed by this trial and especially by her husband's ungodly response to it. She stumbled into her minister's office and cried out that she did not know nor understand. She asked, "What does God want me to do?" Through this trial, she learned that she knew not, and sought God's answer for what she did not know. She went on to become a junior.

The Junior

The junior Christians know hope, but they do not know that they know it. They begin to trust God, His Word, and His provision for victory, but they do not understand the dynamics of why all of this works. Their faith is emerging, but still struggling.

As the testing time for James and May continued, May practiced "tough love," wanting to show her husband that he would lose everything and everyone if he continued drinking. She was deeply concerned, but found hope in God's promise from 1 Corinthians 10:13: "There hath no temptation taken you but such as is common to man: but God is faithful, who will not suffer you to be tempted above that ye are able; but will with the temptation also make a way to escape, that ye may be able to bear it."

May did not understand how God would "make a way to escape," or how He would protect her from being tested beyond what she could bear, but she did trust His promise. She knew hope, but did not know exactly how it would sustain her in the situation currently fac-

ing her. James responded to her tough love and for the first time in their marriage, he said to her, "I need help." James then moved from a freshman to a sophomore, and May began moving from a junior to a senior.

Like Daniel's three friends, when the junior emerges from the furnace, he will know that God provides victory to His trusting and obedient children. He not only knows hope; he now knows that he knows. He is a senior.

The Senior

Philadelphia and Smyrna are examples of senior churches that had endured the trials they encountered with hope and confidence, and with unswerving loyalty to Christ. Seniors have been tested by trials, and they know that they can endure any trial, in faith that God will provide the victory that He has promised to overcomers. Like the good soil, the seniors "by persevering [endurance] produce a crop" (Luke 8:15, *New International Version*). They are overcomers who face trials with *an enduring hope*. Such individuals are the martyrs and overcomers mentioned in Revelation. They are part of the "great multitude," standing "before the throne, and before the Lamb, clothed with white robes, and palms in their hands" (Revelation 7:9). They have come "out of great tribulation, and have washed their robes, and made them white in the blood of the Lamb" (v. 14). They will drink freely from the water of life (Revelation 21:6), inherit all things (v. 7), and enter the city of God, where every tear will be wiped away by God Himself (v. 4). All of the sorrows and trials of earth will be ended forever.

For then the senior will have graduated. Then he will be home.

Answers to Quarterly Quiz
on page 226

Lesson 1—1. Philippi. 2. nurse, children. **Lesson 2**—1. holiness. 2. brotherly love. **Lesson 3**—1. Paul, Silvanus (Silas), Timothy. 2. false. **Lesson 4**—1. the word of the Lord. 2. work, eat. **Lesson 5**—1. Galilee. 2. archangel, trump. **Lesson 6**—1. Patmos. 2. Asia. **Lesson 7**—1. ten days. 2. Balaam. **Lesson 8**—1. Jezebel. 2. repent. 3. rod, iron. **Lesson 9**—1. David. 2. lukewarm, cold, hot, spew. **Lesson 10**—1. a strong angel. 2. Lion, Root. **Lesson 11**—1. their foreheads. 2. great tribulation. **Lesson 12**—1. many crowns. 2. second. **Lesson 13**—1. Jerusalem. 2. tabernacle. 3. kings.

Proclaim the Gospel!

March 2
Lesson 1

DEVOTIONAL READING: 1 Thessalonians 1:1-10.

LESSON SCRIPTURE: 1 Thessalonians 2:1-13.

PRINTED TEXT: 1 Thessalonians 2:1-13.

1 Thessalonians 2:1-13

1 For yourselves, brethren, know our entrance in unto you, that it was not in vain:

2 But even after that we had suffered before, and were shamefully entreated, as ye know, at Philippi, we were bold in our God to speak unto you the gospel of God with much contention.

3 For our exhortation was not of deceit, nor of uncleanness, nor in guile:

4 But as we were allowed of God to be put in trust with the gospel, even so we speak; not as pleasing men, but God, which trieth our hearts.

5 For neither at any time used we flattering words, as ye know, nor a cloak of covetousness; God is witness:

6 Nor of men sought we glory, neither of you, nor yet of others, when we might have been burdensome, as the apostles of Christ.

7 But we were gentle among you, even as a nurse cherisheth her children:

8 So being affectionately desirous of you, we were willing to have imparted unto you, not the gospel of God only, but also our own souls, because ye were dear unto us.

9 For ye remember, brethren, our labor and travail: for laboring night and day, because we would not be chargeable unto any of you, we preached unto you the gospel of God.

10 Ye are witnesses, and God also, how holily and justly and unblamably we behaved ourselves among you that believe:

11 As ye know how we exhorted and comforted and charged every one of you, as a father doth his children,

12 That ye would walk worthy of God, who hath called you unto his kingdom and glory.

13 For this cause also thank we God without ceasing, because, when ye received the word of God which ye heard of us, ye received it not as the word of men, but, as it is in truth, the word of God, which effectually worketh also in you that believe.

GOLDEN TEXT: We were bold in our God to speak unto you the gospel of God with much contention.—1 Thessalonians 2:2.

Hope for the Future
Unit 1: Stand Fast in the Lord
(Lessons 1-5)

Lesson Aims

This lesson should prepare the student to:

1. Name several ways in which Paul and his companions exemplified the spirit of Christ in their teaching ministry at Thessalonica.

2. Show how the character of a teacher affects the students' acceptance of his teaching.

3. Activate a plan to improve his own influence for Christ among the people around him.

Lesson Outline

INTRODUCTION

    A. Defense of the Gospel

    B. A Closer Look at the Work Site

    C. Lesson Background

  I. WORKERS WITH THE WORD (1 Thessalonians 2:1-12)

    A. In the Face of Opposition (vv. 1-3)

    B. In the Sight of God (vv. 4-6)

      Whom Are You Trying to Please?

    C. With Loving Care (vv. 7-9)

      Gentleness

    D. With Parental Patience (vv. 10-12)

 II. WORKING OF THE WORD (1 Thessalonians 2:13)

CONCLUSION

    A. Protecting What?

    B. Prayer for Messengers

    C. Thought to Remember

The visual for Lesson 1 in the visuals packet is a map highlighting significant places covered in this quarter's lessons. It is shown on page 237.

Introduction

A. Defense of the Gospel

The young church at Thessalonica was under attack (1 Thessalonians 1:6). Apparently its members were being ridiculed as deluded followers of crafty and deceptive foreigners who had brought ridiculous tales of a Jewish cult leader called Jesus. These so-called preachers had then skipped town when the pressure became too much for them (probably taking considerable cash from their followers). The Roman world was full of such wandering "philosophers," who were, in reality, swindlers.

What would happen to the cause of Christ in and around Thessalonica if such charges were left unanswered? For the sake of Christians young and mature, in Thessalonica and elsewhere, it was necessary to cite the testimony of the Thessalonian people and the integrity of Paul and his companions. This would show that the church in that city was not a band of deluded sheep trailing after self-serving hirelings. The Christians constituted a company of substantial believers in an established gospel. They were the recipients of a priceless heritage, as seen in the behavior of those who had brought the message. "We preach not ourselves, but Christ Jesus the Lord; and ourselves your servants for Jesus' sake" (2 Corinthians 4:5).

B. A Closer Look at the Work Site

Thessalonica (modern Salonika) was a city of some two hundred thousand residents, located about one hundred miles west of Philippi in the Roman province of Macedonia. It was the capital of the province and thus a strategic center from which to spread the gospel. Paul, Silas, and Timothy arrived there on Paul's second missionary journey after their tumultuous experience in Philippi. There they had established a church, but in the process, Paul and Silas had been arrested, flogged, and imprisoned (all unlawfully) for healing a demon-possessed girl (Acts 16:16-40).

In Thessalonica, the missionaries found a Jewish synagogue. There Paul taught on three successive Sabbaths, winning converts but making some bitter foes among the Jews. Their opposition was not eased by Paul's success in winning Gentiles who had come to respect the Old Testament Scriptures but were not full proselytes to Judaism. Paul's antagonists finally stirred up a mob and stormed the house of a man named Jason, with whom Paul and his companions had lodged. The Jews brought charges before the city rulers that the apostles had "turned the world upside down," teaching against the decrees of Caesar and promoting another King called Jesus. For the safety of all persons involved, the Christians sent Paul and Silas on to Beroea, where they received a far more positive response (Acts 17:1-12).

How long were the apostles in Thessalonica? It is hard to arrive at a specific time, but they were there long enough for the following to occur: (1) they established a viable church and built some lasting friendships (1 Thessalonians 1:2-4); (2) Paul established himself in a self-sustaining occupation (1 Thessalonians 2:9); and (3) Paul received financial gifts at least twice from the saints at Philippi (Philippians 4:16).

C. Lesson Background

Paul was deeply concerned for the welfare of the Thessalonian church and expressed that concern in making plans to visit it (1 Thessalonians 2:17, 18). When those plans did not materialize, he sent Timothy so that he could encourage the believers and then report to Paul on their condition (1 Thessalonians 3:1-8). Paul was in Athens when he dispatched Timothy on this mission (3:1, 2). Apparently Silas accompanied Timothy, because Acts 18:5 records that both Timothy and Silas rejoined Paul in Corinth, having come from Macedonia. Their good news concerning the Thessalonians' continued faithfulness in the face of persecution (1 Thessalonians 3:6-8) was most encouraging to Paul. The report also seems to have included bad news of the Jews' ongoing campaign to discredit the church by slandering the apostles who had brought it into being. So Paul—joined by Silas and Timothy (1 Thessalonians 1:1)—wrote what is perhaps the earliest written material in the New Testament, to strengthen and encourage the beleaguered young church in Thessalonica. The year was approximately A.D. 51, and the place of writing was Corinth.

I. Workers With the Word (1 Thessalonians 2:1-12)

The Thessalonian Christians were committed to Christ, in accordance with the gospel preached by Paul and his partners. To protect these saints from the slanderous attacks of Paul's opponents, the gospel had to be firmly defended and established. One way of doing this was to demonstrate that the teachers of that gospel were men of integrity, known to be speakers of truth.

A. In the Face of Opposition (vv. 1-3)

1. For yourselves, brethren, know our entrance in unto you, that it was not in vain.

The readers were able to draw from their own experience and memory the facts that would establish confidence in their teachers and what they had been taught. The *entrance* into

VISUALS FOR THESE LESSONS

The Adult Visuals packet contains classroom-size visuals designed for use with the lessons in the Spring Quarter. The packet is available from your supplier. Order No. 392.

How to Say It

AGONIA (Greek). ag-owe-*nee*-uh.
BEROEA. Buh-*ree*-uh.
CAESAREA. Sess-uh-*ree*-uh.
EPHESUS. *Eff*-uh-suss.
MACEDONIA. Mass-uh-*doe*-nee-uh.
PHILIPPI. Fuh-*lip*-pie or *Fill*-uh-pie.
SALONIKA. Suh-*lahn*-ik-uh or Sal-uh-*nee*-kuh.
THESSALONICA. *Thess*-uh-loe-*nye*-kuh (strong accent on *nye*).

Thessalonica of Paul, Silas, and Timothy had been as a team of like-minded equals. They had come into the city investing themselves and becoming involved in the lives and experiences of the people they taught. This whole procedure had not been *in vain;* it was not an empty show, nor a failure. It had resulted in the establishment of a growing and influential church in an essentially heathen city.

The phrase *in vain* could also mean empty or empty-handed. The missionaries did not come with hands outstretched to receive material benefits; they came bearing gifts of themselves and the gospel.

2. But even after that we had suffered before, and were shamefully entreated, as ye know, at Philippi, we were bold in our God to speak unto you the gospel of God with much contention.

The wounds from Paul and Silas's flogging at *Philippi* (Acts 16:22, 23) may not have been fully healed when they arrived at Thessalonica. In any case, their embarrassing treatment by the authorities in Philippi was well known (Acts 16:35-40).

Also well known in Thessalonica was the way in which Paul and his partners had plunged into their work, making themselves just as vulnerable as they had in Philippi. Their Christlike example was most evident in their endurance of affliction. Such circumstances served to strip away any veneer of piety, so that the real substance of their faith appeared.

We were bold in our God to speak unto you. Because of their confidence in the divine source of their message, they did not hesitate to deliver it, in spite of opposition similar to what they had faced previously in other cities. The Greek term for *contention* in this verse is *agonia*, from which we get our English word "agony." It implies a strenuous struggle against strong opposition.

3. For our exhortation was not of deceit, nor of uncleanness, nor in guile.

This suggests the kind of charges being brought against the apostles and their teaching. Accustomed to the kind of roaming charlatans and swindlers who victimized the Roman world (Acts 8:9; 13:6-10), Jewish opponents could easily accuse Paul and his partners of being "cut from the same cloth." Nothing could be farther from the truth.

Instead, the *exhortation* (urging or admonition) of the gospel message called hearers to a higher way of life. It did not spring from *deceit,* as do the works and words of the arch deceiver, Satan (2 Corinthians 11:13-15; Revelation 12:9), but from the established facts of Jesus' life, death, and resurrection. It was not motivated by desires rooted in *uncleanness* or *guile.* Here the word *guile* translates a word that originally described a fisherman's method of enticing his catch. Paul and his companions did not "bait" their appeal with promises to potential converts of health, wealth, and happiness. Instead they preached Christ in plain terms, relying for success on the power of the Holy Spirit rather than the wisdom of men (1 Corinthians 2:1-5). They did not try to hide some of the harsher aspects of following Jesus, such as the fact that the believers would suffer persecution (1 Thessalonians 3:4).

B. In the Sight of God (vv. 4-6)

Here Paul outlined the basic motivation that compelled him and his companions to serve as they did.

4. But as we were allowed of God to be put in trust with the gospel, even so we speak; not as pleasing men, but God, which trieth our hearts.

Allowed means being approved after testing. Thus, Paul and others like him were entrusted to deliver the gospel to the Gentiles, much as a bank representative is commissioned to deliver items of great value only after being subjected to close scrutiny. Paul acknowledged his commission as a solemn trust, so he spoke with a constant awareness of his accountability before God. This did not mean that he acted without regard to the feelings of those about him. After all, "Love thy neighbor" is commanded by Him who claims our first devotion.

WHOM ARE YOU TRYING TO PLEASE?

It is a characteristic of our age that we eagerly seek to please others. Commercially, this is obvious. When an automobile is advertised by its manufacturers, great pains are taken to show how "pleasing" it is. The seats are comfortable and adjustable, the ride is very smooth, and the brakes stop the car quickly but without "grabbing." One will be happy with the many miles it will run on a gallon of gas. The appearance of the car in your driveway will make all your neighbors envious.

It is also true that many churches publicize how "user friendly" they are. They feature services at different hours to make them more convenient to attend, facilities so children (or even babies) can be cared for during worship or study periods, and ample parking close at hand. Some even advertise that one can dress informally and feel more relaxed and comfortable while in worship.

Of course, it is not necessary to stress that a church has uncomfortable seats, long, boring services, or inadequate parking space in order to show that it is not being influenced by "worldly" distractions. But we must be concerned in all our decisions that our primary motive is the desire to please *God.* We must find a way to emphasize consecration rather than comfort; God's way, not the easy way; and eternal ends instead of merely temporal means. After all, we are following the way of the cross, not the way of the cushion.   —J. G. V. B.

5. For neither at any time used we flattering words, as ye know, nor a cloak of covetousness; God is witness.

The Thessalonian Christians were fully aware that Paul was not among those who "by good words and fair speeches deceive the hearts of the simple" (Romans 16:18). He was not given to flattery, seeking the favor of persons by extravagant praise. On the other hand, he was generous with words of real appreciation, as in the first chapter of this epistle, where he begins with the typical Pauline prayer: "We give thanks to God always for you all" (v. 2). He to whom the prayer was addressed knew its sincerity. He was *witness* to the fact that the apostles did not use words as a *cloak of covetousness,* to hide a greedy purpose.

6. Nor of men sought we glory, neither of you, nor yet of others, when we might have been burdensome, as the apostles of Christ.

It is noteworthy that Paul considered not only himself, but also Timothy and Silas, as *apostles of Christ.* Although the term *apostle* is usually applied to one of Jesus' twelve disciples, it is used of others outside that group (see Acts 14:14) and even of Jesus (Hebrews 3:1). In such passages (as well as in the verse before us), the word carries its basic meaning of "one who is sent forth."

Paul, Silas, and Timothy, working together as equals in the apostolic task of evangelism, could have trumpeted their right to respect and honor. They could have demanded special recognition and unquestioned obedience, using a heavy hand. But they preferred the way of self-forgetful service and gentle persuasion. The Thessalonians could reasonably infer that they had worked in the same manner elsewhere.

C. With Loving Care (vv. 7-9)

Paul had just explained how his ministry was *not* conducted; he now turned from this negative perspective to a more positive one.

7, 8. But we were gentle among you, even as a nurse cherisheth her children: so being affectionately desirous of you, we were willing to have imparted unto you, not the gospel of God only, but also our own souls, because ye were dear unto us.

The apostles' ministry resembled a family relationship more than it did a business or form of government. Just because a *nurse,* or nursing mother, is *gentle* does not mean that her influence is substandard. She pours herself into the life of her infant without thought of advantage to herself. She directs that life by her constant care and consistent teaching. This was the kind of self-investment practiced by the apostles, because they were *affectionately desirous* (literally "filled with earnest love") toward the people among whom they labored.

GENTLENESS

How many times is the soft touch the means by which change, growth, and blessing are furthered! We know that one cannot cause plants to grow by pulling them up in impatient haste. They must be gently placed in the earth, carefully nurtured, and tenderly cultivated. Sometimes a child will be given a puppy for a present and will want to maul and pinch and pummel it. This only scares and alienates the new pet. The child should be taught to pat the dog softly and be "nice" to it, not rough and harsh.

Surely in spiritual matters, Paul's example of gentleness has much to teach us. Some have used a "fire and brimstone" approach in the teaching of Christian truth. This usually includes a fierce denunciation of certain sins, a stern warning about the consequences of dis-

obedience, and a vehement cry that all such conduct is cursed, doomed, and well-nigh unforgivable. The calm, considerate, and concerned attitude with which Jesus treated the woman caught in adultery should encourage us to show the gentleness that characterized Paul's treatment of the Thessalonians.

Such gentleness does not imply indifference to sin, but confidence in the truth and a loving desire to encourage and build up others in a teaching situation. As Robert Browning observed,

"The great mind knows the power of gentleness,
Only tries force, because persuasion fails."

—J. G. V. B.

9. For ye remember, brethren, our labor and travail: for laboring night and day, because we would not be chargeable unto any of you, we preached unto you the gospel of God.

The missionaries' self-giving included manual *labor* by which they supported themselves while preaching in Thessalonica, as Paul also did in Corinth (Acts 18:1-3; 1 Corinthians 9:14-19) and in Ephesus (Acts 20:34). Paul did not hold to the Greek and Roman disdain for manual labor and laborers. Instead he accepted the God-ordained respect for work and workers (Exodus 20:9; 31:1-5; Proverbs 6:6-11; 24:30-34), and he urged the same upon his converts (Ephesians 4:28). This was true especially in Thessalonica, where he cited more than once his own example and declared that "if any would not work, neither should he eat" (2 Thessalonians 3:10).

Paul insisted that those who preach the gospel have a right to live of the gospel (1 Corinthians 9:4-14), for "the laborer is worthy of his hire" (Luke 10:7). As for himself, however, he chose to work a double shift, *night and day,* in order to provide an example for others and to deprive his critics of any excuse for charging him or his companions with mercenary motives (1 Corinthians 9:15-19).

D. With Parental Patience (vv. 10-12)

10. Ye are witnesses, and God also, how holily and justly and unblamably we behaved ourselves among you that believe.

Again the writers cited the testimony from their readers, who were *witnesses* in matters observable to all, and from *God,* who knew what was not evident to human eyes. The apostles' integrity and generosity were evident in their daily dealings with those about them. No fault could be reasonably charged or proved against them. They provided for things honest in the sight of both God and men (Romans 12:17; 2 Corinthians 8:20, 21). This is the course that

visual for
lesson 1

every Christian—especially every parent, leader, and teacher—would do well to follow.

11, 12. As ye know how we exhorted and comforted and charged every one of you, as a father doth his children, that ye would walk worthy of God, who hath called you unto his kingdom and glory.

With tenderness (v. 7), the apostles had met the immediate needs of the infant church. With the teaching, exhortation, and supportive encouragement of a *father*, they had pointed the developing church toward maturity in Christ.

II. Working of the Word
(1 Thessalonians 2:13)

13. For this cause also thank we God without ceasing, because, when ye received the word of God which ye heard of us, ye received it not as the word of men, but, as it is in truth, the word of God, which effectually worketh also in you that believe.

Paul's constant prayerful concern for his Christian friends is again evident. The epistle began with an expression of thanks for the people's response to the ministry rendered among them (1:2-10). A second cause for thanks was now introduced: their understanding and attitude toward the message itself—*the word of God*. The Thessalonians had heard and accepted the spoken word of God, telling of the living Word of God—the Lord Jesus Christ. The spoken word was respected for its divine source and received as something that possessed the power to work *effectually* in those who *believe*. Thus received, it did its appointed work within the Thessalonians, giving them purpose and hope, and radiating out to their neighbors, both near and far (1 Thessalonians 1:5-10).

The Word of God still works when it is presented, accepted, and followed as such, in spite of imperfections in the messengers. "We have this treasure in earthen vessels," Paul said, "that the excellency of the power may be of God, and not of us" (2 Corinthians 4:7). This is not an excuse for carelessness or irresponsibility in the Christian leader or follower. One's "vessel," or body, should be a tool to magnify the message, not cheapen it. The Word of God is a word of life and a word for living. In Thessalonica it was lived by both messengers and hearers.

Conclusion
A. Protecting What?

What did the apostle Paul accomplish by penning the passage we have just reviewed? If it was meant to protect himself from criticism and

mistreatment, it failed badly. He was haled before the authorities in Corinth, mobbed in Ephesus, attacked in Jerusalem, imprisoned in Caesarea and Rome, and (if we may believe the strongest of implications) was finally executed as a criminal.

If, however, this passage was written to protect the church and the gospel, setting an example and precedent for Christian ministry in ages to come, it succeeded mightily indeed. The church at Thessalonica was strengthened to overcome its obstacles, and succeeding generations of churches have partaken of that comfort. Succeeding generations of gospel messengers also have been strengthened to overcome difficulties and to share in the ultimate victory won by Paul. They recognized that Paul and his partners were not presenting something they had invented or had trimmed to suit their hearers.

Sadly, all too many messengers have placed self-protection and self-promotion ahead of protecting the gospel and the church. May we be willing, like Paul and his companions, to pay any price to keep the gospel pure and untarnished.

B. Prayer for Messengers

We praise and thank You, our Father God, for the word of life in Christ Jesus. Thank You for faithful messengers who brought the word to us —in writing, in speaking, and in living demonstration. May we in our turn be faithful in conveying the word to others, that they too may live in Christ, in whose blessed name we pray, amen.

C. Thought to Remember

Apostles preached and lived their message. Believers heard and responded. The Word of God worked.

Home Daily Bible Readings

Monday, Feb. 24—Serve the True God (1 Thessalonians 1:1-10)
Tuesday, Feb. 25—Witness of the Prophets (1 Peter 1:1-12)
Wednesday, Feb. 26—Confess Jesus Christ (Romans 10:1-13)
Thursday, Feb. 27—Be Guardians of God's Word (Acts 20:25-38)
Friday, Feb. 28—Keep Your Ministry Honest (2 Corinthians 4:1-6)
Saturday, Mar. 1—Make Your Message Clear (1 Corinthians 14:18-25)
Sunday, Mar. 2—All People Should Praise God (Psalm 67:1-7)

Learning by Doing

This page contains an alternate lesson plan emphasizing learning activities.
Classes desiring such student involvement will find these suggestions helpful.

Learning Goals

This lesson should help students:

1. Name several ways in which Paul and his companions exemplified the spirit of Christ in their teaching ministry at Thessalonica.

2. Show how the character of a teacher affects the students' acceptance of his teaching.

3. Put in action a plan to improve his own influence for Christ among those around him.

Into the Lesson

Begin the class by asking students to name a preacher, teacher, or other Christian leader whom they think was or is especially effective in sharing the Word of God with others. This should be someone who had (or is still having) significant influence on their lives. Ask, "What made that person so effective?" Get as many people as possible involved in this activity. Make the transition into the lesson by pointing out that the positive influence and example of mature Christians is absolutely necessary for the growth of individuals and the church.

Into the Word

Divide the class into several groups and ask them to read 1 Thessalonians 2:1-13. Give each group a sheet of paper and a pen or pencil. Have the group designate a "secretary" to take notes. Ask each group to write down a list of as many of the positive characteristics and qualities of Paul, Silas, and Timothy (who are mentioned in the first verse of the book) as they can find stated or implied in this passage. Give them only *one minute* to do this (this exercise is also in the student book). After one minute, stop the writing and see which group has the longest list, giving small prizes to the group with the most items (such as a bag of candy). Answers would include: bold (v. 2), truthful and honest (vv. 3, 5), trustworthy (v. 4), focused on pleasing God (v. 4), gentle and loving (vv. 7, 8), hard-working (v. 9), holy (v. 10), just (v. 10), blameless (v. 10), encouraging (vv. 11, 12), and thankful (v. 13). Allowing each group to contribute, write a complete list of all their responses on a chalkboard or on poster board.

Now ask the class members to express out loud some of the stated and implied characteristics in this passage that are the opposite of the ones just listed. Some answers would be: con-tentious (v. 2), deceitful, unclean, and tricky (v. 3), focused on pleasing men (vv. 4, 6), flattering and covetous (v. 5), and burdensome (v. 6).

Next, have the women in the class work together, using vv. 7-9, to explain why a preacher, teacher, or church leader would be much more effective by demonstrating the positive characteristics of a "nurse" (point out, as the commentary does, that this term probably means "nursing mother"). The men should likewise work together, using vv. 10-12, to explain why a leader would be more effective by demonstrating the positive qualities of a father. Choose spokespersons for each group carefully, and have some fun as they share their insights.

Into Life

The character of a teacher often determines whether others listen to and accept what is being taught. Ask the class to give illustrations of people who have led others with "ulterior motives" or selfish ambitions. Avoid any gossip or unkind words. The idea is to note that people of this type are still around. In contrast, our goal should be to influence *positively* those around us. This means that we must purposefully conduct ourselves in ways that increase our influence for Christ, avoiding any behavior that sours that influence.

Ask each class member to restudy the list of positive characteristics and qualities listed earlier, and identify two or three on which he or she is "doing well" and one or two on which he or she "needs work" (this activity is in the student book). Remind the class that accountability to others is helpful and ask each person to share his or her conclusions with another person. Give them a few minutes to do this.

Now ask the students to identify specific people with whom they have influence (this is also in the student book.) This could include children, neighbors, fellow employees, and relatives, among others. Have them meet in twos again, with the same partner as before. Ask this final question: "What one thing will you do this week to improve your influence with the people you named?" Encourage them to be specific.

Close with prayer for God's help in becoming people who are committed to living blameless and positive lives, so that we can have the greatest possible influence for our Lord.

Let's Talk It Over

The questions on this page are designed to encourage review of the lesson Scriptures and to promote discussion of the lesson by the class. The answers provided are only discussion starters. Let your class talk it over from there.

1. Paul may have been able to show the Thessalonians the wounds he had received at Philippi for his faithfulness to the gospel. What kinds of wounds may we have as a result of our commitment to Christ?

Paul was able to testify in Galatians 6:17: "I bear in my body the marks of the Lord Jesus." We probably have no physical wounds we can attribute to people's reaction to our faith and witness. However, we are likely to bear in our spirits some very real wounds. Perhaps we have experienced rejection and ridicule because of our stand for Christ. We may have had doors slammed in our faces or telephones hung up abruptly on us when we tried to speak to people about Christ and His church. Of course, we must always distinguish between wounds received for Christ and those that result from efforts to protect or promote ourselves.

2. How can we avoid the trap of giving flattery to others rather than genuine praise? How does this apply to our life in the church?

What is our motive for speaking positive words to others? Do we want to "win friends and influence people" in order to gain a personal advantage? Where the church is concerned, are we tempted to use flattery to influence people to attend services, give more generously, or take a position of responsibility? In his writings, Paul frequently makes reference to the principle of edification. For example, in Romans 14:19 he writes, "Let us therefore follow after the things which make for peace, and things wherewith one may edify another." Genuine praise edifies or builds up the person to whom it is given. In contrast, flattery is given for the benefit of the flatterer. It is obvious that Paul himself had no use for flattery, but was consistently concerned with building others up in the Lord.

3. It is interesting to contrast Paul's relationship to the churches he served with the kind of leadership exercised in the modern cults. What are some contrasts we can note?

Cult leaders usually seek to dominate their followers and exercise control over their behavior. In contrast, Paul stressed that he and his companions did not aim to "lord it over your faith, but we work with you for your joy" (2 Corinthians 1:24, *New International Version*). Cult leaders also engage in self-glorification. Paul, however, expressed his hope that "Christ shall be magnified in my body, whether it be by life, or by death" (Philippians 1:20). Some cult leaders live in luxury, while their followers sacrifice for them. A passage such as 2 Corinthians 11:23-29 makes it clear that Paul knew nothing of luxury as he labored for Christ.

4. Paul was determined to make clear that financial gain was not the purpose of his ministry. How can the church demonstrate the priority of spiritual goals, while acknowledging its need for financial support?

Some churches include a note in their Sunday bulletins, pointing out that while visitors are welcome to contribute to the offering, they are in no way obligated to do so. This is a way of emphasizing that the church's ministries are supported by the faithful giving of its members. Many churches make a monthly statement of income and expenditures available to anyone who wishes to inspect it. This statement can demonstrate that moneys received are being used to fund spiritual labors both within the local congregation and outside of it.

5. The Word of God works in people's lives. How can we picture this power?

The Bible describes itself by the use of several helpful symbols. For example, it is seed (Luke 8:11). We know how seed works in the earth, generating the tiny plant that ultimately produces our food. The seed of the Word works similarly within our hearts and minds, producing holiness of life, faithful service, and a Christlike character. Another symbol the Bible uses for itself is light (Psalm 119:105). Light works in illuminating darkness, revealing potential hazards, and showing us how to proceed. The light of God's Word enables us to proceed safely along life's dark, dangerous pathways. In addition, the Bible compares itself more than once with a sword (Ephesians 6:17; Hebrews 4:12). In the hand of an ancient warrior, a sword worked to fend off and defeat a foe. We can work with the sword of the Spirit to ward off the devil's attacks and to defeat him in his efforts to destroy our faith.

Live in Love and Holiness!

DEVOTIONAL READING: 1 Peter 1:13-22.

LESSON SCRIPTURE: 1 Thessalonians 3:6— 4:12.

PRINTED TEXT: 1 Thessalonians 3:12—4:12.

1 Thessalonians 3:12, 13

12 And the Lord make you to increase and abound in love one toward another, and toward all men, even as we do toward you:

13 To the end he may stablish your hearts unblamable in holiness before God, even our Father, at the coming of our Lord Jesus Christ with all his saints.

1 Thessalonians 4:1-12

1 Furthermore then we beseech you, brethren, and exhort you by the Lord Jesus, that as ye have received of us how ye ought to walk and to please God, so ye would abound more and more.

2 For ye know what commandments we gave you by the Lord Jesus.

3 For this is the will of God, even your sanctification, that ye should abstain from fornication:

4 That every one of you should know how to possess his vessel in sanctification and honor;

5 Not in the lust of concupiscence, even as the Gentiles which know not God:

6 That no man go beyond and defraud his brother in any matter: because that the Lord is the avenger of all such, as we also have forewarned you and testified.

7 For God hath not called us unto uncleanness, but unto holiness.

8 He therefore that despiseth, despiseth not man, but God, who hath also given unto us his Holy Spirit.

9 But as touching brotherly love ye need not that I write unto you: for ye yourselves are taught of God to love one another.

10 And indeed ye do it toward all the brethren which are in all Macedonia: but we beseech you, brethren, that ye increase more and more;

11 And that ye study to be quiet, and to do your own business, and to work with your own hands, as we commanded you;

12 That ye may walk honestly toward them that are without, and that ye may have lack of nothing.

GOLDEN TEXT: The Lord make you to increase and abound in love one toward another, and toward all men, . . . to the end he may stablish your hearts unblamable in holiness before God, even our Father, at the coming of our Lord Jesus Christ with all his saints.—1 Thessalonians 3:12, 13.

> ### Hope for the Future
> Unit 1: Stand Fast in the Lord
> (Lessons 1-5)

Lesson Aims

After completing this study, the student should:

1. Know the importance of personal purity and of brotherly love in the Christian life.

2. Know how a person may rejoice in present spiritual accomplishments and yet still see the need for ongoing development in Christian maturity.

3. Set and pursue a specific goal for his own expressions of Christian love.

Lesson Outline

INTRODUCTION
    A. Christians in the World
    B. Lesson Background
I. PRAYER FOR GROWTH (1 Thessalonians 3:12, 13)
    A. Growth in Love (v. 12)
      Love: Increasing and Abounding
    B. Growth in Holiness (v. 13)
II. PLEA FOR PURITY (1 Thessalonians 4:1-8)
    A. Live to Please God (vv. 1, 2)
    B. God Commands Sexual Purity (vv. 3-5)
      Abstain From Fornication
    C. God Punishes the Impure (v. 6)
    D. God Calls All to Holiness (vv. 7, 8)
III. PLEA FOR THE PRACTICE OF LOVE (1 Thessalonians 4:9-12)
    A. You Were Taught Love by God (v. 9)
    B. You Have Made a Good Start (v. 10)
    C. You Must Put Love to Work (vv. 11, 12)
CONCLUSION
    A. Of Goals and Plans
    B. Prayer for Improvement
    C. Thought to Remember

Use the visual for Lesson 2 in the visuals packet to highlight today's golden text from 1 Thessalonians 3:12, 13. It is shown on page 245.

Introduction

A. Christians in the World

An ancient Greek writing, entitled "Address to Diognetus," and apparently from the third century A.D., provides a vivid description of how Christians lived and behaved among their fellowmen at that time. Here are some of its contents:

"[Christians] live in their native lands, but like foreigners. They take part in everything like citizens, and endure everything like aliens. Like everyone else they marry, they have children, but they do not expose their infants. They set a common table, but not a common bed. They find themselves in the flesh, but they do not live after the flesh . . . They obey the established laws, and in their own lives they surpass the laws. They love all men and are persecuted by all men . . . are insulted, and they do honor."

Here were people who had taken seriously the instructions of Christ and the apostles concerning love and purity!

B. Lesson Background

The opening of Christian gatherings with a word of prayer is more than a good habit; it is an expression of our basic faith and character. Our study today begins with a word *on* prayer from 1 Thessalonians 3.

The opening verses of 1 Thessalonians 3 record the apostle Paul's concern for his friends in Thessalonica, his sending of Timothy to encourage them (since he could not go himself), and his rejoicing at Timothy's return, with good news of their steadfastness. "Now we live," he exults, "if [or since] ye stand fast in the Lord" (v. 8). With verse 9 comes the mention of specific prayer. Paul gives thanks to God for the Thessalonian Christians and for the joy they have brought him, and he continues with a petition that he may revisit them and supply what is still lacking in their faith and life (vv. 10, 11).

This shift from thanks to petition, and from rejoicing in his friends' accomplishments to concern for their maturity in Christ, reflects an attitude that is critically important in kingdom labors. Is God's messenger never satisfied and always asking for more? Yes, he is never satisfied! Pleased with the good—certainly! Satisfied with an unchanging level in that good—certainly not! One might as well expect a proud parent to be satisfied with two-year-old behavior in a four-year-old child.

There is a difference, however, between our children on the one hand and God's children on the other. In this world we reach physical maturity and cease growing. Our minds slow down, and we quit learning. But in Christ we never reach the end of opportunity for development, and we always have eternity to anticipate. Our text this week deals with carrying out our earthly responsibilities while looking past them to Heaven.

I. Prayer for Growth
(1 Thessalonians 3:12,13)

The apostle was thankful to hear of his friends' faithfulness to the gospel. Yet there was still room for growth.

A. Growth in Love (v. 12)

12. And the Lord make you to increase and abound in love one toward another, and toward all men, even as we do toward you.

And links the following petition to the request made in the preceding verse for a future visit to Thessalonica. Paul's prayer was that the believers' love, both among themselves and toward all other persons, should *increase and abound* until it overflowed. As love was the identifying badge of Jesus' disciples (John 13:35), so the ongoing development of that love became the central element in growth toward the likeness of Christ (Ephesians 4:15). The missionaries' Christlike devotion to the Thessalonians (*even as we do toward you*) constituted an example of the love they recommended.

LOVE: INCREASING AND ABOUNDING

For centuries the Nile River has flowed north from the mountains of Africa through the desert regions of the Sahara and emptied into the Mediterranean Sea. Each year the river has overflowed its borders. The flood waters contain heavy amounts of rich, fertile soil, which is then deposited along the banks of the river. This soil has in turn produced an abundance of crops and vegetation. Winding like a long green serpent across the reddish brown dullness of the desert, the Nile has made possible continued civilization for millennia.

Paul urged the Thessalonian Christians to allow God to make them "increase and abound in love one toward another" (3:12). The *New International Version* renders this, "Make your love increase and overflow for each other." The love that God has manifested to us in Jesus is to

stimulate us not only to love Him in return, but to love all who are in Him.

But even this is not the whole story. Verse 12 adds that this love is to abound not just "to one another," but "toward all." Thus, our love is to overflow like the Nile to refresh and renew all the lives we touch in the process. Christian living should not be constricted and directed as if being forced through a concrete sluiceway. Rather, it must be allowed to expand and to enrich art, literature, civic concerns, commerce, medicine, political life—indeed, everything we touch as Christians.   —J. G. V. B.

B. Growth in Holiness (v. 13)

13. To the end he may stablish your hearts unblamable in holiness before God, even our Father, at the coming of our Lord Jesus Christ with all his saints.

The Christian's love for others will lead toward increasing *holiness*. Thus, the monastic life, in which one withdraws from social contacts, is not the way to godliness. While holiness must affect our *hearts*, a key to one's acceptance before Jesus will be the practical expression of love to the sick, the sorrowing, the hungry, and the homeless (Matthew 25:31-46).

The final judgment on holiness will take place at the *coming of our Lord Jesus Christ* in His glory. Accompanying Jesus at His appearing will be a vast retinue of *saints*—those holy people who have departed "to be with Christ" (Philippians 1:23) and who will participate in the glory of His triumphant return. Some believe that the word *saints* includes the angels, who are described as "holy" (Matthew 25:31; Mark 8:38) and who are also associated with the return of Christ (Matthew 13:41; 2 Thessalonians 1:7).

II. Plea for Purity
(1 Thessalonians 4:1-8)

The apostle now began to exhort the Thessalonians concerning the subjects about which he had been praying.

A. Live to Please God (vv. 1, 2)

1, 2. Furthermore then we beseech you, brethren, and exhort you by the Lord Jesus, that as ye have received of us how ye ought to walk and to please God, so ye would abound more and more. For ye know what commandments we gave you by the Lord Jesus.

Paul sought to *beseech . . . and exhort* the Thessalonians in their growth. He and his partners pleaded and urged, but they did not compel. Once again they pointed to their on-site

---

How to Say It

ACHAIA. Uh-*kay*-uh.
BEROEA. Buh-*ree*-uh.
CONCUPISCENCE. con-*kew*-pih-sunce.
DIOGNETUS. Dye-ahg-*nee*-tus.
MACEDONIA. Mass-uh-*doe*-nee-uh.
PHILIPPI. Fuh-*lip*-pie or *Fil*-uh-pie.
PORNEIA (Greek). pore-*nay*-uh.
THESSALONICA. *Thess*-uh-loe-*nye*-kuh
(strong accent on *nye*).

teaching, by word and by example, which had dealt with the kind of everyday living that will prepare one for the day when Jesus returns.

B. God Commands Sexual Purity
(vv. 3-5)

3. For this is the will of God, even your sanctification, that ye should abstain from fornication.

The will of God may be seen at two levels: what He *determines* and what He *desires.* We cannot change what He determines, but we can thwart His desires for us by our own rebellious choices. God earnestly desires our *sanctification* —that we be set apart and steadfastly committed to Him and His way. Many acts, attitudes, and principles are included under sanctification. Perhaps the most significant one is the avoidance of sexual immorality. One Christian educator summed up his own teaching on this matter in these words: "Purity before marriage; faithfulness in marriage."

The opposite viewpoint is captured in the Greek word, *porneia,* rendered in this verse as *fornication.* The word is the basis for our term "pornography," which depicts and promotes *porneia,* both mentally and physically. Such *porneia* was a major component of pagan religion in Corinth, the city from which Paul wrote the Thessalonian letters. He did not for a moment compromise with this immoral lifestyle, but brought up his heaviest spiritual artillery to establish God's position on this sensitive personal matter. The Thessalonians were to *abstain from fornication.* This is similar to the counsel given in 1 Corinthians 6:18-20.

ABSTAIN FROM FORNICATION

Solomon is revealed to us in Scripture as one of the wisest men who ever lived. The range of his understanding was remarkable. The writer of 1 Kings says of him, "He spoke three thousand proverbs and his songs numbered a thousand and five. He described plant life [botany]. . . . He also taught about animals [zoology] and birds [ornithology], reptiles [herpetology] and fish [ichthyology]. Men of all nations came to listen to Solomon's wisdom" (1 Kings 4:32-34, *New International Version*).

While all this is true, it is also recorded that "he had seven hundred wives, princesses, and three hundred concubines: and his wives turned away his heart" (1 Kings 11:3)

How similar is Solomon's position to that in which modern society finds itself. We exalt wisdom in the study of nature and in the creation of literary and cultural productions. We have beautiful buildings and all sorts of mechanical

and electronic devices. Yet, as in the case of Solomon, all of our remarkable accomplishments tend to be foiled and soiled by our sexual profligacy. A chaste, controlled, wholesome married life would have crowned Solomon's career with beauty and blessing. His tragic example has much to say to our times. We must not let the temptations and trends of modern life drown out the words of Paul's solemn warning: "Abstain from fornication."   —J. G. V. B.

4, 5. That every one of you should know how to possess his vessel in sanctification and honor; not in the lust of concupiscence, even as the Gentiles which know not God.

Every Christian is to accept and use the gift of sex responsibly, as a gift from God. One is to *possess* and control—not be possessed and controlled by—the physical body. The victim of sensual passion ceases to be master of his own person (see Romans 1:24-27).

Vessel signifies an instrument, or container. The body is the container of our abilities and emotions, the instrument through which we serve God in the world: "We have this treasure in earthen vessels" (2 Corinthians 4:7). On the other hand, some commentators and even translators (as in the *Revised Standard Version*) consider the *vessel* to be a man's wife (as in 1 Peter 3:7). Thus, what Paul is telling the Thessalonians would be similar to his teaching in 1 Corinthians 7:2: "Nevertheless, to avoid fornication, let every man have his own wife, and let every woman have her own husband."

Either way, the *vessel* is to be employed honorably to the glory of God, *not in the lust of concupiscence.* The word *concupiscence* means "strong desire." It comes from the same word that is the basis of the name Cupid, the Roman god of sexual love. The *New International Version* renders the word, "passionate lust." In a society filled with various abuses of God's precious gift of sex, the gospel called men and women to lives of purity and faithfulness, both to God and to spouse. Needless to say, Paul's teaching possesses great relevance to modern society, which seems obsessed at times with "passionate lust." This is an area where Christians must determine to live differently from those who *know not God.*

C. God Punishes the Impure (v. 6)

6. That no man go beyond and defraud his brother in any matter: because that the Lord is the avenger of all such, as we also have forewarned you and testified.

Sexual sins constitute an attempt to *go beyond* the bounds of what is right in the eyes of God.

Whoever commits such sins is trespassing in areas where he has no right to be and taking what he has no right to possess. He is seeking to *defraud,* or cheat, another, with destructive consequences to the families involved. In this matter, the Lord will act on behalf of the persons who have been cheated, and also in reprisal for the commandments violated. God's judgment is a powerful motivation to purity!

This teaching was not new to the Thessalonians. The apostles had *forewarned* them of these truths when the church was established. They had not waited until they were at a safe distance to broach these sensitive subjects.

D. God Calls All to Holiness
(vv. 7, 8)

7, 8. For God hath not called us unto uncleanness, but unto holiness. He therefore that despiseth, despiseth not man, but God, who hath also given unto us his Holy Spirit.

The letter before us was addressed to folk who had heard and responded to being *called* of God through the gospel. That call is consistently in the upward direction, on the highway of *holiness.* The Christian's choices are not to be based on what he feels or thinks, what is statistically popular, or what the counsel of "professionals" and "experts" may dictate, but on the Word of God.

God has not left His hearers without help in carrying out His instructions. He has *given unto us his Holy Spirit.* The motivations to purity are firmly established by the command of God, the judgment of God, the upward call of God, and the empowering presence of God through His Holy Spirit.

III. Plea for the Practice of Love
(1 Thessalonians 4:9-12)

The apostle now returned to the subject he had introduced in 3:12—the practice of Christian love.

A. You Were Taught Love by God (v. 9)

9. But as touching brotherly love ye need not that I write unto you: for ye yourselves are taught of God to love one another.

Brotherly love should be at least as natural among the children of God as among children of the same parents in a home. In Christ there is an even greater impulse toward such love, for we are *taught of God* to do so. This teaching has come from God through Jesus, who was love personified (John 3:16; 1 John 4:8-10). It is received individually through the presence of God's Spirit (Romans 5:5).

B. You Have Made a Good Start (v. 10)

10. And indeed ye do it toward all the brethren which are in all Macedonia: but we beseech you, brethren, that ye increase more and more.

Paul had already noted the Thessalonians' expressions of love both among themselves and toward others (3:6, 12). Now he acknowledges that it has extended throughout *all* Macedonia to other *brethren.* Acts records the establishment of three churches (Philippi, Beroea, and Thessalonica) in Macedonia; however, in 1:8 Paul stated that the impact of the Thessalonians' faith had been felt in Achaia as well.

This should cause us to examine our own interest in, and love for, Christians outside our immediate circle or community. Some folk seem to fear that spreading their Christian compassion and fellowship too widely might cause it to thin out at home. But this is not the way the love of Christ works. Love is like light, and the light that shines farthest is the one that is brightest near its source. So Paul had no hesitation in urging the Christians in Thessalonica to *increase,* intensify, and expand their love *more and more.* A few years later, he would write to the Christians in Corinth, calling their attention to the relatively poor churches in Macedonia who were demonstrating an overflowing generosity toward their still poorer brethren in Judea (2 Corinthians 8:1-7). The apostle's exhortation toward continual growth in love was not in vain.

C. You Must Put Love to Work
(vv. 11, 12)

Christian love is found, not only in material generosity, but in the unassuming toil that earns what is to be given.

11. And that ye study to be quiet, and to do your own business, and to work with your own hands, as we commanded you.

Perhaps Paul had received word from Timothy and Silas of a problem that he now proceeded to address. It appears that the Thessalonians were given to wandering about and meddling in the affairs of their neighbors,

visual for
lesson 2

The Lord make you to **increase** and **abound in love** one toward another, and toward **all men, even as we do** toward you: to the end he may stablish your hearts **unblamable in holiness** before **God,** even our **Father,** at the coming of our **Lord Jesus Christ** with all his saints.

1 Thessalonians 3:12, 13

and that they were quick to excuse themselves from hard work while they let someone else support them. These admonitions were just what the Thessalonians needed.

Study is rendered in other versions as "give diligence," "make it your aim," or "be ambitious." The ambitious person is not usually thought of as *quiet,* but ambitious love directs one's attention to the qualities that make for peace (1 Corinthians 13:4-7).

That the Thessalonians should mind their *own business* is an admonition hard to misunderstand. He who is occupied with his own work has little time left to become meddlesome. Paul repeats this point in 2 Thessalonians 3:10-12 and 1 Timothy 5:11-14. The hard-working Christian is not unmindful of his brothers' needs, however. Ephesians 4:28 stipulates that a part of the earnings from his work should go to help others.

12. That ye may walk honestly toward them that are without, and that ye may have lack of nothing.

At least two desirable results would come from the kind of daily diligence just prescribed. Those who are *without* (non-Christians), whether pagan or Jewish, would have to respect that kind of behavior. They would appreciate dependable integrity, and would likely take note of the fact that the people involved were Christians. Such honest behavior in a dishonest society had the potential to open doors of opportunity for witnessing—a lesson that should not go unnoticed by modern believers!

The industrious Christian, moreover, would enjoy the same kind of honorable independence that Paul found so satisfying for himself (1 Corinthians 9:14-19). He would not be in need of daily requirements, nor stagger under the pressure of excessive debt. Neither would he need help from people around him. However, when such a quiet, clean-living, hard-working, helpful person falls prey to illness or accident, he often finds others quick to lend him a hand (Luke 6:38). Love is a two-way street, and it is never overcrowded.

Conclusion

A. Of Goals and Plans

At both the beginning and the end of our Scripture text for today is the apostle's injunction to "increase and abound . . . more and more" in the practice of Christian virtue (3:12; 4:1, 10). The Thessalonian Christians were doing well; they must continually do better. They must "keep on keeping on." But to what end? What is the goal?

The Christian's goal is clear: it is the perfection of God (Matthew 5:48) as it is revealed in His Son Jesus Christ (Ephesians 4:15). This is enough to keep one going and growing for a lifetime, until he reaches the perfection of Heaven.

The whole of Jesus' perfection cannot be grasped in a single concept. Today's lesson has dealt with two outstanding concepts, so important that they are sometimes said to be largely responsible for the wide acceptance of the gospel during the first centuries of the Christian era. These are the Christians' remarkable love for one another and their pure and holy manner of life.

Even these, however, are too broad to provide single, reachable steps in the upward path. So today we have been challenged regarding certain important parts of the whole: *purity* in using God's gift of sex and in following His provision for the marriage relationship; and *love* represented by minding one's own business, while earning a living through honest toil and behaving with integrity before the pagans.

Now, what specific goals in Christlike love and purity will *you* strive to attain this week?

B. Prayer for Improvement

We bring joyful thanks, dear heavenly Father, for the revelation of Your grandeur through our Lord Jesus and the written Word that tells of Him. May we understand Him more fully and follow Him more faithfully, step by step, in purity and in patient, unassuming service. In Jesus' name we pray, amen.

C. Thought to Remember

"Let the beauty of Jesus be seen in me,
All His wonderful passion and purity."
—T. M. Jones

Home Daily Bible Readings

Learning by Doing

This page contains an alternate lesson plan emphasizing learning activities.
Classes desiring such student involvement will find these suggestions helpful.

Learning Goals

As a result of participating in today's lesson, a student will be able to:

1. Show the importance of personal purity and of brotherly love in the Christian life.

2. Show how a person may rejoice in present spiritual accomplishments and still see the need for ongoing development in Christian maturity.

3. Set and pursue a specific goal for his own expressions of Christian love.

Into the Lesson

Ask the students to think of as many items as they can for which the following statement would be true: "A little is good, but a lot is terrible." Have some of them share their answers, which may include: castor oil, time spent with your in-laws, food (overeating), debt, exercise, dieting, sermons (long ones!), and talking. Have some fun with this and get class members involved.

Make the transition into the lesson by pointing out that there are other items that are good and of which it could be said, "The more, the *better*."

Into the Word

Read 1 Thessalonians 3:12—4:12 aloud to the class. Ask them to separate into two teams. Give one team the assignment of developing reasons why *purity* is the most important goal of the Christian life, using 3:13 and 4:3-8. The other team is to develop reasons why *love* is the most important goal of the Christian life, using 3:12 and 4:9, 10. (This activity is also in the student book.) Allow several minutes for this. Call on one or two individuals from each group to share its responses. At some point in the discussion, raise these questions: "If holiness is pursued, will love naturally follow?" "If love is pursued, will holiness automatically follow?" Have the class address these issues for a few minutes.

Ask the class, "Why do you think Paul places such an emphasis on increasing our love and holiness? Why is increasing them so important?" Have them search the text from 1 Thessalonians for answers, and as each of the following responses is suggested, write it on a chalkboard or on poster board: the resulting positive relationships in the church (see the "one another" passages in 3:12 and 4:9); the expanded testimony to other believers (4:10); our witness to non-Christians (4:12); our readiness for Christ's return (3:13); our having received the Holy Spirit (4:8); being pleasing to God (4:1, 3, 8); distinguishing ourselves from those who do not know God (4:5); avoiding punishment (4:6); and obeying God's instructions (4:1, 2, 7-9). You may want to refer to the commentary for assistance in defining and discussing such words as sanctification (4:3, 4) and concupiscence (4:5).

Now have the class work in teams again, and give each team one of the following questions:

1. What do the actions described in 4:11 have to do with love and purity? How can we be loving if we are quiet and attending to our own business?

2. What is the effect of one's sexual conduct on his or her spiritual life? Why is this such a crucial issue in today's world? How can the church more effectively address it?

Give each group time to develop a response, then ask a spokesperson to summarize its conclusions for the benefit of the other group.

Into Life

Ask the class, "To what extent do you feel you are growing in your love and purity as a Christian?" Ask several class members to share personal responses. Give people time to think, and prompt them if necessary. Encourage them to praise God for the growth that has been seen and to celebrate that level of achievement, no matter how small or slow that growth might have been. Some might be hesitant or shy about responding to this exercise, so be patient and let this work.

Next, give each person a sheet of paper (or do this exercise out of the student book). Ask students to write a brief paragraph on: "How do you know when you have grown enough in love and purity?" After a few minutes, ask for responses. The point is that everyone needs to be striving toward greater love and holiness. We never "arrive."

Finally, ask each person to write a brief paragraph naming one specific step that he or she will take this week to move forward in the expression of Christian love and/or personal purity. If time allows, ask class members to share their goals. Close by dividing the class into pairs and having each partner pray for the other.

Let's Talk It Over

The questions on this page are designed to encourage review of the lesson Scriptures and to promote discussion of the lesson by the class. The answers provided are only discussion starters. Let your class talk it over from there.

1. Why should we be grateful for preachers and teachers who will not allow us to become self-satisfied with the spiritual level we have attained?

The Christian life has often been compared with climbing a mountain. Such a challenge involves reaching ever higher plateaus, where we may rest briefly before resuming our ascent. Sometimes, however, we are content to remain on a certain plateau. It is vital that someone stir us to return to our climbing. Our preachers and teachers are God's messengers in urging us to "grow in grace, and in the knowledge of our Lord and Saviour Jesus Christ" (2 Peter 3:18). Our response to their efforts should be one of thanksgiving.

2. As Christians we are not only to love one another, we are to "increase and abound in love . . . toward all men" (1 Thessalonians 3:12). What are some ways in which we demonstrate that love?

Galatians 6:10 contains a similar challenge: "As we have therefore opportunity, let us do good unto all men, especially unto them who are of the household of faith." This verse tells us what our priorities in regard to benevolent work should be. When fellow Christians are in need of food or clothing or financial assistance, our first obligation is to help them. In that sense the often repeated statement, "Charity begins at home," is true. But it should not be used as an excuse for neglecting the needy outside the church. We should consider it a privilege to demonstrate the love of Christ by supplying material aid, comfort, and care to our neighbors both nearby and throughout the world. Of course, we show our love best when we share the message of eternal salvation.

3. It is interesting to read Paul's concern that a Christian "know how to possess his vessel [body]" (1 Thessalonians 4:4), in regard to sexual desires. How does this contradict much of today's popular thinking?

While there is a growing movement toward sexual abstinence among teenagers, some influential people still suggest that it is unrealistic to expect young people to resist sexual urges. The content of most movies and television programs seems to accept this latter viewpoint. When heroes and heroines become attracted to one another, they almost invariably end up in bed together. This sometimes happens in shows that are otherwise reasonably wholesome. Believers in Christ have an extra incentive for practicing sexual purity. But surely the principle that we can exercise discipline in handling physical appetites and desires is one that applies to all people.

4. In what ways does the Holy Spirit help us to live holy lives?

The Holy Spirit brings glory to Jesus (John 16:13, 14). When He dwells in us, He influences us also to seek to please, magnify, and glorify our Savior. A holy and pure life is one way we can do this. The Holy Spirit has given us the Word of God, "the sword of the Spirit" (Ephesians 6:17), which helps us to combat Satan in his efforts to lure us into sin. In Romans 8:26 Paul tells us that the Spirit helps us with our prayers. When we pray for strength to resist temptation, we can be sure He is present, making intercession for us. Galatians 5:22, 23 describes "the fruit of the Spirit." The indwelling Spirit makes it possible for us to produce the Christlike fruit, or characteristics, mentioned in these verses. He will aid us in overcoming those trademarks of ungodliness known as "the works of the flesh" (Galatians 5:16-21).

5. Why is it especially vital today that all Christians practice integrity in their business dealings?

How tragic it is when non-Christians can say, "Christians are no different from anyone else! They will lie and cheat and take advantage of you!" Unfortunately some church members have been guilty of such charges, and that reflects badly on all of us. Among the principles we Christians are supposed to stand for is the superiority of spiritual and heavenly treasures over the material and temporal variety. If we "bend the rules" and "cut corners" like everyone else to increase our material wealth, it makes our testimony about Heaven's greater blessings seem a farce. On the other hand, with honesty and integrity we underscore our spiritual witness.

Pray for Others!

March 16
Lesson 3

DEVOTIONAL READING: 1 Timothy 1:1-8.

LESSON SCRIPTURE: 2 Thessalonians 1.

PRINTED TEXT: 2 Thessalonians 1.

2 Thessalonians 1

1 Paul, and Silvanus, and Timothy, Unto the church of the Thessalonians in God our Father and the Lord Jesus Christ:

2 Grace unto you, and peace, from God our Father and the Lord Jesus Christ.

3 We are bound to thank God always for you, brethren, as it is meet, because that your faith groweth exceedingly, and the charity of every one of you all toward each other aboundeth;

4 So that we ourselves glory in you in the churches of God, for your patience and faith in all your persecutions and tribulations that ye endure:

5 Which is a manifest token of the righteous judgment of God, that ye may be counted worthy of the kingdom of God, for which ye also suffer:

6 Seeing it is a righteous thing with God to recompense tribulation to them that trouble you;

7 And to you who are troubled rest with us, when the Lord Jesus shall be revealed from heaven with his mighty angels,

8 In flaming fire taking vengeance on them that know not God, and that obey not the gospel of our Lord Jesus Christ:

9 Who shall be punished with everlasting destruction from the presence of the Lord, and from the glory of his power;

10 When he shall come to be glorified in his saints, and to be admired in all them that believe (because our testimony among you was believed) in that day.

11 Wherefore also we pray always for you, that our God would count you worthy of this calling, and fulfil all the good pleasure of his goodness, and the work of faith with power:

12 That the name of our Lord Jesus Christ may be glorified in you, and ye in him, according to the grace of our God and the Lord Jesus Christ.

GOLDEN TEXT: Wherefore also we pray always for you, that our God would count you worthy of this calling, and fulfil all the good pleasure of his goodness, and the work of faith with power.—2 Thessalonians 1:11.

Hope for the Future
Unit 1: Stand Fast in the Lord
(Lessons 1-5)

Lesson Aims

This study should prepare the student to:

1. Tell briefly what the apostles gave thanks for, and what they requested, in their prayers for the Thessalonian Christians.

2. Show how the experience of the Thessalonian Christians served to establish the certainty of divine justice.

3. Identify some point at which the student will proceed immediately to glorify God more fully in his or her daily conduct.

Lesson Outline

INTRODUCTION
   A. Prayer Lists
   B. Lesson Background
  I. GREETING (2 Thessalonians 1:1, 2)
 II. THANKS FOR STEADFASTNESS (2 Thessalonians 1:3-5)
   A. Occasion for Rejoicing (vv. 3, 4)
   B. Preview of the Kingdom (v. 5)
    Being Worthy
III. COMFORT IN DIVINE JUSTICE (2 Thessalonians 1:6-10)
   A. Correcting the Balances (vv. 6, 7)
   B. Punishment of the Wicked (vv. 8, 9)
    Obeying the Good News
   C. Christ's Glorious Return (v. 10)
IV. PRAYER FOR FULFILLMENT (2 Thessalonians 1:11, 12)
   A. Fulfillment of God's Pleasure (v. 11)
   B. Fulfillment of Glory (v. 12)
CONCLUSION
   A. When the Going Gets Tough
   B. Who Benefits From Prayer?
   C. Prayer for Maturity in Praying
   D. Thought to Remember

The visual for Lesson 3 in the visuals packet focuses on the priority that prayer should receive. It is shown on page 252.

Introduction

A. Prayer Lists

Church publications often include prayer lists, naming persons for whom prayer is suggested. These often deal with matters of sick-ness, sorrow, or safety. While Scripture encourages that kind of concern among God's family (James 5:14, 15; 3 John 2), matters of health and safety are not ends in themselves. They are related to the more important issues of an individual's faith and his relationship with God.

Today's lesson addresses this subject through the words of the apostle Paul, who prayed continually for many fellow Christians. In addition, his other writings were filled with expressions of prayer and exhortations to prayer on behalf of others. For what did he pray? Seldom did he mention physical health. On one occasion he prayed three times for his own relief from an unnamed "thorn in the flesh," and God responded, "My grace is sufficient for thee" (2 Corinthians 12:9). The thorn remained as a reminder that the Lord's presence was more important than physical comfort. That may have helped to shape Paul's priorities in prayer.

Jesus' life and teaching reflected such spiritual priorities. He taught, "Fear not them which kill the body, but are not able to kill the soul: but rather fear him which is able to destroy both soul and body in hell" (Matthew 10:28). Perhaps we should invite the Lord and His apostles to shape our prayer lists, first personally and then publicly. Today's lesson may help.

B. Lesson Background

The setting of 2 Thessalonians is virtually the same as that of 1 Thessalonians. Written from Corinth, and addressed by the same three messengers to the same body of believers, it recognizes the same steadfast faithfulness and spiritual growth in the face of persecution. It also acknowledges a similar need for additional instruction and maturity, thus justifying the composition of a second letter.

Interim reports from Thessalonica had reached Corinth. The Thessalonian Christians, already anticipating Christ's coming in glory and judgment, had seized on Paul's instruction about this matter in 1 Thessalonians 4 and 5 to create a misguided excitement about the event.

How to Say It

APOKALUPSIS (Greek). uh-*pock*-uh-*loop*-sis (strong accent on *loop*).
LYSTRA. *Liss*-truh.
PAROUSIA (Greek). par-oo-*see*-uh.
SHALOM (Hebrew). shah-*lome*.
SILVANUS. Sil-*vay*-nus.
THESSALONICA. *Thess*-uh-loe-*nye*-kuh (strong accent on *nye*).

Some had even ceased their daily work to wait in idleness for the final day (2 Thessalonians 3:11). The church needed assurance of God's perfect justice, and the understanding that glorifying Jesus through continued faithful service was the best way to prepare for His return.

I. Greeting
(2 Thessalonians 1:1, 2)

The apostle opened this prayerful epistle by invoking God's blessing on his readers.

1, 2. Paul, and Silvanus, and Timothy, Unto the church of the Thessalonians in God our Father and the Lord Jesus Christ: Grace unto you, and peace, from God our Father and the Lord Jesus Christ.

In writing to the *Thessalonians, Paul* was joined by *Silvanus* (Silas), his companion throughout his second missionary journey. *Timothy* had joined the missionary party at Lystra (Acts 16:1-3). The three had worked together at Thessalonica, and Timothy had maintained the communication between Paul and *the church of the Thessalonians* (1 Thessalonians 3:2, 6).

The apostles' blessing was meaningful to both Greeks and Jews. *Grace*, or favor, is a Christian application of a common Greek greeting of good wishes. *Peace* is the traditional Jewish greeting (the Hebrew word is *shalom*), indicating wholeness in God. The source of these blessings is spiritual; they can come only *from God our Father and the Lord Jesus Christ.*

II. Thanks for Steadfastness
(2 Thessalonians 1:3-5)

Paul's gratitude shows that he considered the people of God more important than anything else in creation. He was thankful for the growing faith and love of the Thessalonian believers.

A. Occasion for Rejoicing (vv. 3, 4)

3. We are bound to thank God always for you, brethren, as it is meet, because that your faith groweth exceedingly, and the charity of every one of you all toward each other aboundeth.

The obligation of being *bound* to give thanks does not come from an outward compulsion; it springs from within. The apostles recognized that all credit for the Thessalonians' enthusiastic response to earlier teachings had to go to God. They had prayed that He would "perfect that which is lacking in your faith" (1 Thessalonians 3:10), and that He would "make you to increase and abound in love one toward another" (1 Thessalonians 3:10, 12).

Concerning the great triad of faith, hope, and love (1 Corinthians 13:13; 1 Thessalonians 1:3), these brethren matched ongoing persecution with expanding *faith,* and they supported one another with abundant *charity,* or love. Their hope, especially in expectation of Christ's immediate return, needed some additional sharpening and training. But thanks be to God, they were growing up! Nothing is said about prayers for the Thessalonians' physical safety or relief from persecution. Would an easier life really have been that beneficial to them?

4. So that we ourselves glory in you in the churches of God, for your patience and faith in all your persecutions and tribulations that ye endure.

Pursued by enemies as a hare is chased by hounds, the Christians in Thessalonica encountered all kinds of *persecutions and tribulations.* But Paul did not ask God to make their situation easier for them; he thanked God for their *patience and faith* through it all! Perhaps Christians today should not complain too loudly when the public media make uncomplimentary remarks about them.

B. Preview of the Kingdom (v. 5)

5. Which is a manifest token of the righteous judgment of God, that ye may be counted worthy of the kingdom of God, for which ye also suffer.

A faith that triumphs over difficulties becomes a clear indication that the *judgment of God* is *righteous.* Contrary to the world's opinion, it proves the power of godliness, surviving and advancing in the face of all odds and foreshadowing the ultimate defeat of God's enemies (see Philippians 1:28). Furthermore, it declares the necessity of final judgment, in which the scales of justice, so long apparently unbalanced in the suffering of innocent folk at the hands of the wicked, will at last be set right. What seems to be the status quo will be reversed in accord with eternal truth. Tried, purified, and proved in the fires of affliction, the saints will be *counted worthy of the kingdom of God*—a worthiness bestowed by divine grace through Christ.

The suffering of the Thessalonian Christians linked them with the apostles who had suffered earlier for the same cause. Together they were participants in an ongoing fellowship of saints.

BEING WORTHY

We all have had experiences that have caused us to evaluate the worthiness or unworthiness of some activity or product. Sometimes we have attended a lecture or gone to a party that turned out to be hardly worth our time and the effort.

Perhaps we purchased a new, highly advertised pen and found that it failed to write any better than some we already had. It "wasn't worth what we paid for it."

At times, however, our evaluations are quite different. We may go reluctantly to some gathering and find it inspiring, uplifting, and invigorating. "My," we say, "that was worth more than all the effort we made to be present." We all know of different items we purchased that ended up lasting far longer than we anticipated, thereby giving us "our money's worth."

Paul prayed that the Thessalonian Christians would be "counted worthy of the kingdom of God" (2 Thessalonians 1:5). The great blessings of this kingdom are ours as well. Our past sins have been forgiven. We have a fellowship with people of honest hearts, devoted wills, transformed minds, and spiritual purposes. We have hope for an eternity full of gladness, grace, and glory. Surely we can believe that inconveniences, persecution, difficulties, and even disasters are not too much to pay so that we too "may be counted worthy."   —J. G. V. B.

III. Comfort in Divine Justice (2 Thessalonians 1:6-10)

There was more to be said about the sustaining assurance of God's righteous judgment.

A. Correcting the Balances (vv. 6, 7)

6. Seeing it is a righteous thing with God to recompense tribulation to them that trouble you.

"For after all it is only just for God to repay with affliction those who afflict you" (*New American Standard Bible*). This theme is at least as old as the cry of Abraham: "Shall not the Judge of all the earth do right?" (Genesis 18:25). There is no other way for us to be sure that sin will be punished and righteousness rewarded, except by the *righteous* nature of God.

One of the purposes of divine justice is to *recompense*, or provide compensation for, the injustices of this life. This involves retributive justice, which will punish *them that trouble you*. Such judgment is infinitely better than the awkward, sin-tainted efforts of men to work personal vengeance on private enemies. "I will repay, saith the Lord" (Romans 12:19). God's justice is also remunerative, supplying to His people what they have lacked.

7. And to you who are troubled rest with us, when the Lord Jesus shall be revealed from heaven with his mighty angels.

Besides bringing trouble upon the troublers, God will provide *rest*, or relief, to those who

visual for lesson 3

have been *troubled*. This rest will be enjoyed along *with us*, for Paul and his companions also anticipated the coming rest. Rest for God's people is a prominent theme in Scripture, as Hebrews 3:7—4:11 explains.

The promised rest will come *when the Lord Jesus shall be revealed from heaven*. The Greek word used to describe this revelation is not *parousia*, which signifies a coming or an appearing (and was used in 1 Thessalonians 3:13). Here the term is a form of the word *apokalupsis*, meaning a disclosure or uncovering, such as is accomplished by removing the covering from a long-concealed work of art. Then and only then will human eyes see the Lord Jesus as He comes *from heaven*. "Behold, he cometh with clouds; and every eye shall see him" (Revelation 1:7).

The accompanying *angels* are described in this verse not as "holy" (Matthew 25:31), but as *mighty*. They will be active participants in the events of judgment, gathering the weeds for destruction, and gathering the good grain for the Lord's use (Matthew 13:30, 41).

B. Punishment of the Wicked (vv. 8, 9)

8. In flaming fire taking vengeance on them that know not God, and that obey not the gospel of our Lord Jesus Christ.

Flaming fire may describe either the brilliant glory of the revealed Judge, or the instrument of punishment meted out to those who have rejected His mercy. In either case, we may be sure that the ultimate reality is greater and far more severe than the material figure in which it is expressed. The fire of Sinai (Exodus 19:18) signified the glory of God's presence to the children of Israel. An even greater display of fire will be most appropriate for the hour of Christ's return.

Those who *know not God* and those *that obey not the gospel of our Lord Jesus Christ* may well describe the same individuals, who have taken the fatal step of rejecting the final revelation of God's grace through His Son. Others believe that the first phrase is describing pagan Gentiles who have stubbornly refused to acknowledge God, while the second includes Jews who rejected Jesus as Messiah and became persecutors of His followers.

OBEYING THE GOOD NEWS

I know a pair of grandparents who came up with an interesting idea. They wanted to leave some money for their grandchildren when they died. But since they were growing older and older, as were their grandchildren, they decided that the grandchildren should have the money earmarked for them now instead of after their death. They believed that these grandchildren, most of whom were married and rearing children, or in college, could better use this money now than at some future time.

The immediate reception of the thousands of dollars involved in this decision was, of course, great news to the grandchildren. However, while the money was a "free gift," the gifts were in the form of checks. These had to be endorsed in order to make the money available to the grandchildren. So conditions had to be met, even though the money was a gift.

Surely we have "good news," or the gospel, which tells us of Jesus' coming as our Redeemer, His life of goodness, His death on the cross, and His resurrection. This is good news of salvation that is a gift, "not of works, lest any man should boast" (Ephesians 2:9).

Yet this is a gospel that must be "obeyed," as verse 8 of our printed text affirms. As Christians we proclaim "good news," but it is something that not only must be heard, but also heeded. Confession of faith, baptism, and Christian living are all responses that show one is "obeying the gospel." —J. G. V. B.

9. Who shall be punished with everlasting destruction from the presence of the Lord, and from the glory of his power.

The faithless and disobedient ones will receive the penalty of *everlasting destruction*, being banished forever from God's *presence* and *glory*. Fulfilled in them will be the words of Matthew 25:41: "Depart from me, ye cursed, into everlasting fire, prepared for the devil and his angels." Having rejected God and the gospel, they will be shut out forever from the presence of the One whom they have spurned.

C. Christ's Glorious Return (v. 10)

10. When he shall come to be glorified in his saints, and to be admired in all them that believe (because our testimony among you was believed) in that day.

The revelation of Christ *in that day* of judgment will occur with glory indescribable, as He comes from Heaven with a full retinue of angels and saints. Yet He will be *glorified* even more, as He is met by saints arising from the dead (1 Thessalonians 4:16). Added to that will be the praise originating from saints living at the time of His return. Among this glory-giving throng will be many Thessalonians, because they also believed the *testimony* of the gospel as it was preached by Paul and his companions.

The judgment-day glory of the Lord will terrify the unbelieving and the rebellious. His people will rejoice in the greater glory of His saving grace as He glorifies and is *glorified in His saints* who greet Him at His coming.

IV. Prayer of Fulfillment (2 Thessalonians 1:11, 12)

From an assurance that God will set all things right by His judgment, the apostle now turned to a prayer that the Thessalonians might enjoy a full portion of the blessings prepared for the saints.

A. Fulfillment of God's Pleasure (v. 11)

11. Wherefore also we pray always for you, that our God would count you worthy of this calling, and fulfil all the good pleasure of his goodness, and the work of faith with power.

Paul's continual prayers constituted a very important part of his ministry to his converts. Here his prayer was that God would *count* (some versions say *make*) *you worthy of this calling*. Either translation is accurate, for if a person is to be counted worthy in God's sight, it is because he has been made worthy by God's grace. The believer remains in this God-provided worthiness as he continues to accept the power and guidance of God's Word for his spiritual nourishment.

The *calling* Paul mentions comes through the gospel. Let the hearer honor that call, making it his vocation to live so as to show a proper respect for it: "I . . . beseech you that ye walk worthy of the vocation wherewith ye are called" (Ephesians 4:1). If we do this, we will *fulfil all the good pleasure of his goodness*. Such should be the resolute purpose of every sincere believer.

Paul then prayed that God would fulfill *the work of faith with power*. Once again the emphasis is upon the need for divine aid in pleasing God. The Christian needs such power, not only during times of suffering, but in carrying out the daily responsibilities of *goodness* and *faith*. The

New International Version renders the second portion of this verse, "That by his power he may fulfill every good purpose of yours and every act prompted by your faith." Perhaps the *power* of the Holy Spirit to enable Christian living may be compared with power steering in an automobile. The person at the wheel (the Christian) chooses to walk in a direction pleasing to God; the machinery (the Holy Spirit) provides the energy to follow the chosen course.

B. Fulfillment of Glory (v. 12)

The theme of verse 10 is repeated in the conclusion to which this chapter has been building.

12. That the name of our Lord Jesus Christ may be glorified in you, and ye in him, according to the grace of our God and the Lord Jesus Christ.

A *name* in Biblical usage represents the essence of the person who is named. To honor the name is to honor the person. When God's purpose is fulfilled through the life and testimony of the saints, *the name of our Lord Jesus Christ* is *glorified*. In addition, when the believer develops a character reflecting the qualities of Christ, that believer is *glorified . . . in him*. Here the emphasis is upon the present glory of the Christian life, as experienced by one who knows and walks with Christ. Could a greater request than this be made for one's friends?

Conclusion

A. When the Going Gets Tough

"When the going gets tough, the tough get going!" The high school football coach drummed this slogan into his players from the first practice session to the last game of the season. Never did he say, "Take it easy." Comfort was not the goal. The team was not content with victories over weak opponents. The players went out to win over teams that would try their mettle. Nothing less would satisfy the purpose for which they donned their gear and ran onto the field.

Should we be satisfied with a lesser commitment as we engage in God's eternal campaign for human redemption? Paul was never so easily satisfied, and his readers seemed to get the idea. How about us?

B. Who Benefits From Prayer?

"Pray for Others!" So exhorts our lesson title in developing the larger theme of this unit, "Stand Fast in the Lord." Our text makes it clear that Paul and his partners spent much time in prayer for the folk among whom they labored. Their prayers brought many benefits to those for whom they prayed. We may be sure that their praying brought many benefits to the "pray-ers" as well—Paul, Silas, and Timothy. They were saved from any pride in their accomplishments among the Thessalonians. They were prevented from losing sight of their priorities. Their focus was kept on Christ and on the building of His church.

Paul also requested prayer for himself, not that he would be kept safe or be blessed physically or materially, but "that utterance may be given unto me, that I may open my mouth boldly, to make known the mystery of the gospel . . . as I ought to speak" (Ephesians 6:19, 20). That kind of praying was clearly effective for Paul, and it surely benefited those who responded to his appeal.

Praying for preachers, teachers, missionaries, and Christian writers and editors—both home and abroad—is surely in order. Paul's request to the Ephesians is an ideal guide for the content of such praying. A major benefit may be expected for all, including the one who prays.

C. Prayer for Maturity in Praying

We give You thanks, our heavenly Father, for the courage of faithful saints, and for the apostles whose Word instructed them and us. May we become increasingly mature in making our prayer requests. May we honor You as we continually accept Your gracious provisions for our spiritual growth. We glorify Your name and the name of Your Son, Jesus Christ, in whose name we pray. Amen.

D. Thought to Remember

"Keep alert and never give up; pray always for all God's people" (Ephesians 6:18, *Today's English Version*).

Home Daily Bible Readings

Monday, Mar. 10—Pray in Humility (2 Chronicles 7:11-18)

Tuesday, Mar. 11—Pray As Jesus Prayed (John 17:6-12)

Wednesday, Mar. 12—Pray in Private (Matthew 6:5-15)

Thursday, Mar. 13—Pray in the Holy Spirit (Jude 17-23)

Friday, Mar. 14—Pray for the Sick (James 5:13-16)

Saturday, Mar. 15—Pray for Friends (Acts 8:14-24)

Sunday, Mar. 16—Pray for the Penitent (1 Samuel 12:19-25)

Learning by Doing

This page contains an alternate lesson plan emphasizing learning activities.
Classes desiring such student involvement will find these suggestions helpful.

Learning Goals

As a result of participating in today's lesson, a student will be able to:

1. Tell briefly what the apostles gave thanks for, and what they asked for, in prayers concerning the Thessalonian Christians.

2. Show how the experience of the Thessalonian Christians served to establish the certainty of divine justice.

3. Identify some point at which the student will proceed immediately to glorify God more fully in his or her daily conduct.

Into the Lesson

Begin the class in a more lighthearted manner by asking specific people to respond to the following questions:

1. Would you rather be dressed in formal attire among casually dressed people, *or* dressed casually in the middle of a formal setting?

2. Would you rather listen to someone else who is very boring, *or* talk on and on even though you know you are boring others?

Allow some responses and comments from others in the class, then move into the lesson.

Into the Word

Have someone read 2 Thessalonians 1:1-12, then ask for responses to these questions:

1. Would you rather be rich and lonely *or* poor with many friends?

2. Would you rather be spiritually healthy and persecuted *or* spiritually stagnant and comfortable?

Next, ask students to make the connection between these two questions, the responses they have just given, and the Scripture that was just read. Possible answers include: we should appreciate and value our Christian friends; we often grow more during difficult times than easy times; and persecution is a real possibility (probability?) for Christians, especially when they are growing in faith and love.

Point out that the Thessalonian Christians had suffered much persecution. Ask, "For what did Paul, Silas and Timothy specifically thank God concerning the Thessalonians?" Answers they should find in this passage are: their growing faith and love (v. 3), and their patience and faith in the midst of suffering (v. 4). (This question is in the student book.)

Ask individuals to share their testimonies of how their faith in God and their love for others was actually made stronger through trials and suffering. Perhaps two or three will offer to share meaningful experiences of growth.

Continue by asking, "For what did the apostles specifically ask in prayer concerning these Christians?" Answers should include: that they would be counted worthy of their calling, that they would please God, that they would do the work of faith with power (these three are found in v. 11), and that God would be glorified (v. 12). (This question is also in the student book.)

Use the lesson commentary to clarify any of the above phrases, particularly the reference to being "counted worthy" (in both verses 5 and 11). Be prepared to explain this idea of being found worthy by having triumphant faith in hard times. Make the point that when those who do good suffer, it only emphasizes the rightness and necessity of God's final judgment.

Into Life

Divide the class into small groups and give each of the groups one of the following situations to consider. For each situation, they are to: (1) find specific reasons why they could give thanks to God, and (2) identify what they would pray for on behalf of the people in that situation. (This activity is also in the student book.)

1. A group of Christian students in a local school are being ridiculed for having a Bible study before school in the lunchroom.

2. A church member has just been fired for refusing to falsify his company's tax reports.

3. After counseling a separated couple, a minister has been falsely accused of being involved with the woman.

4. The local newspaper has run a series of articles and editorials that question the methods and motives of a local ministry to women with crisis pregnancies.

After several minutes, ask for someone from each group to present its responses. Then ask the class to consider whether similar situations actually exist around them. Challenge them to consider how they can glorify God by demonstrating faith and love in their conduct and in their prayers for others. Ask them to identify and share a specific action that they are prepared to take in order to follow through on this.

Let's Talk It Over

The questions on this page are designed to encourage review of the lesson Scriptures and to promote discussion of the lesson by the class. The answers provided are only discussion starters. Let your class talk it over from there.

1. We pray often for the physical health of loved ones, but perhaps much less often for their spiritual health. How can we combine these two elements of intercessory prayer?

It is interesting to note John's concerns for his friend Gaius, recorded in 3 John 2: "Beloved, I wish above all things that thou mayest prosper and be in health, even as thy soul prospereth." Here John combines the elements of physical health and spiritual well-being. When we pray for a Christian friend who is ill, we do not want to neglect the spiritual aspects of the situation. On the one hand, we may ask that his or her faith will remain strong in the face of suffering. On the other hand, we may ask that if God has specific lessons He wants our friend to learn through suffering, he or she will have the perceptiveness to profit from them. Let us emphasize not only the healing of the body, but of the soul as well.

2. When Christians persevere in the face of trials, it testifies to the authenticity of their faith. But why must we be cautious in applying this principle?

We should note that followers of heathen religions and members of pseudo-Christian cults have frequently stood firm in the midst of persecution. Yet they adhere to certain doctrines that are far from the pure doctrines of the gospel. It is clear that the testimony we offer when we handle hardships well is but one of several ways of demonstrating the authenticity of our faith. Our love for one another (John 13:34, 35), our faith in the historical truth of Christ's death and resurrection, and our practice of holy, Christlike living are other ways.

3. The idea of God's giving rest or relief to His people is an appealing one. What kind of rest does God promise us?

A key verse is Revelation 14:13: "And I heard a voice from heaven saying unto me, Write, Blessed are the dead which die in the Lord from henceforth: Yea, saith the Spirit, that they may rest from their labors; and their works do follow them." However, this does not mean that we will be lying down on a cloud for an eternal nap. We will *serve* God in Heaven (Revelation 22:3). This seems to suggest work, but it will definitely not be the back-breaking, sweat-generating toil of earth. Since Revelation is a book that depicts the persecution of Christians, it is clear that the *rest* in the verse above suggests relief from the trials to which unbelievers subject us. We will no longer hear the Bible attacked, be ridiculed for trusting in Jesus, or be threatened by people who reject our witness.

4. Second Thessalonians 1:7-9 speaks clearly of a fiery, eternal punishment for the wicked. Why is it important to emphasize this today?

The subject of Hell will never be a tremendously popular one. Today many pulpits are silent regarding it. Even people who are otherwise sound in doctrine seem inclined to explain this one away. They embrace the doctrine of universalism, which maintains that all people will ultimately be saved; or they will merely affirm that they believe that "God is too loving to condemn anyone to an eternal Hell." But if we are to be faithful to Biblical teaching, we must affirm the reality of Hell and urge people to turn to the Christ who saves from Hell. Paul referred to the evangelistic impact of the doctrine of Hell when he wrote, "Knowing therefore the terror of the Lord, we persuade men" (2 Corinthians 5:11). That knowledge should motivate us in our evangelism as well.

5. We should aim to have the name of the Lord Jesus Christ glorified in us, in line with Paul's prayer for the Thessalonians (2 Thessalonians 1:12). How can this aim inspire and uplift us?

Truly Jesus Christ is Savior, Lord and King, whether or not human beings acknowledge Him as such. However, the name of Jesus is glorified each time an individual comes to trust in Him and be obedient to Him. We seek to win people to the Lord for their own sakes, that they may escape the punishment of Hell and obtain the joys of Heaven. We engage in evangelism also for the sake of our church, that it may grow and be filled with excitement. But we find even greater joy in bringing others to salvation, when we see it as a way of glorifying the name of Jesus Christ. How gratifying to know that we are pleasing Him, helping others to know Him, and thereby giving Him increased honor and praise.

Do What Is Right!

**Mar
23**

DEVOTIONAL READING: Ephesians 4:25-32.

LESSON SCRIPTURE: 2 Thessalonians 3.

PRINTED TEXT: 2 Thessalonians 3:1-16.

2 Thessalonians 3:1-16

1 Finally, brethren, pray for us, that the word of the Lord may have free course, and be glorified, even as it is with you:

2 And that we may be delivered from unreasonable and wicked men: for all men have not faith.

3 But the Lord is faithful, who shall stablish you, and keep you from evil.

4 And we have confidence in the Lord touching you, that ye both do and will do the things which we command you.

5 And the Lord direct your hearts into the love of God, and into the patient waiting for Christ.

6 Now we command you, brethren, in the name of our Lord Jesus Christ, that ye withdraw yourselves from every brother that walketh disorderly, and not after the tradition which he received of us.

7 For yourselves know how ye ought to follow us: for we behaved not ourselves disorderly among you;

8 Neither did we eat any man's bread for nought; but wrought with labor and travail night and day, that we might not be chargeable to any of you:

9 Not because we have not power, but to make ourselves an ensample unto you to follow us.

10 For even when we were with you, this we commanded you, that if any would not work, neither should he eat.

11 For we hear that there are some which walk among you disorderly, working not at all, but are busybodies.

12 Now them that are such we command and exhort by our Lord Jesus Christ, that with quietness they work, and eat their own bread.

13 But ye, brethren, be not weary in well doing.

14 And if any man obey not our word by this epistle, note that man, and have no company with him, that he may be ashamed.

15 Yet count him not as an enemy, but admonish him as a brother.

16 Now the Lord of peace himself give you peace always by all means. The Lord be with you all.

GOLDEN TEXT: But ye, brethren, be not weary in well doing.—2 Thessalonians 3:13.

Hope for the Future
Unit 1: Stand Fast in the Lord
(Lessons 1-5)

Lesson Aims

This study should prepare the student to:

1. Tell briefly why the apostle Paul did not accept support from the Thessalonians while he worked in their city.

2. Describe the disciplinary action Paul recommended for "disorderly" church members.

3. Initiate a pattern of action by which the student will seek to do his share of work in the church and the community.

Lesson Outline

The visual for Lesson 4 features examples of good deeds, thus illustrating today's golden text. It is shown on page 261.

Introduction

A. "Take Me Out to the Ball Game"

Most baseball fans are acquainted with this popular tune. It contains casual lyrics about peanuts and Cracker Jack, to be munched without thought of healthful diets, and with the attitude, "I don't care if I never get back." The fan has come to the ball park for a day of fun and relaxation and a break from the daily routine.

The same fan, however, expects something different on the field. The players are to perform to perfection—hitting line drives, pitching with pinpoint accuracy, and turning the quick double play. Woe to the umpire who is less than perfect in seeing and calling the close pitch or play. Woe to the base runner who gets picked off base. And all who are present expect the game to be played by the rules with which they are acquainted. Three strikes means "you're out," no matter who the batter is. No one can avoid the need for order and discipline, even in a place where one goes to "lighten up."

The need for order also holds true in religion, despite the insistence of some who may question the importance of time schedules, prepared lessons, meaningful songs, understandable speech, or correct grammar. "Disorderly" is not a compliment in Scriptural language, at least not in 2 Thessalonians 3:1-16.

B. Lesson Background

The Thessalonian letters deal extensively with Jesus' future coming in glory and judgment. The expectation of His return is presented in 1 Thessalonians 4:13-18 as a prime source of comfort for afflicted believers. Chapter five then warns that the time of the Lord's coming is totally unknown, so Christians must always be ready. Some in Thessalonica seem to have assumed that the Lord would appear almost immediately. From this they concluded that they need not make any further provisions for life on earth, and ceased any productive labor. They lived only on what they and their brethren had at hand and likely engaged in much excited discussion of the subject of Christ's return.

In 2 Thessalonians 2:1-12, the apostle writes a vigorous correction: "Be not soon shaken in mind . . . as that the day of Christ is at hand" (v. 2). First, there must come a falling away and the appearance of the Lord's ultimate enemy, the "man of sin" (v. 3). Then, lest his description of such a powerful enemy overly frighten his readers, Paul reminds them of God's still greater protective power and saving grace. The chapter concludes with a prayer that God will "comfort your hearts, and stablish you in every good word and work" (v. 17).

How to Say It

THESSALONICA. *Thess*-uh-loe-*nye*-kuh (strong accent on *nye*).

I. Prayer Requested
(2 Thessalonians 3:1-5)

Chapter 3 opens with a request for prayer that God's power would meet the apostles' continued needs.

A. Apostles in Need (vv. 1, 2)

1. Finally, brethren, pray for us, that the word of the Lord may have free course, and be glorified, even as it is with you.

Finally provides a transition from the previous statements in chapter 2 to the request now being made. Brothers and sisters in Christ are asked to pray for their teachers in the faith. The appeal is not merely for personal advantage, but for success in God's work. The *word of the Lord* is viewed as something alive and powerful (Hebrews 4:12); "his word runneth very swiftly" (Psalm 147:15). Paul's prayer is that obstacles may not prevent the word from accomplishing its goal in the saving of many, and that, like an athlete winning a race, it may be honored (*glorified*) in the accomplishment. If God's word continues to triumph, the apostles will count themselves blessed and their work a success.

2. And that we may be delivered from unreasonable and wicked men: for all men have not faith.

Here the element of personal safety enters into the request, but only for the sake of the gospel. Opposition from men who hated the gospel and its messengers were well known to the Thessalonian Christians. Such men had persecuted Paul and his partners before, during, and after their ministry in Thessalonica. Even as he wrote this letter, unbelieving Jews were making life difficult for Paul in Corinth (Acts 18:5, 6, 12-17).

All men have not faith. Paul did not expect pagans to act like Christians, nor Jewish opponents of Christ to love His ambassadors. The best Paul could expect was that God would keep him going in spite of their opposition. In Corinth, he received that assurance (Acts 18:9, 10). Paul also met with resistance from folk who acknowledged Jesus as Messiah, but continued to indulge in habits from their former life-styles. In addition, he suffered "perils among false brethren" (2 Corinthians 11:26).

B. God Sufficient for All Needs
(vv. 3-5)

3, 4. But the Lord is faithful, who shall stablish you, and keep you from evil. And we have confidence in the Lord touching you, that ye both do and will do the things which we command you.

In contrast to the faithless men just mentioned stands *the Lord*, who is always faithful. Here Paul expresses his confidence that his prayer at the conclusion of the previous chapter (2:16, 17) would be answered. The request to *keep you from evil* echoes the prayer that Jesus taught His disciples (Matthew 6:13), and applies both to Satan and to his works—to evil in all its manifestations.

Confidence in the Lord becomes confidence in the Lord's people. Their steadfastness depends on their identification with Him. As they dwell in Him they will be found doing, both now and in the future, what He desires. God's resources are entirely sufficient to sustain His people.

5. And the Lord direct your hearts into the love of God, and into the patient waiting for Christ.

The Thessalonian Christians needed to be guided (as do all of us) into a continually deeper understanding of God's all-sufficient *love*—both His love for us and our love in responding to Him. We also need a deeper understanding of Jesus' patience—both the patience He exhibited and the patience He creates in His followers. We are to love because God loves us; we are to be patient because Jesus endured for us.

LOOKING TO THE LORD

In a certain retirement home, there are many rooms and apartments where the residents live. These are cleaned once a week. Each resident has certain items he wants "left alone," certain ways he wants things rearranged, and other preferences. He leaves these directions with the "executive housekeeper," who tells the various cleaning women how these rooms or apartments are to be treated. The individual workers follow the directives given them. Occasionally one will hear an employee say, "I wouldn't really do it this way on my own, but Eva says this is how it has to be done." ("Eva" is the executive housekeeper.)

In his letters to the church at Thessalonica, Paul is telling the believers there how Jesus wants them to order and arrange their lives. Again and again he refers to "the Lord" because He is the One who has given Paul the authority to tell them how they are to act. In the section covered in today's lesson text, we see evidence of Paul's constant awareness of the presence, purpose, and power of the Lord Jesus. Notice especially verses 1-6, 12, and 16.

Certainly this says something significant to us. We are to clean up and order our lives as our Lord directs us. We are not to do as we please, but as He pleases. We are not "on our own"; we are servants and workers in the house of faith which we inhabit. He is a co-worker with us, aware of our tasks. He is not just an austere authoritarian, but a loving, joyous comrade in an eternal quest.   —J. G. V. B.

II. Idleness Rebuked
(2 Thessalonians 3:6-13)

Now Paul turns his attention to a specific area in which a lack of Christ's perseverance was found in Thessalonica.

A. Avoid the Unruly Brother (v. 6)

6. Now we command you, brethren, in the name of our Lord Jesus Christ, that ye withdraw yourselves from every brother that walketh disorderly, and not after the tradition which he received of us.

Command is a military term, used in the manner of a commissioned officer speaking with the authority of the highest commander (Matthew 28:18). It contrasts with the milder words "beseech" and "exhort" (used in 1 Thessalonians 4:1 and 5:14), but it deals with the same problem: unruly or undisciplined behavior, such as that of a soldier who has broken ranks. The earlier admonition in 1 Thessalonians 5:14 was to "warn" any such brother. This passage, addressed to a worsening situation, directs the church to *withdraw yourselves from* the offender, in order to avoid any appearance of approving his behavior. 1 Corinthians 5:11 commands such social discipline, or peer pressure, to be used in the case of a "brother" flagrantly disregarding the Lord's directives. No one in the church is to coddle the offender with misplaced sympathy, thus creating division and destroying the corrective power of the action. The word must go out clearly: such undisciplined behavior is simply not tolerated in the body of Christ!

The pattern of acceptable behavior was established in the teaching delivered by the apostles of Christ. Here it is called *tradition*, or that which is handed down, or conveyed. In this case, Christ is the divine source, and His chosen messengers are the channel of conveyance.

B. Follow Paul's Example (vv. 7-9)

Here we begin to see more clearly the kind of unruliness occurring in Thessalonica.

7, 8. For yourselves know how ye ought to follow us: for we behaved not ourselves disorderly among you; neither did we eat any man's bread for nought; but wrought with labor and travail night and day, that we might not be chargeable to any of you.

In Thessalonica, the Lord's messengers had conducted themselves "holily and justly and un-

blamably" (1 Thessalonians 2:10) among the citizens, while showing genuine affection for them. The apostles' behavior had been anything but *disorderly*.

To *eat . . . bread* means to procure one's livelihood (as in Genesis 3:19; Amos 7:12). Paul was not claiming that he had never accepted any "free lunches" from anyone, but that he had refused to receive any kind of assistance in earning a living. No one could ever call him a freeloader. To avoid this, he worked a double shift, *night and day,* first at preaching and teaching and then at earning an income, perhaps making tents as he did at Corinth (Acts 18:3).

9. Not because we have not power, but to make ourselves an ensample unto you to follow us.

Paul was the kind of leader who stayed ahead of the competition, doing more than he expected of others. His right to live at the expense of those he served was established by Jesus Himself, who said, "The laborer is worthy of his hire" (Luke 10:7). God established that they who preach the gospel should live of the gospel (1 Corinthians 9:14). Yet in order to avoid any hint of appearing to be self-serving and to offer the strongest possible influence by *ensample* ("example"), Paul refused to exercise the laborer's right to his salary. He was willing to go far beyond what was required of him in order to persuade his Gentile converts to do the same in overcoming their aversion to manual labor. Such was the intensity of Paul's desire to become "all things to all men" (1 Corinthians 9:22).

C. An Important Principle (v. 10)

10. For even when we were with you, this we commanded you, that if any would not work, neither should he eat.

This teaching concerning the importance of honest labor had been emphasized in the first Thessalonian letter (2:9; 4:11). Such an attitude toward work is grounded in God's earliest dealings with mankind (Genesis 2:15; 3:19). It is stressed in various portions of the Old Testament, especially in the book of Proverbs with its repeated injunctions against slothfulness and the careless attitude of the sluggard. Jesus enforced this principle with His condemnation of the "wicked and slothful servant" (Matthew 25:26). He declared, "My Father worketh hitherto, and I work" (John 5:17).

Adherence to this principle does not imply the denial of help to those who are unable to help themselves. Paul promoted the most generous giving to Jewish Christians who were experiencing severe poverty (Romans 15:26, 27; 2 Corinthians 8, 9). But for those who choose to live at public expense because it is easier or more lucrative than working at an available job, there is no word of approval in Scripture.

Productive labor is something any Christian can do to the glory of God (1 Corinthians 10:31). It builds and fulfills one's physical, mental, and emotional capacities. It produces a sense of satisfaction and worth never available to those who deliberately avoid productive exertion. Besides this, honest labor makes one's bread taste better.

D. Command to the Idle (vv. 11, 12)

11. For we hear that there are some which walk among you disorderly, working not at all, but are busybodies.

Once again a charge of *disorderly* conduct is addressed. Engaged in no productive work of their own, the idle ones were spending their time meddling in their neighbors' business—the definition of *busybodies* (see 1 Timothy 5:13). Such individuals had become a hindrance to ordinary accomplishment and a source of disturbance to the church.

12. Now them that are such we command and exhort by our Lord Jesus Christ, that with quietness they work, and eat their own bread.

Corrective measures are addressed directly to the offenders, no matter what their number may have been. The orders are couched in whatever terms may be most effective, whether brotherly exhortation or authoritative *command* in the full name and power of Heaven's King. The careless ones are to cease their idle chatter, calm their turbulent spirits, and settle down to work, so as to earn an honest living and bring credit rather than shame to Him whose name they wear (1 Thessalonians 4:11, 12).

E. Continue in Good Works (v. 13)

13. But ye, brethren, be not weary in well doing.

Faithful *brethren* are not to give up on *well doing*, simply because some people live bountifully and gain notoriety by doing wrong. Paralyzing weariness comes more often from discouragement or despair than from physical exhaustion. Nothing so clogs the channels of honest charity as the demands of human parasites who think the world owes them a living. Nothing so destroys incentives to honest labor as the advertised fact that some people do live in luxury through dishonest dealing. Temptations to such discouragement demand steadfast resistance, through constant prayer (Luke 18:1; 1 Thessalonians 5:17) and constant attention to the goal in Christ (Philippians 3:13, 14). "Let us not be weary in well doing: for in due season we shall reap, if we faint not" (Galatians 6:9).

visual for lesson 4

As for you..., never tire of doing what is right.

Well doing is much more than the avoiding of wrongdoing. It is a fulfilling, positive, and active life-style. The Scripture describes Dorcas as "full of good works" (Acts 9:36) and Jesus as someone "who went about doing good" (Acts 10:38). "Lord, please help me to be good—for something" is the prayer of a Christian who recognizes that, while *being* is the foundation for *doing*, *being* is not complete without the *doing*.

TIRED OF GOODNESS

Sometimes while one is standing in line at a salad bar in a restaurant, he hears complaints from those ahead of him as they look over the available foods. "Oh, it's the same old thing—lettuce, tomatoes, green peppers, etc." No one denies the tomatoes are red and luscious, the lettuce green and crisp, the peppers fresh and spicy. The items are both nutritious and delicious. The problem is that these patrons have become tired of good things.

In the same way, it is possible to become tired of helping others, weary of trying to cheer the disturbed, and discouraged about giving help to the needy. It may well be as harmful to be bored about doing good as it is to be inclined to do evil. So it is that Paul writes to the Thessalonians, "Be not weary in well doing" (2 Thessalonians 3:13). The same challenge is offered in Galatians 6:9.

Have we ever felt "weary in well doing"? Perhaps many times we become bored simply because of repetition. We take people with us in our car—the same people, to the same place, at the same time. We give, as individuals or as a church, to someone who does not seem to be appreciative or who seems to be taking advantage of our generosity.

An anonymous poet has written in a poem entitled "How Long Shall I Give?":

"Go break to the needy sweet charity's bread;
For giving is living," the angel said.
"And must I be giving again and again?"
My peevish and pitiless answer ran.
"Oh, no," said the angel, piercing me through,
"Just give till the Master stops giving to you."
—J. G. V. B.

III. Discipline for the Disorderly (2 Thessalonians 3:14, 15)

The saints also have some responsibility beyond their own good behavior. They are to take specific action concerning the lazy and meddlesome brethren.

A. Withdraw Social Contacts (v. 14)

14. And if any man obey not our word by this epistle, note that man, and have no company with him, that he may be ashamed.

If someone in the church ignored what Paul had just written, and continued to be a meddlesome freeloader, others in the church were to *note* this and take appropriate action. Elders in particular are directed to "take heed . . . to all the flock, over the which the Holy Ghost hath made you overseers" (Acts 20:28), but the action commanded in the verse before us cannot be accomplished by the elders alone. Disapproval of the offender's behavior is to be made obvious enough to embarrass him and thus turn him toward more appropriate conduct.

B. Warn the Erring Brother (v. 15)

15. Yet count him not as an enemy, but admonish him as a brother.

The offender is still a *brother*—a member of the family of God—and is to be disciplined as such. The purpose is not to destroy him or drive him away, but to motivate him to repentance and to restore him, as directed in Galatians 6:1: "If a man be overtaken in a fault, ye which are spiritual, restore such a one in the spirit of meekness." Such discipline is not only for the sake of the disciplined one. It also affects the church and its influence on its members and on the community. In addition, it conveys a message to prospective members, so that they do not gain a distorted view of the gospel, the body of Christ, or the demands of the Christian life.

IV. Benediction (2 Thessalonians 3:16)

16. Now the Lord of peace himself give you peace always by all means. The Lord be with you all.

Peace does not mean the avoidance of difficult situations, such as the one just addressed by Paul. Peace comes when such situations are handled in a manner pleasing to the *Lord of peace*. Such a blessing is not limited to the mature and well-disciplined saints; it is asked for *you all*—the ones commanded with rebuke as well as those commended with praise.

Conclusion

A. Keeping the Body Healthy

Disorders in the body of Christ are certainly not limited to the problem of freeloading busybodies. This problem and others may become especially acute where stirred up by obsessive speculation about the "end times"—the schedule and specific details of the Lord's appearing in glory and judgment. Other disorders, such as sexual immorality, greed, gossip, drunkenness, extortion, and strife (1 Corinthians 5:11; Galatians 5:19-21), do not seem limited to certain times and seasons.

Biblical prescriptions for these ailments include many of the same ingredients. One is a firm rejection of such evils, from oneself and from within the family of Christ. Another is regular exercise in godliness (1 Timothy 4:7, 8), in an atmosphere of prayer and with nourishment from God's Word. Also crucial is the encouragement that comes from Christian fellowship. Expectant waiting for the Lord's return is not to be spent in idleness, but rather in diligent pursuit of the Lord's business (Matthew 25:14-46). The same may be said of waiting for the arrival of a loved one coming from a distance. The time goes much better if spent in productive work rather than in clock-watching, nail-biting worry!

B. Prayer for Partnership

Heavenly Father, we pray that when Jesus returns, He may find us steadily engaged in fruitful service for Him and His people. In His name we pray. Amen.

C. Thought to Remember

Doing right includes doing my share of the Lord's work.

Home Daily Bible Readings

Monday, Mar. 17—Turn Away From Evil (Colossians 3:1-11)

Tuesday, Mar. 18—Do Everything in Jesus' Name (Colossians 3:12-17)

Wednesday, Mar. 19—Be Gracious to Others (Colossians 4:1-5)

Thursday, Mar. 20—Live in Harmony With Others (Romans 15:1-6)

Friday, Mar. 21—Live Peacefully Within the Church (Ephesians 4:1-6)

Saturday, Mar. 22—Live Peacefully Within the Family (Ephesians 5:22—6:4)

Sunday, Mar. 23—Rules for Christian Living (1 Peter 3:8-12)

Learning by Doing

This page contains an alternate lesson plan emphasizing learning activities. Classes desiring such student involvement will find these suggestions helpful.

Learning Goals

As a result of participating in today's lesson, a student should be able to:

1. Tell briefly why the apostle Paul did not accept support from the Thessalonians while he worked in their city.

2. Describe the disciplinary action Paul recommended for "disorderly" church members.

3. Initiate a pattern of action by which the student will seek to do his share of work in the church and community.

Into the Lesson

Write this statement on a chalkboard or poster board: "No matter what else is going on, it is always right to _____." Ask people to complete the sentence. Do not ask for the "correct" answers; ask for "possible" answers, whether serious or humorous, such as: *love, honor your parents, pay your debts, blow your nose,* etc. Make the transition into the lesson by pointing out that the challenge (and the title) of today's lesson is, "Do What Is Right!"

Into the Word

Ask the class members to work individually or in small groups to study 2 Thessalonians 3:1-5, and determine how Paul would have completed the above sentence (this exercise is also in the student book). After a few minutes, ask for responses and for the specific verse on which each response is based. Answers include: *pray* (v. 1), *glorify God and His Word* (v. 1), *have faith* (v. 2), *avoid evil* (v. 3), *have confidence in the Lord* (v. 4), *obey commands* (v. 4), *love* (v. 5), and *patiently wait for Christ's return* (v. 5). Summarize by saying that God's people must always be ready to do what is right rather than what is convenient, easy, or popular.

Next, ask someone to read 2 Thessalonians 3:7-13. Again, either individually, in small groups, or as a class, determine what the Scripture says is right to do (this also is in the student book). Answers include: *behave in an orderly fashion* (v. 7), *eat one's own bread* (v. 8), *work hard* (v. 8), *be a good example* (v. 9), *mind one's own business* (v. 11), and *continually do good* (v. 13). Mention that Paul worked as a tentmaker so that he could model this teaching.

Now go back to address 2 Thessalonians 3:6 and 3:14, 15. Read 3:6, 11, 14, and 15. Raise

these questions: (1) What was the apparent problem? (2) Why was this so bad? (3) What was Paul's solution? (4) What was the desired result? Point out that Paul was talking about unruly, undisciplined behavior, not just differences of opinion. Some in the Thessalonian church were not just "not working"; they were being "busybodies." Also ask whether there is a difference between the disorderly of verse 6 and the disobedient of verse 14. Refer to the lesson commentary for helpful insights. Emphasize the attitude of brotherly concern (seen in verse 15), and the desire for repentance and restoration.

Into Life

Have the class form groups of three to five. Ask each group to develop a role play for presentation to the rest of the class. The "cast" should include: one person who is a hard worker, one who is a nonworking busybody, and one who is an observer. Each group should come up with a plausible situation and dialogue, then carry its play to a conclusion. After each group presents its play, lead the rest of the class in applause, and then ask them to respond briefly to what they saw. Was it realistic? Did they relate to one of the characters? Would they handle the situation in the same way as the characters did? The point is to develop an awareness of how we can best implement what Paul is telling us to do (shun the disorderly and the disobedient), with attitudes and approaches that will be the most productive.

As time allows (or if class members bring it up), address the question: What about those who truly cannot work? Focus on those who, for legitimate reasons, cannot support themselves or their families. Discuss the church's responsibility to help those who cannot help themselves. Refer to Acts 2:44-46; 4:34-37; and 6:1 for additional Biblical teaching on this topic.

In closing, ask each person to answer the following questions personally: (1) To what extent am I focused on doing what is right, rather than easy, convenient, or popular? (2) Do I work hard at home, on the job, and in the church? (3) What specifically can I do to improve my conduct and example to others? (These questions are in the student book.) Allow several minutes for reflection. Conclude the session by reading 2 Thessalonians 3:16.

Let's Talk It Over

The questions on this page are designed to encourage review of the lesson Scriptures and to promote discussion of the lesson by the class. The answers provided are only discussion starters. Let your class talk it over from there.

1. Why should we pray that the word of the Lord may "have free course" (2 Thessalonians 3:1) or "spread rapidly" (*New International Version*) among us and among other people?

God's Word is active and powerful (Hebrews 4:12). If given the opportunity it will work mightily in human lives. However, both in Paul's time and in our own, Satan has worked to erect barriers against the Word. He has used godless governments to oppose the preaching of the gospel. He has inspired unbelievers to sow seeds of doubt in regard to the authenticity of the Bible. He has enticed human beings into such preoccupation with material pleasures that they are disinclined to give heed to God's Word. Our prayers for the "free course" of the Word can break up these barriers and open the way for it to touch human hearts.

2. The New Testament practice of withdrawing fellowship from an erring church member is difficult to apply today. Why is this true, and what can we do about it?

Were we to attempt such a disciplinary action today, it could result in division in the church. Family members and friends of the offending brother might rally to his side without thinking of the good of the church. Leaders and members could forget the importance of doctrinal soundness and moral purity. Another possible result of such action would be the offending brother's transfer to another congregation, where he might repeat his error. It is obvious that in this era of doctrinal compromise and moral relativism, we must be extremely diligent in teaching church members the New Testament principles regarding doctrinal truth and personal holiness. And we must do a better job of communicating with sister congregations, so that erring members can not easily escape disciplinary action.

3. What can we do to reawaken our society to the values of working for a living?

Perhaps in our community there are employers who are desperate for workers, yet many potential employees would rather accept welfare payments than work. This is obviously a drain on our society, and it is clearly not what God intended for human beings. Some critics scoff at the "work ethic," but it is clear that honest work offers many benefits. From the beginning of the Bible, when Adam was assigned the task of working in and caring for the garden of Eden (Genesis 2:15), work has been seen as a grand cooperation with our Creator. Even the curse that came through sin (Genesis 3:17-19) did not change that basic truth.

4. "Be not weary in well doing" (2 Thessalonians 3:13). Why do we need this exhortation?

Paul must have considered it an important exhortation, since he also challenged the Galatians (6:9) with the same words. It is needed, partly because we have a very human tendency to become slack in our labors. We see other church members shirking responsibility, and we ask ourselves why we should not do the same. We receive unfair criticism for the way we have performed our duties, and we wonder if it is really worth it. We work diligently at such projects as evangelism, teaching, and improving the church's worship, and we grow discouraged at the lack of fruit from our labors. So we must heed Paul's exhortation, and we must stir up one another with similar words: "However much or little others are doing, let us press on with the Lord's work."

5. How can we make our church a haven of godly peace?

This world is a place of continual stress, and it is tragic when the church also becomes such a place. Paul urged the Romans to "follow after the things which make for peace, and things wherewith one may edify another" (Romans 14:19). We tend to think of peace as the absence of conflict, but this verse seems to be speaking of something much more positive. It is dangerous to seek a peace that consists only in avoiding conflict, for then we may allow problems to grow and fester until they finally break out into unmanageable conflict. It is better if we emphasize a positive peace that involves edifying, or building up, one another. Then, when we encounter negative attitudes and unholy habits among members, we will be better prepared to deal with them. This distinction is important: we do not merely want to live at peace with other members; we want to build them up in the Lord.

The Resurrection Hope

DEVOTIONAL READING: Romans 5:1-11.

LESSON SCRIPTURE: Matthew 28:1-10; 1 Thessalonians 4:13-18.

PRINTED TEXT: Matthew 28:1-10; 1 Thessalonians 4:13-18.

Mar 30

Matthew 28:1-10

1 In the end of the sabbath, as it began to dawn toward the first day of the week, came Mary Magdalene and the other Mary to see the sepulchre.

2 And, behold, there was a great earthquake: for the angel of the Lord descended from heaven, and came and rolled back the stone from the door, and sat upon it.

3 His countenance was like lightning, and his raiment white as snow:

4 And for fear of him the keepers did shake, and became as dead men.

5 And the angel answered and said unto the women, Fear not ye: for I know that ye seek Jesus, which was crucified.

6 He is not here: for he is risen, as he said. Come, see the place where the Lord lay.

7 And go quickly, and tell his disciples that he is risen from the dead; and, behold, he goeth before you into Galilee; there shall ye see him: lo, I have told you.

8 And they departed quickly from the sepulchre with fear and great joy; and did run to bring his disciples word.

9 And as they went to tell his disciples, behold, Jesus met them, saying, All hail. And they came and held him by the feet, and worshipped him.

10 Then said Jesus unto them, Be not afraid: go tell my brethren that they go into Galilee, and there shall they see me.

1 Thessalonians 4:13-18

13 But I would not have you to be ignorant, brethren, concerning them which are asleep, that ye sorrow not, even as others which have no hope.

14 For if we believe that Jesus died and rose again, even so them also which sleep in Jesus will God bring with him.

15 For this we say unto you by the word of the Lord, that we which are alive and remain unto the coming of the Lord shall not prevent them which are asleep.

16 For the Lord himself shall descend from heaven with a shout, with the voice of the archangel, and with the trump of God: and the dead in Christ shall rise first:

17 Then we which are alive and remain shall be caught up together with them in the clouds, to meet the Lord in the air: and so shall we ever be with the Lord.

18 Wherefore comfort one another with these words.

GOLDEN TEXT: For if we believe that Jesus died and rose again, even so them also which sleep in Jesus will God bring with him.—1 Thessalonians 4:14.

Hope for the Future
Unit 1: Stand Fast in the Lord
(Lessons 1-5)

Lesson Aims

This study should prepare students to:

1. Show how the resurrection account in Matthew lays the groundwork for Paul's letter of assurance to the Thessalonian Christians.

2. Show how 1 Thessalonians 4:13-18 offers courage and strength to Christians of all times and places.

3. Name one way in which Jesus' resurrection and His coming again will make a difference in their lives during the coming week.

Lesson Outline

INTRODUCTION
  A. A Matter of Death and Life
  B. Lesson Background
 I. JESUS IS RISEN (Matthew 28:1-10)
  A. The Empty Tomb (vv. 1-4)
  B. An Angel Explains and Directs (vv. 5-8)
  C. Jesus Assures and Commands (vv. 9, 10)
II. JESUS IS RETURNING (1 Thessalonians 4:13-18)
  A. Paul's Purpose in Writing
  B. The Source of Our Hope (vv. 13, 14).
    No Hope
  C. The Events at His Return (vv. 15-17)
    Together
  D. The Assurance We Receive (v. 18)
CONCLUSION
  A. A Positive "Uplook" On Life
  B. Prayer of Expectation
  C. Thought to Remember

The Easter message is a message of hope and victory in Jesus. The visual for lesson 5 seeks to convey this. It is shown on page 269.

Introduction

A. A Matter of Death and Life

The telephone crackles with the 911 plea for help. Before long, the sirens of ambulances are demanding the right of way. It is a matter of life and death. When the paramedics get to the scene, every ounce of effort and every available piece of technology is employed to prolong human life.

Man has always sought to keep death under control and to stave off its arrival for as long as possible. The reason for this is quite simple: death is a fearful and frightening prospect. Unless an individual is prepared to face death through the victory secured by Jesus' resurrection, that dismal prospect still looms before him.

Before the Christian gospel "turned the world upside down" (Acts 17:6), it turned the most important human experiences inside out. Life and death matters were turned into matters of *death and life*; for death no longer signaled the end of life, but the passageway *to* life. Jesus Himself blazed the trail (John 10:17, 18). Through Him, the dread of physical decline and death is transformed into the glad expectation of life eternal with Him.

B. Lesson Background

Since today is Easter Sunday, our focus in today's lesson is quite naturally upon the resurrection of Jesus. Our text from the Thessalonian epistles is taken from 1 Thessalonians 4:13-18. Paul penned these words in order to allay fears among some of the Thessalonian believers that those of their number who had died would be excluded from the events surrounding the return of Christ. While Paul's teaching offers much that is important to an understanding of the doctrine of Jesus' second coming, he also meant for his words to provide practical help to the Thessalonians: "Wherefore comfort one another with these words" (v. 18). Such comfort can sustain believers today as well.

The first portion of our printed text records the account of Jesus' resurrection as found in the Gospel of Matthew. It is this event that gave to Paul and the Thessalonians, and gives to today's Christian, the assurance that the future is filled with hope, not despair. Death may close the door to earth; but in Christ, it opens another door—to Heaven!

I. Jesus Is Risen
(Matthew 28:1-10)

A. The Empty Tomb (vv. 1-4)

1. In the end of the sabbath, as it began to dawn toward the first day of the week, came Mary Magdalene and the other Mary to see the sepulchre.

After Jesus died, His body was entombed before *the sabbath* began on Friday evening. The Galilean women then left Golgotha and returned home to prepare spices to embalm the body (Luke 23:56). They observed the Sabbath rest, and then came at the earliest opportunity to visit the *sepulchre* on the morning of *the first day of the week*. Mark 16:1 and Luke 24:10 mention other women as participating in the visit, in addition to those named here. The name of *Mary Magdalene,* out of whom Jesus had cast seven devils (Mark 16:9), figures prominently in John's account of the resurrection (John 20:1-18). The *other Mary* was probably the mother of James and Joses (Matthew 27:56, 61).

2-4. And, behold, there was a great earthquake: for the angel of the Lord descended from heaven, and came and rolled back the stone from the door, and sat upon it. His countenance was like lightning, and his raiment white as snow: and for fear of him the keepers did shake, and became as dead men.

The women discovered what had already happened. As an *earthquake* had marked the death of Jesus (Matthew 27:51), so now an earthquake marked His resurrection, terrifying the guards (*keepers*) who had been posted to prevent Jesus' body from being removed.

A large *stone* was sometimes placed in a groove before the entrance of a tomb, to keep animals or thieves from going inside. Such a stone had been rolled into place by Joseph of Arimathea after he laid the body of Jesus in "his own new tomb" (Matthew 27:57-60). That it became a seat for *the angel of the Lord* showed dramatically who was now in charge.

The angel's brilliant appearance brings to mind the description of Jesus at His transfiguration (Matthew 17:1, 2). Luke 24:4 mentions "two men in clothes that gleamed like lightning" (*New International Version*) at the tomb. Matthew writes of the one who spoke to the women. These heavenly visitors terrified the guards to such an extent that they *did shake, and became as dead men.* These men seem to have recovered enough to return to Jerusalem (vv. 11-15) before the women arrived.

B. An Angel Explains and Directs
(vv. 5-8)

Mark 16:5 and Luke 24:3, 4 indicate that the angels were not on the doorway stone, but had moved inside the tomb when one of them spoke to the women.

5, 6. And the angel answered and said unto the women, Fear not ye: for I know that ye seek Jesus, which was crucified. He is not here: for he is risen, as he said. Come, see the place where the Lord lay.

The angel responded, not to anything the women had said, but to their unspoken fears and questions. He whose appearance had struck terror to the soldiers now spoke comfort to the friends of Jesus: *He is not here: for he is risen.* Jesus could not and cannot be found among the dead. Both the cross and the tomb were and are empty. He arose as He had repeatedly predicted

(Matthew 16:21; 17:9, 23; 20:19), but the predictions were not comprehended by the disciples until after they were fulfilled. Since then, however, there is no question that He is truly Lord. *The place where the Lord lay,* its grave clothes now empty and its head covering neatly folded (John 20:6, 7), still bears the kind of testimony that cannot be successfully contested or denied. The stones did indeed cry out (Luke 19:39, 40), as the rock-hewn tomb opened its mouth to herald Jesus' lordship in a shout that will not be stilled.

7. And go quickly, and tell his disciples that he is risen from the dead; and, behold, he goeth before you into Galilee; there shall ye see him: lo, I have told you.

Having seen the evidence that the *disciples* had not yet seen, these women were commissioned as the first human proclaimers of the great news. Their glad tidings, however, would be met with disbelief (Luke 24:10, 11).

Next came word that Jesus would be going to *Galilee.* This region was home to most of the apostles. Jesus and they had worked there throughout most of their time together. There the living Lord would give instructions for the ongoing ministry that they would carry out in His name.

I have told you concluded the angel's message to the women. Extending it to answer any questions they may have had would have been unwise at this point. The women simply needed to convey the information they had been given.

8. And they departed quickly from the sepulchre with fear and great joy; and did run to bring his disciples word.

The women followed the angel's instructions, driven by a mixture of emotions as well as by the heavenly command. *Fear* forbade them to tell anyone along the way about the resurrection, but *joy* led them to seek out the disciples and convey their message. Would that we possessed such excitement, instead of the dull indifference that characterizes all too much of religion in our present time!

C. Jesus Assures and Commands

(vv. 9, 10)

9. And as they went to tell his disciples, behold, Jesus met them, saying, All hail. And they came and held him by the feet, and worshipped him.

"Suddenly Jesus met them," says the *New International Version*. Exactly at what point in the women's journey to the city this occurred is uncertain. John 20:11-18 speaks of Jesus' appearance to Mary Magdalene, who was alone. *Hail* is not the usual Jewish greeting of peace (which is *shalom*). It calls on the hearer to "rejoice" or "be glad." The mood of the women's morning visit to the sepulchre had been completely reversed.

The women seem to have recognized Jesus immediately, but knelt to clasp Him *by the feet*. By this gesture of worship, they could assure themselves that His risen body was real and tangible. Thus they experienced the kind of proof that was similar to that which was granted to Thomas and which brought his confession, "My Lord and my God" (John 20:28).

10. Then said Jesus unto them, Be not afraid: go tell my brethren that they go into Galilee, and there shall they see me.

The angel's earlier message was now reinforced with the highest possible authority. With the women now fully convinced of the reality of Jesus' triumph over death, they were filled with an even greater zeal to convey the news of His resurrection to the disciples.

That Jesus referred to His disciples as *brethren* speaks of His tenderness toward them. It also foreshadowed the special relationship that all future believers would have with Him (Hebrews 2:11, 12).

II. Jesus Is Returning
(1 Thessalonians 4:13-18)

A. Paul's Purpose in Writing

Forty days after the events recorded in Matthew 28:1-10, the ascension of Jesus into Heaven took place. Two angels who were standing near the amazed apostles told them what they needed to know about the event unfolding before them: "This same Jesus, which is taken up from you into heaven, shall so come in like manner as ye have seen him go into heaven" (Acts 1:11). Ten days later the church was born and the apostles went forth preaching the Christ who died for our sins, arose from the tomb, and is coming in judgment. Paul became one of those apostles, and Thessalonica was one of the cities where he planted a church. Through his writings to the Thessalonians, he earnestly desired to complete "that which is lacking in your faith" (1 Thessalonians 3:10). One area in which they were lacking in understanding was the doctrine of Jesus' "appearing" or coming in glory to receive His own to Himself. It is significant that every one of the five chapters in 1 Thessalonians closes with a positive reference to the Lord's return.

A misunderstanding that Paul had to address was the fear that anyone who died before Jesus' return would have no part in that glorious occasion. The passage before us was written to correct that error.

B. The Source of Our Hope (vv. 13, 14)

13. But I would not have you to be ignorant, brethren, concerning them which are asleep, that ye sorrow not, even as others which have no hope.

The apostle was not willing to leave his readers *ignorant*, or without instruction, on such an important theme. In several other passages Paul introduces new or important subjects in the same manner (Romans 1:13; 11:25; 1 Corinthians 10:1; 12:1; 2 Corinthians 1:8). The phrase *them which are asleep* refers to those who have died. Jesus used it concerning Lazarus (John 11:11). It suggests rest from one's labors and the expectation of resurrection.

One may question Paul's desire that the Thessalonians *sorrow not*, for even Jesus wept at the tomb of Lazarus (John 11:35). Paul himself experienced sorrow over the illness of a friend (Philippians 2:27). There is a great difference, however, between the bitter emptiness of those who see only the end of everything with the final heartbeat, and those whose faith in Jesus provides an infinitely joyous expectation of a new beginning. The sorrow of the latter group is vastly different in every way from those who have *no hope*. Such a difference, when exhibited in circumstances of death or suffering, can provide a persuasive testimony to the power of Christian faith.

NO HOPE

In his work, *An Essay on Man*, Alexander Pope wrote, "Hope springs eternal in the human breast." This may well be true, but the "hope" about which he spoke was the hope of many blessings and favorable outcomes in this life. It is immeasurably more difficult for man, in the limits of his own intelligence, to entertain a valid hope for anything *beyond* this life.

G. K. Chesterton, the British essayist, said, "The fierce poet of the Middle Ages [Dante] wrote, 'Abandon hope, all ye who enter here,' over the gates of the lower world. The emancipated poets of today have written it over the gates of this world." Paul indicated that such was certainly true of the Graeco-Roman world in which he and his readers lived.

How closely are these two realities linked together—"having no hope" and "without God" (Ephesians 2:12)! Godlessness and hopelessness will always be twins. Only those who have faith in Jesus as God's Son—living, loving, crucified, risen, and returning—can have genuine hope.

—J. G. V. B.

14. For if we believe that Jesus died and rose again, even so them also which sleep in Jesus will God bring with him.

Here Paul begins to address the primary question troubling the Thessalonians. What had become, and what would become, of those who had already died in Christ? The answer is this: *them also which sleep in Jesus will God bring with him.*

This statement can be understood one of two ways. The first possibility is that those who *sleep in Jesus* will be included among those "saints" who will return with Jesus when He comes (1 Thessalonians 3:13). The second possibility involves taking the word *bring* to refer to what will happen to the dead *after* Jesus has returned; that is, God will *bring* them back to Heaven with Jesus. With either understanding comes the assurance that the future of those who die in Christ is secure. Believing that God will bring Christians from the grave is surely not difficult after knowing that He has brought Jesus from the tomb.

C. The Events at His Return (vv. 15-17)

15. For this we say unto you by the word of the Lord, that we which are alive and remain unto the coming of the Lord shall not prevent them which are asleep.

The highest possible authority is cited for what is to follow. It comes from *the Lord,* whether by some otherwise unrecorded teaching of Jesus during His earthly ministry (compare the statement cited in Acts 20:35), or by direct revelation to Paul himself (note 1 Corinthians 11:23; Galatians 1:11, 12; 2:2; Ephesians 3:3).

The *word* is this: at *the coming of the Lord,* those who are *alive* will not *prevent* those who have already died (or *are asleep*) in Christ. The word *prevent* literally means "to go before"; the *New International Version* reads "precede." Thus, those Christians who have died will share fully in the glory of Christ's return.

Some believe that this statement reveals Paul's belief that the return of Jesus would take place in his lifetime. However, it is more accu-

visual for
lesson 5

For if we believe that Jesus died and rose again, even so them also which sleep in Jesus will God bring with him.

rate to say that he believed that it *could* take place in his lifetime; on the other hand, were Paul to die before that day, he was perfectly content to "depart, and to be with Christ" (Philippians 1:23).

16, 17. For the Lord himself shall descend from heaven with a shout, with the voice of the archangel, and with the trump of God: and the dead in Christ shall rise first: then we which are alive and remain shall be caught up together with them in the clouds, to meet the Lord in the air: and so shall we ever be with the Lord.

Observe the dominant theme: *the Lord himself shall descend . . . the dead in Christ shall rise . . . meet the Lord . . . ever be with the Lord.* No heavenly representative or emissary will come. Jesus *himself* will one day come down from Heaven, fulfilling what the angels had spoken at His ascension (Acts 1:10, 11). The *shout* is the bold command of an officer addressing his troops. Thus Jesus called Lazarus forth from the grave (John 11:43). This command probably will be uttered by Jesus, although it may be the same sound as *the voice of the archangel,* heralding the coming of Jesus. The sound of *the trump of God* will call forth those who sleep (1 Corinthians 15:52).

The *dead in Christ* are *in Christ* as surely in death as they were in life. Death cannot separate anyone from the love of God (Romans 8:38, 39). The spirits of these who have died in Christ will have been alive all the time, although absent from their bodies (see 2 Corinthians 5:8; Philippians 1:23). At Christ's return, their bodies will arise and will "put on immortality" (1 Corinthians 15:53). These saints will thus be prepared to "inherit the kingdom of God" (v. 50). They will then be joined by the saints who are living at Jesus' return, but who will be instantly changed into their glorified spiritual bodies (vv. 51, 52). Together, both the dead and the living will *meet the Lord in the air,* and will be *with the Lord* forever.

It should be noted that this is not meant to be a full treatise on Christ's return. Certain subjects (for example, what will happen to the earth itself) are not covered. It was enough for Paul to deal with the Thessalonians' most pressing question: will a believer miss out on the glory of Christ's return if he dies before it happens? Clearly he will not.

TOGETHER

To those whose relationship is characterized by genuine love, the most glorious word in all our human vocabulary is the word *together*. Many times those who love are separated—by illness, for example. One person is confined to a hospital; the spouse must remain at home. While they can see each other whenever the spouse visits the hospital, the yearning of both is for a degree of recovery that will allow them to be together in the manner to which they have become accustomed.

Perhaps the clouds of war gather overhead and a responsibility in terms of military service must be met. The tides of war pull a couple apart, but letters and telephone calls make some communication possible. One can be sure that a predominant wish is expressed again and again: "Someday, before long, we can be *together* again."

When our loved ones are severed from us by death, we find the separation a source of bitterness and grief. We cry, with Tennyson,

"But O for the touch of a vanish'd hand,
And the sound of a voice that is still!"

The greatest wish we have, however, is not to know what all the conditions of a future life may be. We desire to know one thing above all: "Can we be *together* again?" If we can, love is content with that assurance alone.

Home Daily Bible Readings

Monday, Mar. 24—Jesus Christ Died for Sinners (Romans 5:1-11)
Tuesday, Mar. 25—God's Gift of Grace for All (Romans 5:12-19)
Wednesday, Mar. 26—The Fact of the Resurrection (1 Corinthians 15:1-11)
Thursday, Mar. 27—The Need for the Resurrection (1 Corinthians 15:12-19)
Friday, Mar. 28—The Assurance of the Resurrection (1 Corinthians 15:20-28)
Saturday, Mar. 29—The Nature of the Resurrection (1 Corinthians 15:35-44)
Sunday, Mar. 30—The Victory of the Resurrection (1 Corinthians 15:51-58)

Paul writes, regarding those who have gone before in relation to those who are left, "We . . . shall be caught up *together* with them" (1 Thessalonians 4:17). For love, this is enough!

—J. G. V. B.

D. The Assurance We Receive (v. 18)

18. Wherefore comfort one another with these words.

It is not enough for the words of Scripture to instruct, establish, and encourage the people who read them. Those same Scriptures are to be shared, reviewed, and discussed in gatherings of the church (Hebrews 10:25) and in personal contacts, so that all may receive *comfort*. Let us use the Word to quiet anxieties over the fate of departed saints, to strengthen faith in the promises of God, and to encourage the kind of living that is prepared to receive those promises.

Conclusion

A. A Positive "Uplook" on Life

Many church buildings have been designed to highlight the essential facts of the gospel message and to call the worshipers' attention to them. In the building where this writer worships, the Communion table is centrally located on the worshipers' level. Behind the table is the pulpit, dedicated to the unashamed proclamation of Jesus Christ as the way, the truth, and the life. Highly visible behind the pulpit is the baptistery, where believers, dying to sin in repentance, are buried with their Lord in baptism, that they may rise to walk with Him through time and eternity. Having understood the purpose of His first coming, they are now fully prepared for His second.

Someone has said, "If the outlook is bad, try the 'uplook'." Because of Jesus' resurrection and promised return, our future is certain. May we, like the Thessalonians, learn to "wait for his Son from heaven, whom he raised from the dead, even Jesus" (1 Thessalonians 1:10).

B. Prayer of Expectation

Thanks and praise to You, dear God, for the fulfilled promises that provide a sure and certain hope. You have promised a Savior and given Your Son. You promised His resurrection and raised Him in power. Thank You beforehand for Your presence in all of life, for Your comfort in death, for Jesus' coming in glory, and for the endless, glorious joy of Your dwelling place in Heaven. Amen.

C. Thought to Remember

Because Jesus lives, I too shall live.

Learning by Doing

This page contains an alternate lesson plan emphasizing learning activities.
Classes desiring such student involvement will find these suggestions helpful.

Learning Goals

As a result of today's lesson, students will be able to:

1. Show how the resurrection account in Matthew lays the groundwork for Paul's letter of assurance to the Thessalonian Christians.

2. Show how 1 Thessalonians 4:13-18 offers courage and strength to Christians in any age.

3. Name one way in which Jesus' resurrection and His coming again will make a difference in their lives during the coming week.

Into the Lesson

Ask for volunteers among the class to tell briefly about a time when they were very joyful. Then ask for responses relating a time when someone was scared, very sad, or felt left out. Take as many brief responses as possible, then make the transition into today's lesson by saying that many of those same emotions were at work when Jesus rose from the dead.

Into the Word

Divide the class into four groups. Each group should be assigned one of the following passages: Matthew 28:1-10; Mark 16:1-11; Luke 24:1-12; and John 20:1-18. Ask for someone to serve as the class "scribe," writing on a chalkboard or on poster board a chronological outline of the resurrection narrative as each group tells its story. (The student book includes this exercise.) The Matthew group should retell in their own words the narrative of Christ's resurrection as it appears in that Gospel. Whenever another group's passage gives additional information, that group should interrupt and continue the narrative with their material. For example, the Mark group should interrupt with the question the women asked as they neared the tomb (Mark 16:3). Each group should add what its passage says about the names of the women, what the angel said to the women, etc., at the appropriate time. Make this both an enjoyable and informative process as the entire story unfolds. Be ready to resolve the differences in the four narratives (for instance, Luke and John specify two angels at the tomb, while Matthew and Mark mention only one). The lesson commentary should help you prepare for some of these differences, but don't allow the class to get too sidetracked on these details.

Make the transition from Jesus' resurrection to His promised return by reading Acts 1:6-11. The clear teachings of Jesus and the apostles were that He would come again. Ask volunteers to read Matthew 24:42-44, 25:31, and 1 Corinthians 15:51, 52. Now ask someone to read 1 Thessalonians 4:13-18. Explain that some in Thessalonica were alarmed that those Christians who had already died would somehow miss Jesus' return and its blessings. Paul wrote this passage to correct this misunderstanding and to comfort the Thessalonians' fears.

Now, using the chalkboard or poster board, list the events described in 1 Thessalonians 4:13-18 in chronological order (this activity is also in the student book). Entertain questions and comments, but do not allow the discussion to move too far from the major focus of the lesson (in other words, consideration of topics such as Armageddon, the antichrist, and other "end times" issues will have to wait).

Ask the class to explain the connection between our faith, the resurrection, and the second coming of Jesus. Point out that the assurance of Jesus' resurrection and ascension in the *past* is our assurance of what He will do for us in the *future*. His personal triumph over death is the foundation of our hope of resurrection and ascension into Heaven.

Into Life

Ask one half of the class to review Matthew 28:1-10, and the other half of the class to review 1 Thessalonians 4:13-18. Each group is to look for any references that deal with emotions, attitudes, feelings, or other states of mind. After a few minutes, ask for their findings. Matthew 28:1-10 includes instances of grief, paralyzing fear, fear mixed with joy, and adoration. 1 Thessalonians 4:13-18 contains references to ignorance, sorrow, hopelessness, and confidence.

Continue the discussion of these Scriptures with these questions: How do these passages help us when a family member dies? When a job is lost? When a family is breaking apart? As Christians we are not insulated from sadness, grief, and fear, but we are equipped with a certainty of "long-range" victory. The joy and assurance we receive from knowing that the past and the future are in God's hands will help us confront present situations from His perspective.

Let's Talk It Over

The questions on this page are designed to encourage review of the lesson Scriptures and to promote discussion of the lesson by the class. The answers provided are only discussion starters. Let your class talk it over from there.

1. Matthew's Gospel emphasizes only Jesus' meeting in Galilee with His disciples after His resurrection. But we know from the other Gospels that Jesus appeared more than once to disciples in and around Jerusalem. How do we explain this difference?

Matthew does not state that the appearances in Galilee were Jesus' *only* appearances after His resurrection, so there is no contradiction involved. Matthew was from Galilee, as were most of the apostles, and that may have given an appearance in Galilee a special significance to them. Another factor may have been that much of Jesus' ministry of teaching and healing took place in Galilee. Perhaps it was in Galilee that Jesus did most of His post-resurrection teaching, referred to in Acts 1:1-3. It is frequently suggested that Jesus' appearance to more than five hundred disciples (1 Corinthians 15:6) took place in Galilee. Some Bible teachers believe that this is the same appearance Matthew records.

2. Another curious difference in the New Testament's resurrection accounts pertains to the role the women played. The Gospels describe the women as significant witnesses, while Paul in 1 Corinthians 15:1-8 does not mention them. How do we explain this difference?

Paul was obviously not concerned about giving a complete summary of resurrection appearances. For example, he mentions only one early appearance to the band of apostles, whereas John's Gospel describes two appearances one week apart. Thomas was absent during the first of these (John 20:19-23), but present at the second (John 20:24-29). In writing to the Corinthians, Paul seems to focus on resurrection witnesses with whom they would be most familiar, such as Peter and Paul himself.

3. What are some ways in which the sorrow of a Christian at the death of a loved one differs from the sorrow of a non-Christian?

We may wonder how a non-Christian can bear the death of someone dear to him or her. To have absolutely no hope of ever seeing that deceased person again would seem devastating. However, we have surely noticed that often even

people who show little interest in the gospel will speak of going to Heaven and being reunited there with deceased family members and friends. Theirs is only a desperate kind of hope, little more than wishful thinking, since they do not know Him who called Himself "the resurrection, and the life" (John 11:25). We possess not only a solid hope of Heaven—we also know "the Father of mercies, and the God of all comfort" (2 Corinthians 1:3). Even when Christians lose an unsaved family member or friend to death, they are able to conduct themselves with the dignity of believers. They rest in the comfort only God can give.

4. It is interesting that Paul closes 1 Thessalonians 4 with the exhortation to "comfort one another with these words." How can we gain comfort from a passage that has often caused debate among believers with differing views regarding Christ's return?

That Jesus Christ *will* return is the unquestionable message of 1 Thessalonians, Revelation, and the rest of the New Testament. While we may differ on our interpretation of certain passages, that should not divide us, as long as we agree on the basic fact of His return. This is not to say that it is unimportant for us to study the doctrine of the second coming and come to our own understanding of the relevant passages. But in forming our convictions let us never lose sight of the comfort.

5. What can we do to maintain a constant sense of expectancy regarding Christ's return?

Do we still sing the gospel songs that declare, "Jesus may come today, Glad day!" and "Jesus is coming again!"? We should, for they contribute to that sense of expectancy. Do those who preside at the Lord's table remind us regularly of Paul's words: "For as often as ye eat this bread, and drink this cup, ye do show the Lord's death till he come" (1 Corinthians 11:26)? They should, because we need that reminder. Do we hear frequent sermons on the second coming? We should, for these fix in our minds the key Biblical passages on this topic. Do we read books on the subject of Christ's return? We should, although it is wise to consult the Bible as we read such literature.

Commanded to Write

DEVOTIONAL READING: Revelation 21:1-4.

LESSON SCRIPTURE: Revelation 1.

PRINTED TEXT: Revelation 1:4-15.

Revelation 1:4-15

4 John to the seven churches which are in Asia: Grace be unto you, and peace, from him which is, and which was, and which is to come; and from the seven Spirits which are before his throne;

5 And from Jesus Christ, who is the faithful witness, and the first-begotten of the dead, and the prince of the kings of the earth. Unto him that loved us, and washed us from our sins in his own blood,

6 And hath made us kings and priests unto God and his Father; to him be glory and dominion for ever and ever. Amen.

7 Behold, he cometh with clouds; and every eye shall see him, and they also which pierced him: and all kindreds of the earth shall wail because of him. Even so, Amen.

8 I am Alpha and Omega, the beginning and the ending, saith the Lord, which is, and which was, and which is to come, the Almighty.

9 I John, who also am your brother, and companion in tribulation, and in the kingdom and patience of Jesus Christ, was in the isle that is called Patmos, for the word of God, and for the testimony of Jesus Christ.

10 I was in the Spirit on the Lord's day, and heard behind me a great voice, as of a trumpet,

11 Saying, I am Alpha and Omega, the first and the last: and, What thou seest, write in a book, and send it unto the seven churches which are in Asia; unto Ephesus, and unto Smyrna, and unto Pergamos, and unto Thyatira, and unto Sardis, and unto Philadelphia, and unto Laodicea.

12 And I turned to see the voice that spake with me. And being turned, I saw seven golden candlesticks;

13 And in the midst of the seven candlesticks one like unto the Son of man, clothed with a garment down to the foot, and girt about the paps with a golden girdle.

14 His head and his hairs were white like wool, as white as snow; and his eyes were as a flame of fire;

15 And his feet like unto fine brass, as if they burned in a furnace; and his voice as the sound of many waters.

GOLDEN TEXT: What thou seest, write in a book, and send it
unto the seven churches.—Revelation 1:11.

Hope for the Future
Unit 2: Letters to Churches
(Lessons 6-9)

Lesson Aims

This study should equip the student to:

1. Describe the circumstances under which the book of Revelation was received and recorded.

2. Explain briefly the items in the description of the One who told John to record his vision.

3. Accept added responsibility for serving Him who saved us by His blood.

Lesson Outline

INTRODUCTION
    A. It Is Written!
    B. Lesson Background
  I. GREETING TO THE CHURCHES (Revelation 1:4, 5a)
    A. Writer and Readers (v. 4a)
    B. Blessings and Their Source (vv. 4b, 5a)
    Attention to Tenses
  II. GLORY TO THE SAVIOR (Revelation 1:5b-8)
    A. He Is Blessed (vv. 5b, 6)
    B. He Is Coming (v. 7)
    C. He Is Eternal (v. 8)
  III. ASSIGNMENT TO JOHN (Revelation 1:9-11)
    A. The Man and the Place (v. 9)
    The Patience of Jesus Christ
    B. The Preparation (v. 10)
    C. The Assignment (v. 11)
  IV. DESCRIPTION OF THE SAVIOR (Revelation 1:12-15)
    A. His Place With the Churches (vv. 12, 13a)
    B. His Robe of Authority (v. 13b)
    C. His Countenance of Purity (v. 14)
    D. His Posture of Power (v. 15)
CONCLUSION
    A. What to Do With This Writing
    B. Prayer of Thanks for God's Word
    C. Thought to Remember

The visual for Lesson 6 is an artist's depiction of the apostle John on the island of Patmos. It is shown on page 277.

Introduction

A. It Is Written!

What a marvelous gift is the ability to write, and thus to convey information, thoughts, and feelings to people you may never see! From ear- liest times God made certain that His people wrote down what He deemed essential for them to remember, since it contained a message for all people in all times (Romans 15:4). These writ- ings, which became part of the Scriptures, were preserved, often with great difficulty.

In the New Testament, writing was crucial to the preservation of the life and message of Jesus. Two Gospel writers, Luke and John, offer personal testimony as to the process and pur- pose of their efforts (Luke 1:1-4; John 20:30, 31). Luke continued his "treatise" of the life of Christ with the book of Acts (Acts 1:1, 2). The New Testament epistles gave encouragement and instruction to both congregations and indi- viduals, and were meant to be distributed for the benefit of others (Colossians 4:16). As we will see in today's lesson, it was vital that John *write* what Jesus wanted to be conveyed to the seven churches in Asia.

The commonly used phrase, "It is written," reflects the consistent concern of God through- out Scripture that His revelation be carefully copied and preserved. Let us never take for granted our precious privilege of being able to read and to know the *Word* of God.

B. Lesson Background

God's people are no strangers to difficulty. They have frequently endured physical persecu- tion, exile, and the demand that they renounce their God and swear allegiance to lesser deities, including the human rulers of lesser kingdoms. Apocalyptic (that is, highly figurative and sym- bolic) literature has often appeared as a kind of "code" writing during times of severe persecu- tion. By this means, the faithful have been en- couraged and instructed in terms that made no sense at all to their oppressors. The Old Testa- ment books of Daniel and Zechariah abound in such language.

The earliest persecutions of the church came from Jewish sources that were familiar with the Old Testament apocalyptic material. Thus, for a time, plain language served best in strengthen- ing the church. However, when the Roman Em- pire sought to require all its subjects to worship the emperor, and intensified its persecution of the church, apocalyptic symbolism again be- came the style in which God's Word was com- municated to God's people. This is the style that is found throughout most of the book of Revela- tion.

Most scholars believe that Revelation was written during the persecution mounted by Domitian, the Roman emperor from A.D. 81 to 96. The writer of Revelation identifies himself as John (most likely the apostle John, son of

Zebedee). The style of writing differs considerably from that of his Gospel and his three brief epistles; however, one must keep in mind that the circumstances behind the writing of Revelation differed considerably. John was already separated from his friends by exile because of his preaching. How would he communicate to them a written message of ultimate triumph over their Roman oppressors without getting himself and them into greater difficulties? The Holy Spirit was wise to provide John with visions of the victory of Christ in words and symbols familiar to those who know the Scripture, but meaningless to the literal Roman mind.

I. Greeting to the Churches (Revelation 1:4, 5a)

The message to be delivered took the form of an extensive letter to groups of Christians in the Roman province of Asia.

A. Writer and Readers (v. 4a)

4a. John to the seven churches which are in Asia.

John, who had served for years among the churches around Ephesus (the principal city of *Asia*), was known well enough among them to require no further introduction. The province of Asia occupied much of the western one-fourth of Asia Minor, or modern Turkey. As part of the Roman Empire Asia and its people came under the imperial edict that anyone who accepted the protection of Rome must participate in the forms of worship to the Roman emperor.

Churches were found in at least ten cities of Asia in New Testament times. The *seven* mentioned here and addressed individually in Revelation 2 and 3 may represent all churches in every place and time, since *seven* in the Bible frequently symbolizes perfection or completeness. The book of Revelation is applicable to all congregations, but its message speaks particularly to those suffering under conditions similar to those experienced by the seven churches.

B. Blessings and Their Source (vv. 4b, 5a)

4b, 5a. Grace be unto you, and peace, from him which is, and which was, and which is to come; and from the seven Spirits which are before his throne; and from Jesus Christ, who is the faithful witness, and the first-begotten of the dead, and the prince of the kings of the earth.

John's petition for *grace* and *peace* upon his readers combines the Greek wish for goodness and beauty with the Jewish prayer for God's

wholeness. The New Testament (as in Ephesians 2:7) adds the assurance of God's love in Jesus Christ to *grace*, and the wholeness that can come only from Jesus (John 14:27) to the idea of *peace*.

John also includes a majestic description of the Trinity within his greeting. The words *which is, and which was, and which is to come* are reminiscent of the name by which God revealed Himself in Exodus 3:14, 15 (I AM THAT I AM).

The Holy Spirit is identified by the term *seven Spirits*. Again this conveys the idea of completeness. Perhaps the number *seven* was used in conjunction with the seven churches to which the letter was being sent. Yet just as the seven churches would be considered one body, the seven Spirits designated the one Spirit (Ephesians 4:4).

The primary focus of the book of Revelation is *Jesus Christ* (see 1:1, 2). Here three aspects of His ministry are highlighted. Jesus told Pilate that He had come to "bear witness unto the truth" (John 18:37), and His *faithful* commitment to this mission led to His death. Death, however, could not hold Him. Through His resurrection He became *the first-begotten of the dead*. Similar titles are "the firstfruits of them that slept" (1 Corinthians 15:20) and "the firstborn from the dead" (Colossians 1:18). Jesus was the first to be brought back to life, never to die again. This makes Him *the prince of the kings of the earth*. He is the supreme Ruler over all earthly rulers— "Lord of lords, and King of kings" (Revelation 17:14; see also Ephesians 1:20, 21).

ATTENTION TO TENSES

John begins the book of Revelation with greetings from the One "which is, and which was, and which is to come." This is an interesting

---

How to Say It

AEGEAN. A-*jee*-un.
APOCALYPTIC. uh-*pock*-uh-*lip*-tik (strong accent on *lip*).
COLOSSAE. Kuh-*lahss*-ee.
DOMITIAN. Doe-*mish*-un.
EPHESUS. *Eff*-uh-suss.
HIERAPOLIS. High-er-*ap*-uh-liss.
JOSEPHUS. Joe-*see*-fuss.
LAODICEA. Lay-*odd*-uh-*see*-uh (strong accent on *see*).
MILETUS. My-*lee*-tuss.
PERGAMOS. *Per*-guh-muss.
SMYRNA. *Smur*-nuh.
TROAS. *Troe*-az.

sequence to apply to our own lives. We are what we are, and are doing what we are doing, in terms of right now. Yet all that we are now has grown out of what we were and did in the past. Likewise, it is true that what happens in the future will be in large part determined by what we are and what we do in the present.

We also find this to be true occupationally. If one is a secretary to an important businessman, usually he or she has concentrated on the study of typing, shorthand, and other business subjects in the past. If more career advances take place in the future, they will be based on the work being done now.

In our Christian lives, the same sequence of verb tenses comes into play. Our sense of forgiveness, fellowship, and fruitfulness in the present is dependent on the past. What Jesus did for us enables us to stand as we do—complete in Him. All the benefits and bliss of the future come from the life and joy we find in Him in our life's present. The One who is, and was, and is to come makes *us* what we are and were and are to become! —J. G. V. B.

II. Glory to the Savior (Revelation 1:5b-8)

Christ, the source of blessing to the saints in the seven churches, is now presented as the object of adoration among those communities of faith.

A. He Is Blessed (vv. 5b, 6)

5b, 6. Unto him that loved us, and washed us from our sins in his own blood, and hath made us kings and priests unto God and his Father; to him be glory and dominion for ever and ever. Amen.

Loved us is more accurately rendered, based on the Greek text, in the ongoing present tense: *loves us.* Jesus' love is not limited to the sacrifice of His life on Calvary that cleansed us from our sins, but it continues in that "he ever liveth to make intercession" for His own (Hebrews 7:25; 1 John 2:1). He is continually with His dedicated disciples (Matthew 28:20).

A choice between two words found in ancient manuscripts (both of which sounded much the same) has persuaded many translators (as in the *New International Version*) to say that Christ has *freed us* (by paying the ransom price) rather than *washed us, from our sins.* Either word expresses a glorious truth.

The word rendered *kings* in this verse is the Greek word that means *kingdom.* Christ has established His people as a *kingdom,* made up of *priests* who have direct access to God in Jesus'

name (see 1 Peter 2:5). All this is reason to celebrate and to give Him *glory and dominion for ever and ever.*

B. He Is Coming (v. 7)

7. Behold, he cometh with clouds; and every eye shall see him, and they also which pierced him: and all kindreds of the earth shall wail because of him. Even so, Amen.

Just as a cloud was present when Jesus ascended (Acts 1:9), so will *clouds* be part of the background when He returns (Matthew 26:64). Paul mentions *clouds* in his description of Christ's return in 1 Thessalonians 4:17.

That *every eye shall see him* means that His audience will include reluctant foes (they who *pierced him,* as predicted in Zechariah 12:10), as well as eager friends. The word *wail* pictures the bitter cry of those who must confront divine judgment unprepared (Matthew 13:42, 50).

C. He Is Eternal (v. 8)

8. I am Alpha and Omega, the beginning and the ending, saith the Lord, which is, and which was, and which is to come, the Almighty.

Alpha, or A, is the first letter of the Greek alphabet, and *Omega,* or long O, is the last. Thus, *the Lord* declares Himself to be the eternal One (as He did in v. 4), living before all else began and after all created matter has been extinguished. Near the end of Revelation, Jesus describes Himself with the words *Alpha and Omega,* and uses other titles that affirm His deity (Revelation 22:13, 16).

III. Assignment to John (Revelation 1:9-11)

A. The Man and the Place (v. 9)

9. I John, who also am your brother, and companion in tribulation, and in the kingdom and patience of Jesus Christ, was in the isle that is called Patmos, for the word of God, and for the testimony of Jesus Christ.

Although he was an elderly and respected apostle at this point, John did not consider himself above or superior to those he addressed. He was their *brother,* sharing their experiences. He understood what it was like to experience *tribulation* for one's faith. He, along with Peter, had suffered persecution not long after the church began (Acts 4:18-21; 5:40-42). Later he had lost his brother James during the persecution initiated by King Herod Agrippa I (Acts 12:1, 2). Now, after many years, John had insisted on preaching that God, as revealed in Jesus Christ, was the only deity to be worshiped, while the emperor Domitian demanded that any worship be directed toward himself. For that reason, John had been exiled—separated from his people and confined to a desolate island.

Among the islands in the Aegean Sea, *the isle that is called Patmos* is a rough and irregular cluster of three sections linked by narrow necks of land. Its total tortuous shoreline is comparable with its distance from the Asian coast—some forty miles, though Patmos contains not more than twenty-five square miles in total area. John's stay there is believed to have lasted about eighteen months and to have been concluded by the emperor Nerva after the death of Domitian in A.D. 96.

More meaningful to us is John's introduction of the threefold Christian experience of *tribulation*, *kingdom*, and *patience*. These themes echo throughout Revelation: *tribulation* for the faith, the triumph of Heaven's *kingdom* over worldly realms, and the *patience*, or steadfast endurance, that enables the saints to achieve Heaven's victory. This triumphant trio makes the book of Revelation of special value in times of hardship.

THE PATIENCE OF JESUS CHRIST

Would it ever be possible for anyone who examined our lives and conduct closely to refer to "the patience of Mary White" or "the patience of Frank Brown"? If we are honest about ourselves, we will likely be embarrassed by the frequency of our impatience and the sad infrequency of our patience. We lose our temper with our children, or we find ourselves becoming argumentative with our spouse.

Our comfort and encouragement is that Jesus is the very personification of patience. Again and again He had to urge His disciples to love and forgive and to realize that they were exhibiting the wrong attitude. Their impatience with those who brought their children to see Jesus is a prime example. In time, these men were changed and became models of patience. James and John, the "sons of thunder," became loving and forgiving men. The blundering, impulsive Peter began to exhibit "rock-like" qualities.

Perhaps the greatest motivation any of us has to be patient toward others is the patience that Jesus has to exercise with us—on a daily basis! May each of us think more and exhibit more of "the patience of Jesus Christ."   —J. G. V. B.

B. The Preparation (v. 10)

10. I was in the Spirit on the Lord's day, and heard behind me a great voice, as of a trumpet.

Following Jesus' resurrection on the first day of the week, and the establishment of the church on the first day of the week (Pentecost), Christians chose that day to meet at the Lord's table (Acts 20:7) and to bring offerings for the needy (1 Corinthians 16:2). The term *Lord's day* does not appear in Scripture until this passage in Revelation, but soon afterward Christians in general were known to call the first day of the week the Lord's Day.

John's exile kept him from meeting with fellow believers for worship (Hebrews 10:25), but he could still engage in prayer and meditation. The *great voice* that he heard from *behind* him reminded him in an impressive way that, though in exile, he was by no means alone.

C. The Assignment (v. 11)

11. Saying, I am Alpha and Omega, the first and the last: and, What thou seest, write in a book, and send it unto the seven churches which are in Asia; unto Ephesus, and unto Smyrna, and unto Pergamos, and unto Thyatira, and unto Sardis, and unto Philadelphia, and unto Laodicea.

The order in which the *seven* cities are named form a kind of circuit, from *Ephesus* northward, then eastward and southward to *Laodicea*, east of Ephesus, which is the last city mentioned. Why other cities in the region, such as Troas, Miletus, Colossae, and Hierapolis were omitted can only be surmised. Churches anywhere, however, could profit from the seven messages John was to receive.

IV. Description of the Savior (Revelation 1:12-15)

A. His Place With the Churches (vv. 12, 13a)

12, 13a. And I turned to see the voice that spake with me. And being turned, I saw seven golden candlesticks; and in the midst of the seven candlesticks one like unto the Son of man.

John gave immediate attention to *the voice* coming from behind him. Immediately he noticed *seven golden candlesticks*. Revelation 1:20

visual for
lesson 6

What thou seest, write in a book, and send it unto the seven churches which are in Asia.   Revelation 1:11

states that these candlesticks symbolized the churches to which the writing was addressed. Coming immediately to mind is Matthew 5:14, 15: "Ye are the light of the world. . . . Neither do men light a candle, and put it under a bushel, but on a candlestick." Each congregation brings the light of the gospel to its community. Jesus is then described as present in the midst of His beleaguered churches.

Son of man is a title introduced in Daniel's night vision: "One like the Son of man came with the clouds of heaven" (7:13). Jesus referred to Himself frequently by that title (Matthew 8:20; Mark 2:10; Luke 22:69; John 1:51), emphasizing His identity with humanity while at the same time affirming His divinity.

B. His Robe of Authority (v. 13b)

13b. Clothed with a garment down to the foot, and girt about the paps with a golden girdle.

Exodus 28 gives instructions on the preparation of robes for Aaron and his sons, which served to distinguish them as priests in Israel. All were to wear a specially designed *girdle* (Exodus 39:27-29). Aaron in particular, as high priest, was to be recognized by his robe and by a specially ornamented girdle (Josephus says that it had "a mixture of gold interwoven") that was wound around the chest (the area designated by the word *paps*). Thus, what John saw in his vision was the familiar attire of the priesthood. How fitting for our great High Priest, who "hath made us . . . priests unto God" (v. 6) to be clothed in such garments!

C. His Countenance of Purity (v. 14)

14. His head and his hairs were white like wool, as white as snow; and his eyes were as a flame of fire.

Pure, glistening *white* is the symbol of utmost purity and of the holiness of God. Such a one, whose *eyes were as a flame of fire*, could see and understand the inmost thoughts of the human heart.

D. His Posture of Power (v. 15)

15. And his feet like unto fine brass, as if they burned in a furnace; and his voice as the sound of many waters.

When the Lord takes a stand He will not be moved. The appearance of the Son of man's feet resembled *fine brass*—imperishable metal, refined and burnished to a glow. In addition, His words were spoken with authority. The *sound* of His *voice* was not an intimidating shout, but a naturally dominant sound, like that of waves crashing on a rocky seacoast or of a mighty wa-

terfall. Ezekiel 43:2 also speaks of such a sound coming forth from the "God of Israel."

Thus did John's vision come to his readers through figures familiar from other portions of the Scriptures. The living Lord Jesus was revealing Himself to the churches through revealing Himself to His exiled apostle.

Conclusion

A. What to Do With This Writing

John obeyed the Lord's command to write what he saw and to convey the writing to the churches. What were they to do with it? Read it? Accept it and use it for their encouragement, spiritual growth, and victory over present and future afflictions? All this and more. They passed it along to us for the same ongoing uses.

God's purpose for the book of Revelation was only partly accomplished when John completed his work and passed it on to the seven churches. The promise of Revelation 1:3 is addressed to us as well: "Blessed is he that readeth, and they that hear the words of this prophecy, and keep those things which are written therein."

B. Prayer of Thanks for God's Word

We thank You, God our Father, for the gift of communication, by which You have revealed Your nature and Your will. Thank You especially for revealing Yourself through Jesus our Lord. Thank You for putting Your "thoughts" and Your love in writing. In His name we pray. Amen.

C. Thought to Remember

God, unchanging and eternal, has revealed Himself through the timeless truth of His Son and His written Word.

Home Daily Bible Readings

Monday, Mar. 31—Jesus, God's Eternal Word (John 1:1-4)

Tuesday, Apr. 1—Jesus, the Light of the World (John 1:5-18)

Wednesday, Apr. 2—We Live Through Jesus Christ (Romans 6:1-11)

Thursday, Apr. 3—Christ, the Head of All Things (Colossians 1:15-20)

Friday, Apr. 4—Give Thanks to the Lord (Psalm 100)

Saturday, Apr. 5—God Honors Those Who Serve Him (John 12:20-26)

Sunday, Apr. 6—A Savior for All People (Luke 2:25-32)

Learning by Doing

This page contains an alternate lesson plan emphasizing learning activities. Classes desiring such student involvement will find these suggestions helpful.

Learning Goals

As students participate in today's class session, they should:

1. Express the primary purpose of the book of Revelation.

2. Explain how the introductory portion of the book contributes toward this purpose.

3. Be more compassionate toward those who have experienced adversity for their faith, and do something specific to minister to them.

Into the Lesson

Begin the class by distributing three or four slips of paper to certain individuals (select those who won't mind reading aloud in class). On each slip you will have written a potentially discouraging piece of news. Include such incidents as: a major car repair bill, a layoff from work, losing a championship game, or a break-in at your home. After each has been read, ask, "How would you try to encourage the person facing this particular situation? What would you say?" Be sure that the final slip read has something like, "Losing a friend because of your stand for Christ," or "Being taunted at school because of your involvement in the church."

Point out that the book of Revelation was written primarily to provide encouragement to suffering believers in the first century. In spite of the high degree of controversy that often surrounds the study of Revelation, this theme should not be overlooked. Emphasize the relevance of the book to someone who has experienced some degree of ridicule or rejection as a result of his faith.

Into the Word

Today's lesson is the first in a series of studies from Revelation. Thus it will be important to provide a good introduction to the book. Use the information in the Lesson Background (p. 274) to explain why Revelation was written in the style (apocalyptic) that it was. Note also the period in which Revelation is believed to have been written (around A.D. 95 during the reign of Emperor Domitian). In referring to the "seven churches in Asia," use the map provided for Lesson 6. Also point out the location of the isle of Patmos on this map, and use the information in the lesson commentary under Revelation 1:9 to provide additional details about Patmos.

Ask the class, "What word would you use to describe the book of Revelation?" Possible responses may include: *confusing, frightening, complicated, encouraging*. Point out that this series of eight lessons will focus on the practical purpose of encouraging believers, rather than the theories of interpretation.

Next, divide the class into two groups for the study of today's Scripture. Have each group designate a "reporter" to record the group's answers to its questions. Give each group its set of questions (or refer to the student book, where these are also written).

The Savior (Revelation 1:4-8, 12-15)

1. List all the titles for Jesus in this section of Scripture. How would these titles offer encouragement to suffering Christians?

2. List all that Jesus has done for us or promises to do for us, according to this passage. What encouragement does this offer?

3. What do the "seven golden candlesticks" (1:12) symbolize (see 1:20)? What does Jesus standing "in the midst" of the church mean? How would this be encouraging for the church? Why could it be reason for concern?

The Sufferer (Revelation 1:9-11)

1. Why do you think John introduced himself as a "brother" (v. 9) rather than an apostle?

2. What is there about tribulation that can strengthen one's faith? How can it draw Christians closer to each other?

3. Do you know of someone who has experienced severe treatment because of his Christian faith? Why do such individuals often have the most inspiring testimonies?

After about fifteen minutes, have the class reconvene, and allow each group's reporter to share its responses to its questions.

Into Life

Ask, "How can adversity or persecution strengthen a church?" Point out how the persecution of the church in Acts seemed to produce greater growth. Is it true, as someone has observed, that, "The best thing we could do for the church today would be to start a persecution"?

Close with a time of silent prayer. Have the class members focus: (1) on Christians who are suffering throughout our world, and (2) on people they are aware of who have experienced ridicule or rejection because of their faith.

Let's Talk It Over

The questions on this page are designed to encourage review of the lesson Scriptures and to promote discussion of the lesson by the class. The answers provided are only discussion starters. Let your class talk it over from there.

1. Revelation 1:7 promises that at Christ's second coming, "every eye shall see him." How can this be?

This is a prospect that perhaps we can envision more easily than Bible students of past generations. Satellite communication by way of a television screen can transmit up-to-the-moment images to us from around the world. But aside from this, we must remember that Christ is no longer bound by space and time. He is capable of appearing in the skies over New York and Los Angeles in the same instant. He can descend from the heavens over Chile and China, or over Alaska and Argentina, simultaneously. Even in our electronic age this promise is one that boggles the mind. But we accept it by faith and anticipate it with a sense of wonder.

2. John's mention of being "in the Spirit on the Lord's day" (Revelation 1:10) provides a good example for us. How can we apply this personally?

John may have been referring to the level of communion with the Holy Spirit that made it possible for him to receive divine revelation and record it accurately for his readers. That kind of contact with the Spirit is not available to us. However, we can and should be enjoying regular communion with the Holy Spirit (note 2 Corinthians 13:14). It is especially important that we prepare ourselves on the Lord's Day to be receptive to the Holy Spirit. If we are preoccupied with thoughts of ballgames, picnics, or television shows, we will have difficulty deriving benefit from the congregational worship. But if we prepare our hearts with prayer and meditation on the Word, our worship will be more pleasing to God and more fulfilling for us.

3. Why is it helpful to think of our church as being like a candlestick?

In Indianapolis, Indiana, "The Light of the World Christian Church" serves within the African American community. It would be well if every church, whatever name it uses, would think of itself as "The Light of the World Church." We present Jesus Christ, who is "the light of the world" (John 8:12; 9:5). Furthermore, He said of His followers, "Ye are the light of the world" (Matthew 5:14). Our church is needed as a candlestick for our Lord, because it is clear that our world, our nation, and our community are dwelling in darkness. The symbol of the candlestick serves as a reminder of that spiritual and moral darkness around us. It also calls attention to our evangelistic obligations. We must be very diligent in shining the light of the gospel into the minds and hearts of those people who are groping in darkness.

4. In John's vision of Christ, the whiteness of His hair symbolized His purity and holiness. Why would this be a frightening aspect of the vision?

Perhaps we have experienced a measure of discomfort while being in the presence of a missionary, minister, or other Christian who was known for his purity of life. We felt our own lack of holiness more keenly because of the contrast between our life and that of the other individual. This discomfort in being near an apparently holy believer would be multiplied many times over if we were in the presence of Christ. When we ponder it, the prospect of appearing before a holy God and our pure Savior is indeed frightening. However, John reminds us of how "perfect love casteth out fear" (1 John 4:18). We realize that God loves us in spite of our impurities, and that realization reduces our fear.

5. What are some benefits of reading and studying the book of Revelation?

Note that this book begins with a pronouncement of blessing upon all who read, hear, and heed it (1:3). Revelation encourages Christians of every era to be faithful, because it demonstrates vividly the ultimate victory of Jesus Christ and those who follow Him. In that connection we can gain a benefit from meditating on the further pronouncements of blessing found within it. These appear in 14:13; 16:15; 19:9; 20:6; 22:7, 14. They speak in various ways of the victory we shall achieve through Christ. Chapters 21 and 22, with their detailed description of the new Jerusalem, are among the most cherished chapters in the Bible. Meditating on them will aid us in fulfilling Paul's exhortation in Colossians 3:1: "If ye then be risen with Christ, seek those things which are above, where Christ sitteth on the right hand of God."

To Smyrna and Pergamos

DEVOTIONAL READING: 1 Corinthians 8:1-13.

LESSON SCRIPTURE: Revelation 2:8-17.

PRINTED TEXT: Revelation 2:8-17.

Revelation 2:8-17

8 And unto the angel of the church in Smyrna write; These things saith the first and the last, which was dead, and is alive.

9 I know thy works, and tribulation, and poverty, (but thou art rich) and I know the blasphemy of them which say they are Jews, and are not, but are the synagogue of Satan.

10 Fear none of those things which thou shalt suffer: behold, the devil shall cast some of you into prison, that ye may be tried; and ye shall have tribulation ten days: be thou faithful unto death, and I will give thee a crown of life.

11 He that hath an ear, let him hear what the Spirit saith unto the churches; He that overcometh shall not be hurt of the second death.

12 And to the angel of the church in Pergamos write; These things saith he which hath the sharp sword with two edges.

13 I know thy works, and where thou dwellest, even where Satan's seat is: and thou holdest fast my name, and hast not denied my faith, even in those days wherein Antipas was my faithful martyr, who was slain among you, where Satan dwelleth.

14 But I have a few things against thee, because thou hast there them that hold the doctrine of Balaam, who taught Balak to cast a stumblingblock before the children of Israel, to eat things sacrificed unto idols, and to commit fornication.

15 So hast thou also them that hold the doctrine of the Nicolaitans, which thing I hate.

16 Repent; or else I will come unto thee quickly, and will fight against them with the sword of my mouth.

17 He that hath an ear, let him hear what the Spirit saith unto the churches; To him that overcometh will I give to eat of the hidden manna, and will give him a white stone, and in the stone a new name written, which no man knoweth saving he that receiveth it.

GOLDEN TEXT: Be thou faithful unto death, and I will give thee a crown of life.
—Revelation 2:10.

Hope for the Future
Unit 2: Letters to Churches
(Lessons 6-9)

Lesson Aims

This lesson should equip students to:

1. Name the outstanding characteristics of the churches in Smyrna and Pergamos.

2. Compare these two congregations with theirs.

3. Name a way in which the messages to Smyrna and Pergamos will affect their lives.

Lesson Outline

INTRODUCTION

  A. Worth Dying For

  B. Lesson Background

I. ENCOURAGEMENT TO SMYRNA (Revelation 2:8-11)

  A. From the Living Lord (v. 8)

  B. He Understands Their Trials (v. 9)

    Dangerous Deceit

  C. He Promises Life Beyond Affliction (v. 10)

    Those Things Which Thou Shalt Suffer

  D. He Assures the Hearers (v. 11)

II. WARNING TO PERGAMOS (Revelation 2:12-17)

  A. From the Well-Equipped Lord (v. 12)

  B. He Understands Their Surroundings (v. 13)

  C. He Condemns False Teachings (vv. 14, 15)

  D. He Commands Correction (v. 16)

  E. He Challenges All to Overcome (v. 17)

CONCLUSION

  A. Filling the Real Need

  B. Prayer of Thanks for Revelation

  C. Thought to Remember

The visual for Lesson 7 in the visuals packet highlights the truth that the way to the crown is the way of the cross. It is shown on page 284.

Introduction
A. Worth Dying For

Several candidates for an attractive position with a prominent business firm appeared before the board of examiners. One friendly applicant centered his preparation on finding out all he could about the members of the board, and he gave every questioner the answers he wanted to hear. One of the examiners later remarked that the man obviously did not believe anything strongly enough to stake his life on it.

The Lord is conducting an examination to determine whether those who claim to believe in Him are willing to stake their lives on it. This is the message of Revelation 2:10. Christians may not be called upon to die for their faith, but they are expected to live for it, making each of their daily choices from that perspective. Having found something worth dying for, they have also established themselves in something that is worth living for.

B. Lesson Background

It had been approximately forty years since the apostle Paul had spent three years preaching and teaching in Ephesus, the chief city of the province of Asia (Acts 20:17, 31). From there the gospel had gone throughout all Asia (Acts 19:10, 26), including the cities to which the letters of Revelation were addressed. The first letter was addressed to the church at Ephesus (2:1-7) where John (according to tradition) had served in recent years. The church there was praised for its faithfulness to the gospel, but was rebuked for having left its "first love" (v. 4), that is, its early warmth and enthusiasm. Such a condition could be fatal if not corrected. The second letter was addressed to Smyrna, on the seacoast to the north.

I. Encouragement to Smyrna (Revelation 2:8-11)

Only two of the seven churches in Revelation were commended without any rebuke. Smyrna was one of the two.

A. From the Living Lord (v. 8)

8. And unto the angel of the church in Smyrna write; These things saith the first and the last, which was dead, and is alive.

The *angel of the church* would seem to refer to the "messenger" (this is the basic meaning of the word *angel*), who usually addressed the congregation with God's message. Perhaps we should think of someone similar to a minister or an elder of a church. This individual would be the person who would receive and convey to the people what the Lord said in this letter.

Smyrna (its modern name is Izmir) was a proud and beautiful city with an important commercial harbor on the Aegean Sea about forty miles north of Ephesus. Smyrna was noted for its impressive temples erected to a variety of Roman gods, and also for its willingness to meet the demands of Rome for worship of the emperor. These factors, along with a large Jewish population hostile to Christianity, made Smyrna a difficult place to live as a Christian.

The source of the letter to Smyrna is identified here as *the first and the last*. God speaks as such an eternal One in Isaiah 44:6 and 48:12. Jesus referred to Himself by this title when He first appeared to John (Revelation 1:17). The words are similar in meaning to *Alpha and Omega* (1:11). That Jesus *was dead, and is alive* was also impressed upon John (1:18). Such a declaration was especially meaningful in Smyrna, which preserved a myth that the god Dionysus had come back from the dead.

B. He Understands Their Trials (v. 9)

9. I know thy works, and tribulation, and poverty, (but thou art rich) and I know the blasphemy of them which say they are Jews, and are not, but are the synagogue of Satan.

The words *thy works* do not appear at this point in the oldest manuscripts; thus they do not appear in many of the later translations. The phrase *I know thy works* is found at the beginning of each of the other letters, except the one to Pergamos.

The believers at Smyrna could take comfort from the fact that the Lord knew the circumstances (*tribulation, and poverty*) that made living the Christian life so challenging in their city. Relatively few wealthy or powerful individuals were found in the first-century churches (1 Corinthians 1:26-29; James 2:5). *Poverty* is not specifically mentioned in the other six letters; perhaps it was especially severe in Smyrna, where the hard-pressed Christians obviously did not share in the prosperity of their commercially thriving city.

However, Jesus reminded the Christians in Smyrna that they were *rich*. Perhaps they did not fully appreciate what they possessed. They were "heirs of the kingdom which he hath promised to them that love him" (James 2:5). Their wealth was the kind not suspected by careless observers with more worldly pursuits. Heaven's bank account never can be overdrawn, and when spiritual wealth is shared with others, it becomes even more treasured.

The injurious speaking referred to here as *blasphemy* was not uttered directly against God, but was rather a program of slander against His people. The false *Jews* who conducted it resembled the "children of Abraham" who opposed Jesus and to whom He said, "If ye were Abraham's children, ye would do the works of Abraham" (John 8:39). He later added, "Ye are of your father the devil, and the lusts of your father ye will do" (v. 44). By their lack of inward commitment to the Law of Moses (Romans 2:28, 29) and by their stubborn rejection of the Messiah whom God promised to Abraham, these Jews had forfeited their claim to be God's people and had become instead a congregation (*synagogue*) *of Satan.*

DANGEROUS DECEIT

John André became a faithful and distinguished British soldier, joining the army in 1771. He was sent to Canada and rapidly rose through the ranks. Eventually he was appointed an aide to Sir Henry Clinton, an important British general. It was in 1780 that Benedict Arnold negotiated with General Clinton to betray the fort of West Point to the British. Major André was disguised as a civilian and tried to pass through the colonial forces. He carried the plans of West Point, furnished by Arnold, in his boots. André was captured near Tarrytown, New York, and taken to General George Washington. A military court appointed by Washington sentenced André to be executed as a spy and he was hanged at Tappan, New York, on October 2, 1780.

Jesus said to Smyrna, "I know the blasphemy of them *which say they are Jews, and are not, but are the synagogue of Satan*" (Revelation 2:9). To pretend in time of war to be for one side while actually being a combatant for the enemy is indeed punishable by death.

In its conflict with evil and with the evil one, the church is engaged in a life-and-death struggle; it is nothing less than a spiritual war. There are forces ("principalities and powers") that seek not just to damage or demean Christianity, but to destroy it. The call is not to be faithful until difficulties arise, or until it is unpleasant to be a Christian; we must be faithful "unto death." Counterfeit Christianity plays right into the hands of the enemy.   —J. G. V. B.

C. He Promises Life Beyond Affliction (v. 10)

10. Fear none of those things which thou shalt suffer: behold, the devil shall cast some of you into prison, that ye may be tried; and ye shall have tribulation ten days: be thou faithful unto death, and I will give thee a crown of life.

Although the saints at Smyrna had already been introduced to *tribulation*, they were to encounter more of it. *Prison* would be the trying experience of some, as it had been for the apostles (Acts 4:3; 5:17, 18; 12:1-4; 16:19-24). Through such surroundings the Christians would be *tried* by *the devil*. These same circumstances also had the potential, however, to strengthen the believers (James 1:12; 1 Peter 4:12-19), even as steel gains strength through the heat of its tempering.

The *ten days* of tribulation is subject to various interpretations. Is it a literal time period, is it symbolic for a longer period (ten years perhaps), or is it a general term, indicating a significant, but not unending, period of time (note the use of *ten* in Numbers 14:22; Nehemiah 4:12; Daniel 1:20)? In historical context, the last option seems most reasonable. If one dates the book of Revelation at around A.D. 95, as many scholars do, then Domitian's reign and attendant persecution would end in a matter of months. At the same time, any persecution a Christian endures is minor, when viewed in light of his eventual reward. (See 2 Corinthians 4:17.)

The phrase *faithful unto death* is rendered as "even if it means death" in *Today's English Version* and as "even to the point of death" in the *New International Version*. This is plainly what it meant to Stephen (Acts 7:59, 60) and to James the brother of John (Acts 12:1, 2). Faithfulness to Christ does not always hasten death, but it must never stop short of it.

To the faithful ones, Christ promises eternal life as a crown. The Greek word for crown is not the royal *diadema* worn by emperors (from which we get our word "diadem"); it is the *stephanos*—the garland or wreath awarded to the winner in a great athletic contest. Paul referred to it as an "incorruptible crown" (1 Corinthians 9:24, 25) and anticipated it as a "crown of righteousness" to be shared by all who love and anticipate Christ's final appearing (2 Timothy 4:8).

THOSE THINGS WHICH THOU SHALT SUFFER

Revelation 2:10 is one of several places in Revelation where the experience of tribulation is predicted for Christians. We know from both New Testament accounts and post-Biblical his-

torical records that many followers of Jesus were terrorized and tortured for their faith.

Yet it is not just first-century martyrs who have suffered for Jesus' sake. What about the harsh treatment many receive in Islamic countries around the world? Who can deny the grave consequences of seeking to lead people to Christian conversion in Hindu-controlled areas of India? What about the many who have given their lives for Christ in Communist China?

Throughout the world many have faced suffering for the Lord Jesus. In 1956 five missionaries were killed by Auca Indians in western Ecuador. They were well-educated, enthusiastic servants of our Lord whose tragic deaths taught us that many of Jesus' disciples must still suffer as they seek to advance His kingdom. Speaking for all the widows of the slain men, Elisabeth Elliot (wife of martyr Jim Elliot) wrote in her powerful book *Through Gates of Splendor*, "To the world at large this was a sad waste of five young lives. But God has His plan and purpose in all things."
         —J. G. V. B.

D. He Assures the Hearers (v. 11)

11. He that hath an ear, let him hear what the Spirit saith unto the churches; He that overcometh shall not be hurt of the second death.

Jesus frequently concluded His parables by admonishing His hearers to use their ears for their intended purposes—receiving and considering what He had just said (Matthew 11:15; Mark 4:9, 23; Luke 14:35). Here He repeats the injunction, not only to the saints in Smyrna, but to all who would hear the words anywhere else at any time.

He that overcometh is the believer who remains steadfast through all his trials without giving in or giving up, as Jesus remained faithful all the way to the cross and was given Heaven's highest accolade (Philippians 2:5-11). His followers will be out of reach of *the second death*, which is Hell, the final and eternal separation from God and His grace (Revelation 20:6, 14;

visual for
lesson 7

21:8). To be twice born, first physically, then spiritually, is to die but once—physically. To be once born, only physically, is to die twice—physically and spiritually. This is the ultimate tragedy.

II. Warning to Pergamos (Revelation 2:12-17)

A. From the Well-Equipped Lord (v. 12)

12. And to the angel of the church in Pergamos write; These things saith he which hath the sharp sword with two edges.

Whereas the opening words to Smyrna were triumphant and inspiring, here we find the makings of a full-fledged confrontation. The city of *Pergamos* (or Pergamum), which today is known as Bergama, was made the capital of Asia by the Romans. It stood on a cone-shaped hill rising a thousand feet above the surrounding valley, some fifty miles north of Smyrna. It was, according to one writer, "a sort of union of a pagan cathedral city, a university town, and a royal residence." Here people came to worship at the temple of Zeus, to seek healing at the temple of Aesculapius (the Roman god of medicine), and to conduct emperor worship. It is not accidental therefore that the letter to Pergamos challenges the sword of the emperor with the *sword* of the Spirit: the word of God which is "quick, and powerful, and sharper than any two-edged sword" (Hebrews 4:12; see also Ephesians 6:17).

B. He Understands Their Surroundings (v. 13)

13. I know thy works, and where thou dwellest, even where Satan's seat is: and thou holdest fast my name, and hast not denied my faith, even in those days wherein Antipas was my faithful martyr, who was slain among you, where Satan dwelleth.

The *works* accomplished by the church in Pergamos included their faithful testimony to Christ under trying circumstances. Their location constituted a notable handicap. The reference to *Satan's seat* (his throne or dwelling place) may allude to the city's cluster of pagan temples, or it may reflect its position as the official center of emperor worship in Asia. Any church whose community draws heavily on gambling or the liquor business for its revenue will know something of Pergamos's predicament.

The believers in Pergamos had held *fast* and had *not denied* their *faith* in Christ. A believer's confession made before baptism may be the easiest one he will ever make. Spoken before supportive friends, it is encouraged by the whole church. To speak up for Christ among scoffing unbelievers or zealots of an opposing religion is much more challenging, and that is what the Christians in Pergamos had done. They had not forsaken their testimony, even when *Antipas* became a *faithful martyr* because of his. Concerning this man, we know nothing except what is written here, but those in Pergamos knew all about his courage. According to one tradition, he was slowly roasted to death in a bronze kettle during the reign of Domitian. Such a violent death attested to Pergamos's reputation as a city *where Satan dwelleth.*

C. He Condemns False Teachings (vv. 14, 15)

The Lord's fervent appreciation of the Christians' steadfastness in Pergamos did not prevent His equally loving rebuke of their toleration of false teaching.

14. But I have a few things against thee, because thou hast there them that hold the doctrine of Balaam, who taught Balak to cast a stumblingblock before the children of Israel, to eat things sacrificed unto idols, and to commit fornication.

The account of *Balaam* and *Balak* is found in Numbers 22:1—24:25 and 31:15, 16. It is alluded to in 2 Peter 2:15 and Jude 11. Balak, king of Moab, feared the forces of Israel, advancing under Moses' leadership. So Balak hired the prophet Balaam to pronounce a curse upon Israel. Instead, God caused Balaam to bless Israel. Balaam, however, showed the Moabites another way to weaken Israel. They succeeded in enticing the Israelites to engage with them in idolatrous feasts and immoral acts.

15. So hast thou also them that hold the doctrine of the Nicolaitans, which thing I hate.

Three of the seven letters in Revelation mention false teachings that led to a toleration and even an encouragement of sexual immorality and the eating of foods dedicated to idols. The details of the beliefs and practices of the *Nicolaitans* have been the subject of much conjecture, but specific information is limited. Apparently they were condoning and encouraging acts similar to those mentioned in the previous verse. Perhaps they argued that Christian liberty included the freedom to participate in such hitherto-forbidden practices. The church at Ephesus was complimented for rejecting the Nicolaitan heresy (Revelation 2:6); the church at Pergamos is rebuked for tolerating it. *Which thing I hate* is a phrase that does not appear in the oldest manuscripts or the newer translations, but such a fact is evident (the words do appear in 2:6).

D. He Commands Correction (v. 16)

16. Repent; or else I will come unto thee quickly, and will fight against them with the sword of my mouth.

The most pressing need of the believers in Pergamos was simple: *Repent!* Change your mind and change your ways! God's people must cease to tolerate and harbor among themselves teachers who disseminate teachings that God abhors. Repentance, however, is not a harsh and punitive requirement; instead, it is offered in love by the Lord of the church as the tool that will make it a stronger church.

The alternative is the sudden and unannounced arrival of Christ as the instrument of judgment. He will make war against the offending false teachers if they refuse to repent. His weapon will be the *sword* of His *mouth*, the same sword mentioned at the beginning of this letter (v. 12).

E. He Challenges All to Overcome (v. 17)

17. He that hath an ear, let him hear what the Spirit saith unto the churches; To him that overcometh will I give to eat of the hidden manna, and will give him a white stone, and in the stone a new name written, which no man knoweth saving he that receiveth it.

Again comes the admonition that concludes all seven letters: Let all people of all churches in all times and all places listen to what the Lord says to you. This applies both to the foregoing warnings and to the promises about to be heard. Those who use God's available power to triumph over the trials and temptations of life will be welcomed to feast in Heaven with God.

The *hidden manna* brings to mind the miraculous supply of food provided to the people of Israel as they journeyed toward the promised land (Exodus 16:14, 15; Psalm 78:24). A memorial portion of this was kept in the ark of the covenant in the tabernacle (Exodus 16:33, 34; Hebrews 9:3, 4). Jesus contrasted Israel's manna with Himself as the bread of life (John 6:48-51), thus declaring Himself to be the true nourishment from Heaven. This manna is *hidden* from the world, but will be given to those who have refused to participate in the feasts associated with idol worship.

Ancient tradition identifies a *white stone* or its equivalent as a token of acceptance or approval. It could be used as a sign of acquittal by a judge in court, as an admission to a wedding feast, or as an indication of purchasing power in the marketplace. The engraving of a secret symbol or name on such a stone would give it immeasur-

able value to the recipient. Thus the promise before us is a way of saying that each faithful saint among the multitudes of the saved will have a special and personal invitation to Heaven. No promise could be more meaningful.

Conclusion

A. Filling the Real Need

The saints in Smyrna lived in poverty, while those in Pergamos were oppressed by unfriendly forces all around them. The Lord could have provided relief supplies to Smyrna and could have worked miracles on behalf of those in Pergamos, persuading pagans there to treat Christians respectfully. But He did neither. These saints in Asia needed something else far more important. They needed to be right with God. They needed inner strength to overcome their difficulties and remain faithful, a strength that is the product of close fellowship with the Lord who bore our difficulties without seeking relief for Himself. Their ultimate relief would be found with Him who won glory for Himself through His suffering. Sharing in that glory is the "blessed hope" of all the faithful, both then and now.

B. Prayer of Thanks for Revelation

Thank You, God, for this marvelous book of Revelation, with its display of the divine love. Please give us hearing ears, receptive spirits, and willing hearts, to receive and claim Your promises. In Christ we pray. Amen.

C. Thought to Remember

"If we be dead with him, we shall also live with him: if we suffer, we shall also reign with him" (2 Timothy 2:11, 12).

Home Daily Bible Readings

Monday, Apr. 7—Repent and Return to God (Acts 3:17-26)

Tuesday, Apr. 8—Pray for Spiritual Wisdom (Colossians 1:9-14)

Wednesday, Apr. 9—Use Your Faith to Overcome (1 John 5:1-5)

Thursday, Apr. 10—Have Faith in Jesus Christ (1 John 5:6-12)

Friday, Apr. 11—Hold Firm Your Hope (Hebrews 3:1-6)

Saturday, Apr. 12—Be Wise in the Lord (Proverbs 4:1-9)

Sunday, Apr. 13—Be Faithful and Righteous (Proverbs 28:20-28)

Learning by Doing

This page contains an alternate lesson plan emphasizing learning activities.
Classes desiring such student involvement will find these suggestions helpful.

Learning Goals

As students participate in today's class session, they should:

1. Recognize the need to maintain solid convictions based on the truth of God's Word.

2. State the perspective from which Christians should view suffering.

3. Resolve to remain faithful to Jesus in spite of pressures to conform to the world or to compromise one's convictions.

Into the Lesson

Arrange a few days ahead of class for two of the more expressive members of your class to help you stage a mock debate between themselves. One person will represent the position: "The truth of God's revealed Word must never be subject or secondary to our traditions and methods." The other person will represent the viewpoint: "Our methods must always take precedence over the message, and we must go with what seems to work." Let each person speak for two to three minutes, then open the debate to the class and allow questions.

Point out that today's lesson from Revelation is a call to two churches to be faithful to their message, in spite of the threat of persecution and the attractiveness of false teaching.

Into the Word

To begin this session, use the Lesson Background to provide information about the cities of Smyrna and Pergamos. Refer to the map that accompanied last week's lesson to locate them.

Following these comments, give each class member an index card or a piece of paper or cardboard of similar size. One side of each card should have the letter S (for Smyrna) on it; the other side should be marked with the letter P (for Pergamos). Be sure to have enough for your usual attendance (plus a few more for any guests).

Read the Scripture text from Revelation 2:8-17, telling the class to listen carefully. Then read the following statements. Have the class members respond by showing you the S side of their card (if they think Jesus said that to the church at Smyrna) or the P side (if they think Jesus was speaking to the church at Pergamos).

1. "Ye shall have tribulation ten days." (S)

2. "I have a few things against thee." (P)

3. "Antipas was my faithful martyr." (P)

4. "I will give thee a crown of life." (S)

5. "Thou hast there them that hold the doctrine of Balaam." (P)

6. "Fear none of those things which thou shalt suffer." (S)

7. "I know thy works." (Both).

8. "He that hath an ear, let him hear." (Both)

Note that the final two statements are addressed to *both* churches and are certainly applicable to *all* churches.

Next, lead in a discussion of the following questions:

1. Discuss how Jesus assured the Christians at Smyrna that they would suffer. Use the commentary's discussion of v. 10 to explain the reference to "ten days." What truths are most important to remember when suffering for Jesus' sake?

2. For what was the church at Pergamos commended? For what was it rebuked? Point out that the acceptance of false teaching had severely crippled this church's progress. Why is sound doctrine so important to the church? How does the church most effectively guard against false doctrine?

Into Life

Refer to the key verse for today's lesson, found in the last part of Revelation 2:10. Ask, "What blessings are promised to Smyrna and to Pergamos if they remain faithful?" You may wish to comment further on the "hidden manna" and the "white stone" of v. 17, using the material in the lesson commentary. Point out that the invitation to Heaven is a personal one from Jesus to every Christian.

Bring the class session to a close by asking, "What can our Sunday school class do to encourage Christians to remain faithful?" List these ideas on the blackboard or on poster board. Perhaps this would be a good time to stress the need to keep in touch with absentees. Have cards ready with names, addresses, and/or phone numbers on them, to distribute to volunteers who will make contacts in the coming week.

Ask for two volunteers to lead in closing prayers. Have the first pray for the faithfulness of the class to God and His Word. The second should focus on the efforts the class will make to contact others in the coming week and encourage them toward greater faithfulness.

Let's Talk It Over

The questions on this page are designed to encourage review of the lesson Scriptures and to promote discussion of the lesson by the class. The answers provided are only discussion starters. Let your class talk it over from there.

1. According to the *King James Version,* Jesus said to all of the seven churches, "I know thy works." In some cases that was good, while in other cases it was cause for rebuke. How may it be helpful for our church to ponder the fact that Jesus knows our works?

It should stimulate us to ask ourselves certain important questions: "Are we doing what Jesus wants us to be doing?" "Are we engaging in our spiritual labors for God's glory or for self-promotion?" Jesus knows what our church is doing, and He knows what kind of contribution each member is making. If our zeal is giving way to indifference (as in the church at Ephesus), He knows it. If we have become materially comfortable but spiritually lukewarm (as the church at Laodicea), He knows it. Once we examine our works in the light of these questions and compare our condition with that of each of the seven churches, it will be time to make any appropriate changes.

2. The letters to the seven churches feature a strong emphasis on believers as overcomers (Revelation 2:7, 11, 17, 26; 3:5, 12, 21). In what ways must we be overcomers?

First John 5:4 speaks of "the victory that overcometh the world, even our faith." We must be overcomers in maintaining our faith. Unbelievers seem to be working overtime today in attacking the Bible as the basis of our faith. They try to undermine our confidence in its historical character and timeless authority. Through our faith we must overcome these attacks. Also, we must be overcomers as far as the world's allurements are concerned. We are under constant assault from worldly values based upon power, money, sex, and manipulation of the truth. In our commitment to righteousness and holiness we must overcome these temptations.

3. Is there a "Satan's seat" (Revelation 2:13) in our community? If so, what should we do?

The *New International Version* renders this term as "where Satan has his throne." It must refer to a place or situation in which Satan is able to exercise a significant rule over people's lives. The lesson writer suggests that in Pergamos this may have referred to pagan temples or the presence of emperor worship. In modern communities it could apply to a business establishment that deals in occult objects or literature. A store that sells pornographic materials or a place where gambling is practiced could properly be termed "Satan's seat." It is important that we show from the Scriptures how such items are part of Satan's agenda. We should also publicize the statistics, examples, and personal testimonies available that demonstrate how destructive these elements can be within a community.

4. The lesson writer indicates that "the doctrine of the Nicolaitans" (Revelation 2:15) probably involved a misapplication of Christian liberty. How are Christians today tempted to abuse the freedom they have in Christ?

We hear frequently of Christians who have experienced a moral downfall and then have come back to the Lord. Through repentance they have been restored to fellowship with the Lord and His people. Perhaps other believers see this, overlook the pain involved in the process, and reason that if they sin similarly, they can also repent and return. It is tempting to think this way, but it is dangerous. We cheapen God's grace when we treat it like this. Another way we may abuse our freedom in Christ is by exposing ourselves to temptations while assuming they will not affect us. Christians may view highly questionable movies or television shows on this basis, or they may indulge in social drinking or "recreational drugs." Again, this is flirting with danger.

5. How is the promise of "hidden manna" (Revelation 2:17) an appealing one?

It may raise the question, "Will we eat and drink in Heaven?" In John's vision of the new Jerusalem, he mentions the abundant fruits yielded by the tree of life (Revelation 22:2). Perhaps these references do not imply actually eating in Heaven, but have a symbolic meaning. Even if the "hidden manna" describes not literal food, but God's abundant supply of all our heavenly needs, it is still very encouraging. We remember that the original manna sustained the wandering Israelites over a period of forty years. The "hidden manna" speaks of God's power to provide for our needs eternally.

To Thyatira

DEVOTIONAL READING: Romans 2:1-11.

LESSON SCRIPTURE: Revelation 2:18-29.

PRINTED TEXT: Revelation 2:18-29.

Revelation 2:18-29

18 And unto the angel of the church in Thyatira write; These things saith the Son of God, who hath his eyes like unto a flame of fire, and his feet are like fine brass.

19 I know thy works, and charity, and service, and faith, and thy patience, and thy works; and the last to be more than the first.

20 Notwithstanding I have a few things against thee, because thou sufferest that woman Jezebel, which calleth herself a prophetess, to teach and to seduce my servants to commit fornication, and to eat things sacrificed unto idols.

21 And I gave her space to repent of her fornication; and she repented not.

22 Behold, I will cast her into a bed, and them that commit adultery with her into great tribulation, except they repent of their deeds.

23 And I will kill her children with death; and all the churches shall know that I am he which searcheth the reins and hearts: and I will give unto every one of you according to your works.

24 But unto you I say, and unto the rest in Thyatira, as many as have not this doctrine, and which have not known the depths of Satan, as they speak; I will put upon you none other burden.

25 But that which ye have already, hold fast till I come.

26 And he that overcometh, and keepeth my works unto the end, to him will I give power over the nations:

27 And he shall rule them with a rod of iron; as the vessels of a potter shall they be broken to shivers: even as I received of my Father.

28 And I will give him the morning star.

29 He that hath an ear, let him hear what the Spirit saith unto the churches.

GOLDEN TEXT: All the churches shall know that I am he which searcheth the reins and hearts: and I will give unto every one of you according to your works.
—Revelation 2:23.

Hope for the Future
Unit 2: Letters to Churches
(Lessons 6-9)

Lesson Aims

This study should prepare the student to:
1. Tell briefly what Jesus commended and what He condemned in the church at Thyatira.
2. Tell what qualifies Jesus to speak as He does, using the description of Him in this text.
3. Show how the message to Thyatira speaks to the student's own life as a Christian.

Lesson Outline

INTRODUCTION
    A. Politically Incorrect
    B. Lesson Background
  I. THE SON OF GOD SPEAKS (Revelation 2:18)
 II. HE COMMENDS STEADFAST DEVOTION (Revelation 2:19)
    The Last More Than the First
III. HE CONDEMNS ACCEPTANCE OF WRONG (Revelation 2:20-23)
    A. Jezebel and Her Influence (vv. 20, 21)
    Space to Repent
    B. Jezebel's Punishment (vv. 22, 23)
IV. HE COMMANDS AND ASSURES THE FAITHFUL (Revelation 2:24-29)
    A. Hold to What You Have! (vv. 24, 25)
    B. Reign With Christ! (vv. 26-28)
    C. Hear and Heed! (v. 29)
CONCLUSION
    A. How Is Your Hearing?
    B. Prayer of a Hearer
    C. Thought to Remember

The visual for Lesson 8 in the visuals packet illustrates the cost of taking a stand for what is right. It is shown on page 293.

Introduction

A. Politically Incorrect

God is not politically correct. He does not adjust His being, His behavior, His expectations, or His manner of expression to avoid irritating those who would seek to remake Him into their own image. Instead, He insists on being the same I AM that He has been since before there was anything else.

God created mankind in His own image. From the first, people have not been satisfied with that, but have shown a distressing tendency to make gods in their own image. Some have fashioned gods of wood or stone, which they have worshiped by acts of their own lust. Others have invented deities who became personalities larger and more lustful than themselves (as did the Greeks and Romans). Man's tendency in our time is to worship gods that reflect his technological progress and his fascination with the latest fads in entertainment. Even users of the Bible may seek to make God in their own image. "My God would never do that," they say in response to Biblical warnings of judgment. But will God be manipulated and told what He may or may not do?

"That's my kind of church," one will say after shopping around for and finding a congregation that reflects his or her own special preferences in worship style or interpretation of Scripture. The Lord still makes it clear, however, that *His* kind of church—not yours or mine—is the one we should seek. "Shopping" is an inappropriate term to describe the search for eternal truth.

"But that is intolerant!" cries the anything-goes multitude to whom tolerance is held as the highest virtue. Apparently the one thing they will not tolerate is intolerance. Yet these same people depend on mechanics and engineers who limit their tolerances to the thousandth part of an inch! It should not surprise us, then, that the Engineer of the universe cannot approve or welcome into His presence that which flouts and violates His plan and His very being. Neither should it surprise us that He should say to His people, "You are too tolerant of corruption among you." Let us choose acceptability with Him (Romans 12:1, 2), as we are encouraged to do in today's lesson.

B. Lesson Background

Thyatira should not be entirely unknown to readers of the New Testament. Lydia, the "seller of purple" who was Paul's first convert in Philippi of Macedonia (Acts 16:11-15), came from Thyatira. This detail fits well with the fact that many highly organized trade guilds were present in Thyatira. Membership in these guilds posed special problems to those who, like Lydia, became followers of Jesus. This is because the trade guilds were closely associated with heathen worship, which included feasts in honor of idols, and the accompanying immoral practices. To live as a Christian businessman or businesswoman in Thyatira demanded real commitment! We can only surmise the pressures that Lydia may have faced if she returned to her home and sought to share her new-found faith with others.

Thyatira was located on the Lycus River in northern Asia, on the road between Pergamos (the capital of Asia) and Sardis. Its principal deity was Apollo, the mythical Roman god of light and learning. Its modern name is Akhisar, or "White Castle," so named for the rocky hill overhanging it.

I. The Son of God Speaks (Revelation 2:18)

18. And unto the angel of the church in Thyatira write; These things saith the Son of God, who hath his eyes like unto a flame of fire, and his feet are like fine brass.

Once again the *angel,* or messenger (apparently one of the leaders of the congregation), was to receive, deliver, and circulate the letter. *Thyatira* was the first of four inland cities of Asia to be addressed by the Lord of the church. Earlier letters (to Ephesus, Smyrna, and Pergamos) had gone to towns located closer to the seacoast. It should be noted that this letter to Thyatira is the longest of the seven.

The title *Son of God* is not used anywhere else in Revelation. It emphasizes Christ's deity, perhaps as a direct response to the aforementioned tendency of the trade guilds to promote idol worship. The description of Jesus as having *eyes like unto a flame of fire* is reminiscent of how He first appeared to John as the Son of man (Revelation 1:14). In addition, it further challenged the belief that the god Apollo was the source of light. It emphasized that Christ is not only ever-present with His own, but also perceives their inmost thoughts. The *feet . . . like fine brass* again recalls Christ's initial appearance to John (Revelation 1:15).

How to Say It

AKHISAR. Ahk-iss-*ar.*
ASHERAH. Uh-*she*-ruh.
BALAAMITES. *Bay*-luh-mites.
ETHBAAL. Eth-*bay*-ul.
GNOSTICS. *Nahss*-ticks.
LAODICEA. Lay-*odd*-uh-*see*-uh (strong accent on *see*).
LYCUS. *Like*-us.
MACEDONIA. Mass-uh-*doe*-nee-uh.
NICOLAITANS. Nick-oh-*lay*-ih-tunz.
PERGAMOS. *Per*-guh-muss.
PHILIPPI. Fuh-*lip*-pie or *Fill*-uh-pie.
SIDONIANS. Sigh-*doe*-nee-uns.
SMYRNA. *Smur*-nuh.
THYATIRA. Thy-uh-*tie*-ruh.

II. He Commends Steadfast Devotion (Revelation 2:19)

19. I know thy works, and charity, and service, and faith, and thy patience, and thy works; and the last to be more than the first.

One may question why the phrase *thy works* is used twice in this verse. A clearer reading, with the second usage appearing in its correct place, is given in the *American Standard Version*: "I know thy works, and thy love and faith and ministry and patience, and that thy last works are more than the first." This made Thyatira's pattern of growth the very opposite of that of Ephesus, which had lost its "first love" and had fallen from its "first works" (Revelation 2:4, 5).

The believer's *works* should include such inner qualities as *charity* (love) and *faith,* along with the more visible attributes of *service* to others and *patience* when suffering affliction. At the same time, love cannot be expressed without action (1 John 3:17, 18), and neither can faith (James 2:14-18).

Thyatira's crowning achievement lay in a level of maturity that produced more and better accomplishments for Christ as the years went on. Like a good fruit tree, these believers brought forth a better crop each season. Could that be said of us?

THE LAST MORE THAN THE FIRST

In many areas of life it is essential to recognize how important the final stages of any activity or project can be. In athletic competitions, quite often a team will start out like a whirlwind. The actions of the players seem almost effortless. Shots, strokes, or passes are crisp and accurate. But as the end of the game or match nears, the same team may appear droopy, dispirited, and inept, particularly if they are losing or have fallen far behind. Teams that win and are used to winning will approach the end of the game still alert, focused, and enthusiastic. Their last is "more than the first."

This principle also holds true in nature: the oak is much greater than the acorn, the rose is more attractive than the bud, and the mature racehorse is much more graceful than the awkward, stumbling colt. It is good to begin with enthusiasm and excitement, but only persistence and disciplined growth lead to achievement and victory.

This is what the apostle John was saying about the Christians at Thyatira. Their love, service, faith, patience, and their works in general were "more" than they were at the beginning of their Christian walk. Sadly, this is contrary to the condition of many in our churches today. As Jesus said, testings and persecution cause some to be offended, while the "deceitfulness of riches" causes others to become unfruitful (Matthew 13:20-22). It is one thing to accept Christ and begin the Christian life with enthusiasm. It is quite another to maintain steady growth and to do and to be "more than the first."

—J. G. V. B.

III. He Condemns Acceptance of Wrong (Revelation 2:20-23)

A. Jezebel and Her Influence (vv. 20, 21)

20. Notwithstanding I have a few things against thee, because thou sufferest that woman Jezebel, which calleth herself a prophetess, to teach and to seduce my servants to commit fornication, and to eat things sacrificed unto idols.

Again, let us note the contrast with Ephesus: Ephesus had been found at fault for letting its "first love" diminish while resisting evil (Revelation 2:2-5). Thyatira is rebuked for tolerating false doctrine while increasing in good works. The saints were suffering persecution patiently, and that was to their credit. But they were also suffering (in the sense of permitting, tolerating, or allowing) abominable teachings, and that was a serious error.

The *few things* wrong in Thyatira stemmed from one source. *That woman Jezebel* brings to mind the daughter of Ethbaal, king of the Sidonians, who became the wife of Israel's King Ahab (1 Kings 16:30, 31). She also became the merciless enemy of God's prophets, and supporter of the prophets of Baal and Asherah (1 Kings 18:3, 4, 13, 19). Her counterpart in Thyatira has been variously identified as: (1) the wife of the *angel* or leader of the church; (2) a woman of influence in the church and community; or (3) the leader of a group of persons similar to the Nicolaitans in Ephesus and Pergamos or the Balaamites in Pergamos (Revelation 2:6, 14, 15).

This Jezebel *calleth herself a prophetess.* Apparently she claimed supernatural guidance in teaching and persuading the Christians in Thyatira to engage in those acts specifically forbidden to Gentile converts among the churches: *fornication*, and eating of *things sacrificed to idols* (Acts 15:28, 29). Both of these were essential parts of the pagan worship festivals associated with the various trade guilds in Thyatira. But Christian belief and conduct cannot include teachings and practices that God abhors.

21. And I gave her space to repent of her fornication; and she repented not.

God's grace provides time and opportunity to acknowledge sins, to seek forgiveness, and to change direction. Some, like Thyatira's Jezebel, spurn the offer.

SPACE TO REPENT

Repentance involves change of direction. Essentially it means making an "about face," turning from one way to go in the opposite way. Many times people are confronted with the need for change. An overweight person may continue to gain pounds, as repeated trips to the scales indicate. Someone is smoking and becomes concerned about how many packs of cigarettes he is using. A college student needs to complete an assignment or prepare for an exam, but continues to neglect his responsibilities. In all such cases, there is usually a margin or space of time that is available for a change of direction.

However, there comes the point when the excess weight leads to clogged arteries, heart trouble, or breathing problems. The smoking may lead to lung or heart damage. The academic neglect can result in lower grades, possible failure of a class, and inability to achieve a degree or to graduate.

The Son of God told the Christians at Thyatira that they had been given "space to repent" (Revelation 2:21). Jesus had shown great patience with their departure from God's ways as expressed in their toleration of false teaching. This patience was not to be disregarded or misunderstood. The problems in Thyatira were known; the punishment was deferred in the hope that the church would respond accordingly.

As Jesus said to all Christians in Revelation 3:20, "Behold, I stand at the door, and knock." While He is at the door, there is a waiting period as He seeks a response. There is "space for repentance," but it is an opportunity to be embraced *now*, not neglected or postponed.

—J. G. V. B.

B. Jezebel's Punishment (vv. 22, 23)

22. Behold, I will cast her into a bed, and them that commit adultery with her into great tribulation, except they repent of their deeds.

Behold is designed to call attention to the severe punishment that is imminent. Jezebel will be *cast . . . into a bed*, apparently indicating some form of sickness. Thus, the place where Jezebel and her followers experienced their sinful pleasure will be changed into an instrument of punishment. In this instance, physical punishment is indicated (perhaps symbolically) for sins. Such are the consequences, not only for the false teacher, but also for her followers. Yet their punishment stops short of death, and the opportunity to *repent* remains. Manuscript evidence leads recent translators of this verse to indicate that the wicked *deeds* for which the followers in unfaithfulness must repent are *hers*—Jezebel's. They must reject her counsel and return to the right kind of leadership!

23. And I will kill her children with death; and all the churches shall know that I am he which searcheth the reins and hearts: and I will give unto every one of you according to your works.

Here *children* probably refers to those who practice the false doctrines Jezebel has promoted (see Isaiah 57:3; John 8:44). While to *kill . . . with death* seems redundant, it is a way of depicting the severity of the coming punishment. It means "to totally destroy." Perhaps some kind of violent or painful death is implied. At any rate, the evident punishments will demonstrate to *all the churches* throughout Asia and elsewhere that the Lord is fully aware of all that has been going on in His church.

The word *reins* is actually a word meaning "kidneys." It reflects the belief that this portion of the body was the seat of one's emotions (we still refer to someone's "gut feeling"). The heart is often associated with reasoning or thinking (see Mark 2:8). Thus, the phrase *reins and hearts* means that every emotion and every thought is open to Jesus' inspection.

IV. He Commands and Assures the Faithful (Revelation 2:24-29)

Jesus did more than just point out the problems present in Thyatira. He proceeded to tell them what to do to correct them and to make their "candlestick" burn brightly again. He also promised that perseverance on their part would be richly rewarded.

A. Hold to What You Have! (vv. 24, 25)

24, 25. But unto you I say, and unto the rest in Thyatira, as many as have not this doctrine, and which have not known the depths of Satan, as they speak; I will put upon you none other burden. But that which ye have already, hold fast till I come.

The ones here addressed should not be considered two separate groups; the *American Standard Version* reads, "But to you I say, to the rest that are in Thyatira." Jesus was now directing His words to all those saints in Thyatira who had not followed the *doctrine* of Jezebel, and thus had not been involved in the so-called *depths of Satan*. Perhaps the faithful recognized this teaching as coming from the pit, or the underworld (Revelation 9:1, 2). However, it may

visual for
lesson 8

also refer to claims made by Satan and his followers to offer *depths* of secret wisdom, such as those offered to Eve in Eden (Genesis 3:4-6). *Deep* was a commonly used term among the Gnostics (or "knowing ones"), a heretical group just beginning to make its troublesome presence known. One of their teachings was that in order to defeat Satan a person must enter his stronghold; that is, he must experience evil deeply. This was knowledge *as they speak*; it was knowledge only in the perverted thinking of these deceivers.

None other burden seems to echo the decision of the apostles and elders in Jerusalem concerning the Law and its application to Gentile Christians. These believers were directed to avoid fornication and the eating of meats dedicated to idols (Acts 15:28, 29). The letter to Thyatira warns against these same sins, as we have seen from verse 20.

The Phillips translation, however, points in a different direction, saying, "I will lay no further burden upon you, except that you hold on to what you have until I come!" To what must the saints at Thyatira hold with a firm grip? Certainly the virtues already commended in verse 19: their ongoing works of faith, love, service, and patient endurance. These virtues gave evidence of their loyalty to Christ and prepared them for the day when He would *come*. They were to live with the hope of Christ's return as their primary source of motivation.

B. Reign With Christ! (vv. 26-28)

26. And he that overcometh, and keepeth my works unto the end, to him I will give power over the nations.

The Lord's promise, here as in the other letters, is to the one who overcomes the temptations to defect or to simply remain neutral. Such a person continues in the *works* of Christ, heeding what He commands and commends. This is in direct contrast with those who are condemned for the *deeds* of Jezebel (v. 22).

Having been fully tried and found faithful to *the end* amidst the fires of affliction and controversy, the saints at Thyatira will then be ready to accept from their Lord *power over the nations*. How this power will be exercised is explained in the next two verses.

27. And he shall rule them with a rod of iron; as the vessels of a potter shall they be broken to shivers: even as I received of my Father.

As Jesus *received* authority to *rule* from His *Father*, so will He convey to His faithful ones a share in that rule. Christians will even participate in the judgment of the world (1 Corinthians 6:2).

The Greek word for *rule* in this verse literally means "to shepherd." This brings to mind the shepherd's most important piece of equipment: his *rod*, used in both directing and protecting his flock. But since this rod is made of *iron*, we are to think of an authority that is firm and unyielding. An iron rod will not bend. In the hands of God's Messiah it will accomplish His judgment, destroying the wicked and rebellious, as prophesied in Psalm 2. Our text quotes from Psalm 2:9: "Thou shalt break them with a rod of iron; thou shalt dash them in pieces [this is the meaning of the word *shivers*] like a potter's vessel."

28. And I will give him the morning star.

In the last chapter of Revelation are these words of the Lord Jesus: "I am the root and the offspring of David, and the bright and morning star" (22:16). This continues the promise of future authority granted to believers. As the *morning star* rules the heavens, so will believers reign with Jesus. A star is linked with the scepter in Numbers 24:17 and with kingship in Matthew 2:2.

Such a promise as this possessed special meaning for the saints in Thyatira. It assured them that the *morning star*, eternal in Heaven, would forever extinguish the imaginary luster of Apollo, the city's deity of light and learning. It assures us that the spiritual darkness that seems to overwhelm us at times is not permanent. The darkness will be forever vanquished when the Light of the world returns.

C. Hear and Heed! (v. 29)

29. He that hath an ear, let him hear what the Spirit saith unto the churches.

In the first three letters to the seven churches, the promise to the faithful overcomers appeared *after* the admonition to listen to the divinely given message. Here, and in the letters to Sardis, Philadelphia, and Laodicea, these words constitute a firm and final command. It applies not only to the congregations immediately addressed, but to the Lord's people in all churches, and in all times. Listen!

Conclusion

A. How Is Your Hearing?

Grandpa was hard of hearing. Almost everything you said to him had to be repeated in response to his habitual, "Huh?" But if you were patient and did not repeat what you had said, he might reply in a way that indicated he had heard you the first time. He also had a strong tendency to hear what he wanted to hear, but to be utterly oblivious of matters distasteful to him. In that respect, he was somewhat like his granddaughter, who could hear only the first half of her mother's statement: "You may watch your television program *after your homework is done.*"

Most of us tend to hear clearly God's promises of abundant and eternal blessings, but to be oblivious to the conditions on which these blessings are based: "*He that overcometh . . . to him will I give . . . .*" Because the Lord knows our "hearing problem," along with everything else about us and within us, He repeats, "If you have ears, listen!" Perhaps if we formed a habit of listening carefully to what we *don't* want to hear as well as to what we *do*, our total hearing would improve.

B. Prayer of a Hearer

Thank You God for the words Jesus speaks to us from the book of Revelation, even though at times they are strict and demanding. Help us to recognize His absolute right to speak, to be heard, and to be obeyed. Please help us to listen with open ears and receptive hearts to all that He says, and to live by it. Amen.

C. Thought to Remember

God's people can ill afford to be tolerant of what God Himself abhors.

Home Daily Bible Readings

Monday, April 14—God Searches Our Hearts (Romans 8:26-30)

Tuesday, April 15—God Shows No Partiality (Romans 2:1-11)

Wednesday, April 16—God Rewards According to Works (Psalm 62:8-12)

Thursday, April 17—God Rescues the Godly From Trial (2 Peter 2:4-10)

Friday, April 18—Hold Fast to Freedom in Christ (Galatians 5:1-14)

Saturday, April 19—Rejoice in the Lord (Philippians 4:1-9)

Sunday, April 20—Test Your Faith (2 Corinthians 13:5-10)

Learning by Doing

This page contains an alternate lesson plan emphasizing learning activities.
Classes desiring such student involvement will find these suggestions helpful.

Learning Goals

Students in today's class should:

1. Understand the need for faithfulness to Christ even in difficult surroundings.

2. See the need to cooperate more fully with the Lord in their spiritual growth.

3. Hold fast to their faith, regardless of the challenge or affliction.

Into the Lesson

Use one of the following two activities to begin this week's lesson.

Activity One. On a chalkboard, poster board, or flip chart, draw a line down the middle, dividing it into two sections. On the left, write the date 1960; on the right, put the year 1997. Ask class members to give you examples of sin or evil from that era. Then ask for examples of sin or evil from the present day. After you have received several responses, compare the two lists, asking the following questions:

1. Has our society become more tolerant of evil? In what ways?

2. Have we become more idolatrous in the present day? If so, give some evidences of this.

Activity Two. Begin by reading Revelation 2:19: "I know thy works, and charity, and service, and faith, and thy patience, and thy works; and the last to be more than the first." Then ask the class to consider your congregation. If Jesus were to speak to it, what do you think would be the first statement He would make about it? What would catch His attention most of all? Have several people respond.

Today's lesson deals with a church under great pressure to conform to its corrupt surroundings. As was the case with all the churches in Revelation, this one was promised a rich reward, if it remained faithful to Christ.

Into the Word

Use the information in the Lesson Background (p. 290) to set the stage for the study of Jesus' message to the church in Thyatira. Ask the class if they know which New Testament character made her home in Thyatira (the answer is Lydia, who was Paul's first convert in the city of Philippi). Mention the existence of the trade guilds in Thyatira, also noted in the Lesson Background. Membership in these frequently involved participation in pagan practices. The pressure upon Christians to conform to these practices must have been great.

Divide the class into two groups. If the class is too large for two groups, assign the same series of questions to more than one group. You will need to go to each group to give it its assignment and to make sure its assignment is understood.

Group One. Ask this group to consider the pressures that Christians likely faced because of the trade guilds in Thyatira. Refer to the lesson commentary as needed to explain this. Then ask the group: "What would be some situations on the job today that would pose a dilemma for a Christian?" Some members may be able to offer personal illustrations. Have the group use one or two of the examples and discuss it further, asking, "What should a Christian's response be to such a situation?"

Group Two. Have this group consider the phrase, "the depths of Satan" in Revelation 2:24. Again, use the lesson commentary to explain to the group its possible meanings. Have the group discuss this question: "The church in Thyatira had become tolerant of false teachings. When a church member is suspected of holding to a false teaching, what should be the response of individual Christians or of the leadership?"

After a short discussion, bring the class together. Point out that both groups were dealing with situations that tested a congregation's or a Christian's *faithfulness.* Then ask, "What was going to happen to those who followed the false teaching of Jezebel (vv. 22, 23)? What would happen to the followers of Jesus (vv. 26-28)? What part should reward and punishment play in motivating us to serve Jesus?"

Into Life

Lead the class into a time of silent prayer, using the following open-ended statements. Encourage them to finish the statements, expressing their own needs and requests to the Lord.

The areas of my life where I often resist You are . . .

One part of a Christlike character with which I struggle is . . .

Purge from my life the evil of . . .

Help me to be more patient with . . .

As I try to put You first in my life, give me the courage to loosen my grip on . . .

One way I am committed to obeying You is . . .

Let's Talk It Over

The questions on this page are designed to encourage review of the lesson Scriptures and to promote discussion of the lesson by the class. The answers provided are only discussion starters. Let your class talk it over from there.

1. Many unbelievers accuse Christians of being intolerant. How do we respond to this charge?

For a large segment of society, tolerance is the cardinal virtue of our time. It is often referred to in connection with attitudes toward people of differing races and nationalities. From the Christian standpoint, tolerance should be considered a very weak response to people who differ from us. Instead, Jesus commanded us to love them: "Thou shalt love thy neighbor as thyself" (Matthew 22:39). Tolerance is also urged in attitudes toward homosexuals, women who choose abortion, and criminals who have become what they are, supposedly because of the effects that a painful childhood has had on them. Again, these are neighbors we must love, but that does not mean we must accept the legitimacy of their behavior. Our response to the charge of intolerance must finally be, "If it is intolerant to label sin as sin, then so be it!"

2. "I know . . . that you are now doing more than you did at first" (Revelation 2:19, *New International Version*). Why is this an attribute of the church at Thyatira that we would do well to imitate?

It is easy for a church to fall into a rut, putting on the same old programs in the same old way. The leaders and the members may assume they are doing God's will, simply because they are keeping up with their past performances. But Christ calls us to continual improvement of our work and expansion of our efforts. We need to ask ourselves on a regular basis, "How can we do better what we are doing now?" and, "What should we be doing that we are not presently doing?" When we merely maintain the status quo, we rob ourselves of some significant spiritual benefits. By looking for fresh challenges, undertaking new projects, and going after loftier goals, we strengthen our faith and lay hold of the excitement that should characterize our Christianity.

3. What are "the depths of Satan" (Revelation 2:24)? Why must we be wary of them?

The *New International Version* speaks of "Satan's so-called deep secrets" in this verse. Whatever these were, they probably have their counterpart in the occult practices commonly seen today. Some Christians feel it is harmless to dabble in astrology, spiritism, fortune-telling, and other such practices. But both Old and New Testaments contain stern warnings about these activities (Deuteronomy 18:9-14; Isaiah 8:19, 20; Galatians 5:19, 20; Revelation 21:8). These passages indicate that we should stay away completely from the occult. Even supposedly innocent dabbling in certain aspects of the occult could lure us into deeper involvement. Paul told the Romans, "I want you to be wise about what is good, and innocent about what is evil" (Romans 16:19, *New International Version*). This is wise counsel when applied to the occult.

4. How is the promise of receiving "the morning star" (Revelation 2:28) an especially appealing one?

Since the morning star offers the promise of a new day, Jesus' giving of the morning star seems to symbolize the great eternal day that we shall share with Him. Many people find it exciting to view the morning star, watch the sunrise, and anticipate what the new day may bring. How much more exciting it is to contemplate the joys, blessings, and glories of that eternal day!

5. The seven letters to the churches all contain a strong admonition to hear the Spirit's message. Why is this admonition especially important in our time?

We live in what must be the noisiest era in history. Depending on where we live, we may regularly hear automobile traffic on roads and highways, trains rumbling down a track, or airplanes soaring overhead. Radios and television sets are constantly pouring out a flood of music and spoken words. Often we encounter people who enjoy lengthy conversations. With all that we hear, it can be difficult to appreciate the fact that what we hear from the pulpit and in the classroom on Sunday is of supreme importance. Jesus advised us to "take heed therefore how ye hear" (Luke 8:18). We must practice a "stewardship of our ears." It is important for us to close our ears to what is unimportant or unwholesome, so that they may be alert to hear what God wants to tell us. Psalm 46:10 reminds us of the virtues of silence: "Be still, and know that I am God."

To Philadelphia and Laodicea

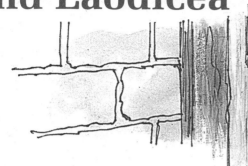

Devotional Reading: 2 Peter 2:4-10.

Lesson Scripture: Revelation 3:7-22.

Printed Text: Revelation 3:7-10, 14-21.

Revelation 3:7-10, 14-21

7 And to the angel of the church in Philadelphia write; These things saith he that is holy, he that is true, he that hath the key of David, he that openeth, and no man shutteth; and shutteth, and no man openeth.

8 I know thy works: behold, I have set before thee an open door, and no man can shut it: for thou hast a little strength, and hast kept my word, and hast not denied my name.

9 Behold, I will make them of the synagogue of Satan, which say they are Jews, and are not, but do lie; behold, I will make them to come and worship before thy feet, and to know that I have loved thee.

10 Because thou hast kept the word of my patience, I also will keep thee from the hour of temptation, which shall come upon all the world, to try them that dwell upon the earth.

. . . .

14 And unto the angel of the church of the Laodiceans write; These things saith the Amen, the faithful and true witness, the beginning of the creation of God.

15 I know thy works, that thou art neither cold nor hot: I would thou wert cold or hot.

16 So then because thou art lukewarm, and neither cold nor hot, I will spew thee out of my mouth.

17 Because thou sayest, I am rich, and increased with goods, and have need of nothing; and knowest not that thou art wretched, and miserable, and poor, and blind, and naked:

18 I counsel thee to buy of me gold tried in the fire, that thou mayest be rich; and white raiment, that thou mayest be clothed, and that the shame of thy nakedness do not appear; and anoint thine eyes with eyesalve, that thou mayest see.

19 As many as I love, I rebuke and chasten: be zealous therefore, and repent.

20 Behold, I stand at the door, and knock: if any man hear my voice, and open the door, I will come in to him, and will sup with him, and he with me.

21 To him that overcometh will I grant to sit with me in my throne, even as I also overcame, and am set down with my Father in his throne.

Apr
27

Golden Text: I know thy works.—Revelation 3:8, 15.

Hope for the Future
Unit 2: Letters to Churches
(Lessons 6-9)

Lesson Aims

This study should prepare students to:

1. Explain the self-descriptions of Jesus that appear in the introductions to the letters before us.

2. Compare and contrast the churches at Philadelphia and Laodicea.

3. Name adjustments that they will make in claiming for themselves the promises that conclude these letters.

Lesson Outline

INTRODUCTION
    A. What Are Muscles For?
    B. Lesson Background
  I. PHILADELPHIA'S STEWARDSHIP (Revelation 3:7-10)
    A. The Voice of Authority (v. 7)
    B. Commending Faithfulness (v. 8)
      A Little Strength
    C. Rewarding Faithfulness (vv. 9, 10)
 II. LAODICEA'S COMPLACENCY (Revelation 3:14-21)
    A. The Voice of Eternal Truth (v. 14)
    B. Complacency Exposed (vv. 15-18)
    C. Love Seeks Reconciliation (vv. 19, 20)
      To Sup With Jesus
    D. Victory and Glory Beckon (v. 21)
CONCLUSION
    A. "I Will"
    B. Thanks for Chastening Love
    C. Thought to Remember

Introduction

A. What Are Muscles For?

A familiar picture in many popular magazines is that of a man posed to display bulging and rippling muscles. What, we wonder, does he do with those muscles, except to develop them and display them for the admiration of viewers, beginning with himself?

Perhaps more familiar to many of us is the mental picture of a slender man, clad in overalls and toiling to coax a livelihood from his family farm. He may have walked with a limp, but this did not keep him from carrying out his daily tasks. We could not see his muscles, for they were covered by his work clothes. But they were constantly in use, laboring for those he loved. Isn't that really what muscles are for?

Today's lesson from Revelation tells of two more churches in the Roman province of Asia that were addressed by the Lord Jesus. One was limited in its size and resources, perhaps like the churches in which many of us came to Christ, but it used what it had to the glory of God. The other was wealthy, but seems to have spent its energy on posing for the admiration of its audience. And that is not what the church's resources are for.

B. Lesson Background

Philadelphia and Laodicea, the cities to which the last two of the seven letters in Revelation were written, lie farthest inland of the seven cities. Both occupied commanding positions on important trade routes, and both were subject to occasional earthquakes. Philadelphia was located almost directly on a line between Sardis and Laodicea. Today it is known by the name Alashehir.

In Roman times, Laodicea was known as the richest city in the district of Phrygia. Its major commodity was a glossy black textile made from the soft black wool of a now-extinct breed of sheep. Its famous medical college developed a "Phrygian powder" that was used to make a widely exported eyesalve. These and other businesses developed banking establishments that dominated the area and made the city of Laodicea wealthy and powerful. Ironically, its site is now deserted.

Laodicea, however, had a problem with its water supply. The city of Hierapolis, six miles northward, was the home of an abundant supply of mineral springs, which provided hot, healing waters. Colossae, ten miles to the east, was famous for its clear, cold water. But Laodicea's supply, delivered by aqueduct from both directions, was tepid and distasteful when it arrived. We will see that many of these aspects of life in Laodicea were incorporated into the language Jesus used to address the church and appeal to its spiritual needs. He wanted the Laodiceans to see that the items in which they took such great pride were actually worthless, when compared to what He could give them.

Colossians 4:13-16, written some thirty years before Revelation, expressed Paul's concern for all the Christians in the cities of Hierapolis, Colossae, and Laodicea. He urged that his letter to Colossae be shared with the other two churches. Through the book of Revelation, Jesus' letters to Philadelphia and Laodicea are shared with us.

I. Philadelphia's Stewardship (Revelation 3:7-10)

Two of the seven letters in Revelation express approval without any rebuke. Both of the letters are addressed to "poor" churches. One is to Smyrna (Revelation 2:8-11). The other is to Philadelphia.

A. The Voice of Authority (v. 7)

7. And to the angel of the church in Philadelphia write; These things saith he that is holy, he that is true, he that hath the key of David, he that openeth, and no man shutteth; and shutteth, and no man openeth.

In most of the letters to the seven churches, Jesus introduces Himself in terms found in His earlier self-revelation to John (Revelation 1:12-16). This is not the case here, although the words used carry the same tone of divine authority. *Holy* and *true* are used in Revelation as attributes of God (4:8; 6:10; 15:3; 16:7).

The phrase *key of David* calls to mind the words of Isaiah 22:22: "And the key of the house of David will I lay upon his shoulder; so he shall open, and none shall shut; and he shall shut, and none shall open." This passage was originally addressed to a man named Eliakim, whom God had designated to replace Shebna as King Hezekiah's steward in Jerusalem. Now, Jesus applies the words to Himself and draws attention to His authority to open and close doors on behalf of His church. The next verse applies this specifically to the church in Philadelphia.

B. Commending Faithfulness (v. 8)

8. I know thy works: behold, I have set before thee an open door, and no man can shut it: for thou hast a little strength, and hast kept my word, and hast not denied my name.

Whereas Jesus had "a few things against" Pergamos (2:14) and Thyatira (2:20), He found in Philadelphia a band of saints who had remained faithful. Other churches had succumbed to the pressures of persecution from without and corruption from within, but the believers in Philadelphia had stood firm.

What was the *open door* that Christ had *set before* this church? Was it an opportunity for fruitful service and evangelism such as Paul found at Ephesus (1 Corinthians 16:9) and Troas (2 Corinthians 2:12), and desired to find in a Roman prison (Colossians 4:3)? Or was it the *door* through which they were able to enter by faith, in order to find salvation and life eternal (Acts 14:27)? In either case, *no man can shut* the door that Jesus opens to those who are willing to follow Him without reservation.

What made the faith of these disciples even more noteworthy was the fact that they possessed only *a little strength.* Apparently they were severely limited in numbers or resources, yet they faithfully used what they had. The small, struggling congregation has the same Lord as the large, multistaffed one!

The accolade that *thou . . . hast not denied my name* was another testimony to Philadelphia's tenacity. An integral part of the Roman persecution of Christians was the demand that the accused believer recant his faith and curse the name of Jesus. Those who persistently refused to do so were charged with treason and counted worthy of death.

A LITTLE STRENGTH

Recently a story on television dealt with a young girl who had developed herself as a weight lifter. She was just five feet tall and weighed 119 pounds, yet she could lift barbell weights of about 117 pounds. Of course, she could not lift weights the way three-hundred-pound men can, but for her size she possessed considerable strength.

Jesus spoke of the church at Philadelphia as having "a little strength" (Revelation 3:8). This did not automatically make the church ineffective. In fact, Philadelphia was one of only two churches among the seven (Smyrna was the other) with which Jesus did not find fault. Philadelphia's strength may have been little, but it was enough to keep the word of Christ and not deny His name.

This concept of a little strength is very helpful to us as Jesus' followers today. We may not have such a dynamic faith that we can move mountains or achieve impossible victories for our Lord. Perhaps our tasks are not enormous and our challenges are rather modest. We need to realize that, whatever our level of strength,

---

How to Say It

ALASHEHIR. *Al*-uh-shuh-*here* (strong accent on *here*).
COLOSSAE. Kuh-*lahss*-ee.
ELIAKIM. Ee-*lye*-uh-kim.
HIERAPOLIS. High-er-*ap*-uh-liss.
LAODICEA. Lay-*odd*-uh-*see*-uh (strong accent on *see*).
PERGAMOS. *Per*-guh-muss.
PHRYGIA. *Frij*-ee-uh.
SHEBNA. *Sheb*-nuh.
SMYRNA. *Smur*-nuh.
THYATIRA. Thy-uh-*tie*-ruh.
TROAS. *Troe*-az.

God can help us greatly if we dedicate what we have to His cause. We may have just "a little strength," but it is more than enough for the many little tasks, crises, and opportunities we usually face. Even a little strength applied at the right time and place can accomplish great things for God.   —J. G. V. B.

C. Rewarding Faithfulness
(vv. 9, 10)

9. Behold, I will make them of the synagogue of Satan, which say they are Jews, and are not, but do lie; behold, I will make them to come and worship before thy feet, and to know that I have loved thee.

The synagogue of Satan, introduced previously in the letter to Smyrna (Revelation 2:9), was apparently a community of unbelieving, hostile Jews, who had forfeited their right to be called the people of God by their cold formalism (Romans 2:28, 29) and their rejection of the Jews' Messiah. By thus serving their father, the devil (John 8:44), they earned the identification of their assembly with the devil. Eventually these enemies will bow humbly at the *feet* of their former victims (see Isaiah 60:14).

10. Because thou hast kept the word of my patience, I also will keep thee from the hour of temptation, which shall come upon all the world, to try them that dwell upon the earth.

The Christians in Philadelphia had exhibited unshakable *patience* in keeping Jesus' commands and enduring affliction for His sake. This enabled them to receive His promises of preservation *from* an even greater *hour of temptation* (better understood as testing or trial) yet to *come upon all the world.* The Greek word rendered *from* can mean either kept from undergoing the coming trials or kept through or during them.

One may recall a similar promise of preservation given to the apostles: "Ye shall be hated of all men for my name's sake. But there shall not a hair of your head perish" (Luke 21:17, 18). Yet James, like John the Baptist and Stephen before him, met a martyr's death (Acts 12:1, 2). Others like the apostle Peter (Acts 12:6-11) experienced a miraculous deliverance from prison and death. The New Testament contains accounts of both deliverances *from* and deliverances *through* affliction.

The specific trial referred to in this verse is not known. More important is the promise of Christ's presence in the hour of trial—a promise that has sustained believers throughout the history of the church. The promise may well include the great final trial of judgment, which will be an occasion of rejoicing for the faithful ones (Matthew 25:31-34).

II. Laodicea's Complacency
(Revelation 3:14-21)

In contrast to Philadelphia, the last of the letters to the seven churches contains only rebuke and correction. Even so, it expresses the love of Jesus for His church.

A. The Voice of Eternal Truth (v. 14)

14. And unto the angel of the church of the Laodiceans write; These things saith the Amen, the faithful and true witness, the beginning of the creation of God.

The church in Laodicea is addressed, as are the other six churches, through the *angel* or messenger who was expected to carry the words to the congregation. Here Jesus emphasizes eternal truth as His credential. He calls Himself *the Amen,* a title based on a Hebrew word that means "in truth" or "truly" (the Greek form is generally translated "verily"). He also refers to himself as *the faithful and true witness.* The importance of this title will be seen when Jesus unmasks the Laodicean church and confronts the believers there with the truth about their sad condition.

In addition, Jesus calls Himself *the beginning of the creation of God.* The Son was present at the creation of the heavens and the earth and was the instrument of their creation (John 1:1-3; Colossians 1:15-17). He is Lord of the church *and* Lord of creation!

B. Complacency Exposed (vv. 15-18)

15, 16. I know thy works, that thou art neither cold nor hot: I would thou wert cold or hot. So then because thou art lukewarm, and neither cold nor hot, I will spew thee out of my mouth.

The church in Laodicea was not charged with any great wickedness, or even with tolerating false doctrine. The Lord simply found this church disgustingly self-satisfied and lacking in genuine motivation and commitment. The phrase *neither cold nor hot* brings to mind the problems with Laodicea's water supply, mentioned in the Lesson Background. The city's *lukewarm* water illustrated perfectly the spiritual condition of the church. It was not cold like the waters at Colossae, nor was it hot like the springs at Hierapolis. We can understand why Jesus would say, *I would thou wert . . . hot.* It is easy to relate spiritual heat to the kind of fervency mentioned in Romans 12:11: "Fervent in spirit; serving the Lord." We still speak of someone being "on fire" for the Lord.

But why would Jesus say, *I would thou wert cold?* How could this be more pleasing to God than a neutral, *lukewarm* stance? Perhaps the bitter atheist or the hardened sinner, like the publicans and harlots of Jesus' day, may be led to recognize his need and turn to Christ more readily than the self-satisfied nominal Christian. It may also be that the nominal Christian is so unattractive that he hurts the cause of Christ more than does the outspoken enemy of the church. In any case, the Lord says He is sick enough to vomit (*I will spew thee out*) at the Laodiceans' tepid Christianity.

There was, however, a ray of hope for the Laodiceans. The Greek text literally reads, "I am about to spit you out." Prompt repentance, such as that urged in all the letters directed to churches with problems, would avert final judgment.

17. Because thou sayest, I am rich, and increased with goods, and have need of nothing; and knowest not that thou art wretched, and miserable, and poor, and blind, and naked.

When Laodicea suffered major damage in an earthquake some thirty years before this letter was written, the city was so financially secure that it refused assistance from the empire. They had *need of nothing*, or so they thought.

In reality, the Christians in Laodicea were sadly impoverished. They failed to recognize the need for the kind of wealth that their banks could not handle, the kind of eyesight their "Phrygian powder" could not provide, and the kind of clothing not available in their fine fabrics. Until they learned to depend on God, they would be eternally helpless and pathetic. They would have no assets beyond the grave, no ability to see beyond temporary material things, and no covering for their sins. "There is that maketh himself rich, yet hath nothing: there is that maketh himself poor, yet hath great riches" (Proverbs 13:7). Christ offers real wealth.

18. I counsel thee to buy of me gold tried in the fire, that thou mayest be rich; and white raiment, that thou mayest be clothed, and that the shame of thy nakedness do not appear; and anoint thine eyes with eyesalve, that thou mayest see.

Buy of me, invites Jesus, for He is the only source of the riches, clothing, and vision needed by the Laodiceans. Not from deposits in their banks, but from depending upon Him, would come the riches of faith "much more precious than of gold that perisheth, though it be tried with fire" (1 Peter 1:7). Not from their supplies of black textiles, but from the Savior with whom they had clothed themselves at baptism (Galatians 3:27), could they receive the pure *white raiment*, signifying purity and forgiveness from the blackness of their sin and shame. Not from

their famous *eyesalve*, but from Him who had given sight to a blind man with an ointment of spittle and clay (John 9:6, 7), could they receive the ability to see God and Heaven. Jesus is still willing to bestow spiritual sight on any willing patient (John 9:39-41).

It should be noted that this was not the first message about spiritual wealth addressed to the Laodiceans. Read Colossians 2:1-3.

C. Love Seeks Reconciliation
(vv. 19, 20)

19. As many as I love, I rebuke and chasten: be zealous therefore, and repent.

Purposeful chastening is one of the clearest expressions of love (see Proverbs 3:11, 12; Hebrews 12:5-11). It is not the loving parent or teacher, but the selfish seeker of ease and comfort, who withholds correction. He does not care enough to endure the stress involved in administering discipline. He would rather avoid the pain of confrontation or the possibly negative reaction his efforts might produce.

Thus, to this church that has made Jesus sick by bragging that it does not need Him or what He has to offer, Jesus declares His *love*. It is the love that prunes the fruit-bearing branch to make it still more fruitful (John 15:1, 2). As for the Laodiceans, only when their smug complacency was shattered could they effectively repent, shake off their apathy, and become *zealous* to serve the Lord with their considerable resources. The command to *repent* is not only for the unsaved; this church needed to do it! The repentance that preceded baptism in Christ must be followed with repentance whenever the Christian has failed to follow his Lord in the way of life.

20. Behold, I stand at the door, and knock: if any man hear my voice, and open the door, I will come in to him, and will sup with him, and he with me.

There is no more touching picture than the one that shows Jesus knocking patiently at a door that must be opened from within. This is not the knock of a stranger. This is not an appeal to sinners to be saved. Jesus is addressing a church, or perhaps a church member who has come to feel that he can get along without Jesus. Jesus will not enter where He is not welcomed, even though He is the Lord of glory and is Himself the door by which any person must enter life eternal. If the occupant does respond to the voice and the knocking, and will *open the door* to welcome Jesus, He will make Himself at home and will stay to *sup*—a word that pictures the intimate fellowship and friendship around a table at mealtime.

TO SUP WITH JESUS

The invasion of the island of Sicily and the mainland of Italy was one of the most significant campaigns toward the close of World War II. Among the thousands of American soldiers were many troops with an Italian background. Every once in a while a young man would enter a town where a close relative of his father or mother lived. While on a brief leave, such a soldier would visit his relatives. What a joyous meeting that would be!

Usually the hosts of these gatherings would bring out their scanty resources of bread and few scraps of food to celebrate the occasion. Not much was available, for times were hard in Italy during the Fascist occupation of their country. Very often, however, their visitor had in his knapsack supplies that he had brought with him, such as canned meat, dried vegetables, and perhaps cheese and macaroni. Many times candy bars were given to the children that were present. Everyone enjoyed a time of sharing and fellowship.

Jesus promises that the one who will "open the door" and let Him in will experience rich fellowship and sharing as well. It does not matter if our resources are meager, for He will share His great gifts with us. He will pour out upon us His mercy, grace, peace, and inner spiritual power. He will indeed sup with us and we with Him. And as precious as this is, it is only a foretaste of the greater supper yet to come!

—J. G. V. B.

D. Victory and Glory Beckon (v. 21)

21. To him that overcometh will I grant to sit with me in my throne, even as I also overcame, and am set down with my Father in his throne.

Home Daily Bible Readings

Monday, Apr. 21—Love One Another (1 John 3:11-24)

Tuesday, Apr. 22—Listen to God's Call (Isaiah 55:1-9)

Wednesday, Apr. 23—Expect Christ's Coming (2 Thessalonians 1:3-10)

Thursday, Apr. 24—Endure Trials to the End (Matthew 24:4-14)

Friday, Apr. 25—Trust God, Not Wealth (Proverbs 10:11-24)

Saturday, Apr. 26—Bless the Lord for His Care (Deuteronomy 8:1-10)

Sunday, Apr. 27—Do All for God's Glory (1 Corinthians 10:23-33)

The believers in Laodicea had to overcome their pride and their self-satisfaction with their wealth. Perhaps this was harder than other churches' having to overcome poverty, persecution, false doctrine, or blatant sin. But if they failed to do so, the rewards of victory could never be theirs.

The word *throne* indicates power and authority. Jesus *overcame* all opposition to the fulfillment of His Father's plan and was then "exalted" and given "a name which is above every name" (Philippians 2:9). Likewise, His disciples must follow the same path of first overcoming on earth and subsequently reigning with Christ in Heaven.

With such a future awaiting, who could be content with earth's vanishing riches?

Conclusion

A. "I Will"

Usually a person prepares for his departure from this life by expressing his desires concerning the distribution of his belongings. He writes a *will*—a document that says, "I will," or, "It is my serious desire." A will reveals a great deal about what an individual desires his family to have and to be.

In the same way, we learn about the Lord Jesus from the "I wills" written within the letters to the seven churches. There is, however, a significant difference between what He wills to the church and what people will to their families. The Lord's desires are not left for someone else to carry out. He continues to be in control. When He says "I will," it means that He is going to do it, according to the conditions He has set forth. Thus, to the churches at Philadelphia and at Laodicea—and to us on the same conditions—He says, "*I will* make them . . . to know that I have loved thee," "*I also will* keep thee from the hour of temptation," "If any man hear my voice, and open the door, *I will* come in to him, and will sup with him," and "To him that overcometh *will I* grant to sit with me in my throne." What *will* we let Him do for us?

B. Thanks for Chastening Love

Thank You, God our Father, for the love that seeks us and finds us where we are, and chastens and changes us according to our needs. Thank You especially for Jesus our Savior and King, who offers His love and companionship forever. Amen.

C. Thought to Remember

For lasting strength and wealth we have only one source: Jesus Christ our Lord.

Learning by Doing

This page contains an alternate lesson plan emphasizing learning activities.
Classes desiring such student involvement will find these suggestions helpful.

Learning Goals

As students participate in today's class session, they should:

1. Understand more clearly what constitutes a "strong" church in the eyes of Jesus.

2. Dedicate their resources, or lack of resources, and both their strengths and their weaknesses to the Lord's glory.

Into the Lesson

Begin class with two questions. First, ask how many grew up in a large church, with an impressive budget, many people on the staff, and a wide range of programs and activities. Second, ask how many grew up in a small church, where financial struggles were common and where it was difficult, for example, to maintain a steady youth program.

You will likely have both kinds of churches represented in your class. Point out that while a large church might be considered more "efficient" in the Lord's work, there is a place for the small, struggling church. Today's lesson tells of one church with "a little strength" and one that was "rich." The first was commended by Jesus; the second made Him sick.

Into the Word

Use the Lesson Background to provide information on the cities of Philadelphia and Laodicea. This is especially important with Laodicea, because much of what Jesus said to this church contains references to life in Laodicea that its residents would readily understand.

Next, lead the class in one of the following two activities:

Activity One. Show the class a copy of the church's "annual report" (obtain this ahead of time from the minister or church secretary). Divide the class into two groups. Tell one group to write an "annual report" for the church in Philadelphia, and have the other group do the same for the church in Laodicea. Have the groups first read carefully what Jesus had to say to these churches. Knowing what Jesus said, what would you emphasize in your report? What would be the positive and the negative news? Have the groups work for about fifteen minutes, then let each group choose someone who will read its report to the rest of the class.

Point out the tragic irony of a church with but "a little strength," which was commended by Jesus (Philadelphia), and a church that was "rich" and yet turned His stomach (Laodicea). Ask, "What does this tell us about what Jesus seeks in a church? What really makes a congregation 'strong' or 'weak'?"

Call attention to the fact that despite Laodicea's sorry condition, Jesus still appealed to the Christians there to "open the door." Ask, "How does a church go about 'opening the door' to Jesus? What steps must it take?"

Activity Two. Divide the class into two groups. One will study Jesus' message to the church in Philadelphia; the other will examine His words to Laodicea. Move between the groups to offer assistance with any questions a group may have.

The Philadelphia Group.

1. To what may the "open door" (Revelation 3:8) refer? How does a church know when such a door is open? How does an individual know?

2. What is the meaning of the phrase, "Thou hast a little strength"? Was this a positive or a negative quality? What does this tell you about what makes a church "strong"?

The Laodicea Group.

1. Why would Jesus prefer a "cold" church to a lukewarm one (Revelation 3:15, 16)?

2. How can material abundance cause a church's spiritual zeal to decline?

3. What steps can a church take to allow Christ to "come in," in response to His invitation? How can an individual do this? How can a family?

Give the groups about fifteen minutes to answer their questions. Have each group designate a "reporter," then bring the class together to hear a summary of each group's discussion.

Into Life

Many Christians minimize their effectiveness by reasoning, "If only I had more _____, or were more _____, I would be able to serve Jesus better." Have the class offer suggestions for filling in these blanks, then allow them time to provide responses to counter their suggestions.

Have the groups that worked together earlier reconvene for closing prayer. Tell each group to form a prayer circle, offering sentence prayers that focus on the lessons learned from the two churches in today's Scripture.

Let's Talk It Over

The questions on this page are designed to encourage review of the lesson Scriptures and to promote discussion of the lesson by the class. The answers provided are only discussion starters. Let your class talk it over from there.

1. The "open door" that Christ had set before the church at Philadelphia may have been a door of opportunity for evangelism. How is this an appropriate symbol for evangelism?

This language in Revelation 3:8 sounds similar to Paul's mention in 2 Corinthians 2:12 of an open door of opportunity to preach in Troas. It is exciting when we find a similar door of opportunity for evangelism, but we must be prepared to enter it. A literal open door is of no use to us if we are too lazy, indifferent, or clumsy to enter it. An open door for the gospel may also prove useless unless we enter it prepared with a Biblically sound, thoughtful, loving presentation of Jesus Christ and His salvation.

2. Why does the Lord prefer a "cold" response to Him rather than one that is lukewarm?

This reference in Revelation 3:15 is consistent with two familiar pleas made to the Israelites in Old Testament times. One was Joshua's challenge offered late in his life: "Choose you this day whom ye will serve . . . but as for me and my house, we will serve the Lord" (Joshua 24:15). The second came from Elijah at Mount Carmel: "How long halt ye between two opinions? if the Lord be God, follow him: but if Baal, then follow him" (1 Kings 18:21). These examples illustrate how God prefers that a person be a committed foe rather than a half-hearted follower, for a half-hearted follower is really not a true follower. If a person claims to be a Christian, but is lukewarm about such vital areas as worship, Bible study, prayer, and evangelism, he is obviously too far removed from the concerns of Christ to be a true disciple. His lukewarmness is dangerous in that it may affect other believers. It will also have no appeal to unbelievers.

3. Are there churches today, like Laodicea, that regard themselves as being rich while they are actually poor? How does this happen?

Some churches are materially rich, but spiritually poor. The possession of a fine building with elaborate furnishings can delude a congregation into thinking that it is pleasing the Lord. But the members may be neglecting spiritual growth, evangelism, ministry to the needy, or other vital aspects of their responsibility to

Christ. Other churches are rich in programs, but spiritually poor. They may offer activities to meet the needs of all age groups. Perhaps they are very strong in building ties of fellowship within the congregation. But at the same time they may be weak in outreach. Some churches are even doctrinally rich, but spiritually poor. They may pride themselves on the Biblical purity of their teaching. But it is possible for them to drift into a legalism devoid of love.

4. It is noteworthy that Christ emphasizes His love for the lukewarm Laodicean church in Revelation 3:19. What does this show us regarding the nature of loving rebuke?

Could we say in sincere love to an erring Christian, "You are wretched and miserable and poor and blind and naked"? Christ could, and we must be able to do so also. On a number of occasions during His earthly ministry, Jesus spoke bluntly, as He did to the Laodiceans. Matthew 23, for example, contains His withering indictment of the obstinate Jewish leadership ("Woe unto you, scribes and Pharisees, hypocrites!"). Did Jesus say all this merely to "get it off His chest"? No, He was speaking in love, using strong words in an effort to shake these men out of their smug, sinful attitudes. We also must develop the ability to speak in love the kind of blunt reproof that some non-Christians and lukewarm believers need to hear. It is the only kind of language that can awaken them to their perilous state.

5. The picture in Revelation 3:20 of Christ knocking at the door is one that has appealed to artists, hymn writers, and Christians in general. What are some elements of its appeal?

Christ is knocking at the door, rather than forcing His way in, which He has the authority to do. He gives us the opportunity to respond. He asks for admission. We can imagine a tender, pleading voice calling upon us to give up our resistance and throw open the door. He will be prompt to enter once the door is open. When He comes into our lives, He comes to sup with us. No description of intimate fellowship with our Savior could be more vivid than this. Any person who studies Revelation 3:20 will surely be moved by the invitation offered there.

The Redeeming Lamb

DEVOTIONAL READING: Revelation 4:1-11.

LESSON SCRIPTURE: Revelation 4, 5.

PRINTED TEXT: Revelation 5:1-10.

Revelation 5:1-10

1 And I saw in the right hand of him that sat on the throne a book written within and on the back side, sealed with seven seals.

2 And I saw a strong angel proclaiming with a loud voice, Who is worthy to open the book, and to loose the seals thereof?

3 And no man in heaven, nor in earth, neither under the earth, was able to open the book, neither to look thereon.

4 And I wept much, because no man was found worthy to open and to read the book, neither to look thereon.

5 And one of the elders saith unto me, Weep not: behold, the Lion of the tribe of Judah, the Root of David, hath prevailed to open the book, and to loose the seven seals thereof.

6 And I beheld, and, lo, in the midst of the throne and of the four beasts, and in the midst of the elders, stood a Lamb as it had been slain, having seven horns and seven eyes, which are the seven Spirits of God sent forth into all the earth.

7 And he came and took the book out of the right hand of him that sat upon the throne.

8 And when he had taken the book, the four beasts and four and twenty elders fell down before the Lamb, having every one of them harps, and golden vials full of odors, which are the prayers of saints.

9 And they sung a new song, saying, Thou art worthy to take the book, and to open the seals thereof: for thou wast slain, and hast redeemed us to God by thy blood out of every kindred, and tongue, and people, and nation;

10 And hast made us unto our God kings and priests: and we shall reign on the earth.

GOLDEN TEXT: Thou wast slain, and hast redeemed us to God by thy blood out of every kindred, and tongue, and people, and nation.—Revelation 5:9.

Lesson Aims

This study should enable the student to:

1. Explain the titles and characteristics of Jesus that appear in Revelation 5.

2. Tell the reasons given by the twenty-four elders and the four living creatures for worshiping the Lamb.

3. Examine his own worship and make it more meaningful.

Lesson Outline

INTRODUCTION
    A. Cause for Weeping
    B. Lesson Background
  I. THE CLOSED BOOK (Revelation 5:1-4)
    A. The Book Itself (v. 1)
    B. The Crucial Question (v. 2)
    C. The Fruitless Search (vv. 3, 4)
 II. THE ONE WHO IS ABLE (Revelation 5:5-7)
    A. The Elder's Assurance (v. 5)
    B. The Lamb Is Able (vv. 6, 7)
        Slain, Yet Standing
III. HONORING THE LAMB (Revelation 5:8-10)
    A. Bowing in Adoration (v. 8)
        The Fragrance of Heaven
    B. Singing in Praise (vv. 9, 10)
CONCLUSION
    A. All Join in Singing!
    B. Prayer of Thanks and Praise
    C. Thought to Remember

The visual for Lesson 10 is an artist's conception of Jesus as both Lion and Lamb. It is shown on page 308.

Introduction

A. Cause for Weeping

"I wept much," said John, while experiencing visions of Heaven's utmost glory. Why was he crying? Because no one worthy could be found to do the task at hand! His tears have been shared by God's people throughout the ages.

Consider the "weeping prophet" Jeremiah, who had to tell his beloved countrymen in Judah that their sins had brought them to defeat and captivity at the hands of the idolatrous Babylonians. Our language preserves his name in the word *jeremiad,* meaning a prolonged complaint and lamentation.

Consider the apostle Paul. This man, who coldly and brutally oversaw the killing and imprisonment of believers in Jesus, became a believer himself. He was transformed into a man of compassion, whose tears reflected his burden for a lost world and his desire that others know the Christ who had done so much for him (see Acts 20:19, 31; 2 Corinthians 2:4; Philippians 3:18). Paul's own tears gave him a keen awareness of the tears of others (2 Timothy 1:4).

It is not hard to find cause for weeping in the present day. Anyone can find an abundance of causes in the daily newspaper, at the grocery store magazine rack, or on the television screen.

Is the situation hopeless? No, as long as the Lamb of God is still available to take away the sin of the world (John 1:29), and to lead us back to the Father, who will one day wipe away all tears from His children's eyes (Revelation 7:17; 21:4).

B. Lesson Background

During his exile on the rocky island of Patmos, John was given a series of messages and visions to convey to the seven churches in Asia (Revelation 1:11). First came the letters to the churches (Revelation 2 and 3). Chapter 4 begins with the opening of a door in Heaven, after which John hears a voice: "Come up hither, and I will show thee things which must be hereafter" (v. 1). The rest of the chapter then presents a description of the glory of God seated upon His throne and of the response of reverent worshipers to His glory. Our lesson text for today is taken from chapter 5, which introduces God's worthy Lamb.

I. The Closed Book (Revelation 5:1-4)

A. The Book Itself (v. 1)

1. And I saw in the right hand of him that sat on the throne a book written within and on the back side, sealed with seven seals.

The one holding this *book* is referred to as *him that sat on the throne.* He is the One who has just received worship and adoration in chapter four, and before whom the elders have cast their crowns. The *book* that He holds should not be thought of as the kind to which we are accustomed. This was a scroll, rolled together and *sealed with seven seals.*

Rolled documents of papyrus, parchment, or vellum (a more durable form of parchment) were usually inscribed on only the smoother face of the material, which became the inside of the scroll as it was unfolded and read. Only if a great amount of material had to be recorded would *the back side* be used as well, and this would become immediately evident to even the casual observer. Clearly, there was much to say in the book that John saw! The prophet Ezekiel was offered a similar scroll, also with writing on both sides, and was commanded to eat it (Ezekiel 2:9—3:2).

Seals, commonly of wax, were affixed to important documents to: (1) indicate ownership, (2) assure genuineness of authorship, (3) protect against any change or abuse of the contents, and (4) conceal the contents until a properly authorized person was present for the opening. The use of *seven* seals indicates complete and perfect security against such tampering. The seven seals seem to have been immediately visible, which suggests that they were aligned along the outside of the scroll. This would lead one to believe that all the seals had to be broken before any of the contents could be read.

However, the impression given in the following chapter is that as each seal was opened, a new vision was revealed to John. It appears more likely that the scroll consisted of seven separate sheets, and that when a seal was opened, a sheet was unfolded before John. At any rate, this document was secured in a manner appropriate for the wondrous mysteries of God that it contained.

B. The Crucial Question (v. 2)

2. And I saw a strong angel proclaiming with a loud voice, Who is worthy to open the book, and to loose the seals thereof?

The business of one of God's messengers (an *angel*) is not a work for weaklings. An angel rolled the huge stone away from the entrance to Jesus' tomb (Matthew 28:2). Another angel is seen tossing a "great millstone" into the sea (Revelation 18:21). The angel introduced here may have been Michael or Gabriel, but his question is more important than his name. The candidate for breaking the seven seals and revealing its mysteries had to be *worthy* in every way: ability, character, and standing with God and man.

C. The Fruitless Search (vv. 3, 4)

3, 4. And no man in heaven, nor in earth, neither under the earth, was able to open the book, neither to look thereon. And I wept much, because no man was found worthy to open and to read the book, neither to look thereon.

Strong repetition of the negatives in this verse emphasizes the hopelessness John felt in the search for one qualified to receive, open, and ex-

amine the scroll extended by the Ruler of the universe. The word *man* does not appear in the Greek: "No one in heaven, no one in earth, and no one under the earth" was worthy. Such was the report after searching high and low in all the places where someone might possibly be found (see Exodus 20:4; Philippians 2:10).

John's frustration caused him to burst into tears and to continue weeping (he *wept much*). Did his tears express his disappointment in not being able to see what would happen in the future (Revelation 4:1)? Did he cry out of a sense of hopelessness in realizing the present unworthiness of everything that God had originally created good and perfect, or for His "pleasure," as 4:11 says? In that, we share his tears.

II. The One Who Is Able (Revelation 5:5-7)

At this point John experienced the fulfillment of the promise recorded in one of Jesus' Beatitudes: "Blessed are they that mourn: for they shall be comforted" (Matthew 5:4).

A. The Elder's Assurance (v. 5)

5. And one of the elders saith unto me, Weep not: behold, the Lion of the tribe of Judah, the Root of David, hath prevailed to open the book, and to loose the seven seals thereof.

The word of assurance came to the apostle, not from one of the angels, but from an unidentified representative of the twenty-four *elders*. His admonition was, *Weep not*; his gentle assurance was that someone worthy was indeed at hand.

The phrase *the Lion of the tribe of Judah* recalls the patriarch Jacob's reference to his son Judah as a "lion's cub," and his prophecy that "The scepter will not depart from Judah . . . until he comes to whom it belongs" (Genesis 49:9, 10, *New International Version*). Jesus, descended from the tribe of Judah (Hebrews 7:14), fulfilled this prophecy. As *the Lion*, He was the most noble of all the kings from that tribe.

The phrase *Root of David* recalls another Messianic prophecy, found in Isaiah 11:1: "There shall come forth a rod out of the stem of Jesse,

---

How to Say It

APOCALYPTIC. uh-*pock*-uh-*lip*-tik (strong accent on *lip*).
ARNION (Greek). ar-*nee*-ahn.
EPHESUS. *Eff*-uh-suss.
JEREMIAD. jer-uh-*mee*-ud.

and a Branch shall grow out of his roots." *Jesse,* as David's father, identifies the same ancestry. The word *root* can mean either a source, or an outgrowth from a root (such as a shoot, stem, or branch). Near the end of the book of Revelation, Jesus refers to Himself as "the root and the offspring of David" (Revelation 22:16). Thus, the verse before us reflects Old Testament prophecies that highlighted: (1) the specific tribe from which the Messiah would come, and (2) the specific individual in that tribe from whom He would be descended.

This prophesied One *hath prevailed* (triumphed) over Satan, sin, and even death itself. He is therefore unquestionably worthy to *open the book* and reveal the mysteries therein.

B. The Lamb Is Able (vv. 6, 7)

6. And I beheld, and, lo, in the midst of the throne and of the four beasts, and in the midst of the elders, stood a Lamb as it had been slain, having seven horns and seven eyes, which are the seven Spirits of God sent forth into all the earth.

The visions in Revelation are designed primarily to convey important spiritual messages. One must keep in mind the nature of its apocalyptic contents. The language is predominantly symbolic, and the symbols can change rapidly, with little warning. So we should not be too taken aback when the *Lion* mentioned by the elder appears as a *Lamb.* In addition, the four beasts, who had formerly occupied the position *in the midst of the throne* (4:6), are now overshadowed by the presence of the Lamb.

It is with good reason that the Lamb now occupies center stage in John's vision. He bears the marks of having been *slain* (perhaps showing a healed scar across the throat, according to the manner of slaying the Passover sacrifice). Now, however, this Lamb is very much alive, and is not even identified by the same term as the lamb on the altar. Twenty-nine times in Revelation the Lamb is mentioned, and always with a term (Greek, *arnion*) that is found elsewhere only in John 21:15, where Jesus tells Peter, "Feed my lambs." The term seems to designate Jesus as the risen and triumphant Lamb; He appears as though slain, yet He still stands!

The *seven horns* and *seven eyes* are also strongly symbolic. As noted already, *seven* indicates completeness or perfection. *Horns* symbolize power, representing an animal's primary means of defending himself and his flock. The Psalms (along with other poetic passages in the Old Testament) also use *horns* in several instances as a symbol of strength. See examples recorded in Psalms 18:2; 75:10; Jeremiah 48:25; Micah 4:13.

The characteristic of having *seven eyes* indicates the ability to observe fully and to know completely. "They are the eyes of the Lord, which run to and fro through the whole earth" (Zechariah 4:10). The Lamb sees, knows, and understands everything. These eyes are identified with the *seven Spirits of God*, a phrase used in the introductory greeting to the book (1:4) and in the introduction to the letter to Sardis (3:1). It suggests the thoroughness of the work of the Holy Spirit, whose presence in Christians all over the world and in the inspired Word extends His influence *into all the earth*. The capability of this Lamb is complete!

SLAIN, YET STANDING

A 1994 report by the National Opinion Research Center at the University of Chicago told of a study conducted in Russia. This involved three thousand persons who until recently had spent their entire lives under a Communist system where religion was banned and ridiculed. A third of these Russians under twenty-five indicated that they had come to a belief in God. Seventy percent of those surveyed expressed a confidence in church leaders, while forty percent believed in miracles. The *World Christian Encyclopedia*'s editor, David Barrett, stated that these numbers reflected "one of the most enormous swings in the history of Christianity."

John tells us in verse six of our text for today that "in the midst of the elders, stood a Lamb as it had been slain." One would expect a slain lamb to lie fallen and lifeless. Yet here was one that to all appearances was indeed slain, but remained standing. This is a picture of the Lamb of God, Jesus of Nazareth, standing victorious after paying the ultimate price for the sins of the world.

Throughout the long history of the church, the death of Christianity has often been announced. It has appeared to be slain, but has remained standing. Such was the case in ancient Rome and most recently in Communist Russia. Where Marx was exalted, our Master is proclaimed. Where the church was mocked and

visual for
lesson 10

scorned, now Christ is preached and believers are multiplied. Behold the Lamb—slain, yet *standing!* —J. G. V. B.

7. And he came and took the book out of the right hand of him that sat upon the throne.

This brief verse provided the answer John was seeking to the question raised by the strong angel (v. 2). It also calmed John's anxieties concerning the book he had been shown. The Lamb, having been introduced and shown to be qualified, will do what no other being in all the world could do.

We should keep in mind as we study these symbols that the items that were part of John's vision were not as limited as the same items in the material world might be. The seven Spirits were described as "seven lamps of fire" in chapter 4 (v. 5); in chapter 5 they are "seven eyes." After taking the book, the Lamb proceeds to open one of the seals (in chapter 6), and one of the beasts speaks to John. Such is the nature of apocalyptic literature: it is highly symbolic, but beneath the figures and symbols lies an important message. The remainder of our lesson text provides the message that gave John, and can give believers today, assurance and hope.

III. Honoring the Lamb (Revelation 5:8-10)

Revelation 4 concluded with expressions of thanks and praise to "him that sat on the throne" (v. 10). Now similar expressions from the same worshipers burst forth in recognition of the Lamb.

A. Bowing in Adoration (v. 8)

8. And when he had taken the book, the four beasts and four and twenty elders fell down before the Lamb, having every one of them harps, and golden vials full of odors, which are the prayers of saints.

Celebration began immediately, once it had been established that *the Lamb* was worthy to open the sealed scroll. The *four beasts* and the *elders* encircling the throne prostrated themselves in worship, expressed not only in the act but also with traditional accompaniment. *Harps,* or lyres held in the hands, were commonly associated with songs of joyful praise, as indicated in Psalms 33:2; 43:4; 71:22; 147:7; 149:3; 150:3.

The rising of the *odors* of incense, which was to be burned on an altar in the tabernacle for its fragrance (Exodus 30:7, 8), came to symbolize the *prayers of the saints* ascending toward God: "Let my prayer be set forth before thee as incense" (Psalm 141:2). Incense also could be carried and burned in small bowls, referred to here as *vials. Every one* present joined in the celebration; no one was a mere spectator, depending on another to express praise on his behalf.

THE FRAGRANCE OF HEAVEN

Throughout his letters, the apostle Paul refers to his prayer life (Romans 1:9; 1 Corinthians 1:4; 2 Corinthians 13:7; Ephesians 1:16; 3:14-19; Philippians 1:4, 9-11; Colossians 1:3; 1 Thessalonians 1:2, 3; 2 Thessalonians 1:3; 2 Timothy 1:3; Philemon 4). He indicates that he prayed for both churches and individuals with intensity and continuity. Interest in and petition for the success and stability of God's work in the world should be a constant Christian practice. We tend to emphasize the power of prayer. It is indeed "mighty through God to the pulling down of strongholds" (2 Corinthians 10:4). It can provide healing and strength in many crises of life. Yet prayer is not only a source of power; it is a source of fragrant beauty as well.

Our text for today tells us that the ruling Lamb had seven horns and seven eyes. The horn signifies power while the eyes stand for perception and perfect understanding. The church praises the risen Lord for His ability to understand our needs, our opportunities, and our victories. This is supplemented with perfect power to effect changes in us and in our world in proportion to our trust in Him and our compliance with His will.

The four beasts and the twenty-four elders around the Lamb's throne held harps and golden vials. The harps stand for Heaven's harmony and beautiful music. The vials are sources of "odors," produced by their incense as it rises toward Heaven. These odors represent "the prayers of the saints," through which God is glorified and His church purified. Our prayers are not only an evidence of reliance on God, but are a fragrance that permeates the precincts of paradise. —J. G. V. B.

B. Singing in Praise (vv. 9, 10)

9, 10. And they sung a new song, saying, Thou art worthy to take the book, and to open the seals thereof: for thou wast slain, and hast redeemed us to God by thy blood out of every kindred, and tongue, and people, and nation; and hast made us unto our God kings and priests: and we shall reign on the earth.

Next, the twenty-four elders and the four living creatures lifted their voices in a song of celebration to the victorious Lamb. A *new song* is usually composed to celebrate a great victory and honor a notable hero. We should recall the praise song of Moses and of Israel after the crossing of the Red Sea (Exodus 15:1-21). In Scripture a *new song* is addressed always to God (Psalms 33:3; 96:1; Isaiah 42:10).

Thou art worthy. What was the basis of the Lamb's worthiness? The primary qualification was suggested earlier when the Lamb first appeared as though *it had been slain* (v. 6). The Lamb had willingly sacrificed Himself for others (Isaiah 53:7). By the shed blood of that sacrifice, He has *redeemed* (purchased and brought to God) all those from all times and all places who have accepted His sacrifice in obedient faith (John 3:16).

Not all of those invited accept the blood-bought gift of life, but some from every distinguishable group among humankind are described as having done so. They come from every *kindred* (blood-related family, clan, or tribe), *tongue* (language or dialect), *people* (identifiable cultural group), and *nation* (governmental unit). These divisions, which often erect barriers and create animosities among warring factions, are erased in Christ. In Him such distinctions are no longer important.

In making all believers *kings and priests* of God, the Lamb has expanded upon God's promise to Moses at Sinai: "Ye shall be unto me a kingdom of priests, and a holy nation" (Exodus 19:6). Concerning Christians' priestly access to God, we read, "Ye also . . . are built up a spiritual house, a holy priesthood, to offer up spiritual sacrifices, acceptable to God by Jesus Christ" (1 Peter 2:5).

To enjoy such a standing as *priests* and to *reign on the earth* is a marvelous privilege. "All things are yours," Paul told the Corinthians (1 Corinthians 3:21). It is also an awesome responsibility with great obligations. Just as King Herod and King Agrippa in Palestine were answerable to their emperor in Rome, so anyone who would reign in the name of Christ is answerable totally to Him. He is King of kings and Lord of lords (1 Timothy 6:14, 15). To reject His authority is high treason!

Conclusion
A. All Join in Singing!

Jim traveled widely in his work for a Christian organization, and so he had occasion to meet on the Lord's Day with many congregations in many cities. Not surprisingly, he encountered a variety of styles in church music, some traditional and others contemporary. On one occasion he heard an excellent choral presentation from Handel's *Messiah*. Afterward he introduced himself to the choir director and said, "I like praise choruses." A shadow of disappointment clouded the director's eyes until Jim added, "Such as the ones I heard this morning!"

Christians of all musical tastes can join wholeheartedly in the hymn to Christ that we have just examined. We can join the white-robed elders and the living creatures, along with the multitude of angels that immediately added their voices in singing, "Worthy is the Lamb that was slain to receive power, and riches, and wisdom, and strength, and honor, and glory, and blessing" (Revelation 5:11, 12). Even that was not enough, for following this tribute, all creation blended its voices to join the chorus: "Blessing, and honor, and glory, and power, be unto him that sitteth upon the throne, and unto the Lamb for ever and ever" (5:13).

Whether we prefer the grand repetitions of the classic hymns, or the simpler repetitions of the choruses we first learned in Christian service camp, we will find ways to lift our voices together in praise to the Lamb of God who loved us and bought us for the Father at the price of His own precious blood. The unity of Heaven's choir should be anticipated by voices united in praise on earth.

B. Prayer of Thanks and Praise

Thank You, our Father, for the spotless and death-conquering Lamb who brings us into Your presence. May we praise Him in joyous harmony with all who love Him truly, and may we serve Him with selfless abandon. Amen.

C. Thought to Remember

"Unto him that loved us, and washed us from our sins in his own blood, and hath made us kings and priests unto God and his Father; to him be glory and dominion for ever and ever. Amen" (Revelation 1:5, 6).

Home Daily Bible Readings

Monday, Apr. 28—The Lamb Sacrificed (Isaiah 53:4-9)

Tuesday, Apr. 29—The Lamb Receives a Kingdom (Daniel 7:9-14)

Wednesday, Apr. 30—Sinners Ransomed by the Blood of Christ (1 Peter 1:18-25)

Thursday, May 1—The Lamb, the Light of Jerusalem (Revelation 21:22-27)

Friday, May 2—The Lamb, Worthy of Praise (Revelation 4:1-11)

Saturday, May 3—The Redeemed Worship the Lamb (Revelation 14:1-5)

Sunday, May 4—The Lamb, Our Final Judge (Romans 14:1-11)

Learning by Doing

This page contains an alternate lesson plan emphasizing learning activities. Classes desiring such student involvement will find these suggestions helpful.

Learning Goals

As a result of this study, the student should be able to:

1. List and elaborate upon the symbols used in Revelation 5 to portray the One who redeems.

2. Tell the reasons given by the twenty-four elders and the four living creatures for worshiping the Lamb.

3. Commit to implementing ideas that will make the student's own personal worship more meaningful.

Into the Lesson

Prepare for this lesson by securing several well-known symbols to show the students. You may wish to use some of the following examples from the secular world: a dollar bill, a wedding ring, a picture of an eagle, an American flag, the insignia of a sports team that has a rich tradition (New York Yankees, Dallas Cowboys, University of Notre Dame, for examples) or a picture of the McDonald's arches. In addition to these, bring in some of the following Christian symbols: a cross, a Bible, a picture of a dove, or the emblems of Communion.

Spread the symbols out on a table so that students can see them as they enter the classroom. Lead into the lesson by saying, "We've gathered several well-known symbols that are important in our society today. What is a symbol?" Point out that a symbol is simply an item that stands for something else. Have students look at the examples that you have brought to class and offer their explanations of what these symbols represent. Save the Christian symbols that you have brought for last. As you discuss these, ask the class to comment on how these symbols better help us understand truths about God, Christ, and the church.

Conclude this introduction by pointing out that many people are hesitant to study the book of Revelation, for they are afraid that it contains too many strange descriptions that cannot be understood. While it is true that the book contains difficult passages, we must keep in mind that the book describes certain sights and events too awesome for literal words. The symbols that John uses are in some ways like the ones we have just discussed: symbols that communicate ideas much deeper and richer than mere words can convey.

Into the Word

Divide the class into three or four small groups for the purpose of studying today's text and examining some of the symbols that appear there. Give each group these phrases from Revelation 5: "Lion of the tribe of Judah," "Root of David," "seven," and "the Lamb." Tell the groups to discuss what makes each of these symbols so significant (for example, as they discuss "Lion," they should consider what characteristics of a lion could be applicable to Jesus).

Next, raise the following questions with the class (answers are given in parentheses). "Where are the events mentioned taking place?" (Around the throne of God). "What images come to mind when the throne of God is mentioned?" (The place where God dwells, where He makes His judgments, and where He rules over His creation). "What is happening as the chapter begins?" (A strong angel is seeking one who would be found worthy to open a book.) "Is anyone found worthy to open the book?" (An elder mentions that One has been found worthy to open the book and break its seals.) "How is this One described?" (He is depicted as a Lion from the tribe of Judah, as the Root of David, and as a Lamb having been slain.) "What happens after this worthy One takes the book?" (The elders and the four beasts fall down before the Lamb, and they sing a song of praise to Him.) "What are the reasons that the elders and the four beasts give for worshiping the Lamb?" (He is worthy of worship because He has been slain, and He has redeemed us to God.)

Into Life

Conclude by encouraging the students to make a commitment to deepen their own personal worship time by taking advantage of the dimensions of worship that are most meaningful to them. These could include music, personal prayer, or a time of meditation on God's Word. Challenge them to take time out of each day during the coming week to focus on God—who He is, what He has done for them in the past, and how He continues to care for them in the present. End the study with a time of prayer, asking students to offer short sentence praises to God for the great things He has done. Perhaps a student could close by leading the class in a stanza of "Holy, Holy, Holy!"

Let's Talk It Over

The questions on this page are designed to encourage review of the lesson Scriptures and to promote discussion of the lesson by the class. The answers provided are only discussion starters. Let your class talk it over from there.

1. The angelic question, "Who is worthy?" was answered by the heavenly choir's song to the Lamb: "Thou art worthy." How may we compare Christ's worthiness for His mission with our worthiness for our earthly tasks?

Jesus Christ was perfectly suited for His mission as Savior and Redeemer. In His identity as the Son of God and by His sinless life, He was worthy to fulfill that mission. We also have been given the kinds of talents and experiences that make us worthy to fulfill God's task for us. Jesus did not back away from His mission, difficult though it was. Neither should we shrink from our duties by protesting our unworthiness, our lack of ability, or our lack of time. If God has equipped us and made us worthy for a specific task, we should acknowledge our God-given worthiness and get to work.

2. Why is Jesus' title, "the Lion of the tribe of Judah," so significant?

Satan is compared to a "roaring lion" in 1 Peter 5:8. To combat him requires a strong, courageous effort, and Jesus as the Lion of the tribe of Judah is capable of such an effort. Frequently writers and artists have chosen to portray Jesus as meek and gentle. As Matthew 11:28-30 demonstrates, this is a legitimate portrayal. But some of the images of Jesus that become fixed in our mind from an early age depict these "kinder, gentler" qualities to the extent that we may have only a dim perception of His boldness and strength. Satan's power and the power of evil in general are very much in evidence today. We need reminders that Jesus is strong enough to overcome the most powerful attacks Satan can muster. This description in Revelation 5:5 is one such reminder.

3. What important lessons can we learn from Jesus' title of "the Lamb"?

As we mentioned in the preceding question, Jesus is strong as a lion in combating the evil assaults of Satan. However, the fact that the figure in Revelation 5 quickly changes from the Lion to the Lamb reminds us that we can compare Jesus with a lion only in a limited way. A lion is a predator—a beast that uses speed, strength, and cunning to destroy other beasts. That aspect is applicable to Satan, but not to Jesus. Instead, the source of Jesus' power is His identity as the Lamb of God. When He became outwardly weak and allowed His blood to be shed, He demonstrated the kind of power needed to take away sins and to defeat any Satanic assault (Hebrews 2:14, 15). The wounded but living Lamb in Revelation 5 also testifies to the power of Jesus' resurrection, a victory that delivered a crushing blow to Satan (Genesis 3:15; Romans 16:20).

4. What does the connection between prayer and the burning of incense teach us about prayer?

The burning of incense was a kind of offering. It is helpful for us to think of our prayers as offerings. The incense that was to be offered in the tabernacle was a divinely prescribed blend of spices (Exodus 30:34-38). If our prayers are to be most pleasing to God, they should be carefully and reverently presented, in harmony with the Biblical principles regarding prayer (Matthew 6:5-15; Philippians 4:6, 7; James 1:5-8). Another aspect of the burning of incense that applies to prayer is its continual rising toward Heaven. We are to "pray without ceasing" (1 Thessalonians 5:17). It is important to observe special times of prayer, such as those we have at mealtimes or at bedtime. But it is equally vital to lift up constant praise for blessings we experience and constant petition for problems we encounter.

5. The book of Revelation shows us that Heaven will be a place of singing. How can we make our earthly music more of a foretaste of heavenly singing?

The lesson writer mentions the difference of taste between believers who prefer traditional hymns and those who favor simpler choruses. Heavenly singing will surely transcend these and all other categories we use on earth. It will be God-centered and Christ-centered. It will be a wholehearted act of worship and not merely a means of showing off a ringing soprano voice or a powerful bass voice. We will sing, not merely because it is an essential part of a Scriptural worship service, but because we will want to express our joy, our gratitude, and our praise for the eternal salvation we have received. Let us put these principles into practice in our present worship.

Provision for the Redeemed

DEVOTIONAL READING: Hebrews 9:7-14.

LESSON SCRIPTURE: Revelation 7.

PRINTED TEXT: Revelation 7:1-3, 9, 10, 13-17.

Revelation 7:1-3, 9, 10, 13-17

1 And after these things I saw four angels standing on the four corners of the earth, holding the four winds of the earth, that the wind should not blow on the earth, nor on the sea, nor on any tree.

2 And I saw another angel ascending from the east, having the seal of the living God: and he cried with a loud voice to the four angels, to whom it was given to hurt the earth and the sea,

3 Saying, Hurt not the earth, neither the sea, nor the trees, till we have sealed the servants of our God in their foreheads.

. . . .

9 After this I beheld, and, lo, a great multitude, which no man could number, of all nations, and kindreds, and people, and tongues, stood before the throne, and before the Lamb, clothed with white robes, and palms in their hands;

10 And cried with a loud voice, saying, Salvation to our God which sitteth upon the throne, and unto the Lamb.

. . . .

13 And one of the elders answered, saying unto me, What are these which are arrayed in white robes? and whence came they?

14 And I said unto him, Sir, thou knowest. And he said to me, These are they which came out of great tribulation, and have washed their robes, and made them white in the blood of the Lamb.

15 Therefore are they before the throne of God, and serve him day and night in his temple: and he that sitteth on the throne shall dwell among them.

16 They shall hunger no more, neither thirst any more; neither shall the sun light on them, nor any heat.

17 For the Lamb which is in the midst of the throne shall feed them, and shall lead them unto living fountains of waters: and God shall wipe away all tears from their eyes.

GOLDEN TEXT: For the Lamb which is in the midst of the throne shall feed them, and shall lead them unto living fountains of waters: and God shall wipe away all tears from their eyes.—Revelation 7:17.

Hope for the Future
Unit 3: A Message of Hope
(Lessons 10-13)

Lesson Aims

This study should equip class members to:

1. Explain the relationship between the assurances found in Revelation 7 and the final judgment.

2. Name one assurance that is most meaningful to them.

3. Understand how the reference to "great tribulation" can apply to suffering believers throughout the history of the church.

Lesson Outline

INTRODUCTION
    A. Security for Mothers
    B. Lesson Background
I. SECURITY FOR GOD'S SERVANTS (Revelation 7:1-3)
II. PRAISE FROM GOD'S SERVANTS (Revelation 7:9, 10)
III. BLESSINGS TO GOD'S SERVANTS (Revelation 7:13-17)
    A. They Are Kept and Cleansed (vv. 13, 14)
       White Robes
    B. They Serve in God's Presence (v. 15)
    C. They Continue in God's Care (vv. 16, 17)
       Tears Wiped Away
CONCLUSION
    A. No Fatherless Children
    B. Prayer of a Trusting Child
    C. Thought to Remember

Use the visual for Lesson 11 to focus on God's wonderful promise to "wipe away all tears." It is shown on page 317.

Introduction

A. Security for Mothers

"Well, I'm not buying any green bananas." That's the way one mother answered a friend who wanted to know how she felt about future prospects for herself and her family. And who of us would be inclined to argue with her about it? Her concern for her own advancing years and for the uncertainties facing her children and grandchildren, gave her an uneasy feeling about what lay ahead. Any of us could respond with our own litany of insecurities relating to crime, national debt, moral decay, family breakdown, and other special items of concern. How about our green bananas? Will they have the opportunity to ripen and be enjoyed by others?

What lasting gift can we bestow on Mother on this, her day? In addition to the assurance of our love and prayers and our pledge of lasting support, what security can we provide or promise?

Perhaps we can begin by remembering that this particular first day of the week was the *Lord's Day* long before it became *Mother's Day.* God's revelation of eternal triumph and lasting security came to an apostle, and thus to the church, on a Lord's Day (Revelation 1:10) long ago, amid circumstances that were much less secure than ours. To all mothers and all their children of all generations, God offers the abiding security of His unchanging love and eternal presence.

B. Lesson Background

The vision recounted in Revelation 7 seems to interrupt a series of events recounted in chapters 4-6. Yet it is built on what is found in those chapters. Chapters 4 and 5 describe the throne room of Heaven, focusing on the glorious One who is seated on the central throne. Accompanying Him is the Lamb, standing after having been slain, who alone was found worthy to open the sealed scroll of eternal mysteries. Surrounding the central throne appear four living creatures, suggesting the totality of created beings. Encircling all these are twenty-four thrones occupied by twenty-four white-robed elders, symbolizing either the leaders of believers from both Old and New Covenants or the believers themselves. Surrounding all of these is a throng of angels, joining in praise to God.

Chapter 6 presents a series of visions occurring with the opening of six of the seven seals on the scroll. Each of the first four visions consists of a horse with its rider. First comes a victorious rider on a white horse, followed by one on a red horse (representing war), another on a black horse (representing pestilence or famine), and a fourth rider (whose name was Death) on a "pale" horse. The opening of the fifth seal results in a vision of "the souls of them that were slain for the word of God, and for the testimony which they held" (Revelation 6:9). The sixth introduces the terrors of final judgment, from which multitudes try to hide themselves.

The vision of the sixth seal closes (as does the sixth chapter of Revelation) with a penetrating question: "For the great day of his wrath is come; and who shall be able to stand?" Who will be able to endure the release of divine wrath against human sin? And by what means? At this point, Revelation pauses from the opening of the seals to provide the answer. The seventh and final seal will not be opened until the beginning of chapter 8.

I. Security for God's Servants (Revelation 7:1-3)

1. And after these things I saw four angels standing on the four corners of the earth, holding the four winds of the earth, that the wind should not blow on the earth, nor on the sea, nor on any tree.

Matthew 13:39, 41, 42, and 24:29-31 refer to *angels* as agents of judgment. In the present vision John saw God's agents *standing on the four corners of the earth*, thus controlling all the earth. The task of these angels was to hold *the four winds of the earth*. They were to prevent the destructive hurricanes of judgment from being released too quickly to work their devastation. For similar language used of divine judgment, see Jeremiah 49:35, 36. This act by the angels protected, at least for a time, the *earth* and *sea* and the kind of growth (trees) that normally bears the brunt of destructive storms.

2, 3. And I saw another angel ascending from the east, having the seal of the living God: and he cried with a loud voice to the four angels, to whom it was given to hurt the earth and the sea, saying, Hurt not the earth, neither the sea, nor the trees, till we have sealed the servants of our God in their foreheads.

This next *angel* appeared *from the east*, as does the rising sun. His mission was one of light and preservation. He carried the evidence of authority from God Himself—an official *seal* such as that identifying the ambassador of a nation and serving to authenticate his message. This angel demonstrated his authority by delivering his message to the four angels *with a loud voice.*

The angel's cry kept the effects of the four winds from being felt by the *earth*, *sea*, and *trees.* His words also reveal why the opening of the seventh seal had been delayed. The pause was a pause of grace, allowing the angels to seal *the servants of our God in their foreheads.* Revelation 14:1 and 22:4 also refer to this marking as an important means of identifying the faithful.

Ezekiel 9:3-6 tells of a similar marking of the faithful before the punitive slaughter of those who were guilty of abominations in Jerusalem. Both markings are reminiscent of the procedure followed during the Israelite Passover. A mark was placed on the doorposts of the Israelites' homes in Egypt before the Lord struck the Egyptians with the plague of death on the firstborn (Exodus 11:1—12:30).

> **How to Say It**
>
> SHEKINAH (Hebrew). shih-*kye*-nuh.

The *forehead* was an appropriate place to carry the *seal* identifying those belonging to God. Associated with the intellect, the forehead indicates a willing commitment. It is prominent and easy to see. Deuteronomy 6:4-9 directs that God's words be worn as "frontlets between thine eyes."

Rather than an actual physical mark, a spiritual identification is indicated in 2 Timothy 2:19: "The foundation of God standeth sure, having this seal, The Lord knoweth them that are his." The seal of God's ownership may not be physically visible on our brows, but His ownership of our lives will become evident as His will guides our thoughts, directs our attention, and determines the course of our actions.

Verses 4-8, not included in our printed text, describe those who were sealed as 144,000 descendants of Jacob, with 12,000 from each of twelve tribes. The twelve tribes named are not identical with the ones who were assigned territories in the promised land. This, along with the precise pattern of exact numbers, suggests that these numbers are symbols rather than literal statistics.

What do these numbers symbolize? Some believe that the 144,000 of verses 4-8 refer to the saved who are Jews, while the "great multitude" described in verse 9 includes Gentiles who have turned to Christ. It is more likely, however, that the 144,000 and the great multitude refer to the same group of people. This understanding is in line with the tendency of the New Testament to apply Old Testament language to the church (see Hebrews 12:22-24; 1 Peter 2:9). Those who belong to the "Israel of God" (Galatians 6:16) are pictured in Revelation as the Israel of God in glory with Him.

II. Praise From God's Servants (Revelation 7:9, 10)

9, 10. After this I beheld, and, lo, a great multitude, which no man could number, of all nations, and kindreds, and people, and tongues, stood before the throne, and before the Lamb, clothed with white robes, and palms in their hands; and cried with a loud voice, saying, Salvation to our God which sitteth upon the throne, and unto the Lamb.

What John had earlier *heard* (v. 4) as the sealing of the 144,000 from the tribes of Israel, he now *beheld* as an innumerable throng of saints coming from all imaginable categories of humanity (political units, families, clans, cultural groups, races, languages and dialects) and gathering *before the throne, and before the Lamb*. In Christ there is neither Jew nor Greek, slave nor freeman, male nor female, but all share a common relationship to God (Galatians 3:28). While that unity remains imperfect here on earth, in spite of our efforts to achieve it, in Heaven it will be complete. We will be one!

The unity of the redeemed is reflected in the similarity of their clothing, equipment, and activity. *White robes* signified a God-given purity, innocence, and righteousness. The redeemed also carried *palms*, indicating a festive occasion such as that which occurred during Jesus' triumphal entry into Jerusalem (John 12:12, 13; see also Leviticus 23:39, 40). Thus equipped, this throng became a mighty choir declaring praise to the Ruler of Heaven and earth, and to the Lamb who had risen in power and glory after dying as a sacrifice for the sins of the world.

The promise that such an all-inclusive throng will gather around the throne in Heaven, challenges the church to take seriously Christ's command to go into all the world and make disciples of *all nations* (Matthew 28:18-20). If that throng will indeed be one, without divisions into separate cultural, racial, and language groups, some mingling of these within congregations and choirs here on earth would be a most appropriate preparation.

Verses 11 and 12, not included in our printed text, tell us that the multitude of redeemed persons were then joined in their praises by "all the angels." The angels' sevenfold tribute of praise is similar to that found in Revelation 5:12.

III. Blessings to God's Servants (Revelation 7:13-17)

God's devoted servants have reason enough to praise Him on earth for blessings they experience in their daily walk with Him. They have immeasurably greater blessings yet to come.

A. They Are Kept and Cleansed (vv. 13, 14)

13, 14. And one of the elders answered, saying unto me, What are these which are arrayed in white robes? and whence came they? And I said unto him, Sir, thou knowest. And he said to me, These are they which came out of great tribulation, and have washed their robes, and made them white in the blood of the Lamb.

At this point, John's role changed from that of an observer of the events in Heaven, and he be-

came an invited participant. An otherwise unidentified member of the twenty-four *elders* may have noticed some confusion in John's expression, so he left the assembly around the throne to help this observer understand what was happening. He spoke the question that was evidently on John's mind: "Who are all these white-robed folk singing God's praises, and how did they get here?" John could have suggested an answer, but he preferred to learn from one who knew. So with appropriate respect he said, in effect, "I'm listening; tell me." The instructive elder responded by answering the question and going on to tell what these assembled saints could expect in the future. His response continues to the end of the chapter.

Two characteristics identified the members of the throng first mentioned in verse 9. They had endured *great tribulation* for the sake of Christ, and they had been cleansed by "him that loved us, and washed us from our sins in his own blood" (Revelation 1:5). The term *great tribulation* is made more specific in the Greek text, which reads, *the great tribulation*. It implies a definite period of affliction, perhaps calling to mind Daniel's prophecy of "a time of trouble, such as never was since there was a nation" (Daniel 12:1). One may also think of Jesus' words to His disciples: "For then shall be great tribulation, such as was not since the beginning of the world to this time, no, nor ever shall be" (Matthew 24:21; see also Mark 13:19).

Many have suggested a specific period of intense suffering as the fulfillment of this time of tribulation. Some believe that it refers to a period of extreme opposition shortly before Christ's second coming. It is believed that this hostility will accompany the appearance of the "man of sin," whose coming will precede Christ's return (2 Thessalonians 2:3). However, it is also possible that *the great tribulation* is a general reference to any form of persecution of believers. This would make the message concerning tribulation pertinent to suffering Christians of any era and in any country, whose sufferings may well be for them *the great tribulation*. The important point then becomes the assurance offered to the oppressed believer, not the discovery of the clue to a particular theory of interpretation.

Thus, whatever the immediate reference may have been, this passage bears a close and timeless relationship to the assurances of Romans 8:35-37 and 2 Corinthians 4:16-18 that no difficulty on earth can separate God's people from His love, and that the worst of present afflictions for Christ's sake is insignificant when compared with future blessings.

While the idea of whitening robes with blood seems impossible from a human perspective, spiritually there is no difficulty with bleaching one's garments *white* by applying the sacrificial *blood of the Lamb*. Those who may feel uneasy about singing, "Are You Washed in the Blood of the Lamb?" need to reconsider Ephesians 1:7; 1 Peter 1:18, 19; 1 John 1:7; and Revelation 1:5.

WHITE ROBES

You can always tell who the graduates are at any high school or college commencement. They are the ones dressed in robes. Wearing a robe indicates that a milestone in one's academic career has been reached.

John tells us that the multitude of the redeemed were distinguished by the white robes that they wore. They are said to have "washed their robes, and made them white in the blood of the Lamb" (Revelation 7:14). They have responded in faith and obedience to the Son of God's sacrifice for them.

Those in the church at Sardis are told that the white garments promised to them are a token of the fact that they have overcome (3:5). Jesus tells them that "they shall walk with me in white" (3:4). In Revelation 19 we are given a vision of the Lamb's wife who is clothed "in fine linen, clean and white." We are also informed that "the fine linen is the righteousness of saints" (v. 8).

Just as academic achievement involves overcoming certain obstacles and challenges, spiritual achievement means conquering the daily challenges to our growth in Christ. The robe of academic accomplishment is a beggar's garment compared with the white robes awaiting those who have overcome in Jesus' name. The congratulatory words from a dean or president pale in comparison with the Master's commendation of "Well done." What a glorious "graduation ceremony" that will be!   —J. G. V. B.

B. They Serve in God's Presence
(v. 15)

15. Therefore are they before the throne of God, and serve him day and night in his temple: and he that sitteth on the throne shall dwell among them.

Because the saints have availed themselves of Christ's cleansing sacrifice and have remained faithful through the most severe afflictions, they will experience the joy of serving God face to face without the limitations of *day and night*. It is difficult to know exactly how the saints will *serve* God in Heaven, beyond expressions of worship and praise. Since there will be no poverty or pain, acts of mercy to the needy will not be necessary. The eternal activities are a part

visual for lesson 11

God shall wipe away all tears.

of the divine provision that we cannot begin to fathom (1 Corinthians 2:9).

In its references to the *temple*, Revelation uses a Greek word that indicates the inner shrine, symbolizing the very presence of God, rather than the outer courts. So intimate is His presence that Revelation 21:22 says of the new Jerusalem, "I saw no temple therein: for the Lord God Almighty and the Lamb are the temple of it."

Heaven's most essential ingredient (that is, what will make Heaven *Heaven*) will be the very presence of the Almighty—*among* His people rather than on a distant throne. The word translated *dwell* speaks literally of God's *spreading His tent* among His people and sheltering them with His presence (compare the promises of Ezekiel 37:27 and Zechariah 2:10). In the Old Testament, the Hebrew word *shekinah* described the glory of God that appeared over the mercy seat in the tabernacle, indicating the presence of God among His people. The eternal reality will be infinitely greater.

C. They Continue in God's Care
(vv. 16, 17)

16. They shall hunger no more, neither thirst any more; neither shall the sun light on them, nor any heat.

The elder found it easier to describe Heaven by its relief from familiar problems and difficulties than by its positive provisions. We know what hurts us here; Heaven is a place where none of that will be present. *Hunger* and *thirst* are universal and sometimes critical problems, especially among the poor. There will be no such deprivations in Heaven.

In many areas where John had ministered, the discomforts and dangers of desert *heat* were closely related to hunger and thirst. Isaiah 49:10 promised freedom from all of these: "They shall not hunger nor thirst; neither shall the heat nor sun smite them: for he that hath mercy on them shall lead them, even by the springs of water shall he guide them." The new Jerusalem is described as having no need of the *sun*, "for the glory of God did lighten it, and the Lamb is the light thereof" (Revelation 21:23).

17. For the Lamb which is in the midst of the throne shall feed them, and shall lead them unto living fountains of waters: and God shall wipe away all tears from their eyes.

The *Lamb*, who had been shown worthy to open the book with the seven seals, now becomes the Good Shepherd of His flock (John 10:11-14). The promises of Psalm 23 reach their ultimate fulfillment, as do the words of Ezekiel 34:23: "I will set up one shepherd over them, and he shall feed them, even my servant David; he shall feed them, and he shall be their shepherd." The reason that hunger is absent is that the Lamb *shall feed them*; the reason there is no thirst is that He *shall lead them unto living fountains of waters*.

Perhaps the tenderest picture presented in the Bible is that of Almighty God tenderly caressing one of His faithful ones and wiping away his *tears*. Again, this was foretold in Isaiah 25:8: "He will swallow up death in victory; and the Lord God will wipe away tears from off all faces . . . for the Lord hath spoken it."

TEARS WIPED AWAY

People around the world live without many possessions that we believe to be essential to our life and work. But something all peoples seem to have in common is tears. At some time or in some circumstance, everyone needs to cry.

We know that we cannot escape tears in our own lives. When loved ones die, when tragedies invade the lives of those near to us, when we know bitter defeats or disappointments, or when some utterly unbelievable blessing comes our way, we know the presence of tears. Even the Son of God, whom we usually think of as the master of every emergency, cried unashamedly at Lazarus's grave. The shortest verse in the Bible speaks volumes: "Jesus wept."

Because tears are such a universal language, the promise in today's text becomes one of the most comforting in the entire Bible: "God shall wipe away all tears from their eyes" (Revelation 7:17). This is reinforced by a later assurance: "And God shall wipe away all tears from their eyes; and there shall be no more death, neither sorrow, nor crying" (21:4).

Here in this present life there is no place *without* tears. In that future life in Heaven, there shall be no place *with* tears. Fear, frustration, failure all gone; pain, parting, pathos unknown; death, defeat, disappointment forever past. "God shall wipe away all tears."   —J. G. V. B.

Conclusion

A. No Fatherless Children

The process of becoming a mother is in a way comparable to the experience of the white-robed saints of Revelation—there is joy after tribulation. Jesus said, "A woman when she is in travail hath sorrow, because her hour is come: but as soon as she is delivered of the child, she remembereth no more the anguish, for joy that a man is born into the world" (John 16:21).

Childbirth is not, of course, the end of difficulties or problems for a mother; it is the beginning of altogether new ones. This is especially true for those mothers in today's society who must take on the challenge of bringing up a fatherless child. How important it becomes for such children to learn and understand that God is their heavenly Father. Where He lives, there are no fatherless children. Lonely mothers and orphaned children, adopted into God's family, are included in the fatherly embrace of Him who will one day wipe all tears forever from their eyes.

B. Prayer of a Trusting Child

We are frightened, O God, by circumstances around us and by our inability to overcome our own "great tribulations." Constantly we need Your loving care, Your guidance, and Your power to gain the victories You have in store for us. May we never stray from the security of Your presence. We pray in Jesus' name. Amen.

C. Thought to Remember

"Be ye steadfast, unmovable, always abounding in the work of the Lord, forasmuch as ye know that your labor is not in vain in the Lord" (1 Corinthians 15:58).

Home Daily Bible Readings

Monday, May 5—Worship in Spirit and in Truth (John 4:19-26)

Tuesday, May 6—The Lord, Your Keeper (Psalm 121:1-8)

Wednesday, May 7—The Lord, Your Shepherd (Psalm 23)

Thursday, May 8—The Lord, Your Comforter (Isaiah 25:6-9)

Friday, May 9—Jesus, the Good Shepherd (John 10:11-16)

Saturday, May 10—The Lord, Worthy of Worship (1 Chronicles 16:28-36)

Sunday, May 11—Jesus Rewards Faithfulness (John 14:15-21)

Learning by Doing

This page contains an alternate lesson plan emphasizing learning activities.
Classes desiring such student involvement will find these suggestions helpful.

Learning Goals

This study should enable students to:

1. Point to portions of our text assuring them that God cares for His people.

2. Name one assurance that is most directly related to them.

3. Understand the urgency of taking the gospel to all mankind.

Into the Lesson

Prepare for today's class by gathering several items to bring to class that symbolize security for different people. Some of these might include: money, an old teddy bear or blanket, a picture of a strong athlete, a picture of a sports car, or perhaps an insurance policy. Display these items for students to see as they enter.

To begin, ask students, "Can you see anything that these items have in common?" As members offer answers, see if you can steer the thinking to the fact that these are items to which people look for security. Continue by asking, "What makes many feel secure in today's world?" (Possible answers are a good job, a nice house, health, friends, family, possessions, money in the bank, or a relationship with God.)

Now focus the discussion of the class on their relationship with God. "What makes you feel secure in your relationship with God? What makes you feel insecure?" Note that God wants us to be confident and secure in our relationship with Him (Hebrews 4:16; 1 John 5:13). Conclude this introduction by saying, "Today we are going to look at God's provision for the redeemed, as seen through John's vision in Revelation 7."

Into the Word

Supply the context of Revelation 7 by using the material under the Lesson Background in the commentary. Have three good readers in the class read today's text in the following sections: Revelation 7:1-3; Revelation 7:9, 10; and Revelation 7:13-17. Summarize these passages, using the outline provided in the commentary.

Have students look back through the text for assurances that God cares for His people. You may wish to list them on a chalkboard or on poster board. The pictures that stand out in this text are: (1) the "angel . . . having the seal of the living God" (7:2), signifying that God's messengers are watching His servants in a special way;

(2) "Hurt not the earth" (7:3), showing God's ability to stop the trauma and calamity that the four angels were prepared to bring upon the earth; (3) "a great multitude, which no man could number" (7:9), presenting the vast number of God's people and His desire for salvation to include all nations; (4) "arrayed in white robes" (7:13), describing God's desire to clothe His people with forgiveness through Jesus' blood; (5) "they which came out of great tribulation" (7:14), showing that God can protect His children from even the worst of tribulations; (6) "washed their robes, and made them white in the blood of the Lamb" (7:14), focusing on God's provision of salvation for His people; (7) "They shall hunger no more, neither thirst any more; neither shall the sun light on them, nor any heat" (7:16), showing that God takes care of the basic needs of His followers; (8) "For the Lamb . . . shall feed them" (7:17), reemphasizing God's care for His people's needs; (9) "shall lead them unto living fountains of waters" (7:17), representing the fulfillment of God's salvation; (10) "God shall wipe away all tears" (7:17), showing that God will eliminate all that causes sorrow and pain; and (11) "he that sitteth on the throne shall dwell among them" (7:15), showing that God cares for His people enough that He actually dwells in their midst.

Ask students to take a moment and decide which of these portraits is most meaningful to their own lives. Suggest that they highlight or underline the passage in their Bibles.

Into Life

Perseverance through tribulation involves recognition of certain factors: *security* (I am confident in my relationship with God and in His ability to see me through any of my circumstances); *praise* (I am willing to focus my attention on my Creator rather than on my circumstances); and a proper *perspective* on my circumstances (do I look at them as opportunities for God to work, or as situations through which I must work on my own?).

Encourage students to have a time each day during which they can: (1) deepen their security in their relationship with God, (2) express their praise to God, and (3) meditate on their circumstances in order to see God's fingerprints of blessing upon their lives.

Let's Talk It Over

The questions on this page are designed to encourage review of the lesson Scriptures and to promote discussion of the lesson by the class. The answers provided are only discussion starters. Let your class talk it over from there.

1. In what way can we say that we have been sealed in our foreheads?

Paul speaks in Romans 8:6 of our being "spiritually minded," or of having "the mind controlled by the Spirit," as the *New International Version* renders it. The symbolism of being sealed on the forehead most likely refers to a mind that has come under the authority and guidance of the Holy Spirit. Do we have a hunger for the Word of God? Are we glad for the opportunity to join with other Christians in worship and fellowship? Do we desire a holier, purer life, and are we growing into such a life? Are we eager to share with others our faith in Jesus Christ and our gratitude for His salvation? If we can answer "yes" to questions like these, it indicates that we have the seal of God's Spirit on our foreheads, for His interests have become our interests.

2. The scene in Revelation 7:9, 10, with the worshiping multitudes assembled from all races and nations before God's throne, should inspire us to missionary zeal. Why is this so?

This scene reminds us that the gospel is intended for people of all races and nations. In many communities and in many churches, we have become accustomed to encountering people from only our own racial background. It is easy to lose sight of the fact that "God is no respecter of persons: but in every nation he that feareth him, and worketh righteousness, is accepted with him" (Acts 10:34, 35). The scene also indicates that the gospel will find success among all races and in all nations. Some peoples may be strongly resistant to the Word of God today. But we should still endeavor to present it to them, knowing it has power to overcome whatever barriers men may raise against it.

3. Many students of Bible prophecy hold rather strong convictions regarding the "great tribulation" referred to in Revelation 7:14. Without getting into the various opinions regarding the tribulation, can we list some indications that a time of great tribulation for Christians could be drawing near?

In our society we have witnessed an increasing abandonment of Biblical principles of right and wrong. Whenever Christians speak against the rising acceptance of abortion, homosexuality, sexual relations outside of marriage, and the like, they are being subjected to increasing ridicule and even hostility. Also, we see anti-Christian groups and individuals who are working to limit the rights of Christians to practice their faith publicly. Such trends illustrate that the cost of following Jesus is becoming much greater, possibly producing a time of "great tribulation" for believers in our society. We should keep in mind, however, that throughout the history of the church, Christians somewhere in the world have had to suffer what for them must have seemed like "great tribulation." The promises of Revelation 7:15-17 are for all those believers who remain faithful through such periods of trial.

4. The lesson writer refers to "those who may feel uneasy about singing, 'Are You Washed in the Blood of the Lamb?'." How do we respond to those critics who object to our emphasis on blood atonement?

From a Biblical perspective, Christian faith is pointless if it is separated from the blood atonement: "Without shedding of blood is no remission" (Hebrews 9:22). Romans 3:23-26 describes the universality of sin and points to Jesus' blood as the only source of grace and redemption. While the world often makes light of sin, Christians know how serious and destructive it is. It is foolish to think that sin can be overcome by education, psychology, or mere human goodness. Only something as drastic as the shedding of Christ's blood could provide an answer to the horror of sin.

5. In Heaven we will continuously serve God. What can we do now to prepare for that service?

We must keep in mind that our present service should be done for God and His glory (Colossians 3:23). The point of this is that we learn to serve, not for human applause, but for the joy of pleasing our heavenly Father. When we contemplate Heaven, the prospect of mansions, fine robes, and crowns should be secondary to hearing those blessed words: "Well done, thou good and faithful servant" (Matthew 25:21).

The Victorious Christ

DEVOTIONAL READING: Revelation 19:1-10.

LESSON SCRIPTURE: Revelation 19, 20.

PRINTED TEXT: Revelation 19:11-16; 20:11-15.

Revelation 19:11-16

11 And I saw heaven opened, and behold a white horse; and he that sat upon him was called Faithful and True, and in righteousness he doth judge and make war.

12 His eyes were as a flame of fire, and on his head were many crowns; and he had a name written, that no man knew, but he himself.

13 And he was clothed with a vesture dipped in blood: and his name is called The Word of God.

14 And the armies which were in heaven followed him upon white horses, clothed in fine linen, white and clean.

15 And out of his mouth goeth a sharp sword, that with it he should smite the nations; and he shall rule them with a rod of iron: and he treadeth the winepress of the fierceness and wrath of Almighty God.

16 And he hath on his vesture and on his thigh a name written, KING OF KINGS, AND LORD OF LORDS.

Revelation 20:11-15

11 And I saw a great white throne, and him that sat on it, from whose face the earth and the heaven fled away; and there was found no place for them.

12 And I saw the dead, small and great, stand before God; and the books were opened: and another book was opened, which is the book of life: and the dead were judged out of those things which were written in the books, according to their works.

13 And the sea gave up the dead which were in it; and death and hell delivered up the dead which were in them: and they were judged every man according to their works.

14 And death and hell were cast into the lake of fire. This is the second death.

15 And whosoever was not found written in the book of life was cast into the lake of fire.

GOLDEN TEXT: He [the rider] hath on his vesture and on his thigh a name written, KING OF KINGS, AND LORD OF LORDS.—Revelation 19:16.

Hope for the Future
Unit 3: A Message of Hope
(Lessons 10-13)

Lesson Aims

Participation in this lesson should prepare the student to:

1. Cite those characteristics of Christ that qualify Him to be Conqueror and Judge of all the earth.

2. Tell how we must adjust our ways so as to enjoy His eternal reign over us.

3. Name a specific adjustment that is needed now in his or her life.

Lesson Outline

INTRODUCTION
 A. What Price Victory?
 B. Lesson Background
I. THE VICTOR (Revelation 19:11-16)
 A. The Mighty Warrior (vv. 11-13)
  A Vesture Dipped in Blood
 B. His Troops (v. 14)
 C. His Victorious Reign (vv. 15, 16)
II. THE JUDGMENT (Revelation 20:11-15)
 A. The Judge (v. 11)
 B. The Books and the Book (vv. 12, 13)
  The Books Were Opened
 C. The Outcasts (vv. 14, 15)
CONCLUSION
 A. Happy Ending
 B. Prayer of Expectation
 C. Thought to Remember

The visual for Lesson 12 in the visuals packet focuses on the final judgment that will take place when Jesus returns. It is shown on page 325.

Introduction

A. What Price Victory?

You can find them all over the world, wherever a nation has gained its independence or achieved a major triumph on the field of battle. Such nations have erected statues, monuments, or other impressive structures to celebrate their victories. Included among these are memorials honoring those who made the ultimate sacrifice and "who more than self their country loved, and mercy more than life." Victory comes only through conflict and sacrifice. The more meaningful victories come at the greater costs.

The theme of the book of Revelation is *victory!* It announces the decisive conquest of our most bitter foes: Satan, sin, and death. It tells that the victory has been won by Jesus our Lord at the cost of suffering and death to Himself.

For every victor in conflict there must be someone or something vanquished. Many gentler folk shudder at the thought of eternal defeat and destruction for anyone. But Satan and his minions wage their warfare relentlessly against God, seeking to destroy His influence and His people as thoroughly as possible. Victory for one side cannot be achieved without the destruction of the other. The book of Revelation faces honestly the impossibility of compromise in this arena of spiritual warfare. Victory can come no other way.

B. Lesson Background

Last week's lesson from Revelation 7 dealt with God's "sealing" or identifying His people to protect them from the coming judgment. They are described as having emerged from "great tribulation," which is part of the continuing warfare between God and Satan. Chapters 8-18 depict that warfare in dramatic visions that are puzzling in detail but very clear in showing the ferocity of the conflict. Chapters 19 and 20, from which today's lesson comes, depict the end of that warfare through Christ's coming in glory and judgment. The outcome is eternal joy for His people and the consignment of His enemies to the eternal lake of fire.

Chapter 19 opens with thunderous hymns of praise by the multitudes in Heaven (vv. 1-8), followed by the grand announcement of the marriage supper of the Lamb and His bride (v. 9). It then depicts the victorious Christ coming forth to judge the earth.

I. The Victor
(Revelation 19:11-16)

A. The Mighty Warrior (vv. 11-13)

11. And I saw heaven opened, and behold a white horse; and he that sat upon him was called Faithful and True, and in righteousness he doth judge and make war.

That John *saw heaven opened* signaled that something dramatic and climactic was about to unfold before him. Ezekiel 1:1 speaks of the heavens being opened so that the prophet might see "visions of God," and Matthew 3:16 says that "the heavens were opened" to Jesus at the time of His baptism.

As John watched in amazement, there appeared before him *a white horse*. The color *white* is a symbol of both righteousness and purity (see Revelation 7:9-14 and 19:8). The horse is associated with conquest and the capability of making *war* (see 6:2). The primary focus then turns to the identity of the Rider, and the horse is quickly forgotten.

Faithful and True are such essential characteristics of the living Christ that they serve as His name. Jesus is described in John's initial greeting to the seven churches as the "faithful witness" (1:5). He later refers to Himself as "true" (3:7) and as the "faithful and true witness" (3:14). These are the qualities of divinity, for God is eternally faithful (Deuteronomy 7:9; 1 Corinthians 10:13) and true (Revelation 6:10).

The ability to *judge and make war* with *righteousness* is one that is sadly lacking in today's world. Only Jesus possesses such an ability. In one of Isaiah's numerous Messianic prophecies, he declared, "With righteousness shall he judge the poor, and reprove with equity for the meek of the earth: and he shall smite the earth with the rod of his mouth, and with the breath of his lips shall he slay the wicked" (Isaiah 11:4). Jesus' parables of judgment, such as those recorded in Matthew 24 (vv. 45-51) and 25 (vv. 1-30) echo the same theme. The era of grace and reconciliation will end when Jesus returns to hold both Satan and the sinner accountable for their endless rebellion and to pronounce judgment (Matthew 25:41; Hebrews 9:27). God's righteous judgment is as real as His love and mercy; Hell is as real as Heaven.

12. His eyes were as a flame of fire, and on his head were many crowns; and he had a name written, that no man knew, but he himself.

The description of *eyes . . . as a flame of fire* calls to mind Jesus' first appearance to John on Patmos (1:14) and his later introduction to the church at Thyatira (2:18). Such eyes as these could penetrate the dark recesses of the human mind and perceive what is normally invisible. They are fully capable of rendering final judgment.

Whereas John's vision of Jesus in Revelation 1 contained details associated with the priesthood (see the commentary on 1:13 in Lesson 6), this vision magnifies His position as King. An ancient king having power over more than one country would sometimes wear a crown for each territory. Thus it is fitting that Christ, as Ruler over all kingdoms and all His enemies (Philippians 2:5-9; 1 Corinthians 15:24-28), should wear *many crowns.*

Was the *name written, that no man knew,* written on a crown or garment worn by the royal rider, or upon His person? How does it relate to the name given to faithful overcomers and

---

How to Say It

Hades. *Hay*-deez.
Thyatira. Thy-uh-*tie*-ruh.

---

known by no one but the recipients (Revelation 2:17)? In any case, the writing could not be read. The Lord's unknown name is in addition to all the familiar titles He holds: Savior, Redeemer, Master, Lord, Christ, Son of man, Son of God, and others.

We should keep in mind that names or titles are sometimes given in conjunction with new accomplishments or changes in our social or educational status. In parts of Africa a man becomes *Mr.* when he marries, just as his bride becomes *Mrs.* We are all familiar with titles such as Doctor, Professor, General, or President. Of course, there is that most meaningful name (Christian) for the believer in Jesus (see Isaiah 62:2). Apparently Jesus' name will be one appropriate for His triumphant return in glory.

13. And he was clothed with a vesture dipped in blood: and his name is called The Word of God.

The Rider's *vesture,* or robe, bore evidence of the conflict through which He had gained a great victory. Manuscripts and translations differ as to whether this robe was *dipped in blood,* or *sprinkled* or *spattered* with blood. If the blood was Jesus' own blood freely given at the cross, the rendering of *dipped* would be most acceptable. However, if this was the blood of conquered enemies, a translation of *sprinkled* or *spattered* would be appropriate. Either interpretation describes a significant aspect of the warfare waged by our Lord. Isaiah 63:3 gives this vivid account of God's wrath manifested in judgment: "I have trodden the winepress alone; and of the people there was none with me: for I will tread them in mine anger, and trample them in my fury; and their blood shall be sprinkled upon my garments, and I will stain all my raiment." The Lamb's victory was accomplished through a life-and-death (or, more accurately, death-and-life) struggle.

This verse adds yet another title to those already given to Jesus: *his name is called The Word of God.* In John 1:1-3, 14-18 and 1 John 1:1, Jesus is referred to as the *Word*—the means by which God communicates His nature and His love to mankind. Only in this passage, however, does the full title, *The Word of God,* appear in Scripture. Some believe that this is the *name* mentioned in verse 12. But John mentions still another name for Jesus in verse 16, as well as other names and titles in the remaining chapters. The name of verse 12 is something that simply lies beyond our grasp, known only to Jesus.

A VESTURE DIPPED IN BLOOD

When Winston Churchill became Prime Minister of Great Britain, he said in his first statement to the House of Commons (May 13, 1940), "I have nothing to offer but blood, toil, tears, and sweat." Victory in World War II was achieved at just such a cost. It seems strange that the victorious Monarch of Heaven, riding in triumph and leading "the armies which were in heaven" (Revelation 19:14), should be wearing a bloody garment. His vesture, or robe, is "dipped in blood" (v. 13).

Some scholars believe that this blood is that of Christ's enemies. Others point to the emphasis throughout the book of Revelation upon the victory of the Lamb secured through the shedding of His own blood. He has "washed us from our sins in his own blood" (1:5). "Thou . . . hast redeemed us to God by thy blood" (5:9).

The prominence of the blood of Christ in Revelation (and throughout the New Testament) teaches us that winning people to Christ is achieved only at a great cost. The victorious Lamb of God is the Lamb that was slain. Jesus instituted the New Covenant with His own blood. Great multitudes are pictured in Revelation as having made their robes "white in the blood of the Lamb" (7:14).

It is through the blood, sweat, and tears of dedicated servants of God that people of every tongue, tribe, and nation can be saved from sin and liberated to walk with God. God's victories are great and lasting, but their price is also great.

—J. G. V. B.

B. His Troops (v. 14)

14. And the armies which were in heaven followed him upon white horses, clothed in fine linen, white and clean.

This description does not satisfy our curiosity as to exactly who comprised *the armies which were in heaven*. They may have been angels; we know that Jesus will be accompanied by "all the holy angels" when He comes in glory to judge all nations (Matthew 25:31).

Perhaps these *armies* also included the saints—those faithful ones cited and commended in Revelation 7:14. The garments (*fine linen, white and clean*) are exactly what the wife of the Lamb (the church) will be wearing, according to Revelation 19:8. Here they follow their blood-stained Captain, sharing His victory and riding on *white horses* similar to His. They carry no weapons; they bear no visible stains of battle. *He* bears the marks of battle—the blood and the crowns of triumph. By *His* power, they have come through their great tribulation, and have washed their garments and made them white in His blood. Now they are prepared to ride in triumph behind their Captain.

C. His Victorious Reign (vv. 15, 16)

15. And out of his mouth goeth a sharp sword, that with it he should smite the nations; and he shall rule them with a rod of iron: and he treadeth the winepress of the fierceness and wrath of Almighty God.

Jesus introduces Himself, in Revelation 1:16 and 2:12, as the One with a *sharp* two-edged *sword* coming *out of his mouth*. Ephesians 6:17 identifies the Word of God as the sword of the Spirit, and Hebrews 4:12 says that the Word of God is "quick and powerful and sharper than any two-edged sword." According to our text, the sword is used to *smite the nations*. The outcome of this onslaught is that the kingdoms of the world will "become the kingdoms of our Lord, and of his Christ" (Revelation 11:15).

To *rule* these nations *with a rod of iron* calls to mind the punishment predicted for God's enemies in Psalm 2:9: "Thou shalt break them with a rod of iron; thou shalt dash them in pieces like a potter's vessel." A similar promise was given to the church in Thyatira to anyone who would overcome and keep the "works" of Christ (Revelation 2:26, 27). The theme of judgment continues in the striking reference to treading *the winepress of the fierceness and wrath of Almighty God*. Here, as in Isaiah 63:3, 4, divine judgment is compared with the trampling of grapes into a dry pulp as their juice is crushed out of them. So shall God's enemies be trampled and crushed in the end.

There is another side, however, to the use of the *rod of iron*. The Greek word translated *rule* literally means "to shepherd." For God's people His unchanging purpose is their safety. The rod that destroys the predators is a source of constant comfort to the sheep (Psalm 23:4). Only those who are not a part of the flock have something to fear from the Shepherd's rod.

16. And he hath on his vesture and on his thigh a name written, KING OF KINGS, AND LORD OF LORDS.

The *name* that proclaims total sovereignty for the victorious Christ appears where it would be most visible on the rider of a horse—on the *thigh*. No one could escape noticing that He has been declared superior to all other rulers.

The remainder of Revelation 19 elaborates on the utter defeat of the Lord's enemies, including the beast, those who have worshiped his image, the kings of earth and their armies, and the false prophet. Revelation 20:1-10 speaks of a much-discussed thousand-year period when Satan is to be bound, just before the consummation of all history. Then comes the vision of final judgment.

II. The Judgment
(Revelation 20:11-15)

A. The Judge (v. 11)

11. And I saw a great white throne, and him that sat on it, from whose face the earth and the heaven fled away; and there was found no place for them.

The judgment throne that John saw was *white* (symbolic of the purity and impartiality of this judgment), and sufficiently *great* to accomplish the evaluation of all the earth. The One whom John saw sitting on the *throne* during his first vision of "things which must be hereafter" (4:1) now prepares to conduct a worldwide, history-encompassing judgment.

Terror at the prospect of such judgment will cause men of the earth to hide themselves and pray for the mountains to cover them, crying, "Hide us from the face of him that sitteth on the throne, and from the wrath of the Lamb: for the great day of his wrath is come; and who shall be able to stand?" (Revelation 6:16, 17). Such an attempt will be futile, for even the *the earth and the heaven* will not stand in the presence of the One who created them and now removes them.

An end to the material world in a cataclysm of fire is associated with Christ's coming again (2 Peter 3:5-13). John's final vision begins in this manner: "I saw a new heaven and a new earth: for the first heaven and the first earth were passed away" (Revelation 21:1). The old order is to be swept away to make way for the new one. There will be no *place* for it; its purpose in the Creator's plan will have been fulfilled.

B. The Books and the Book
(vv. 12, 13)

12. And I saw the dead, small and great, stand before God; and the books were opened: and another book was opened, which is the book of life: and the dead were judged out of those things which were written in the books, according to their works.

The judgment scene will bring all mankind alike *before God.* Whoever is alive at the return of Christ must stand in judgment with those who have lived and died in all preceding generations. King and peasant, rich and poor, philosopher and laborer, will all be present.

We often think of *books* as the records of important transactions or financial matters. Heaven's records preserve the "official" account of our *works,* on the basis of which we shall be *judged.* We should recall the words that frequently introduced the messages of Jesus to the seven churches: *I know thy works.*

Another book, later *opened,* is also important, for it is the *book of life,* bearing the names of those whom God recognizes as living in Him. Those who have worshiped the beast will not be recorded there (Revelation 13:4, 8; 17:8), for such individuals have chosen the path of Satan and death rather than God and life. This book contains the names of those who have overcome their trials for Jesus' sake (Revelation 3:5).

13. And the sea gave up the dead which were in it; and death and hell delivered up the dead which were in them: and they were judged every man according to their works.

No one is excused from the judging process. Those who have been lost or buried at *sea,* whose bodies have been consumed, will be restored and will be present for the event.

The word *hell* in this verse (and in the next one as well) is actually the Greek word *hades,* which signifies the intermediate state for the spirits of those awaiting judgment. When Jesus returns, both the wicked and righteous dead will arise (Acts 24:15), or be *delivered up* to face the final judgment. There the public, worldwide vindication of God's eternal purpose will occur.

The basis of judgment will be the same for all: *according to their works.* These *works* include those expressions of faith that lead one to accept Christ, and those that accompany a fruitful Christian life. By such deeds one identifies himself as a child of God and is enrolled in the book of life.

THE BOOKS WERE OPENED

One of the interesting technological marvels of our time is the increasing development of "information retrieval" systems. Due to computers and the marvels of various "chips," it is now possible to store millions of factual items and to "call them up" at will. For example, one can

visual for
lesson 12

drop a postcard to an address in Baltimore and request a report on one's contributions to and status with the Social Security system. The report comes back with a detailed summary of contributions and of the projected amounts to be paid at certain intervals.

We are told that when the dead "stand before God," the "books" will be opened (Revelation 20:12). This means that there will be an accurate accounting of our actions on file in the memory system of Heaven. Paul says in Romans 14:12, "Every one of us shall give account of himself to God." He states that those who have been faithful workers in God's kingdom are those "whose names are in the book of life" (Philippians 4:3).

If men can make instruments that can record, keep, and recall millions of acts and facts, why should anyone think it impossible for God to do the same?

In a sense, we stand before God every day that we live, for in Him we indeed "live, and move, and have our being" (Acts 17:28). The time will come, however, when each one of us will actually stand before Him. There the "books" will be opened, and we will be confronted with all we did, said, thought, and were. If our names are in the book of life, our sins will have been forgiven. By grace our record will be clear, and we will be assured of a blessed future.   —J. G. V. B.

C. The Outcasts (vv. 14, 15)

14, 15. And death and hell were cast into the lake of fire. This is the second death. And whosoever was not found written in the book of life was cast into the lake of fire.

First Corinthians 15:26 describes *death* as the last enemy that shall be destroyed. Hades, or the repository of the dead, is death's partner. Both are vanquished by Jesus (Acts 2:27, 31, where *hades* is again translated as *hell* in the *King James Version*). Both are *cast into the lake of fire* following God's judgment. Thus, our experience with Christ is a matter of death and life, with life having the final and victorious word.

Jesus' description of judgment included this preliminary reference to the lake of fire: "Depart from me, ye cursed, into everlasting fire, prepared for the devil and his angels" (Matthew 25:41). This is the place of utter and eternal terror referred to in the verses before us and in Revelation 21:8: "The fearful, and unbelieving, and the abominable, and murderers, and whoremongers, and sorcerers, and idolaters, and all liars, shall have their part in the lake which burneth with fire and brimstone: which is the second death."

If the lake of fire is the *second death*, the first death would appear to be the process of physical death that places a person in Hades. Since no one will suffer the first death anymore after Jesus returns, both death and Hades will be eliminated. Along with those *not found written in the book of life*, they will be cast into the lake of fire.

Conclusion
A. Happy Ending

Today's text ends on a negative note, describing the tragic destiny of those who have neglected enrollment in the Lamb's book of life and have followed instead the road to destruction with the beast and the false prophet. There remains, however, "the rest of the story." That will come with next week's lesson, when we conclude the quarter by considering "A New Heaven and Earth." The grace of God provides a victorious conclusion for those who will receive His grace and the blessings that accompany it. This includes a share in the eternal reign of Christ Himself. Through all the difficulties of an uncertain life in an unfriendly world, we can be "more than conquerors through him that loved us" (see Romans 8:35-39).

B. Prayer of Expectation

You are to be praised above measure, O God, for paying the price of victory for us—a victory that lasts through time and eternity. May we grow in our thanks, shaping our lives toward the eventual coming of Your kingdom. We pray and trust in Jesus' name. Amen.

C. Thought to Remember

"The kingdoms of this world are become the kingdoms of our Lord, and of his Christ; and he shall reign for ever and ever" (Revelation 11:15).

Home Daily Bible Readings

Monday, May 12—Praise God for His Judgments (Revelation 19:1-5)
Tuesday, May 13—Power Belongs to God (Revelation 19:6-10)
Wednesday, May 14—Punishment of False Prophets (Revelation 19:17-21)
Thursday, May 15—Reigning With Christ One Thousand Years (Revelation 20:1-6)
Friday, May 16—A Kingdom That Cannot Be Shaken (Hebrews 12:22-29)
Saturday, May 17—Our Bodies Will Be Changed (Philippians 3:17-21)
Sunday, May 18—Jesus Shall Abolish Death (2 Timothy 1:8-12)

Learning by Doing

This page contains an alternate lesson plan emphasizing learning activities.
Classes desiring such student involvement will find these suggestions helpful.

Learning Goals

After this study, students should be able to:

1. Describe what today's text says about the return of Christ and the thorough nature of God's judgment on the wicked.

2. Resolve to live so that Judgment Day will be a day of triumph, not terror.

Into the Lesson

Start today's lesson with an examination of what it costs to achieve victory. Have some examples of victory for the students to see as class begins. If you have time and resources, show a video of a championship being won in a particular sport. Video rental stores should have a number of these. If such a project is not possible, bring in a newspaper clipping describing a championship sporting event, or a triumph in battle (such as World War II or the Gulf War). Whatever you use should portray personal or collective victory. After showing this, ask, "What does it take to achieve victory? To win a sports championship? To win a war? While the cost to the loser is clear, what does victory cost the winner?"

As the class responds to the question, expect to hear the following suggestions: dedication; discipline; sacrifice of time, energy, or resources; money or other physical resources; training, practice, or rehearsal; and mental preparation. Sacrifice is to be expected when one contemplates success in an undertaking.

Explain to the class that today's lesson focuses on "The Victorious Christ," as portrayed in Revelation 19 and 20. The battle between Christ and Satan, and good and evil, builds throughout the book of Revelation, with its culmination coming in these two chapters. Use the material in the Lesson Background of the commentary to prepare for discussion of today's text.

Into the Word

Divide the class into three groups. (If you have a large class, form additional groups that will work on the same assignment as another group.) Prior to class, prepare three worksheets and distribute one to each group. Label one worksheet, "The Victor—Revelation 19:11-13," another, "The Victor's Troops—Revelation 19:14," and the last, "The Victor's Sacrifice—Revelation 19:15, 16." On the sheet labeled "The

Victor," make three columns with these headings: "His Name," "His Actions," and "The Cost of Victory." List the following Scriptures in each column: "His Name" (Matthew 1:21; Acts 4:12; Philippians 2:9-11); "His Actions" (Isaiah 11:4; 2 Timothy 4:1); and "The Cost of Victory" (Luke 9:51; Luke 22:63-65; Luke 23:44-46). On the sheet labeled "The Victor's Troops," make two columns with these headings: "Clothing" and "Character." List the following Scriptures in each column: "Clothing" (Isaiah 61:10; Ephesians 6:13-17; Revelation 3:5); and "Character" (Matthew 16:24; John 8:31; John 15:8). On the sheet labeled "The Victor's Sacrifice," make two headings: "Christ" and "Followers." List the following Scriptures in each column: "Christ" (Isaiah 53:5; Matthew 27:30, 31; Mark 15:24-27; John 19:1-3); "Followers" (Matthew 16:24; Romans 6:2, 6; Galatians 2:20; Philippians 3:8). (This exercise is found in the student book.)

Have the groups look at their portion of Revelation 19. Tell them to list phrases that fit the column headings on their paper. Then have them look up the additional Scriptures and add words or phrases drawn from these passages to their lists. After giving them enough time to look up their Scriptures and fill their lists, give each group the opportunity to report on its findings.

Next, have a good reader in the class read Revelation 20:11-15. Ask the class, "What details of the final judgment stand out most prominently in these verses?" The class should respond with such answers as: the great white throne, the judgment books of God, the book of life, and the lake of fire (the second death).

Into Life

Have students look up Matthew 25:34-40, and have someone read it. According to this passage, how we respond to the needs of others will affect our standing in the final judgment. Have the students mention words or phrases that would characterize each of the needs that Jesus singles out. Next to each, have the class list ways that your congregation is attempting to meet those needs. Can your class think of additional ways that your church could do this?

Close your session with a time of prayer for "the least of these my brethren" in your congregation and community. Pray about ways that your class can meet their needs.

Let's Talk It Over

The questions on this page are designed to encourage review of the lesson Scriptures and to promote discussion of the lesson by the class. The answers provided are only discussion starters. Let your class talk it over from there.

1. How is the description "Faithful and True" (Revelation 19:11) a fitting title for Jesus?

In the Gospels we witness Jesus' faithfulness to His mission. The records that Matthew (4:1-11) and Luke (4:1-13) give us of His temptation in the wilderness show how Satan attempted unsuccessfully to divert Him from that mission. John 6:14, 15 demonstrates how easily Jesus could have become an earthly king, and how He rejected that temptation. The Gospel writers tell of His emotional struggles in Gethsemane, as He prayed for the possible removal of His impending cup of suffering. But He remained true to His Father's purpose, giving Himself for the sins of the world. Three days later, faithful to His word and true to His promise, He rose from the dead. And Christians throughout the centuries have testified to His faithfulness in fulfilling the last promise in Matthew's Gospel: "Lo, I am with you alway, even unto the end of the world" (28:20).

2. Our lesson text depicts a warlike Christ. Why is this an aspect of Christ that must be emphasized today?

The world seems eager to make Jesus Christ a symbol only for world peace. In recent years, for example, political cartoonists have tried to influence parents to refrain from buying toy weapons for their children at Christmastime. Their cartoons have been designed to show the incongruity of giving warlike gifts to celebrate the birthday of the Prince of Peace. Of course, such items as toy guns, tanks, and warplanes have little in common with Christ, but He does make war, using truth as a mighty weapon. As long as falsehood, immorality, injustice, violence, and other evils beset our world, we need to emphasize a Christ who brings peace by warring against those evils that destroy peace.

3. The sharp sword by which Christ is able to "smite the nations," according to Revelation 19:15, is obviously His Word. How does this help us to appreciate the power of His Word?

This description reminds us of one piece of our spiritual weaponry listed in Ephesians 6: "the sword of the Spirit, which is the word of God" (verse 17). Perhaps we do not ponder often enough the fact that the Word of God is a sword we can wield for God and against Satan. When we think of a sword fight as portrayed in the movies, we recall that one stroke or blow has little discernible effect on the outcome. It is also true that no single sermon, Bible lesson, or personal sharing of the plan of salvation may visibly shake Satan's kingdom. But each time we wield God's Word faithfully, we make a thrust toward the victory that Christ will ultimately win. By the same token, each time we have an opportunity to teach God's Word or witness of its truth, but remain silent, we contribute to the advancement of Satan's interests. Any weapon is useless if not handled competently, and the same is true of the sword of the Spirit.

4. Perhaps no title of Jesus given in Revelation is more awesome than "KING OF KINGS, AND LORD OF LORDS" (19:16). What are some reasons why this title is so striking?

This title occupies a prominent place in one of the most dramatic pieces of sacred music: the great "Hallelujah Chorus" in Handel's *Messiah*. According to tradition, even the king of England was moved to rise in tribute to the true "King of kings" when he heard this music. Today, through the marvel of television, we are able to view heads of state as they meet in their summit conferences. We are awed by the display of splendor, pomp, and power, until we remember that Jesus is far greater than all of this. His authority far surpasses that of any earthly potentate. His rule transcends any earthly display of political power or military might.

5. Heaven's record books describe all our deeds, and these books will be opened on the Day of Judgment. How should that fact affect the way we live now?

Most of us take various precautions to avoid embarrassment. In the morning, before going off to work, we check our appearance in the mirror, so that we may be certain that our clothing and hair are presentable. We weigh our words carefully, so that we will not say something foolish. We practice good table manners and other forms of etiquette, so as to appear courteous. How much more important it is to avoid the kind of behavior that is hidden now from human view, but will be revealed on the Judgment Day!

A New Heaven and Earth

DEVOTIONAL READING: Revelation 22:1-9.

LESSON SCRIPTURE: Revelation 21:1—22:5.

PRINTED TEXT: Revelation 21:1-7, 22-27.

Revelation 21:1-7, 22-27

1 And I saw a new heaven and a new earth: for the first heaven and the first earth were passed away; and there was no more sea.

2 And I John saw the holy city, new Jerusalem, coming down from God out of heaven, prepared as a bride adorned for her husband.

3 And I heard a great voice out of heaven saying, Behold, the tabernacle of God is with men, and he will dwell with them, and they shall be his people, and God himself shall be with them, and be their God.

4 And God shall wipe away all tears from their eyes; and there shall be no more death, neither sorrow, nor crying, neither shall there be any more pain: for the former things are passed away.

5 And he that sat upon the throne said, Behold, I make all things new. And he said unto me, Write: for these words are true and faithful.

6 And he said unto me, It is done. I am Alpha and Omega, the beginning and the end. I will give unto him that is athirst of the fountain of the water of life freely.

7 He that overcometh shall inherit all things; and I will be his God, and he shall be my son.

. . . .

22 And I saw no temple therein: for the Lord God Almighty and the Lamb are the temple of it.

23 And the city had no need of the sun, neither of the moon, to shine in it: for the glory of God did lighten it, and the Lamb is the light thereof.

24 And the nations of them which are saved shall walk in the light of it: and the kings of the earth do bring their glory and honor into it.

25 And the gates of it shall not be shut at all by day: for there shall be no night there.

26 And they shall bring the glory and honor of the nations into it.

27 And there shall in no wise enter into it any thing that defileth, neither whatsoever worketh abomination, or maketh a lie: but they which are written in the Lamb's book of life.

GOLDEN TEXT: I saw a new heaven and a new earth: for the first heaven and the first earth were passed away; and there was no more sea.—Revelation 21:1.

May 25

Lesson Aims

This study should enable the student to:

1. Describe briefly the holy city that John saw.
2. Tell why some will live in the holy city and some will not.
3. Set his own course toward the enjoyment of life eternal.

Lesson Outline

INTRODUCTION
  A. "Talkin' About Heaven"
  B. Lesson Background
  I. THE HOLY CITY (Revelation 21:1-7)
    A. God's New Jerusalem (vv. 1, 2)
      Dwelling in the City of God
    B. God With His People (vv. 3, 4)
    C. God's Faithful Promise (v. 5)
    D. God's Eternal Provision (vv. 6, 7)
  II. THE CITY OF GOD AND THE LAMB (Revelation 21:22-27)
    A. The City's Temple (v. 22)
      No Temple Therein
    B. The City's Light (vv. 23, 24)
    C. The City's Security (vv. 25-27)
CONCLUSION
  A. Frustration and Certainty
  B. Prayer of Anticipation
  C. Thought to Remember

The visual for Lesson 13 is an artist's portrayal of John's vision of the new Heaven and earth. It is shown on page 333.

Introduction

A. "Talkin' About Heaven"

"It was like I'd died and gone to Heaven."

How often have you heard that from someone who had just experienced something remarkably exciting or pleasant, whether it was making a hole-in-one on the golf course or seeing some breathtakingly beautiful scenery? Seldom is the "heavenly" experience related to God or to Jesus, and even more seldom is it anything like the holy city described in Revelation.

Each person is inclined to invent his or her own "Heaven," based on whatever the inventor most enjoys: a hobby, a family reunion, or even,

as in Muslim tradition, a luxurious harem. In some cases, such thinking has invaded the songs we sing in church and the sermons we hear about Heaven, telling us much about the enhancement of earthly pleasures and little about the glories of God that await us.

This kind of speculation is understandable. It illustrates our human limitations as we try to grasp something beyond our ability to describe or comprehend. A more harmful side of this is the tendency of some to invent a heavenly gatekeeper who admits or rejects applicants to Heaven on the basis of the inventor's opinions. Some would make the Lamb's wedding feast an open affair, ushering in even those who have never indicated that they wanted to come!

Everyone talks about Heaven, but distressingly few pay much attention to what is said in the Bible. After all is said, the Bible is our only word from God about the only Heaven He has to offer. We need to respect His description and what He says about how to get there.

B. Lesson Background

Our lesson title for today, "A New Heaven and Earth," recalls Genesis 1:1, which records the creation of the Heaven and earth that have "fled away" in the book of Revelation (19:11). That creation was a long time ago, and it may be a long time yet before God establishes the new Heaven and earth. But no matter how many years may be involved, the whole is but a fleeting interlude within the eternity of Him who was forever before He created the world, and will be forever after this world is gone. That new Heaven and its inhabitants, however, will share the eternity of their Maker.

The more immediate background of our lesson this week is found in the judgment scene of last week's lesson. The verses immediately preceding our printed text tell of judgment for all mankind according to what was written in the "books" (the records of each person's "works") and in the Lamb's book of life. God's enemies are cast into the lake of fire (Revelation 20:14, 15). Today's lesson ends our quarter on a note of victory, as we consider what God has prepared for those who love and serve Him.

I. The Holy City (Revelation 21:1-7)

A. God's New Jerusalem (vv. 1, 2)

1. And I saw a new heaven and a new earth: for the first heaven and the first earth were passed away; and there was no more sea.

And I saw introduces a new vision, by which John is allowed to see *a new heaven and a new earth.* The word *new* stands in deliberate contrast with the old, or, as this verse reads, *the first heaven and the first earth.* But exactly what does this contrast involve? Does this speak of the cleansing and renovation of the existing heaven and earth, or of a total replacement? In the light of 2 Peter 3:10-13, which predicts the dissolution of the earth with a "great noise" and "fervent heat," a total replacement would seem reasonable. This is also implied in one of the texts studied last week, which notes that "the earth and the heaven fled away" from the One who sits upon the great white throne (Revelation 20:11). The *heaven* that will pass away is clearly not the place of God's eternal presence (Matthew 6:9), but rather the area including the atmosphere and what we consider outer space, with its sun, moon, and stars.

John also notes that *there was no more sea.* John on the island of Patmos and his readers in Asia might have considered the sea a turbulent barrier between them, as it is between many nations even now. It will not divide the new earth from the new Heaven.

It is also noteworthy that in Revelation the *sea* is the symbol of unrest and turmoil. The beast with seven heads and ten horns arises from out of the sea (13:1). The absence of the sea indicates the presence of peace in the new Heaven and earth.

2. And I John saw the holy city, new Jerusalem, coming down from God out of heaven, prepared as a bride adorned for her husband.

The holy city, new Jerusalem stands in vivid contrast to *Babylon,* the "unholy city" representing all wickedness, which had been destroyed in God's judgment (Revelation 18:1-8). The significance of Jerusalem can be traced to the influence and efforts of David and Solomon. David made the city his capital, and Solomon added various improvements to it, including the building of his magnificent temple. Because of the temple's presence, Jerusalem came to hold a special place as "the city which the Lord did choose out of all the tribes of Israel, to put his name there" (1 Kings 14:21). In the New Testament, Jerusalem becomes a symbol for the church (see Galatians 4:26; Hebrews 12:22-24). Its appearance in John's vision tells us that Heaven is the true holy city, the one that Abraham "looked for . . . whose builder and maker is God" (Hebrews 11:10).

To this holy city, God gave a purity and a beauty like that of a radiant *bride* on her wedding day. The Bible often uses the symbol of marriage to portray the relationship between God and His people. Isaiah 54:5-8 and Hosea 2:19, 20 speak of Israel's relationship with the

Lord using the language of marriage, and Ephesians 5:23-32 uses the ties of marriage to illustrate the special relationship between Christ and His church. The Ephesians passage tells of Christ's desire to cleanse the church, that His bride might be "holy and without blemish" (v. 27). Now, in Revelation, that bride appears fully *adorned,* prepared for the great marriage supper of the Lamb (19:9). Her radiance and purity present a contrast to the corruption of Babylon the Great (17:5), to whom God promises, "The voice of the bridegroom and of the bride shall be heard no more at all in thee" (18:23).

DWELLING IN THE CITY OF GOD

All the cities of men have been *built up.* However, John saw the holy city *"coming down* from God out of heaven" (Revelation 21:2). The cities of earth are places from which many have fled because of the congestion, crime, and the confusion of moral and spiritual values that one finds in most cities. The movement of masses of people to the suburbs in countries around the world has been spurred by a belief that it is important to get away from the city.

Several decades before Christ, a Roman writer named Marcus Terentius Varro, wrote in his work *On Agriculture,* "It was divine nature which gave the country, and man's skill that built the cities." A similar sentiment was expressed by William Cowper in his long poem, *The Task* (1785): "God made the country, and man made the town." When we think about it, the reasons we run from the city are related, not to "man's skill," but to man's flaws and imperfections.

We have in the picture of the city "coming down" from God a perfection in beauty, glory, and holiness that can thrill and encourage us. The city is "holy" because its inhabitants are redeemed, free from sin, purified in character, and alive with the radiance of the love of God in Jesus. How wonderful it will be to move away from the "city of man" and dwell forever in the "city of God"!   —J. G. V. B.

B. God With His People (vv. 3, 4)

3. And I heard a great voice out of heaven saying, Behold, the tabernacle of God is with men, and he will dwell with them, and they shall be his people, and God himself shall be with them, and be their God.

The *great voice out of heaven* may have come from an angel assigned to make the ensuing announcement. The message is that God is to place His *tabernacle* (literally, to "spread His tent") forever among the people who have sought His presence while on earth.

The desire of God to be *with* His people is one of the most prominent themes in all of Scripture. The purpose of the tabernacle in the wilderness was to provide a place where God's presence would be recognized by the Israelites (Leviticus 26:11, 12). Later God's presence was associated with Solomon's temple (1 Kings 8:12, 13). After this temple was destroyed by the Babylonians, the prophet Ezekiel reassured those who wondered whether this meant that God had forsaken His people: "And the heathen shall know that I the Lord do sanctify Israel, when my sanctuary shall be in the midst of them for evermore" (Ezekiel 37:28).

When Jesus came to earth, He was designated as Immanuel, meaning "God with us" (Isaiah 7:14; Matthew 1:23). Christians are to recognize that the Spirit of God dwells in them, making their bodies His temple (1 Corinthians 3:16; 6:19). The perfect and eternal fulfillment of God's plan to dwell with His people will come only when His presence is directly experienced by all, without the limitations of time or space. In the Greek text, the final clause before us is emphatic in declaring this fulfillment: "God *Himself* shall be with them—their God!"

4. And God shall wipe away all tears from their eyes; and there shall be no more death, neither sorrow, nor crying, neither shall there be any more pain: for the former things are passed away.

Where is there in Scripture a picture in words to match that of the heavenly Father drying the *tears* of His children? The primary cause of tears (and the first mentioned here) is *death*—the last enemy to be destroyed when Jesus returns (1 Corinthians 15:24-26). Those tears include the "crocodile tears" of a little child whose pet has died as well as the uncontrolled sobbing caused by the death of an aged one's infant grandchild. From such circumstances, and from lesser causes, springs much of our *sorrow* and the *crying* that expresses grief and frustration. Also removed in Heaven is that nagging companion of advancing age—the *pain* that reminds us when our physical machinery is worn. All of these difficulties will be in the forgotten past, wholly replaced by the glory of God in the endless future of the holy city.

C. God's Faithful Promise (v. 5)

5. And he that sat upon the throne said, Behold, I make all things new. And he said unto me, Write: for these words are true and faithful.

God Himself speaks from the central *throne* of Heaven to make one brief, but all-inclusive statement and promise: "*I make all things new.*"

He is not only the architect and builder, but the furnisher and decorator, of every detail in the new Jerusalem.

What more could He say at this point? We know the harsh reality of death, grief, and pain, but how could we even begin to understand what totally new experiences will replace them? All our efforts to describe Heaven in terms of earthly delights simply reveal the scope of our limitations.

The final words of this verse seem to be a directive from God Himself. Apparently seeing some hesitancy in John (perhaps John was expecting to hear more at this point), He commands, "Write that down! It's important! I will do exactly as I have promised." The words *true and faithful* appear as divine trademarks in Revelation (3:14; 19:11; 22:6).

D. God's Eternal Provision
(vv. 6, 7)

6. And he said unto me, It is done. I am Alpha and Omega, the beginning and the end. I will give unto him that is athirst of the fountain of the water of life freely.

Again we hear the words of God. The making of all things new for the children of God is complete: *It is done. Alpha and Omega* are the first and last letters of the Greek alphabet. The phrase is God's declaration that He is eternal; He is the One "which was, and is, and is to come" (Revelation 4:8). Thus, the God who introduces Himself at the beginning of this book as *Alpha and Omega* (1:8) now speaks again as the book nears its conclusion. Jesus refers to Himself by the same title (22:13, 16).

The presence of the *water of life* in the city calls to mind Jesus' discussion with the Samaritan woman at the well of Sychar (John 4:10-15). He is as essential for spiritual life as water is for physical life. Later John sees "a pure river of water of life, clear as crystal, proceeding out of the throne of God and of the Lamb" (Revelation 22:1). Here is one good hint of what to expect in Heaven: provisions for life and refreshment given *freely* out of the loving Father's care for His children.

7. He that overcometh shall inherit all things; and I will be his God, and he shall be my son.

The overcoming ones are identified in the letters to the seven churches as those who remain faithful to Christ amidst persecution, evil influences, and false teaching, even to the point of dying for His sake. Every letter concludes with a promise to him *that overcometh* (Revelation 2:7, 11, 17, 26; 3:5, 12, 21). Now the patience and diligence of the saints are rewarded. At the same time, they are not said to have earned what they receive; they *shall inherit all things*. They enter the holy city, not because of their virtue, but by their relationship to the Father as His children (see John 1:12). While every Christian is a *son* or child of God through faith in Christ (Galatians 3:26), both His fatherhood and our sonship will take on a new dimension when we enter the city where He resides.

visual for
lesson 13

And I saw a new heaven and a new earth: for the first heaven and the first earth were passed away.
Revelation 21:1

II. The City of God and the Lamb (Revelation 21:22-27)

Verses 9-21 (not in our printed text) describe what might be called (for lack of a better term) the "material" aspects of the holy city as John saw it from a distance. Its walls, gates, and streets are made of the most precious items known to man. Its vast measurements show it to be a cube, just as the Holy of Holies in Solomon's temple was equal in all three dimensions (1 Kings 6:19, 20). Such a mind-boggling description of the city should convince us that we are viewing something that is actually immeasurable and indescribable. The city's true glory, however, is the very presence of God within. To this John now returns.

A. The City's Temple (v. 22)

22. And I saw no temple therein: for the Lord God Almighty and the Lamb are the temple of it.

The word translated *temple* refers to the inner portion, or sanctuary. The Old Testament equivalent would be the Holy Place in the tabernacle, where only priests were permitted to enter. In Heaven's immeasurable city, the true Holy Place (see Hebrews 9:24), no such special area was needed or appropriate, since *God* and *the Lamb* were everywhere, and totally accessible to all.

Glimpses of this degree of access to God had been seen in Jesus' teaching that worship is not a matter of special places, but of spirit and of truth (John 4:21, 23), and in Peter's statement that all Christians comprise a "holy priesthood, to offer up spiritual sacrifices, acceptable to God by Jesus Christ" (1 Peter 2:5). Our access to God will reach its highest level when we "see his face" (Revelation 22:4).

No Temple Therein

Our world contains many beautiful and striking edifices of worship. These include the Church of St. Peter's in Rome, the Cathedral of Notre Dame in Paris, and the Cathedral of St. Mark in Venice. Simpler, yet possessing elegance and charm, are the white spires of wooden church buildings that beautify New England colonial towns.

Perhaps it comes as something of a shock to learn that there is "no temple" in the city of God that descends before John and glistens with the eternal luster of Heaven. However, this city is His home, so it is not necessary to invite Him to be present. He Himself is with the city's inhabitants. His glory is everywhere. Where He lives, there is nothing "that defileth, neither whatsoever worketh abomination, or maketh a lie" (Revelation 21:27). His servants are always blessed by the light of His presence, and their thirst for God's beauty and bounty is forever quenched.

Our earthly "temples" and sanctuaries speak of our need to worship God and of our testimony to and for Him. "No temple therein" assures us that what these temples mean to us will be everlastingly fulfilled. —J. G. V. B.

B. The City's Light (vv. 23, 24)

23. And the city had no need of the sun, neither of the moon, to shine in it: for the glory of God did lighten it, and the Lamb is the light thereof.

Heaven will offer a manifestation of *the glory of God* unlike anything ever witnessed by man. Isaiah foretold this: "The sun shall be no more thy light by day; neither for brightness shall the moon give light unto thee: but the Lord shall be unto thee an everlasting light, and thy God thy glory" (Isaiah 60:19).

24. And the nations of them which are saved shall walk in the light of it: and the kings of the earth do bring their glory and honor into it.

The light of the gospel will have made it possible for those of many *nations* to be enrolled in the Lamb's book of life and to experience the *light* of God shining in the holy city. The phrase, *of them which are saved*, does not appear in the best New Testament manuscripts and thus is not found in more recent English translations.

The term *nations* implies the far-reaching impact of the church and its saving message. The members of this diverse multitude add their tributes of *glory and honor* to God. The *kings of the earth* are in attendance as well, acknowledging that they are in the presence of the King of kings. This, too, was foretold by the prophet of old: "It shall come to pass in the last days, that the mountain of the Lord's house shall be established in the top of the mountains, . . . and all nations shall flow unto it" (Isaiah 2:2). "The Gentiles shall come to thy light, and kings to the brightness of thy rising" (Isaiah 60:3).

C. The City's Security (vv. 25-27)

Locked gates and doors, alarm systems, and security guards and patrolmen will be unnecessary and inappropriate in the holy city. The acknowledged presence of God and the Lamb provides all the security it needs.

25, 26. And the gates of it shall not be shut at all by day: for there shall be no night there. And they shall bring the glory and honor of the nations into it.

The holy city is described as having twelve *gates*, three on each of its four sides, but there is never any reason to close any of them. The light of God's presence is constant, never to be extinguished, so there is no darkness from which to be protected. There is no danger from enemies, for the archenemy (Satan) and his minions have been cast into the lake of fire.

Once more the presence of *nations* in the holy city is emphasized. Here too the prophet Isaiah looked ahead, by God's Spirit, to "the glory that should follow" (1 Peter 1:11): "Thy gates shall be open continually; they shall not be shut day nor night; that men may bring unto thee the forces of the Gentiles, and that their kings may be brought" (Isaiah 60:11).

27. And there shall in no wise enter into it any thing that defileth, neither whatsoever worketh abomination, or maketh a lie: but they which are written in the Lamb's book of life.

Here is why Heaven deserves the title of the holy city. Everything evil—everything contrary to God's righteous character and standards—will have no opportunity to *enter* that city.

Not only is this verse *exclusive*; it is also *inclusive*, telling us how to plan and live so that we may enter there. Enrollment in *the Lamb's book of life* is a lifelong commitment to learning the love and the way of God, that we may be prepared for the utmost pleasure of His eternal presence. Enroll, and don't become a dropout!

Conclusion

A. Frustration and Certainty

You may have heard the classic story of the mother who tried for years to tell her blind daughter about the world she could not see. Then came that wonderful day when a newly developed surgical procedure brought sight to the girl and gave her the opportunity to view her world for the first time. She could not understand why her mother had not told her that the world was so beautiful. Tenderly the mother replied, "I did my best, honey, but you just didn't have any way to understand."

Through the book of Revelation, God's apostle has done his best to depict Heaven through the visions of the holy city. We gain a strong impression of the grandeur and glory that await us in the presence of God and our Savior, but we simply do not have any way to understand fully those spiritual delights that are beyond our experience or imagination. Truly a vast array of delightful surprises await the faithful followers of Christ.

We are given a clear understanding, however, about the means of access to Heaven. We must go through Him who is the way, the truth, and the life (John 14:6)—believing, loving, trusting, obeying, and following Jesus. That information is beyond question!

B. Prayer of Anticipation

We praise You, our Father eternal, as the Giver of life, for time and eternity. Increase our desire for life everlasting with You, so that we may have a contagious excitement for it. Preserve us from counterfeit "heavens," and give us patience as we approach what Christ has gone to prepare for us. This we pray in His precious name. Amen.

C. Thought to Remember

"God himself shall be with them, and be their God" (Revelation 21:3).

Home Daily Bible Readings

Monday, May 19—The New Jerusalem (Revelation 21:9-14)

Tuesday, May 20—The City's Measurements (Revelation 21:15-21)

Wednesday, May 21—The City's Blessings (Revelation 22:1-5)

Thursday, May 22—A Trustworthy Book (Revelation 22:6-14)

Friday, May 23—A Certain Return (Revelation 22:16-20)

Saturday, May 24—Zion's Future Glory (Isaiah 60:1-5)

Sunday, May 25—Grow in Knowledge As You Wait (2 Peter 3:8-18)

Learning by Doing

This page contains an alternate lesson plan emphasizing learning activities.
Classes desiring such student involvement will find these suggestions helpful.

Learning Goals

Today's lesson should enable students to:

1. Describe briefly the holy city that John saw.

2. Understand that eternal life is a quality of life that begins when one becomes a Christian.

3. Set the course of their lives toward the goal of enjoying eternal life each day.

Into the Lesson

Today's lesson should be one of the most exciting, because it focuses on "the prize before us"—Heaven. Although John tries to describe its grandeur and splendor, Heaven is a place that actually defies description in human language. In our study today, we want to reflect upon what Heaven will be like, and how we can best prepare ourselves to go there.

During the week before class, contact several students and ask them to bring in pictures of the most beautiful place they have ever visited. Have a couple of tables set up to display the pictures. As class begins, have those who brought these items tell about the place they visited and what impressed them most concerning it. If this is not possible in your setting, bring in some pictures of a place that you think is especially beautiful.

After people have talked about these places, ask, "Why is it sometimes hard to capture how wonderful something is when you try to describe it to someone else?" After hearing responses, say, "Perhaps you can begin to imagine the problems that John had trying to convey the glory of Heaven to people who had never been there. Let's take some time this morning to look at what John said Heaven would be like, what changes will be in store for us when we get there, and what eternal life is really all about."

Into the Word

Before class begins, secure several Bible concordances for the class to use. Have the students break into small groups. Give each group a concordance and the instructions to find passages that portray what Heaven is like. Be sure to have them look under both *heaven* and *heavenly*. (Some in the class may know certain Scriptures without the aid of a concordance.) No doubt many of their references will come from Revelation, including the portion covered in today's lesson.

After giving the students time to compile the Scriptures, have the class reconvene. Ask for some from each group to mention a couple of verses they discovered. Mention that it is difficult for us to grasp what Heaven will be like; thus the Bible describes Heaven by highlighting many of the problems and woes that will *not* be present.

Next, on the blackboard or on poster board, make two columns, labeling one "The First Creation" and the second "The New Creation." Ask the class to turn in their Bibles to today's Scripture text from Revelation 21:1-7, 22-27. Tell the class that you are going to list characteristics of God's first creation (in the first column), and ask them to supply the contrast in the new Heaven and earth, using our text (this will go in the second column).

1. The sun and moon are created (Genesis 1:16). *Contrast*: There is no need for the sun or the moon (Revelation 21:23).

2. People sin (Genesis 3:6). *Contrast*: Sin is no longer present (Revelation 21:27).

3. People hide themselves from God (Genesis 3:8). *Contrast*: God is in the midst of His people (Revelation 21:3).

4. Death takes hold of man (Genesis 2:17; 3:19). *Contrast*: There is no more death (Revelation 21:4).

5. Pain and sorrow are part of life (Genesis 3:16). *Contrast*: Pain and sorrow are no longer present (Revelation 21:4).

6. The entrance into the Garden of Eden is guarded (Genesis 3:24). *Contrast*: Heaven's gates are never shut (Revelation 21:25).

Into Life

Next, read John 17:3. Ask, "According to these words of Jesus, when does eternal life begin?" Answer: At the moment we begin our walk with God through accepting Jesus. How does knowing this help us deal with everyday problems and pressures? How does it help us prepare for death? Encourage specific and practical answers.

Conclude today's session by saying, "One of the best ways to make our eternal life real on a daily basis is to remind ourselves constantly that Jesus is coming again." Read Revelation 22:12-17, then offer a prayer thanking God for all that He has done to prepare Heaven for us.

Let's Talk It Over

The questions on this page are designed to encourage review of the lesson Scriptures and to promote discussion of the lesson by the class. The answers provided are only discussion starters. Let your class talk it over from there.

1. What are some popular, but erroneous, views about Heaven?

Some people, weary from this life's labors, view Heaven as a place of uninterrupted rest. Revelation 14:13 does speak of rest for those who "die in the Lord," but worship and service for God will also be features of the heavenly life. Other people hold a rather shallow view regarding degrees of reward in Heaven. They feel that some citizens will have better mansions, richer robes, or brighter halos, than others. Perhaps the most tragic of the erroneous views regarding Heaven is that people can get there on the basis of their good deeds or their generally decent lives. On that basis it would seem that almost everyone will be in Heaven, because everyone has at least some worthwhile qualities. But Jesus Christ is the only way to Heaven (John 14:6), and that is a fact we must constantly repeat.

2. Why is the symbolism of marriage, a bride, and her husband appropriate for representing Heaven?

This symbolism points to the preparedness, purity, and faithfulness of the bride of Christ, which is the church. Ephesians 5:25-27 pictures the church in this way. When we think of Christ as the husband, we are reminded of His sacrificial love for the church. As Revelation demonstrates, the love that caused Jesus Christ to die for our sins will be a glorious theme of heavenly worship. His bride will be dressed in garments appropriate for the occasion: "fine linen, clean and white: for the fine linen is the righteousness of saints" (Revelation 19:8). In Bible times and in our time, marriage stands out as an occasion of great celebration. This makes it appropriate as a symbol for Heaven. The fullness of God's love, grace, wisdom, and power will offer us cause for eternal celebration.

3. Revelation 21:4, with its promise of the cessation of death, sorrow, crying, and pain, is one of the Bible's most precious verses. And yet, why are some Christians unable to appreciate it fully?

Many Christians have an unsaved spouse, or unsaved parents or children. Some of these believers have difficulty seeing Heaven as a place without sorrow, for they fear that the absence of an unsaved loved one will cause bitter sorrow. But God's promise is clear: there will be no sorrow and no tears in Heaven. The all-sufficiency of God's love, the joy of personal fellowship with Jesus, and the glorious reunion with those friends and loved ones who *are* in Heaven will surely transcend any inclination to sorrow.

4. How are the references to the fountain of the water of life (Revelation 21:6) and the river of the water of life (Revelation 22:1) especially appealing?

Jesus spoke frequently about quenching the thirst of the human spirit (John 4:13, 14; 6:35; 7:37-39). His statements illustrate how a thirst for water has a spiritual counterpart in the longing for hope, strength, guidance, love, and eternal life that only He can supply. The references to water in Revelation remind us that Jesus will supply our every need throughout eternity on a far grander scale than anything we could ever experience on earth. We gain refreshment for our weary souls through occasions of Christian worship and fellowship; ultimately we shall experience an even more satisfying and lasting supply of such refreshment.

5. The gates of the new Jerusalem will never be shut (Revelation 21:25). Why is this a promise that offers particular reassurance to people today?

Locks, watchdogs, and sophisticated security systems are indicative of the lack of security about which many today are greatly concerned. Newspaper stories and television reports call attention to the seriousness of this matter. It seems that no community is immune to the ravages of crime and violence. Burglary, rape, and murder frequently take place within the homes of the victims. Elderly people, no longer strong enough to defend themselves, are especially fearful concerning the dangers that threaten their safety. But in Heaven such fears will vanish. No locks or security systems will be needed. The gates will be opened wide and left open, for no criminals or vandals will exist to enter and prey upon the citizens. In that place we will experience the ultimate fulfillment of Proverbs 29:25: "The fear of man bringeth a snare: but whoso putteth his trust in the Lord shall be safe."

Summer Quarter, 1997

Special Feature

Lessons

Guidance for Ministry

A Call to Faithfulness

Unit 1: The Greatness of Christ

Unit 2: Be Faithful Followers of Christ

About these lessons

The lessons for this quarter are divided into two main studies. The first five lessons are taken from 1 and 2 Timothy and Titus. They focus on what it means to be a true servant of Christ, particularly when circumstances are less than ideal. The remaining nine lessons are taken from the book of Hebrews. Emphasis is placed upon Jesus as the superior revelation of God to man, and upon how we can serve Jesus faithfully and responsibly.

Jun 1
Jun 8
Jun 15
Jun 22
Jun 29
Jul 6
Jul 13
Jul 20
Jul 27
Aug 3
Aug 10
Aug 17
Aug 24
Aug 31

Christian Theology and Christian Living

by John W. Wade

This is a rather unusual quarter, in that it includes fourteen lessons instead of the ordinary thirteen. What is not unusual is the balance that you will find in this quarter between a strong emphasis on theology and an equally strong emphasis on practical Christian living. Christian theology and Christian living go together. Whenever one is separated from the other, problems are certain to arise.

Guidance for Ministry

The first five lessons of this quarter form the first unit, entitled "Guidance for Ministry." They are based on what we call the Pastoral Epistles—1 and 2 Timothy and Titus. These epistles were written by the apostle Paul to two of his younger co-workers. The title for this unit could very well have been "Christ's Servant," for each lesson deals with some aspect of the duties and responsibilities of those who would serve Christ.

Lesson 1, "Christ's Servant Sets an Example," urges His servants to be an example to others in sound doctrine and in living a godly life.

Lesson 2 focuses on Christ's servant as a teacher of godliness. True godliness means more than just a pious life. It involves sound teaching and the avoidance of "profane and vain babblings" (1 Timothy 6:20).

In **Lesson 3** the emphasis is on suffering as a servant of Christ. Timothy is encouraged to "endure hardness, as a good soldier of Jesus Christ" (2 Timothy 2:3). While Christians are not to deliberately seek suffering, they must be prepared to accept it joyously if it comes upon them because of their faith.

Lesson 4 continues this theme, stressing faithfulness on the part of the Christian servant.

Lesson 5, "Christ's Servant Encourages Community," discusses how a Christian ought to respond to the society about him. While he must be "subject to principalities and powers" (Titus 3:1) and deal gently with all, he must never compromise the faith.

A Call to Faithfulness

The remaining two months of the quarter cover the topic, "A Call to Faithfulness." This is a study based upon selected Scriptures from the epistle to the Hebrews. The nine lessons are divided into two units, the first of which is entitled, "The Greatness of Christ."

Lesson 6 begins this unit by affirming that "Jesus Is God's Son." This lesson should provide strength for those who feel threatened by so many today who deny the deity of Jesus.

Lesson 7 presents Jesus as Savior. He became human and suffered death, in order to free men from the power of sin and the fear of death.

Jesus is next seen as our great High Priest. **Lesson 8** highlights one of the main thrusts of the book of Hebrews, which is to show the superiority of the priesthood of Christ.

In **Lesson 9** Jesus is seen as the sacrifice. Since the blood of animals cannot take away sin, it was necessary for Jesus to come to earth as the perfect sacrifice who died in our place.

The unit containing the final five lessons of the quarter is entitled, "Be Faithful Followers of Christ." In **Lesson 10** the writer urges the Hebrew Christians to "Grow in Faithfulness." He rebukes them because they are content to live on milk (that is, the first principles of the gospel), when they ought to be maturing by eating strong meat.

Lesson 11 urges the Hebrew Christians to "Remain Near to God." These believers were being tempted to return to Judaism, their former faith. The writer warns of the dire consequences that await those who turn back.

"Remember the Past" is the theme of **Lesson 12,** which is based on Hebrews 11. The readers are reminded of the great faith of those who had preceded them, and they are encouraged to exhibit similar faith in their lives.

In **Lesson 13** the Hebrew Christians are exhorted to "Renew Commitment." The writer depicts the Christian life as a race. To succeed, believers must run with patience and strength.

Lesson 14 urges Christians to "Live Responsibly"—a much-needed lesson in our age, when so many avoid responsibility for their actions.

These lessons, particularly those from the book of Hebrews, build upon one another, and so summer vacations may make it difficult to maintain the kind of continuity you desire in your teaching. However, there is enough power in each lesson for it to stand alone. So don't be discouraged! Teach faithfully, and then let God's Word work on the hearts of your students!

Christ's Servant Sets an Example

DEVOTIONAL READING: Psalm 37:1-11.

LESSON SCRIPTURE: 1 Timothy 4:6-16.

PRINTED TEXT: 1 Timothy 4:6-16.

1 Timothy 4:6-16

6 If thou put the brethren in remembrance of these things, thou shalt be a good minister of Jesus Christ, nourished up in the words of faith and of good doctrine, whereunto thou hast attained.

7 But refuse profane and old wives' fables, and exercise thyself rather unto godliness.

8 For bodily exercise profiteth little: but godliness is profitable unto all things, having promise of the life that now is, and of that which is to come.

9 This is a faithful saying, and worthy of all acceptation.

10 For therefore we both labor and suffer reproach, because we trust in the living God, who is the Saviour of all men, specially of those that believe.

11 These things command and teach.

12 Let no man despise thy youth; but be thou an example of the believers, in word, in conversation, in charity, in spirit, in faith, in purity.

13 Till I come, give attendance to reading, to exhortation, to doctrine.

14 Neglect not the gift that is in thee, which was given thee by prophecy, with the laying on of the hands of the presbytery.

15 Meditate upon these things; give thyself wholly to them; that thy profiting may appear to all.

16 Take heed unto thyself, and unto the doctrine; continue in them: for in doing this thou shalt both save thyself, and them that hear thee.

GOLDEN TEXT: Bodily exercise profiteth little: but godliness is profitable unto all things, having promise of the life that now is, and of that which is to come.
—1 Timothy 4:8.

Guidance for Ministry
(Lessons 1-5)

Lesson Aims

After this lesson, each student should:

1. Know the background of the book of 1 Timothy.

2. Appreciate more fully the importance of being a consistent Christian example for others.

3. Be able to state a specific way in which he or she will be a better example for others.

Lesson Outline

INTRODUCTION

  A. A Careful Example

  B. Lesson Background

 I. THE SERVANT'S TRADEMARKS (1 Timothy 4:6-8)

  A. Faithfully Instructs Others (v. 6)

  B. Shuns Useless Myths (v. 7)

  C. Strives for Personal Piety (v. 8)

    Fit or Fat

 II. THE SERVANT'S EXAMPLE (1 Timothy 4:9-14)

  A. Suffers Reproach (vv. 9, 10)

  B. Persists Despite His Youth (vv. 11, 12)

    Follow the Pattern

  C. Reads and Exhorts (v. 13)

  D. Exercises His Spiritual Gift (v. 14)

III. THE SERVANT'S GROWTH (1 Timothy 4:15, 16)

  A. Obvious to Others (v. 15)

  B. To Be Rewarded (v. 16)

CONCLUSION

  A. Models

  B. Despised Youth

  C. Let Us Pray

  D. Thought to Remember

The visual for Lesson 1 stresses the importance of exercising oneself "unto godliness" (1 Timothy 4:7). It is shown on page 343.

Introduction

A. A Careful Example

Several years ago we were leading a group of young people on a backpacking trip along the Appalachian Trail. At one point we came to a fork in the trail. The shorter route led up the side of the mountain, almost reaching its summit before coming down and rejoining the longer trail. This shorter trail was a challenge even for experienced hikers, for it was narrow and led over large boulders, some of which had to be scaled with the aid of a rope.

I preferred to follow this trail because it was two miles shorter and would have taken me less time, had I been alone. But I took the longer trail because some of the younger members of the party would have had great difficulty on the steeper trail.

This is the way a good Christian ought to lead. He should not choose the path that best satisfies himself. Instead, he should lead along the trail that best protects and guards those who look to him for guidance. This was the kind of ministry that Paul urged Timothy to pursue.

B. Lesson Background

By the time of Paul's writing of 1 Timothy, Timothy, although a young man, had been recognized for some time as someone with great potential for Christ and His kingdom. He had been a trusted co-worker with Paul in many of his missionary endeavors. Paul had often dispatched Timothy to provide counsel for troubled churches (see 1 Corinthians 4:17; Philippians 2:19-23; 1 Thessalonians 3:1-3).

Timothy was the child of a mixed marriage; his father was a Greek pagan, while his mother Eunice was a devout Jewish woman who (along with his grandmother Lois) taught him the Hebrew Scriptures. Timothy joined Paul during Paul's second missionary journey (Acts 16:1-3), and continued to be his faithful companion until the apostle's death. So strong was the bond between the two men that Paul often referred to Timothy as his "son" (1 Corinthians 4:17; Philippians 2:22; 1 Timothy 1:2, 18; 2 Timothy 1:2; 2:1).

Most scholars believe that 1 Timothy was written after Paul's house arrest in Rome (Acts 28:16, 30, 31) had ended (about A.D. 63). It may have been written in Macedonia after Paul left Rome (1 Timothy 1:3). Although the letter is addressed to Timothy, whom Paul calls "my own son in the faith" (1 Timothy 1:2), it seems that much of its content was designed to be shared with other Christians and churches. In the first chapter, Paul warns against false doctrines that were already beginning to assail the faith of new Christians. In the second chapter, he gives instructions about prayer. In the third chapter, he sets forth the qualifications of bishops, or overseers, and deacons. In the fourth chapter, from which today's lesson text is taken, Paul offers some practical counsel that Timothy needed to heed if he wanted to become an effective servant of Christ. These suggestions are just as important to us today as they were when Paul penned them.

I. The Servant's Trademarks (1 Timothy 4:6-8)

A. Faithfully Instructs Others (v. 6)

6. If thou put the brethren in remembrance of these things, thou shalt be a good minister of Jesus Christ, nourished up in the words of faith and of good doctrine, whereunto thou hast attained.

The word translated here as *minister* is the Greek word *diakonos*. It does not refer to a professional clergyman as we tend to think of a "minister" today, but simply means "servant." It is the word used in the previous chapter (vv. 8-13) to refer to the office of deacon.

Part of being a *good minister* (servant) *of Jesus Christ* is to communicate *the words of faith and of good doctrine*. The knowledge of the Scriptures had been an instrumental part of Timothy's upbringing (2 Timothy 3:15). He had not outgrown his need for them. The Scriptures were still his most important tool in serving Christ and building His church. To fail to be *nourished* by their words would lead to an inferior ministry.

B. Shuns Useless Myths (v. 7)

7. But refuse profane and old wives' fables, and exercise thyself rather unto godliness.

Paul urged Timothy to reject all forms of false teaching. The teachings mentioned here were not necessarily blasphemous or sacrilegious; they did, however, turn one's attention away from the gospel. For that reason Timothy was to *refuse* or reject them. The Greek word translated *fables* is the plural of the word *muthos*, from which comes our word "myth." These fables may have included either some of the tales that had become a part of the Jewish literature of that day, or the pagan stories that abounded in the Graeco-Roman literature. Instead of wasting time on these, Paul urged Timothy to make personal *godliness* a priority. Christ's servant cannot afford to be distracted by trivial matters.

C. Strives for Personal Piety (v. 8)

8. For bodily exercise profiteth little: but godliness is profitable unto all things, having promise of the life that now is, and of that which is to come.

Paul often made reference to athletic activities to illustrate a spiritual point. We know that proper physical *exercise* can help us maintain good health. Such exercise is especially important to those of us who follow a more sedentary life-style. It is likely to make us feel better and prolong our lives.

While these benefits are indeed important, Paul states that *bodily exercise profiteth little*. Just how little becomes apparent when it is compared with the joys that *godliness* can bring not only in this life, but, more important, in the life *to come*. At best, physical exercise can prolong our lives only a few years, but godliness can prepare us for an eternity of bliss.

Physical exercise and the effort to attain godliness offer some interesting parallels. First of all, one who trains for an athletic contest must subject his body to hours of strenuous and exhausting exercise. In the same way, one must exert himself spiritually to grow in godliness. We should not expect to be lifted to Heaven on "flowery beds of ease," but should expect to agonize as we struggle against sin and temptation. Second, the athlete who is successful must have a goal, whether it be winning a race, jumping higher than the other contestants, or hurling the discus farther than his competitors. To train without a goal would be foolish. In the same way, the Christian must keep ever before him the ultimate goal—Heaven. Finally, the athlete who expects to succeed in his contest must lay aside other conflicting interests that will keep him from his goal. The Christian who expects to see his Lord face to face someday, must turn aside from the distractions of the world and give himself exclusively to that one goal.

While physical exercise and spiritual exercise are similar in these respects, they are quite different in one very important respect. The rewards for physical exercise are temporal. In the Olympic games of Paul's day, the prize was a simple wreath. Today the prize for a successful athlete may amount to worldwide fame and an annual income of millions of dollars. As impressive as this may seem, it is just as temporal as the Olympic wreath; it will all too quickly pass away. Spiritual exercise promises blessings not only during *the life that now is*, but eternal joy in that life *which is to come*.

FIT OR FAT

Covert Bailey has become one of the most popular fitness experts in America. His book *Fit or Fat* and his lectures carried over the public television network have exposed his insights to millions. Bailey has popularized what health experts have known for years: that small daily changes in diet and exercise determine whether a person is fit or fat.

A slim, energetic young man does not go to bed with 150 pounds of solid muscle and wake up to find that he has gained fifty pounds of fat and has become out of shape overnight. We gain weight and become flabby over time, one cheeseburger or one donut at a time. We lose our muscle tone and fitness gradually, one missed workout at a time.

We also regain or maintain fitness in the same way—by small daily acts. If you eat a low-fat diet of moderate portions today, tomorrow, and the next day, and if you exercise regularly this week, next week, and the next, then over time you will be fit. Patience in following a prescribed routine is essential.

In several New Testament passages, the apostle Paul uses sports and fitness analogies to teach us about the Christian life, as he does in 1 Timothy 4:8. Like physical fitness, spiritual fitness comes through small daily habits maintained diligently and consistently over a period of time. A daily time of prayer and Bible study, and a consistent application of the spiritual disciplines prescribed in God's Word make us spiritually fit. And the lack thereof makes us spiritually fat. —C. B. Mc.

II. The Servant's Example (1 Timothy 4:9-14)

A. Suffers Reproach (vv. 9, 10)

9, 10. This is a faithful saying, and worthy of all acceptation. For therefore we both labor and suffer reproach, because we trust in the living God, who is the Saviour of all men, specially of those that believe.

Verse 9 seems to be a formula used by Paul when he wanted to call a reader's attention to something important (see 1 Timothy 1:15; 2 Timothy 2:11; Titus 3:8). Whether it refers here to what Paul had just said in verse 8 or to what he was about to say is uncertain.

The price that Paul paid for being a committed spokesman for the gospel included strenuous *labor* that was often accompanied by *reproach* from those he sought to win. For Paul this involved physical suffering that on more than one occasion almost led to his death. He assures Timothy that as a true minister of Christ, he may very well have to face a similar set of circumstances.

Across the centuries, such has been the experience of countless numbers of Christians who have stood against false religions and violent rulers. The valorous deeds of these faithful may be hidden in the dusty pages of history, but God has not forgotten them. Furthermore, these martyrs are not limited to the past; our own times have produced their share.

The phrase *the Saviour of all men* is sometimes quoted to prove that God will save all, regardless of the lives they have lived. This kind of universalism flies in the face of many other

teachings in the Bible. It is best to understand Paul's words in the sense that God is *potentially* the Savior of all men. That potential is realized only in the lives of those who *believe* in Him.

B. Persists Despite His Youth (vv. 11, 12)

11, 12. These things command and teach. Let no man despise thy youth; but be thou an example of the believers, in word, in conversation, in charity, in spirit, in faith, in purity.

Paul urged Timothy to *teach* that which he had learned from Paul. In doing this, one of the barriers Timothy might encounter was his *youth.* Timothy was probably in his thirties at this time, not a mere teenager as some have suggested. But in a culture that had great respect for the elderly, Timothy was considered a young man. Since Christianity was still a relatively new religion at this point, many would be especially reluctant to receive it from someone as young as he. To overcome this obstacle, Timothy had to speak and act carefully and with patience. Timothy could command respect from those he taught, because he came to them with the authority vested in him by Paul (see 2 Timothy 1:6). But he still had to *earn* their respect by his own conduct. Paul proceeded to highlight some areas that Timothy needed to attend to if he was to do this.

He was to be an example in *word,* that is, in his speech. One can offend others, not only by the words he uses, but also by the tone of voice with which he speaks. Timothy was to avoid giving offense in this way. The word translated *conversation* in this verse is rendered "conduct" or "behavior" in other translations. Timothy was to embrace a life-style that reflected his Christian calling. He was to act *in charity,* or love, toward the people he was serving. Timothy was to act *in faith,* for what one believes determines in a large measure how he will behave. Timothy must not only uphold sound doctrine; he must translate sound doctrine into a godly life.

How to Say It

DIAKONOS (Greek). dee-*ah*-kuh-nawss.
EPHESUS. *Eff*-uh-sus.
EUNICE. *You*-niss.
GRAECO. *Greck*-owe.
LYSTRA. *Liss*-truh.
MACEDONIA. Mass-uh-*doe*-nee-uh.
MUTHOS (Greek). *moo*-thawss.
PRESBYTERY. *prez*-bih-tare-ee.

Finally, Paul concluded with an admonition to live a life of *purity*. This admonition was especially necessary for those who lived in the Graeco-Roman world—a culture that was saturated with all kinds of illicit sexual activities. Such an admonition is certainly needed today, because the same problems persist in our society. Unfortunately, many Christian leaders have failed to heed Paul's warning and have succumbed to impurity, thereby destroying their ministries.

FOLLOW THE PATTERN

In 1859 an American manufacturer named Ebenezer Butterick invented the first standardized paper pattern for clothing. Ten years later Butterick's factory in Brooklyn, New York, was turning out dress patterns by the thousands. He even founded a fashion magazine, *Metropolitan*, to promote pattern sales.

More than one hundred years later, seamstresses still use Butterick patterns to sew clothing. The pattern is pinned to a piece of fabric, which is then cut and sewn according to the pattern. The end product is a dress or shirt or suit that looks just like the original design.

A pattern serves as a plan or model to be followed in making something. In 1 Timothy 4:12 Paul reminds Timothy that because he is in the disciple-making business, he is to be a pattern or example for the church he is leading. In speech, in life, in love, in faith, and in purity, church leaders and mature believers should be models worthy of imitation.   —C. B. Mc.

C. Reads and Exhorts (v. 13)

13. Till I come, give attendance to reading, to exhortation, to doctrine.

Paul anticipated joining Timothy in Ephesus. Until he arrived, Timothy was to give particular attention to *reading*, which refers to the public reading of the Scriptures. Since few persons owned copies of the Scriptures in that day, it was a common practice for someone to read them aloud for the benefit of others. In the *New International Version* the pair, *to exhortation, to doctrine*, is translated "to preaching and to teaching." This accurately describes the activities to which Timothy was to devote himself.

D. Exercises His Spiritual Gift (v. 14)

14. Neglect not the gift that is in thee, which was given thee by prophecy, with the laying on of the hands of the presbytery.

This *gift* was probably not a miraculous gift. In the context, it seems to refer to those activities mentioned in verse 13: reading, preaching, and teaching.

The *laying on of the hands of the presbytery* apparently refers to Timothy's ordination by the presbytery (or "elders," as the word is rendered in some other translations). This most likely occurred in Lystra during Paul's second missionary journey. It was a public service before fellow Christians, setting Timothy apart to accompany Paul on his missionary endeavors. By reminding Timothy of that special moment in his life, Paul hoped to encourage him not to *neglect* the gift he had received at that time. Many a dispirited Christian leader has found renewed courage by reflecting on his ordination and on those men who prayerfully laid hands on him.

III. The Servant's Growth (1 Timothy 4:15, 16)

A. Obvious to Others (v. 15)

15. Meditate upon these things; give thyself wholly to them; that thy profiting may appear to all.

Paul urged Timothy to give himself *wholly*, or totally, to his growth in the ministry. A variety of obstacles could turn him aside from this path. He could be distracted by the cares of the world, or his success in the ministry could turn his head and cause him to become a victim of his own pride. In his own ministry, Paul knew just one pace—full steam ahead—and he wanted every other servant of the Lord to serve with the same level of commitment. In this he was echoing the words of the Master: "No man, having put his hand to the plow, and looking back, is fit for the kingdom of God" (Luke 9:62). If Timothy committed himself to his personal spiritual growth with a similar zeal, his *profiting* would be obvious to others. This did not imply that Timothy should call attention to his growth. Genuine maturity in Christ should speak for itself without having to be "advertised."

B. To Be Rewarded (v. 16)

16. Take heed unto thyself, and unto the doctrine; continue in them: for in doing this thou shalt both save thyself, and them that hear thee.

visual for
lesson 1

Godliness is profitable unto all things, having promise of the life that now is, and of that which is to come.
1 Timothy 4:8

The final victory belongs to the person who persists to the end. Those who turn back or are distracted by the allurements of this world will never stand in the victor's circle. But there was more at stake here than Timothy's own salvation. By his faithful teaching and preaching, he could offer others the hope of salvation that he himself enjoyed. By the same token, a leader who is unfaithful not only stumbles himself, but causes others to stumble.

Conclusion

A. Models

We are hearing much these days about the importance of children having good models as they grow up. Most children do pattern their lives after some person they look up to or even idolize. Such an individual may be a parent, an older brother or sister, or a sports hero. Children often try to imitate their heroes in the way they walk or talk, the way they play a game, or in their values. This is a perfectly healthy, acceptable thing for children to do—unless the hero turns out to be less than heroic. Unfortunately, in recent years we have seen several of these heroes betray the trust others have placed in them by becoming involved in drugs and violent crimes. This has led to the disillusionment of many young people, or worse, their own tragic downfall as they tried to imitate their fallen heroes.

Some seem to think that "role modeling" is a new concept just recently discovered by child psychologists. Of course they are wrong, for this is exactly what Paul was talking about when he encouraged Timothy to be "an example of the believers" (1 Timothy 4:12). Paul knew quite well that Christ was the perfect example. On one occasion he wrote, "Walk in love, as Christ also hath loved us" (Ephesians 5:2). To the Corinthians he wrote "Be ye followers of me, even as I am of Christ" (1 Corinthians 11:1). But Paul also recognized that people need someone close at hand "with skin on"—someone they can watch daily to see Christian principles at work. For many in Ephesus, Timothy was that person.

Timothy was not to be a one-dimensional model as some of our contemporary heroes are. He was to be a model in his correct doctrine. He was to demonstrate moral purity in his life—a quality that was rare in the lives of most people in that day. He was to show other believers how to handle rejection and persecution. He was to use the spiritual gift that God had given him, thereby encouraging other Christians to use their gifts.

What Paul wrote to Timothy applies with equal force to us. After all, we really do not have much choice about being models. Whether we like it or not or are even aware of it, others are looking to us as models. The real issue is what kind of models we will be.

B. Despised Youth

Paul was concerned that the Christians in Ephesus might reject Timothy's teaching because of his youth. Older people today sometimes have a similar problem when younger people suggest new ideas or desire to start new programs. "We've never done it that way before," they complain. They then proceed to oppose or reject the idea.

Youthfulness on the part of the messenger may be one barrier to the transmission of the gospel, but there are others. Some may reject a messenger because he speaks with a different accent. Others may have trouble accepting a message from a man who has long hair or is not dressed in a suit and tie. There is no way that a messenger can overcome all of the biases of his listeners. But when we go out as ambassadors of our Lord, we should make every accommodation we can to the sensitivities of our hearers. At the same time, we must never compromise sound doctrine in order to please others.

C. Let Us Pray

Help us, dear Father, that we may all become good and effective ministers for You. Help us to keep our lives pure, our message true, and our commitment untiring, that we may save ourselves and those who hear us. In our Master's name we pray. Amen.

D. Thought to Remember

Be a good example!

Home Daily Bible Readings

Monday, May 26—Set a Good Example (Psalm 37:1-11)

Tuesday, May 27—Be Wise (Proverbs 23:15-25)

Wednesday, May 28—Be Trustworthy (1 Corinthians 4:1-5)

Thursday, May 29—Be Humble (1 Corinthians 4:6-13)

Friday, May 30—Be Faithful As God Is Faithful (1 Thessalonians 5:23-28)

Saturday, May 31—Beware of False Doctrines (1 Timothy 4:1-5)

Sunday, June 1—Preach Christ Crucified (1 Corinthians 1:10-25)

Learning by Doing

This page contains an alternate lesson plan emphasizing learning activities. Classes desiring such student involvement will find these suggestions helpful.

Learning Goals

After this study in 1 Timothy 4, each student will be able to:

1. List the characteristics of the Christian servant as enumerated in the text and outline.

2. Give a short "biography" of Timothy, especially his relationship to Paul and the gospel.

3. Identify and commit to applying personally at least one of the ministry characteristics that needs to be developed in his or her own life.

Into the Lesson

Recruit a young man in his thirties to come to your class, preferably in Biblical garb, either to deliver a monologue on "I am Timothy" in which he answers all the following questions, or to answer these questions, which you will have prepared and given to class members for use in an "interview of Timothy." (1) "What is your religious background?" (2) "What was your first experience with Paul?" (3) "What are some of the experiences you shared with Paul as you traveled with him?" (4) "Where were you when you received this letter (1 Timothy) from Paul?" (5) "How would you characterize your relationship with Paul?" (6) "What in this letter was most surprising to you, if anything?" (7) "Why would Paul caution you about your youth? You aren't all that young!" Feel free to develop other questions that you believe to be relevant and answerable. Advise your role-player to read the lesson writer's commentary, Acts 16, and 2 Timothy 1:5, 6.

Into the Word

Though the following activity can be done on a chalkboard, it might have greater instructional effect as word strips mounted one by one on the wall or line by line on an overhead projector. Prepare a title, "THE TRUE MINISTER," for whichever format you choose, then reveal each of the following phrases, in random order, and ask your students to identify a verse that says something relevant to that phrase. (Verse numbers are given here after each phrase for your convenience.) (1) "instructs others," v. 6; (2) "avoids false doctrine," v. 7; (3) "strives for personal piety," v. 8; (4) "suffers reproach," vv. 9, 10; (5) "persists in spite of obstacles," vv. 11, 12; (6) "reads and exhorts," v. 13; (7) "exercises gifts given," v. 14; (8) "considers the life to come," v.

8; (9) "is rewarded," v. 16. As each is introduced and matched with the text, you will have opportunity to expand upon the meaning of the text.

To help define the concept of what we call a full-time *minister,* ask your class to help you prepare an acrostic for the word. On the chalkboard (or poster board or an overhead) put the letters of the word vertically. Ask students to look directly at the text to identify "what a minister does," beginning with each letter. Here is a sample of key words that may be suggested: M—models, meditates; I—ignores (fables), instructs; N—nourished; S—suffers, saves (himself); T—trusts, teaches; E—exhorts, exemplifies, exercises; R—reads, reminds. Once you complete your acrostic, ask the class, "What does a minister do that our acrostic does not represent?" List these answers, and as you do, try to fit each under one of the descriptions already given.

Paul's admonition to Timothy is full of warning. Hand out index cards with the word WARNING printed with black marker on each. Ask the adults, individually or in pairs, to write out a WARNING sign related to the text. Give them two to three minutes and then have all the signs read. Post them outside your classroom where passersby will be duly warned. Some samples: "WARNING: Bodily exercise profits less than godly exercise!" or "WARNING: Do *not* neglect your gift!"

Into Life

Most congregations have one or more "Timothys"—former members who went on to prepare for and then enter the full-time ministry. Gather names and addresses and make these available to the class. Encourage each to take one (or more) name(s) and write a short "epistle" to someone involved in ministry. Have the class look at the text once again to find ideas that might be appropriate for such a note. For example, "Be careful not to get bogged down in the subjects men love to argue" (based on v. 7), or, "Remember the trust our elders expressed in you when they set you apart for ministry" (based on v. 14), or, "Don't forget: you must *save yourself* as well as those to whom you minister" (based on v. 16). You might want to begin your note with the short explanation: "Our Bible class just finished a study of 1 Timothy 4 and we thought of you. So I am writing to. . . ."

Let's Talk It Over

The questions on this page are designed to encourage review of the lesson Scriptures and to promote discussion of the lesson by the class. The answers provided are only discussion starters. Let your class talk it over from there.

1. What are some popular myths and erroneous viewpoints that are a threat to true Christian doctrine today?

There have always been competing religious ideas that are at odds with true Christian faith and doctrine. Perhaps the most dangerous are those that have the most in common with Christianity, so that believers are ensnared without recognizing the heresy. The "health and wealth" gospel and the "name it and claim it" theology are examples. The New Age Movement, which teaches reincarnation and makes all people gods unto themselves, constitutes another threat to true doctrine. Such views seem to abound in current society, for we are living in the midst of a cultural relativity that accepts every religious claim as equally valid and has no regard for truth. This makes the warnings issued by Jesus and the apostles about being deceived highly relevant to our surroundings.

2. What are some comparisons that can be made between physical exercise and spiritual exercise?

First, it is important to do some personal study on the subject, or get some sound advice from someone else, before beginning an exercise regimen. A person can seriously injure himself if he does not follow good technique. Likewise, spiritual exercise should be undertaken with a foundation of personal Bible study, or with the counsel of someone more mature in the faith. Second, physical exercise requires personal discipline or commitment. If we exercise only when it is convenient and never exert ourselves beyond what is comfortable, the benefits of our efforts will be minimal. Engaging in spiritual exercise also requires an intentional decision backed by determined effort. The benefits of physical exercise are realized only after consistent application over time. Again this is true with spiritual exercise; over time, our character is transformed to be more like Jesus as we consistently apply spiritual disciplines. The rewards of physical exercise are both noticeable and measurable: greater strength, loss of body fat, increased circulation, and lower blood pressure, to name just a few. The rewards of spiritual exercise can be measured in terms of the fruit of the Spirit (Galatians 5:22, 23).

3. Paul calls God the "Saviour of all men" (1 Timothy 4:10). If all men will not be saved, then what does Paul mean?

Paul was not advocating a form of universalism, which teaches that everyone will eventually be saved. The message of the gospel is that salvation and eternal life are *conditional*, and a relationship with Jesus as Savior and Lord is the condition. This is the clear message of the New Testament. "Whosoever will may come" is the invitation, but everyone must come to God to be saved. Furthermore, everyone must come to God only through His Son Jesus. Jesus' sacrifice is sufficient to forgive everyone's sins; however, only those who respond in faith are forgiven. There is no other source of salvation.

4. How does a leader gain moral authority? How does that increase effectiveness?

We are always disappointed when someone we respected as a leader is convicted of a crime, is guilty of an abuse of power, or displays some moral weakness. We consider this a compromise of their integrity and a violation of the trust we have placed in them. Leaders, especially spiritual leaders, gain moral authority by living the kind of life they are advocating that others should live. If their lives bear evidence of the consistent application of God's moral standard, people will be more apt to heed what they say. Thus did Paul tell Timothy, "Take heed unto *thyself*, and unto the doctrine" (1 Timothy 4:16).

5. Paul tells Timothy to make preaching and teaching a priority. In what ways can a church protect its minister's preparation time for preaching and teaching?

Today we often lay many expectations upon our ministers. Sometimes these responsibilities can be overwhelming. Your minister may need some help reestablishing the priority of preaching and teaching. Are the members willing to help with some of the support ministries like shepherding, music, youth programming, stewardship, and other areas? Have you provided sufficient secretarial help? Do you encourage your preacher by your careful attention to and thoughtful comments on his messages? We must never forget that the minister needs to be ministered to as much as any Christian.

Christ's Servant Teaches Godliness

DEVOTIONAL READING: 1 Timothy 6:12-20.

LESSON SCRIPTURE: 1 Timothy 6:2b-21.

PRINTED TEXT: 1 Timothy 6:2b-21.

1 Timothy 6:2b-21

2b These things teach and exhort.

3 If any man teach otherwise, and consent not to wholesome words, even the words of our Lord Jesus Christ, and to the doctrine which is according to godliness;

4 He is proud, knowing nothing, but doting about questions and strifes of words, whereof cometh envy, strife, railings, evil surmisings,

5 Perverse disputings of men of corrupt minds, and destitute of the truth, supposing that gain is godliness: from such withdraw thyself.

6 But godliness with contentment is great gain.

7 For we brought nothing into this world, and it is certain we can carry nothing out.

8 And having food and raiment, let us be therewith content.

9 But they that will be rich fall into temptation and a snare, and into many foolish and hurtful lusts, which drown men in destruction and perdition.

10 For the love of money is the root of all evil: which while some coveted after, they have erred from the faith, and pierced themselves through with many sorrows.

11 But thou, O man of God, flee these things; and follow after righteousness, godliness, faith, love, patience, meekness.

12 Fight the good fight of faith, lay hold on eternal life, whereunto thou art also called, and hast professed a good profession before many witnesses.

13 I give thee charge in the sight of God, who quickeneth all things, and before Christ Jesus, who before Pontius Pilate witnessed a good confession;

14 That thou keep this commandment without spot, unrebukable, until the appearing of our Lord Jesus Christ:

15 Which in his times he shall show, who is the blessed and only Potentate, the King of kings, and Lord of lords;

16 Who only hath immortality, dwelling in the light which no man can approach unto; whom no man hath seen, nor can see: to whom be honor and power everlasting. Amen.

17 Charge them that are rich in this world, that they be not high-minded, nor trust in uncertain riches, but in the living God, who giveth us richly all things to enjoy;

18 That they do good, that they be rich in good works, ready to distribute, willing to communicate;

19 Laying up in store for themselves a good foundation against the time to come, that they may lay hold on eternal life.

20 O Timothy, keep that which is committed to thy trust, avoiding profane and vain babblings, and oppositions of science falsely so called:

21 Which some professing have erred concerning the faith. Grace be with thee. Amen.

GOLDEN TEXT: Follow after righteousness, godliness, faith, love, patience, meekness.
Fight the good fight of faith.—1 Timothy 6:11, 12.

Lesson Aims

After studying this lesson, each student should:

1. Understand that the standards for godliness are set by God, not by man, and are not subject to change.

2. Have a growing concern to manage his or her possessions in keeping with God's personal standards.

3. Be able to avoid foolish disputes over insignificant issues, and focus instead on developing true godliness.

Lesson Outline

INTRODUCTION
  A. You Can't Take It With You
  B. Lesson Background
  I. THE DANGER OF FOOLISH DISPUTES (1 Timothy 6:2b-5)
    A. Disputers Described (vv. 2b-4)
    B. Warning to Withdraw (v. 5)
  II. THE SECRET OF CONTENTMENT (1 Timothy 6:6-8)
    A. The Reward of Godliness (v. 6)
    B. Material Gain Is Temporary (v. 7)
    C. True Contentment (v. 8)
  III. THE DANGERS OF DESIRING WEALTH (1 Timothy 6:9, 10)
    A. A Deadly Snare (v. 9)
    B. The Root of All Evil (v. 10)
    How Much Land Does a Man Need?
  IV. THE PURSUIT OF TRUE WEALTH (1 Timothy 6:11-20)
    A. Seek Godliness (v. 11)
    B. Fight the Good Fight (v. 12)
    Fight One More Round
    C. Be Faithful (vv. 13-16)
    D. Teach the Rich (vv. 17-19)
    E. A Final Charge (vv. 20, 21)
CONCLUSION
    A. Whose Ruler?
    B. The Bottom Line
    C. Let Us Pray
    D. Thought to Remember

The visual for Lesson 2 focuses on what we should "flee" and "follow," according to today's lesson text. It is shown on page 351.

Introduction

A. You Can't Take It With You

Jack Benny, a popular comedian of a generation ago, was usually depicted on stage as a penny-pinching tightwad. During one performance, another character asked him what would happen to all his money when he died.

"I intend to take it with me," replied Jack.

"But, Jack," replied his questioner, "you can't take it with you."

"Well, then," said Jack, "I just won't go!"

Of course, Jack Benny eventually did go, and he did *not* take his money with him. No one can, for in the words of a portion of today's text, "We brought nothing into this world, and it is certain we can carry nothing out" (1 Timothy 6:7). Generosity with material possessions is not the only mark of godliness, but it is an important one, for one's attitude toward possessions will determine how conscientious and successful he is in developing other marks of godliness. Jesus' question should still disturb us: "What shall it profit a man, if he shall gain the whole world, and lose his own soul?" (Mark 8:36).

B. Lesson Background

The theme of last week's lesson was the example of a Christian leader; the theme of today's lesson is godliness. Several verses in our text give special attention to riches and the danger they pose to godliness. This was a much-needed emphasis, since Ephesus, where Timothy was serving, was a very wealthy city. It was located in western Asia Minor, which is now a part of modern Turkey. Ephesus was the western terminus of an important trade route that originated in the East. Trade items passed through its port to destinations all over the Mediterranean world. In addition, the famous temple of the Roman goddess Diana (also known by her Greek name Artemis) was located there. Her presence brought a booming business to the silversmiths, who made images of the goddess to sell to her worshipers (see Acts 19:24, 25).

I. The Danger of Foolish Disputes (1 Timothy 6:2b-5)

A. Disputers Described (vv. 2b-4)

2b-4. These things teach and exhort. If any man teach otherwise, and consent not to wholesome words, even the words of our Lord Jesus Christ, and to the doctrine which is according to godliness; he is proud, knowing nothing, but doting about questions and strifes of words, whereof cometh envy, strife, railings, evil surmisings.

The phrase *these things* may refer to the verses that precede it, or it could just as appropriately apply to the teachings that follow. Regardless, this was Paul's way of calling Timothy's attention to that which needed to receive priority. From Paul's words it is obvious that the church in the first century faced some of the same problems that the church faces today. Then, as today, foolish and misguided individuals disturbed the church with their false teachings. Sound *doctrine* is not an "elective" course for Christians; it is essential to the health of the church. One may hold to sound doctrine and still not display other essential marks of *godliness*, but he certainly will not possess godliness if he does not hold to sound doctrine.

The word *doting* accurately pictures the attitude of these teachers toward the viewpoints they defended. We sometimes speak of parents or grandparents *doting* on their children or grandchildren, meaning that they give them special attention that they give no one else. So it was with these false teachers; they loved to treat their "pet" theories and speculations with "tender loving care."

We do not know for certain the content of these disputes. Some of the false teachers may have come from Jewish backgrounds. Rabbis in that day loved nothing better than to engage in lengthy, intricate, hair-splitting debates. However, since the membership of the church in Ephesus was drawn largely from pagan backgrounds, this seems the more likely source of the contentions. Ultimately their source lay in human pride and ignorance (*proud, knowing nothing*), a combination that almost always spells trouble. The bitter fruit of these deliberations is seen in the list of negatives at the end of verse 4. It includes *revilings*, which renders a Greek word that is the source of our word "blasphemies."

B. Warning to Withdraw (v. 5)

5. Perverse disputings of men of corrupt minds, and destitute of the truth, supposing that gain is godliness: from such withdraw thyself.

Paul's denunciation of these false teachers is not what we would call gentle, indicating that we today must deal firmly with such teachers lest they beguile the innocent. In this verse Paul reveals their motivation: *supposing that gain is godliness.* In other words, they are in it for the money. Paul's counsel on how to deal with these charlatans is quite blunt: *from such withdraw thyself.* Many manuscripts do not contain these instructions, and thus they are omitted from most modern versions. Yet they do seem appropriate to this situation, and in keeping with Paul's instructions given elsewhere (see 2 Corinthians 6:17; 2 Thessalonians 3:6; 2 Timothy 3:5).

II. The Secret of Contentment (1 Timothy 6:6-8)

A. The Reward of Godliness (v. 6)

6. But godliness with contentment is great gain.

The godly person has learned to resist the enticements of material gain. He knows how fragile and temporary such wealth can be. He also knows that it tends to cause strife and envy. Today, more than at any time in history, we have allowed ourselves to be seduced by the idolatry of *things.* We plunge hopelessly into debt to buy items that in the end can never bring real *contentment.* People are willing to sell their bodies and even their souls to accumulate *things*, only to have these so-called treasures turn to ashes in their hands. Never has a society had so much and yet enjoyed so little.

B. Material Gain Is Temporary (v. 7)

7. For we brought nothing into this world, and it is certain we can carry nothing out.

A Brinks truck never follows a hearse to the cemetery. Nothing should be more obvious than the fact that "you can't take it with you." Yet Satan with his clever enticements keeps many blinded to this truth.

C. True Contentment (v. 8)

8. And having food and raiment, let us be therewith content.

We live in a world where many lack enough *food and raiment*, or clothing, to sustain life. Television has made us aware of people by the millions, especially children, who are starving to death. Ironically, one of the biggest health problems in our land is overeating. In a nation that God has blessed with such abundance, how can we learn to be *content* with just the necessities of life? It is vital that we keep the "big picture" in view and give eternal matters priority. Paul "learned, in whatsoever state I am, therewith to be content" (Philippians 4:11).

III. The Dangers of Desiring Wealth (1 Timothy 6:9, 10)

A. A Deadly Snare (v. 9)

9. But they that will be rich fall into temptation and a snare, and into many foolish and hurtful lusts, which drown men in destruction and perdition.

How to Say It

ARTEMIS. *Ar*-tuh-miss.
CAESAREA PHILIPPI. Sess-uh-*ree*-uh Fuh-*lip*-pie or *Fill*-uh-pie.
EPHESUS. *Eff*-uh-sus.
GNOSIS (Greek). *no*-sis.
GNOSTICISM. *Nahss*-tuh-sizz-um.
MEDITERRANEAN. *Med*-uh-tuh-*ray*-nee-un (strong accent on *ray*).

A *snare* is a trap used to catch birds or small animals. In its simplest form it is nothing but a loop of wire or a strong cord anchored to a stake, tree, or rock. Without even being aware of it, the animal passes through the loop, causing it to draw tightly about its neck or leg. As the animal tries to escape, its struggles only cause the loop to draw tighter and tighter, making the animal's escape almost impossible. The desire for wealth operates in much the same way. Without even realizing what is happening, we allow ourselves to be drawn into the loop. Once snared, we find it increasingly difficult or even impossible to break free.

The desire for money often leads to other and more destructive sins. It may cause a company to produce a shoddy product or misrepresent its value. It may cause a person to enter an agreement he has no intention of fulfilling. One may be led to steal, commit armed robbery, or traffic in illegal drugs to gain money. People will even kill for it. The desire for money or the things it will buy has become so pervasive in our society that many tend to consider this desire "normal," rather than a deadly sin.

Jesus directed some of his most pointed warnings toward the rich (Luke 6:24; Matthew 19:23-26). But as Paul indicates, the dangers are great, not just for the rich, but for those who *will*, or want to, become rich. The desire for wealth does not produce godliness, but a godlessness that will lead to ultimate *destruction*.

B. The Root of All Evil (v. 10)

10. For the love of money is the root of all evil: which while some coveted after, they have erred from the faith, and pierced themselves through with many sorrows.

The *New International Version* translates the first part of this verse more accurately as, "The love of money is a root of *all kinds of evil*." Obviously, evil arises from other sources. Sexual lust or pride have their origins in something other than a love for money. At the same time, we must recognize that greed is not totally unrelated to sexual lust, pride, and a lust for power. Where greed is present, these other sins are likely to be lurking nearby. Greed frequently leads to a departure from *the faith* and numerous other *sorrows*. The testimonies of the wealthy tell of loneliness, restlessness, and sadness, even leading in some cases to suicide.

HOW MUCH LAND DOES A MAN NEED?

The Russian author Leo Tolstoy wrote a short story that tells of a rich peasant who was never satisfied. He was consumed with the desire for more and more. One day he heard of a wonderful offer to acquire more land. For a thousand rubles he could have all the land that he could cover on foot in a day. But he had to return to the starting point by sundown or lose everything.

The man arose early and began his journey. He walked on and on, always thinking he could go just a little farther and get just a little more land. Eventually he went so far that he realized he would have to walk very fast if he was to return to the starting point in time to claim the land.

As the sun sank lower in the sky, he quickened his pace. Then he began to run. As he came within sight of the starting point, he expended his last energies, plunged over the finish line—and dropped dead.

The man's servant then took a spade and dug a grave for his master. He made it just long and wide enough to bury the man. The title of Tolstoy's story is, *How Much Land Does a Man Need?* Tolstoy concludes by saying, "Six feet from his head to his heels was all he needed."

We do well to remember that this world is not our home. The great aim of life is not found in amassing possessions. We are here to know God and to prepare to spend an eternity with Him.

—C. B. Mc.

IV. The Pursuit of True Wealth (1 Timothy 6:11-20)

A. Seek Godliness (v. 11)

11. But, thou, O man of God, flee these things; and follow after righteousness, godliness, faith, love, patience, meekness.

In the previous verses, Paul had warned against a number of vices that Timothy was not just to avoid but to *flee*. Now He spells out a number of virtues that Timothy is to *follow after*, not treating them passively, but pursuing them vigorously. These virtues are some of the attributes one must possess if he is to become an effective leader in the Lord's church. The need for such men of God is as crucial to today's church as it was in the first century.

B. Fight the Good Fight (v. 12)

12. Fight the good fight of faith, lay hold on eternal life, whereunto thou art also called, and hast professed a good profession before many witnesses.

Depicting the pursuit of eternal life as an athletic contest, Paul encourages his young comrade to enter the struggle with fervor. Timothy first entered this contest when he made a *good profession* (that is, professed or confessed his faith) *before many witnesses*. At an early date in the history of the church, one who desired to become a Christian made a public confession of his faith. We do not know what form this public statement may have taken, but it was probably a simple statement, similar to that of Peter at Caesarea Philippi: "Thou art the Christ, the Son of the living God" (Matthew 16:16). This reminder of Timothy's earlier statement of faith would give him strength for the struggles that lay ahead in his ministry. That it was made before witnesses helped him to realize that he did not stand alone.

Fight One More Round

On September 7, 1892, in New Orleans, James Corbett and John L. Sullivan fought for the world's heavyweight boxing title. Their match was the first in which the boxers used gloves rather than "bare knuckles." "Gentleman Jim" Corbett, as he was known, became the American heavyweight champion when he knocked out Sullivan in the twenty-first round. Corbett held the title for five years until 1897.

When asked later for his advice on becoming a champion, Corbett said:

"Fight one more round. When your feet are so tired that you have to shuffle back to the center of the ring, fight one more round. When your arms are so tired that you can hardly lift your hands to come on guard, fight one more round. When your nose is bleeding and your eyes are black and you are so tired that you wish your opponent would crack you in the jaw and put you to sleep, fight one more round. Remember that the man is never whipped who always fights one more round."   —C. B. Mc.

C. Be Faithful (vv. 13-16)

13, 14. I give thee charge in the sight of God, who quickeneth all things, and before Christ Jesus, who before Pontius Pilate witnessed a good confession; that thou keep this commandment without spot, unrebukable, until the appearing of our Lord Jesus Christ.

Paul presents Timothy with a solemn *charge* —solemn because it was made *in the sight of God*, the Giver of all life (to *quicken* means to give life), and *before Christ Jesus*, whose *confession* affirmed His authority. Jesus acknowledged before *Pontius Pilate* that He was a king, and that His kingdom was not of this world (John 18: 36, 37). Christians (both then and now) are called to confess Jesus without hesitation when confronted by hostility or skepticism.

Paul charges Timothy to keep the commitment he had made without compromise and in a manner that was above reproach *until the appearing of our Lord Jesus Christ.* Many in that day anticipated an early return of Christ, perhaps within a generation. Nothing in Paul's statement (or in any of his other teachings) necessarily indicates belief in an early return. The thrust of what he says here is that Timothy is to remain faithful, regardless of when Christ returns.

15, 16. Which in his times he shall show, who is the blessed and only Potentate, the King of kings, and Lord of lords; who only hath immortality, dwelling in the light which no man can approach unto; whom no man hath seen, nor can see: to whom be honor and power everlasting. Amen.

In the midst of his exhorting Timothy to faithfulness, Paul suddenly breaks into a doxology of praise to Almighty God. The word *Potentate* means Sovereign, or Ruler (something that is "potent" has power). Some have suggested that these words may have been part of a hymn used by the early Christians. Regardless of their source, Paul so lived in the presence of God that such words of praise seemed appropriate at almost any time (see 1 Timothy 1:17).

D. Teach the Rich (vv. 17-19)

17-19. Charge them that are rich in this world, that they be not high-minded, nor trust in uncertain riches, but in the living God, who giveth us richly all things to enjoy; that they do good, that they be rich in good works, ready to distribute, willing to communicate; laying up in store for themselves a good foundation against the time to come, that they may lay hold on eternal life.

visual for lesson 2

In verses 9 and 10, Paul had warned against the dangers of *riches*. Now he discusses this issue further. It is noteworthy that while Paul warns against the dangers of wealth, he does not condemn wealth as such. He condemns *trust* in wealth, which becomes a substitute for trust *in the living God*. In addition, wealth often causes people to become *high-minded*, or arrogant, toward others. Possessing wealth gives them power over people—a power that many do not hesitate to use. The Christian's perspective is that if God has blessed him with material wealth, he is to use that wealth to help others, thereby glorifying God.

Some have used verse 19 as a basis upon which to build a theology of salvation by works. Such a theology flies in the face of other Scriptures and is certainly not Paul's emphasis here. One cannot buy his way into Heaven. The point is that one who shows true generosity with his wealth is investing in spiritual riches, and will thus be better prepared to enjoy the blessings of *eternal life*.

E. A Final Charge (vv. 20, 21)

20, 21. O Timothy, keep that which is committed to thy trust, avoiding profane and vain babblings, and oppositions of science falsely so called: which some professing have erred concerning the faith. Grace be with thee. Amen.

Paul shows his deep affection for Timothy as he closes this letter with some words of wisdom and warning. These words were necessary, for some had already *erred concerning the faith* and had fallen away (see 1 Timothy 1:19, 20). The word translated *science* is actually a form of the Greek word *gnosis*, meaning "knowledge." This was not what we today would call science. It may well have been the beginnings of a heretical teaching called Gnosticism, which posed a serious threat to the church toward the close of the first century. In order to *keep* the faith that had been entrusted to him, Timothy had to live it, preach it, and defend it against its enemies. One can scarcely imagine more timely advice than this for our age—a time when all kinds of strange teachings are drawing men and women away from the true faith.

Grace be with thee. In one form or another, the blessing of *grace* appears at the close of all of Paul's epistles.

Conclusion

A. Whose Ruler?

A friend of mine once had a "fisherman's ruler." It was only about six inches long, but the markings on it indicated that it was eighteen inches long. When he used this ruler, even a good-sized minnow would be long enough legally to keep. When he came back from fishing trips, he could boast that he had caught several fish more than eighteen inches long, according to his special ruler. Of course, all of this was a joke, and we always got a good laugh out of it.

Sometimes, however, we are guilty of a similar form of deception when it comes to evaluating godliness. We convince ourselves that God's standards for morality revealed in the Bible are too limited and too narrow, and so we use our own ruler marked off according to our own standards. An unborn baby we now call a "product of conception," not a human being, and thus there is nothing wrong in destroying it. Alcoholism is now a "disease," so an alcoholic has no moral responsibility for his sad plight. Homosexuality is just an "alternative life-style," so it should no longer be condemned by obvious Biblical teachings.

Although this list could be easily enlarged, these examples demonstrate how all too often we establish our own moral values. Today's lesson emphasizes the importance of godliness. The question we must answer is simple: do we measure godliness by our ruler, or by the ruler God has given us in the Bible?

B. Let Us Pray

Thank You, dear God, for inspiring the apostle Paul to write this letter to Timothy, setting forth Your standards for godliness. As we study and meditate upon them, give us the wisdom and courage to apply them to our lives. Amen.

C. Thought to Remember

"Godliness with contentment is great gain" (1 Timothy 6:6).

Home Daily Bible Readings

Monday, June 2—Keep Above Reproach (1 Timothy 6:13-21)

Tuesday, June 3—Keep Yourself Pure (1 Timothy 5:17-22)

Wednesday, June 4—Approve That Which Is Good (Philippians 1:3-11)

Thursday, June 5—Do Not Love the World (1 John 2:12-17)

Friday, June 6—Accept the Love of Christ (Ephesians 3:14-21)

Saturday, June 7—Follow Christ's Example (John 13:12-17)

Sunday, June 8—God's Divine Power Grants Godliness (2 Peter 1:3-11)

Learning by Doing

This page contains an alternate lesson plan emphasizing learning activities.
Classes desiring such student involvement will find these suggestions helpful.

Learning Goals

After this study, each adult will:

1. Clearly define the role of contentment in godliness.

2. Identify what the godly person is to flee and what he is to follow.

Into the Lesson

Prepare for this class by cutting out some small arrows, six or eight inches long, from either paper or cardboard. On half of these write the word *flee*; on the other half, write *follow*. Place one of these on each of the seats where your class members will sit. The arrows will be used to divide your class for the first group activity. They will also be useful during the "Into Life" activity at the end of class.

Enlarge the following word find puzzle onto a chalkboard, poster board, or overhead transparency (this is also included in the student book).

```
R T C O N T E N T M E N T
I F R N O I T P U R R O C
G L L U E E S F E O Y L P
H O L O T W F C L E T R E
T V D F O H N H L T I L O
E E W L F E T L E D S E F
O O L L I I O E E W R U E
U F L T A N E E F F E N L
S O A F L L E O L I V E W
N P U R I T Y S F Y R L E
E M E E K N E S S F E T O
S L L G N I L I A R P O S
S W F L E C N A R O N G I
```

Divide your class into two groups, according to the FLEE and FOLLOW arrows. The FLEE group is to find words in the puzzle related to ungodliness; the FOLLOW group is to locate words related to godliness. There are ten of the former: *corruption, envy, evil, ignorance, lust, perversity, pride, railing, sin, strife.* There are eight in the latter: *contentment, faith, godliness, meekness, patience, purity, righteousness, truth.* List the words as they are noted, in separate columns.

Into the Word

Divide your class into three to seven work groups (depending on your class size). Give each group one (or more) of the following statements, each of which is a comment by the lesson writer. Tell all groups, "Decide if you agree or disagree with the statement, and how and to what extent it is accurate, based on the Scripture verse(s) listed with each." (1) "The church in the first century faced some of the same problems that the church faces today"— vv. 2b-4; (2) "We today must deal firmly with [false] teachers lest they beguile the innocent . . . they are in it for the money"—v. 5; (3) "Today, more than at any time in history, we have allowed ourselves to be seduced by the idolatry of *things*"—v. 6; (4) "One of the biggest health problems in our land is overeating"—v. 8; (5) "The desire for money . . . has become so pervasive in our society that we tend to consider this desire 'normal,' rather than a deadly sin"—v. 9; (6) "Greed is not totally unrelated to sexual lust, pride, and a lust for power. Where greed is present, these other sins are likely to be lurking nearby"—v. 10; (7) "Wealth often causes people to become *high-minded*, or arrogant, toward others. Possessing wealth gives them power over people—a power that many do not hesitate to use"—vv. 17-19. After groups have a few minutes to discuss, have each report in the order of the lesson text. This will give you opportunity to add explanations and insights as you choose. (A similar agree/disagree activity is included in the student book.)

Into Life

Read 1 Timothy 6:15, 16. The lesson commentary notes that these verses were possibly "part of a hymn used by the early Christians." Divide the class into the *flee* and *follow* groups used earlier. Have one group try to think of as many hymns, Christian songs, or choruses as possible that use the word *King* in the title. Have the other group do the same with the word *Lord.* Give each group five minutes to complete its list, then call time and see which team has won.

Close the class session by singing a stanza of one song or hymn from each group. Encourage class members to hum, sing, or reflect on the words of one of these songs during personal devotions this week.

Let's Talk It Over

The questions on this page are designed to encourage review of the lesson Scriptures and to promote discussion of the lesson by the class. The answers provided are only discussion starters. Let your class talk it over from there.

1. How can believers recognize the difference between true and false doctrine?

In today's text Paul is warning Timothy, and all of us, about the dangers of those who teach false doctrines. In 1 Timothy 6:3-5 Paul gives several tests for identifying false teaching. First, any teaching that does not agree with the words of Jesus is false. We must examine every teaching in light of what Jesus clearly taught, in order to judge its validity. Second, rather than producing positive, constructive results, false teaching will generally lead to arguments, quarrels, and even malicious personal attacks. Finally, Paul contends that false teachers generally have selfish motives and are promoting their cause for personal (sometimes financial) benefit.

2. What does our text teach us about refuting the error of false religions and cult groups?

To expose something as counterfeit, we must be thoroughly familiar with the genuine article. As we gain a solid understanding of all that Jesus taught, we will be equipped not only to recognize error, but to refute it with the very words of Jesus. Given Paul's counsel here, we should spend little time in arguments or quarrels, and focus on the godliness of a changed character that results from true doctrine. That level of maturity is attained through serious systematic Bible study and consistent personal discipline. It is ironic that many cult members are far better students of their false religion than Christians are of the Bible.

3. Who are those today who are seeking financial gain out of godliness?

The most notable example in recent years of one who tried to turn godliness into gold is Jim Bakker. There are undoubtedly others who have had similar motives, but have not amassed such great amounts of wealth or made such a show of it. Most people who enter the ministry have a strong sense of calling and an overwhelming desire to serve God. They are not immune, however, to the temptation to materialism and greed. Churches can help their ministers deal with these temptations by being sensitive to their material needs, and by compensating them generously, according to prevailing standards of the community.

4. How is a person of modest means who is content richer than a wealthy business tycoon who is still ambitious to get more?

The person who is content is richer because he realizes that true wealth is not a matter of money or material possessions. Contentment brings a sense of peace and freedom to the soul, and this is wealth indeed. The contented person is at peace with his circumstances, and is free to receive whatever increase he gets as a gift that should be accepted with gratitude. The contented person is also free to share more generously with others in need. The person who is ambitious for more wealth sees every request as an imposition, and sharing as a burden instead of a blessing. Often he is in a state of constant anxiety, worrying about his wealth.

5. How could we, who are so richly blessed, prove to ourselves that we could be content with food and clothing only?

Believers over the centuries have used fasting as a way of gaining mastery over physical appetites. Perhaps we could prove (or improve) our mastery over material things by doing without them for selected periods. Could we stand an entertainment fast (no television, radio, movies, stereo, etc.)? Could we go for a week with one less vehicle? After such an experience, we should be able to receive every comfort as a gift and with deeper appreciation.

6. Short of armed robbery or murder, what are some of the evils into which the lover of money may fall?

The pursuit of money can cause us to neglect other values that ought to take priority. Neglect of worship, neglect of spouse, neglect of children, or neglect of personal health for the sake of making money are all evils that carry tragic consequences. The compromise of ethical and moral standards for the sake of profit is also evil. Would you misrepresent a product, lie about a delivery date, or exaggerate quality test results for the sake of money? Would you betray a confidence, embarrass a friend, or slander someone in order to benefit your own standing? Would you steal office supplies or time from the company that employs you? The love of money creates many temptations.

Christ's Servant Endures Suffering

DEVOTIONAL READING: 2 Timothy 2:14-26.

LESSON SCRIPTURE: 2 Timothy 2:1-13.

PRINTED TEXT: 2 Timothy 2:1-13.

2 Timothy 2:1-13

1 Thou therefore, my son, be strong in the grace that is in Christ Jesus.

2 And the things that thou hast heard of me among many witnesses, the same commit thou to faithful men, who shall be able to teach others also.

3 Thou therefore endure hardness, as a good soldier of Jesus Christ.

4 No man that warreth entangleth himself with the affairs of this life; that he may please him who hath chosen him to be a soldier.

5 And if a man also strive for masteries, yet is he not crowned, except he strive lawfully.

6 The husbandman that laboreth must be first partaker of the fruits.

7 Consider what I say; and the Lord give thee understanding in all things.

8 Remember that Jesus Christ of the seed of David was raised from the dead, according to my gospel:

9 Wherein I suffer trouble, as an evildoer, even unto bonds; but the word of God is not bound.

10 Therefore I endure all things for the elect's sake, that they may also obtain the salvation which is in Christ Jesus with eternal glory.

11 It is a faithful saying: For if we be dead with him, we shall also live with him:

12 If we suffer, we shall also reign with him: if we deny him, he also will deny us:

13 If we believe not, yet he abideth faithful: he cannot deny himself.

GOLDEN TEXT: Endure hardness, as a good soldier of Jesus Christ.—2 Timothy 2:3.

Guidance for Ministry
(Lessons 1-5)

Lesson Aims

After studying this lesson, each student should:

1. Understand that being a Christian sometimes involves suffering.

2. Have a growing appreciation for those who have suffered for their faith.

3. Be better able to face the challenges to faith in the modern world.

Lesson Outline

INTRODUCTION
  A. No Pain, No Gain
  B. Lesson Background
 I. EXHORTATION TO FAITHFULNESS (2 Timothy 2:1-7)
  A. Be Strong (v. 1)
  B. Be a Teacher (v. 2)
  C. Be Tough (vv. 3, 4)
  D. Be Fair (v. 5)
  E. Be Blessed (vv. 6, 7)
    Don't Be Cheap With the Seed
II. ENCOURAGEMENT TO ACCEPT SUFFERING (2 Timothy 2:8-13)
  A. Remember Jesus Christ (v. 8)
  B. Paul's Example (vv. 9, 10)
    No Reserves, No Retreats, No Regrets
  C. A Faithful Saying (vv. 11, 12)
  D. A Faithful Savior (v. 13)
CONCLUSION
  A. Hang Tough!
  B. Passing the Baton
  C. Winning Is the Only Thing
  D. Let Us Pray
  E. Thought to Remember

The visual for Lesson 3 (shown on page 359) highlights the occupations used by Paul in our text to illustrate Christian commitment.

Introduction

A. No Pain, No Gain

One often sees the words, "No Pain, No Gain," posted on the walls of locker rooms in gymnasiums. This slogan suggests that if team members in any sport are going to accomplish anything worthwhile, they must be willing to suffer the rigors of training and practice, and the aches and sprains that are part of athletic competition.

Few athletes may recognize that this is a thoroughly Christian concept. It is a point stated clearly by the apostle Paul in our text for today's lesson. Paul knew from personal experience what he was talking about (read his personal litany of suffering in 2 Corinthians 11:24-29). With such credentials, Paul was certainly qualified to explain to Timothy the suffering he was likely to experience as a servant of the Lord. The apostle's words are just as applicable to us today.

B. Lesson Background

Paul's first imprisonment in Rome occurred in about A.D. 61. It appears that, following a two-year period under house arrest (Acts 28:16, 30, 31), he was released. Paul then resumed his travels, visiting such places as Macedonia (1 Timothy 1:3). He may even have made his way to Spain, fulfilling a desire he had expressed in Romans 15:24, 28. During this period, he wrote the letters of 1 Timothy and Titus. However, the great apostle's activities came to an abrupt end around A.D. 67, when he was seized by the emperor Nero and once more imprisoned in Rome. Conditions this time were far worse than during the first imprisonment; one of Paul's friends had difficulty even locating him (2 Timothy 1:17). The second epistle to Timothy was written during this second imprisonment, as Paul awaited his execution.

I. Exhortation to Faithfulness (2 Timothy 2:1-7)

A. Be Strong (v. 1)

1. Thou therefore, my son, be strong in the grace that is in Christ Jesus.

At the beginning of this epistle, Paul addressed Timothy as "my dearly beloved son" (1:2). In the first chapter he mentioned that he prayed for Timothy "night and day" (1:3). He reminded Timothy of his upbringing, and the faith Timothy had received from his mother and grandmother (1: 5). Paul encouraged him to stir up the gift of God that he had received (v. 6). Paul's admonition to *be strong* was based on these factors in Timothy's background.

It is difficult to overestimate the importance of early training and loving guidance in helping one develop the character necessary to stand strong in the faith. One of the reasons for the growing problems among so many of the young people in our churches today is that we have neglected to provide them the right kind of training. Until we are committed to making the sacrifices necessary to bring our children up in the faith, we cannot expect to find a solution to these problems.

Timothy had the background to stand strong in the faith, but still he needed this encouragement from Paul. Such encouragement is something that leaders in Christian work frequently need. The question, "Who ministers to the minister?" remains valid. All Christians can and should participate in this ministry.

B. Be a Teacher (v. 2)

2. And the things that thou hast heard of me among many witnesses, the same commit thou to faithful men, who shall be able to teach others also.

This charge that Paul gave to Timothy applies to all Christians. One does not have to be a Sunday school teacher in order to pass his faith along to others. Teaching is not confined to a formal classroom setting. In fact, often the most effective teaching occurs in one-on-one situations. Any Christian may find himself with ample opportunities to share his faith with family members, friends, or co-workers—opportunities that no one else has.

Timothy is instructed to impart what he has *learned* from Paul to *faithful men*, but Paul's instructions do not stop there. Timothy is to *commit* these truths to those who in turn will convey them to the next generation. The Christian faith is not like stocks, bonds, or other valuables that must be locked up in a vault to protect them. The only way that the faith can be preserved is by sharing it with others, not by locking it up.

C. Be Tough (vv. 3, 4)

3, 4. Thou therefore endure hardness, as a good soldier of Jesus Christ. No man that warreth entangleth himself with the affairs of this life; that he may please him who hath chosen him to be a soldier.

In verses 3-6, Paul uses the illustrations of a soldier, an athlete, and a farmer to impress upon Timothy his responsibilities. During his many labors for Christ, Paul had had a number of encounters with soldiers. Even as he wrote this letter from prison, he was probably guarded by one. Certain aspects of a soldier's life parallel those of a Christian. The life of a soldier is not easy, especially under combat conditions.

Military training is designed to make a soldier not only physically tough, but also mentally tough. A *good soldier* is prepared not only for the expected; he must also be prepared for the unexpected.

Being a soldier in the Lord's army is no different. As Christians most of us are not called upon to endure physical hardships, but we certainly need to be mentally tough to resist all the threats and challenges to our faith that we face almost daily. Just as it takes a soldier months of preparation and continuous training to be ready to meet the enemy, so we must be prepared to spend much time in study and in the proper spiritual disciplines, in order to be able to fend off Satan and his cohorts.

A soldier's first responsibility is to carry out the orders he is given. When he allows himself to become entangled *with the affairs of this life*, he loses his effectiveness. He cannot live as both a civilian and a soldier. In the same way, a Christian is likely to be ineffective if he allows himself to become engrossed in seeking pleasure, fame, money, or anything else that might turn his focus from the Lord. The Christian may live in this world, but his allegiance is to the kingdom "not of this world" (John 18:36).

D. Be Fair (v. 5)

5. And if a man also strive for masteries, yet is he not crowned, except he strive lawfully.

An athlete must prepare himself for competition by strenuous practice, proper diet, and adequate rest. Even such conscientious preparation, however, is not enough. If the athlete expects to receive the wreath of victory, he must compete *lawfully*, or according to the rules. Some modern athletes have attempted to enhance their prowess by the use of illegal drugs. When they are caught, they often must give up their awards, and in some cases they are barred from future competition.

In the same way, a servant of the Lord must conduct himself properly. He will not cut corners to achieve success, nor serve for gain or fame. And he certainly will not compromise the faith in order to please others.

E. Be Blessed (vv. 6, 7)

6, 7. The husbandman that laboreth must be first partaker of the fruits. Consider what I say; and the Lord give thee understanding in all things.

The third figure that Paul offers as a model for Timothy is that of a *husbandman*, or farmer. Farming has always been hard work. Furthermore, it involves numerous risks. The weather must be just right in order for the farmer to work up the soil to sow the seeds. Then the rains must come at the right time and in the right amounts. If the rains come too soon, the seed may rot in the ground. If they come too late, the plants will be stunted. If there is too little rain, the crops will be dry and parched. If it rains too much, the crops will be washed out or drowned. There are also various insects and diseases about which to be concerned.

If all goes well, however, the farmer's hard work and risk-taking will be rewarded. He is then entitled to *be first partaker of the fruits.* Just as the farmer is nourished by the crops he raises, so the Christian worker is spiritually nourished and sustained by his labor. This may refer to the joys that come to a Christian as he sees the kingdom of the Lord grow. It may also refer to the reward of Heaven that lies in his future.

DON'T BE CHEAP WITH THE SEED

In 2 Timothy 2:6, Paul compares Christian service with the intensive labor of a "husbandman" or farmer.

How do successful farmers plant seed? They do not reach into a bin, pull out an ear of corn, pop out the kernels, and plant them one by one. No, they take a double tandem truck, fill it with certified seed, back it up to a thirty-foot-wide distributor, open the slots, and pour in the seed. The rule for successful farming is: "If you're ever going to be cheap, *don't be cheap with the seed.*" One bushel of seed planted, yields (in a good year) thirty bushels of grain harvested. Thirty to one—not a bad return, if you are ready and willing to invest and work hard.

Likewise, the Christian life can yield a number of great rewards. But what we get out of it will depend in large part on what we are willing to put into it.   —C. B. Mc.

II. Encouragement to Accept Suffering (2 Timothy 2:8-13)

A. Remember Jesus Christ (v. 8)

8. Remember that Jesus Christ of the seed of David was raised from the dead, according to my gospel.

In the previous verses, Paul had tried to prepare Timothy for the suffering that he, like Paul, would probably face. Now, to provide further encouragement, the apostle challenges Timothy to *remember . . . Jesus Christ.* Jesus was of *the seed of David*; that is, he was descended from King David. Timothy, as a keen student of the Old Testament, knew some of the prophecies indicating that the Messiah would be a descendant of David. One of the most significant was this promise from God to David: "I will set up

thy seed after thee, which shall proceed out of thy bowels, and I will establish his kingdom. He shall build a house for my name, and I will establish the throne of his kingdom for ever" (2 Samuel 7:12, 13).

At the heart of the *gospel* that Paul preached were the foundational truths that Jesus had died, was buried, and *was raised from the dead.* If Timothy were to face suffering or even death for the cause of Christ, he could find assurance in the fact that his Master had also suffered and died, yet the tomb could not hold Him. Christ's resurrection gives a similar hope to every Christian.

B. Paul's Example (vv. 9, 10)

9, 10. Wherein I suffer trouble, as an evildoer, even unto bonds; but the word of God is not bound. Therefore I endure all things for the elect's sake, that they may also obtain the salvation which is in Christ Jesus with eternal glory.

Paul discusses the subject of suffering in other passages in this epistle (1:8, 12; 3:11, 12; 4:5). This does not suggest that Paul had some kind of psychotic fixation about suffering. He never implies that Christians ought to seek suffering for suffering's sake. He was trying to prepare Timothy and other Christians for the suffering that they were likely to face in the future. With the words, *I suffer trouble, as an evil doer,* Paul was not saying that he was a criminal, but that he was suffering the same punishment meted out to criminals. Suffering had been and still was a fact of life for him. Peter viewed suffering in much the same way, encouraging believers not to consider their "fiery trial" a "strange thing," but to look at the larger picture —the "exceeding joy" awaiting the faithful sufferer (1 Peter 4:12, 13).

Paul's play on words in this verse is noteworthy, and is conveyed in the English translation as well as in the original Greek. Although he has been placed in *bonds,* yet *the word of God is not bound.* When Paul had been imprisoned the first time in Rome, he continued to teach and preach (Acts 28:23-31). His opportunities to do so were greatly restricted during his second imprisonment in Rome, but even there he was not completely silenced. Though in chains, he could still write to those outside, as this epistle shows. Furthermore, the word that he had proclaimed earlier was still loose in the world, touching the lives of people all across the Roman Empire. Men may bind the messenger, but the message continues to run free!

I endure all things for the elect's sake. Again, Paul is not boasting of his efforts or exhibiting a "martyr complex." Rather, he is calling Timothy's attention to the higher purpose of suffering: that others might have the opportunity to receive *the salvation which is in Christ Jesus.* When viewed from the perspective of *eternal glory,* suffering for Christ is never in vain.

NO RESERVES, NO RETREATS, NO REGRETS

In 1904 William Borden, heir to the Borden Dairy estate, graduated from a Chicago high school as a millionaire. As a graduation present, his parents gave him a trip around the world. Traveling through Asia, the Middle East, and Europe gave Borden a burden for the world's hurting people. Writing home, he said, "I'm going to give my life to prepare for the mission field." When he made this decision, he wrote in the back of his Bible two words: "No Reserves." After graduating from Yale University, he continued to turn down high-paying job offers, entering two more words in his Bible: "No Retreats."

Following completion of his studies at Princeton Seminary, Borden sailed for China to work with Muslims there. While on the mission field, Borden was stricken with cerebral meningitis and died within a month. Many of his family and friends thought, "What a tragedy—such a promising young man, dying in a foreign place so far from home!" But shortly before he died, underneath the words "No Reserves" and "No Retreats," Borden had written in his Bible two more words: "No Regrets."

In 2 Timothy 2:3 Paul tells Timothy to "endure hardness, as a good soldier of Jesus Christ." No matter what obstacles or hardships we may face, we must serve Christ with no reserves, no retreats, and no regrets.

—C. B. Mc.

C. A Faithful Saying (vv. 11, 12)

11, 12. It is a faithful saying: For if we be dead with him, we shall also live with him: if we suffer, we shall also reign with him: if we deny him, he also will deny us.

These two verses, along with verse 13, have given rise to two different interpretations. Some see these verses as parallel to Paul's teaching in Romans 6:1-11, in which he spells out the significance of baptism. One who decides to become a Christian, figuratively dies to sin and is symbolically buried with Christ in baptism. Then, just as Christ arose from the tomb, the Christian arises from his watery grave to walk in a new life with Christ. Such an interpretation would not be foreign to Paul's thought.

Others suggest that these verses are from an ancient Christian hymn. It is true that their

visual for lesson 3

Endure hardship as a good soldier of Jesus Christ.... If anyone competes in athletics, he is not crowned unless he competes according to the rules. The hard-working farmer must be first to partake of the crops. ...May the Lord give you understanding in all things.

structure seems poetic. The theme of this hymn is that those who suffer martyrdom for Christ's sake will be made alive in Him and will reign with Him. Since in the immediate context of these verses, Paul has been discussing suffering, this second view may be preferable.

D. A Faithful Savior (v. 13)

13. If we believe not, yet he abideth faithful: he cannot deny himself.

The Scriptures affirm that God is *faithful* and that He cannot go back on His promises (1 Thessalonians 5:23, 24; 1 John 1:9). In this verse, however, the reference is to Jesus Christ. In His very character He shares in the faithfulness of His Father. Such faithfulness does not depend upon our faithfulness. Even if we become faithless, He will not *deny himself.* What He has promised us He will provide. If we remain faithful, He has promised us eternal life. If we deny Him, He has promised that He will deny us (Matthew 10:33).

Conclusion

A. Hang Tough!

When Paul wrote his second letter to Timothy, he was in prison facing execution because of his proclamation of the gospel. Paul knew that his death could present a rather serious test of Timothy's faith. Timothy, on learning of the death of his mentor and father in the faith, might be tempted to abandon his faith, or at least compromise his message so that it would be more acceptable to the Roman authorities. So Paul, instead of wallowing in self-pity, sent words of encouragement to Timothy. Simply put, his message was this: "Hang tough!"

Timothy was urged to "endure hardness." These words apply equally to us today, but we often have difficulty in accepting them. We have tried to remove the idea of hardship from our vocabulary and experience. Our culture has surrounded us with so many "creature comforts," that any suggestion that we break out of our cocoons and confront a hostile world sends shock waves through our systems.

We should also recognize that the lack of physical comforts is not the only source of suffering. Indeed, some of our most painful experiences result from "people problems." Many of us have been so conditioned to avoid anything that might be offensive to anyone, that we are afraid to speak to others about the Lord and His kingdom. Or we so compromise our Christian commitment that no one, not even a total worldling, will take offense.

We need to hear and heed Paul's challenge to Timothy. Most of us do not face situations where we are physically threatened for defending our faith, but we do live in a culture that is increasingly antagonistic to Christians who take their Bible seriously enough to try to live by its teachings. We often hear the challenge: "When the going gets tough, the tough get going!" Hang tough, Christians!

B. Passing the Baton

Many of us have watched track and field events in which runners, both individuals and members of a relay team, competed for honors. The relay teams that won not only had to have fast runners; they also had to pass the baton from one member to another quickly and smoothly. The act of passing a baton may seem simple enough, but teams spend many hours practicing it in order to do it more effectively.

Sharing our Christian faith with others is in some ways like passing the baton to the member of a relay team. Runners are often awkward at it the first time they try, but they gain experience through practice. So it is when we try to communicate our faith to non-Christians. Expert soul winners did not start out that way. They gained their ability through experience, and so must we.

Often when we try to share our faith, we fail miserably. We drop the baton. It is likely that members of a championship relay team all experienced at some time the frustration that comes from dropping the baton. But they refused to quit! They came back and practiced harder, and eventually became winners. Let us take courage and learn from them.

C. Winning Is the Only Thing

Vince Lombardi, who became a legend in football as coach of the Green Bay Packers, once remarked, "Winning isn't everything; it's the only thing!" Unfortunately, some have taken this to mean that one should do anything he can to win, ignoring whatever regulations exist. "Win at all costs" is the only standard many seem to know. Professional athletes have been fined and suspended for breaking the rules.

Prominent universities have had their athletic programs restricted or even terminated, because the pressure to win was more important than doing what was right.

What has all this to do with our lesson today? Just this: Paul went all out to achieve victory for the Lord, and he expected other Christians to do the same. For Paul, to "win at all costs" meant that he was willing to suffer any personal inconvenience or loss of freedom, if it resulted in the further progress of the gospel (1 Corinthians 9:12).

In his zeal to win, however, Paul insisted that we must "strive lawfully" (2 Timothy 2:5). At times we may be tempted to take shortcuts in our efforts to advance the Lord's kingdom. In the past, men have mistakenly used military might, clever promises, or political pressure to accomplish this. When Satan tempted Jesus, he offered Him shortcuts that would have allowed Jesus to establish His kingdom without having to confront the cross. Of course, Jesus resisted such temptations to "bargain" over His Father's will, and so should we.

D. Let Us Pray

We thank You, Father, that Christians who have lived before us were willing to suffer so that we today may enjoy the blessings of the faith. We pray that we may not have to face such suffering. But, Father, if suffering should be our lot, give us the strength to face it courageously as did Paul. In Jesus' name we pray. Amen.

E. Thought to Remember

"I reckon that the sufferings of this present time are not worthy to be compared with the glory which shall be revealed in us" (Romans 8:18).

Home Daily Bible Readings

Monday, June 9—Jesus' Suffering Foretold (Luke 9:18-27)

Tuesday, June 10—Christ Suffered for Us (1 Peter 2:18-25)

Wednesday, June 11—Suffer for Righteousness (1 Peter 3:13-22)

Thursday, June 12—Be Proud to Suffer for Christ (1 Peter 4:12-19)

Friday, June 13—Rejoice in Suffering (Colossians 1:24-29)

Saturday, June 14—Suffering Produces Character (Romans 5:1-11)

Sunday, June 15—God Is Our Comforter (2 Corinthians 1:3-11)

Learning by Doing

This page contains an alternate lesson plan emphasizing learning activities.
Classes desiring such student involvement will find these suggestions helpful.

Learning Goals

Having studied 2 Timothy 2:1-13 with the class, each adult will:

1. Be able to explain why suffering for one's faith is to be expected.

2. Be able to enumerate Paul's basic exhortations to Timothy in this text.

3. Serve Christ effectively in one's daily position or occupation.

Into the Lesson

As class members arrive, hand each a small peel-and-stick label with one of these words written on it: *soldier, athlete, farmer.* Attempt to use an equal number of each; these will be used to divide the class for a later activity.

Give class members the following list of "Reasons a Christian Should Expect and Accept Suffering." (This list is included in the student book.) Direct the class to number the reasons from one to eight as "most significant" to "least significant." (Though the list is numbered here, if you reproduce it, do not number the entries.) (1) Suffering offers an example to others. (2) Christ suffered on our behalf. (3) Suffering builds personal faith and strength. (4) Suffering can strengthen and reinforce one's witness. (5) Paul and other first-century Christians suffered. (6) Suffering is only temporal. (7) Evil resents the presence of righteousness and always reacts to it with violence. (8) Suffering is evidence that one's witness is being noticed by the world. Do not expect complete agreement in these ratings. Briefly discuss the validity of the statements and the reasons the students give for their rankings. Ask if there are other statements that should be in the list.

Into the Word

Take some time to provide the background of 2 Timothy (use the Lesson Background on page 356). Mention how much Paul's surroundings had changed since the time he wrote 1 Timothy. Note that even though Paul was facing certain death when he wrote 2 Timothy, the letter begins with a reference to "the promise of life which is in Christ Jesus" (2 Timothy 1:1).

Divide the class into three groups, according to the stickers used earlier. (If groups exceed five or six each, consider splitting each group into two other groups.) Direct each group to make two lists: how the occupation on the sticker is an appropriate description of a Christian and how it is not. If your groups need assistance with this, use the lesson writer's insights in the commentary or suggest the following: (1) *Soldier*—must submit to the authority above him/must face the possibility of violence or death; (2) *Athlete*—must train and abide by the rules/considers a healthy body a priority; (3) *Farmer*—gets to enjoy the fruit of his work/suffers from the uncertainty of weather patterns. Add this directive: "Be sure to include the similarities that the Scripture text notes." Let the groups work for five minutes or so, then add this challenge: "Now select another occupation that might offer other comparisons with being a Christian. Make the same lists you have made for the three occupations mentioned by Paul." If your groups need help, offer these suggestions: *carpenter, fireman, electrician, stonemason, physician.* After four or five minutes, ask the groups to give their responses. As comparisons are identified, list them on the chalkboard or on poster board. (The five occupations mentioned above are included in an activity in the student book. Suggest, whether they use the list as distributed or in the student books, that your students do this exercise on their own. Such consideration will keep the concepts of today's text in their minds. The "Into Life" activity is similar and can also be a part of such review and reinforcement.)

Into Life

Display the following incomplete statement: "Being a Christian is like being a _____." Ask each person to fill in his or her own vocation or position in life and then to consider the way(s) it is an appropriate symbol. For example, if one filled in *retiree*, he could say it is appropriate in that he is living on an investment made earlier, much as a Christian is living on an investment that God made earlier. If someone says *housewife*, she could make the comparison with the Christian life, since both involve caretaking, managing, and nurturing (plus a lot of hard work!). Encourage your class members to continue developing their personal parallelism this coming week. Lead in a closing prayer that each may use his or her position in life as a means of glorifying God and serving Him.

Let's Talk It Over

The questions on this page are designed to encourage review of the lesson Scriptures and to promote discussion of the lesson by the class. The answers provided are only discussion starters. Let your class talk it over from there.

1. How does grace make it easier for us to "be strong" (2 Timothy 2:1)?

Grace is often described as God's "unmerited favor" toward us, whereby He promises to forgive our sins if we trust in Jesus. After we have become Christians, God's grace continues to be effective in our lives, giving us power to do His will. Grace gives us a new relationship with God, a new status, and a new hope that should be a source of strength for us each day. It is God's grace that forgives us and restores our relationship with Him after every confession of sin (1 John 1:9). Grace also sustains us when we undergo difficult circumstances. In response to the apostle Paul's appeal for physical healing, the Lord told him, "My grace is sufficient for thee: for my strength is made perfect in weakness" (2 Corinthians 12:9). Paul learned the power of grace to overcome weakness. When we demonstrate such grace in the midst of difficult circumstances, it can be a compelling testimony to unbelievers of the difference that faith in Christ can make in our daily lives.

2. What provision have you made in your church to train up those who will be able to teach God's truth to the next generation?

Have you heard the saying, "Sunday school is the only school you never graduate from"? If the implied meaning of this is that we always have more to learn from God's Word, this is a true and positive message. If the statement is a comment upon an apparent lack of direction or progress toward some specific learning objectives, then it is a severe criticism. Unfortunately, such criticism may be deserved in many places. The writer of Hebrews complained to his readers, "For when for the time ye ought to be teachers, ye have need that one teach you again which be the first principles of the oracles of God" (Hebrews 5:12). Churches must intentionally provide opportunities to prepare those who want to teach, but there must also be Christians willing to step forward, study, and prepare themselves to be teachers. We should be quick to recognize and encourage those who do. Another way we can be obedient to training faithful teachers is by supporting Bible colleges and seminaries, and by encouraging the students who attend them. Does your church have a scholarship fund for students pursuing full-time ministry or missionary service?

3. How did the resurrection of Christ cause Paul trouble? How does it cause Christians trouble today?

The death and resurrection of Christ was central to the gospel message Paul preached (1 Corinthians 15:3, 4), although it was not always accepted by those who heard him. In Athens Paul was "mocked" because of his preaching of the resurrection (Acts 17:32). His mention of the resurrection caused an uprising within the Jewish council (Acts 23:6-8). It is the resurrection, however, by which Jesus was "declared to be the Son of God with power" (Romans 1:4). The resurrection gives hope to every believer (1 Corinthians 15:19-22). The resurrection of Jesus is a unique claim among world religions. Because of the resurrection, Christians claim preeminence for Jesus as the Son of God and the only way to God. Unbelievers react to this claim as exclusionary and intolerant—two of the greatest "sins" of this postmodern world.

4. In what circumstances might Christians be treated as evildoers in our culture?

In recent years there has been a growing contempt expressed for what is referred to as "the religious right." The Christian element of the culture remains ignored, while the media has consistently portrayed a Christianity that is either laughable, contemptible, or both. When Christians uphold and promote absolute values such as the sanctity of life or the Biblical view of marriage, those who disagree paint us as judgmental and as enemies of personal rights.

5. Does 2 Timothy 2:11 ("For if we be dead with him, we shall also live with him") mean that anyone who expects eternal life must be a martyr for Jesus? Explain.

In Galatians 2:20 Paul writes, "I am crucified with Christ: nevertheless I live; yet not I, but Christ liveth in me." Since Paul was very much alive when he wrote these words, the call to die with Christ pertains to the surrender of private desires and agendas in favor of God's will. That will *may* include a martyr's death, but it *must* include a life of faithful obedience to Jesus.

Christ's Servant Teaches Faithfulness

DEVOTIONAL READING: Philippians 4:8-20.

LESSON SCRIPTURE: 2 Timothy 4:1-18.

PRINTED TEXT: 2 Timothy 4:1-8.

2 Timothy 4:1-8

1 I charge thee therefore before God, and the Lord Jesus Christ, who shall judge the quick and the dead at his appearing and his kingdom;

2 Preach the word; be instant in season, out of season; reprove, rebuke, exhort with all longsuffering and doctrine.

3 For the time will come when they will not endure sound doctrine; but after their own lusts shall they heap to themselves teachers, having itching ears;

4 And they shall turn away their ears from the truth, and shall be turned unto fables.

5 But watch thou in all things, endure afflictions, do the work of an evangelist, make full proof of thy ministry.

6 For I am now ready to be offered, and the time of my departure is at hand.

7 I have fought a good fight, I have finished my course, I have kept the faith:

8 Henceforth there is laid up for me a crown of righteousness, which the Lord, the righteous judge, shall give me at that day: and not to me only, but unto all them also that love his appearing.

GOLDEN TEXT: I charge thee therefore before God, and the Lord Jesus Christ, who shall judge the quick and the dead at his appearing and his kingdom; preach the word; be instant in season, out of season; reprove, rebuke, exhort with all longsuffering and doctrine.—2 Timothy 4:1, 2.

Guidance for Ministry
(Lessons 1-5)

Lesson Aims

After studying this lesson, each student should:

1. Understand the importance of sound doctrine.

2. Come to accept the fact that all of us must eventually face death.

3. Appreciate Paul's example of calm acceptance and trust in God as he faced impending death.

4. Be able to share Paul's hope of eternal life.

Lesson Outline

INTRODUCTION
    A. Faithful Unto Death
    B. Lesson Background
I. PAUL'S CHARGE TO TIMOTHY (2 Timothy 4:1-5)
    A. Authority for the Charge (v. 1)
    B. Five Imperatives (v. 2)
        It Is Always Too Early to Quit
    C. Beware of False Teachers (vv. 3, 4)
    D. Endure Afflictions (v. 5)
        Deep Water
II. PAUL'S ACCEPTANCE OF DEATH (2 Timothy 4:6-8)
    A. His Departure Is at Hand (v. 6)
    B. He Has Finished His Course (v. 7)
    C. The Crown Awaits Him (v. 8)
CONCLUSION
    A. It Is Inevitable
    B. "Semper Fidelis"
    C. Let Us Pray
    D. Thought to Remember

Paul's charge to Timothy emphasized preaching the Word. So does the visual for Lesson 4. It is shown on page 367.

Introduction

A. Faithful Unto Death

When Italy's Mount Vesuvius erupted in the year A.D. 79, the volcanic ashes completely covered the nearby town of Pompeii. Centuries later the town was excavated. Among other finds, the archaeologists uncovered the remains of a Roman soldier standing erectly at his post. Though his body has long since disintegrated, the impression of his body can be seen in the lava that surrounds him. His helmet, armor, and sword are still in place just as they were when he died. Other inhabitants of the town escaped, and the soldier might have been able to escape had he been willing to leave his post. But he was willing to die rather than disobey his orders.

The apostle Paul displayed similar bravery. He was under orders to carry the gospel to the world. He was busy carrying out these orders when the persecution of Christians intensified. No doubt he could have gone into hiding and escaped the persecutors, but to do so would have meant betraying his Commander, Jesus Christ. This kind of faithfulness gave him a calm assurance as he faced death, knowing that there was a "crown of righteousness" awaiting him.

B. Lesson Background

In A.D. 64 Rome was swept by a terrible fire. The people blamed the emperor Nero for the inferno, but he accused Christians of the deed. Many of them were subsequently arrested and executed. Whether Paul was in Rome when he was captured we do not know, but in any event he was held in prison in Rome awaiting his execution.

It is likely that Timothy was in Ephesus when Paul wrote 2 Timothy. We may very well refer to the closing chapter of 2 Timothy as Paul's "farewell address." There we learn that except for Luke he was alone, everyone else having left him (2 Timothy 4:11). Some apparently had been sent away to carry out other tasks in the service of the Lord. A tragic note surrounds the absence of Demas who had forsaken Paul, "having loved this present world" (4:10). While urging Timothy to join him in Rome and to "come before winter" (v. 21), Paul also encouraged his "dearly beloved son" (1:2) to remain faithful in his ministry.

I. Paul's Charge to Timothy
(2 Timothy 4:1-5)

A. Authority for the Charge (v. 1)

1. I charge thee therefore before God, and the Lord Jesus Christ, who shall judge the quick and the dead at his appearing and his kingdom.

Paul lays upon Timothy the solemn *charge* of faithfully carrying out his ministry. This sacred responsibility is not based upon any personal whim of Paul. It is made *before God, and the Lord Jesus Christ.* Thus it is based upon the highest authority available.

Numerous passages in the New Testament declare that Jesus will *judge* the world when He returns (Matthew 25:31-33; John 5:22, 25-27;

Acts 10:40-42; Romans 2:16; 2 Corinthians 5:10). The phrase *the quick and the dead* means that both those who are alive when Jesus returns and those who have already died will be subjected to His judgment. *His appearing* refers to the return of Jesus at some point in the future. That glorious event will signal the consummation of Christ's *kingdom*. All Christians are in that kingdom now (Colossians 1:13); they look forward to its magnificent, heavenly fulfillment (2 Timothy 4:18; 2 Peter 1:10, 11).

B. Five Imperatives (v. 2)

2. Preach the word; be instant in season, out of season; reprove, rebuke, exhort with all longsuffering and doctrine.

Paul specifies five ways in which Timothy is to be faithful to his charge. The first is to *preach the word*. The proclamation of the good news is basic to the other four. This phrase may also be translated, "herald the word" or "proclaim the word publicly." A herald is under orders to proclaim a message just as he has received it. To argue, debate, or change it is not his prerogative.

The command *be instant in season, out of season* speaks of Timothy's preparation to preach the word. He should be prepared at all times to serve as God's herald. One commentator has rendered this, "Be on duty at all times." In the front lines, a soldier is not entitled to any vacations or time off. Certainly Timothy was in a combat zone, surrounded by a hostile world that seemed intent upon silencing the gospel. Every Christian worker knows from experience that there are times when people appear receptive to the gospel; at other times they are completely negative and unresponsive. "Never mind the situation," Paul advises Timothy. "Proclaim the good news at all times."

For the word *reprove*, the *New International Version* reads, "correct." This suggests that the herald is to make his proclamation clear enough so that his hearers will understand the changes that the gospel demands of those who hear it. He is also to correct any misunderstandings they might have. In a world that has little or no understanding of true Christianity, we need to exercise the same care in presenting the message of salvation.

The term *rebuke* indicates stronger action than reproving. It urges one to refute error when it arises. This was no minor matter, for elsewhere in this epistle Paul mentions a number of errors creeping in among the believers (2:14, 16-18, 23; 3:5-8).

Timothy is also to *exhort*; that is, to urge or encourage his listeners to respond to the gospel and to apply it to their lives so that changes are

---

How to Say It

DAMASCUS. Duh-*mass*-cus.
DEMAS. *Dee*-mus.
EPHESUS. *Eff*-uh-sus.
POMPEII. Pom-*pay* or Pom-*pay*-ee.
THESSALONICA. *Thess*-uh-loe-*nye*-kuh (strong accent on *nye*).
VESUVIUS. Veh-*soo*-vee-us.

obvious. To know the truth is not enough; we must live the truth for it to be effective.

Timothy is to carry out these mandates *with all longsuffering and doctrine.* He is to exercise patience with those under his care. Probably no advice to a preacher, elder, deacon, or teacher is more important than this. Some people may be slow to accept some of the obligations attached to the gospel message. There may be any number of misconceptions or assumptions that have formed a "wall" in the thinking of an individual. And so the teacher must be patient, teaching "precept upon precept; line upon line, line upon line; here a little, and there a little" (Isaiah 28:10). Furthermore, he must not neglect sound doctrine in his teaching. Many today would try to separate Christian life and doctrine, insisting that a fruitful life is more important than doctrine. But a Christian life-style must be built on a foundation of sound doctrine, else it will collapse in times of stress.

IT IS ALWAYS TOO EARLY TO QUIT

Paul instructed Timothy to carry out his ministry with "all longsuffering" (2 Timothy 4:2), even to the point of enduring "afflictions" (v. 5). Paul's words echo numerous Biblical teachings on the necessity of perseverance.

In Luke 18 Jesus tells the story about a persistent widow who finally received justice from an unjust judge because she continually confronted him with her request. Jesus told His disciples this story "to show them that they should always pray and not give up" (Luke 18:1, *New International Version*).

In Luke 11:5-8 Jesus tells about a persistent man who woke up his neighbor in the middle of the night to borrow three loaves of bread. From behind a locked door, the neighbor refused and told the man to go away. However, said Jesus, because the man persisted in his request for bread, the neighbor got up and gave him as much as he needed.

General Douglas MacArthur once observed, "Americans never quit." That should be doubly true of Christians. We should remember that in ministry, as in baseball, stopping at third base adds no more to the score than striking out at the plate.

When you are doing God's work, it is always too early to quit. Never, never give up.

—C. B. Mc.

C. Beware of False Teachers
(vv. 3, 4)

3, 4. For the time will come when they will not endure sound doctrine; but after their own lusts shall they heap to themselves teachers, having itching ears; and they shall turn away their ears from the truth, and shall be turned unto fables.

Some think that the phrase *the time will come* refers to the "last days" mentioned in 3:1. It must be recognized, however, that a lack of *sound doctrine* has always been a problem against which the church has had to struggle. Acts 20:29, 30 records Paul's words to the elders of the church at Ephesus, warning them that "of your own selves shall men arise, speaking perverse things, to draw away disciples after them."

The response described in these verses is one often encountered by God's messengers. Isaiah met with a similar reaction when his hearers, stung by his preaching, responded, "Prophesy not unto us right things, speak unto us smooth things, prophesy deceits" (Isaiah 30:10). We still have our share of church members who prefer to have their ears tickled, their wrongs approved, and their egos stroked. At least preachers today who stand for the truth do not have to fear the violent consequences their predecessors did centuries ago. Usually we don't behead preachers, exile them, or throw them to the lions; we just fire them.

D. Endure Afflictions (v. 5)

5. But watch thou in all things, endure afflictions, do the work of an evangelist, make full proof of thy ministry.

The behavior of Timothy's fickle audience is now contrasted with the behavior Paul expects from Timothy. Although Timothy may encounter stiff resistance to his preaching, he is to carry on his *ministry*, even as Paul's own ministry is coming to an end.

Watch thou in all things. The *New International Version* reads, "Keep your head in all situations." We might speak of "keeping your cool" no matter what happens. This is sound advice, especially for a church leader who finds himself surrounded on every side by frustrating problems.

The phrase *endure afflictions* repeats the instructions Paul had given earlier (2 Timothy

2:3); in fact, the same Greek word is used in both passages. Paul urges Timothy to toughen himself against the trials and tribulations, both mental and physical, that he would have to endure.

Do the work of an evangelist. The work of an evangelist is to share the good news of salvation with sinners, in order to bring them into a saving relationship with Jesus Christ. Ephesians 4:11 regards this as a specific office, including it among the tasks of apostles, prophets, and pastors and teachers. While some may indeed be specially gifted to carry on this responsibility, evangelism should also be the concern of every Christian.

DEEP WATER

It is interesting that in his instructions to Timothy, Paul says, "endure afflictions" and, "do the work of an evangelist" in the same breath (2 Timothy 4:5). Evangelism is often hard work.

Luke tells about the day that Jesus called His disciples from their boats and nets by the Sea of Galilee to follow Him. Though they had been fishing all night and had caught nothing, Jesus told them, "Put out into deep water, and let down the nets for a catch" (Luke 5:4, *New International Version*).

When these fishermen followed the Lord's instructions and cast their nets in the deep water, they caught such a large number of fish that their nets began to break. When they called for another boat to come and help them, both boats became so full of fish that they began to sink. Afterward, Jesus told Simon Peter that from then on he and his partners would catch men.

Evangelism, or "fishing for men," often requires us to launch out into deep water. Sometimes it can stretch our nets to the breaking point. Ask anyone involved in a rapidly growing church. Reaching and teaching new people is a challenge. But Jesus calls us to "do the work of an evangelist" and to join Him in the great adventure of fishing for men.   —C. B. Mc.

II. Paul's Acceptance of Death
(2 Timothy 4:6-8)

A. His Departure Is at Hand (v. 6)

6. For I am now ready to be offered, and the time of my departure is at hand.

By this time, perhaps the Roman government had set the date for Paul's execution, or God may have given him a special revelation that his death was imminent. This added an extra measure of urgency to Paul's advice to Timothy.

I am now ready to be offered. The *New International Version* renders this in a more specific manner: "I am already being poured out like a drink offering." This interesting figure calls to mind certain practices under the Old Testament Law. Numbers 15:1-10 states that when an animal was offered on the altar, a vessel of wine was poured out beside the altar as the final act of the sacrificial ceremony. Timothy, who had been taught the Old Testament by his mother and grandmother, would appreciate this striking figure. By its use here, Paul is indicating that the final act of his personal sacrifice had begun. Earlier Paul had stated that a Christian's whole life ought to be considered a "living sacrifice" (Romans 12:1). Now, even as Paul had offered his life to Jesus, he offers his death in one final expression of devotion.

B. He Has Finished His Course (v. 7)

7. I have fought a good fight, I have finished my course, I have kept the faith.

Here, as in his other writings, Paul uses language drawn from the athletic arena and from the battlefield. The phrase *fought a good fight* probably would have called the attention of Paul's readers to a wrestling or boxing match, or perhaps a contest between gladiators. The participants in these events strained every muscle to gain victory or avoid defeat. This was especially true of the gladiators' competition, where defeat might very well mean death.

In fighting the good fight, Paul had many opponents. Satan and his cohorts were the primary foes. Satan had used a variety of people and situations to try to overwhelm and frustrate Paul. His own people, the Jews, sought his life, and the Judaizers, who sought to make the laws of Moses binding upon Gentiles, created serious problems in many churches. Paul often struggled against the presence of worldliness, divisiveness, and false teaching. Even among his friends he experienced conflict (as his dispute with Barnabas about John Mark indicates) and betrayal (as the example of Demas, mentioned in verse 10 of this chapter, demonstrates). In addition to all these challenges, he constantly sought to keep himself from becoming spiritually careless and straying into the category of "castaway" (1 Corinthians 9:27).

Yet in this lifelong struggle against numerous opponents, Paul had never quit and had never given less than his best. When he affirms that he had fought the good fight, this was not bragging; this was a fact.

I have finished my course. For Paul, life was not only a fight, it was also a race to be completed. We are reminded of the language used in

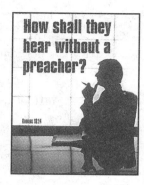

visual for lesson 4

Hebrews 12:1: "Wherefore, seeing we also are compassed about with so great a cloud of witnesses, let us lay aside every weight, and the sin which doth so easily beset us, and let us run with patience the race that is set before us." Now the apostle prepares to cross the finish line and receive the reward that is promised to all who have completed their race.

I have kept the faith. Paul may be referring to his faithful proclamation of the gospel. He had not been intimidated into silence by his foes, nor had he compromised the gospel when threatened by them. Paul may also be alluding to his own personal commitment to the Lord. After his conversion in Damascus, the Lord had called him to become an apostle to the Gentiles. He was warned that accepting this call would mean much suffering (Acts 9:15, 16). Knowing this, Paul still accepted the call, and from that point on he never looked back. Now he was on the verge of receiving "the prize of the high calling of God in Christ Jesus" (Philippians 3:14).

C. The Crown Awaits Him (v. 8)

8. Henceforth there is laid up for me a crown of righteousness, which the Lord, the righteous judge, shall give me at that day: and not to me only, but unto all them also that love his appearing.

The word rendered *crown* does not refer to the gem-encrusted symbol of royalty, but to the simple laurel wreath that was awarded to a victorious athlete. While its intrinsic worth was negligible, symbolically its value was immeasurable. The *crown of righteousness* was much more than a simple wreath of leaves. It symbolized eternal life (Revelation 2:10), and would never wither or fade, as the athlete's crown eventually would. Paul's crown came, not as a reward for his efforts, but as a gift from *the Lord, the righteous judge.*

Whereas in most races there is only one winner, in the race of life there are many winners. Paul has no exclusive claim on the crown, but it is reserved for *all them also that love his appearing*; that is, for those who look forward to Christ's return. What a triumphant note to sound in the face of certain death!

Conclusion

A. It Is Inevitable

Occasionally we hear people say that the only things certain in this life are death and taxes. For many persons this may be only a half-truth. While there are some situations under which one may never have to pay taxes, *every* person who has ever lived has had to face death.

In spite of death's inevitability, our culture has attempted to remove it from any serious consideration. Of course, we read or hear about death every day in our newspapers and on our televisions, but for most of us those incidents remain nothing more than dramas played out on the tube, remote from our snug little worlds. In previous generations people died at home, not in hospitals, and funerals were community affairs that almost everyone attended. It is not unusual today to find college-age persons who have never attended a funeral; if they have, it has probably been the funeral of a family member. Many parents have the notion that they need to shield their children from the harsh realities of life, and this includes death.

The Bible speaks often about death, and we need to help people learn the Biblical view of death. Today's lesson has given us a brief glimpse of the apostle Paul, who, after a life of faithful service to the Lord, could calmly face his approaching death without fear or remorse. For Paul, death was not the end, but was, instead, a graduation to a higher realm. His was not some vain, empty hope that one grasps in desperation as death approaches. It lay at the very foundation of the apostle's unshakable faith (1 Corinthians 15:54, 55).

B. "Semper Fidelis"

The motto of the United States Marine Corps is "Semper Fidelis," which means "Always Faithful." This might also have served as the apostle Paul's motto. Many years earlier he had made a life-changing decision. He was transformed from a persecutor of Christians to a proclaimer of Christ. The honors that he had gained as a devout Jew became nothing but garbage to him after his conversion. Once that decision had been made, he held to it without wavering for the rest of his life.

Such unwavering faithfulness seems strangely out of place in our age. We live in times that make easy compromise a virtue and waffling an art form. What was the key to Paul's tenacity? First of all, he knew what he believed, or more precisely, *whom* he believed. Second, he had clear-cut goals for his life. He knew that Christ had called him to become an apostle to the Gentiles. He knew that Christ had commissioned His followers to carry the gospel to the "uttermost part of the earth." Paul could not rest until the Lord's orders, sweeping though they were, had been carried out. Third, Paul surrounded himself with comrades who shared his views, and who, with few exceptions, remained as faithful as Paul himself.

Paul's life serves as a sterling example for us today. Like him, we must know whom we believe. This involves more than just an academic belief in Jesus; it means that we must accept Him as Lord of our lives. Like Paul, we must have definite goals in life. God has a plan for every one of us. We may have to struggle and search to find that plan, but when we have, we must pursue it with uncompromising vigor. Finally, like Paul, we need to surround ourselves with fellow Christians who will provide help and support when we are tempted to compromise or turn back. May our motto become "Semper Fidelis"—Always Faithful—to Jesus.

C. Let Us Pray

Dear Lord, help us give heed to Paul's example as we strive to live lives that will be pleasing to You. Give us knowledge and courage in this effort. Above all, help us come to life's close with a spirit of triumph. In the name of the Lord of life, even Jesus. Amen.

D. Thought to Remember

"To me to live is Christ, and to die is gain" (Philippians 1:21).

Home Daily Bible Readings

Monday, June 16—The Lord's Laws Are Forever (Psalm 119:89-96)

Tuesday, June 17—Praise the Lord for His Faithfulness (Psalm 31:19-24)

Wednesday, June 18—Faithful in Spite of Trials (2 Timothy 4:9-18)

Thursday, June 19—Be Faithful As God's Child (Romans 8:12-17)

Friday, June 20—Be Faithful Over Small Things (Luke 16:1-13)

Saturday, June 21—The Lord Requires Faithfulness (Deuteronomy 10:12-22)

Sunday, June 22—Faithfulness Will Be Rewarded (1 Peter 5:1-11)

Learning by Doing

This page contains an alternate lesson plan emphasizing learning activities.
Classes desiring such student involvement will find these suggestions helpful.

Learning Goals

With today's study, each adult will possess and express:

1. An admiration for Paul's calm and godly attitude toward death.

2. A personal hope of eternal life.

3. A desire to accept personal responsibility for a faithful life of service, incorporating all the elements of Paul's charge to Timothy in our text.

Into the Lesson

Begin today's session by asking, "Has anyone ever been to an ordination service for a minister?" It is likely that some have. Ask what those who have witnessed such a service found most impressive or meaningful about it. Point out that most ordination services include a section known as a "charge" (if you can secure a bulletin from an ordination service, it should include a place where the charge is to be presented). Ask the class to define a charge and to tell what it should include. Explain that a charge to a new minister is a challenge often delivered by someone who has been especially close to the person being ordained or has been a strong spiritual influence.

Lead into today's Scripture by pointing out that Paul gave to Timothy a "charge" in the concluding chapter of 2 Timothy—Paul's final letter to his "son" in Christ. This charge contains much that is timely for today's Christian leader.

Into the Word

Provide students with a brief review of the background of 2 Timothy, noting that Paul is writing from a Roman prison. His death is imminent—a fact that will become especially clear in today's Scripture.

Read (or have someone read) 2 Timothy 4:1-8, then divide the class into two groups. Provide each group with one of the following sets of questions for discussion. Have each group designate a reporter who will summarize the group's answers when you reconvene.

Group One: The Message. This group will focus on Paul's challenge to Timothy in verse 2 by considering the following questions:

1. What does "preach the word" mean? Is this something that all Christians can do? What are some ways that the church can fulfill this command?

2. Discuss the words "reprove, rebuke, exhort." What does each mean? Why are all of these important? What happens in a church if too much attention is given to reproof and rebuke without exhortation? What if too much attention is given to exhortation without reproof and rebuke?

Group Two: The Man. This group will discuss Paul's challenge in verse 5, using the following questions:

1. What are some "afflictions" that church leaders today may frequently "endure"? How are these similar to or different from those that Timothy would have faced?

2. What is "the work of an evangelist"? Should this be a paid position? If so, what would such a person do? Isn't evangelism something for all Christians to do? How can our church carry out this task more effectively?

Be sure to move between the groups to offer any insights or answer questions that arise. Use the material in the lesson commentary as needed. Then, after fifteen to twenty minutes, bring the groups together and have each group's reporter summarize its answers.

Into Life

Many refer to these verses as "Paul's last words," and appropriately so, as Paul realizes he is about to die. He includes both last words concerning himself and last words for his son in the faith. Give each person in the class a sheet of paper, and tell them to fold the sheet to create two columns to be headed "*I*" and "*YOU*." Direct students to put this sheet in their Bibles. During the coming week, they should review Paul's convictions about himself (for example, "I have fought a good fight" and "There is laid up for me a crown") and then write statements (under "*I*") regarding themselves and their understanding of or preparation for death. Also direct them to review Paul's challenge to Timothy and to write similar statements (under "*You*") that they would choose to leave for those working in Christ's service. A similar exercise is included in the student book.

Close the class session with a time of silent prayer. Have the students focus on thanking God for the hope we have in Christ and for the difference that it makes in our outlook on the future.

Let's Talk It Over

The questions on this page are designed to encourage review of the lesson Scriptures and to promote discussion of the lesson by the class. The answers provided are only discussion starters. Let your class talk it over from there.

1. Paul made Timothy answerable to God for the "charge" he gave him (2 Timothy 4:1). What are the tasks or responsibilities for which Christians today are answerable to God?

Those who are ordained to the ministry certainly must consider that they are responsible to God for the fulfillment of the task to which they have committed themselves. In addition, however, every Christian has received a call to service for which he will be held accountable. "Each one should use whatever gift he has received to serve others, faithfully administering God's grace in its various forms" (1 Peter 4:10, *New International Version*). God desires that all Christians bear fruit (John 15:1, 2). Jesus uses the parable of the talents (Matthew 25:14-30) to warn that an accounting of the resources and opportunities entrusted to us will be required. We may not all be ordained to full-time ministry, but every Christian has a service to contribute and a share in the commission to be the light of the world (Matthew 5:14) and to make disciples (Matthew 28:19, 20).

2. Timothy was to "reprove, rebuke, [and] exhort" (2 Timothy 4:2). Under what circumstances are you willing to receive a word of reproof or rebuke from your minister? Have you told him that?

It takes a good deal of maturity to receive reproof or rebuke without resorting to defensive measures like denial, justifying, or blaming. We are most likely to accept reproof when we agree that we have done something wrong, or failed to do something we should have done. Occasionally a minister may have to do some persuading concerning an issue, and may need to confront us directly with the sin of our actions and the consequences they have caused. The Bible is specific about confronting one in error privately as a first step, then, if necessary, before others (Matthew 18:15-17). Reproof is always easier to accept when we respect the character and the motives of the one reproving.

3. What are some of today's popular "fables" that have distracted people from true doctrine?

In Paul's day some embraced the Epicurean philosophy, which taught, "Let us eat and drink; for tomorrow we die" (1 Corinthians 15:32).

Variations of this have been adopted by many today; they believe, "You only go around once, so grab all the gusto you can!" Others would argue that you "go around" many times, for New Age philosophy has adopted the Hindu doctrine of reincarnation and other aspects of Eastern mysticism. Humanism has elevated humanity to the position of a god, and celebrates cultural diversity and the supposed relativity of all truth. Advocates of this position believe that there is no absolute truth, especially in the realm of religion. Those who hold such a position find the absolute claims of Christianity very offensive.

4. What "afflictions" are common to the ministry in today's churches? How can you help your minister cope?

Timothy was serving at the church in Ephesus when he received the letters we call 1 and 2 Timothy. During Paul's first visit to Ephesus, he became the center of a riot instigated by businessmen who opposed his preaching (Acts 19:23-41). Fortunately, that level of conflict is rare, but there are common "afflictions" severe enough that many of the ordained leave the ministry prematurely. Often ministers are underappreciated or misunderstood, both by those outside and within the church. They can be overwhelmed by a task that never appears finished and by all the demands for their time, attention, and emotional support. You can help your minister by upholding him in prayer, and by being available to serve where needed. You can also allow or encourage him to define and communicate the boundaries of what he is personally capable of doing, and what he cannot or should not do. Respect those boundaries, and make sure that he does as well.

5. Of the future benefits of faith in Christ, which are the most appealing to you? Why?

This question calls for a very personal response. Paul looked forward to the victor's crown. Others will look forward to the release from physical suffering or impairment. Freedom from want or worry may be the most appealing promise for many. Being rid of Satan's destructive temptations will bring great joy to others. You may have another favorite benefit of your future hope. There are many of them!

Christ's Servant Encourages Community

DEVOTIONAL READING: Romans 13:1-10.

LESSON SCRIPTURE: Titus 3:1-11.

PRINTED TEXT: Titus 3:1-11.

Titus 3:1-11

1 Put them in mind to be subject to principalities and powers, to obey magistrates, to be ready to every good work,

2 To speak evil of no man, to be no brawlers, but gentle, showing all meekness unto all men.

3 For we ourselves also were sometime foolish, disobedient, deceived, serving divers lusts and pleasures, living in malice and envy, hateful, and hating one another.

4 But after that the kindness and love of God our Saviour toward man appeared,

5 Not by works of righteousness which we have done, but according to his mercy he saved us, by the washing of regeneration, and renewing of the Holy Ghost;

6 Which he shed on us abundantly through Jesus Christ our Saviour;

7 That being justified by his grace, we should be made heirs according to the hope of eternal life.

8 This is a faithful saying, and these things I will that thou affirm constantly, that they which have believed in God might be careful to maintain good works. These things are good and profitable unto men.

9 But avoid foolish questions, and genealogies, and contentions, and strivings about the law; for they are unprofitable and vain.

10 A man that is a heretic, after the first and second admonition, reject;

11 Knowing that he that is such is subverted, and sinneth, being condemned of himself.

GOLDEN TEXT: I will that thou affirm constantly, that they which have believed in God might be careful to maintain good works. These things are good and profitable unto men.—Titus 3:8.

Guidance for Ministry
(Lessons 1-5)

Lesson Aims

After studying this lesson, each student should:

1. Remind himself of the "amazing grace" he has received.

2. Be able to mention some specific ways in which he will provide a model of Christian behavior.

3. Desire to avoid any issues that would distract him from serving Jesus.

Lesson Outline

INTRODUCTION
- A. An Ambassador of the King
- B. Lesson Background
- I. A CHRISTIAN'S BEHAVIOR (Titus 3:1, 2)
  - A. Toward Government (v. 1)
    Seek the Peace of the City
  - B. Toward Others (v. 2)
- II. A CHRISTIAN'S TESTIMONY (Titus 3:3-7)
  - A. Once a Slave (v. 3)
  - B. Saved Through God's Love (v. 4)
  - C. Not by Works (v. 5a)
  - D. Through Regeneration (vv. 5b, 6)
  - E. The Hope of Eternal Life (v. 7)
- III. A CHRISTIAN'S FAITHFULNESS (Titus 3:8-11)
  - A. Doing Good Works (v. 8)
  - B. Avoiding False Doctrine (vv. 9-11)
CONCLUSION
- A. A Kinder, Gentler Society
- B. The Heretic Detector
- C. Let Us Pray
- D. Thought to Remember

Introduction

A. An Ambassador of the King

J. Hudson Taylor, founder of the China Inland Mission, was once making a trip to a town in China that he had never visited before. He wanted to examine the possibility of starting a church there. On his way he came to a river, and since there was no bridge, he bargained with a man in a boat to ferry him across. Taylor paid the man and was just ready to step aboard when another man rushed forward, pushed him aside, and started to step onto the boat. Taylor, who had a quick temper, started to shove the rude intruder

into the river. Then he realized how foolish that would be. Instead, he gently tapped the man on the shoulder.

"Sir," said Taylor, "I have already hired this man and his boat to take me across the river. But if you would be willing to be my guest, I would be happy to have you accompany me."

The man was so taken aback by Taylor's offer that he questioned him as they crossed the river: "Why did you invite me aboard after I treated you so rudely?"

"Sir," Taylor replied, "I have been sent here on extremely urgent business. I am on a mission for King Jesus, and so I must behave as one of His ambassadors."

"Who is this King Jesus?" asked the man. "I have never heard of Him. What country does He rule?" That was all the invitation that the missionary needed to witness to the man about Christ. It has always been the case that even the smallest acts of love and kindness can open up opportunities for witnessing that we could never have imagined.

B. Lesson Background

The epistle to Titus was apparently written some time between Paul's release from his first imprisonment in Rome in A.D. 63 and his second imprisonment there in A.D. 67. We know little about Titus himself. Although he accompanied Paul on some of his missionary travels, Titus is not even mentioned in the book of Acts. He was heavily involved in the work in Corinth and must have served as a link between Paul and the church, keeping Paul informed of the church's condition (2 Corinthians 2:12, 13; 7:6, 13-15). In 2 Corinthians 8:23, Paul refers to Titus as "my partner and fellow helper concerning you." Titus is also mentioned in Galatians 2:1-3, in connection with Paul's stand for Christian liberty in the face of false teachers. There Paul notes that Titus was not "compelled to be circumcised" (v. 3).

At the time of the writing of Paul's letter to Titus, Titus was serving on the Mediterranean island of Crete (Titus 1:5). Paul had first visited Crete during his voyage to Rome (Acts 27:7-12), but at that point he had not had the opportunity to carry on any evangelistic work. Later, after Paul's house arrest in Rome was ended, he was able to stop at Crete and witness the work being done. When he departed, he left Titus there to continue the ministry, setting "in order the things that are wanting" and ordaining elders in every city (Titus 1:5). In Paul's final letter of 2 Timothy, Paul writes that Titus had gone "unto Dalmatia" (4:10), which is part of modern Croatia.

I. A Christian's Behavior
(Titus 3:1, 2)

A. Toward Government (v. 1)

1. Put them in mind to be subject to principalities and powers, to obey magistrates, to be ready to every good work.

Put them in mind. The Greek verb literally means, "Keep on reminding them." Christian teaching is not something that is done once and is then completed. It is an ongoing process, not only for new students who may be hearing such teaching for the first time, but also for the most mature Christians, who still need frequent reminders of their responsibilities.

The specific teaching about which Titus needed to remind the believers in Crete was their duty *to be subject to* the governing civil *powers*. Paul had addressed this subject earlier (Romans 13:1-7). Thus far, the Roman government had not severely persecuted Christians. The time was approaching, however, when the emperor Nero would unleash his fury against the Christians in Rome. Other more severe and widespread persecutions would soon follow. Paul was helping Titus to prepare the Christians in Crete for this coming storm, when they would be called upon to obey officials who were determined to destroy the church. Of course, Paul is not suggesting that Christians give absolute and unquestioning support to governments—even governments that are generally favorable to Christianity. Whenever the laws of man violate the laws of God, the Christian must choose to obey God (Acts 5:29).

In the context, the phrase *be ready to every good work* may refer specifically to a Christian's relationship to government, but it certainly has a more general application. Under all circumstances, Christians are to do good works, not only because such action is right in the eyes of God, but also because it bears witness to Christ in the eyes of unbelievers.

SEEK THE PEACE OF THE CITY

In 597 B.C. Nebuchadnezzar and his Babylonian army invaded Jerusalem. They took King Jehoiachin of Judah prisoner, plundered the temple, and carried off some ten thousand captives to spend the rest of their lives in a foreign land. Four months later, following a nearly one-thousand-mile journey, the Jewish exiles entered Babylon.

Although the Jews may have been tempted to withdraw from such a pagan society, God gave a different set of instructions to His people through the prophet Jeremiah: "Seek the peace of the city whither I have caused you to be carried away captives, and pray unto the Lord for it: for in the peace thereof shall ye have peace" (Jeremiah 29:7).

Like the Jews in Babylon, we Christians have been called to be a positive influence on our surroundings—to be in the world but not of it. Unlike them, Christians in democratic societies have a far greater opportunity to set the moral direction of their nation and its government. As citizens we choose the national, state, and local legislators who make our laws. We select the representatives, governors, mayors, and other officials who administer those laws. We set the course of our judicial system by electing judges, or those who appoint them. We should seek to use these privileges to fulfill our Lord's command to be the salt and light of our surroundings. And, as Israel was commanded, let us pray for the peace of the country where we live.

—C. B. Mc.

B. Toward Others (v. 2)

2. To speak evil of no man, to be no brawlers, but gentle, showing all meekness unto all men.

The word translated *speak evil* literally means "to blaspheme." This is language that slanders a person or intends to do him harm. Such language does not have to be false for it to be damaging. The truth deliberately told to hurt someone can be even more devastating than lies. Of course, there are exceptions to this prohibition. A person asked to give a recommendation for another, or a witness under oath in court must tell the truth, even though it may harm the individual in question. The motive behind what we speak is all-important.

The word *brawlers* suggests those who are given to physical violence. This particular word, however, may be more accurately translated "uncontentious," giving a broader meaning to Paul's admonition.

The alternative to such behavior is found in Paul's counsel to be *gentle, showing all meekness unto all men.* This summarizes what Paul has written in the first two verses of the chapter. One who is gentle and meek will subject himself to the secular powers, and he will not speak or act violently against his fellowman. The statement is doubly inclusive—*all meekness unto all men.* It is easy enough to be gentle to some people some of the time, but to everyone all of the time? Humanly speaking, this is impossible. Obedience to such a comprehensive commandment is possible only through God's grace and the renewing of the Holy Spirit. These are themes to which Paul now turns.

II. A Christian's Testimony
(Titus 3:3-7)

A. Once a Slave (v. 3)

3. For we ourselves also were sometime foolish, disobedient, deceived, serving divers lusts and pleasures, living in malice and envy, hateful, and hating one another.

The sins listed here cover a broad range, including sins against God, against self, and against other persons. The picture of a person so enmeshed in sin contrasts starkly with that of a person who has been redeemed by grace.

B. Saved Through God's Love (v. 4)

4. But after that the kindness and love of God our Saviour toward man appeared.

Even though man had fallen into the depths of sin and disgrace, God did not give up on him. He showed His matchless *kindness and love* by sending His Son into the world to die for us. "While we were yet sinners, Christ died for us" (Romans 5:8). Such love is beyond our understanding, but we are not required to understand all that occurred at the cross. We are challenged to believe and accept the fact that what happened there was done on our behalf.

C. Not by Works (v. 5a)

5a. Not by works of righteousness which we have done, but according to his mercy he saved us.

Earlier in his ministry Paul had confronted and resisted the Judaizers, who taught that Gentiles must become obedient to the Law of Moses before they could be considered true Christians. Paul emphatically rejected this doctrine, as well as any teaching that sought to advocate salvation by works rather than by grace. This is most clearly taught in Romans and Galatians. Throughout its history, however, the church has been plagued by variants of this heresy that somehow we can be saved by our good works. The good works prescribed have differed from age to age, but the idea persists that there exists a set of scales in Heaven that

---

How to Say It

CRETE. Creet.
CROATIA. Crow-*a*-shuh.
DALMATIA. Dal-*may*-shuh.
JUDAIZERS. *Joo*-deh-eye-zers.
MEDITERRANEAN. *Med*-uh-tuh-*ray*-nee-un
(strong accent on *ray*).

God will use in administering judgment. As long as the good works we do outweigh the bad, we are "in."

According to his mercy he saved us. The idea that we are saved by grace seems too good to be true. Yet that is exactly what this verse states. "Amazing Grace," we sing, and rightly so, for this is the very heart of God's wonderful plan of salvation. We are saved, not because of our worthiness, but in spite of our unworthiness.

D. Through Regeneration (vv. 5b, 6)

5b, 6. By the washing of regeneration, and renewing of the Holy Ghost; which he shed on us abundantly through Jesus Christ our Saviour.

The washing of regeneration refers to the act of Christian baptism, which brings a penitent believer into the fellowship of the church. Paul uses similar language in speaking of Christ's relationship to the church: "That he might sanctify and cleanse it with the washing of water by the word" (Ephesians 5:26). Jesus also addressed this matter in speaking to Nicodemus: "Except a man be born of water and of the Spirit, he cannot enter into the kingdom of God" (John 3:5). Baptism is much more than just a ceremony or ritual. It marks the beginning of the new life in Christ; it is a time of *regeneration*, or "rebirth" (*New International Version*).

The Holy Ghost is the One who brings about our *renewing* or rebirth when we accept Christ. Baptism is the moment at which a person receives the gift of the Spirit (Acts 2:38) and is "raised up" to "walk in newness of life" (Romans 6:4). The Spirit then becomes actively involved in the process known as sanctification, by which one who has experienced rebirth continues to grow toward maturity in Christ. That the Holy Spirit was *shed on us abundantly* may mean that God has given us a generous portion of the Holy Spirit, or that the Holy Spirit assists us in many different ways in the process of sanctification.

E. The Hope of Eternal Life (v. 7)

7. That being justified by his grace, we should be made heirs according to the hope of eternal life.

To be *justified* means that though we are guilty of many sins, we are by the grace of God declared not guilty. We thus escape the penalty of death accompanying these sins, because Christ suffered that penalty for us at the cross. Because we are justified, we have *the hope of eternal life.* Though we may be tested and sorely tempted during the storms of life, this hope serves as a guiding lighthouse, providing direction through the turbulence. When everything about us seems to be falling apart, such hope can give us the calming assurance that we need. Although we may possess little in terms of this world's goods, we have been *made heirs* of God's immeasurable riches.

III. A Christian's Faithfulness (Titus 3:8-11)

A. Doing Good Works (v. 8)

8. This is a faithful saying, and these things I will that thou affirm constantly, that they which have believed in God might be careful to maintain good works. These things are good and profitable unto men.

This is a faithful saying. Paul uses this expression several times in the Pastoral Epistles to emphasize a particular point (1 Timothy 1:15; 3:1; 4:9; 2 Timothy 2:11). In this case he is probably calling attention to the teachings he has just set forth in verses 3-7. But the expression could also apply to the words that follow, for the emphasis Paul makes on good works in the succeeding verses would certainly constitute a *faithful saying.*

To some, Paul might seem to be contradicting himself within the verses we are studying. In verse 5 he rejected "works of righteousness" as a basis of salvation, yet in this verse he urges those *which have believed in God . . . to maintain good works.* But there is really no contradiction. As Christians we do not do good works *in order* to be saved, but *because* we are saved. A person who has been saved by God's grace feels joy and gratitude toward God. It is only natural that he wants to share that joy and gratitude with others. What better way to do this than to help others in every way he can?

The good works that Paul had in mind included more than works of benevolence. They included every aspect of a noble life-style. The Christians on the island of Crete lived in a world steeped in paganism (see Paul's description of the people in Titus 1:10-13). It was important that the believers set good examples for those about them. Even though pagans might condemn the Christians for some of the beliefs that they held, it was important that the life-style of believers be above reproach. Many Christians apparently followed Paul's advice, for numerous pagan writers took note that Christians were different.

We live in an increasingly pagan world, and, like those Christians in the first century, we need to live so that those about us will observe a clear difference. One of the most serious problems the church faces today is that most non-Christians cannot tell any significant difference between the way Christians live and the way pagans live. We would do well to take heed to Paul's words. In a world that has all kinds of needs, a Christian should have no trouble finding a place where he may give his service to the glory of God. Often a good work need be nothing more than a kind word to one who is discouraged, or a listening ear to one whose heart is burdened. Any congregation should be able to recognize opportunities for its members to participate in various demonstrations of *good works.*

B. Avoiding False Doctrine (vv. 9-11)

9. But avoid foolish questions, and genealogies, and contentions, and strivings about the law; for they are unprofitable and vain.

Most of us would prefer to be positive about everything all the time, but in reality this is impossible. There is much evil and foolishness loose in the world, and there comes a time when Christians must take a stand and oppose such things.

Foolish questions refers to all kinds of fruitless discussions in which Christians sometimes engage. These deliberations are foolish, because they have nothing to do with vital issues in living the Christian life. For example, we may think of the great energy and countless hours that were wasted by many scholars in the Middle Ages, arguing about how many angels could dance on the head of a pin.

The *strivings about the law* apparently dealt with matters concerning the Jewish law. Probably most of the Christians on Crete came from Gentile backgrounds. But the Jewish influence was evidently widespread enough to create problems within the church.

The reference to *genealogies* likely reflects the fondness of many Jewish teachers for taking an individual from a list of names (such as one finds in the "begats" of Genesis) and composing a story around that person. Such efforts only served to draw attention away from the true, God-ordained purpose of Scripture.

10, 11. A man that is a heretic, after the first and second admonition, reject; knowing that he that is such is subverted, and sinneth, being condemned of himself.

Today a *heretic* is one who dissents from accepted doctrines. While the term is usually restricted to theological issues, the Greek word is broader in meaning. The *American Standard Version* translates it "a factious man," while the *New International Version* renders it "a divisive person." Thus Paul is referring not only to theological dissenters, but also to those who create controversies and quarrel over issues that are unprofitable. When these controversies disrupt the peace of the church or hinder its efforts to evangelize, then the troublemakers must be dealt with. In so doing they are to be confronted patiently and lovingly, not in some arbitrary, heavy-handed way. Such persons are to be admonished twice, according to Paul's counsel. The purpose is to save them if at all possible, not expel them. Jesus outlined a similar approach to handling situations where one brother has sinned against another (see Matthew 18:15-17).

Church discipline of this sort is, for several reasons, rarely administered today. Certainly it should not be administered arbitrarily. It should be reserved for only the most serious cases, involving one who *is subverted, and sinneth*, or, as the *New International Version* renders this "warped and sinful."

Conclusion

A. A Kinder, Gentler Society

Paul presents to Titus a picture of what a servant of Christ ought to be: a gentle person who is devoted to doing good deeds for others. At first glance the emphasis seems to be on personal virtues, which may appear to clash with the lesson title, "Christ's Servant Encourages Community." But there is no conflict here. To suppose that we can build a solid community or a stable society except upon a foundation of upright individuals is sheer folly. Our society is in serious trouble because we have ignored this obvious truth. We have spent billions of dollars trying to eliminate poverty, supposing that if we created a better environment, we would automatically create better people.

Two thousand years ago, Paul knew that the corruption that had permeated the Roman Empire could be eliminated only one way. A law-abiding citizen who shows gentleness and meekness toward his fellow men, who avoids the lusts of the flesh, and who gives himself to good works, all because he has been given new life in the Lord, will provide a firm foundation for a stable society. The same holds true today. Passing laws and appropriating money may at times be helpful, but if we truly hope to change our society for the better, we must realize that this will happen only when the hearts of people are changed.

In such a setting, the message of the gospel could not be more timely. When people experience the "washing of regeneration" and the "renewing of the Holy Ghost," then they will come to know the "hope of eternal life." What is more, they will help make ours a kinder, gentler, and safer society.

B. The Heretic Detector

The Heretic Detector was the name of a nineteenth-century religious publication. As the title indicates, the editor spent a good deal of time exposing what he believed to be heresies among church members. Perhaps a similar publication is needed today, for various heresies are rife among church members. Such a publication might appear to be carrying out the instructions that Paul gave to Titus, warning him about the dangers of heretics (Titus 3:10, 11).

However, if we engage in the practice of "heretic detection," we must exercise great caution. Across the centuries, many who were actually sincere believers were branded as heretics and severely persecuted by those who claimed to be defending the truth. Most certainly, Paul's instructions do not authorize the use of physical intimidation or violence to insure doctrinal orthodoxy. At the worst, heretics are to be cast out of the fellowship of the church, and only after patient and loving admonition. Those who shatter the tranquillity of the church must be confronted, but the purpose of such admonition is to save them, not destroy them.

C. Let Us Pray

Dear Lord, we pray for Your guidance as we try to live lives that are pleasing to You in a world that is becoming increasingly hostile to Your kingdom. Help us to walk wisely and humbly, knowing that we are saved by grace, not by our good works. Through our Master we pray. Amen.

D. Thought to Remember

Although our home is in Heaven, our present responsibilities are on earth.

Home Daily Bible Readings

Monday, June 23—Avoid Disputes (2 Timothy 2:14-19)
Tuesday, June 24—Support Faithful Workers (Philippians 4:10-20)
Wednesday, June 25—Teach Sound Doctrine (Titus 2:1-8)
Thursday, June 26—Teach With Authority (Titus 2:9-15)
Friday, June 27—Forgive One Another (2 Corinthians 2:5-11)
Saturday, June 28—All Are Guilty Under the Law (Romans 3:9-20)
Sunday, June 29—All Are Justified by God's Grace (Romans 3:21-31)

Learning by Doing

This page contains an alternate lesson plan emphasizing learning activities.
Classes desiring such student involvement will find these suggestions helpful.

Learning Goals

Having participated in a study of today's text, each adult will:

1. Briefly describe Titus, his relationship with Paul, and his ministry.

2. Use the verses in today's text to confront and counter beliefs or actions that are improper for Christians.

Into the Lesson

Find and display a map of the Mediterranean world during the time of Paul. Locate Crete (the site of Titus's ministry), along with other locations relevant to Titus's relationship to Paul and the churches in that area.

Give the class the following quiz on Titus. Indicate that it is a *True/False/Don't Know* (*T* or *F* or *DK*) quiz, with the *Don't Know* response to be given for statements for which the Scriptures provide no specific information. (Provide paper if the class does not use the student book, which includes this quiz.) (1) Paul baptized Titus; thus he could call him "mine own son" (Titus 1:4). *DK* (2) Titus is described in the book of Acts as being very active with Paul. *F, Titus is not mentioned at all in Acts.* (3) Titus was a native of Crete. *DK* (4) Paul left Titus in Crete to assist the churches there. *T, Titus 1:4, 5.* (5) Titus carried encouraging news from the Corinthian church to Paul in Macedonia. *T, 2 Corinthians 7:5, 6.* (6) Titus, being a Greek, was required to be circumcised by Paul when they visited Jerusalem. *F, Galatians 2:1-3.* (7) Paul used Titus as one of his "collectors" of an offering for some needy Christians. *T, 2 Corinthians 8:1-6.* (8) Titus was involved in taking the gospel to Dalmatia. *T, 2 Timothy 4:10.* (9) Titus was Timothy's half-brother. *DK* (10) Titus was martyred in Spain by the Roman governor there. *DK.* As you discuss these statements, your class will be provided with a good introduction to Titus.

Into the Word

Have each of the following series of statements prepared on a separate sheet or card. Ask for volunteers to stand and read them. Distribute, give a couple of minutes for your readers to review their assignments, and then have the statements read, in no particular order. Direct listeners to identify a verse in today's text that addresses in some way the comments made.

Verses are noted in parentheses after each statement. (1) "This new city leash law for dogs is stupid! No way am I going to drag my little Fifi around by the neck!" (v. 1) (2) "Those Smiths down the street are low-life scum who live like pigs. Their yard's a mess. Their car's a disgrace." (v. 2) (3) "You know this UFO thing? I'm convinced those aliens are up to no good. What about you?" (v. 9) (4) "A person's got to stand up for himself. If I've got to get angry and lash out, I'll get angry and lash out!" (v. 2) (5) "I don't need a preacher or any other authority to keep reminding me of what I'm supposed to do and not to do. I'm an adult!" (v. 1) (6) "Well, I know Johnson's come and gone regarding his faith several times. But everybody deserves one more chance. I say we make him a deacon." (v. 10) (7) "Why shouldn't I go to Heaven? I think I've been pretty good, and I've done a lot of things here at church over the years." (v. 5) (8) "If I had half of the money Elder Jones has, I'd give a lot more to the church. He ought to share some of that with the rest of us. If I had it, I would." (v. 3)

Call the students' attention to Titus 3:4-7. You may want to write these verses on the chalkboard or on erasable marker board ahead of time. Have your group read the verses together. Take a few moments to discuss the meaning of the words *regeneration*, *renewing*, and *justified*, using the lesson commentary as needed. These words convey some very crucial doctrines.

Into Life

Read Titus 3:8, in which Paul stresses the importance of *good works* in the life of a Christian. Ask, "Why are good works so important to 'maintain,' as Paul states in this verse? Is there a contradiction between this verse and verse 5?" Use the material in the lesson commentary under verse 8 to help explain the critical relationship between verses 5 and 8.

Now ask, "What are some examples of 'good works' in which we as a class could participate as a class project?" Make a list of these ideas, based on both church needs and community needs. Try to be as creative as possible. If interest in a specific project seems to surface, meet later to pursue this. Encourage the class to devote a few moments at the beginning of each class period to monitoring the progress of their project. Be sure to stick with it!

Let's Talk It Over

The questions on this page are designed to encourage review of the lesson Scriptures and to promote discussion of the lesson by the class. The answers provided are only discussion starters. Let your class talk it over from there.

1 What is wrong with Christians openly opposing a government that does not acknowledge God?

Paul says in Romans 13:1, 2, "Let every soul be subject unto the higher powers. For there is no power but of God . . . Whosoever therefore resisteth the power, resisteth the ordinance of God." The events recorded in the Bible demonstrate how God is able to use even pagan governments to accomplish His purposes. When governments demand something that is in direct opposition to the express will of God, then we must obey God's higher authority. As a general principle, however, Christians should respect authority and should be careful not to deserve a reputation as rebellious.

2. If Christians are always "gentle, showing all meekness unto all men" (Titus 3:2), won't unbelievers take advantage of us? How can we protect ourselves from this?

The people of Crete, where Titus was serving, had a reputation for being "liars, evil brutes, lazy gluttons" (Titus 1:12, *New International Version*). Paul was anxious for the Christians of Crete to overcome these habits. Showing constraint and responding gently, however, is not the same as conceding to the weaknesses of others. A gentle and restrained response can still be firm, but with a greater respect and understanding of the other's point of view. There are times when the loudest, most obnoxious, or most violent party seems to win the day, but remember: "Recompense to no man evil for evil . . . Vengeance is mine; I will repay, saith the Lord" (Romans 12:17, 19).

3. How would you respond to someone who says, "Christians think they are better than anyone else"?

It is certainly possible that among people who have struggled to apply or maintain Christian standards of right and wrong, some may yield to the temptation of spiritual pride. Most, however, will gladly attribute any moral improvement to the grace of God at work in a repentant and pliable character. Furthermore, it should take but a little effort to remind ourselves of times when we have been foolish and disobedient. Christians enjoy the blessings of forgiveness

and spiritual renewal, but those are not reasons for pride in ourselves and contempt for others. The work of God's grace in us should motivate us to compassionate sharing of the good news of forgiveness and new life available in Christ.

4. How good do we have to be to deserve Heaven and eternal life? What is our only hope of being accepted by God?

"The wages of sin is death" (Romans 6:23), and it takes only one sin to condemn us. In a permissive age when school grading is done on a curve, when guilty defendants are allowed to bargain their way out of going to prison, and when all manner of reprehensible behavior is blamed on external factors or defended in the name of personal rights, many people have a hard time understanding God's righteous standard. The standard is constant perfection. Today's obedience cannot make up for yesterday's sin. No matter how devoted or righteous we become, we can never "deserve" acceptance by God. There is no such thing as "extra credit." Our only hope is in God's mercy, and in the application of Christ's righteousness to our account. Praise God for the second half of Romans 6:23: "The gift of God is eternal life through Jesus Christ our Lord."

5. For a Christian, what is the motivation to "maintain good works" (Titus 3:8)?

Paul taught that we cannot hope to be saved by works of righteousness that we do; we must depend upon the mercy and grace of God. He knew that some would misunderstand this teaching and rush to the conclusion that good works make no difference, if God's grace freely forgives. In Romans 6 Paul is adamant that the Christian cannot presume upon God's grace by continuing in sin. Here in Titus 3:8 he commends good works because they are "profitable," or advantageous. There are many practical benefits to the good works we may do. Personally we receive a sense of peace and fulfillment, plus the admiration and goodwill of others. Others benefit from our kindness extended to them. Finally, God receives glory through our obedience: "Let your light so shine before men, that they may see your good works, and glorify your Father which is in heaven" (Matthew 5:16).

Jesus Is God's Son

DEVOTIONAL READING: Hebrews 1:6-14.

LESSON SCRIPTURE: Hebrews 1:1—3:6.

PRINTED TEXT: Hebrews 1:1-5; 3:1-6.

Hebrews 1:1-5

1 God, who at sundry times and in divers manners spake in time past unto the fathers by the prophets,

2 Hath in these last days spoken unto us by his Son, whom he hath appointed heir of all things, by whom also he made the worlds;

3 Who being the brightness of his glory, and the express image of his person, and upholding all things by the word of his power, when he had by himself purged our sins, sat down on the right hand of the Majesty on high;

4 Being made so much better than the angels, as he hath by inheritance obtained a more excellent name than they.

5 For unto which of the angels said he at any time, Thou art my Son, this day have I begotten thee? And again, I will be to him a Father, and he shall be to me a Son?

Hebrews 3:1-6

1 Wherefore, holy brethren, partakers of the heavenly calling, consider the Apostle and High Priest of our profession, Christ Jesus;

2 Who was faithful to him that appointed him, as also Moses was faithful in all his house.

3 For this man was counted worthy of more glory than Moses, inasmuch as he who hath builded the house hath more honor than the house.

4 For every house is builded by some man; but he that built all things is God.

5 And Moses verily was faithful in all his house as a servant, for a testimony of those things which were to be spoken after;

6 But Christ as a son over his own house; whose house are we, if we hold fast the confidence and the rejoicing of the hope firm unto the end.

GOLDEN TEXT: Wherefore, holy brethren, partakers of the heavenly calling, consider the Apostle and High Priest of our profession, Christ Jesus; who was faithful to him that appointed him.—Hebrews 3:1, 2.

A Call To Faithfulness
Unit 1: The Greatness of Christ
(Lessons 6-9)

Lesson Aims

After studying this lesson, students should:

1. Have a better understanding of Jesus Christ as the unique Son of God.

2. Have a desire to trust Christ more fully and to treat Him as unique.

3. Resolve to remain firm in their commitment to follow and serve Jesus.

Lesson Outline

INTRODUCTION
  A. Communicating With Ants
  B. Lesson Background
I. GOD HAS SPOKEN (Hebrews 1:1-5)
  A. Through the Prophets (v. 1)
  B. By His Son (v. 2)
  C. The Son's Relationship to the Father (v. 3)
  D. The Son's Superiority (vv. 4, 5)
    Lord, Liar, or Lunatic?
II. CHRIST, THE FAITHFUL ONE (Hebrews 3:1-6)
  A. Our High Priest (v. 1)
  B. Compared With Moses (v. 2)
  C. Superior to Moses (vv. 3-6)
    Greater Than Moses
CONCLUSION
  A. Who's in Charge?
  B. "What Think Ye of Christ?"
  C. Let Us Pray
  D. Thought to Remember

The visual for Lesson 6 (page 382) points out that Jesus is the superior revelation of God.

Introduction

A. Communicating With Ants

A Christian and an atheist were once discussing the existence of God. The atheist offered this challenge: "If there is a God like the one you claim to worship, how could He possibly communicate with us? His intellect would be so vastly superior to ours that we couldn't begin to understand Him." As they walked along, they came upon an anthill. "Look at those ants," said the atheist. "How could we possibly speak to them in a way that they could understand us? Why, we would have to become an ant and live among them to be able to speak to them!"

"You are quite correct," responded the Christian. "And that's exactly what God did. When He wanted to speak to us in a way that we could really understand, He sent His Son as a man."

B. Lesson Background

The first five lessons of this quarter, drawn from 1 and 2 Timothy and Titus, dealt with the topic, "Guidance for Ministry." Today's lesson begins a new unit entitled, "The Greatness of Christ." The four lessons in this unit are based upon the book of Hebrews.

While most of the epistles of the New Testament begin by identifying the writer, Hebrews is quite different. In fact, it begins more like a tract than a letter. The writer is not identified. This has led to abundant speculation as to the author's identity; among the most frequent suggestions are Paul, Apollos, and Barnabas. On the other hand, the destination of the book seems certain: it was directed to Jewish, or Hebrew, Christians. Exactly where these believers lived is yet another mystery. Some scholars suggest Palestine, while others believe the book was destined for Alexandria (in Egypt) or Rome.

These questions concerning the book's authorship and destination should not be allowed to detract from its great value to us. Hebrews is both a theological treatise and a guidebook for practical Christian living. Christians today can find valuable instruction and encouragement from both of these emphases.

I. God Has Spoken
(Hebrews 1:1-5)

A. Through the Prophets (v. 1)

1. God, who at sundry times and in divers manners spake in time past unto the fathers by the prophets.

A fundamental proposition of Christianity is that God has spoken to man. That revelation has come at *sundry*, or various, *times*. Since the writer was addressing Hebrew Christians who were familiar with the Old Testament, they would immediately call to mind how God spoke to Adam in the Garden of Eden, how He called Abram from Ur of the Chaldees, and how He thundered forth His commandments on Mount Sinai. They would also remember how He spoke to kings, such as David and Solomon, and to *prophets*. The writer focuses particularly on the prophets, perhaps because of their role in preparing for the coming of God's Son into the world.

The phrase *in divers manners* highlights the many different ways in which God spoke to man. Sometimes He spoke in audible words. On other occasions He spoke through dreams, visions, signs, or miracles. Expressions found in the prophets, such as "Thus saith the Lord," "The word of the Lord came unto me," and "Hear the word of the Lord," indicate that God communicated more directly to these specially chosen spokesmen.

B. By His Son (v. 2)

2. Hath in these last days spoken unto us by his Son, whom he hath appointed heir of all things, by whom also he made the worlds.

Frequently the Bible divides the history of God's redemptive work into two segments of time. The Old Testament era is considered the "former days," or, as in Hebrews 1:1, "time past." The New Testament era, beginning with Christ's first coming and ending with His return, is viewed as the *last days.* For other uses of this phrase and similar terminology in the New Testament, see Acts 2:16, 17; 1 Corinthians 10:11; Hebrews 9:26; 1 Peter 1:20; and 1 John 2:18. While we do not know when Jesus will return, we know that when He does come back, He will judge the nations (Matthew 25:31-33). We need to pay special attention to God's message for the *last days,* just as the Hebrew Christians did. This message is found only in *his Son.*

Jesus has been *appointed heir of all things.* We are not to think of this inheritance as one in which the father must die before the son can receive it. This expression indicates the close relationship of the divine Son to the heavenly Father. One aspect of this kinship is the Son's participation in the creation of *all things.* This doctrine is stated, not only in this verse, but in other New Testament passages as well (see John 1:1-3; 1 Corinthians 8:6; and Colossians 1:14-17). *All things* will one day come under the dominion of Jesus, and then of the Father, when Jesus returns (1 Corinthians 15:24-28).

The term *worlds* apparently refers to the extent of God's creation through all time and space; thus, some versions render this "universe" (*New International Version, Today's English Version*).

C. The Son's Relationship to the Father (v. 3)

3. Who being the brightness of his glory, and the express image of his person, and upholding all things by the word of his power, when he had by himself purged our sins, sat down on the right hand of the Majesty on high.

The writer expresses the Son's relationship to the Father through a series of striking phrases. The Son is *the brightness of his glory.* Translators have struggled to find a way to express this idea in English. The *New International Version* uses, "the radiance of God's glory"; the *Revised Standard Version,* "He reflects the glory of God"; and the *New English Bible,* "the effulgence of God's splendour." John 1:14 tells us, "And the Word was made flesh, and dwelt among us, (and we beheld his glory, the glory as of the only begotten of the Father,) full of grace and truth."

The unity of the Father and the Son is also expressed in the next phrase: *the express image of his person.* The Son "bears the very stamp of his [God's] nature" (*Revised Standard Version*), much as the image on a coin is an exact match of the image on the die. Hear Jesus' own words: "He that hath seen me hath seen the Father" (John 14:9).

Furthermore, the Son is described as *upholding all things by the word of his power.* To the Colossians Paul wrote that through Jesus, "all things consist" (Colossians 1:17). He is not only our Creator; He is also our Sustainer.

The writer then notes that as majestic as the Son was, He humbled Himself and came to earth for the purpose of purging, or cleansing us of, *our sins.* Once this was accomplished by His death on the cross, He returned to His proper place *on the right hand of the Majesty on high.*

D. The Son's Superiority (vv. 4, 5)

4. Being made so much better than the angels, as he hath by inheritance obtained a more excellent name than they.

Angels were held in high regard because of their participation in the giving of the Law at Mount Sinai (Acts 7:53; Galatians 3:19). They also enjoyed a prominent place in first-century Jewish thought. Yet the Son was superior to any of the angels, not only because of His obedience in carrying out God's will in human redemption, but because of the *more excellent name* he had *obtained* as a result. The verses following this one show this name to be *Son.*

How to Say It

ALEXANDRIA. Al-iks-*ann*-dree-uh.
APOLLOS. Uh-*pahl*-us.
CHALDEES. Kal-*deez*.
DARIUS. Duh-*rye*-us.
MACEDONIANS. Mass-uh-*doe*-nee-unz.
MELCHIZEDEK. Mel-*kizz*-ih-deck.

5. For unto which of the angels said he at any time, Thou art my Son, this day have I begotten thee? And again, I will be to him a Father, and he shall be to me a Son?

The writer of Hebrews quotes from the Psalms five times in this first chapter, one of those occurring in this verse. The book of Psalms was the hymnbook used in the Jewish synagogue. When Jews became Christians, they no doubt continued to use these songs in their worship. Thus, these quotations would be quite familiar to them. This one is taken from Psalm 2:7.

The second half of the verse contains a quotation from 2 Samuel 7:13, 14, where God promised that David's seed would be given an everlasting kingdom. The writer of Hebrews declares its fulfillment to be in Jesus Christ. When God proclaimed Jesus to be His *Son*, this relationship made Christ superior to the angels, for no angel was ever addressed by such a distinguished title.

LORD, LIAR, OR LUNATIC?

The great confession that sets a Christian apart from adherents to other religions is that *Jesus Christ is God's Son.* Throughout history, unbelievers have attempted to portray Jesus as something other than the Son of God. Many will readily accept Him as a good man or a great teacher, but not as God in the flesh. The problem with such an approach is that Jesus never left any of those options open to us.

In John 5:25 and 11:4, Jesus referred to Himself as "the Son of God." Jesus said that to know Him is to know God (John 8:19). He said that to believe in Him is to believe in God (John 14:1). He said that to receive Him is to receive God (Mark 9:37). When Philip said, "Show us the Father," Jesus answered, "He that hath seen me hath seen the Father" (John 14:9). Jesus continually equated a person's attitude toward Him with that person's attitude toward God.

The noted author C. S. Lewis stated the issue of Jesus' identity and our response to it in these powerful words:

> A man who was merely a man and said the sort of things Jesus said would not be a great moral teacher. He would either be a lunatic—on a level with the man who says he is a poached egg—or else he would be the Devil of Hell. You must make your choice. Either this man was, and is, the Son of God: or else a madman or something worse. You can shut Him up for a fool, you can spit at Him and kill Him as a demon; or you can fall at His feet and call Him Lord and God. But let us not come up with any patronizing nonsense about His being a great human teacher. He has not left that open to us. He did not intend to.
> —C. B. Mc.

II. Christ, the Faithful One
(Hebrews 3:1-6)

A. Our High Priest (v. 1)

1. Wherefore, holy brethren, partakers of the heavenly calling, consider the Apostle and High Priest of our profession, Christ Jesus.

In the closing verses of chapter 1, the writer of Hebrews uses other Old Testament quotations to support his argument that Christ is superior to the angels. His readers needed such teaching, because chapter 2 indicates that they were becoming somewhat lax in their commitment. He urges them to "give the more earnest heed to the things which we have heard, lest at any time we should let them slip" (v. 1). He warns about neglecting "so great salvation" (v. 3). In the later verses of chapter 2, he deals with the incarnation of Christ, explaining that He had to be "made a little lower than the angels," so that He could suffer and die for our sins (v. 9). Thus He became our "merciful and faithful high priest" (v. 17).

The designation of Christians as *holy brethren* is based on the fact that they have been made holy by the sacrificial death of Christ. This special relationship to Jesus makes them more than mere followers. They are His brothers! As such they are *partakers of the heavenly calling.* Our calling is heavenly, because it originated in Heaven and because it directs people to Heaven.

The word *Apostle* means "one who is sent." We think immediately of the twelve whom Jesus sent out with the good news of the gospel, and of the apostle Paul, who was sent to the Gentiles with the same message. Here it is applied to *Christ Jesus,* whom God sent into the world to bring salvation (see John 20:21).

Christ is also our *High Priest.* Under the Law of Moses, the high priest was an intermediary between God and man. One of his duties was to offer sacrifices to God, as prescribed by the Law. The Jewish readers of this letter would be quite

visual for
lesson 6

familiar with this function. According to the Law, the high priest had to come from the tribe of Levi. This meant that Jesus, since He was from the tribe of Judah, was not eligible to be a priest under the Old Covenant (Hebrews 7:14). However, Jesus' priesthood was not of the Levitical order, but of the order of Melchizedek —that mysterious priest who appears rather suddenly in the Old Testament to bless Abram after his victorious return from battle (Genesis 14:17-20).

B. Compared With Moses (v. 2)

2. Who was faithful to him that appointed him, as also Moses was faithful in all his house.

The faithfulness of any person is measured by how completely he carries out the responsibilities that are assigned to him. In these verses the writer compares the faithfulness of Moses with the faithfulness of Christ. Moses was declared by God to be faithful (Numbers 12:7). That faithfulness was displayed in the two capacities that the writer of Hebrews has already applied to Christ: an apostle and a priest. Moses was an apostle, in the sense that he was sent by God to free the Israelites from Egyptian bondage. Moses also on occasion acted as a priest (see Psalm 99:6), interceding before God for the people. It is true that Aaron, Moses' brother, was actually designated high priest. Yet, when Aaron consented to the making of the golden calf, it was Moses who stood before God and pleaded for the people (Exodus 32:31, 32).

Jesus functioned in these same two capacities, as the writer has already observed. He was an apostle, sent from God to bring the message of salvation to the world. He was also a High Priest, who offered Himself as the perfect sacrifice for the sins of all.

C. Superior to Moses (vv. 3-6)

3, 4. For this man was counted worthy of more glory than Moses, inasmuch as he who hath builded the house hath more honor than the house. For every house is builded by some man; but he that built all things is God.

Although both Moses and Christ were faithful in their duties, Christ was *counted worthy of more glory than Moses.* The writer uses the analogy of a *house* and its builder to make his point. A house that is both sturdy and attractive is worthy of honor, but the individual who built the sturdiness and attractiveness into the house is worthy of *more honor.*

The writer then applies his analogy to Moses and Christ. The *house* that Moses built was the Hebrew nation. At the same time, Moses himself was a part of that house and a part of the vast universe created by *God,* who *built all things.* Earlier we learned that Jesus the Son participated with God in the creative process. Thus, as the builder, He is superior to others (such as Moses) who are but a part of what has been built.

5, 6. And Moses verily was faithful in all his house as a servant, for a testimony of those things which were to be spoken after; but Christ as a son over his own house; whose house are we, if we hold fast the confidence and the rejoicing of the hope firm unto the end.

Here the writer continues to affirm the superiority of Jesus to Moses. Moses was but a *servant,* who ministered *in all his* (God's) *house.* Note the prepositions used in the verse: Moses served *in* God's house, but Christ is *over* His house. As a faithful servant, Moses was given considerable responsibility, yet he still remained only a servant. Christ is superior because *as a son* He exercises authority over the servants in God's house. Moses' ministry also constituted *a testimony of those things which were to be spoken after.* His ministry prepared for the superior ministry of Jesus and His New Covenant.

With the phrase *whose house are we,* the writer now turns from his theological discussion to its practical implications. Christians are now Christ's *house.* They became His house by believing in and obeying Him. That relationship, however, is conditional. It is in force only as long as *we hold fast* in our faith and obedience. This warning is in harmony with the major thrust of the book of Hebrews, which is to encourage Jewish Christians to stand firm in their new faith. To abandon Christianity is to abandon the *rejoicing* that their *hope* has given them.

GREATER THAN MOSES

He was raised in Pharaoh's house. He was quite possibly an adopted heir to the throne of Egypt. He was skilled in all the arts, languages, and wisdom of one of the greatest nations of the ancient world.

Yet God had an even greater calling for Moses. He led an entire nation out of bondage in Egypt. He became recognized as Israel's lawgiver, having received God's commandments on Mount Sinai.

When the day of God's deliverance of Israel came, He sent Moses to confront Pharaoh. At that time Egypt was at the pinnacle of her power and influence in world affairs. Pharaoh himself was considered to be a god by his own people. No other king could match the strength of his armies or the size of his wealth. When Moses strode into Pharaoh's court to demand, "Let my people go," he was confronting the most powerful man on earth.

Without question, Moses was the greatest figure of the Old Testament. Yet Moses was only a man—an extraordinary man for certain, but still just a man. In these latter days, the writer of Hebrews says, God has spoken to us through one far greater than Moses: His own Son. With power, wisdom, and glory far beyond that of Moses, Jesus came to make of us what no one else could: a people prepared to live for eternity with God.   —C. B. Mc.

Conclusion

A. Who's in Charge?

One of the decisive battles of the ancient world pitted Alexander the Great against Darius III, king of Persia. Darius had carefully selected the site of the battle—a level plain where he could most effectively deploy his cavalry and chariots. His forces outnumbered Alexander and the Macedonians four or five to one. To strike fear into the hearts of his enemies, Darius lined up his troops in battle array the night before the battle and reviewed them by torchlight. The ploy seemed to work, for Alexander's generals came to him in a state of panic. Some urged a retreat, while others suggested a surprise attack by night. To the latter suggestion Alexander supposedly replied, "I will not steal a victory. We will attack in the morning as planned!" The generals were then sent back to their tents for a good night's rest, reassured that they had nothing to fear. The attack was carried out according to plan, and it was so successful that Darius fled from the field of battle. The Macedonians were victorious because they knew Alexander was in charge. They had enough confidence in him to follow him wherever he led them.

In today's world, the forces of evil seem to be winning against the forces of good on every hand. We seem to be hopelessly outnumbered. But before we flee in panic, we need to stop and consider who is in charge. Christ Jesus is our Commander and *He* is in charge! This lesson has reminded us that He "made the worlds," and that He upholds "all things by the word of his power." Knowing this, we can enter the fray with renewed confidence, realizing that temporary losses will not alter the fact that the ultimate victory belongs to Him and His kingdom.

B. "What Think Ye of Christ?"

The writer of Hebrews makes a concerted effort to convey what the deity of Christ encompasses. He does this, not by offering a detailed analysis of Christ's deity, but by demonstrating that Jesus is far superior to any other means by which God has communicated with mankind.

First of all, we are told that Christ is God's final revelation to us. In earlier ages God spoke through the prophets, whose messages prepared the way for Jesus to come as the culmination of all that they prophesied. We are told also that Jesus is the "heir of all things." Furthermore, Christ was active with God in the creation of all things, and with God He continues to sustain all things.

Second, as noble as the angels might be, Christ is superior to them. He is our great High Priest. Through His death on the cross, He has purged us of our sins, and now He sits at the right hand of God the Father in a position of absolute authority.

On one occasion Jesus asked the Pharisees, "What think ye of Christ? whose son is he?" (Matthew 22:42). Unwilling to acknowledge Him as the Son of God, they refused to answer. We, on the other hand, are quick to affirm with our lips that Jesus is God's Son, but with our actions we often deny what our lips affirm. The Pharisees stood condemned for their unbelief. Can we expect to escape similar condemnation for our practical denial?

C. Let Us Pray

Gracious God and heavenly Father, teach us how to understand and accept the fact that Jesus Christ is Your divine Son, that He is the Creator and Sustainer of the universe, that He has made atonement for our sins, and that even now He sits at Your right hand. In His blessed name we now pray. Amen.

D. Thought to Remember

If Christ is not divine, every impulse of the Christian world falls to a lower octave.

      —Henry Ward Beecher

Home Daily Bible Readings

Monday, June 30—Christ Is Eternal (Hebrews 1:5-14)

Tuesday, July 1—Christ Is Over All (Ephesians 1:15-23)

Wednesday, July 2—Christ Has Come From God (John 8:37-42)

Thursday, July 3—Christ, Son and Heir of God (Galatians 4:1-7)

Friday, July 4—To Know Christ Is to Know God (John 14:1-11)

Saturday, July 5—Confess Christ As God's Son (1 John 4:13-21)

Sunday, July 6—Christ Has Come to Do God's Will (John 6:35-40)

Learning by Doing

This page contains an alternate lesson plan emphasizing learning activities.
Classes desiring such student involvement will find these suggestions helpful.

Learning Goals

By completing this study, students will:

1. Be able to enumerate at least five examples of the ways God spoke in the Old Testament era.

2. Explain how Jesus the Son is superior to Moses.

3. Refute specific doctrinal errors, using today's text.

Into the Lesson

Read (or have someone read) Hebrews 1:1, 2. Ask, "What is the primary subject and verb of this sentence?" Point out that even though Hebrews 1:1-5 constitutes one sentence in our text (as it appears in the *King James Version*), its main thought is: "God hath spoken!"

As class members arrive, give name tags, each with a string attached so it can be worn around the neck, to the first ten. Each tag should have one of the following names written boldly on it: ADAM, BALAAM, BELSHAZZAR, DAVID, ELI-JAH, EZEKIEL, ISAIAH, JOB, JONAH, MOSES. On the back of each tag, print the appropriate Scripture reference (given here in the order of the above names): Genesis 3:8-13; Numbers 22:21-31; Daniel 5:1-6; 2 Samuel 12:1-14; 1 Kings 19:1-13; Ezekiel 1:1-3; Isaiah 1:1 and 6:1-8; Job 38:1-3; Jonah 1:17, 3:1, and 4:6-11; Exodus 3:1-6. Make the suggestion that each "necklace wearer" check the text that is related to his or her Bible character.

As class begins, ask each "character" to stand and say, "I am ____, and God spoke to me." Respond by asking, "And how did God speak to you, ____?" Let the person respond, using insights drawn from his Scripture passage, and move immediately to the next. After all ten speak in this manner, read Hebrews 1:1, 2 and highlight the primary truth: "God hath spoken!" Ask the class to note other Old Testament examples of how God spoke to others. Also, you might like to use the lesson writer's story, "Communicating With Ants" (p. 380), as a transition to the fact that God ultimately and decisively spoke through His Son.

Into the Word

Have each person write the letters of the alphabet vertically on a sheet of paper. Direct them to find or determine words from today's text for as many letters as they can, which will complete the sentence, "*Jesus is . . .*" (They should not expect to find something for every letter.) Give them ten to fifteen minutes and then compare/contrast lists orally. The following may be found in the text (verse numbers indicated): Apostle (3:1), Begotten (1:5), Better (1:4), Christ (3:1), Faithful (3:2), Glory (1:3), Heir (1:2), Image (1:3), Majesty (1:3), Priest (3:1), Son (1:2), Worthy (3:3). Such designations as the following might be used (based on words or thoughts in the text): Excellent (1:4), Householder (3:6), Inheritor (1:4), Upholder (1:3), Word (1:2), Creator (1:2). Expect and accept other reasonable ones.

The epistle to the Hebrews combats many of the false doctrines of the first century and of centuries since. Give your class members each of the following "statements of faith," and ask them to refute them from today's texts. Appropriate verses are given following each statement. (1) "Jesus was only a man, adopted by God to be His Son" (1:2-4). (2) "Jesus did not do exactly what God wanted Him to do" (3:2). (3) "God may have created us, but if He did, He left us on our own to resolve the issues of life" (1:1, 2). (4) "Angels, as heavenly spiritual beings, deserve reverence and honor" (1:4, 5). (5) "All of creation can be explained in purely scientific terms" (1:2). (6) "Moses, as a prophet of God, should be counted equal with Jesus, another of God's prophets" (3:3). (7) "I accepted Christ years ago—that's all that really affects how I stand with God" (3:6). As each statement is discussed and refuted, note or ask how these doctrines have been or are promoted today. For example, the sixth statement expresses a belief of the Muslim faith, but it is wholly contrary to what Hebrews 3:3, 4 says.

Into Life

Give a copy of the preceding seven false doctrinal statements to each student. Challenge them to consider one a day throughout the next week and, in their personal Bible study, to find other key Bible verses that refute the statement. Suggest that they look for expressions of any of these erroneous ideas in what they read or hear this week.

Have the class members form a prayer circle, and close with a prayer of thanks that "God hath spoken" through His Son Jesus.

Let's Talk It Over

The questions on this page are designed to encourage review of the lesson Scriptures and to promote discussion of the lesson by the class. The answers provided are only discussion starters. Let your class talk it over from there.

1. What are some of the truths that God revealed about Himself through the prophets of old?

During Old Testament times, the religious speculations of the cultures surrounding Israel led to far different beliefs from those of the Israelites. This was because of God's revelation of Himself through history and through the word of the prophets. The Israelites knew, for example, that God is one; there is not a host of deities. The one God is the all-powerful Creator. He is all-knowing, and aware of the details of our lives. God is also faithful and completely righteous in His dealings. He is a God of covenants, and He is explicit about His expectations and about the way of life that leads to blessing. He is a God of love and mercy, and He desires to bless His people. He makes provision for forgiveness; but He is also a God of justice, and He will punish unconfessed and unforgiven sin.

2. How was the revelation of God in Jesus an improvement over the prophets?

Jesus was the "express image" of God, as Hebrews 1:3 says. What Jesus did to reveal God to us may be likened to the difference between a blind man having someone describe a rainbow to him, or being given sight to see it himself for the first time. Jesus furnished us a living illustration of how God relates to us and to this world. He showed us what righteousness looks like and how perfect love behaves. Jesus taught us of the inclusive nature of God's love as He reached out to tax collectors and other sinners. He taught us of God's willingness to forgive as He pardoned the woman taken in adultery and the thief on the cross. He demonstrated God's power over the elements as He calmed the storm, walked upon the water, and caused a fig tree to wither. His living illustration was worth more than all the words of all the prophets.

3. Why is it important that the Son is superior to angels or other heavenly beings?

An angel would have nothing to give on behalf of human sin that could make any difference. If Jesus were just one of thousands of angels, or if He were any part of the created order, He would not be unique, and His intercession for us would not satisfy the claims of

justice against sinners. The fact that Jesus was and is the unique and perfect Son of God—God incarnate—and that He laid down His life for unworthy sinners, makes His story not just *good* news but *great* news.

4. Jesus had apostles. Why is He described in our text as "the Apostle" (Hebrews 3:1)?

The term "apostle" literally means "one who is sent." Certainly Jesus sent out apostles to spread the news of His kingdom. We must remember that the Son also was sent by the Father with a mission to fulfill for our sake (John 4:34). At one point He prayed that He might not be required to die, but then surrendered to the Father's will (Matthew 26:39). On the cross He indicated that His mission was complete when He uttered the words, "It is finished" (John 19:30). Jesus was unwavering in His obedience to the will of the Father and to the mission that He had been sent to earth to accomplish.

5. How does Jesus function as a high priest?

A priest ministered on behalf of God to the people and on behalf of the people to God. (The Latin word for priest, *pontifex*, means "bridge builder.") Jesus (as we noted in an earlier question) was the "express image" of God. His name was Immanuel: God with us (Matthew 1:23). He was the Word that was in the beginning with God and was God, but "was made flesh, and dwelt among us" (John 1:1, 2, 14). He said of Himself, "He that hath seen me hath seen the Father" (John 14:9). But not only did Jesus represent God to people; He also intervened to represent people to God. He took the burden of our sins upon Himself, and He accepted the punishment we deserve (Isaiah 53:5). He not only offered the sacrifice for our sins; He *was* the sacrifice for our sins. When Jesus died, the veil that separated the Holy of Holies from the Holy Place in the temple at Jerusalem was torn from top to bottom. This miracle demonstrated that because of Jesus we now have open access to God. Jesus accomplished what no other high priest could. Even now, "he is able also to save them to the uttermost that come unto God by him, seeing he ever liveth to make intercession for them" (Hebrews 7:25).

Jesus Is Savior

DEVOTIONAL READING: Hebrews 10:1-10.

LESSON SCRIPTURE: Hebrews 2.

PRINTED TEXT: Hebrews 2:5-11, 14-18.

Hebrews 2:5-11, 14-18

5 For unto the angels hath he not put in subjection the world to come, whereof we speak.

6 But one in a certain place testified, saying, What is man, that thou art mindful of him? or the son of man, that thou visitest him?

7 Thou madest him a little lower than the angels; thou crownedst him with glory and honor, and didst set him over the works of thy hands:

8 Thou hast put all things in subjection under his feet. For in that he put all in subjection under him, he left nothing that is not put under him. But now we see not yet all things put under him.

9 But we see Jesus, who was made a little lower than the angels for the suffering of death, crowned with glory and honor; that he by the grace of God should taste death for every man.

10 For it became him, for whom are all things, and by whom are all things, in bringing many sons unto glory, to make the captain of their salvation perfect through sufferings.

11 For both he that sanctifieth and they who are sanctified are all of one: for which cause he is not ashamed to call them brethren.

. . . .

14 Forasmuch then as the children are partakers of flesh and blood, he also himself likewise took part of the same; that through death he might destroy him that had the power of death, that is, the devil;

15 And deliver them, who through fear of death were all their lifetime subject to bondage.

16 For verily he took not on him the nature of angels; but he took on him the seed of Abraham.

17 Wherefore in all things it behooved him to be made like unto his brethren, that he might be a merciful and faithful high priest in things pertaining to God, to make reconciliation for the sins of the people.

18 For in that he himself hath suffered being tempted, he is able to succor them that are tempted.

Jul
13

GOLDEN TEXT: We see Jesus, who was made a little lower than the angels for the suffering of death, crowned with glory and honor; that he by the grace of God should taste death for every man.—Hebrews 2:9.

A Call to Faithfulness
Unit 1: The Greatness of Christ
(Lessons 6-9)

Lesson Aims

As a result of studying this lesson, students should:

1. Appreciate more fully what Christ did to obtain their salvation.

2. Realize that only in Christ can a person become what he was created to be.

3. Use to the fullest the resources they have in Christ for living the Christian life.

Lesson Outline

INTRODUCTION
    A. The Murdered Hostage
    B. Lesson Background
I. THE HUMILIATION AND EXALTATION OF CHRIST
    (Hebrews 2:5-11)
    A. God's Purpose for Man (vv. 5-8)
    B. God's Purpose Realized in Christ (v. 9)
    C. Christ Made Perfect by Suffering (v. 10)
    D. We Become Christ's Brethren (v. 11)
II. THE INCARNATION OF CHRIST (Hebrews 2:14-18)
    A. Delivering Us From Bondage (vv. 14, 15)
       Prisoners No More
    B. Becoming Our High Priest (vv. 16, 17)
    C. Helping Us in Our Temptations (v. 18)
CONCLUSION
    A. He Has Been There
    B. Jesus Saves
    C. Let Us Pray
    D. Thought to Remember

The visual for Lesson 7 (seen on page 390) illustrates today's golden text: Jesus suffered, but is now "crowned with glory and honor."

Introduction

A. The Murdered Hostage

According to an old story set in the Middle Ages, a powerful duke rebelled against his king. To advance his cause, the duke took scores of the king's loyal followers hostage. When he threatened to execute them one by one if the king did not give in to his demands, the king sent his son to investigate the situation. When the prince arrived at the duke's castle, he saw how desperate the situation was and offered himself as a hostage if the duke would set the

other hostages free. The duke agreed and the exchange was made, but as soon as he had the prince in his custody, he murdered him.

In a way this resembles how God dealt with us through His Son. We were captives of sin, held hostage by Satan. When God's Son came to rescue us, the forces of evil seized Him and put Him to death. At this point, however, what happened to God's Son and what happened to the prince are noticeably different. Jesus was able to break the shackles of death and rise again. Now He sits at the right hand of God, making intercession for us.

B. Lesson Background

In the previous lesson we learned that angels, although they enjoy an exalted and privileged position in God's order, are still inferior to God's Son (Hebrews 1). Furthermore, we learned that Moses, honored giver of Israel's Law, was also inferior to the Son (Hebrews 3:1-6).

In today's lesson the writer's argument takes a somewhat surprising turn. Instead of providing additional evidence to support the superiority of the Son, he begins to describe the Son's humiliation. When Jesus became a human being, He was "made a little lower than the angels" (2:9). He became subject to the frailties of the flesh, including suffering and death. Therein lies part of the "mystery of godliness" (1 Timothy 3:16). It does not seem rational to the human mind that Christ could be exalted by being humiliated in suffering and death, and yet that is exactly what today's lesson teaches. The Highest and Mightiest laid aside His highness and mightiness to dwell among us, that He might triumph as the Captain of our salvation. We are reminded once more how feeble our wisdom is compared with God's (see 1 Corinthians 1:25).

I. The Humiliation and Exaltation of Christ (Hebrews 2:5-11)

A. God's Purpose for Man (vv. 5-8)

5. For unto the angels hath he not put in subjection the world to come, whereof we speak.

The first four verses of chapter 2 contain an exhortation to the Hebrew Christians to hold fast to the gospel they had received. Apparently there was some danger that they might abandon the salvation offered through the gospel and return to Judaism. Now the writer turns once again to the subject dealt with in the first chapter: the superiority of Christ to *the angels*.

In the present age, angels have certain responsibilities, many of which we are unaware. We are simply told that they are "sent forth to minister for them who shall be heirs of salvation"

How to Say It

ELOHIM (Hebrew). El-owe-*heem*.
JUDAISM. *Joo*-day-izz-um.
RECONCILIATION. *reck*-un-sill-ee-*a*-shun
    (strong accent on *a*).
SEPTUAGINT. Sep-*too*-ih-jent.

(Hebrews 1:14). In *the world to come*, which may refer to the heavenly realm, the angels will no doubt also have responsibilities, but there they will still be subject to the Son.

It is also possible that *the world to come* means the New Covenant system instituted by Jesus, which stands in contrast to the Old Covenant, referred to in verse 2 of this chapter. That word was "spoken by angels," but the salvation of the New Covenant focuses not upon angels, but upon the Son. Whereas Jews who rejected Christ were (and are) still looking for that "world to come," the writer of Hebrews demonstrates that it has come to pass in Jesus.

6, 7. But one in a certain place testified, saying, What is man, that thou art mindful of him? or the son of man, that thou visitest him? Thou madest him a little lower than the angels; thou crownedst him with glory and honor, and didst set him over the works of thy hands.

The writer introduces this quotation from Psalm 8:4-6 with the words, *one in a certain place testified.* Seldom does the writer name the specific author of any Old Testament passage that he quotes. The message of the text is his primary concern. The point of this quotation is to call attention to the fact that man was created by God with great potential: *a little lower than the angels.*

It should be noted that the Hebrew text of this passage in Psalm 8 literally reads, "a little lower than *Elohim.*" *Elohim* is a Hebrew word that is usually translated "God." At times, however, it is used elsewhere in the Old Testament to describe any being who is greater than human beings. The Septuagint (the Greek version of the Old Testament) uses the Greek word for "angels" in this verse, and this is the rendering that the inspired writer of Hebrews uses.

8. Thou hast put all things in subjection under his feet. For in that he put all in subjection under him, he left nothing that is not put under him. But now we see not yet all things put under him.

Thou hast put all things in subjection under his feet. Whereas the previous verse stated man's dominion in terms of what he was *over,* this final sentence from the writer's quotation of

Psalm 8 states that all things were placed *under* man. This changed radically with the entrance of sin into the world. Man lost the dominion he had been given. Death entered, over which man has little or no control. What control man did retain became tainted by sin. The harmony God intended for man to enjoy has not been fully restored: *But now we see not yet all things put under him.*

B. God's Purpose Realized in Christ (v. 9)

9. But we see Jesus, who was made a little lower than the angels for the suffering of death, crowned with glory and honor; that he by the grace of God should taste death for every man.

Let us keep in mind that in Psalm 8, David was celebrating the exalted position of man, who was created *a little lower than the angels* and given *glory and honor.* The writer of Hebrews, however, sees something in this psalm that David did not see: *we see Jesus.* But there is a crucial difference between Jesus and man: when Jesus *was made a little lower than the angels,* this was not a sign of exaltation; it was a mark of humiliation. Christ relinquished His authority, surrendering His dominion over the created world to enter the world as a human being. In thus becoming the true *son of man* mentioned in Psalm 8, Jesus desired to restore to man the dominion lost through sin.

The way in which Jesus made it possible for man to regain his position of dominion was to *taste death for every man.* Death then lost its bitter taste when Jesus arose from the tomb. He returned to Heaven where He was *crowned with glory and honor.* Eventually Jesus' full authority will be restored and His people will reign with Him, but *now we see not yet all things put under him,* as verse 8 states. That time of restoration will occur when Christ returns to claim His own and declare victory over His enemies. The purpose for which God created man will thus be realized when we actually *see Jesus* on that day.

C. Christ Made Perfect By Suffering (v. 10)

10. For it became him, for whom are all things, and by whom are all things, in bringing many sons unto glory, to make the captain of their salvation perfect through sufferings.

The word *became* is used here in its older meaning, "to be fitting or appropriate." God desired to create a family of *sons* who would one day dwell with Him in *glory.* To accomplish this, it was fitting that He *make the captain of their salvation perfect through sufferings.* The idea of a suffering Messiah was repugnant to the Jews;

Paul calls the crucifixion of Christ a "stumbling-block" to them (1 Corinthians 1:23). Thus these Jewish Christians required an explanation as to why the Messiah had to experience this.

That Jesus was made *perfect through sufferings* does not refer to moral perfection, for Jesus was without sin. The word translated here as *perfect* means "to bring to completion." It does not speak of Christ's character as much as it speaks of His calling. "Before the foundation of the world," God already had a plan for human redemption (1 Peter 1:18-20). This plan required that His Son would suffer and die. Until Christ underwent this ordeal, He was incomplete in the sense that His mission to save mankind had not been completed.

D. We Become Christ's Brethren (v. 11)

11. For both he that sanctifieth and they who are sanctified are all of one: for which cause he is not ashamed to call them brethren.

To be *sanctified* means to be holy, or set apart to a holy purpose. Through His sacrifice for us, Christ gave us the opportunity to be set apart for service to God. Being sanctified does not mean that one is perfect, or never sins. It does mean that he has made a commitment to become more Christlike. This thought is captured in the phrase: "Not perfect, but progressing."

The words *are all of one* may mean of one faith, one purpose, or one family. The latter choice may be the best one, for the verse goes on to state that Jesus *is not ashamed to call them brethren*. Under ordinary circumstances we would consider it most unusual for one so holy and exalted as Jesus to accept sinners like us as members of His family. This is what makes Christ's love for us so amazing. Sin-stained creatures that we are, He is still willing to forgive us and to welcome us as His brothers and sisters.

II. The Incarnation of Christ (Hebrews 2:14-18)

A. Delivering Us From Bondage (vv. 14, 15)

14, 15. Forasmuch then as the children are partakers of flesh and blood, he also himself likewise took part of the same; that through death he might destroy him that had the power of death, that is, the devil; and deliver them, who through fear of death were all their lifetime subject to bondage.

The last verse of our printed text affirmed that Christ is our Brother. For that relationship to become a reality, Jesus needed to become fully human, assuming all the weaknesses of the flesh. This verse elaborates on this point.

visual for lesson 7

CROWNED WITH GLORY AND HONOR

Since his fall, man has lived under the curse of sin, which has subjected him to unceasing suffering and sorrow. The most dreadful of all these threats has been the pall of *death* that has cast a shadow over every human being who has set foot on the earth. It was necessary that Christ come in *flesh and blood* and suffer death Himself, in order that the shackles of *the devil* might be broken. Herein lies one of the most striking paradoxes of the gospel: Christ limited Himself that we might be freed from our sin-imposed *bondage*. He was bound that we might be free. He came to die that we might live. It was Christ's death and His resurrection that led Paul to cry out triumphantly, "Death is swallowed up in victory. O death, where is thy sting? O grave, where is thy victory?" (1 Corinthians 15:54, 55).

PRISONERS NO MORE

Thomas Costain's historical adventure, *The Three Edwards*, describes the life of Raynald III, a fourteenth-century duke in what is now Belgium. Raynald was grossly overweight. After a violent quarrel, Raynald's younger brother Edward captured Raynald but did not kill him. Instead, he built a room around Raynald in the Nieuwkerk (*New*-kirk) castle, and promised him he could regain his title and property as soon as he was able to leave the room.

This would not have been difficult for most people, since the room had several windows and a door of near-normal size, and none was locked or barred. The problem was Raynald's size. To regain his freedom he needed to lose weight. But Edward knew his older brother, and each day he sent a variety of delicious foods to him. Instead of dieting his way out of prison, Raynald only grew fatter. When Duke Edward was accused of cruelty toward his brother, he had a ready answer: "My brother is not a prisoner. He may leave when he so wills."

Raynald stayed in that room for ten years and was not released until after Edward died in battle. By then his health was so ruined that he died within a year—a prisoner of his own appetite.

Hebrews 2:14, 15 tells us that Jesus took upon Himself flesh and blood, so that through His death, "he might destroy him that had the power of death, that is, the devil; and deliver them, who through fear of death were all their lifetime subject to bondage." Jesus has provided the way of escape from the vicious cycle of sin and death. We need not be prisoners anymore. We can be freed from the cycle—if we so will.

—C. B. Mc.

B. Becoming Our High Priest
(vv. 16, 17)

16. For verily he took not on him the nature of angels; but he took on him the seed of Abraham.

No doubt Christ could have come to earth as an angel, but this was not God's plan. Centuries before, God had promised Abraham that He would bless him, and through him bless "all families of the earth" (Genesis 12:1-3). That promise was fulfilled in Jesus Christ, through whom Christians are counted as the *seed of Abraham* when they come to Jesus by faith (Galatians 3:29).

What this and the previous two verses describe is often called the *incarnation* of Christ. This word literally means "in flesh." Jesus entered our world, coming to earth at a particular time, to a particular place, and with a specific parentage. It was surely appropriate that He come as a descendant of Abraham, since He lived and taught in the land that had been promised to Abraham. The link with Abraham also possessed a special appeal to Jewish readers. Matthew establishes the same link at the beginning of his Gospel (Matthew 1:1).

17. Wherefore in all things it behooved him to be made like unto his brethren, that he might be a merciful and faithful high priest in things pertaining to God, to make reconciliation for the sins of the people.

In the previous verses the writer has emphasized Jesus' solidarity with His brethren. This was necessary in order for Him to become their *high priest*. Having been one with them in the flesh and having experienced the frailties of the flesh, He could be a *merciful* high priest, sympathetic to their weaknesses (see Hebrews 4:15). He was *faithful* in two ways: to God, because He faithfully carried out the mission that God sent Him to accomplish, and to His brethren, because He faced death on the cross on their behalf.

The writer also notes that Jesus came *to make reconciliation for the sins of the people.* Every sin is an affront to God's holy nature and deserves eternal punishment. Yet God mercifully chose to send His Son into the world to reconcile man to Himself. It is important to note that man does not and cannot reconcile himself to God. Our only hope was for God to take the initiative and send His Son, which He did. Instead of being separated from God, "we have peace with God through our Lord Jesus Christ" (Romans 5:1).

C. Helping Us in Our Temptations
(v. 18)

18. For in that he himself hath suffered being tempted, he is able to succor them that are tempted.

Because Christ *suffered* temptations similar to those that we suffer, He can not only sympathize with us; He can also *succor*, or help, us. We are told of certain temptations that He faced (Matthew 4:1-11; Luke 4:1-13), but certainly there were many others. Indeed, because He was the Son of God, Jesus faced the full fury of Satan in a way that no human being can ever face. At the time the book of Hebrews was written, these Hebrew Christians were being tempted to return to Judaism, thus compromising their Christian commitment. Satan placed a similar temptation before Jesus by encouraging Him to abandon His mission and thus compromise His commitment to His Father's will.

Whatever temptation we encounter, we are assured that Jesus encountered it as well. He was "in all points tempted like as we are, yet without sin" (Hebrews 4:15). Because He passed successfully through the fires of temptation, He can now offer sympathy and support to His brethren who face similar fires. What a glorious blessing to know that there is always "grace to help in time of need" (4:16)!

Conclusion
A. He Has Been There

During the Vietnam War, an American officer compiled an outstanding record of service. He was wounded twice and received a medal for special courage in combat. Furthermore, he received a number of commendations from his commanding officer. But the greatest tribute to his skill and courage was the fact that men asked to be transferred to his unit. This was especially surprising, because his unit was usually given the most hazardous assignments in the area. When one of the men who wanted to be transferred to the officer's unit was asked why, his answer was short and to the point: "He's been there!"

What he meant was that this officer had been in combat, had suffered the difficult conditions in the field along with his men, had been wounded, and had survived. Through his actions he had won the respect and trust of those who served under him in the only way that a combat officer can win genuine respect: he had been there.

This is similar to the reasons that men and women in every age have respected and trusted Jesus Christ. Our Lord is not some remote deity residing in a distant Heaven, isolated from the events of our lives. Christ has been there! He left His heavenly home and became a human being, subject to human problems and limitations. When we suffer, we know that He empathizes, for He has suffered also. When we are tired, He understands, for He has known fatigue. When we are tempted, He can help us because He was tempted. Christ has been there, because He has been *here*!

B. Jesus Saves

Under the Mosaic Law, the high priest was the religious leader of the Israelites. He had many functions, but none more important than his entrance once a year into the Holy of Holies of the tabernacle or temple, where he sprinkled blood upon the ark of the covenant for the sins of the people. In preparation for this, the high priest had to go through a process of ritualistic cleansing that symbolically made him pure when he represented the people before God.

In the Christian era, Christ is our High Priest. In many ways the high priesthood of the Old Testament was similar to Christ's high priesthood. There are, however, striking differences. The Old Testament priest had to come from the tribe of Levi, whereas Christ came from the tribe of Judah. The Old Testament high priest had to purge himself of sin ceremonially before he could stand before God. For Christ, however, no such cleansing was necessary, for He was without sin. The Old Testament high priest entered a physical Holy of Holies, whereas Christ entered the heavenly Holy of Holies (Hebrews 9:24).

In one very important respect, the high priest of the Old Testament and Christ, our great High Priest, have one item in common. Both had to deal with man's universal problem of sin. There has never been an era of human history to which the words of Jeremiah 17:9 have not applied: "The heart is deceitful above all things, and desperately wicked: who can know it?"

Today, however, it is no longer "politically correct" to speak of sin. Those who violate accepted moral codes are said to be "socially maladjusted" or "ethically challenged." Actions that the Bible clearly marks as sinful have now become acceptable by clever changes in terminology. Taking the life of an unborn child has

now become a matter of "choice." Homosexuality, condemned in the Scriptures, has become an "alternate life-style" that is widely defended even in some religious circles.

In all of these discussions, one very important element is often overlooked: personal responsibility for our actions. All of us on occasion have tried to shift the blame for our moral failures onto other persons. or onto society as a whole. Again and again the Bible thunders out the message sounded centuries ago by the prophet Ezekiel: "The soul that sinneth, it shall die" (Ezekiel 18:4). God has never altered or withdrawn that pronouncement. All of us, because of our sins, fall under this death sentence (Romans 3:23; 6:23).

There is no way that we can save ourselves. On the basis of our works we do not deserve salvation. A lifetime of good works cannot atone for even one sin. Our situation is hopeless except for—and what a wonderful exception it is—Jesus Christ, our matchless Lord and Savior. Because He gave Himself as a sacrifice for our sins, He has made reconciliation between God and mankind. He has welcomed us as a part of His family, even calling us brethren. Is there any reason we should not love Him, trust Him, and give our lives in service to Him?

C. Let Us Pray

We give You thanks, dear God, that in Your great mercy You saw fit to send Your Son into the world as a servant, that we might have the hope of eternal life. In the name of our great High Priest, we pray. Amen.

D. Thought to Remember

We are saved because Christ did for us what we could not do for ourselves.

Home Daily Bible Readings

Monday, July 7—Jesus Christ Gives Eternal Life (John 10:22-30)

Tuesday, July 8—Jesus Christ Is of God (1 John 4:1-6)

Wednesday, July 9—Jesus Christ Is Love (1 John 4:7-11)

Thursday, July 10—Jesus Christ Resists Temptations (Matthew 4:1-11)

Friday, July 11—Jesus Christ Was Sent by God (John 3:16-21)

Saturday, July 12—Jesus Christ Is Our Advocate (1 John 2:1-6)

Sunday, July 13—Jesus Christ Was Faithful (Hebrews 3:1-6)

Learning by Doing

This page contains an alternate lesson plan emphasizing learning activities.
Classes desiring such student involvement will find these suggestions helpful.

Learning Goals

Studying today's text should help students:

1. Affirm with assurance that Christ's suffering was to accomplish our reconciliation.

2. Explain in what ways Jesus becoming flesh was a humiliation for Him.

3. State what it means to have Jesus Christ as our High Priest.

Into the Lesson

On eleven index cards, put the word *humiliation*, one letter per card, on one side. On the reverse side, put the word *superiority*, matching the *s* with the *h*, *u* with *u*, and so forth. Display the cards spelling the word *superiority* (the dust tray of a chalkboard might be a good place). Point out to your class that last week's lesson emphasized that Jesus the Son is superior to the angels and to Moses. Then note that this week's emphasis is surprisingly different. Ask class members, one at a time, to select a letter from the word *superiority* (randomly and none in sequence), and as each calls a letter, turn that card over to show the letter on the other side. As the cards are turned, allow guesses as to the word concealed. Once guessed, turn all the cards over to show the word *humiliation*. Note that this is the emphasis of today's study: Christ was humiliated on our behalf.

Into the Word

Introduce the following as "headlines" in a newspaper. Ask your class to examine today's Scripture text from Hebrews 2:5-11, 14-18, and to identify the relevant verse for each headline. Though they are given here in verse order, you will want to mix them up.

2:5—"Angels Not in Charge in Heaven"; 2:6—"Man Hardly Worth God's Time"; 2:7—"Man Created Lower Than Angels"; 2:8—"All Things Are Not Under Man's Authority"; 2:9—"Jesus Tastes Death"; 2:9—"Jesus Made Lower Than Angels"; 2:10—"Jesus Is Declared 'Captain'"; 2:11—"Jesus Calls the Sanctified 'Brethren'"; 2:14—"Jesus: Devil Destroyer"; 2:15—"Fear of Death Subjects Many to Bondage"; 2:16—"Jesus Is Not Like an Angel"; 2:17—"Jesus As High Priest Makes Reconciliation His Goal"; 2:18—"Jesus Just Like Us: Tempted!" Note that headlines sometimes limit or distort the truth to grab attention. It is difficult to capture all the truth

about a certain incident or event in one headline. Ask your class members if any of these "headlines" are incomplete. Note that the one given for verse 14, "Jesus: Devil Destroyer," is true insofar that Jesus has seized control of death; however, the devil still awaits final destruction in the lake of fire. The headline for verse 18, "Jesus Just Like Us: Tempted!" does not imply that Jesus is so human that He sinned. Your class may think of similar examples.

Next, ask the students to suggest other "headlines" that they see within the truths of these verses. They may offer such suggestions as "Jesus Crowned With Glory and Honor" from verse 9, "Deliverance—at Last!" from verse 15, or "Jesus: Helper of the Tempted" from verse 18. Encourage the class to be creative in their ideas.

Display the following list of words related to the concept of *humiliation: disgrace, scandal, shame, embarrassment, contempt, mockery, jeering, insult, subjugation, dishonor, discredit.* Ask the class to identify ways, from the text or otherwise, that Jesus experienced each of these negative results through His humiliation. For example, the suffering of verse 9 relates to *subjugation;* the *jeering* was experienced as Jesus hung upon the cross; *scandal* could easily be related to the circumstances of His birth and His death; and *dishonor* or *discredit* could describe His death between two convicted thieves. Even though He was often *shamed* in the way He was treated, verse 11 affirms that He is *not ashamed* to call us His brethren.

Into Life

Give each student a copy of the following list of seven truths to use, one per day, in their daily devotional time for the next week. Suggest a time of pondering and a time of praying related to each. (1) Jesus was crowned with glory and honor after He had tasted death for everyone. (2) The Captain of our salvation fulfilled His mission by suffering. (3) We are one with Jesus through the process of sanctification; He calls us His "brethren." (4) Jesus became like us in order to die for us. (5) Jesus has destroyed the one who had the power of death, so that we need fear death no longer. (6) Jesus is a merciful and faithful High Priest, reconciling us to God. (7) Jesus has been tempted; thus He can help us in our temptations.

Let's Talk It Over

The questions on this page are designed to encourage review of the lesson Scriptures and to promote discussion of the lesson by the class. The answers provided are only discussion starters. Let your class talk it over from there.

1. In recent years there has been a renewed interest in angels. How important to Christians is the study of angels? How might curiosity about angels be harmful to Christians?

There are enough references in the Bible to angels to give us some idea of their existence, work, and purpose. We know that they were a part of the created order (Psalm 148:2-5). We know that they are capable of carrying out assignments in this world, including fighting battles or delivering messages from God (2 Kings 19:35; Luke 1:11-13). At times they are associated with a brilliant appearance (Luke 2:9); at other times their presence is undetected (Hebrews 13:2). We also understand that angels are capable of rebelling against the rule and will of God (2 Peter 2:4; Jude 6).

While we can know much about angels, there are still many unanswered questions. To be caught up in speculation concerning them, or to make any attempt to communicate with angels, would be insulting to our Lord and Savior Jesus. He is our source of spiritual help, He is our atoning sacrifice, and He stands ready to hear our prayers and intercede for us. It would be idolatrous to let curiosity about angels interfere with our devotion to Christ.

2. Was it a sign of strength or weakness for Jesus to assume a role "a little lower than the angels"? Explain why.

We know that the Son was co-eternal with the Father and that He was the agent of all creation, which would include the angels (John 1:1-3). He certainly holds preeminence over the angels, but He willingly chose to take the role of a mortal for the purpose of redeeming lost mankind. It is always a sign of character strength to voluntarily set aside privilege and position in the interest of serving others. It is a sign of weakness when one must cling jealously to every fragment of honor or prestige for the sake of self-affirmation. Jesus called us to such a model of self-sacrifice when He said, "He that findeth his life shall lose it: and he that loseth his life for my sake shall find it" (Matthew 10:39).

3. How was the "captain" of our salvation made "perfect through sufferings" (Hebrews 2:10)?

Here the word perfect has the sense of being "complete." In order to be our Savior, it was necessary for Jesus to pay an extraordinary price. He suffered and died an undeserved death, and took the judgment that belongs to sinners even though He was innocent. In so doing He completed His role as a Savior.

4. How do you feel about being numbered among Jesus' "brethren" (Hebrews 2:11)? What does that say about our relationship with all other believers?

When we consider the moral differences between ourselves and Jesus, most Christians are filled with wonder that He would call us His brothers and sisters. The Bible makes much of the idea of adoption, and of our being made sons and daughters of God through Christ (Galatians 3:26-29; Romans 8:14, 15). It is a testimony to the love of Jesus and the grace of God that this can be so. If we accept this identity as "brethren" of Jesus, we must also consider that we are therefore related to the millions of others who claim Jesus as Lord. In Christ we have many relatives, and there are some family obligations for us to consider. The New Testament defines those obligations in terms of many "one another" commands: love one another, forgive one another, and pray for one another, to name a few.

5. If you were held hostage by terrorists, is there anyone who would offer to take your place? How would you feel toward that person? Is that how you feel toward Christ? How do you show those feelings?

Many of us have loved ones who would pay a ransom for our return if we were kidnapped, but for someone to offer his life in exchange is a rare love indeed. We would no doubt feel moved to pay tribute to that individual at every opportunity. We might look for a way of honoring his sacrifice through some lasting monument or memorial. Jesus' sacrifice on our behalf should move us in a similar manner. Paul notes that our "reasonable service" is to give ourselves as "living sacrifices" (Romans 12:1). We also pay tribute to Jesus when we worship in His name, when we observe His chosen memorial in partaking of the loaf and the cup of Communion, and when we are obedient to His commands.

Jesus Is the High Priest

DEVOTIONAL READING: Hebrews 7:20-28.

LESSON SCRIPTURE: Hebrews 4:14—5:10; 7.

PRINTED TEXT: Hebrews 4:14—5:10.

Hebrews 4:14-16

14 Seeing then that we have a great high priest, that is passed into the heavens, Jesus the Son of God, let us hold fast our profession.

15 For we have not a high priest which cannot be touched with the feeling of our infirmities; but was in all points tempted like as we are, yet without sin.

16 Let us therefore come boldly unto the throne of grace, that we may obtain mercy, and find grace to help in time of need.

Hebrews 5:1-10

1 For every high priest taken from among men is ordained for men in things pertaining to God, that he may offer both gifts and sacrifices for sins:

2 Who can have compassion on the ignorant, and on them that are out of the way; for

that he himself also is compassed with infirmity.

3 And by reason hereof he ought, as for the people, so also for himself, to offer for sins.

4 And no man taketh this honor unto himself, but he that is called of God, as was Aaron.

5 So also Christ glorified not himself to be made a high priest; but he that said unto him, Thou art my Son, today have I begotten thee.

6 As he saith also in another place, Thou art a priest for ever after the order of Melchizedek.

7 Who in the days of his flesh, when he had offered up prayers and supplications with strong crying and tears unto him that was able to save him from death, and was heard in that he feared;

8 Though he were a Son, yet learned he obedience by the things which he suffered;

9 And being made perfect, he became the author of eternal salvation unto all them that obey him;

10 Called of God a high priest after the order of Melchizedek.

**Jul
20**

GOLDEN TEXT: Let us therefore come boldly unto the throne of grace, that we may obtain mercy, and find grace to help in time of need.—Hebrews 4:16.

A Call to Faithfulness
Unit 1: The Greatness of Christ
(Lessons 6-9)

Lesson Aims

After studying this lesson, each student should:

1. Find comfort in the knowledge that Jesus is our High Priest.

2. Explain what makes Jesus a superior High Priest.

3. Be challenged to share with others their knowledge of Christ as their High Priest.

Lesson Outline

INTRODUCTION
    A. About Priests
    B. Lesson Background
  I. JESUS, OUR HIGH PRIEST (Hebrews 4:14-16)
    A. Has Passed Into the Heavens (v. 14)
    B. Was Tempted As We Are (v. 15)
    C. Provides Mercy and Grace (v. 16)
      Access to the Throne of God
 II. THE WORK OF THE HIGH PRIEST (Hebrews 5:1-3)
    A. Offers Gifts and Sacrifices (v. 1)
    B. Has Compassion on Others (v. 2)
    C. Is Also a Sinner (v. 3)
III. JESUS' HIGH PRIESTHOOD (Hebrews 5:4-10)
    A. Called of God (vv. 4, 5)
    B. Has an Eternal Priesthood (v. 6)
    C. Learned Through Suffering (vv. 7, 8)
      Surrendering to the Will of God
    D. Offers Eternal Salvation (vv. 9, 10)
CONCLUSION
    A. "What a Friend We Have in Jesus"
    B. Let Us Pray
    C. Thought to Remember

The visual for Lesson 8 encourages us to "come boldly unto the throne of grace" (Hebrews 4:16). It is shown on page 399.

Introduction

A. About Priests

For many people, the concept of priest and priesthood often conjures up negative images. We think of ancient pagan religions in which priests wielded almost absolute power, often serving as kings as well as priests. Some of these priests presided over religious rites that included sexual abuses and even human sacrifice.

The Biblical images of priests are sometimes almost as negative. The Old Testament speaks of the priests of the false god Baal (2 Kings 10:19) and of pagan peoples such as the Philistines (1 Samuel 6:2). Even though the Mosaic Law created a priesthood among God's own people, many of these turned out to be scoundrels (see 1 Samuel 2:12-17, 22-24; Jeremiah 2:26, 27). In Jesus' day, the priests were among His most bitter enemies. In fact, the priests, including the high priest, spearheaded the plot to crucify Him. But these negative images of priests are not the whole story. There are many good and noble priests within the pages of Scripture. We read of Jehoiada, who counseled young Jehoash when he became king at age seven (2 Kings 12:2). A high priest named Hilkiah found the book of the Law in the temple of the Lord (2 Kings 22:8). Later, when King Josiah heard what the Law said, he ushered in a period of revival and reformation throughout Judah. We are told that in the early church, many priests became "obedient to the faith" (Acts 6:7).

It is important to note that Christians are called a "holy priesthood" (1 Peter 2:5) and a "royal priesthood" (1 Peter 2:9). Most important of all, Jesus Christ is set forth as our great High Priest. Our Lord bears many different titles and serves in many different capacities, but among the most important of these is His function as High Priest—our mediator before Almighty God.

B. Lesson Background

The Jewish Christians who were the recipients of the book of Hebrews would have been quite familiar with the office of priest. It is likely that many of them had witnessed priests offering sacrifices on the altar. They had probably attended the services led by priests on some of the great Jewish holy days, such as the feasts of Passover and Pentecost. A few may even have witnessed the high priest on the Day of Atonement as he prepared to enter the hidden and mysterious Holy of Holies.

When Jews became Christians, their view of these religious traditions changed. In many cases, however, this did not involve a complete break from their past. Paul, for example, continued to observe the Jewish feasts (Acts 20:16). He even paid the expenses of four men who had taken a Jewish vow (Acts 21:23-26). It should not surprise us that many Jewish Christians still harbored nostalgic feelings about priests and the temple. Their memories of inspiring worship services shared with family and friends likely moved many of them to want to return to Judaism. It was just this situation that served as the occasion for the book of Hebrews. The writer attempts to show his readers that something better had been provided by God to replace the Old Covenant system. By becoming Christians they were not abandoning their Jewish faith; they were simply acknowledging that the New Covenant that God had promised had now arrived. As Christians they could enjoy the benefits of a great High Priest, who is now in Heaven: Jesus the Son of God.

I. Jesus, Our High Priest (Hebrews 4:14-16)

A. Has Passed Into the Heavens (v. 14)

14. Seeing then that we have a great high priest, that is passed into the heavens, Jesus the Son of God, let us hold fast our profession.

In previous lessons we have learned that Jesus serves as our High Priest (Hebrews 2:17; 3:1). Here the writer notes that He has *passed into the heavens*. This contrasts sharply with the practice of the priest under the Old Covenant, who once a year entered the Holy of Holies to make atonement for the people's sins. In the Holy of Holies he was symbolically in the presence of God for a few minutes. On the other hand, Jesus has entered Heaven (the true Holy Place), where He sits at the right hand of God (Hebrews 1:3; 9:24) and enjoys an "unchangeable priesthood" (7:24).

Christ's superior priesthood had important consequences for the recipients of the book of Hebrews. These Jewish Christians, who were thinking about returning to Judaism with its inferior priesthood, needed to be reminded of this and admonished to *hold fast* their *profession*. This profession (translated "confession" in the *American Standard Version*) was mentioned previously in 3:1, where Jesus is called "the Apostle and High Priest of our profession." The term may reflect both the private and the public aspects of one's commitment to Christ. The private aspect is the acceptance of Jesus as Lord and Savior. The public dimension is the acknowledgment of this faith before witnesses.

How to Say It

GETHSEMANE. Geth-*sem*-uh-nee (g as in *get*).
HILKIAH. Hill-*kye*-uh.
JEHOASH. Jeh-*hoe*-ash.
JEHOIADA. Jeh-*hoy*-uh-duh.
JOSIAH. Joe-*sye*-uh.
JUDAISM. *Joo*-day-izz-um.
MELCHIZEDEK. Mel-*kizz*-ih-deck.
PHILISTINES. Fuh-*liss*-teens or *Fill*-us-teens.

B. Was Tempted As We Are (v. 15)

15. For we have not a high priest which cannot be touched with the feeling of our infirmities; but was in all points tempted like as we are, yet without sin.

When we seek someone to represent us before God, we want someone who understands our problems, who has stood where we have stood, and who hurts when we hurt. Were Christ only divine, He could not fully meet this requirement. But He was also human, and this makes the crucial difference. He was *tempted like as we are*. We are told of certain specific temptations that Jesus successfully faced (Matthew 4:1-11; Luke 4:1-13). But Luke's record of these temptations states that the devil "departed from him for a season" (Luke 4:13), indicating that there were other temptations during Jesus' ministry. The important point is that although He suffered these temptations, He was *yet without sin*.

C. Provides Mercy and Grace (v. 16)

16. Let us therefore come boldly unto the throne of grace, that we may obtain mercy, and find grace to help in time of need.

Because Christ is now in the presence of God in Heaven, all Christians enjoy a very sacred privilege. For a sinful human being to be able to come into the presence of Almighty God seems inconceivable. Isaiah felt totally overwhelmed by his experience, recorded in Isaiah 6:1-8. But Jesus our High Priest has changed all of this. Now we can *come boldly unto the throne of grace*. When we do so through our prayers, we are assured that we will receive *mercy* and *help* for whatever *need* we might have. We will discover, as did Paul, that God's grace is sufficient (2 Corinthians 12:9).

ACCESS TO THE THRONE OF GOD

Imagine it is the end of time. From the center of the universe comes the sound of a trumpet so loud and clear that every mortal ear hears its call. From the eastern sky a great archangel descends to declare that time is no more. The earth quakes. The moon darkens. The stars are extinguished. The very sky rolls up like a scroll. All human activity comes to an end, as every man and woman who has ever lived stands before the Creator, either to be separated forever from Him, or to live eternally with Him.

Suddenly you find yourself entering a magnificent city of gold through a gate made of a single pearl. Its walls glimmer with precious stones and gems. There is no sun nor moon, but the city is brighter than a summer noon because the glory of God fills every portion. A magnificent river flows down the great street of the city, and the tree of life blooms on either side.

At the center of the city, behind the sparkling sea of glass, is the throne of Almighty God. At the right hand of God stands our High Priest, Jesus Christ, and with a nail-scarred hand He bids you draw near. As millions of angels and the saints of all the ages look on and lean forward to hear, Jesus calls your name and presents you to your Creator.

Such is the direct access to God awaiting those who confess Christ as their Lord and Savior. Let us come boldly to His throne now, as the writer of Hebrews instructs us to do, that we may come before His heavenly throne and stand in His presence some day.   —C. B. Mc.

II. The Work of the High Priest (Hebrews 5:1-3)

A. Offers Gifts and Sacrifices (v. 1)

1. For every high priest taken from among men is ordained for men in things pertaining to God, that he may offer both gifts and sacrifices for sins.

In this and the verses that follow, the Hebrew Christians were reminded of the "job description" of the Aaronic priesthood. Although they were familiar with these requirements, this reminder served to show that Jesus also met these qualifications. One of the primary functions of a priest is to serve as a mediator between God and man. If he is to do this adequately and thereby represent his fellowmen well, he must share in their experiences; that is, he must be *taken from among men.* Christ fully met this qualification. He was born of a woman, He grew to maturity in a normal way, and He suffered the limitations that beset every other human being.

A very important function of a priest was to *offer both gifts and sacrifices for sins.* Some scholars draw a distinction between the gifts (consisting of grain offerings) and the sacrifices (involving animals whose blood was shed). It seems better, however, to understand *gifts and sacrifices* as simply a summary of the various ceremonial activities of the priest.

B. Has Compassion on Others (v. 2)

2. Who can have compassion on the ignorant, and on them that are out of the way; for that he himself also is compassed with infirmity.

The priest in ancient Israel served not only in formal and public functions; he also had what might be called a pastoral responsibility toward his people. He was to be a teacher and an exam-

ple for them. He was to rebuke the rebellious and wayward. He had a special obligation to those who wandered *out of the way* because they were *ignorant.* For them, patient guidance and loving nurture were more appropriate than stern rebuke. The priest was able to offer this kind of ministry, because he himself was *compassed with infirmity,* or, as the *New International Version* states it, "subject to weakness."

C. Is Also a Sinner (v. 3)

3. And by reason hereof he ought, as for the people, so also for himself, to offer for sins.

Even as the priest offered sacrifices for the *sins* of *the people,* he also had to offer sacrifices *for himself.* Although the priest dealt with holy things every day, this did not exempt him from sin. Indeed, a priest faced certain temptations that were unique to his office. For example, he was tempted to lose his sense of reverence for the holy functions he performed. Furthermore, he was tempted by spiritual pride to feel himself superior to those who were not involved with spiritual activities every day. These are temptations to which Christian leaders can still fall prey. In view of this fact, it is most appropriate and important to keep our leaders in constant prayer.

III. Jesus' High Priesthood (Hebrews 5:4-10)

A. Called of God (vv. 4, 5)

4, 5. And no man taketh this honor unto himself, but he that is called of God, as was Aaron. So also Christ glorified not himself to be made a high priest; but he that said unto him, Thou art my Son, today have I begotten thee.

The priesthood was a part of God's plan to provide spiritual direction to His people. Thus, only *God* had the right to call a person to fill the office. One could not elevate himself to the position, or be voted into office by his friends. To fill the office, one not only had to be a member of the tribe of Levi; he also had to be a member of the family of *Aaron,* the first high priest. Some scholars suggest that the writer had in mind some of the Jewish religious leaders of his own day, who had played politics and connived with the Romans in order to gain their offices.

In contrast, the writer points out that *Christ* did not use political maneuvering to gain the office. Nor did He carry on a political campaign among the people to win their respect. Furthermore, since Jesus was not a descendant of Aaron or a member of the tribe of Levi, He was not qualified according to the Law of Moses to fill the office of priest. The only way He could serve in this capacity was to be specially *called of God*. This is the point that the writer makes, quoting Psalm 2:7 (which he had already quoted in 1:5) to support his case.

B. Has an Eternal Priesthood (v. 6)

6. As he saith also in another place, Thou art a priest for ever after the order of Melchizedek.

Here the writer quotes Psalm 110:4 to show that Christ's priesthood is unique in two respects. First, it lasts *for ever*. Any person called to the Aaronic priesthood held office only until his death. By contrast, Christ's priesthood actually *began* with His death, when He offered Himself as the perfect sacrifice for the sins of the world.

Second, the priesthood of Jesus is *after the order of Melchizedek* rather than the order of Aaron. What little we know about Melchizedek, we learn from Genesis 14:17-20. When Abram returned home after a victory over a coalition of Near Eastern kings, he was met by Melchizedek, who is identified as "king of Salem" and the "priest of the most high God" (Genesis 14:18). In what was apparently some kind of a religious ceremony, Melchizedek "brought forth bread and wine" (v. 18), and Abraham in turn "gave him tithes" (v. 20). Since Melchizedek had obviously been appointed to his office by God and because his priesthood preceded that of Aaron's, the implication is that his priesthood is superior to Aaron's.

C. Learned Through Suffering
(vv. 7, 8)

7, 8. Who in the days of his flesh, when he had offered up prayers and supplications with strong crying and tears unto him that was able to save him from death, and was heard in that he feared; though he were a Son, yet learned he obedience by the things which he suffered.

In the days of his flesh refers to Christ's incarnation, a subject that we saw the writer discuss in last week's text from Hebrews 2:5-11, 14-18. That "the Word was made flesh" (John 1:14) brought many limitations. One of these was the suffering Jesus experienced. The mention of *prayers and supplications with strong crying and tears* brings to mind Jesus' prayers in the Garden of Gethsemane (Matthew 26:36-46; Mark 14:32-42; Luke 22:39-46). Jesus' spiritual and emotional agony during that experience is graphically expressed in Luke's Gospel: "His sweat was as it were great drops of blood falling down to the ground" (22:44).

The mention of Jesus' prayers and suffering is designed to show how completely He identified with the human race. As our great High Priest,

visual for
lesson 8

He knew the agony that we suffer and much more, for His suffering greatly surpassed anything that we might experience. When He prayed in Gethsemane, He prayed for far more than just the avoidance of the pain of physical death. His agony involved bearing the weight of human sin, a burden beyond our ability to comprehend.

The writer then makes the striking observation that Jesus *learned . . . obedience by the things which he suffered*. From our own experience, we know that we learn from painful mistakes. We learn that fire burns, that sharp knives cut, and that icy surfaces are slippery. We also learn that foolish mistakes in our dealings with others are often quite painful. Such experiences teach us that obedience produces greater and longer lasting benefits than disobedience.

But how did Jesus, who was the sinless *Son*, learn obedience? The thought of this verse is similar to that of Hebrews 2:10, which was part of last week's lesson text. There we learned that it was necessary for God to make Jesus, the Captain of our salvation, "perfect through sufferings." More than anything else, Jesus' obedience to the Father's will involved *suffering*. Had He not suffered for the sins of mankind on the cross, His obedience would have been incomplete. That God's Son had to travel such a path as this was meant to offer reassurance to the Hebrew Christians, many of whom had suffered hardships and persecution as a result of their loyalty to Jesus.

Surrendering to the Will of God

Hebrews 5:7 tells us that when Jesus prayed He was heard because of His "reverent submission" (*New International Version*) to His Father's will. What does it mean to pray according to the will of God? It means much more than just mindlessly tacking on the phrase, "if it be Thy will." It involves telling God what we honestly want, but letting Him choose what He will do and how He will answer.

As a young man, Augustine, the brilliant theologian of the early church, led a wild and profligate life. His family was living in North Africa when Augustine told his mother that he was going to Rome to study rhetoric and public speaking. She immediately began to pray for God to keep Augustine from going to Rome. She was sure the evils of that great city would destroy him. But despite his mother's prayers, Augustine went. While there, some of Augustine's friends encouraged him to go to Milan, Italy, to study the great preacher Ambrose, who was acknowledged as the greatest public speaker of his day. Augustine went and returned again and again. Eventually he was converted to Christianity and became a powerful spokesman for the Christian faith.

Scholars today doubt whether anyone else in the world but Ambrose could have reached a brilliant young mind like Augustine's. Yet all that time Augustine's mother was praying, "Don't let Augustine go to Rome."

Did God answer her prayer? Yes. Did God give her what she asked? No, but He gave her something better. We should pray with a willingness to accept the greater good that God may give us when, in His infinite wisdom, His answer comes in a form different from what we have asked. Let us cultivate an attitude of "reverent submission" to Him in our prayer life.   —C. B. Mc.

D. Offers Eternal Salvation
(vv. 9, 10)

9, 10. And being made perfect, he became the author of eternal salvation unto all them that obey him; called of God a high priest after the order of Melchizedek.

Through His obedience Christ *became the author* ("source" in the *New International Version*) of our *salvation*. As the spotless Lamb of God, He provided the perfect sacrifice that was needed to forgive every sin. This offer of

salvation, however, is not for everyone. It is available only to those who *obey him*. The idea that rebellious and unrepentant sinners can receive this salvation finds no basis anywhere in the Scriptures.

The writer of Hebrews mentions *Melchizedek* once again at the end of this verse, and then observes that of him, "we have many things to say, and hard to be uttered" (v. 11). Most of these additional details regarding Melchizedek are found in chapter 7.

Conclusion

A. "What a Friend We Have in Jesus"

Although many church hymnals have been updated and have left out some of the more traditional hymns, most of them still include an old favorite, "What a Friend We Have in Jesus." And for good reason! Countless believers have found strength and reassurance in its words. The hymn also reflects some of the main points of today's lesson. The first stanza reminds us of our Friend, Jesus, who bears "all our sins and griefs." Whereas the Old Testament priest offered "gifts and sacrifices for sins" (Hebrews 5:1), Jesus offered but one sacrifice: His own life, given on the cross as an atonement for our sins.

As our High Priest, Jesus serves as the mediator between man and God. Because of this we may "come boldly unto the throne of grace" (Hebrews 4:16). We often fail to take advantage of this privilege, and as a result we "often forfeit" peace and bear "needless pain . . . All because we do not carry Ev'rything to God in prayer."

In addition, our great High Priest has been "touched with the feeling of our infirmities" (Hebrews 4:15). The hymn reminds us that we can take our problems to Jesus in prayer because He "knows our ev'ry weakness." When we have "trials and temptations," we know that Jesus will understand, because He "was in all points tempted like as we are, yet without sin" (v. 15).

You may want to consider closing the class period by singing this hymn.

B. Let Us Pray

Almighty God, we give You thanks for sending Your Son into the world, not only to die for our sins but to return to Heaven to be our great High Priest before the throne of grace. Give us the wisdom and strength to share this wonderful good news with those all about us. In Jesus' name we pray. Amen.

C. Thought to Remember

Jesus is the author of salvation to all who obey Him.

Home Daily Bible Readings

Monday, July 14—Melchizedek Is King of Peace (Hebrews 7:1-10)

Tuesday, July 15—High Priests Offer Blood Sacrifices (Hebrews 9:1-10)

Wednesday, July 16—Christ's Prayer to Be Glorified (John 17:1-5)

Thursday, July 17—Christ Is High Priest Forever (Hebrews 7:11-19)

Friday, July 18—Christ Sits at God's Right Hand (Hebrews 8:1-6)

Saturday, July 19—Christ Intercedes for Us (Hebrews 7:20-28)

Sunday, July 20—Nothing Can Separate Us From God's Love (Romans 8:31-39)

Learning by Doing

This page contains an alternate lesson plan emphasizing learning activities. Classes desiring such student involvement will find these suggestions helpful.

Learning Goals

Through today's study, students will:

1. State what it means to have Jesus as our High Priest.

2. Explain what qualified Jesus to fill this office.

3. See themselves as filling the role of priest on behalf of others.

Into the Lesson

On three strips of poster board (about eighteen by four inches each) write these three names: AARON, JESUS, MELCHIZEDEK. Show the names and ask for a volunteer to "put the names in order." Do not be any more definite than this. Probably someone will ask, "Alphabetical order?" Have the volunteer do this, then ask, "In what other 'order' could we put the names?" Another person may suggest chronological order. Let him or her do this. Eventually someone should suggest order of importance (although you can prompt the class if necessary). Have someone rank the three according to importance. Point out that Jesus must come first, Melchizedek second, and Aaron third.

Keep in mind that some in your class may have never heard of Melchizedek. Tell them that today's lesson will explain more about who Melchizedek was, and why Jesus is superior to him and to Aaron.

Into the Word

Number the people in your class: 14, 15, 16, and then 1 through 10, so that you can assign the verses of today's text for this activity. Give a student more than one verse if necessary. Have the following questions written on separate cards. There is one question for each verse.

4:14: Since Jesus has passed into the heavens, what should we do? 4:15: What is different about the effects of temptation in our lives and in the life of our High Priest? 4:16: What attitude is appropriate when we approach the throne of God? 5:1: What two items does the earthly high priest offer? 5:2: Why can the priest himself have compassion on the weak? 5:3: For whose sin does the priest make an offering? 5:4: What Mosaic priest is named in today's text? 5:5: What words from the Psalms does the writer of Hebrews say were spoken to Jesus? 5:6: To what Old Testament order of priests does Christ

belong? 5:7: With what did the Son offer up prayers and supplications? 5:8: How did the Son learn obedience? 5:9: How does one gain the eternal salvation Jesus offers? 5:10: Who called Jesus to be High Priest?

Shuffle these question cards, but do not ask them yourself. Call on another class member, especially one who was not given a verse to read. Direct those who were given verse numbers to answer from the appropriate verse. At the end of the question and answer time, ask, "How did this activity resemble the role of a priest?" Answer: "I, the teacher, had someone act on my behalf to ask the questions. This is what a priest does; he acts on behalf of others."

Into Life

Most Scriptures contain "Whats" and "So Whats," or, truths and consequences. Read each of the following "Whats" from today's text and ask the students to identify some of the corresponding "So Whats." If they need help, suggest that they think in terms of, "If Jesus . . . ," then "we ought to . . ."

(1) Jesus is our High Priest. (2) Our High Priest is touched by our infirmities. (3) Jesus learned obedience by the things He suffered. (4) Jesus promises eternal salvation to all who obey Him. (5) Jesus prayed with tears. (6) Jesus is a priest in the order of Melchizedek. (7) A high priest does for another what that person cannot do for himself. (8) Christ did not glorify Himself.

The students should see and offer a variety of responses; the following are given as examples (the numbers match the above statements). (1) We ought to use His services to the fullest. (2) We should never imagine ourselves abandoned or ignored by God. (3) We must continue to trust God, even in the midst of difficult circumstances. (4) We must obey God to please Him. (5) Our prayers must not be casual or thoughtless. (6) We must know and understand Melchizedek's role, according to the Scriptures. (7) We must never be so self-assured that we believe we have no need for Jesus. (8) We must allow God to glorify us, never seeking to glorify ourselves.

The apostle Peter says that all Christians are part of a "royal priesthood" (1 Peter 2:9). In closing, discuss with the class what it means to fulfill that calling on a daily basis.

Let's Talk It Over

The questions on this page are designed to encourage review of the lesson Scriptures and to promote discussion of the lesson by the class. The answers provided are only discussion starters. Let your class talk it over from there.

1. Since Jesus successfully resisted temptation to sin, can he really empathize with us when we succumb to temptation? Explain.

Did the person in your math class who always got an "A" show impatience with those who struggled? Do you know people who are very disciplined about diet and exercise, and are arrogant toward those with poorer habits? Because Jesus never gave in to temptation, we might conclude that He would be impatient with our weaknesses. It would be unjust, however, for us to project the insensitivity we have witnessed in ourselves or others upon Jesus. Even though He succeeded where we fail, He knows the severity of the temptations we face, and He has offered to provide us with grace and strength.

2. Describe why coming "boldly unto the throne of grace" (Hebrews 4:16) is such a privilege.

Did you ever visit Washington, D.C.? Were you able to walk casually into the White House and meet the President? You may have seen your congressman, but not without an appointment. Powerful and important people have a way of insulating themselves from contact. Yet the Creator of the universe, the Sovereign of all space and time, is available to Christians at any time that they breathe the name of Jesus the Savior in prayer. This is one of the rare privileges in which Christians should take great joy.

3. How do you reconcile the fact that your minister, the one who is teaching you the Scriptures, is also a sinner?

Certainly those among us who are considered for ordination and church leadership must be of exemplary character and have recognizable maturity in the faith. Since only Jesus is without sin, of all those who have walked the earth, we know that even ministers are sinners. They, like all Christians, are growing toward maturity. Knowing the frailties of the flesh, we should pray regularly for our ministers, that they may remain faithful in the face of temptation.

4. Most Christians agree that full-time vocational ministry should be a calling from God. How does one recognize that kind of call upon his life?

God calls every believer to be obedient and to serve in ways appropriate to the individual. It is not necessary or expected that we should all have the same ministry for God. The Bible compares the working of Christians in the church with the functioning of the various parts of the human body. Each part fills a particular role. Within God's plan for the church there is a place for leadership ministries that we associate with a full commitment of time and a high degree of formal education and other preparation. In order to recognize God's call to that type of ministry, there are several tests one can apply: (1) personal conviction and passion for the ministry, coupled with a vision of what God wants to accomplish; (2) evidence of aptitude and effectiveness in the various components of the chosen ministry; (3) confirmation from trusted and mature Christian advisors familiar with the person; (4) opportunity for the necessary preparation; and (5) availability of resources or support to pursue the vision.

5. How may we interpret the fact that at times suffering continues, even after we have prayed that God would remove it?

When conditions of suffering continue after we have prayed for their removal, we may be tempted to conclude: (1) that God has not heard our prayers; (2) that He is unwilling to remove the suffering; or (3) that He is unable to do anything about it. Mature faith knows that none of these conclusions is true, so we must look for other answers. It is good for us to recall that Jesus also prayed for the removal of suffering in His life, but suffered a violent death anyway. It is not that God ignored His prayers or that He was uncaring. Jesus framed His request with the condition, "Nevertheless, not my will, but thine, be done" (Luke 22:42). God's greater purpose was served by the suffering that Jesus endured. God does not always intervene to rescue us or to grant us our desired comfort (which may disappoint us), but we must remember that we cannot see the entire picture. We cannot know the complete mind and will of God. We must trust that there is some redeeming virtue even in the experience of suffering (Romans 5:3-5), and that God can work for good even in the midst of trying circumstances (Romans 8:28).

Jesus Is the Sacrifice

DEVOTIONAL READING: Hebrews 9:23-28.

LESSON SCRIPTURE: Hebrews 9:11—10:18.

PRINTED TEXT: Hebrews 10:1-14.

Hebrews 10:1-14

1 For the law having a shadow of good things to come, and not the very image of the things, can never with those sacrifices, which they offered year by year continually, make the comers thereunto perfect.

2 For then would they not have ceased to be offered? because that the worshippers once purged should have had no more conscience of sins.

3 But in those sacrifices there is a remembrance again made of sins every year.

4 For it is not possible that the blood of bulls and of goats should take away sins.

5 Wherefore, when he cometh into the world, he saith, Sacrifice and offering thou wouldest not, but a body hast thou prepared me:

6 In burnt offerings and sacrifices for sin thou hast had no pleasure.

7 Then said I, Lo, I come (in the volume of the book it is written of me) to do thy will, O God.

8 Above when he said, Sacrifice and offering and burnt offerings and offering for sin thou wouldest not, neither hadst pleasure therein; which are offered by the law;

9 Then said he, Lo, I come to do thy will, O God. He taketh away the first, that he may establish the second.

10 By the which will we are sanctified through the offering of the body of Jesus Christ once for all.

11 And every priest standeth daily ministering and offering oftentimes the same sacrifices, which can never take away sins:

12 But this man, after he had offered one sacrifice for sins for ever, sat down on the right hand of God;

13 From henceforth expecting till his enemies be made his footstool.

14 For by one offering he hath perfected for ever them that are sanctified.

**Jul
27**

GOLDEN TEXT: By one offering he hath perfected for ever them that are sanctified.
—Hebrews 10:14.

A Call to Faithfulness
Unit 1: The Greatness of Christ
(Lessons 6-9)

Lesson Aims

After studying this lesson, each student should:

1. Have a better understanding of the relationship between sacrifices and the forgiveness of sin.

2. Possess a deeper appreciation for the sacrifice Jesus Christ made for us.

3. Be able to share with others his or her experience of forgiven sin.

Lesson Outline

INTRODUCTION
    A. To Sacrifice a Son
    B. Lesson Background
  I. IMPERFECT SACRIFICES (Hebrews 10:1-6)
    A. Only a Shadow (v. 1)
    B. Had to Be Repeated (vv. 2, 3)
    C. Could Not Take Away Sin (v. 4)
    D. Did Not Please God (vv. 5, 6)
      The World's Most Expensive Sacrifice
  II. THE PERFECT SACRIFICE (Hebrews 10:7-14)
    A. Offered by Jesus (vv. 7, 8)
    B. Replaces the Old System (vv. 9, 10)
    C. Christ's Superior Priesthood (vv. 11-14)
      Rebel Without a Cross
CONCLUSION
    A. What Sacrifice Means
    B. Once for All
    C. Let Us Pray
    D. Thought to Remember

Use the visual for Lesson 9 to call attention to Jesus' "once for all" sacrifice. The visual is shown on page 407.

Introduction

A. To Sacrifice a Son

Many incidents recorded in the Old Testament prefigure and help us understand many teachings of the New Testament. For example, God gave Abraham a son through Sarah in his old age. No doubt Abraham experienced a sense of pride as he watched Isaac grow to maturity. But then came a commandment from God that must have devastated the aged father: he was ordered to offer Isaac as a sacri-

fice. Although Abraham must have been overwhelmed by his sadness, he prepared to carry out God's order. Isaac, too, was a willing participant in this test of Abraham's faith, for he could easily have run from his father when he realized what was about to happen. Of course, the story had a happy ending: Isaac was not sacrificed, and a substitute was found for him.

This touching story should lead us to a greater appreciation of what Jesus came to do for us. Though we cannot fully comprehend all that occurred at the cross, we know that Jesus was dying there in our place, in obedience to His Father. But whereas God intervened to spare Isaac, He did not spare His own Son, but permitted Him to suffer the agonies of the cross as a sacrifice for our sins.

B. Lesson Background

Jewish Christians in the first century were under various pressures to abandon their Christian faith and return to Judaism. The writer of the epistle to the Hebrews advances several arguments why they should resist this temptation. His major thrust is that Christianity is superior to Judaism. In the first lesson of this unit, we noted that Christianity is superior because it is based on a fuller revelation; in the former days God spoke through the prophets, but in "these last days" He has spoken through His Son (Hebrews 1:1, 2). In the second lesson, Jesus was presented as our Savior, temporarily made a little lower than the angels that He might release mankind from bondage to Satan and to death. In last week's lesson, Jesus was presented as the great High Priest after the order of Melchizedek, and as superior to the Hebrew priests who were descendants of Aaron. Today we focus on still another aspect of Christ's superiority: Jesus was a better *sacrifice*.

I. Imperfect Sacrifices (Hebrews 10:1-6)

A. Only a Shadow (v. 1)

1. For the law having a shadow of good things to come, and not the very image of the things, can never with those sacrifices, which they offered year by year continually, make the comers thereunto perfect.

In previous chapters, the author of Hebrews had set forth Jesus Christ as the perfect sacrifice for man's sins (2:9, 17; 7:26-28). In fact, he had just done so at the conclusion of the preceding chapter (9:26-28). The first eighteen verses of chapter 10 appear to bring to a climax the writer's argument up to this point. *The law* and its various details were but a *shadow of good things to come.* A shadow is never a very good representation of reality, because it does not show color. A shadow provides no details, only an outline of what is real. Furthermore, a shadow is not living; it simply indicates the absence or presence of light.

In this verse the writer of Hebrews sees the shadowy nature of the Law specifically in the sacrifices that it required. He places particular emphasis on the sacrifices associated with the Day of Atonement, which were *offered year by year continually.* The very fact that these had to be repeated is clear evidence that they could not *make the comers thereunto perfect.* Although these ceremonies were impressive, they could not free worshipers from the guilt and the tyranny of their sins. They could only establish the need for a perfect sacrifice, which was offered by Jesus—the "high priest of good things to come" (Hebrews 9:11).

B. Had to Be Repeated (vv. 2, 3)

2, 3. For then would they not have ceased to be offered? because that the worshippers once purged should have had no more conscience of sins. But in those sacrifices there is a remembrance again made of sins every year.

Had the sacrifices required by the Law been able to address man's real need, *the worshippers* would have had *no more conscience of sins.* The *New International Version* reads, "would no longer have felt guilty for their sins." The frequent offerings were a continual reminder of the people's sin and its accompanying guilt.

This point raises an interesting question. We cannot literally forget our sins. In fact, if we make a conscious effort to forget our past sins, we succeed only in embedding them more deeply in our minds. However, there is a very important difference between remembering our sins and having our consciences burdened by the guilt of these sins. The regular sacrifices under the old order served to keep alive both the memory of sins and the sense of guilt that they brought.

Christians have not completely avoided this problem. Many are burdened by a feeling of guilt that has lingered for years. This feeling may deny them the joy that comes from being cleansed from one's sins, and it can very well cripple their effectiveness as servants of the Lord. The proper understanding of two points can perhaps solve this problem. The first point is theological: God has promised, under certain conditions, to remove our sins completely. These conditions are that we trust Him wholly, that we truly repent of our sins, and that we be baptized for the forgiveness of our sins (Acts

---

How to Say It

JUDAISM. *Joo*-day-izz-um.
MELCHIZEDEK. Mel-*kizz*-ih-deck.
SEPTUAGINT. Sep-*too*-ih-jent.

2:38). As Christians we then have "an advocate with the Father" who pleads our case (1 John 2:1). We have this assurance: "If we confess our sins, he is faithful and just to forgive us our sins, and to cleanse us from all unrighteousness" (1 John 1:9).

The second point is more practical. If we are to know the joy of forgiven sins, we must make restitution for them. If we have stolen, we ought to return what we have stolen. If we have cheated, we need to reimburse those whom we have cheated. Of course, no adequate restitution can be made for certain sins, such as murder. It is impossible for one to restore a life he has destroyed. At best, all he can do is to try to alleviate some of the consequences of such a terrible sin.

A note of caution must be inserted here. Restitution must not be seen as a form of paying for one's sins. One should never allow good deeds to serve as a salve to deaden his or her conscience to the seriousness of sin. Yet many forms of restitution, conscientiously pursued, can help restore the joy that sin has stolen and the sense that one's life can still be used of God.

C. Could Not Take Away Sin (v. 4)

4. For it is not possible that the blood of bulls and of goats should take away sins.

It should have been quite obvious that the sacrifice of animals was inadequate. Animals lacked any consciousness of sin; they were but innocent victims of a process that they could not understand. Furthermore, *it is not possible* for such material or "fleshly" items to make any lasting impact on man's standing with God. They are simply a shadow (v. 1), pointing out the need for something more effective.

D. Did Not Please God (vv. 5, 6)

5, 6. Wherefore, when he cometh into the world, he saith, Sacrifice and offering thou wouldest not, but a body hast thou prepared me: in burnt offerings and sacrifices for sin thou hast had no pleasure.

Here the writer turns to the Old Testament Scriptures to strengthen his argument. He quotes from Psalm 40:6-8. Apparently the writer is quoting from the Septuagint (a Greek version of the Old Testament), rather than the Hebrew text. As a result there is a slight difference in the quotation before us. Our translation reads, *but a body hast thou prepared me*, whereas the Psalms passage, based on the Hebrew, reads, "mine ears hast thou opened."

We may question why these translations are so different or why the writer of Hebrews would quote from a reading so different from the Hebrew text. The difference, however, may not be that great. To have one's ears opened suggests two possible interpretations. The first calls to mind the practice, recorded in Exodus 21:5, 6, of boring a hole in the ear of a servant who wanted to remain with his master for life. This would reflect Jesus' singular commitment to His heavenly Father's will. The second is the idea of "opening the ear" to hear an important message (see Deuteronomy 32:44; 1 Samuel 9:15; Job 33:14-16). This too would describe Jesus' devotion to God's will (see the prophecy in Isaiah 50:4). Ultimately that devotion resulted in Jesus giving His *body* as the sacrifice for the sins of the world.

Thus, the writer of Hebrews is taking this passage from the Psalms and declaring its fulfillment in the death of Jesus, by which He carried out His Father's plan and brought salvation to mankind. We can be certain that the writer's use of the Septuagint at this point expressed the Holy Spirit's understanding of Psalm 40.

That God *had no pleasure* in *sacrifice and offering* needs to be studied carefully, in light of the fact that God did command Israel to bring these, and that they constituted a "sweet savor" to Him, as the laws in Leviticus 1-4 state repeatedly. In Old Testament times, God honored offerings and sacrifices when they were brought to Him by a humble and contrite worshiper. But they were absolutely worthless when presented as part of an empty ritual, by those who had no intention whatsoever of obeying God. This fact was recognized by the Old Testament prophets (see Isaiah 1:10-17; Jeremiah 7:22, 23; Hosea 6:6; Micah 6:6-8). These sacrifices could not completely take away sins (as v. 4 states); thus, *when he* [Jesus] came *into the world*, He brought a better sacrifice, for He brought Himself. Ephesians 5:2 says, "Christ . . . hath given himself for us an offering and a sacrifice to God for a sweet-smelling savor."

THE WORLD'S MOST EXPENSIVE SACRIFICE

It is hard to comprehend just how expensive the Old Testament sacrificial system was. Consider the cost of just the ordinary public temple sacrifices offered for the whole community (excluding whatever private sacrifices were made).

Every day of the year the priests sacrificed two lambs: one in the morning and one in the evening. On the Sabbath Day two additional lambs were sacrificed. At each new moon (signifying the beginning of a new month), the priests added two bulls, one ram, one goat, and seven lambs. They added a bull, a ram, a goat, and seven lambs for the Day of Atonement, and seventy-one bulls, fifteen rams, eight goats, and one hundred five lambs for the Feast of Tabernacles.

The Feast of Unleavened Bread (Passover) required another fourteen bulls, seven rams, seven goats, and forty-nine lambs, excluding the thousands of Passover lambs slain in every home in the nation of Israel. (See the requirements for these sacrifices in Numbers 28, 29.) The Jewish historian Josephus estimated that at the Passover in A.D. 70, 256,500 lambs were sacrificed in Jerusalem. At today's current prices, that Passover sacrifice cost almost thirty million dollars.

The world's most expensive sacrifice, however, is the one described in today's text from Hebrews 10. Jesus Christ paid the ransom for our sins, not with the blood of bulls and goats, but with His own blood. His single precious sacrifice cost more and did more than all others ever offered. —C. B. Mc.

II. The Perfect Sacrifice (Hebrews 10:7-14)

A. Offered by Jesus (vv. 7, 8)

7, 8. Then said I, Lo, I come (in the volume of the book it is written of me,) to do thy will, O God. Above when he said, Sacrifice and offering and burnt offerings and offering for sin thou wouldest not, neither hadst pleasure therein; which are offered by the law.

Verse 7 continues the quotation from Psalm 40:6-8. Jesus is speaking: *In the volume of the book it is written of me.* The reference to *sacrifice and offering and burnt offerings and offering for sin* is intended to represent the entire sacrificial system of the Mosaic Law.

B. Replaces the Old System (vv. 9, 10)

9, 10. Then said he, Lo, I come to do thy will, O God. He taketh away the first, that he may establish the second. By the which will we are sanctified through the offering of the body of Jesus Christ once for all.

God's desire has always been for man's obedience rather than sacrifice (1 Samuel 15:22). Through the obedience of Jesus Christ *the first*, that is, the Old Covenant, has been superseded by *the second*, or the New Covenant. This was all part of God's plan.

visual for
lesson 9

The process of being *sanctified*, or set apart, now comes, not through the elaborate rituals that characterized the Old Covenant, but through the offering of *the body of Jesus Christ* as a sacrifice for our sins. This offering was *once for all*; since His sacrifice was perfect, it did not have to be repeated. The finality of this offering has been mentioned in 7:27 and 9:12, 26-28.

C. Christ's Superior Priesthood
(vv. 11-14)

11, 12. And every priest standeth daily ministering and offering oftentimes the same sacrifices, which can never take away sins: but this man, after he had offered one sacrifice for sins for ever, sat down on the right hand of God.

These two verses set forth three ways in which the Aaronic priests differed from Christ. First, the Aaronic priests *standeth* while Christ *sat down on the right hand of God*. This means that their work was never-ending, whereas Christ's work is completed. Second, the Aaronic priests offered *oftentimes the same sacrifices*, whereas Christ *offered one sacrifice*. Third, the many sacrifices of the Aaronic priests *can never take away sins*, while Christ's sacrifice is sufficient to take away sins *for ever*. A thousand years from now, if Christ has not returned, His blood will still "make the foulest clean."

REBEL WITHOUT A CROSS

Barabbas was guilty of insurrection and murder. According to Mark 15:7, he and some of his cohorts had been caught and imprisoned. There Barabbas awaited his execution. As an enemy of the state, he knew he would be crucified.

Day after day Barabbas sat in the darkness of his cell and thought about dying on a cross. But when the Romans came for him, he was led from his cell, not to a cross, but to freedom. An angry mob and a band of religious power brokers had persuaded a spineless governor to nail a Galilean carpenter to a cross that should have belonged to Barabbas.

Looking at the larger picture, Barabbas stands for each of us. He was a condemned criminal who was freed because someone else took his place. Each of us is a condemned sinner who can be freed and forgiven if we accept the Christ who died in our place.

For Jesus did not die only on Barabbas's cross. He died on yours and mine.   —C. B. Mc.

13, 14. From henceforth expecting till his enemies be made his footstool. For by one offering he hath perfected for ever them that are sanctified.

Verse 13 uses the language of Psalm 110:1, a psalm with obvious Messianic implications. This psalm sets forth two aspects of the Messiah's work: the royal and the priestly. On the one hand, the Messiah is viewed as a conquering king, while on the other He is "a priest for ever after the order of Melchizedek" (Psalm 110:4). We see the same two aspects of Christ's ministry in the two verses before us.

Through Christ's *one offering*, He *hath perfected* those who have accepted His sacrifice. They have been cleansed of their past sins, and thus stand *perfected*, or complete, before Him. This does not mean that they are sinless. They *are sanctified*: they have been set apart for the Lord's service, and they are part of the ongoing process by which one becomes more like Jesus.

Conclusion

A. What Sacrifice Means

Years ago it was quite common for farmers to raise animals such as cows or pigs for their meat supply. When cold weather came, the animals would be butchered and the meat preserved by smoking, sugar curing, or canning. (In those days the only way that meat could be preserved by freezing was when the weather turned cold and stayed cold.) I was about six or seven when I first witnessed the butchering process. Late in the winter a calf had been born to one of our neighbor's cows. We watched him the first few days as he awkwardly made his way about the barnyard on unsteady legs. We continued to watch during the spring and summer, and were amazed at how quickly he grew and how agile he became. When fall came, we passed the barnyard each day on our way to and from school. Occasionally we would throw him a handful of grass or an apple. He repaid our kindness by coming to greet us when we came by.

Then came that fateful day. My brother and I did not realize what Dad meant when he said that the calf would be butchered. On a cold morning we witnessed the whole terrible process.

We boys were heartbroken because even though the calf did not belong to us, it had become our pet. Dad tried to explain to us that life was like that—that some things had to be sacrificed in order for others to live. What He said to us did not make much sense to us then, but as the years passed, we ourselves became involved in the fall butchering ritual and came to accept it as just another part of rural life.

Few young people today have this experience. In fact, few farmers do their own butchering these days. When we see cuts of meat neatly displayed in the grocery store, or eat a hamburger or chicken sandwich, we hardly give a thought to the process that was involved in making these foods available to us.

To some degree, this resembles our response to the death of our Lord on the cross. The early disciples who witnessed His crucifixion were overwhelmed by His death. Their leader—the best individual they had ever known—had been brutally slain by His enemies for no other reason than to maintain their control over the people. Only later, when the disciples began to learn the real meaning of Jesus' death, did they begin to understand what seemed at the time to have been a complete tragedy. What a difference it made when they came to realize that He died to save them from their sins! This frightened little band of followers was transformed into a spiritual force that challenged the Jewish leaders, took on the Roman Empire, and eventually spread throughout the whole world.

Insulated by two thousand years of history, have we lost our ability to feel either the tragedy or the power of Jesus' sacrificial death? Many have managed to encase His sacrifice in creeds, rituals, and traditions to the point that they no longer feel the impact of it. The Hebrew Chris-

tians, some of whom may even have witnessed Christ's death, were in danger of falling into the same trap, abandoning their Christian faith and returning to their former way of life.

Perhaps our appreciation of Christ's sacrifice for us would deepen if we could climb into some magical time machine and be transported back to the first century. Standing at the foot of the cross and watching Jesus die there would certainly give a deeper meaning to the words, "We are sanctified through the offering of the body of Jesus Christ once for all" (Hebrews 10:10). Of course, we cannot go back in time. But we can give renewed diligence to our study of the Scriptures that tell us who Jesus is and what He did for us. May we never forget what His sacrifice means.

B. Once for All

Under the Mosaic Law, the priests regularly conducted numerous sacrifices. Across the centuries multiplied thousands of animals were offered, first in the tabernacle worship and later in the temple worship. All of these were limited in their impact, for the blood of animals could not take away sin. At best these sacrifices could only remind the people of their continual guilt before God. From a positive standpoint, the sacrifices looked ahead to the perfect sacrifice of Jesus. As the spotless Lamb of God, Jesus gave Himself "once for all" on the cross. His sacrifice does not need to be repeated.

"Once for all" has another application. Jesus was sacrificed for all—for everyone. The sacrifices in the tabernacle and the temple were primarily for the benefit of the Israelite people. Some allowance was made for "strangers" to participate (see Leviticus 17:8, 9; 22:18, 19), but clearly Gentiles were considered "aliens from the commonwealth of Israel, and strangers from the covenants of promise" (Ephesians 2:12).

In glorious contrast, the benefits of Christ's death on the cross reached beyond the limits prescribed by the Law. The gospel message of hope is for *everyone*. What a wonderful opportunity we have to share this good news: Christ died once for every sin of every person.

C. Let Us Pray

Holy and loving Father, we come before You giving our thanks for sending Your Son to die for us. We thank You that this sacrifice will never have to be repeated. May this wonderful truth be the guiding light of our lives. Amen.

D. Thought to Remember

Jesus, who was innocent, took the punishment that we, who were guilty, deserved.

Home Daily Bible Readings

Monday, July 21—The New Covenant Superior to First (Hebrews 8:7-13)

Tuesday, July 22—Christ Sacrificed One Time Only (Hebrews 9:23-28)

Wednesday, July 23—The New Covenant Verified (Hebrews 9:11-22)

Thursday, July 24—God Does Not Want Sacrifices (Psalm 40:4-10)

Friday, July 25—To Obey Is Better Than Sacrifice (1 Samuel 15:16-23)

Saturday, July 26—To Love Is Better Than Sacrifice (Mark 12:28-34)

Sunday, July 27—Walk Humbly With Your God (Micah 6:1-8)

Learning by Doing

This page contains an alternate lesson plan emphasizing learning activities. Classes desiring such student involvement will find these suggestions helpful.

Learning Goals

From today's study, students should:

1. Identify similarities and differences between Abraham's plan to sacrifice Isaac and God's actual sacrifice of His Son.

2. Identify similarities and differences between the system of Aaronic sacrifices and the sacrifice of Christ.

3. Give thanks that they live, not under the "shadow" of animal sacrifices, but in the full light of Christ's death for their sins.

Into the Lesson

Make five copies of Genesis 22:1-14. Label the copies for five readers: NARRATOR, GOD, ABRAHAM, ISAAC, ANGEL OF THE LORD. Mark the lines in the text that each person should read. Recruit five class members and direct them to look over their parts, then have them stand before the class and read this text, each reading his character's words after the NARRATOR "sets the scene." Direct your readers, either by highlighting their copies or orally (if you can prompt them privately beforehand), to read in unison verse 14. Explain that the name *Jehovah-jireh* (which appears in the *King James Version*) means "The Lord will provide."

At the conclusion of their reading, ask your class to identify <u>S</u>imilarities and <u>D</u>ifferences between this incident and the offering of Jesus at Calvary. The list should include: S—Both are fathers offering prized sons; D—One son is bound; the other, nailed; S—Both sons are to be pierced; D—One event is private; the other, public; S—Both sons appear fully submissive; D—God spoke at the one; at the other He was silent; S—God demanded that each occur; D—One offering was suspended; the other, completed. (You might add a bit more participation by dividing your class into "Similarities" and "Differences" teams. See which team can come up with more responses.)

Into the Word

Give this true-false quiz on today's text aloud (unless your group uses the student book, where it is included). Answers are given here.

(1) The system of Old Testament sacrifices was designed to make the people whole before God. *F* (2) Animal blood fully atoned for the worshiper's sin if he offered it in sincerity. *F* (3) Animal sacrifices were a constant reminder of personal sinfulness. *T* (4) Old Testament priests had a never-ending job. *T* (5) For the sacrifice of Jesus to have effect, the first system of sacrifices had to be taken away. *T* (6) The onetime offering of Jesus as a sacrifice for sin perfects forever those who are made holy through it. *T* (7) The Law was to salvation as a shadow is to the substance creating it. *T* (8) David, in Psalm 40, prophesied the incarnation of Christ. *T* (9) After being offered as a sacrifice for sin, Jesus took His place at the right hand of God. *T*

Once the students have had opportunity to respond, go through the statements for discussion, especially where there is disagreement. Some statements may lend themselves to more disagreement than others. For example, some may put *false* for the fourth statement, because the Old Testament priest's job *did* end when he died. Point out that during the time the priest served in that capacity, he could never consider his job of offering sacrifices "finished." Only Jesus had the right to say, "It is finished."

Into Life

Hand each student seven blank cards (index cards will work fine, or strips of paper cut into rectangles will do). Direct them to take the first card and put *A* on one side, *I* on the other; second card, *D* and *P*; third, *E* and *M*; fourth, *G* and *U*; fifth, *R* and *R*; sixth, *T* and *T*; and seventh, *Y* and *H*. Use one color for the letters on one side and a different color for the letters on the other side. Read aloud or summarize the story found in the first three paragraphs under the heading, "What Sacrifice Means," on page 407 of the lesson commentary; then read aloud the final three paragraphs of that section (beginning, "To some degree, this resembles . . ."). Now ask the students to lay out the seven cards and attempt to form a seven-letter word from the first set of letters they wrote: *A, D, E, G, R, T, Y*. Once someone forms *tragedy*, ask all to thus arrange their cards. At your direction have all turn their cards over, one at a time, to form the word *triumph*. Relate this to the material under "What Sacrifice Means," pointing out that the death of Jesus, which at first seemed an utter *tragedy*, was ultimately seen as a grand *triumph*.

Close with a prayer of thanksgiving for what God has provided through Christ's sacrifice.

Let's Talk It Over

The questions on this page are designed to encourage review of the lesson Scriptures and to promote discussion of the lesson by the class. The answers provided are only discussion starters. Let your class talk it over from there.

1. Is penance an effective way of relieving guilt for sin? Is it effective in relieving guilt feelings? Explain.

Penance generally involves doing acts of devotion to God or kindness to others, in addition to those one might normally do, in order to receive forgiveness for one's sins. Most people view penance as a kind of fine or sentence for sins committed. It is like the hours of "community service" that judges sometimes require from someone convicted of a crime. Guilt cannot be removed, however, by such acts of devotion, but only by the grace of God and His forgiveness. There is no such thing as getting "extra credit," or being devoted today in order to make up for yesterday's sin. God deserves complete devotion and obedience, so we can never earn extra credit. Penance may enforce discipline and remind us of the need to obey God, but it is not effective in removing feelings of guilt. In fact, it may actually stand in the way of finding real forgiveness through the sacrifice of Jesus.

2. Give an example of how someone today might try to atone for personal offenses through material sacrifices or gifts. Why is that repugnant, especially with regard to offenses toward God?

The story is told of a woman who was wearing a beautiful piece of jewelry given to her by her husband. Someone admired it and said, "He must love you very much." With tears in her eyes she replied, "Actually, this gift is an apology for his lack of love." Do you suppose the jewelry could ever truly make up for the husband's lack of attention or affection for his wife? It was presumptuous of him to think it could, and it is presumptuous of anyone to think that he can please God by giving gifts as a substitute for personal devotion and obedience. A materialistic, self-indulgent, "do it my way" person should not think that he can make up for his irreverence and disobedience by making a large contribution to the building fund at church, or by going through the motions of religious ritual. A humble, contrite, and believing heart is what God desires most. Only when we think that we are the most unworthy to come to God, are we really the most prepared to receive His grace. He cannot fill us unless we are empty.

3. If God takes no pleasure in burnt offerings and sacrifices (Hebrews 10:6, 8), why were they required under the Old Covenant?

The sacrificial system prescribed in the Law teaches all of us that God regards sin very seriously, and that justice demands that a penalty be paid for every disobedience. Without an understanding of the demands of justice, we could never appreciate grace. The sacrifices offered under the Law, as ineffective as they were, forecast the day when the perfect sacrifice would be offered for sin once and for all by the Lamb of God.

4. Has anyone, other than Jesus, ever made a great personal sacrifice entirely for your benefit? How does that make you feel? How does that compare with what Jesus has done for you?

Did your parents sacrifice to send you to college? Did they do without Christmas gifts for one another when you were a child, so that you could have some treasured toy? Has your spouse sacrificed security or advancement in a job in order to help you pursue a goal you desired to reach? Has your life been extended because someone donated a kidney or other organ? If you have ever been the recipient of some such act of sacrificial love, you are undoubtedly grateful. I experience a flood of emotion when I think about all that I have received that I can never repay. Jesus gave His all for us. He accomplished something for us that we could never accomplish for ourselves—the forgiveness of our debt before God. If ever we should feel grateful, we should toward Jesus.

5. How can Christ's one sacrifice be sufficient to forgive the sins of the entire world?

The value of Jesus' sacrifice cannot be calculated in terms of any exchange rate. Jesus lived a life of pure obedience to the will of the Father, yet died the death of a common criminal. "The wages of sin is death" (Romans 6:23), but since Jesus had no sin He did not deserve to die. By His death He paid the wages that all of us "owed" before God. That sacrifice does not need to be supplemented or repeated. The testimony of Scripture is that Jesus' sacrifice is "for sins for ever" (Hebrews 10:12).

Grow In Faithfulness

DEVOTIONAL READING: Hebrews 6:13-20.

LESSON SCRIPTURE: Hebrews 5:11—6:12.

PRINTED TEXT: Hebrews 5:11—6:10.

Hebrews 5:11-14

11 Of whom we have many things to say, and hard to be uttered, seeing ye are dull of hearing.

12 For when for the time ye ought to be teachers, ye have need that one teach you again which be the first principles of the oracles of God; and are become such as have need of milk, and not of strong meat.

13 For every one that useth milk is unskilful in the word of righteousness: for he is a babe.

14 But strong meat belongeth to them that are of full age, even those who by reason of use have their senses exercised to discern both good and evil.

Hebrews 6:1-10

1 Therefore leaving the principles of the doctrine of Christ, let us go on unto perfection; not laying again the foundation of repentance from dead works, and of faith toward God,

2 Of the doctrine of baptisms, and of laying on of hands, and of resurrection of the dead, and of eternal judgment.

3 And this will we do, if God permit.

4 For it is impossible for those who were once enlightened, and have tasted of the heavenly gift, and were made partakers of the Holy Ghost,

5 And have tasted the good word of God, and the powers of the world to come,

6 If they shall fall away, to renew them again unto repentance; seeing they crucify to themselves the Son of God afresh, and put him to an open shame.

7 For the earth which drinketh in the rain that cometh oft upon it, and bringeth forth herbs meet for them by whom it is dressed, receiveth blessing from God:

8 But that which beareth thorns and briers is rejected, and is nigh unto cursing; whose end is to be burned.

9 But, beloved, we are persuaded better things of you, and things that accompany salvation, though we thus speak.

10 For God is not unrighteous to forget your work and labor of love, which ye have showed toward his name, in that ye have ministered to the saints, and do minister.

Aug 3

GOLDEN TEXT: Let us go on unto perfection. —Hebrews 6:1.

A Call to Faithfulness
Unit 2: Be Faithful Followers of Christ
(Lessons 10-14)

Lesson Aims

After studying this lesson from Hebrews 5, students should:

1. Have a better understanding of spiritual maturity and be able to recognize some of its evidences.

2. Be aware of the bitter consequences of falling away from their faith.

3. Be motivated to strive for spiritual maturity and to move beyond their present level of growth.

Lesson Outline

INTRODUCTION
    A. Bonsai Christians
    B. Lesson Background
  I. EVIDENCE OF SPIRITUAL IMMATURITY (Hebrews 5:11-14)
    A. Having Dull Hearing (v. 11)
      Lazy
    B. Needing Milk (vv. 12, 13)
    C. Not of Full Age (v. 14)
      An Oak or a Squash?
  II. A CHALLENGE TO CHRISTIANS (Hebrews 6:1-3)
    A. Leaving First Principles (v. 1a)
    B. Not Laying Foundations Again (vv. 1b-3)
  III. THE DANGERS OF TURNING BACK (Hebrews 6:4-10)
    A. Impossibility of Renewal (vv. 4-6)
    B. An Illustration From Nature (vv. 7, 8)
    C. The Writer's Confidence (v. 9)
    D. God's Sure Reward (v. 10)
CONCLUSION
    A. The Slippery Slope
    B. Let Us Pray
    C. Thought to Remember

The visual for Lesson 10 is a unique illustration of today's challenge to grow beyond the need for "milk." It is shown on page 415.

Introduction

A. Bonsai Christians

The Japanese have developed great skill in the art of *bonsai* (bahn-*sye*)—the growing of miniature trees. These trees may be decades old and yet only a few inches tall. Gardeners are able to produce them by using a number of special techniques. The roots are cut and restricted. The branches are carefully trimmed. Then water and fertilizer are withheld. The result is a tree that has many features of a full-grown tree, yet is small enough to sit on a table or shelf.

Many Christians resemble these bonsais. In certain respects they may look like mature believers, but in reality they are miniatures—mere babes in Christ. Satan is a master at growing bonsai Christians. He continually seeks to restrict our progress by keeping us from Bible study, prayer, fellowship, and other means of spiritual nourishment. The result is stunted "bonsai" Christians.

B. Lesson Background

This lesson begins a new unit, "Be Faithful Followers of Christ," which continues our studies from the book of Hebrews. This unit (the final one in this quarter) addresses the problems and obstacles to growth that the Hebrew Christians were facing. They were in danger of succumbing to the temptation to abandon their faith in Jesus and retreat back into Judaism.

Most modern Christians have never been adherents of Judaism and may not be tempted to follow this particular faith. But they are often tempted to surrender to the secularism of the society around them. In some respects the appeal of secularism poses a more dangerous threat to modern Christians than Judaism did to these early Hebrew Christians. When a Hebrew Christian returned to Judaism, he moved from a very small minority group to a group that was larger, but still a minority. He was still considered out of the mainstream of the dominant culture of his day. On the other hand, the modern Christian, when he moves from Christianity back into the secular world, has become a part of the culture that is now dominant. He becomes like his friends and neighbors, and he does not have to feel different or out of place.

Another reason that secularism is so dangerous is that its temptations are so subtle. Secularism does not require its adherents to abandon their previous faith altogether. They can still attend church and be involved in church activities; at the same time, they may live much of their lives according to secular rather than Christian standards. In many instances it becomes difficult to tell Christians apart from non-Christians.

Thus, even though our circumstances today may be quite different from those of the original readers of Hebrews, the five remaining lessons in this quarter speak to some pressing needs within our churches and the lives of Christians.

I. Evidence of Spiritual Immaturity (Hebrews 5:11-14)

A. Having Dull Hearing (v. 11)

11. Of whom we have many things to say, and hard to be uttered, seeing ye are dull of hearing.

In the previous verses of chapter 5, the writer has contrasted the priestly order of Aaron with that of Melchizedek. He has shown that Christ belongs to the order of Melchizedek, which is superior to the order of Aaron. Christ is superior because He "became the author of eternal salvation unto all them that obey him" (v. 9). (You may want to review Lesson 8, which covered Hebrews 4:14—5:10.)

The words of this verse indicate the writer's awareness that many of his readers may not have understood him when he discussed the relationship between the priesthoods of Aaron and Melchizedek. This concept may have been quite new to them, or their minds were so clouded by previous ideas that they could not comprehend what he was presenting to them. The writer challenges their thinking by accusing them of being *dull of hearing*, hoping to prepare them for other truths he wants to explain to them.

LAZY

When the writer of Hebrews interrupts his discussion of Jesus and Melchizedek in chapter 5, he says that he did so because his readers were "dull of hearing" (v. 11).

The word *dull* translates a Greek word *nothros* (*naw*-thross), which means "lazy" or "sluggish." The Greeks used it of lazy workmen. It is also found in Hebrews 6:12: "That ye be not *slothful*, but followers of them who through faith and patience inherit the promises."

Did you ever notice how negative our words for lazy people are: *sluggard, loafer, bum, goldbrick, deadbeat, goof-off, tramp*? These are all hated words—words that none of us want applied to ourselves. Yet this is what the Hebrew Christians had become concerning God's Word. While they had been Christians for some time, they had failed to grow in their faith and in their knowledge of essential spiritual truths.

How to Say It

JUDAISM. *Joo*-day-izz-um.
MELCHIZEDEK. Mel-*kizz*-ih-deck.

Think of how useless *dull* items are. A dull knife will not cut. A dull hoe will not dig. A dull chisel will not hew wood. Any dull tool is useless. We too cannot afford to be dull. We must remain sharp Christians—ready to practice God's Word and teach it to others. We cannot afford to be lazy in studying the Word.

—C. B. Mc.

B. Needing Milk (vv. 12, 13)

12, 13. For when for the time ye ought to be teachers, ye have need that one teach you again which be the first principles of the oracles of God; and are become such as have need of milk, and not of strong meat. For every one that useth milk is unskilful in the word of righteousness: for he is a babe.

Growth toward maturity in the faith seldom appears to progress at a consistent rate; usually it takes place by starts and stops. Still, after a certain lapse of time, some evidence of growth ought to be obvious. Since some of the readers of Hebrews had been Christians for quite some time (as seems the case from Hebrews 10:32), the writer had every reason to expect to see some signs of growth. He laments the fact that some individuals should have been *teachers* at this point, yet they still needed someone to teach them a "remedial" course in basics, or *first principles*.

This assessment sounds very much like the condition of some in our churches today. They have been in Sunday school classes and other Bible study groups all of their lives, and yet they hardly know the fundamentals of the gospel. They have not progressed from the *milk* stage to the level of being able to handle *strong meat*. In some cases, teachers may share some of the responsibility for these Biblical illiterates, for, as someone has observed, "If the student hasn't learned, the teacher hasn't taught."

C. Not of Full Age (v. 14)

14. But strong meat belongeth to them that are of full age, even those who by reason of use have their senses exercised to discern both good and evil.

The diet of small babies is limited to milk, because they lack the ability to chew and swallow *meat*. However, those who are mature, or *of full age*, can find nourishment in meat. Through this illustration, the writer was trying to show why immature Christians were having trouble understanding the doctrine of the superiority of the priesthood of Melchizedek and, as a result, the superiority of Christ's priesthood.

This verse also gives us some insights on how Christians attain maturity. They *have their senses exercised.* The word translated *exercised* is one from which our word "gymnasium" comes. It describes the rigorous exercise by which athletes prepared themselves for their contests. Such physical conditioning cannot be accomplished in one quick burst of activity, nor by a hit-and-miss schedule.

The writer of Hebrews suggests that spiritual maturity is gained in the same way. Occasionally important spiritual insights may seem to come like a brilliant burst of light. In reality, such sudden illumination has been preceded by long periods of study and practice. We know, too, that a high spiritual level can be maintained only by giving regular attention to spiritual disciplines. Occasional prayer, sporadic church attendance, and infrequent instances of Christian service will not accomplish this.

AN OAK OR A SQUASH?

When James A. Garfield was president of Hiram College, a wealthy man brought his son to be enrolled as a student. The man was very impatient for his son to finish college and join him in his business. The man asked if his son could take a shorter course of study than usual so he could get through college quickly. "Yes," Mr. Garfield answered. "He can take a shorter course than usual, but it all depends on what you want to make of him. It takes God a hundred years to produce a mighty oak, but he can turn out a squash in two months."

To be a mature Christian requires discipline and study. Today's text from Hebrews speaks of training and using our spiritual faculties so that we might become mature disciples.

The apostle Peter describes the process this way: "And besides this, giving all diligence, add

---

Home Daily Bible Readings

Monday, July 28—God's Covenant Promise Unchanged (Hebrews 6:13-20)

Tuesday, July 29—Servants Rewarded for Good Work (Matthew 10:34-42)

Wednesday, July 30—By Grace We Are Saved (Ephesians 2:1-9)

Thursday, July 31—Escape Temptations With God's Help (1 Corinthians 10:1-13)

Friday, Aug. 1—God Punishes the Wicked (Job 4:1-9)

Saturday, Aug. 2—Grow in Your Salvation (1 Peter 2:1-5)

Sunday, Aug. 3—Prophecy Came From the Holy Spirit (2 Peter 1:12-21)

---

to your faith virtue; and to virtue, knowledge; and to knowledge, temperance; and to temperance, patience; and to patience, godliness; and to godliness, brotherly kindness; and to brotherly kindness, charity. For if these things be in you, and abound, they make you that ye shall neither be barren nor unfruitful in the knowledge of our Lord Jesus Christ" (2 Peter 1:5-8).

To become a spiritual oak requires great diligence and effort. Shortcuts will yield squashes.

—C. B. Mc.

II. A Challenge To Christians (Hebrews 6:1-3)

A. Leaving First Principles (v. 1a)

1a. Therefore leaving the principles of the doctrine of Christ, let us go on unto perfection.

The writer in the previous verses has rebuked his readers because they were still babes in Christ, not mature enough for anything but milk. Now he challenges them to leave behind the milk of the *principles of the doctrine of Christ* and *go on unto perfection*. Such a challenge indicates that these believers were actually ready to grow; they simply needed someone to encourage them and instill some self-confidence in them.

When the writer tells his readers to leave these principles behind, he does not mean for these principles to be discarded altogether. Instead, they should be used as a starting point for greater knowledge. We do not, for example, forget the ABC's when we learn to read. We use them as building blocks for the development of higher skills.

The *perfection* toward which the Hebrew Christians are urged is not a sinless moral state. The word is better translated "maturity," as several of the more recent versions render it.

B. Not Laying Foundations Again (vv. 1b-3)

1b-3. Not laying again the foundation of repentance from dead works, and of faith toward God, of the doctrine of baptisms, and of laying on of hands, and of resurrection of the dead, and of eternal judgment. And this will we do, if God permit.

Here the writer lists some specific teachings that are included within the "first principles" to which he has referred (5:12). *Repentance from dead works* is a repentance from those evil deeds that lead to spiritual death. This is an essential part of the conversion process (Luke 13:3; Acts 17:30).

Faith toward God is absolutely necessary if one is to become a Christian, but this faith may be quite simple and unsophisticated. The

Hebrew Christians are urged to move beyond their simple faith to a more mature level.

Next, the writer mentions *the doctrine of baptisms*. The presence of the plural has led to a variety of interpretations by scholars and commentators. Some take this to be a reference to the various ceremonial washings associated with Jewish religious practices. On the other hand, *baptisms* may be plural because the people had witnessed many baptisms as the church reached out to the world with its evangelistic message. Still another possibility is that this term refers to the various baptisms associated with the ministry of Jesus: John's baptism (Acts 19:1-5), Christian baptism (introduced on the Day of Pentecost), and the baptism of the Holy Spirit (Acts 1:5; 2:1-4). Whatever the meaning here, the writer urges his readers to progress beyond these teachings.

The *laying on of hands* may refer to ordaining a person to a special ministry. It was also associated with the power of the apostles to impart the Holy Spirit to a person, endowing him with special miraculous gifts (Acts 8:14-24).

The teachings concerning *resurrection of the dead, and of eternal judgment* deal with the future hope possessed by all Christians. Death is not the end for any faithful follower of Jesus. Judgment, which is a dreadful prospect for the lost, holds no fear for Christians, for they will have Jesus as their Advocate on that day.

This will we do refers back to the writer's exhortation in verse 1 to leave the first principles and press on toward maturity.

III. The Dangers of Turning Back (Hebrews 6:4-10)

A. Impossibility of Renewal (vv. 4-6)

4-6. For it is impossible for those who were once enlightened, and have tasted of the heavenly gift, and were made partakers of the Holy Ghost, and have tasted the good word of God, and the powers of the world to come, if they shall fall away, to renew them again unto repentance; seeing they crucify to themselves the Son of God afresh, and put him to an open shame.

These verses provide an additional motivation for the Hebrew Christians to leave the first principles and continue to grow toward maturity. The motivation comes in the form of a solemn warning: to fail to grow is to invite the possibility that they will *fall away*, or reach a stage of apostasy from Christ, from which there is no return. Those in such danger are not described as casual church members who once made only a shallow commitment. The warning is directed

visual for lesson 10

to *those who were once enlightened*; that is, they had a sound understanding of the Christian faith. They *have tasted of the heavenly gift*: they had experienced the blessings that accompany the gift of salvation. They *were made partakers of the Holy Ghost*: they had received the gift of the Holy Spirit that is promised to all who believe in Christ, repent, and are baptized (Acts 2:38). They *have tasted the good word of God, and the powers of the world to come*: they had known the joys that the message of salvation can bring, including the hope of eternal life.

If people who have experienced all these blessings—who, in other words, have become Christians—then *fall away*, the writer says that *it is impossible . . . to renew them again unto repentance*. The reason is this: *they crucify to themselves the Son of God afresh*. Whereas those who partake of the Lord's Supper remember the crucifixion of Jesus, those described in this verse actually reenact the crucifixion, subjecting Jesus *to an open shame*. This is the kind of willful sin discussed in Hebrews 10:26, 27. Such a deliberate rejection of Christ and His salvation brings a person to a point of no return. The problem is not God's inability to help such a person; it is that person's unwillingness to be helped.

Many scholars hold that the writer of Hebrews was not suggesting that such dreadful apostasy had actually occurred among his readers. Verse 9 seems to support this view. Rather, he was pointing out the dreadful results if it should happen. He has already warned his readers of the tragic consequences of unbelief and of their need to maintain their commitment to Jesus (3:7—4:11). He returns to this issue again in 10:26-39, warning them to hold fast and to guard against apostasy.

B. An Illustration From Nature (vv. 7, 8)

7, 8. For the earth which drinketh in the rain that cometh oft upon it, and bringeth forth herbs meet for them by whom it is dressed, receiveth blessing from God: but that which beareth thorns and briers is rejected, and is nigh unto cursing; whose end is to be burned.

To make sure that no one misses his point, the writer offers an illustration from agriculture. He depicts a plot of ground that receives *rain* and is properly *dressed*, or cultivated. This plot in turn brings forth a bountiful crop. He then describes another plot that, although it receives similar treatment, produces nothing but *thorns and briers*. Its *end is to be burned*. The writer suggests that a similar end awaits apostates.

C. The Writer's Confidence (v. 9)

9. But, beloved, we are persuaded better things of you, and things that accompany salvation, though we thus speak.

The previous verses carried a severe warning against apostasy. Now addressing his readers as *beloved*, the writer offers them words of encouragement. He does not believe that they are guilty of such apostasy at this point.

D. God's Sure Reward (v. 10)

10. For God is not unrighteous to forget your work and labor of love, which ye have showed toward his name, in that ye have ministered to the saints, and do minister.

God is not some brutal tyrant who acts whimsically. As a righteous and loving God, He will remember the *work and labor of love* that His people *have showed toward his name*. The Hebrew Christians had demonstrated their love for God by ministering *to the saints*, an activity that they were faithfully continuing.

Conclusion

A. The Slippery Slope

It is an axiom of human behavior that no one becomes good or bad suddenly. On one occasion we were shocked to learn that a bank officer, who was a church member and a highly respected leader in the community where we were living, had absconded with several hundred thousand dollars of the bank's funds. How were we to account for such a sudden breakdown in a person's moral character? The only way to understand such an action is to recognize that it was not *sudden*. Had we been able to look into the man's heart, no doubt we would have discovered that he had toyed with the idea for months or even years.

The first time Satan presented the temptation to this man, it is likely that he recoiled from it in shock. Such an idea was unthinkable! But Satan returned again and again, gradually wearing away the man's resistance. Finally, on that fateful day, the man yielded and the deed was done.

It was this kind of pattern against which the writer of Hebrews was warning. Apparently his readers had not yet reached the critical stage of apostasy from Christ, but he recognized the danger signs. A little turning back here, a tiny stepping aside there, and before long the person or the group has started down the long, slippery slope ending in destruction.

Christians today face a similar threat. At some point in our lives we made a commitment to Jesus Christ. We recognized Him as our Lord and Savior, repented of our sins, and were buried with Him in Christian baptism. As time passed, we grew in our faith and we became more involved in the work of His kingdom.

Then something happened, perhaps something seemingly minor. We missed a church service, or we failed to carry out some assignment we had promised to do for the church. Our conscience probably bothered us, and we promised ourselves that it would never happen again. But it did. It was easier the second time, and the third. The excuses became easier too.

At the time, these departures from what we knew was right did not seem all that serious. After all, we said to ourselves, next month or next year it will be different. What we failed to realize was that we had started down a long, slippery slope—the same slippery slope about which the writer of Hebrews warns.

An airplane that makes a long flight over a large body of water carries enough fuel to make the flight, plus a reserve supply just in case some unanticipated problem arises. On rare occasions a problem does arise, and the plane, if it has flown a hundred or even several hundred miles out to sea, is able to turn back to the airport where it started. But there comes a time in the flight when the plane cannot turn back. It has reached the point of no return. Regardless of the problem, it cannot go back; it must continue its flight. Today's text from Hebrews has warned us about the danger of reaching a similar point of no return in departing from the faith.

Let us move on beyond the first principles, so that we do not fall into similar danger.

B. Let Us Pray

Dear God and heavenly Father, help us to realize that Satan is constantly attacking, seeking to cause us to turn back from our service to You. Give us the wisdom to recognize these temptations when they arise and the strength to resist them. Through Jesus our great High Priest we pray. Amen.

C. Thought to Remember

"No man, having put his hand to the plow, and looking back, is fit for the kingdom of God" (Luke 9:62).

Learning by Doing

This page contains an alternate lesson plan emphasizing learning activities.
Classes desiring such student involvement will find these suggestions helpful.

Learning Goals

Today's study from Hebrews should enable students to:

1. Enumerate the qualities of spiritual maturity found in today's text.

2. Recognize the dangers and consequences of remaining immature in their faith.

3. Make a commitment to acquire the "better things" mentioned in Hebrews 6:9.

Into the Lesson

If you or an acquaintance grows a bonsai plant, bring one to display as class begins. Use the lesson writer's Introduction, entitled "Bonsai Christians," to introduce the concept of "stunted growth."

If such a plant is unavailable, prepare the door frame in the entrance to your room as a height-measuring device. Prominently mark inches and feet, and post a can't-be-missed sign asking the question, "How Tall Are You?" If you think your class would feel comfortable with such an activity, measure each person, write his or her height on a small piece of paper, and hand it to the person.

Into the Word

Collect (during the week before class) eight or more of the following items: (1) a ruler and chalk, (2) an empty milk carton, (3) a sign with the number "10.0," (4) a pair of gloves, (5) a cross in any form, (6) a bottle of spices or herbs, (7) a cupcake or muffin with a candle stuck in the middle, (8) a renewal notice, such as one for a magazine subscription, (9) a thorny branch, such as one from a rosebush, (10) a piece of exercise equipment, such as a small dumbbell, (11) a baby doll, (12) a baptismal certificate, and (13) a rain gauge. Have these ready to display, but keep them hidden until the appropriate time.

Tell the class members that you have some objects you are going to display, which you want them to relate in some way to today's text. Ask them to wait until all objects are displayed before responding. (It is best to have a table on which you can lay each object once you have clearly shown it to the group.) Since the objects are small, present each slowly and carefully, even moving about with it so that all can see. Random order is best, so don't worry about sequence.

Here is the verse to which each of the thirteen objects listed refers (numbered in accordance with how the objects were numbered earlier): (1) teaching (5:12, "ought to be teachers"); (2) immaturity (5:12, "have need of milk"); (3) perfection, as in a perfect score in gymnastics (6:1, "go on to perfection"); (4) hands (6:2, "laying on of hands"); (5) crucifixion (6:6, "crucify to themselves the Son of God afresh"); (6) growth (6:7, "bringeth forth herbs"); (7) birthdays and aging (5:14, "them that are of full age"); (8) renewal (6:6, "to renew them again"); (9) the growth of something useless or unwelcome (6:8, "beareth thorns and briers"); (10) exercising in righteousness (5:14, "senses exercised to discern both good and evil"); (11) infancy (5:13, "he is a babe"); (12) baptism (6:2, "doctrine of baptisms"); (13) being fruitful for God (6:7, "earth which drinketh in the rain").

Once all of your objects have been introduced and displayed, ask the class to establish the relationships. Remember, even if they suggest ideas other than those listed, they *are* considering the text and its ideas closely. As the objects and the text are thus matched, you will have opportunity to ask whatever key questions or make whatever appropriate comments you choose.

Into Life

Have someone dress in exercise clothes ("sweats") and be prepared to give the following "pep talk" on good health and fitness. Ask the person to exaggerate his or her talk in the hyper-active fashion of a TV "infomercial" host or hostess and to include the following statements: (1) "You must eat the right foods . . . in the right amounts!" (2) "You must avoid the wrong foods . . . in any amounts!" (3) "You've got to get the blood pumping!" (4) "Your program must be regular, daily, constant!" (5) "There are no gimmicks, no shortcuts, no magic pills or tonics!" (6) "*So* . . . I am persuaded better things of you!"

Have these statements written on poster board (which you will now display) or on sheets of paper that you will now distribute. Ask how each principle relates to developing *spiritual* health. Point out that spiritual growth is not automatic; it requires disciplined effort.

Close the session by encouraging your class to strive for the "better things . . . that accompany salvation," mentioned in Hebrews 6:9.

Let's Talk It Over

The questions on this page are designed to encourage review of the lesson Scriptures and to promote discussion of the lesson by the class. The answers provided are only discussion starters. Let your class talk it over from there.

1. What can cause us to be "dull of hearing" (Hebrews 5:11) when it comes to spiritual matters?

We are all aware of how difficult it is to hear a whisper when there is a lot of noise around us. The enticements and distractions of this world may capture our attention so that we are less likely to seek out or hear spiritual truth. We get deeply involved in managing and protecting what is ours (family, possessions, health, career). We become preoccupied with the pursuit of material wealth. We begin to cultivate an appetite for entertainment. All of this contributes to a state of being inattentive or even disinterested in spiritual truth or eternal matters. In our culture, it seems that in order to gain a hearing for spiritual truth it must be presented in a sensational or entertaining format. Even then there is resistance to such themes as sacrifice, obedience, and generosity because of prevailing attitudes about personal rights.

2. How would you measure the progress you have made in your spiritual growth since becoming a believer? What has been the greatest help to you? The greatest hindrance?

There are various measures we may apply to spiritual growth. The issue in Hebrews 5 seems to be spiritual understanding. Are you increasing in your knowledge of God's truth and the teachings of the Bible? Can you share what you know with others and make it clear? Another measure of progress has to do with application. Is there evidence in your life of obedience to the commands of Jesus? Are there more acts of love and kindness? Is there more forgiveness? Is there more of genuine worship and prayer? A third measure is the fruit of the Spirit (Galatians 5:22, 23). Are these qualities observable in your life in increasing measure? You may be able to testify that the greatest help in your growth has come from the example of others, the instruction received in Sunday school or other study groups, the encouragement and accountability received in a small group or prayer partnership, the personal discipline of prayer and Bible study, or from service rendered to others. Hindrances will vary, but will include most any item or practice that hampers the growth-producing factors we have mentioned.

3. What is your church doing to encourage spiritual growth in its members? Are these measures effective? What else could be done?

Most churches know that it is important to "make disciples," which includes "teaching them to obey" (Matthew 28:19, 20, *New International Version*). Many churches, however, are not very intentional about getting the task done. Even though they may provide a Sunday school class and/or a midweek Bible study, many churches have not defined how individual Christians will grow, nor have they provided a systematic way for that to be accomplished. It might be helpful to discuss, with your minister and other church leaders, the specific objectives of the church in terms of the personal growth of its members. Just raising the question may challenge them to consider some precise definitions. Are there training opportunities that offer "milk" for the beginner as well as those that offer "strong meat"? Is there a clear progression that members are encouraged to follow so that they do not stay on a constant diet of "milk"?

4. How can we accommodate the needs of seekers or new believers in the church, but still help others move on to maturity?

In recent years the terms "seeker driven" and "seeker sensitive" have become commonly used with regard to church planning. The seeker driven churches plan their Sunday worship with the objective of reaching those who are not yet devoted followers of Jesus. Their services may not follow the traditional worship format. They may use special music, drama, or topical messages to persuade seekers of their need for Jesus as Savior and Lord. Many of these churches then offer a worship service especially for believers at another time in the week. Seeker sensitive churches continue to plan Sunday worship for the benefit of believers, but with special consideration for visitors (for example, giving brief explanations of various elements in the service). What many churches are discovering is that they cannot meet a variety of needs all in one setting. In order to reach the seeker, nurture the new believer, and care for the mature believer's needs, churches must be creative and consider adding ministries or services that address a different or specific set of needs.

Remain Near to God

DEVOTIONAL READING: 1 Corinthians 1:1-10.

LESSON SCRIPTURE: Hebrews 10:19-39.

PRINTED TEXT: Hebrews 10:19-25, 32-39.

Hebrews 10:19-25, 32-39

19 Having therefore, brethren, boldness to enter into the holiest by the blood of Jesus,

20 By a new and living way, which he hath consecrated for us, through the veil, that is to say, his flesh;

21 And having a high priest over the house of God;

22 Let us draw near with a true heart in full assurance of faith, having our hearts sprinkled from an evil conscience, and our bodies washed with pure water.

23 Let us hold fast the profession of our faith without wavering; for he is faithful that promised;

24 And let us consider one another to provoke unto love and to good works:

25 Not forsaking the assembling of ourselves together, as the manner of some is; but exhorting one another: and so much the more, as ye see the day approaching.

. . . .

32 But call to remembrance the former days, in which, after ye were illuminated, ye endured a great fight of afflictions;

33 Partly, whilst ye were made a gazingstock both by reproaches and afflictions; and partly, whilst ye became companions of them that were so used.

34 For ye had compassion of me in my bonds, and took joyfully the spoiling of your goods, knowing in yourselves that ye have in heaven a better and an enduring substance.

35 Cast not away therefore your confidence, which hath great recompense of reward.

36 For ye have need of patience, that, after ye have done the will of God, ye might receive the promise.

37 For yet a little while, and he that shall come will come, and will not tarry.

38 Now the just shall live by faith: but if any man draw back, my soul shall have no pleasure in him.

39 But we are not of them who draw back unto perdition; but of them that believe to the saving of the soul.

**Aug
10**

GOLDEN TEXT: Let us hold fast the profession of our faith without wavering; for he is faithful that promised.—Hebrews 10:23.

A Call to Faithfulness
Unit 2: Be Faithful Followers of Christ
(Lessons 10-14)

Lesson Aims

After studying this lesson, each student should:

1. Appreciate the blessing of being able to come into the presence of God through the blood of Jesus.

2. Recognize how important it is to assemble regularly with fellow Christians.

3. Be better equipped to handle suffering and adversity when we encounter them.

Lesson Outline

INTRODUCTION
    A. Stay Close to Christ
    B. Lesson Background
I. PRACTICAL ADMONITIONS (Hebrews 10:19-25)
    A. Draw Near to God (vv. 19-22)
    B. Hold Fast the Faith (v. 23)
      Holding Fast to Our Promises
    C. Encourage Others (v. 24)
    D. Assemble With Others (v. 25)
      Why I Quit Church
II. LESSONS FROM PAST SUFFERING (Hebrews 10:32-39)
    A. Remembering Afflictions (vv. 32, 33)
    B. Hope Beyond Suffering (v. 34)
    C. Confidence and Patience (vv. 35, 36)
    D. Living by Faith (vv. 37-39)
CONCLUSION
    A. Holding Fast the Profession
    B. Let Us Pray
    C. Thought to Remember

Introduction

A. Stay Close to Christ

A young boy once accompanied his father on a hike up a wooded mountainside. When they returned, the boy's mother asked him if he was afraid at any time during the hike. "The trees were so thick at times that we could hardly see," he replied, "but I wasn't afraid. At other times the trail was so overgrown that we could have gotten lost, but I wasn't afraid. Then one time we came around a curve and there was a big bear and her cub, but I wasn't afraid. Once the trail ran along the top of a cliff, and I could have fallen off, but I wasn't afraid."

"Well, son, it sounds like you had a rather scary morning," said the mother. "Why weren't you afraid?"

"Because, Mommy, I stayed real close to Dad all the way," was his reply.

That is what the writer of Hebrews had in mind when he urged his readers to draw near to Christ. As long as they were close to Him, they had no reason to fear.

B. Lesson Background

In our earlier lessons from Hebrews, we have seen the author's strong doctrinal emphasis. He was intent upon setting forth the superiority of Christianity over the Judaism that his readers had left behind to follow Jesus. He showed how the high priesthood of Christ is superior to the high priesthood under the Mosaic Law. He also showed how Christ's sacrifice of Himself is superior to all the animal sacrifices offered under the Law.

The first eighteen verses of chapter 10 bring the writer's argument to a climax. He concludes his contrast between the Old Covenant priesthood and the priesthood of Jesus. He affirms that the Law was merely "a shadow of good things to come" (v. 1). The sacrifices it prescribed could never fully take away sin; only the "one sacrifice" of Jesus could suffice to forgive all sins (v. 12). Beginning with verse 19 (where the printed text for today begins), the writer turns his focus to exhortations of a more practical and personal nature.

I. Practical Admonitions (Hebrews 10:19-25)

A. Draw Near to God (vv. 19-22)

19-22. Having therefore, brethren, boldness to enter into the holiest by the blood of Jesus, by a new and living way, which he hath consecrated for us, through the veil, that is to say, his flesh; and having a high priest over the house of God; let us draw near with a true heart in full assurance of faith, having our hearts sprinkled from an evil conscience, and our bodies washed with pure water.

The writer shows his warm, personal relationship with his readers by addressing them as *brethren.* He then includes himself with them in his words *let us draw near.* This man is not some distant theologian setting forth his doctrines while isolating himself from his readers. Instead, he is dealing with practical spiritual matters that are as relevant to him as to them.

The writer first calls his readers' attention to the *boldness,* or confidence, that Christians are to have as they *enter into the holiest,* that is, the heavenly sanctuary (see Hebrews 9:24). Under the New Covenant, this is the counterpart of the Holy of Holies in the tabernacle and later the temple. Here the high priest could enter only once a year. Through *the blood of Jesus*, Christians are now granted a privilege that once belonged only to the high priest. Ours is the opportunity to "come boldly unto the throne of grace" (Hebrews 4:16) and to "sit together in heavenly places in Christ Jesus" (Ephesians 2:6). The restrictions of the Old Covenant have been replaced by joyful access to God through *a new and living way*.

Through the veil refers to the veil, or curtain, that separated the Holy Place from the Holy of Holies. The high priest had to pass through this curtain to present his annual offering of blood for the people's sins on the Day of Atonement. The words *his flesh* have created considerable discussion among scholars and commentators. Some take it to refer back to the *way*, indicating that the way by which Christians enter the true Holy of Holies is through the death of Christ's physical body. Others believe that *flesh* refers to the *veil*. They see the veil, not as a barrier to the Holy of Holies, but as a means of entrance into it. Both views recognize the significance of the rending of the veil in the temple (Matthew 27:51), and of the rending of Jesus' body so that man might "enter . . . the holiest" (v. 19). With either interpretation, the intent of this passage is clear: Christ is the *way* to the Father, a truth that Jesus Himself clearly taught (John 14:6).

The writer then uses additional Old Covenant terminology to challenge his readers toward faithfulness to Christ. *Having our hearts sprinkled from an evil conscience* is a blessing not possible under the old sacrificial system, which had no impact upon the evil within man (see Hebrews 9:13, 14, and the prophecy of this sprinkling in Ezekiel 36:25). Being *washed with pure water* calls to mind the various instances in which water was prescribed for cleansing under the Law (see, for example, Leviticus 16:4; Numbers 19). Here the reference is most likely to Christian baptism (see Titus 3:5).

How to Say It

AQUILA. *Ack*-will-uh.
CHALDEANS. Kal-*dee*-unz.
CLAUDIUS. *Claw*-dee-us.
HABAKKUK. Huh-*bak*-kuk.
JUDAISM. *Joo*-day-izz-um.
PRISCILLA. Prih-*sill*-uh.
SEPTUAGINT. Sep-*too*-ih-jent.

B. Hold Fast the Faith (v. 23)

23. Let us hold fast the profession of our faith without wavering; for he is faithful that promised.

The writer has already encouraged his readers to *hold fast* and to follow closely the truth that they have received (2:1; 3:6, 14; 4:14). The same exhortation is given to them in this verse. Their stand for the faith must be without compromise, or *without wavering*. The basis for this exhortation is that God *is faithful*. If He is faithful in His promises to us, then we should make it a matter of top priority to be faithful to Him.

The profession, or confession, *of our faith* is associated with an individual's salvation (Romans 10:9, 10). It must then be expressed through the Christian's life as well as on his lips, and must be made faithfully before others (Matthew 10:32, 33).

HOLDING FAST TO OUR PROMISES

In his book *Up From Slavery*, Booker T. Washington describes meeting an ex-slave from Virginia who, three years before the Emancipation Proclamation, had made a contract with his master to buy his freedom by making an annual payment of a certain sum. While he was paying for his freedom, the slave was permitted to work wherever and for whomever he pleased. Finding that he could secure better wages in Ohio, he went there.

When the Emancipation Proclamation was issued, the slave was still $300 in debt to his master. Even though the Proclamation freed him from any obligation to his master, this slave walked the greater part of the distance back to Virginia and placed the last dollar, with interest, in his former owner's hands.

Booker T. Washington said that this freed slave knew he had no legal obligation to pay the debt, but he did it anyway because he had given his word to his master, and he had never broken his word. He could not enjoy his freedom until he had fulfilled his promise.

When we become Christians, we make a promise to be faithful to Christ, to do His will, and to live by His Word. We have even more reason to be faithful to our Master than the slave did to his. In our Master's service lies the only true freedom.   —C. B. Mc.

C. Encourage Others (v. 24)

24. And let us consider one another to provoke unto love and to good works.

The word *provoke* usually has a negative connotation, meaning to irritate. Sadly, too many Christians hardly need any encouragement to do this, for it occurs all too frequently. Here the word has a positive meaning; other versions render it as "stir up" (*Revised Standard Version*), "arouse" (*New English Bible*), and "spur one another on" (*New International Version*). The idea is that through their words and their actions, Christians are to serve as models to encourage others *unto love and to good works*.

D. Assemble With Others (v. 25)

25. Not forsaking the assembling of ourselves together, as the manner of some is; but exhorting one another: and so much the more, as ye see the day approaching.

One way that Christians can fulfill the exhortation of verse 24 is by setting the example of regular church attendance. While this is certainly not the only mark of a faithful Christian, ordinarily it is a pretty accurate barometer of one's spiritual state. Irregular or infrequent church attendance is usually a sign that a person is not holding fast to his profession of faith. Someone has likened Christians to coals in a fireplace. Lumped together, coals glow and give off light and warmth, but if a coal is removed from the fireplace and placed alone on the hearth, it soon grows cold.

In the early period of the church, following what transpired at Pentecost, the early Christians met every day to worship God and fellowship together (Acts 2:46). Later it became the practice of the church to meet on the first day of the week (Acts 20:7). Believers have a responsibility to exhort their fellow believers not to neglect gathering for worship.

The phrase *as ye see the day approaching* may call attention to the approach of the Lord's Day each week. However, many scholars think it refers to the approaching day of judgment that would soon fall upon the Jewish people. That day came in A.D. 70, when Jerusalem fell to the Roman legions led by the general Titus. The city was destroyed, along with its beautiful temple, which was never rebuilt. Still another view is that *the day* refers to the day of Christ's return. We prepare for that Lord's Day by being faithful in observing the present Lord's Day.

Why I Quit Church

A story from a small-town newspaper carried the headline: "Preacher Quits Sports." In the article, a minister gave ten reasons why he had stopped attending athletic contests. Here they are:

1. Every time I went, they asked me for money.
2. The people sitting near me didn't seem to be very friendly.

3. The games are scheduled when I want to do other things.
4. The seats are too hard and not comfortable.
5. My parents took me to too many games when I was growing up.
6. I don't want to take my children, because I want them to choose for themselves what sport they like best.
7. Some games went into overtime, and I was late getting home.
8. The band played songs I didn't know.
9. The coach never came to call on me.
10. The referee made a decision with which I disagreed.

These would be ridiculous excuses to quit attending sports events. They are even more ridiculous reasons for not being in church. The Bible assumes that the Lord's people will be in the Lord's house on the Lord's Day. If you are a student, you go to school. If you are an employee, you go to work. If you belong to a sports team, you go to practices and games. Likewise, if you belong to the church, you go to church.

—C. B. Mc.

II. Lessons From Past Suffering (Hebrews 10:32-39)

The verses in between the portions of our printed text (26-31) carry a stern warning for those who knowingly and deliberately turn away from Jesus. We saw a similar warning in last week's lesson (Hebrews 6:4-8).

A. Remembering Afflictions (vv. 32, 33)

32, 33. But call to remembrance the former days, in which, after ye were illuminated, ye endured a great fight of afflictions; partly, whilst ye were made a gazingstock both by reproaches and afflictions; and partly, whilst ye became companions of them that were so used.

In the previous verses the writer has warned against the terrible future awaiting those who turn away from the faith. Now he writes words of encouragement to the Hebrew Christians based on their faithfulness under stressful conditions in the past. The Greek word translated *illuminated* is also used in Hebrews 6:4, where it is translated *enlightened*. This apparently refers to the act of becoming a Christian, or "seeing the Light" as revealed through Jesus. In taking this decisive step, these believers had exposed themselves to *a great fight of afflictions*. They had paid dearly for their choice to follow Jesus.

The writer then proceeds to mention some of the afflictions that the Hebrew Christians had suffered. Some commentators believe that, at the time of the writing of Hebrews, these persecutions had not been severe enough to involve martyrdom. This argument is based on Hebrews 12:4: "Ye have not yet resisted unto blood, striving against sin." This was certainly not the case for Christians in Jerusalem. Beginning with Stephen, many had been martyred for their faith. Martyrdom would not have been nearly as common, however, for Jewish Christians living in Rome before A.D. 64. This is one reason some believe that Hebrews was written to Christians living in Rome. Jews had been expelled from Rome by Emperor Claudius in A.D. 49 (see Acts 18:1, 2), affecting in some cases Christians such as Aquila and Priscilla, but there is no evidence that any of them were martyred during this expulsion. The situation changed drastically in A.D. 64, when Nero became emperor. Christians were subjected to unspeakable cruelty, and martyrdom became a common occurrence.

The Hebrew Christians had at one time been a *gazingstock*, meaning that they were the subjects of public ridicule. They were commended by the author, not only because they had remained faithful through such *reproaches and afflictions*, but also because they had provided support and companionship to those *that were so used*. Had they forgotten the thrill of serving Christ and suffering for His sake in those *former days*?

B. Hope Beyond Suffering (v. 34)

34. For ye had compassion of me in my bonds, and took joyfully the spoiling of your goods, knowing in yourselves that ye have in heaven a better and an enduring substance.

These Christians had reached such a level of maturity that they could actually rejoice at the *spoiling* of their *goods*. This means that their belongings had been treated as if they were spoils seized in battle. The believers possessed the faith of the apostles in Jerusalem, who rejoiced "that they were counted worthy to suffer shame for his name" (Acts 5:41). They were willing to suffer such loss with rejoicing, because they knew they had *in heaven a better and an enduring substance*. As long as they held this faith firmly, earthly treasures mattered little. How strikingly different from the attitudes of our materialistic age!

C. Confidence and Patience
(vv. 35, 36)

35, 36. Cast not away therefore your confidence, which hath great recompense of reward. For ye have need of patience, that, after ye have done the will of God, ye might receive the promise.

The Hebrew Christians had come to know Christ and the *confidence* that faith in Him can bring. Now they were in danger of throwing all of that away. Earlier in this epistle, the author had reminded his readers of the fate of those Israelites who left Egypt with Moses and then proved unfaithful, even wishing to return to Egypt. Those who sinned in this fashion fell in the wilderness and were not allowed to enter the promised land "because of unbelief" (Hebrews 3:19). It was this same kind of unbelief that was threatening to shake the confidence of the Hebrew Christians.

In verse 36 the writer pinpoints the believers' problem as a lack of *patience* ("endurance" in the *New American Standard Bible*). They had become Christians and had suffered for their faith. They had fought the good fight for a time, but they had not yet finished the course. Paul had warned the Galatians to beware of becoming "weary in well doing" (Galatians 6:9). It would seem that this lack of endurance was part of the reason that the Hebrew Christians were in danger of falling away.

Many Christians today face this same temptation. Perhaps they have spent many years in the Lord's service, but they feel frustrated because their efforts have begun to appear fruitless or unappreciated. All who are so tempted are encouraged to continue in their good work that they *might receive the promise*.

D. Living by Faith (vv. 37-39)

37-39. For yet a little while, and he that shall come will come, and will not tarry. Now the just shall live by faith: but if any man draw back, my soul shall have no pleasure in him. But we are not of them who draw back unto perdition; but of them that believe to the saving of the soul.

Thus far in our study of Hebrews, we have seen the writer use the Old Testament to make an important point. Here, to further encourage the Hebrew Christians to stand fast, he quotes from Habakkuk 2:3, 4. Since he often quotes from the Septuagint (a Greek version of the Old Testament) in his letter, in some cases his quotations do not coincide word for word with the Old Testament versions that most of us use. We saw this in Lesson 9, where we noted the difference between Psalm 40:6-8 and the way it is quoted in Hebrews 10:5-7.

Habakkuk was called to prophesy to the nation of Judah at a time when the Chaldeans were poised to destroy it. This was God's punishment for His people having turned away from Him. But Habakkuk was troubled by the question of why God would use a people more wicked than Judah to punish Judah (Habakkuk 1:13). God's response was that He was in control, and would make certain that the righteous would be rewarded and the wicked punished. God's people needed to have faith that His purposes would be fulfilled.

The words *he that shall come will come* are used by the writer of Hebrews to refer to the return of Christ. Many of the early Christians looked for Jesus to return very quickly to claim His own. They did not realize that God operates within a different time frame from man's, and so some had become disappointed and discouraged. The example from Habakkuk's experience was meant to bolster their trust in God.

The just shall live by faith. Paul quotes these same words in Romans 1:17. The writer of Hebrews uses them to show that God honors those who trust in Him. At the same time, He has *no pleasure* in those who, because of lack of faith, *draw back.*

In verse 39 the writer again identifies himself with those who stand firmly in their faith. Those who turn back *unto perdition* ("are destroyed," reads the *New International Version*) face a very unpleasant future. Thus there were two options before the Hebrew Christians: continued faithfulness to Christ, leading to salvation, or turning away from Christ, leading to destruction. Is it clear which choice we have made?

Conclusion

A. Holding Fast the Profession

More than fifty years ago, I visited a stretch of beach near Savannah, Georgia. Recently I returned to the same beach, and I hardly recognized it. Much of the beach had disappeared, and the waves were lapping at a road that once

was a quarter of a mile from the water. This change in the beach had not occurred suddenly, but slowly over many years. Although the Corps of Engineers had worked to save the beach, at best they had only slowed the erosion.

This illustrates the process by which Christians sometimes turn from their allegiance to Jesus. The membership roll of almost every church will provide evidence that some Christians do fall away from the faith. Regardless of how we may explain this theologically, the obvious fact is that it does happen. Ordinarily, a Christian does not suddenly turn his back on Christ and return to the world. More often it is a slow erosion that is hardly noticeable until the process is well along. Then it is almost too late to salvage the person.

We see a similar process happening in the area of public morals. Turn back the pages of history only half a century. Murder was uncommon, as were illegitimate births. Divorce was rare, and when one did occur it shocked the entire community. Abortions were illegal, and many of us never bothered to lock our doors at night. One could even attend the movies without being embarrassed at the kind of language used. What happened? What went wrong? Clearly, this decline did not happen all at once, but was the result of a slow erosion that became more rapid as the years passed.

What can we do about it? We could wring our hands in despair and simply give up. But this is not what Christ has commanded us to do. We are to be the salt that has the power to preserve, and the light that has the power to dispel the darkness. If we are to accomplish this task, we must be aware of the dire warnings sounded in this lesson about those who turn away from Christ. More important, we must be encouraged by the promise of rich blessings that await those who patiently and firmly remain faithful, and share their faith and hope with others.

B. Let Us Pray

Dear Father in Heaven, may we draw near to You with a true heart in full assurance of faith, knowing that You have given us Your Son, a High Priest who hears our every prayer. Lift up our hands when we grow weary in well doing. Give us strength when our faith is threatened by forces that tempt us to compromise or turn away from it. In the name of our High Priest we pray. Amen.

C. Thought to Remember

Let us resolve to "draw near" to God (Hebrews 10:22), so that we may not "draw back unto perdition" (v. 39).

Home Daily Bible Readings

Monday, Aug. 4—Power Belongs to God (2 Corinthians 4:7-12)

Tuesday, Aug. 5—Be Born of the Holy Spirit (John 3:1-15)

Wednesday, Aug. 6—Things of the Spirit Are Unseen (2 Corinthians 4:13-18)

Thursday, Aug. 7—Jesus' Prayer for the Church (John 17:20-26)

Friday, Aug. 8—God Speaks Through His Word (Psalm 19:7-14)

Saturday, Aug. 9—A Genuine Faith Is Important (1 Peter 1:3-9)

Sunday, Aug. 10—God Is Faithful (1 Corinthians 1:1-9)

Learning by Doing

This page contains an alternate lesson plan emphasizing learning activities.
Classes desiring such student involvement will find these suggestions helpful.

Learning Goals

By participating in this study from Hebrews 10, students should:

1. Be able to list at least six imperatives given to Christians in the text.

2. Be challenged to become what the Christian must be, in order to "receive the promise."

Into the Lesson

The word *draw*, which is important in today's study, is one of those words that has a variety of uses and meanings. Display the word prominently as the class assembles, and ask, "What does this word mean?" Expect a variety of responses (*Webster's New World Dictionary*, Second College Edition, lists nearly fifty uses of *draw* as a verb and a noun, and includes its use in popular expressions). You may want to have a student skim such a dictionary and give some samples. Indicate that the sense of the word in today's text is, "to make something or someone move toward one or along with one, by or as exerting force."

Next, copy and hand out these riddles, one to a student, on the subject, "Things That Draw." Ask each student to read his or hers aloud and to confirm correct responses. (1) "I am a thing that draws. What am I? I exert invisible forces. I'm handy to carpenters, wilderness hikers, and preschool scientists." Answer: *magnet*. (2) "I am a thing that draws. What am I? Some people have me in their homes. People gather around me in winter." Answer: *fireplace*. (3) "I am a thing that draws. What am I? I make a difference to people who visit the beach. Sailors depend on me. Men have landed on me." Answer: *moon* (clues refer to its effect on tides and time). (4) "I am a thing that draws. What am I? Some people read me every day. I make them laugh, or at least try to." Answer: *cartoonist*. (5) "I am a thing that draws. What am I? I do my drawing by color and by scent. My appeal results in other things growing." Answer: *flowers*. When all riddles are answered, read John 12:32, and note the drawing power of Christ crucified.

Into the Word

Prepare some index cards, half of them with the word *Do* and half with the word *Don't* (written in large letters). Have enough to give one to each class member. Shuffle and distribute the cards. Ask the class to search the text and suggest a *Do* or *Don't*, depending on the card each person holds. As they respond, make a two-column listing on the chalkboard or on poster board. Expect such *Do* entries as: Be bold, v. 19; Draw near, v. 22; Keep a true heart, v. 22; Hold fast, v. 23; Consider one another, v. 24; Exhort one another, v. 25; Remember the past, v. 32; Be patient, v. 36; Live by faith, v. 38. *Don't* entries should include: Don't waver, v. 23; Don't miss church, v. 25; Don't mourn the loss of material goods, v. 34; Don't lose confidence, v. 35; Don't draw back, v. 38. As ideas are presented, you will have occasion to ask questions and make any appropriate comments.

Next, redirect the students' attention to the text by saying, "Now let's leave the *Do's* and *Don'ts* for a series of *twos* and *threes*. Ask them to find and identify each of the following: (1) The three verses that encourage patience, because Christ will return (vv. 35-37). (2) The three verses that picture the negative treatment the Hebrew Christians had received in former days, and their response to it (vv. 32-34). (3) The two verses that picture the joy of faith and the doom of disbelief (vv. 38, 39). (4) The three verses that tell how Christians have a privilege that at one time only the high priest had (vv. 19-21). (5) The two verses that state the necessity and purpose of worship assemblies (vv. 24, 25). Use the lesson commentary to elaborate on any significant words or ideas.

Into Life

Distribute to each student a small (three-or four-inch diameter) geometric shape with seven sides (a heptagon). (You may want to consider having a child or a teen do the geometry and the cutting for you.) Point out that the number *seven* is used in the Bible as a symbol of completeness or wholeness. With your class, make a list of imperatives from today's text in the form "BE ____!" (The student book includes an activity for compiling such a list.) When the list is made, have each student write a large BE in the middle of his or her heptagon. Next, each should select seven of the imperatives that relate most to his or her Christian walk, writing one on each edge of the heptagon. Encourage students to apply one of the imperatives each day this week.

Let's Talk It Over

The questions on this page are designed to encourage review of the lesson Scriptures and to promote discussion of the lesson by the class. The answers provided are only discussion starters. Let your class talk it over from there.

1. Because of Jesus, Christians enjoy the privilege of drawing near to Almighty God without fear. What can we do to make sure that we do not forget the glory of God and what a blessing it is to be able to approach Him freely?

The Jewish believers addressed in Hebrews had a special appreciation for the blessing of approaching God because of their experience of temple worship. The temple construction and pattern of worship there made the separateness of God very clear. The people had to depend upon the priests to intercede for them, and only the high priest was permitted to enter the Holy of Holies where the glory of God resided (and that was but once a year). We today can increase our own sense of wonder at the privilege afforded us, by remembering the limits of temple worship, by exalting God in worship as we sing of His holiness and His mighty acts, and by remembering the awful price that was paid in atonement for our sin.

2. What methods or influences are most effective in encouraging you toward love and good works? How could you be involved in that process on behalf of others?

This is the subject of Hebrews 10:24, in which we find an example of the "one another" commands given to Christians. Ministers, nominating committees, ministry team leaders, Sunday school superintendents, and others charged with recruitment are always looking for the most effective methods for motivating people to love and good works. Too often, perhaps out of desperation, leaders resort to guilt as a lever to get others moving. Guilt may work in the short term, but long-term commitment must depend upon love for God and love for others. If people are persuaded that their service will accomplish something good for others and will glorify God, that is a good beginning. The example of other believers and the expectations set in a fellowship will also help. Newcomers will tend to live up or down to the standards of love and good works already present in a church.

3. What would you lose by not attending corporate worship? What would others lose by your failure to attend? Would you say that church attendance is a matter of desire or duty?

Attending worship every Sunday is a testimony. When believers gather it is a witness to the community, and the larger the number of believers, the greater the impact of the witness. There is strength to be gained when we worship together. One person's testimony of God's blessing may overcome another's discouragement and doubt. God is glorified as we exalt Him in song and in prayer. We receive messages from God as His Word is read and as teaching is shared. If worship has become a dreary duty to you, examine the attitudes you bring to worship and the investment you make in it. Beyond that, offer to discuss with your minister or worship leaders how to improve the experience for everyone. Think about investing more as a church into your worship times, so that they become times of true rejoicing and celebration.

4. What "reproaches and afflictions" (Hebrews 10:33) have you suffered as a Christian? Has the experience given you more or less conviction concerning your faith?

In our culture, Christians have not had to suffer a great deal of direct persecution for their faith. There is, however, an impatience or even intolerance on the part of some in our culture toward people of faith and conviction. Their opposition may take the form of ridicule or contempt ("You're always acting 'holier than thou'"). Jesus warned us that darkness hates the light (John 3:19, 20), so we should not be surprised that those whose deeds are evil (or even shady) oppose those who are committed to a more noble way. Once we have taken a stand and suffered for our faith, the result can be an even stronger conviction.

5. When are you most tempted to cast away your confidence (Hebrews 10:35) or to "draw back" from your faith (v. 39)? How do you overcome such temptations?

The answer to this question will vary with every individual. My greatest temptations to forsake the faith, however, have not come due to opposition, but from the enticements of this world. In order to overcome, I have to be reminded that "the world passeth away, and the lust thereof: but he that doeth the will of God abideth for ever" (1 John 2:17).

Remember the Past

DEVOTIONAL READING: Romans 4:1-15.

LESSON SCRIPTURE: Hebrews 11:1-40.

PRINTED TEXT: Hebrews 11:1, 2, 6-10, 13-16, 39, 40.

Hebrews 11:1, 2, 6-10, 13-16, 39, 40

1 Now faith is the substance of things hoped for, the evidence of things not seen.

2 For by it the elders obtained a good report.

.   .   .   .

6 But without faith it is impossible to please him: for he that cometh to God must believe that he is, and that he is a rewarder of them that diligently seek him.

7 By faith Noah, being warned of God of things not seen as yet, moved with fear, prepared an ark to the saving of his house; by the which he condemned the world, and became heir of the righteousness which is by faith.

8 By faith Abraham, when he was called to go out into a place which he should after receive for an inheritance, obeyed; and he went out, not knowing whither he went.

9 By faith he sojourned in the land of promise, as in a strange country, dwelling in tabernacles with Isaac and Jacob, the heirs with him of the same promise:

10 For he looked for a city which hath foundations, whose builder and maker is God.

.   .   .   .

13 These all died in faith, not having received the promises, but having seen them afar off, and were persuaded of them, and embraced them, and confessed that they were strangers and pilgrims on the earth.

14 For they that say such things declare plainly that they seek a country.

15 And truly, if they had been mindful of that country from whence they came out, they might have had opportunity to have returned.

16 But now they desire a better country, that is, a heavenly: wherefore God is not ashamed to be called their God: for he hath prepared for them a city.

.   .   .   .

39 And these all, having obtained a good report through faith, received not the promise:

40 God having provided some better thing for us, that they without us should not be made perfect.

**Aug
17**

GOLDEN TEXT: Now faith is the substance of things hoped for, the evidence of things not seen.—Hebrews 11:1.

A Call to Faithfulness
Unit 2: Be Faithful Followers of Christ
(Lessons 10-14)

Lesson Aims

After studying this lesson, each student should:

1. Accept the fact that faith is necessary to please God.

2. Have a greater appreciation for the faith of the Bible heroes and heroines referred to in today's text.

3. Be better able to exercise faith in living the Christian life.

Lesson Outline

The visual for Lesson 12 highlights the definition of faith found in Hebrews 11:1. It is shown on page 431.

Introduction

A. Trusting the Compass

Several years ago I was with a group of students on a camping trip. At one point in the trip, we had to canoe across a large lake and up a stream to our next campsite. The lake was so large that we were unable to see the other side, and there were no landmarks to guide us. As we prepared to launch our canoes, thick clouds swept over the lake, obscuring the sun. With no landmarks by which to navigate, and unable to get our directions from the sun, we had no way of knowing just where the stream was.

However, we had a map and a compass, and so we plotted our course and began our journey. Soon a strong wind arose that threatened to blow us off course, but we were able to avoid potential trouble by consulting the compass. At one point our instincts told us that we were going in the wrong direction. Again, we consulted the compass and held to the course we had plotted. After several hours of paddling, we reached our destination. Our journey was successful, because we followed our compass.

The Old Testament heroes we are studying today also embarked on a difficult journey—one of a spiritual nature. They were able to reach their destination because they followed their compass. That compass was their faith in God.

B. Lesson Background

Our lesson today includes several verses from Hebrews 11, known as the faith chapter of the Bible. In this chapter God conducts a "roll call" of faithful men and women. Those who are singled out were not necessarily wiser or more pious than others, but they had one trait that distinguished them: they trusted God! Even when God asked them to perform tasks that must have seemed foolish, they obeyed. God told Noah to build an ark to prepare for a coming flood, and as ridiculous as it certainly must have seemed, he faithfully obeyed. God told Abraham to leave his comfortable home in Mesopotamia and become a wanderer, seeking for a new home. Even without a map or a compass, Abraham acted on faith and obeyed.

God has given us even greater promises. Should we not follow the examples of those cited in Hebrews 11 and live by obedient faith?

I. The Nature and Power of Faith (Hebrews 11:1, 2)

A. The Nature of Faith (v. 1)

1. Now faith is the substance of things hoped for, the evidence of things not seen.

The author begins this faith chapter with a definition of *faith*. This is a general definition of the word and is not necessarily limited to religious faith. The Greek word translated *substance* has a variety of meanings; literally it means "that which stands under" or "foundation." Everyone possesses faith of some kind, and conducts his life on the basis of that belief. The issue then becomes the strength of one's foundation, and no foundation is stronger than faith in God. Such faith gives reality to *things not seen* (as Moses "endured, as seeing him who is invisible," Hebrews 11:27), and gives confidence to the one who is guided by it.

B. The Power of Faith

2. For by it the elders obtained a good report.

To strengthen his point about the necessity of faith, the author now turns to Old Testament history. In the verses that follow, he gives several examples of persons who, through faith, were able to triumph over difficult or seemingly impossible circumstances. These persons were not morally perfect, but in spite of their shortcomings, God was able to use them because they trusted Him. Their faith made them models for all future generations. Beginning with Abel, these heroes and heroines are presented in a somewhat chronological order, culminating in Jesus, "the author and finisher of our faith" (12:2). These examples were meant to encourage the Hebrew Christians, so that they would not "draw back" (10:38, 39).

II. Examples of Faith (Hebrews 11:6-10)

A. The Necessity of Faith (v. 6)

6. But without faith it is impossible to please him: for he that cometh to God must believe that he is, and that he is a rewarder of them that diligently seek him.

Without faith in *God*, these heroes and heroines would not have been pleasing to Him, nor would they have been able to perform their heroic deeds. The twofold aspects of faith expressed in verse 1 are reaffirmed here. Faith provides the evidence for God and the unseen spiritual world. Faith also provides a foundation for the confidence that God will reward those who *diligently seek him*. What was true for these faithful men and women of old was true for the Hebrew Christians, and is also true for us today.

Because faith is so crucial, Satan's severest attacks are often aimed at our faith. He may tempt us to doubt, and when doubt seeps in, it has the potential to dilute our faith and weaken us. Like the father of the boy who was controlled by an evil spirit, we must pray, "Lord, I believe; help thou mine unbelief" (Mark 9:24).

WHAT KIND OF CAR DO YOU DRIVE?

In the 1980s Lee Iacocca, the head of Chrysler Corporation, was easily the most recognized car executive in America, because he personally

How to Say It

CHALDEES. Kal-*deez*.
ENOCH. *E*-nuk.
HARAN. *Hay*-run.
MACHPELAH. Mack-*pea*-luh.
MESOPOTAMIA. *Mes*-uh-puh-*tay*-me-uh (strong accent on *tay*).
RAHAB. *Ray*-hab.

appeared in so many television commercials for Chrysler products. One day a man found himself riding in the same elevator with Iacocca.

"You're Lee Iacocca, aren't you?" the man asked. The auto executive acknowledged that he was.

"Mr. Iacocca," the man said, "I want to tell you how much I enjoy your television commercials."

To this compliment Iacocca replied, "Sir, I couldn't care less what you think of my commercials. What I want to know is: what kind of car do you drive?"

In the automobile business, if you don't buy the car, the commercials don't matter. The same is true of the Christian message. Perhaps, after reading Hebrews 11, we may stand in awe of the great men and women of faith mentioned therein. However, it makes little difference how much we admire these individuals if we fail to exercise faith ourselves. "By faith they" must become "By faith *we*." —C. B. Mc.

B. The Example of Noah (v. 7)

7. By faith Noah, being warned of God of things not seen as yet, moved with fear, prepared an ark to the saving of his house; by the which he condemned the world, and became heir of the righteousness which is by faith.

In verses 4 and 5, Abel and Enoch were cited as men of faith. Here *Noah* is held up as an outstanding example of acting *by faith*. God *warned* Noah that He was preparing a flood to destroy the world because of its unbridled wickedness (Genesis 6:13). Noah was then informed that he was to build an ark by which he and his family were to be saved. It is not hard to imagine the ridicule Noah must have heard as he began this project. At a time when a catastrophic flood was in the realm of *things not seen as yet*, he was to construct a huge boat.

At least two other aspects of this endeavor give us some indication of the strength of Noah's faith. First of all, this was no short-term project; it was to last a hundred and twenty years (according to the figure given in Genesis 6:3), during which time Noah preached to onlookers (2 Peter 2:5). Second, Noah's faith was strong enough that he was able to convert *his house*—his wife, his three sons, and their wives—thus insuring their salvation from the coming judgment.

C. The Example of Abraham (vv. 8-10)

8. By faith Abraham, when he was called to go out into a place which he should after receive for an inheritance, obeyed; and he went out, not knowing whither he went.

God first called *Abraham* when he lived in Ur of the Chaldees (Genesis 11:31; Acts 7:2, 3). Abraham had large flocks and a number of servants, indicating that he was a wealthy man. Archaeologists who have excavated ancient Ur indicate that the wealthy in Abraham's day (approximately 2000 B.C.) lived in an abundance of ease and luxury. From such surroundings of material security, God called Abraham (named *Abram* at the time) to experience the security of living *by faith*. He left his homeland, *not knowing whither he went*. He exchanged the comfort of what he could see and enjoy for the challenge of "things not seen."

9. By faith he sojourned in the land of promise, as in a strange country, dwelling in tabernacles with Isaac and Jacob, the heirs with him of the same promise.

Although Abraham was permitted to live in Canaan, *the land of promise*, he did so as an alien. For Abraham, that land never became a land of possession. After a time he gained the respect of the various tribes among whom he dwelt, yet the only land he actually possessed was the field that included the cave of Machpelah, which he purchased for the burial of his wife Sarah (Genesis 23).

The word *tabernacles* in this verse has nothing to do with the place of worship that God later commanded Moses and the Israelites to construct. It simply means "tents," and indicates that Abraham never considered Canaan a permanent place of residence. He lived *by faith* in the *promise* of a residence far grander than Canaan, as the next verse states. Along the way he received assurances that his faith would be rewarded. The birth of a son in his old age, long promised and long delayed, was certainly a token that other promises would be fulfilled. That son, *Isaac*, and Isaac's son, *Jacob*, also lived in Canaan as *heirs . . . of the same promise*. The most important wealth Abraham bequeathed to them was spiritual.

10. For he looked for a city which hath foundations, whose builder and maker is God.

The secret to Abraham's patience lay in the fact that he was able to see beyond his immedi-

ate horizons far into the future. He could tolerate living as an alien in the land of promise, because he sought an eternal *city . . . whose builder and maker is God*. During Abraham's walk of faith, he lived in a tent—a dwelling without foundations and without permanency. This was only a slight inconvenience, however, compared with the promise of a city with *foundations* as firm as God Himself. There Abraham knew, by faith, that he would dwell some day.

FAITH'S HALL OF FAME

Hebrews 11 can be an intimidating list. Here we find the "all-stars" of faith: Noah, Abraham, Isaac, Jacob, Joseph, and many others. Perhaps you may be tempted to think that the lessons taught here are for extraordinary people, or that someone like you could never have faith enough to become an "all-star."

But consider one of the "stars" of this chapter: Abraham. He was living in Ur of the Chaldees, in southern Mesopotamia, when God first called him. Ur was an important commercial city, whose people had developed a system of writing and an impressive body of literature. But its people were thoroughly pagan. They were polytheistic (worshipers of many gods). This was the kind of atmosphere surrounding Abraham when God called him. With no other guarantee than God's word, Abraham left his home, friends, business, and property to go to a distant land that God had promised him.

But Abraham's faith at times was faulty. At one point, during a famine in Canaan, he fled to Egypt in fear. Then, because he was afraid of the Pharaoh, he lied about Sarah's being his wife. When it seemed that the promised heir would never come, he followed Sarah's urging and fathered a child through her handmaid Hagar.

Yet despite Abraham's failings, God continued promising and Abraham continued believing. He passed the ultimate test of faith by his willingness to offer his son Isaac as a sacrifice. Romans 4:2, 3 tells us that Abraham was not declared righteous by his good works, but by his faith. It ought to encourage us to know that if we are willing to continue believing God and seeking His forgiveness and help, He can make "all-stars" out of us as well.   —C. B. Mc.

III. Lessons From the Patriarchs (Hebrews 11:13-16)

A. Strangers and Pilgrims (vv. 13, 14)

13, 14. These all died in faith, not having received the promises, but having seen them afar off, and were persuaded of them, and embraced them, and confessed that they were

strangers and pilgrims on the earth. For they that say such things declare plainly that they seek a country.

The phrase *these all* refers to Abraham, Sarah, Isaac, and Jacob, because the persons mentioned earlier in this chapter—Abel, Enoch, and Noah —had not received the specific *promises* that came to Abraham and his family. *These all died* before they *received the promises*, but they died firmly believing that they would one day receive them. They had seen them *afar off*, not with physical eyes, but with the eyes of faith. Thus they were content to accept their status as *strangers and pilgrims on the earth.*

B. Seekers of a Better Country
(vv. 15, 16)

15, 16. And truly, if they had been mindful of that country from whence they came out, they might have had opportunity to have returned. But now they desire a better country, that is, a heavenly: wherefore God is not ashamed to be called their God: for he hath prepared for them a city.

Although Abraham and his family considered themselves aliens and sojourners in Canaan, they never really considered Mesopotamia (the territory *from whence they came out*) their home either. Had they considered Ur or Haran (where Abraham later resided) in that manner, they could have returned. In fact, on many occasions they may have been tempted to return, but their faith drove them on to seek *a better country, that is, a heavenly.* We are reminded of the old spiritual: "This world is not my home, I'm just a passing through."

The faithfulness of the patriarchs pleased God; thus He was *not ashamed to be called their God.* "Them that honor me I will honor" (1 Samuel 2:30). He honored them by preparing for them *a city*, the new Jerusalem (Revelation 21:2).

IV. Reward of Faith
(Hebrews 11:39, 40)

39, 40. And these all, having obtained a good report through faith, received not the promise: God having provided some better thing for us, that they without us should not be made perfect.

The intervening verses of Hebrews 11 mention many other champions of faith: Joseph, Moses, Rahab, Gideon, and countless others whom the writer could not take time to name, but whose lives clearly demonstrated great faith. All of these *obtained a good report through faith*, yet they *received not the promise.* Through the

visual for lesson 12

Now faith is the substance of things hoped for, the evidence of things not seen.

eyes of faith they were able to see it from a distance, but they could not fully claim it.

In verse 40 the writer once again uses the word *better*, a key word throughout this epistle. The *better thing* that has been reserved for those who live in the Christian era is God's plan for man's salvation through the high priestly work of His Son, who gave Himself as a sacrifice for us. The benefits of that work, however, are not limited to Christians. Through God's grace they have been extended to the faithful in every age, so that all will one day reside in the city "whose builder and maker is God" (v. 10).

Conclusion
A. "Show Me!"

"I'm from Missouri! Show me!" is a remark that could serve as the motto of our skeptical times. Our scientific age has conditioned us to believe that information about everything that we know and trust must come through the five senses. If we cannot taste it, touch it, smell it, hear it, or see it, then it really cannot exist. In such a system there is no room for a faith that goes beyond the five senses.

Of course, in our daily lives we do not, and in fact cannot, live by this scientific dogma. When we get up in the morning, we turn on the water faucet, trusting that water, not sulfuric acid, will come out. We eat a bowl of cereal, trusting that it is wholesome food, not a deadly poison. We insert the key in the ignition of the car and turn it, fully believing that the car will start (and it does most of the time). We start down the highway, trusting that the oncoming drivers will stay on their side of the road. (If we doubted that they would, we would have to pull off the road every time we met someone, making it impossible to drive anywhere.) We stop at a store, select several items, and hand the clerk a piece of paper money. That piece of paper has little or no intrinsic value, yet the clerk accepts it without hesitation.

It is perfectly obvious that we have to live by these and similar acts of faith on a daily basis. Any person who refused to engage in such acts would quickly be considered a candidate for a mental institution. If we have to act on faith in scores of different ways every day, why should it be any different with our religious lives?

The critics of Christian faith have an answer to this question. They respond that experience leads us to believe that water, not sulfuric acid, will flow out of the tap; that the cereal will be wholesome, not poisonous; that the car will start when we turn it on; that other drivers will stay on their side of the road; that the clerk will accept our money.

But Christians can offer the same kind of argument. All of us who have made a serious effort to live the Christian life can relate numerous experiences as evidence that God can be trusted. We can recount instances of answered prayer. We know the meaning that faith can give to our lives. We know the confidence that comes when we trust God's promises of a glorious life beyond this world. That confidence is strengthened when we study the lives of the great champions of faith in Hebrews 11.

B. "This World Is Not My Home"

Home is one of the richest words we have in the English language. For most of us it brings up warm feelings and many happy memories. For a few, home may be a palatial mansion on a large estate. Others may find their home in a apartment in a crowded city. Many see it as a comfortable suburban dwelling surrounded by grass, flowers, and trees. For others it is a grass hut in a tropical rain forest, while still others call a frequently moved tent in an arid desert their home.

Whether it be a palace or a tent, all of these homes have one thing in common: they are all temporary. A palace may last a thousand years, while a grass hut will be gone in a few months, but sooner or later they will all succumb to the ravages of time and nature.

God promised Abraham and his descendants a land that they could call their own. Abraham was able to live in that land, but he lived there as a stranger and sojourner. Most of his life he lived in a tent, having little opportunity to build a more permanent dwelling. He could have returned to Ur, his original home, with its more comfortable surroundings. But he was content to live as he did, because he was able to see beyond this present world. He sought "a better country, that is, a heavenly" (Hebrews 11:16). He had the faith to forgo present comforts for a far greater comfort in the future.

Today, on every hand we see restless and unhappy people. Many have acquired wealth and the trappings that wealth can bring, yet the happiness they seek has eluded them. Their problems stem from their inability to see beyond this present world. How their outlook would change if only they would realize that this world is not their home! What a difference it would make if they began to seek the city whose builder and maker is God!

C. Women of Faith

We often speak of the men of faith in Hebrews 11, but this chapter also calls our attention to some *women* of faith. Sarah is mentioned because she had faith that God could give her the strength to bear Isaac, even when she was past the childbearing age. Rahab, who protected the Israelite spies, survived the destruction of Jericho because of her faith. Women who "received their dead raised to life again" are mentioned (v. 35). This chapter also describes the suffering and martyrdom of many others, some of whom undoubtedly were women. The point is quite obvious that men have no monopoly on faith. In most cases, behind every faithful man is a faithful, God-fearing woman—usually a wife or a mother.

D. Let Us Pray

Gracious God, we thank You for men and women across the centuries who have faithfully committed themselves to Your service. Kindle within us that same faith that will allow us to look beyond the present to the eternal city that You have promised. Amen.

E. Thought to Remember

Without faith it is impossible to please God.

Home Daily Bible Readings

Monday, Aug. 11—The Faith of Abraham and His Seed (Hebrews 11:17-22)

Tuesday, Aug. 12—The Faith of Moses (Hebrews 11:23-28)

Wednesday, Aug. 13—The Faith of the Israelites (Hebrews 11:29-38)

Thursday, Aug. 14—Abraham Gave God the Glory (Romans 4:13-21)

Friday, Aug. 15—God's Promise to Abraham (Galatians 3:15-22)

Saturday, Aug. 16—Righteousness Comes Through Faith (Romans 9:27-33)

Sunday, Aug. 17—Faith Without Works Is Dead (James 2:14-26)

Learning by Doing

This page contains an alternate lesson plan emphasizing learning activities.
Classes desiring such student involvement will find these suggestions helpful.

Learning Goals

Following today's study, students will:

1. Be able to explain how each of the Old Testament persons mentioned in the text demonstrated faith in God.

2. Realize his firmer basis for faith in God's promises.

3. Express a deeper faith in "things not seen."

Into the Lesson

Set a fan in the front of your classroom. Have it on "low" as your class assembles. Ask the class to identify two "invisible forces" of which the working fan gives evidence. You are looking for the responses: *electricity* and *air*. Note that though both are unseen, the results of their presence are seen daily. Point out that most of us have great faith in both, for we have experienced them repeatedly.

Into the Word

Prepare flash cards (at least five by seven inches), on each of which is written one of the following Old Testament names: ABEL, ABRAHAM, BARAK, DAVID, ELIJAH, ENOCH, ESAU, GIDEON, ISAAC, JACOB, JEPHTHAH, JOSEPH, JOSHUA, MOSES, NEHEMIAH, NOAH, RAHAB, RUTH, SAMSON, SAMUEL, AND SOLOMON. (Adjust the number according to your class size.) Tell the class that you are going to show them names of Old Testament men and women, and that you want them to identify five who are unnamed in Hebrews 11. (You can decide whether students should be given an opportunity to skim the chapter, or whether they should try this activity without any preliminary reading.) Show your flash cards, one at a time. Have students write the names that they believe do *not* appear in Hebrews 11. When you finish, ask for the names that have been written down, and record them for the class to see. Then check the chapter for correct responses (Elijah, Joshua, Nehemiah, Ruth, and Solomon are *not* named in the chapter). You might want to discuss briefly what each of these five did that demonstrated faith in God.

Next, divide the class approximately in half (best if done simply on the basis of seating). Because Noah and Abraham are the two examples found in today's text, designate one half the "Noah Group" and the other, the "Abraham Group." Have the first group review Genesis 6-9, and the second, Genesis 12, 15, 16, and 22 before you ask each group to make a case for its "faith hero" as deserving the title of "Champion of the Faithful." After about ten minutes, write "Noah versus Abraham" on the chalkboard or on a transparency, and call for each group's responses. Though the groups will offer a variety of statements, expect such "proofs" as the following to be offered: "Noah never 'got ahead' of God, as Abraham did concerning Hagar." "Abraham had to leave home immediately when God called him; Noah could stay where he was." "Abraham's faith did not pronounce judgment upon the world; Noah's faith affected the entire world through the flood." "Abraham believed in God's power to resurrect; Noah believed in God's power to destroy." (If your groups seem to need some help to get started, use one or more of the samples given here.) Once the "debate" is over, go directly into the following "Both Are Heroes of Faith" activity.

Read aloud to the class the following propositions based on today's text. Ask students to note how each applies to Noah and Abraham. (1) Faith involves "things hoped for." (2) Faith involves "things not seen." (3) The faithful are given a good report by God. (4) Faith involves being "moved with fear." (5) Faith involves anticipation of reward. (6) There is something "afar off" about faith. (7) Faith in God involves desiring something better than what one has. (8) Faith in God pleases God.

Into Life

If your class members do not use the student book (where the following activity appears), read the following statements of faith aloud and ask the students to reflect briefly and prayerfully on each. (1) I was not present when God created this world, but I believe He did. (2) I am too small to understand the universe, but I believe it is sustained by God's power and grace. (3) I am incapable of fully comprehending how God redeems me through the blood of Christ, but I believe He does. (4) The Holy Spirit is invisible, but I believe He is present. (5) The earth has not yet been destroyed by fire, but I believe it will be. (6) Jesus has not returned yet, but I believe He will. (7) I have not seen Heaven, but I believe it is real.

Let's Talk It Over

The questions on this page are designed to encourage review of the lesson Scriptures and to promote discussion of the lesson by the class. The answers provided are only discussion starters. Let your class talk it over from there.

1. How would you define faith? Can you give an example?

Our text calls faith "the substance of things hoped for, the evidence of things not seen" (Hebrews 11:1). This is not so much a definition as it is an observation about the nature of faith. Faith begins with the element of *belief.* We believe that God is, and we believe certain truths about God because of what has been disclosed through His acts in history, through the prophets, and through Jesus, whom we believe to be the Son of God. There is also a *trust* component to faith. Because of the evidence and the observable revelation of God, we are persuaded to hold certain beliefs about God, but in addition we trust in the continued providence of God and in His promises. This is why the writer of Hebrews speaks of "the substance of things hoped for." A parallel example might be my faith in my marriage. After twenty-five years of experience, I believe certain truths about my spouse and about our relationship, and I trust in the future stability and blessing of our relationship based upon the beliefs I carry from that past experience.

2. Can you name someone in your own experience who is an example of great faith? What remarkable acts did their faith move them to accomplish? What risks is faith calling you to take for God?

Chapter 11 of Hebrews recalls many champions of faith. Each one acted upon his or her faith in some dramatic way. Each of us should be able to point to current saints who have acted boldly out of faith. Among my heroes of faith are my parents. They became Christians as adults, and felt God's call to the ministry after they already had three children. In spite of the risks and the sacrifices, they made a move to a Bible college so Dad could enroll and prepare for the ministry. Following that, he and Mom served in fruitful ministries for forty years, and influenced many people for Christ. Faith in God will prompt believers to undertake some momentous challenges. The question is, will we heed those promptings or resist them? Unfortunately, in too many cases fear overtakes faith. When faith would say, "Yes," do you find yourself saying, "I'm sorry, I can't"?

3. Noah and Abraham acted out of faith in a promise. How do the promises God has made to people of faith today cause us to act differently from those who have no faith?

Because Noah believed God, he built an ark. Because Abraham believed God, he left his home and set out to find the land God promised him. Perhaps the most compelling promise of God to Christians is the promise of eternal life. Any injustice we suffer here will be set right in Heaven. Any sacrifice we make now will be compensated there. If giving full service and obedience to God requires us to forsake some earthly pleasure, we will have all eternity to make up for that loss. It is vanity to pursue wealth that is fleeting and will one day be surrendered or destroyed, when we could be storing up treasure that will last forever. We also have the promise that God will reward the work of His servants (Matthew 25:14-46; 1 Corinthians 3:12-15). This should motivate us to apply ourselves with diligence to seeking and pursuing God's will, and giving priority to the kind of work that will endure. As the apostle Peter asks, "Seeing then that all these things shall be dissolved, what manner of persons ought ye to be?" (2 Peter 3:11).

4. Like Abraham, Christians believe that God will lead them to "a city which hath foundations, whose builder and maker is God" (Hebrews 11:10). How does that change the way we live in this temporal world?

Our faith in God's promises makes us aliens in this world. This raises the question of what our attitude should be toward this world and the people of this world. Should we hold the world in contempt, and despise it for its injustices and for its disregard of God? Certainly our primary loyalty and greatest investment must be in God's eternal kingdom, but we can take our cue for how to regard this world from God Himself. "For God so *loved* the world, that he gave his only begotten Son" (John 3:16). Jesus' prayer for us was not that we should be taken out of the world, but that we should be protected "from the evil" (John 17:15). In fact, He sends us into the world with a mission. We must look upon the people of this world as prospects for the city that God has prepared for all the faithful.

Renew Commitment

DEVOTIONAL READING: 2 Corinthians 4:7-17.

LESSON SCRIPTURE: Hebrews 12:1-11.

PRINTED TEXT: Hebrews 12:1-11.

Hebrews 12:1-11

1 Wherefore, seeing we also are compassed about with so great a cloud of witnesses, let us lay aside every weight, and the sin which doth so easily beset us, and let us run with patience the race that is set before us,

2 Looking unto Jesus the author and finisher of our faith; who for the joy that was set before him endured the cross, despising the shame, and is set down at the right hand of the throne of God.

3 For consider him that endured such contradiction of sinners against himself, lest ye be wearied and faint in your minds.

4 Ye have not yet resisted unto blood, striving against sin.

5 And ye have forgotten the exhortation which speaketh unto you as unto children, My son, despise not thou the chastening of the Lord, nor faint when thou art rebuked of him:

6 For whom the Lord loveth he chasteneth, and scourgeth every son whom he receiveth.

7 If ye endure chastening, God dealeth with you as with sons; for what son is he whom the father chasteneth not?

8 But if ye be without chastisement, whereof all are partakers, then are ye bastards, and not sons.

9 Furthermore, we have had fathers of our flesh which corrected us, and we gave them reverence: shall we not much rather be in subjection unto the Father of spirits, and live?

10 For they verily for a few days chastened us after their own pleasure; but he for our profit, that we might be partakers of his holiness.

11 Now no chastening for the present seemeth to be joyous, but grievous: nevertheless, afterward it yieldeth the peaceable fruit of righteousness unto them which are exercised thereby.

GOLDEN TEXT: Wherefore, seeing we also are compassed about with so great a cloud of witnesses, let us lay aside every weight, and the sin which doth so easily beset us, and let us run with patience the race that is set before us.—Hebrews 12:1.

A Call to Faithfulness
Unit 2: Be Faithful Followers of Christ
(Lessons 10-14)

Lesson Aims

After this lesson, each student should:

1. Appreciate the importance of perseverance and discipline in the Christian life.

2. Be better able to deal with the temptations and problems that arise while living as a Christian.

Lesson Outline

INTRODUCTION
  A. Just Keep Running
  B. Lesson Background
 I. THE CHRISTIAN'S RACE (Hebrews 12:1-4)
  A. Our Witnesses (v. 1)
  B. Our Example (vv. 2-4)
II. TRAINING FOR THE RACE (Hebrews 12:5-11)
  A. The Lord's Chastening (vv. 5, 6)
    The Discipline of Sons
  B. Reason for Chastening (vv. 7, 8)
  C. Example of Fathers (vv. 9, 10)
  D. Rewards of Chastening (v. 11)
CONCLUSION
  A. Lift Up Your Hands
  B. Today's "Cloud of Witnesses"
  C. Let Us Pray
  D. Thought to Remember

Today's visual for Lesson 13 encourages us to "run with patience the race that is set before us." It is shown on page 437.

Introduction

A. Just Keep Running

Years ago I went out for the university track team. I made the team as a distance runner, but after a few weeks I grew tired of the monotony of the training routine. Every day we did warming up and stretching exercises. Then came time with the medicine ball, and other activities to lengthen our stride and to strengthen our ankles and the arches of our feet. We ran against the clock to learn to pace ourselves. Then we ran the usual distance of a race, and on some days the dreaded "over distance." Finally, we finished by running wind sprints, and occasionally running up and down the stadium steps until we almost dropped from exhaustion.

High school track had never been this demanding, and I was looking for an easier way of training. One day I approached the coach and asked about a better way to train for track. I was hoping he would prescribe a special diet or maybe a daily dose of vitamins.

"Son," he replied, "if you want to be a winner, just come out every day like you've been doing and keep going through the exercises." Then pointing to the track, he said, "Then get out there on the track and keep running!"

I can understand how the Hebrew Christians must have felt. They had been through some difficult times. Perhaps they were seeking an easier way. But the writer of Hebrews did not let them "off the hook." He told them to keep on doing what they had been doing, and then get out on the track of life and keep running!

B. Lesson Background

Our previous lesson centered upon Hebrews 11, the great faith chapter of the Bible. In that chapter the writer "calls the roll" of God's faithful—those who had remained true to Him even under very difficult and trying conditions. Their lives served as models for those who came after them. The Hebrew Christians needed these models, for many of them were on the verge of turning back in the face of hardships and persecution. The author acknowledges that they had indeed faced difficulties, but reminds them that they had "not yet resisted unto blood" as had some of the great champions of the faith.

Using an illustration drawn from the races that were held in the great arenas of that time, the writer urges the Hebrew Christians to "run with patience the race that is set before" them. After nearly two thousand years, that advice is still appropriate. Most of us do not face the physical persecutions that the early Christians did (our temptations are of a different order), but often we do become discouraged. We must run our race with patience and consistency if we are to claim the victory.

I. The Christian's Race (Hebrews 12:1-4)

A. Our Witnesses (v. 1)

1. Wherefore, seeing we also are compassed about with so great a cloud of witnesses, let us lay aside every weight, and the sin which doth so easily beset us, and let us run with patience the race that is set before us.

The phrase *so great a cloud of witnesses* suggests the image of a vast stadium filled with fans cheering the athletes on as they run. The witnesses are the champions of the faith mentioned in the previous chapter, who are pictured as watching the Hebrew Christians run their race. However, the writer may not be suggesting that the faithful of the past are actual spectators, but rather that they are witnesses in the sense that their lives bear testimony to the power of faith. Thus do they offer inspiration to Christians.

The words *lay aside every weight* suggest another practice common in the New Testament world. Runners sometimes strengthened their legs by running in practice with weights tied to their legs. In the actual contest, the weights were then removed, giving an added thrust to the runners stride. It is obvious that *sin* is a serious handicap to a runner in the Christian race. *Besetting* speaks of the potential that sin has to neutralize a Christian's effectiveness and to hinder his progress. The *weight* may refer to something that in itself is not sinful. The item in question may even be good, such as concern for family or involvement in one's vocation. But it becomes a hindrance when it takes precedence over one's Christian commitment.

The word translated *patience* is sometimes rendered "endurance" (*New American Standard Bible*) or "perseverance" (*New International Version*). The Christian race is not a one-hundred-meter dash; it is a marathon, requiring a tremendous amount of stamina to complete. Many who start the Christian race drop out because they have not trained in such a way as to build up their endurance.

B. Our Example (vv. 2-4)

2, 3. Looking unto Jesus the author and finisher of our faith; who for the joy that was set before him endured the cross, despising the shame, and is set down at the right hand of the throne of God. For consider him that endured such contradiction of sinners against himself, lest ye be wearied and faint in your minds.

The records set by previous champions in any sport are often held up to challenge and inspire those who come after them. The writer has just challenged his readers (in chapter 11) by highlighting the examples of men and women of great faith. Now he holds up the greatest example of all: *Jesus*, described as *the author and finisher of our faith*. The word translated *author* is the same Greek word rendered "captain" in Hebrews 2:10. The *Revised Standard Version* uses the term "pioneer." We may picture Jesus as "blazing a trail" that has provided the way to salvation. He is the *finisher*, in the sense that He has provided what is essential for the completion of our faith. Even in the suffering and *shame* of *the cross*, Jesus found *joy* because He could look forward to sitting *at the right hand of*

the throne of God. The Hebrew Christians were reminded of this, lest they become *wearied and faint* and drop out of the race.

4. Ye have not yet resisted unto blood, striving against sin.

It seems to be a human trait to think that the hardships we suffer are more severe than the hardships suffered by others. The Hebrew Christians were guilty of this. The writer reminds them that they had *not yet resisted unto blood.* Jesus had died for them, and other Christians had been put to death for Jesus' sake. The Hebrew Christians had suffered various "reproaches and afflictions" for Jesus' sake (Hebrews 10:32-34), but none of them had died for their faith. They were like the man who had no shoes and complained, until he met a man who had no feet.

II. Training for the Race (Hebrews 12:5-11)

A. The Lord's Chastening (vv. 5, 6)

5. And ye have forgotten the exhortation which speaketh unto you as unto children, My son, despise not thou the chastening of the Lord, nor faint when thou art rebuked of him.

The writer now quotes from Proverbs 3:11, 12. The Hebrew Christians would be quite familiar with this Scripture. It would give them a more appropriate perspective from which to view their current hardships.

One of the most serious issues Christians have to face is the problem posed by suffering. We could sense some purpose behind it if only the wicked suffered. The problem arises when we see innocent children and good, decent people suffer. Just because we become Christians does not give us all the answers to these issues. By faith we come to understand the place of suffering in our spiritual growth and in the development of our testimony to the difference our faith in Christ makes. An athlete becomes a champion only after he has suffered intense pain and complete exhaustion in his training program. The coach does not put his players through these stressful regimens because he

visual for
lesson 13

hates them or enjoys seeing them suffer. He does it in order to prepare them for the upcoming contest. When we come to recognize this aspect of suffering, it will help us to see suffering as a means of achieving spiritual maturity.

6. For whom the Lord loveth he chasteneth, and scourgeth every son whom he receiveth.

In a permissive age that has come to reject almost any kind of discipline, this verse may sound harsh and excessive. The Greek word rendered *scourgeth* literally means "to whip." It may refer to the suffering associated with persecution, resulting from the "contradiction of sinners" (v. 3). Whatever the source of the suffering, God would have us keep in mind the purpose of our pain. In "all things," the Scripture tells us, He is at work, molding us into "the image of his Son" (Romans 8:28, 29). Our pain does not have to be in the form of physical suffering, for often the most painful experiences are emotional or spiritual. How we handle them, and whether we seek the heavenly perspective on them, will determine if we are battered or bettered by them.

God disciplines us because He is our Father and He loves us. The most pathetic child is one who grows up without any discipline. A parent who neglects to discipline a child is not showing love, but a selfish disregard for the child's welfare. Certainly our heavenly Father is never guilty of such neglect.

THE DISCIPLINE OF SONS

In his book *The Problem of Pain*, C. S. Lewis says that one of the reasons God permits His people to undergo hardships and suffering is that He desires our perfection. Lewis notes that a key element of all real love is the desire that the thing or person loved be the best it can be.

An artist may not take great care with a simple sketch made to amuse a child. But he will take infinite pains with the great masterpiece of his life. We may not care that a stray dog smells bad or rummages through other people's garbage. But we treat the family dog quite differently. It is washed, house-trained, and taught not to steal or tear up objects. Because we love the dog, we will interfere with its natural state and habits to give it proper instruction and make it even more lovable.

A father who loves a son will discipline him to make him the sort of man he ought to be. It would be odd, even in our permissive age, to hear a man say, "I love my son, but I don't care how rotten a man he becomes just so long as he enjoys himself."

Lewis also compares God's love for us with the love between a man and a woman. When a man falls in love with a woman, does he cease to care what she looks like or how others think of her? Isn't that the time he really begins to care? Does a woman consider it a sign of love in a man that he neither knows nor cares how she looks? Of course not.

When God says that He loves us, He really means it. We are indeed the objects of His love—a love that will not be satisfied until we are the very best we can be.   —C. B. Mc.

B. Reason for Chastening (vv. 7, 8)

7, 8. If ye endure chastening, God dealeth with you as with sons; for what son is he whom the father chasteneth not? But if ye be without chastisement, whereof all are partakers, then are ye bastards, and not sons.

When discipline comes to us because of our own willful disobedience, then we ought to accept it and learn from it. Discipline administered by parents is a normal part of growing up. While some children may rebel at being disciplined, others will receive it and benefit from it.

It is not uncommon for a father to ignore an illegitimate child, thus avoiding any responsibility for disciplining him or her. The writer seems to be suggesting that if we have not experienced suffering, then we are not really God's children. Some of us may have gone through life without experiencing any great tragedies or any severe degree of suffering. Does this mean that we are not God's children? We should keep in mind that the words of our text were directed to the circumstances of Christians who were growing weary of their discipline and considering dropping out of their race. The writer urges them to remain faithful, based on the Scriptural teaching that discipline indicates God's favor. Such teaching is meant to encourage those who are being disciplined. It should not be used to try to evaluate the spiritual condition of believers who are not presently undergoing discipline.

C. Example of Fathers (vv. 9, 10)

9, 10. Furthermore, we have had fathers of our flesh which corrected us, and we gave them reverence: shall we not much rather be in subjection unto the Father of spirits, and live? For they verily for a few days chastened us after their own pleasure; but he for our profit, that we might be partakers of his holiness.

Jewish *fathers* usually took their parenting responsibilities seriously. As a result, Hebrew children, until they reached maturity, were taught to accept the discipline of their fathers and to respect them. However, the fathers were not perfect, and at times their discipline may have been inappropriate. Such is true of any

Home Daily Bible Readings

Monday, Aug. 18—Be Committed to Peace (James 3:13-18)

Tuesday, Aug. 19—In All Things Exercise Self-Control (1 Corinthians 9:19-27)

Wednesday, Aug. 20—Look to God for Wisdom (James 1:1-8)

Thursday, Aug. 21—Every Good Gift Is From God (James 1:12-18)

Friday, Aug. 22—Act Out Your Beliefs (James 1:19-27)

Saturday, Aug. 23—Trust in the Lord (Proverbs 3:1-12)

Sunday, Aug. 24—Pray for Renewal (Psalm 51)

generation of fathers. On occasion they chasten their children *after their own pleasure*; that is, for their own convenience or out of their anger, rather than for the benefit of the children. Still, these fathers are looked upon with *reverence*.

If we respect earthly fathers who are far less than perfect, and whose discipline lasts but *a few days*, how much more should we reverence the perfect *Father of spirits*? His discipline continues throughout our Christian walk, as He prepares us to be *partakers of his holiness*.

D. Rewards of Chastening (v. 11)

11. Now no chastening for the present seemeth to be joyous, but grievous: nevertheless, afterward it yieldeth the peaceable fruit of righteousness unto them which are exercised thereby.

No child enjoys the experience of *chastening*. So it is not surprising that Christians often resent the chastening of the heavenly Father. The writer urges the Hebrew Christians to think in terms of *afterward*—to look beyond their immediate situation and see the long-term results of God's discipline. The athlete, if he is to become a champion, must look beyond the stress and agony of training and see the victor's prize. The Christian must likewise accept any present chastening if he is to receive its positive spiritual benefits, which include the *peaceable fruit of righteousness*.

Conclusion

A. Lift Up Your Hands

Many of the Hebrew Christians had been a part of the Lord's church for some time, during which they had suffered persecution and humiliation (see Hebrews 10:32-34). For many, the Christian race had become long and tiring. The excitement of their earlier commitment had slowly evaporated. Perhaps they had little to show for their efforts. Most of us can identify with this feeling, for sooner or later most of us experience it. This is exactly the kind of situation that Satan knows how to exploit.

In the verses that follow, the writer offers the best solution to this problem: "Wherefore lift up the hands which hang down, and the feeble knees; and make straight paths for your feet" (vv. 12, 13). In other words, get back out on the track, keep running, and take the time to encourage others who are thinking about quitting the race. Usually an individual competing in a race is concerned only with his own progress. He is not expected to stop and help a runner who falls. But the Christian's race is different. To ignore a fallen runner is to score a point for Satan's side, not God's.

B. Today's "Cloud of Witnesses"

Every Christian, unless he happens to be stranded on a deserted island, is surrounded by another "cloud of witnesses" besides the one mentioned in Hebrews 12:1. These witnesses are watching our actions to see whether we translate our faith into real life. Some of these witnesses are hostile. They would like nothing better than to see us stumble. Our failures will give them an opportunity to sneer at Christianity. For this reason we need to run our race with diligence.

Other witnesses, however, will be friendly: other Christians, family members, or those who look to us as examples. While our fundamental commitment is to Christ, we also have a commitment to these who trust us. We must so live that we never cause any of them to stumble. Such a responsibility may seem like a heavy burden, but we need to realize that these friendly witnesses will also become a wonderful blessing to us. They will be there to cheer us on when we become weary, and they will help us up when we stumble.

C. Let Us Pray

Dear Father, when our burdens seem to overwhelm us, remind us that few of us have "resisted unto blood" in our efforts to serve You. Help us to accept present chastening and see beyond it to the glorious future You have in store for us. May we look to Him who is the "author and finisher of our faith" for strength and guidance. In His holy name we pray. Amen.

D. Thought to Remember

The Christian race is a marathon, not a sprint.

Learning by Doing

This page contains an alternate lesson plan emphasizing learning activities.
Classes desiring such student involvement will find these suggestions helpful.

Learning Goals

After this study in Hebrews 12, students should be able to:

1. Accept the discipline and the chastisement of the Christian life with greater patience.

2. Make a commitment to personalizing Hebrews 12:1.

Into the Lesson

Set up your classroom to resemble a race track, with "bleachers" on each side of three running "lanes" that you have marked off on the floor with masking or plastic tape. At the end of the "race track," run a strip of crepe paper between two chairs to symbolize the finish line.

Before your class assembles on Sunday, recruit three class members to be the "runners" in your race. Any appropriate clothing or shoes they choose to wear is optional. Inform your recruits that they will be answering questions on the text of Hebrews 12:1-11, so that they can prepare.

As class begins, introduce your runners and their task, and direct the "fans" to turn to today's text and follow along.

Into the Word

Put each of the following questions and answers on separate cards. Keep them in the verse-by-verse order given here. (Q) What word is used to describe the assembly of witnesses? (*cloud*) (Q) What needs to be laid aside? (*every weight*) (Q) What "doth so easily beset us"? (*sin*) (Q) How are we to run the race? (*with patience*) (Q) Who is the "author and finisher of our faith"? (*Jesus*) (Q) What motivated Jesus to endure the cross? (*the joy ahead of Him*) (Q) What was Jesus' response to the shame of the cross? (*He despised it*) (Q) Where is Jesus now "set down"? (*at the right hand of the throne of God*) (Q) What did Jesus endure? (*the cross, v. 2, or contradiction of sinners, v. 3*) (Q) How are the children of God *not* to react to His chastening? (*despising it*) (Q) When God rebukes His children, what should they *not* do? (*faint*) (Q) What does the Lord do to the one He loves? (*chastens*) (Q) What does the Lord do to every son He receives? (*scourges*) (Q) What is a sign that God is dealing with you as a son? (*you endure chastening*) (Q) What attitude do we have toward earthly fathers who correct us? (*reverence*) (Q)

In contrast to the "fathers of our flesh," what is God called? (*Father of spirits*) (Q) To what purpose do earthly fathers sometimes chasten their children? (*their own pleasure*) (Q) Of what do we partake if God's chastisement works in us? (*His holiness*) (Q) How is chastening always first perceived? (*as grievous*) (Q) What does chastening ultimately yield? (*the peaceable fruit of righteousness*). Mix into your stack, to be selected at random, two cards, each with one of the following messages: (1) "Oops! You've fallen. Miss a turn," and (2) "Ouch! You've twisted your ankle. For the next two turns, all you can do is hop once on one foot."

Ask the questions, in order, of each of your "runners." For each correct answer, allow them to move a short way (you decide) toward the "finish line." Ask your "fans" to encourage the runners. Anticipate that all will finish the race (though you might plan for one to "become discouraged" and take a seat before finishing, to prepare for the "Into Life" section). Award a small trophy or certificate to the runners.

Into Life

Use the two groups of "fans" on either side of the "bleachers" to respond to the following two questions: (1) How was our race *like* the Christian race? and (2) How was our race *unlike* the Christian race? Though you may receive a variety of answers, the following *likes* should be included: there are those who encourage us to finish; occasional setbacks deter our running; one needs to be properly clothed (with Christ, Romans 13:14) to run successfully; one succeeds in the race by knowing Scripture; each who finishes receives a reward. *Unlikes* should include: life is long and hard, not short and easy; much of life is run in secret, rather than on display; some Christians drop out and quit the race (use only if all finish your "race"); in the Christian race, each runner is to help those about him; also in the Christian race, runners jump in at various points and join the race. If your sides need help getting started, give each side one or two of these similarities or differences.

Read Hebrews 12:1 once more as the final challenge to your students. You may want your three "runners" to do so in unison, as they stand at the "finish line."

Close the class session with prayer.

Let's Talk It Over

The questions on this page are designed to encourage review of the lesson Scriptures and to promote discussion of the lesson by the class. The answers provided are only discussion starters. Let your class talk it over from there.

1. How does having an audience watch your performance (in sports, drama, music, etc.) affect what you do? How does it help to think of a "cloud of witnesses" (Hebrews 12:1) watching you live for Christ?

Most of us put pressure upon ourselves to do our best when others are observing us. We do not want to make a mistake or disappoint those who are watching. However, a cheering or otherwise supportive crowd can draw out the best we have to give. Thus we speak of a "home court/field advantage" in sports. The writer of Hebrews is drawing upon that common experience when he refers to the "cloud of witnesses." If we consider that believers of previous generations have an interest in our lives, it may cause us to be more faithful and determined. To think that we are being observed and cheered by those who preceded us in the arena may raise our level of intensity.

2. How is the Christian life similar to a race? What are the lessons for us if we are the "runners"?

People enter a race intentionally, not by accident. People become Christians and set out to follow Jesus intentionally, by faith, repentance, and obedience. People in a race also stay focused. They do not leave the race after a short distance, join the spectators for a while, and then think of reentering the race later. To be authentic Christians, we must continue on the course we have been called to follow. Also, people running a race do not carry extra weight or baggage. Our text challenges us to "lay aside every weight, and the sin which doth so easily beset us" (Hebrews 12:1). If we are serious about living as a Christian, we will be anxious to get rid of the harmful acts or habits that are contrary to Christian character. Finally, to complete a race requires endurance. Every day there are temptations to leave the course, so we must decide every day to keep our eyes upon the goal.

3. How is the example of Jesus' endurance an encouragement to you?

Jesus is the trailblazer and pacesetter for our race as Christians. He is not one to simply point the direction we should go; He goes before us and calls us to follow. Rather than take the easy way, He suffered the worst that the world had to throw at Him, and yet persevered. While we may suffer as we run our race, we know that we will never suffer more than Jesus did. He let the joy that lay ahead be His motivation. We too have a promise of great joy to come, which should make it easier to endure the difficulties of the course we must travel.

4. Do you believe that God sends pain into our lives today to discipline us? Explain why or why not.

The Jews of Jesus' day considered all suffering as God's punishment for sin. This is why the disciples asked Jesus concerning a man born blind, "Who did sin, this man, or his parents, that he was born blind?" (John 9:2). Jesus explained that the man's blindness was not due to sin; thus, we can be assured that whenever we experience pain it is not always God's punishment. Remember that Jesus suffered greatly, yet He was innocent of sin. Our lesson text, however, makes it clear that God does discipline those He loves. It is possible, then, that our sufferings may sometimes be allowed by or used of God to get our attention and to correct some sinful behavior. The law of sowing and reaping alone will dictate some unwelcome results when we ignore God's commands. If we abuse our bodies with drugs, alcohol, or even unhealthy eating habits, we will suffer physical consequences. At other times the connection may not be so direct, but it is observable. For instance, doctors and psychologists often identify such attitudes as worry, bitterness, or envy as the root cause of a variety of ailments. This could be considered God's discipline to direct us away from such attitudes.

5. Which do you think is more important to God—our comfort or our character? Tell why you think so.

God is willing to sacrifice our momentary comfort for the sake of the development of our character, so we must conclude that character is more important. Any parent who applies discipline to a child has made the same choice. A parent makes the choice to "grieve" the child now in order to produce more noble character, and God does the same.

Live Responsibly

DEVOTIONAL READING: James 5:7-16.

LESSON SCRIPTURE: Hebrews 13.

PRINTED TEXT: Hebrews 13:1-16.

Hebrews 13:1-16

1 Let brotherly love continue.

2 Be not forgetful to entertain strangers: for thereby some have entertained angels unawares.

3 Remember them that are in bonds, as bound with them; and them which suffer adversity, as being yourselves also in the body.

4 Marriage is honorable in all, and the bed undefiled: but whoremongers and adulterers God will judge.

5 Let your conversation be without covetousness; and be content with such things as ye have: for he hath said, I will never leave thee, nor forsake thee.

6 So that we may boldly say, The Lord is my helper, and I will not fear what man shall do unto me.

7 Remember them which have the rule over you, who have spoken unto you the word of God: whose faith follow, considering the end of their conversation.

8 Jesus Christ the same yesterday, and today, and for ever.

9 Be not carried about with divers and strange doctrines: for it is a good thing that the heart be established with grace; not with meats, which have not profited them that have been occupied therein.

10 We have an altar, whereof they have no right to eat which serve the tabernacle.

11 For the bodies of those beasts, whose blood is brought into the sanctuary by the high priest for sin, are burned without the camp.

12 Wherefore Jesus also, that he might sanctify the people with his own blood, suffered without the gate.

13 Let us go forth therefore unto him without the camp, bearing his reproach.

14 For here we have no continuing city, but we seek one to come.

15 By him therefore let us offer the sacrifice of praise to God continually, that is, the fruit of our lips, giving thanks to his name.

16 But to do good and to communicate forget not: for with such sacrifices God is well pleased.

GOLDEN TEXT: To do good and to communicate forget not: for with such sacrifices God is well pleased.—Hebrews 13:16.

A Call to Faithfulness
Unit 2: Be Faithful Followers of Christ
(Lessons 10-14)

Lesson Aims

After studying this lesson, each student should:

1. Have a better understanding of what God expects of him or her as a Christian.

2. Appreciate the importance of living responsibly in a world that has lost its moral direction.

3. Be able to mention specific ways in which he or she can demonstrate responsible Christian behavior.

Lesson Outline

INTRODUCTION
    A. Called to Sacrifice
    B. Lesson Background
I. PERSONAL EXHORTATIONS (Hebrews 13:1-6)
    A. To Brotherly Love (vv. 1-3)
    B. To Sexual Purity (v. 4)
        Killer Lust
    C. To Live in Contentment (vv. 5, 6)
II. EXAMPLES TO FOLLOW (Hebrews 13:7, 8)
    A. Teachers of the Word (v. 7)
    B. The Unchanging Christ (v. 8)
III. ADDITIONAL CHALLENGES (Hebrews 13:9-16)
    A. The Danger of Instability (v. 9)
    B. The Christian's Altar (vv. 10, 11)
    C. Following Jesus (vv. 12, 13)
    D. The City to Come (v. 14)
    E. The Proper Sacrifices (vv. 15, 16)
CONCLUSION
    A. The Power of Purity
    B. Change and Decay
    C. Let Us Pray
    D. Thought to Remember

The visual for Lesson 14 illustrates the golden text's emphasis on doing good to others. It is shown on page 444.

Introduction

A. Called to Sacrifice

The Hebrew Christians had gone through some difficult times, although apparently none of them had yet suffered martyrdom (Hebrews 12:4). Still, many were being tempted to abandon their faith in Jesus. We have noticed, beginning with Hebrews 10:19, a more concentrated emphasis by the writer on encouraging the Hebrew Christians to stand fast in their faith. The opening verses of the final chapter (from which today's lesson text is taken) emphasize the importance of living a life that marks Christians as different from persons of the world.

Some in the early church deliberately sought martyrdom, believing it to be a mark of a superior faith. Yet the New Testament nowhere urges people to seek martyrdom. It does talk frequently about sacrifice. Most of us will never be called upon to die for our faith, but all of us have the opportunity to offer service and praise as an acceptable sacrifice to God.

B. Lesson Background

When we first began our studies from the letter to the Hebrews several weeks ago, we observed that it begins like a tract, not a letter. It does not have the salutation or greeting that we normally would expect in a letter. Instead, it begins with a profound theological statement: God has spoken through His Son. The chapters that follow contrast Jesus, the final revelation, with all who had come before. A specific contrast is drawn between the sacrifice of Christ and the sacrificial system of the Old Testament.

All of this profound theology has some practical, down-to-earth implications. Since "our God is a consuming fire" (Hebrews 12:29, the final verse in the chapter), we should expect Him to make ethical demands on those who would follow Him. That is what we see in chapter 13 (the final chapter of this letter). These practical applications are set forth in language that reminds us of the admonitions with which Paul often closes his letters. In addition to these challenges, there is a personal reference to "our brother Timothy" (v. 23) and a final blessing: "Grace be with you all" (v. 25).

I. Personal Exhortations
(Hebrews 13:1-6)

A. To Brotherly Love (vv. 1-3)

1, 2. Let brotherly love continue. Be not forgetful to entertain strangers: for thereby some have entertained angels unawares.

The writer does not supply his readers with a long list of virtues that he expects them to develop. Instead, he concentrates on a few areas of conduct and attitude that seem most appropriate to their situation.

Christians belong to the "household of faith" (Galatians 6:10); thus, it should be a common practice for them to accept and treat one another as brothers and sisters. The Hebrew Christians

**Aug
31**

were also urged to *entertain*, or offer hospitality to, *strangers*. This probably referred to Christians traveling through their vicinity. Such hospitality was especially important in that day. The number of public inns was scarce, and those that existed were likely to have a questionable reputation. The author reminds his readers that some who had offered hospitality in the past had received a very special reward: they had *entertained angels unawares*. The example of Abraham comes to mind (Genesis 18), although there are other incidents recorded in Scripture (Genesis 19:1, 2; Judges 6:11, 19-22). While we may never have the opportunity to "entertain" an angel, many of us have received blessings we were not expecting because we extended kindness to someone in need. We miss such blessings if we consider our homes as solely ours rather than God's.

3. Remember them that are in bonds, as bound with them; and them which suffer adversity, as being yourselves also in the body.

Another special request was that the Hebrew Christians attend to fellow believers who were suffering *bonds*, or imprisonment, because of their faith. Ancient prisons offered no amenities and few necessities. Prisoners were often dependent upon friends for the essentials of food and warm clothing (see Paul's request in 2 Timothy 4:13). Caring for the needs of the imprisoned was a very important ministry that Christians could fulfill. It is interesting to think of how Jesus identified Himself with those in prison (Matthew 25:36). In this verse, Christians are told to identify themselves with those who suffer, *as bound with them*.

B. To Sexual Purity (v. 4)

4. Marriage is honorable in all, and the bed undefiled: but whoremongers and adulterers God will judge.

God demands purity in sexual relations. This was a difficult standard to maintain in the immoral surroundings of the first-century world. We who live in a culture also permeated by sexual license can empathize with these early Christians and the words addressed to them. In spite of the pressures of our times, we need to realize that God's standards have not changed.

Whoremongers is translated as "immoral" in the *Revised Standard Version* and covers a wide range of sexual sins. *Adulterers* are those who violate their marriage vows by becoming intimate with someone other than their spouses. The Scriptures are unanimous in their condemnation of these sins. In the presence of such firm standards, it is amazing that some religious leaders today want to compromise them.

KILLER LUST

An old black-and-white movie showed a group of shipwrecked men drifting aimlessly on the ocean in a lifeboat. As the days passed under the scorching sun, their rations of food and fresh water gave out. The men grew deliriously thirsty. One night while the others were asleep, one man ignored all previous warnings and gulped down some salt water. He quickly died. Ocean water contains seven times more salt than the human body can safely ingest. Drinking it causes a person to dehydrate even faster, because the kidneys demand extra water to flush out the extra salt. The more salt water someone drinks, the thirstier he gets. He actually dies of thirst.

When married people indulge in lust for someone else, they become like the man in the movie. They thirst desperately for something that looks like what they want. They fail to realize, however, that what they seek is precisely the opposite of what they really need. In fact, it is deadly.

God gave us the gift of sexuality to be enjoyed within the married union of one man with one woman for life. This is, and always has been, His loving will for us. It is to our great good to keep the marriage bed pure, and to our great peril to defile it through sexual sin.   —C. B. Mc.

C. To Live in Contentment (vv. 5, 6)

5, 6. Let your conversation be without covetousness; and be content with such things as ye have: for he hath said, I will never leave thee, nor forsake thee. So that we may boldly say, The Lord is my helper, and I will not fear what man shall do unto me.

In the English of the *King James Version*, the word *conversation* was not limited to one's speech, but covered every aspect of a person's life. The word translated *covetousness* refers specifically to the love of money. Greed is an especially dangerous sin, because it leads to

visual for
lesson 14

other sins, such as lying, stealing, and even murder. The exhortation of this verse is appropriate for our materialistic age, driven as it is by the desire for more and more. The problem with greed is that it is never *content*; it always wants more.

In contrast, a Christian possesses spiritual resources that allow him to resist greed. He can be content with what he has, because he has God's assurance: *I will never leave thee, nor forsake thee.* This is not a license for us to relax and do nothing, expecting God to feed and clothe us. The contentment comes from knowing that God is in control of our resources and has promised to supply our needs if we order our priorities according to His will (see Matthew 6:31-33; 1 Timothy 6:6-8).

II. Examples to Follow (Hebrews 13:7, 8)

A. Teachers of the Word (v. 7)

7. Remember them which have the rule over you, who have spoken unto you the word of God: whose faith follow, considering the end of their conversation.

The expression *have the rule over you* is literally "your leading ones." The phrase also appears in verses 17 and 24 of this chapter. In those two verses it refers to the current leaders of the congregation. However, in the verse that is before us it seems to call attention to former leaders, since the Hebrew Christians are asked to *remember them* and to consider the *end* of their *conversation* (way of life). It is possible that these were the individuals who had led many of the Hebrew Christians to Christ through the *word of God*. If these had remained faithful to the end, the Hebrew Christians could also. All of us would do well to consider where we would be without the influence of faithful teachers of God's Word.

B. The Unchanging Christ (v. 8)

8. Jesus Christ the same yesterday, and today, and for ever.

The Hebrew Christians were urged to follow the example of their former leaders; however, these men were no longer available to speak the word of God to them. In contrast, *Jesus Christ,* the perfect leader, remains unchanged. *Yesterday*—in the past—He had died on the cross for their sins. *Today* He was guiding them through faithful leaders and through His presence in their lives. His influence is not subject to the limitations that affect human leaders; it lasts *for ever*. By following Him, the Hebrew Christians are assured that they will not be led astray.

III. Additional Challenges (Hebrews 13:9-16)

A. The Danger of Instability (v. 9)

9. Be not carried about with divers and strange doctrines: for it is a good thing that the heart be established with grace; not with meats, which have not profited them that have been occupied therein.

The picture here is of a ship without a helmsman, *carried about* by changing winds. The same Greek word is used in Ephesians 4:14, where Paul warns the Ephesian Christians not to be "carried about with every wind of doctrine." The Hebrew Christians were in danger of being driven back to the Judaism from which they had come.

Some commentators see the reference to *meats* as part of an unorthodox Jewish sect that put great emphasis on the eating of certain foods. But the reference to an "altar" in verse 10 seems to refer to the ceremonial sacrifices under the Mosaic Law. The point the writer is making here is that the *heart* is nurtured by *grace*, not by the sacrifices prescribed in the Law. These sacrifices had not really *profited* those who had offered them.

B. The Christian's Altar (vv. 10, 11)

10. We have an altar, whereof they have no right to eat which serve the tabernacle.

Since the early Christians had no visible idols, their pagan neighbors often accused them of being atheists. Jews, who had no idols, criticized Christians because they had no altar on which to offer sacrifices for sin. The author answers this charge by pointing out that Christians certainly do *have an altar*. That altar is the cross upon which God's own Son was offered. The term *tabernacle* refers here to the system of sacrifices instituted by Moses along with the tabernacle itself. As long as the Jews continued to cling to this system, they had *no right to eat* from the Christian's altar; that is, they could not receive the benefits of Jesus' death.

11. For the bodies of those beasts, whose blood is brought into the sanctuary by the high priest for sin, are burned without the camp.

The Hebrew Christians were reminded of the ceremony that took place on the Day of Atonement. The priests were allowed to eat of ordinary sacrifices, but on the Day of Atonement the regulations were different. The blood of the animals was sprinkled in the Holy of Holies, and the carcasses were then taken outside *the camp* and *burned*.

C. Following Jesus (vv. 12, 13)

12, 13. Wherefore Jesus also, that he might sanctify the people with his own blood, suffered without the gate. Let us go forth therefore unto him without the camp, bearing his reproach.

Just as the sacrificial animals were burned outside the camp on the Day of Atonement, Jesus *suffered without the gate*, that is, outside the walls of Jerusalem. In so doing, He accomplished *with his own blood* what the sacrifice on the Day of Atonement could never do: *sanctify the people* (Hebrews 10:10). The Hebrew Christians were urged to *go forth* to Jesus, leaving behind the old system under the Law of Moses.

D. The City to Come (v. 14)

14. For here have we no continuing city, but we seek one to come.

When Jews became Christians, they turned their backs upon Jerusalem as the center of true worship. For them Jerusalem was *no continuing city*—a truth that would become tragically evident when the Roman army destroyed the city in A.D. 70. But Christians had no need to fear, for their destination was the "city which hath foundations, whose builder and maker is God" (Hebrews 11:10).

E. The Proper Sacrifices (vv. 15, 16)

15, 16. By him therefore let us offer the sacrifice of praise to God continually, that is, the fruit of our lips, giving thanks to his name. But to do good and to communicate forget not: for with such sacrifices God is well pleased.

Although animal sacrifices are no longer required, God still expects His people to offer *sacrifices*. These sacrifices are the joyous words of *praise* and thanksgiving that we speak and sing to Him. In addition, we are to offer our bodies a "living sacrifice" (Romans 12:1), to be consumed in service to God and to our fellowmen.

Conclusion

A. The Power of Purity

Just as the Jewish priests had to cleanse themselves before they served at the altar, so Christians must also be cleansed before they can render acceptable service to God. Through Christ's blood we are sanctified, or set apart, and we are required to maintain that purity by constantly renewing our commitment to Him.

Personal purity is a critical part of our witness for Christ. We live and serve in a lost and evil world that can ensnare and corrupt even the most mature Christian. For that reason we must turn again and again to Christ's sanctifying power to protect us. We should never underestimate the impact of a consistently holy life, nor should we minimize our need for divine strength in living that life.

B. Change and Decay

Many of us are familiar with the old hymn, "Abide with Me." One line in particular contains a sobering truth: "Change and decay in all around I see." These words express the feelings of many of us, especially those of us who have lived half a century or more. We have witnessed unbelievable changes in so many areas of life. Some of the changes are disheartening and threatening: the breakup of the traditional family, the rising crime rate, the declining moral standards, and the excessive materialism.

In the face of all these changes, we could easily give way to hand-wringing despair. But before we do, let us consider the next line of that inspiring hymn: "O Thou who changest not, abide with me!" Jesus Christ is the same yesterday, today, and forever.

C. Let Us Pray

Loving Father, we thank You for the perfect sacrifice that You have offered up for our sins. Cleanse us from our sins and send us forth to labor wherever You may need us. May we always give You the glory for the opportunities we have to serve. In Jesus' name we pray. Amen.

D. Thought to Remember

The world may not always understand a Christian's profession of faith, but it should be able to see a Christian's pure life and his unselfish service to others.

Home Daily Bible Readings

Monday, Aug. 25—Be Responsible Husbands and Wives (Ephesians 5:22-33)

Tuesday, Aug. 26—Be Responsible Parents and Children (Ephesians 6:1-4)

Wednesday, Aug. 27—Be Responsible Citizens (Matthew 22:15-22)

Thursday, Aug. 28—Be Responsible To God (Hebrews 4:1-10)

Friday, Aug. 29—Be Responsible Leaders (Hebrews 13:17-25)

Saturday, Aug. 30—Be Responsible for What You Say (James 3:1-12)

Sunday, Aug. 31—Be Responsible With Your Wealth (Luke 12:13-21)

Learning by Doing

This page contains an alternate lesson plan emphasizing learning activities.
Classes desiring such student involvement will find these suggestions helpful.

Learning Goals

As a result of today's study, students will:

1. Summarize the practical advice for Christian living and growth in Hebrews 13:1-16.

2. See how relevant this advice is to today's world, and commit themselves to applying it in their own lives.

Into the Lesson

Remember is a key word in today's text. Prepare pieces of yarn or string (six to eight inches long), and hand one to each class member. Do not comment, other than to say, "Keep this for something we will do later." As class assembles, display these letters on the chalkboard or on a transparency: *B, E, E, E, M, M, R, R.* Ask the class to reassemble the letters to make a word. *Remember* should be recognized easily and quickly. Note that this is a key word in today's text. Note also how appropriate a call to *remember* key truths is, in closing a letter such as Hebrews.

Into the Word

Buy enough small stick-on notes about two inches square, to allow you to give five to ten pieces to each student. Leave the pieces that you give each person stuck together as a small pad.

Assign the odd-numbered verses of today's text to half of your group; assign the even-numbered to the other half. Direct students to look at their verses, and to prepare five or more statements on their stick-on sheets (one per sheet). They should use "Don't forget" or "Remember" to preface each statement they write. Give them two examples, if needed, to get them started: "Remember that Jesus never changes" (from verse 8) and "Don't forget to praise God" (from verse 15). After a few minutes, direct students to take their "memos" and stick them all over the classroom at random. (Those who finish early could precede those who are working more deliberately, to avoid too much traffic.) Once your assortment of reminders is in place, have students go back to where they are posted, so they can get a good look at all of them.

After students are seated again, turn to today's text from Hebrews 13:1-16 and, after you read a verse, ask them to recall "Remembers" and "Don't forgets" that they saw for that verse. As you proceed, remove and reassemble the memos into groups for each verse. If you come to a verse for which no one can identify a related memo, stop and ask the class to suggest a possibility. (For example, if none is seen for verse 10, suggest, "Remember: we have privileges others do not!")

When you have completed verse 16, be sure to move any "leftovers" to their proper places, and then ask, "Is there any reason why some verses elicited many memos and some only a few?" Ask whether the verses that produced the most memos were chosen because of ease in preparation or because of a particular need in the lives of today's Christians for the reminders in those verses. Follow up on this point by asking why these subjects covered in today's text are especially relevant for Christians in today's society: hospitality (v. 2), helping the imprisoned and the suffering (v. 3), moral purity (v. 4), contentment (vv. 5, 6), respect for church leaders (v. 7), and false doctrine (v. 9). Ask, "What current trends or attitudes in society make it a challenge to practice each of these?" For example, the tendency of many to isolate themselves from others has made hospitality less common than it once was. Christians can make a difference in this area.

Into Life

Have the adults pull out the pieces of string or yarn that you distributed at the beginning of the session. Ask each to tie the piece loosely around a finger. Call for volunteers to hold up their "tied" finger and give a "Remember" or "Don't forget" from today's study. Get a sampling of six to eight. Suggest that your students also wear their reminder until at least one person asks what it means. They can then select a key truth from the lesson to share with that person.

(If time allows, you may want to include a few moments of review of this quarter's lessons or of this study in Hebrews. Ask class members what truths have stood out most to them. How were they encouraged? Challenged? Warned? Rebuked? What specific verses from the lessons can they recall?)

To close the lesson and this unit on Hebrews, call attention to the beautiful benediction found in Hebrews 13:20, 21. Have your class stand, form a circle, and hold hands, as you conclude by reading this blessing.

Let's Talk It Over

The questions on this page are designed to encourage review of the lesson Scriptures and to promote discussion of the lesson by the class. The answers provided are only discussion starters. Let your class talk it over from there.

1. Can you give an example of how you have received "brotherly love" from other Christians? What are the practical expressions of love between Christians that you believe are most valuable?

Most Christians should be able to testify to having received such love. For me, many remarkable expressions of love came at the death of my mother. The prayers, cards, visits, and meals given by Christian friends were a great consolation. Other very valuable and practical expressions of love may include greeting cards, gifts, or meals shared at significant events, such as a baptism, wedding, birth, graduation, special birthday, anniversary, promotion, or retirement. Assistance offered at a time of unemployment, prolonged illness, accident, or other personal crisis also expresses love and should be common among Christians. We may see such acts occurring spontaneously between Christian friends, but it may also be necessary for a church to be more intentional and organize its efforts.

2. How is the Biblical view of marriage different from society's current attitude toward it?

We believe that God is the author of marriage, and that when it is entered into according to His intention and design, it is the source of manifold blessings. Unfortunately, many in our culture view marriage with contempt as an outdated arrangement that is too confining. Some of these are persuaded that falling in love or falling out of love is something over which they have no control, so they are unable to make a lifelong commitment. They may claim that they cannot predict where their heart will lead them. Christians can prove the foolishness of such thinking by providing a counter example of the true beauty of marriage. God has created us with the capability of making well-reasoned choices and enduring commitments. It is the unreserved commitment of marriage vows, sincerely given and acted upon, that creates the climate for true intimacy between a couple. All other forms of sexual intimacy are subject to God's judgment.

3. In a society that promotes covetousness, how can Christians learn contentment?

To enjoy contentment, you may have to adjust your focus. If your attention is primarily upon possessions that you do not have but desire to have, you will be discontented. Instead of fantasizing about what life might be like with someone else's wealth, concentrate upon the value of what you possess. Commit to being the best manager or steward of what God has already given. A second step to contentment is to include in your list of assets those that cannot be seen as well as those that can be seen. How can you put a value upon the love of God, the gift of eternal life, the presence of the Holy Spirit, and the privilege of prayer? A third step is to remember that all material blessings of this world are destined to perish. They are temporary at best.

4. To what extent does any spiritual leader "have the rule over you" (Hebrews 13:7)?

Many people in our culture recoil at the idea of anyone ruling over them. We put such a high value upon individual freedom and rights that we resist being accountable to anyone or receiving direction from anyone. Our text has in view, however, a relationship as leader to followers between the one speaking the Word of God and the ones receiving it. Hebrews 13:17 makes clear that these spiritual leaders will be called to give account for those who have been entrusted to their care. For that reason we are commanded to obey these leaders.

5. What altar is exclusive to Christians? How do baptism and Communion make us participants in that altar?

The Old Covenant called for the frequent offering of blood sacrifices upon the altar of the tabernacle or temple. Such sacrifices could never completely forgive sin. When Jesus gave His life upon the cross of Calvary, that rugged cross became the most important altar of all time. His blood is still the one and only sacrifice that can completely blot out the guilt of our sin. That altar and that sacrifice, however, belong only to those who accept Jesus as Savior and Lord. We identify ourselves as trusting Jesus by first receiving Christian baptism, and then by partaking of Communion as a continuing memorial and reaffirmation of our faith. Baptism involves the symbols of death, burial, and resurrection. The bread and cup of Communion testify of the body and blood of Jesus given for us.